Praise for

Vicksburg

Winner of the Fletcher Pratt Award and the Laney Prize

"A superb account of both military leadership and soldierly warfare. . . . Books like *Vicksburg* are exactly what Thomas Hardy had in mind when he wrote that 'war makes rattling good history.'"

—John Steele Gordon, *The Wall Street Journal*

"Carefully researched and written with sizzling and persuasive prose, Miller has found the way to write both military and emancipation history in one profound package. Never have headquarters, slave quarters, and the ultimate purpose of the war been so seamlessly and brilliantly demonstrated."

—David W. Blight, Sterling Professor of History,
Yale University, and Pulitzer Prize–winning Author of
Frederick Douglass: Prophet of Freedom

"Miller does an excellent job of illustrating Grant's growth as a commanding general. . . . Well-written and narrative-driven, Donald Miller has provided a book that offers a thoughtful reconceptualization of the Vicksburg Campaign."

—John McMillan, *Civil War Times*

"Miller deftly conjures the campaign's uncertainty and drama—the surprises that lay around every bend of the region's forbidding terrain and swampy waterways. At the heart of his story is U.S. Grant, who emerges here as a master of maneuver and improvisation, and a hero made human and real. This is military history at its best."

—Elizabeth R. Varon, author of
Armies of Deliverance: A New History of the Civil War

"This superbly written narrative is a portrait of America's greatest soldier, warts and all, an accounting of Grant's moral evolution on the slave question, of his many tactical gambles and errors, as well as his strategic triumph in the decisive campaign of America's most important war. . . . Most remarkably, we are guided up and down the Mississippi over the course of the greatest amphibious campaign of the nineteenth century."

—Cathal J. Nolan, author of *The Allure of Battle*,
winner of the 2018 Gilder Lehrman Prize for Military History

"This is a magnificent book, certainly one of the very best ever written about the Civil War. It has breadth and depth, and it is written in a way that makes the reader truly understand not only the battle and siege of Vicksburg, not only the Civil War, but war itself."
—John M. Barry, author of *Rising Tide*

"An insightful and striking look at the actions of General Grant at a turning point not only of the Civil War but also of American history."
— Greg A. Romaneck, *Civil War Courier*

"Renowned historian and author Donald Miller recounts the Vicksburg campaign with astonishing authenticity."
—*Mississippi Magazine*

"An expert, detailed account that should remain the definitive account for quite some time."
—*Kirkus Reviews* (starred review)

"Authoritative, complete, engaging, and enjoyable. . . . *Vicksburg* will become a Civil War standard."
— Jonathan R. Allen, LearnCivilWarHistory.com

"Elegant. . . . Enlightening. . . . Well-researched and well-told."
—*Publishers Weekly*

"Grant has had his biographers over the years, but in Miller he has finally found a writer who captures him in his completeness as a man and a military leader, overcoming heavy odds and repeated failures to win the decisive campaign of the war."
—Rob Citino, Executive Director,
Institute for the Study of War and Democracy, and
Samuel Zemurray Stone Senior Historian,
The National World War II Museum

"Miller provides important context for the final siege of Vicksburg by explaining why the city was vital to control of the Mississippi. . . . Highly recommended."
—*Library Journal*

ALSO BY DONALD L. MILLER

Supreme City: How Jazz Age Manhattan Gave Birth to Modern America

*Masters of the Air: America's Bomber Boys Who
Fought the Air War Against Nazi Germany*

D-Days in the Pacific

The Story of World War II

City of the Century: The Epic of Chicago and the Making of America

Lewis Mumford: A Life

The Lewis Mumford Reader

*The Kingdom of Coal: Work, Enterprise, and Ethnic
Communities in the Mine Fields* (with Richard Sharpless)

The New American Radicalism: Non-Marxian Radicalism in the 1930s

VICKSBURG

GRANT'S CAMPAIGN THAT
BROKE THE CONFEDERACY

DONALD L. MILLER

Simon & Schuster Paperbacks

NEW YORK   LONDON   TORONTO
SYDNEY   NEW DELHI

Simon & Schuster Paperbacks
1230 Avenue of the Americas
New York, NY 10020

First Simon & Schuster paperback edition October 2020

SIMON & SCHUSTER PAPERBACKS and colophon are registered trademarks
of Simon & Schuster, Inc.

For information about special discounts for bulk purchases,
please contact Simon & Schuster Special Sales at 1-866-506-1949 or
business@simonandschuster.com.

The Simon & Schuster Speakers Bureau can bring authors to your
live event. For more information or to book an event contact
the Simon & Schuster Speakers Bureau at 1-866-248-3049
or visit our website at www.simonspeakers.com.

Design by Paul Dippolito

Manufactured in the United States of America

1   3   5   7   9   10   8   6   4   2

The Library of Congress has cataloged the hardcover edition as follows:
Names: Miller, Donald L., 1944– author.
Title: Vicksburg : Grant's campaign that broke the Confederacy / Donald L. Miller.
Description: New York : Simon & Schuster, 2019. |
Includes bibliographical references and index.
Identifiers: LCCN 2019010269 | ISBN 9781451641370 (hardback) | ISBN 1451641370
Subjects: LCSH: Vicksburg (Miss.)—History—Siege, 1863. | Grant, Ulysses S.
(Ulysses Simpson), 1822–1885. | Strategy—History—19th century. | BISAC:
HISTORY / United States / Civil War Period (1850–1877). | HISTORY /
Military / United States. | HISTORY / United States / State & Local /
South (AL, AR, FL, GA, KY, LA, MS, NC, SC, TN, VA, WV).
Classification: LCC E475.27 .M65 2019 |
DDC 973.7/344—dc23 LC record available at https://lccn.loc.gov/2019010269.

ISBN 978-1-4516-4137-0
ISBN 978-1-4516-4139-4 (paperback)
ISBN 978-1-4516-4140-0 (ebook)

To Sophie, who lights up our days

CONTENTS

Author's Note   xi

Prologue   xiii

— PART ONE —

CHAPTER 1 Cairo   3

CHAPTER 2 River Warrior   12

CHAPTER 3 Winter Fortress   42

CHAPTER 4 A Tremendous Murder Mill   62

— PART TWO —

CHAPTER 5 "The Battle for the Mississippi"   97

CHAPTER 6 "These Troublous Times"   119

CHAPTER 7 Secessionist Citadel   135

CHAPTER 8 Rebel Victory   147

— PART THREE —

CHAPTER 9 Anxiety and Intrigue   175

CHAPTER 10 Revolution   198

CHAPTER 11 Grant's March   214

CHAPTER 12   The Chickasaw Slaughter Pen   236

CHAPTER 13   Mud and Misery   263

CHAPTER 14   "Things Fall Apart . . ."   277

CHAPTER 15   Steele's Bayou   292

CHAPTER 16   Crisis   309

CHAPTER 17   The Entering Wedge   325

CHAPTER 18:   This One Object   351

— PART FOUR —

CHAPTER 19   Pursuit   369

CHAPTER 20   The Hill of Death   391

CHAPTER 21   A Circle of Fire   416

CHAPTER 22   "The Crisis is on Us"   443

CHAPTER 23   "It is great, Mr. Welles."   471

Epilogue   499

Appendix : Vicksburg Battlefield Casualties   501

Acknowledgments   503

Notes   507

Bibliography   597

Illustration Credits   635

Index   637

AUTHOR'S NOTE

"With me, a story usually begins," William Faulkner once said, "with a single idea or memory or mental picture."[1] In *Absalom, Absalom!*, his epic tale of slavery and plantation culture, Faulkner created a picture in my mind that shaped this book. I had already decided to write a history of the Vicksburg campaign before reading *Absalom, Absalom!*, but the novel took my book in an entirely new direction.

In 1833, Thomas Sutpen, a big-framed, young stranger rides into the barely developed town of Jefferson, Mississippi, in Faulkner's fictional Yoknapatawpha County, his only possessions his horse, a small saddlebag containing some personal items, and two holstered pistols. He acquires land from an Indian tribe, clears it with twenty slaves he brings over from Haiti, builds a sprawling house, and puts in a cotton crop. He does this with unflagging resolve and ruthless disregard for his work force, driving them, Faulkner writes, "like a pack of hounds." Sutpen works beside them, all of them naked, "plastered over with mud against the mosquitoes" as they haul clay and timber out of a malarial swamp.

The house is impressively large but crude, "unpainted and unfurnished, without a pane of glass or a doorknob or hinge in it."[2] Three years later, Sutpen, now a prosperous frontier farmer, heads into town in search of a wife. To prepare the house for the bride he has yet to meet he installs windows and doors and sends his slaves to meet a steamboat on the distant Mississippi. They return in wagons piled high with mahogany furniture, woven rugs, and crystal chandeliers. Sutpen then marries a local woman of some prominence and sets himself up as a plantation grandee, a member of the local cotton aristocracy.

Faulkner's Jefferson, closely modeled on Oxford, Mississippi, is more than a hundred miles north and east of Vicksburg but its development mirrored that of the Yazoo Delta, located directly north of Vicksburg and connected to it by a lively steamboat trade. Beginning in the 1830s, this wilderness was cleared for cultivation by restless frontier capitalists like Sutpen, most of them from newly settled Vicksburg. With battalions of slaves they carved out cotton plantations in the muddy bottomlands formed by the annual overflows of the Mississippi River, working under the same appalling conditions Faulkner described in *Absalom, Absalom!*

Sutpen and his son, Henry, along with the real-life planters of Vicksburg and Yazoo country, marched off to war in 1861 to save what they had only recently built, an empire founded upon cotton and slaves.

Ulysses Grant does not appear in Faulkner's novel, but when his Army of the Tennessee invaded Mississippi in late 1862 it pushed all the way to Oxford before Confederate cavalry severed its supply line, forcing it to fall back to Tennessee. Yet while in Mississippi, Grant's soldiers had begun tearing at slavery, disastrously weakening it along their line of advance. For Mississippians, the end came when Grant returned in January of 1863 and began sending raiding parties into the Yazoo Delta and other concentrations of cotton and slaves in the Vicksburg region. They burned and plundered and by the time Vicksburg surrendered in July 1863, they had destroyed slavery and its economic underpinnings in Mississippi and great parts of eastern Louisiana. Sutpen returns from the war to find his plantation in ruins, his fields fallow, and his slaves gone.

This is the story that began forming in my mind as I read *Absalom, Absalom!*—a tale of the meteoric rise of a slave-based civilization that was dismantled by military might only three decades after its birth.

Absalom, Absalom! was published in 1936, the same year as Margaret Mitchell's *Gone With the Wind*. No two books about the antebellum South are less alike—one a translucent defense of a culture built upon slavery, the other an indictment of the blighting effects of bondage on Southern society. Faulkner's novel convinced me that a history of Grant's Mississippi Valley campaign would be incomplete without an account of the war waged on slavery by his army and the slaves that audaciously escaped to its lines.

PROLOGUE

"The war history of Vicksburg has more about it to interest the general reader than that of any other of the river towns. . . . Vicksburg . . . saw warfare in all its phases, both land and water—the siege, the mine, the assault, the repulse, the bombardment, sickness, captivity, famine."[1]

—Mark Twain, *Life on the Mississippi*

"Will it not be the unquestioned sentiment of history that the liberty which Mr. Lincoln declared with his pen General Grant made effective with his sword."[2]

—Frederick Douglass, "U.S. Grant and the Colored People"

In January 1863, Vicksburg, Mississippi, was the most important strategic point in the Confederacy. A fortified town on commanding bluffs above the Mississippi River, it was the last obstacle facing Union forces struggling to regain control of the great river of America and split the Confederacy in two, separating Arkansas, Texas, and much of Louisiana from secessionist states east of the Mississippi. A smaller Confederate river bastion, Port Hudson, in Louisiana, was one hundred and thirty miles downriver from Vicksburg. It was an integral part of Vicksburg's river defense system and could not survive on its own if Vicksburg fell.

Employing steam-driven riverine warfare, Federal amphibious forces had retaken the Mississippi from Cairo, a Union naval base at the confluence of the Ohio and Mississippi Rivers in southern Illinois, to the Yazoo River, which emptied into the Mississippi a few miles north of Vicksburg. The saltwater fleet of Flag Officer David Glasgow Farragut controlled the river south of Port Hudson to the Gulf of Mexico. In April 1862, Farragut had steamed upriver from the Gulf, seized New

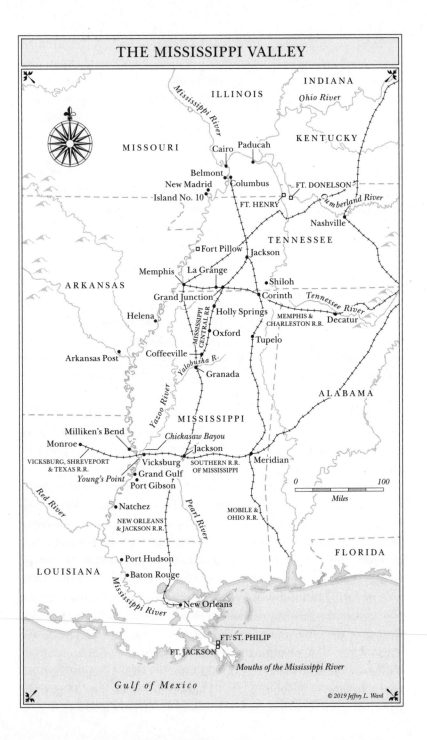

THE MISSISSIPPI VALLEY

Orleans, the South's largest city and leading cotton port, and captured Baton Rouge, Louisiana, and Natchez, Mississippi, without a fight. Farragut stalled in front of lightly defended Vicksburg, however, when hardened secessionists defiantly refused to surrender. The fleet's three-masted sloops-of-war, steam-driven wooden ships built for battles at sea, were unable to elevate their guns to bombard the city effectively. Fearing his big vessels would go aground when water levels dropped rapidly in late spring, Farragut headed back to New Orleans.

Under intense pressure from the Lincoln administration, he returned in mid-June towing a flotilla of wooden schooners commanded by his foster brother Captain David Dixon Porter. The scows, as they were called, carried mammoth seacoast mortars capable of firing two-hundred-pound shells over four thousand yards. After the Union's new ironclad fleet, based at Cairo, subdued Memphis on June 5, it joined Farragut and Porter in front of Vicksburg, and the combined force—the most powerful concentration of brown-water naval power in history—bombarded Vicksburg remorselessly but ineffectively into late July. The weather was abysmally hot, and malaria and dysentery reached plague proportions on the ships and in the camps of the small infantry force that had accompanied Farragut from New Orleans. In late July, after Farragut returned to New Orleans, the ironclad fleet, with hundreds of deathly sick sailors aboard, pulled back toward Memphis. Vicksburg became a symbol of rebel resolve. "Everyone is elated and astonished at the daring achievement," wrote a Mississippi soldier.[3]

The following month rebel troops from Vicksburg marched down-river, recaptured Baton Rouge, and emplaced cannon at Port Hudson, just upriver from the Louisiana capital. It was an inspired move. The hamlet of Port Hudson was strategically located a few miles south of where the Red River, Vicksburg's economic lifeline to the trans-Mississippi west, flowed into the Mississippi. Shielded by the heavy guns of Port Hudson, Confederate steamboats continued to carry essential military provisions to Vicksburg: salt, molasses, cattle, and British rifles smuggled into Galveston, Texas. From Vicksburg, they were trans-shipped by rail to other points in the Confederacy.

When the Union navy left Vicksburg, the rebels retained control of the river from Vicksburg to Port Hudson, but they had only a few lightly armed wooden gunboats to defend it. Vastly superior Federal naval forces had annihilated the Confederate River Defense Fleet at New Orleans and Memphis. Expecting Vicksburg to be attacked again, and soon, the government in Richmond sent reinforcements and a new commander, Lieutenant General John C. Pemberton, a Philadelphian who had resigned from the United States Army to take up the cause of his Newport, Virginia, bride. By late 1862, Vicksburg was one of the most heavily fortified cities on the continent. Batteries lined its riverfront for a distance of seventeen miles, the guns positioned at the base and near the heights of the city's sharply terraced bluffs. The river defenses were thought to be impassable, and thickly armored ironclads had yet to challenge them. Behind the hill city, on its landward side, engineering officer Samuel Lockett began constructing with slave labor a semicircular defensive line: thick, high-sitting earthen forts connected by miles of rifle pits and cannon emplacements.

But Vicksburg relied more on geography than firepower for survival. It was a natural citadel surrounded by terrain of appalling difficulty, a menacing combination of deeply eroded hills, flooded bottomlands, stagnant bayous, and a dense Delta forest that spread northward from the Yazoo River all the way to Memphis, two hundred and fifty land miles north of Vicksburg.

In November 1862, the Federals tested Vicksburg again, this time with Ulysses S. Grant's Army of the Tennessee, undefeated in battle. Eager to avenge his failure in front of Vicksburg that summer, David Dixon Porter agreed to assist Grant with his fleet of newly built ironclads. That October Porter had been appointed commander of the Union's Mississippi Squadron, with the rank of (acting) rear admiral. He and Grant were a formidable combination, hyperaggressive and strategically astute. After taking command of a small army at Cairo in September 1861, Grant captured Forts Henry and Donelson—the Union's first clear victories of the war—and defeated the strongest rebel army in the Deep South at the Battle of Shiloh. He had made monumental mistakes at Donelson and Shiloh but recovered smartly and established himself as the finest general in the west, a ground commander with an inborn understanding of topography and a river warrior masterful at using enemy waters to his advantage. And he had as his second in command his fellow Ohioan and West Point friend

William Tecumseh Sherman, one of the outstanding military minds of that time.

In November 1862, Grant was assembling a strike force in southwestern Tennessee, near Mississippi's northern border. The objective was Vicksburg. His army would follow the line of the Mississippi Central Railroad, which ran southward for nearly two hundred miles to Jackson, the state capital. From there it would swing westward and storm Vicksburg from its landward side. The campaign fell apart, however, when Grant failed to properly cover his supply line. Rebel cavalry severed it and destroyed Grant's forward supply base at Holly Springs, Mississippi. With his army stalled near Oxford, Mississippi, Grant came up with a new plan. He would hold in place Pemberton's army, which was guarding the approaches to Vicksburg, and send Sherman with a division to Memphis, where Grant had arranged for him to rendezvous with Porter and his gunboat fleet. Sherman hijacked troops already in Memphis waiting to be assigned to another commander and headed downstream to the Yazoo River, where he attempted to break into the city by surmounting a rugged line of bluffs that rose precipitously from a swamp on the banks of Yazoo. Rebel scouts had tipped off Vicksburg's defenders, and they slaughtered Sherman's army during Christmas week at a godforsaken place called Chickasaw Bayou.

In late January 1863, Grant came down from Memphis to assume personal command of his dispirited army, camped in the miasmic swamps and bayous of Louisiana, roughly twenty miles upriver and across from Vicksburg. The winter weather was wretched: torrential rains, blowing snow and hail, ripping winds, and lightning storms that split the sky. The swollen river overflowed its banks. The only dry ground in the camps was the high earthen levees along the shoreline. Soldiers camped on them, beside the shallow graves of their comrades, felled in alarming numbers by dysentery, smallpox, and measles. When a levee was split open by the pressure of the fast-rising Mississippi, crude wooden coffins would spill into the river and be swept downstream on the swift current.

The troops were discouraged and there were thousands of desertions, encouraged by Copperheads—anti-war Democrats who had infiltrated the camps. Lacerating criticism of Grant's incompetence and rumors of his drinking filled Northern newspapers. Prominent politicians called for his head. Only victories could save him, but there were none. Grant sent expedition after expedition against Vicksburg through the wild Yazoo Delta and also ordered two gigantic water-moving projects in Louisiana. These were designed to bypass the city's river batteries and carry an army inland on small boats to a spot below Vicksburg, where it would cross the Mississippi and attack the city from below. Lincoln disapproved, and the public failed to comprehend what Grant was up to. "The people of the East, knowing about as much of the geography of the region of Grant's meandering as they did of Japan, were utterly bewildered by reports of his actions in places like Lake Providence, Steele's Bayou, the Yazoo and the Yalobusha," wrote Albert D. Richardson of the *New-York Daily Tribune*, who was with Grant at Vicksburg. "They only knew that months dragged wearily by . . . and that the soldiers were reported dying from disease."[4]

On the last of these desperately launched expeditions, a long-shot effort to get to dry land on Vicksburg's eastern flank by way of a network of shallow, tortuously narrow forest waterways, Grant nearly lost Sherman, Porter, and a good part of the indispensable ironclad fleet to rebel ambushers. By the time the failed expedition backed out of the Yazoo morass into the Mississippi, it was late March of 1863 and Grant looked to be out of options. Infuriated by the general's lack of progress, Secretary of War Edwin Stanton sent a government spy, the noted newspaper editor Charles A. Dana, to infiltrate Grant's inner circle and report back if he was either drinking, incompetent, or both. Dana arrived on April 6. Three months later, on July 4, Grant captured Vicksburg, bagged an entire enemy army, opened the Mississippi from its source to the Gulf, and severed the Confederacy. This is the story of how he did it.

This book takes in the full compass of Grant's Mississippi Valley campaign, from Cairo to Vicksburg, along with Farragut's capture of New Orleans and his frustrating summer in front of Vicksburg in 1862, which is an essential part of the Union's Vicksburg campaign and not a mere prelude to it. Based on letters, diaries, memoirs, and official reports collected over the course of twenty-two years in over forty major archives, it is emphatically a military history, but one that moves out from the fighting and the inner world of the common soldier to take in the experiences of noncombatants: war correspondents and newspaper editors; doctors, nurses, and Northern relief workers; plantation masters, mistresses, and their diary-writing daughters; and tens of thousands of African American slaves who were freed by Grant's army of liberation, which first entered Mississippi one month before Lincoln's Emancipation Proclamation became the law of the land.

And, whether slaveholders or not, the soldiers and civilians who defended Vicksburg form an integral part of the story. Hemmed in for forty-seven days by a circle of fire—guns trained on them from the Mississippi River and batteries positioned on the city's landward side—Vicksburg families took refuge in earthen caves that their slaves dug into the city's steep hillsides. There they withstood, with amazingly few casualties, a relentless, nerve-rattling bombardment in which churches, hospitals, and private homes were deliberately targeted by Union gunners. Toward the end of the siege, the most unfortunate of them subsisted on a starvation diet of peas, fried cornmeal, and mule meat.

I have stitched their stories into those of Confederate soldiers on the line. Boys from the bayous and backwater towns of the South withstood an ever-tightening siege in which they were compelled to sleep on their guns, in the open, exposed to wasting heat and summer storms. They had no backup, no reinforcements, and were required to stay in their trenches and earthen forts without an hour's relief. Yet they fought persistently and "valiantly," in Grant's words, for a "cause" that was "one of the worst for which a people ever fought."[5]

At Vicksburg, Southern nationalism reached new heights, and the diaries and letters of its uniformed defenders and the fervently committed civilians who backed them bring into sharp focus the reasons the garrison held on for so long against surpassing odds. This rich record also helps explain why the Confederate people fought with such resolve and at horrific cost into 1865. There were dissenters and doubters, and large pockets of Union sentiment in the Confederate states, but what stands out are these astonishing numbers: Over three quarters of a million men served in the Confederate army. That is over 75 percent of the Confederacy's available draft-age white population. One in three of these men died.[6]

When Vicksburg surrendered, the war did not end for most of the citizens and soldiers who had fought to turn back the Yankee tide. They remained determined secessionists, seeing themselves as a conquered, not a subdued, people. Plantation slavery was dead in those parts of Mississippi, Tennessee, and Louisiana in which Grant's army had encamped, marched through, or occupied, but areas outside fortified garrison towns and outposts, to which recently freed black people fled for protection and sustenance, were the province of intransigent guerrilla bands and marauding cavalry units. They regularly raided black agricultural settlements established by the national government and sacked and torched the homesteads of white families who made cause with the occupiers.

For thousands of Grant's soldiers who had signed on to crush the secessionist revolution, the Vicksburg campaign ended where it had begun, in Cairo, Illinois, where vast hospitals had been built for the sick and wounded. Cairo was the epicenter for all Union military activity in the Mississippi Valley. The navy's Mississippi River Squadron was formed there in the summer of 1861, one month before Ulysses Grant took command of the troops pouring into that desolate river town by rail from every northwestern state, from Ohio to Minnesota. Before arriving at Cairo that September as a newly minted brigadier general, he marked on a map with red crayon amphibious thrusts into the Mississippi Valley, using as his avenues of invasion the Cumberland and Tennessee Rivers, which flowed northward into the Ohio just east of Cairo. Shortly after taking command at Cairo, Grant helped turn the unpromising town into the supply center and originating point for expeditions he would lead down these western river systems. From Cairo came the ironclads and mortars, the soldiers and sailors who would reopen the Mississippi. The Vicksburg story begins at Cairo.

— PART ONE —

CHAPTER 1

Cairo

"The Mississippi River will be a grand theater of war."[1]

—William Tecumseh Sherman, May 13, 1861

"At length . . . we arrived at a spot so much more desolate than any we had yet beheld. . . . At the junction of the two rivers, on ground so flat and low and marshy, that at certain seasons of the year it is inundated to the house-tops, lies a breeding-place of fever, ague, and death." This was Cairo, Illinois, in 1842, captured with undiminished disgust by Charles Dickens in his travelogue, *American Notes*.[2]

"I do not think that I shall ever forget Cairo," wrote British novelist Anthony Trollope twenty years later in his travel book, *North America*.[3] Chartered in 1818 by speculators hoping to exploit its unrivaled location at the confluence of the great rivers of the west—the Ohio and the Mississippi—Cairo had never lived up to the extravagant expectations of those who invested in it. It languished for decades as a torpid, mosquito-ridden mudflat. But by the time Trollope's ship dropped anchor near its high earthen levees—built to hold back the surging river waters that regularly submerged it—the languid little town of some two thousand souls had been transformed into a surging military metropolis.[4] War made Cairo one of the most prized possessions on the North American continent.

When South Carolina secessionists fired on Fort Sumter on the morning of April 12, 1861, Cairo took on "a fearful new significance."[5] It had become "the nucleus or pivot," Trollope wrote, "of all really strategic movements in this terrible national struggle."[6] Situated on a narrow neck of land projecting deep into slave territory, it was the southernmost town in the Union, located farther south than Richmond. This "frontier town on the very borders of 'Secessia'" was flanked by two slave states—Missouri to the west and Kentucky to the east—"border" states that had declared their neutrality but would eventually have both pro-Union and pro-Confederate governments.[7]

Since early in the century, river towns south of Cairo had engaged in a thriving steamboat trade with St. Louis, Cincinnati, and Louisville, passing dismal Cairo along the way. When the war came, the national government feared that these riverine trade routes would be exploited by Confederate raiding parties intent on doing harm in southern Illinois, Indiana, and Ohio. Tiny Cairo was "the key to the lower Mississippi Valley," wrote journalist Albert D. Richardson, ". . . the most important strategic point in the West."[8] Confederate newspapers concurred. "It is the key to the upper, as New Orleans . . . [is] to the lower Mississippi," said the Jackson *Mississippian*.[9]

In the very first weeks of the war, secessionist sentiment ran strong in the town. Located in that part of Illinois called Egypt for its fertile, flood-enriched soil, it was a community "Southern in interests and feeling," said a Northern reporter. "The great bulk of the Egyptians are of Southern origin, from Virginia, and Tennessee and Kentucky, and a large number of them are actually pro-slavery in sentiment."[10] When war broke out, Cairo was unguarded, vulnerable, and infested with Southern spies. Prominent politicians in the west feared it was about to be stormed by rebel forces from Tennessee, moving through neutral Kentucky, and aided, on arrival at Cairo, by armed and aggressively disloyal townspeople, determined to keep all of southern Illinois free of black labor. Linked to Chicago by the Illinois Central Railroad, Cairo would eventually become the forward supply base and naval station for Union campaigns into cotton country, but in April 1861, the Lincoln administration's first concern was to secure and defend it.

One week after Fort Sumter, Secretary of War Simon Cameron ordered Illinois governor Richard Yates to rush troops to Cairo.[11] A hastily assembled expedition of six hundred volunteers left Chicago by train on the evening of April 21 and rolled into Cairo, 363 miles to the south, twenty-four hours later, just in time to prevent rebel sympathizers from tearing up rail tracks and cutting the levees to flood the town.[12] It was a coup de main. Cairo was placed under martial law and became then and for the remainder of the war an armed camp.

"Our reception by the citizens was not the most cordial and it was plainly evident that they would have been pleased if the occupying forces had come from the opposite direction," recalled a volunteer artilleryman from Chicago.[13] The upstate troops set up camp on mudflats along the Ohio River levee. Reinforcements soon arrived. By mid-June twelve thousand western troops were garrisoned in or around the town, with eight thousand more on the way; and cannon lined the levees, sweeping the Ohio and Mississippi Rivers. "Cairo . . . is now impregnable," declared the *New York Times*.[14]

While there were still "plenty of Secessionists at Cairo," the sight of armed soldiers drilling on the town commons and mounting their brass cannon on the levee caused a noticeable change in sentiment, said one reporter.[15] Dozens of Jeff Davis partisans "are now Union men."[16] The town remained militantly pro-slavery, but most citizens were unwilling to take up arms against their state and country.[17]

Cairo was miserable military duty. Some regiments brought lager beer from home, drinking up to a barrel a day, and the whiskey saloons that lined the top of the Ohio River levee, the "one great street of the town," did a spectacular business.[18] Alcohol, however, was an inadequate antidote to the stink and squalor of the town. From the levee, one descended a long flight of wooden stairs to the downtown, a treeless, saucer-shaped basin, rimmed by earthen embankments that encircled it.[19] The only building of note was the five-story St. Charles Hotel, located on the levee, near the loading platforms of the Illinois Central Railroad. Rats swarmed out of holes underneath the planking. "Cairo is of all towns in America the most desolate, so is its hotel the most forlorn and wretched," wrote Anthony Trollope.[20]

With the saloons on the levee packed to the doors with river men, gamblers, and whores, Brigadier General Benjamin M. Prentiss, the post commander, forbade his troops from frequenting them, fearing a wholesale breakdown of discipline.[21] Armed sentries were stationed at the door of every liquor dispensary, depressing soldier morale even more dangerously.[22] The men were bored out of their minds, eager to take the fight to the enemy.

• • •

Morale shot up on August 12, 1861, when a flotilla of three gunboats—*Tyler, Conestoga,* and *Lexington*—tied up at Cairo.[23] These "timberclads," as they were called, were wooden commercial steamboats—side-wheelers—that had been purchased in Cincinnati by naval commander John Rodgers, who had converted them into "bullet proof" warships by wrapping their decks with thick, eight-foot-high wooden bulwarks. These ungainly looking shields would provide protection from small arms fire from shore but not from the cannon fire of forts the Confederates had begun building along the river.[24]

The Lincoln administration had decided to make Cairo its principal base for military operations on the Mississippi, and these were the first three ships of what would soon become the most formidable brown-water navy in the world. Their arrival at Cairo that August afternoon was a signal to the troops that offensive operations were imminent.

Rodgers, a deep-water sailor unacquainted with riverine warfare, had been sent west by Secretary of the Navy Gideon Welles to create a fresh-water gunboat fleet. The boats, however, were under army control in order to ensure that the resolutely independent navy cooperated closely with its military operations.[25] Rodgers had recruited commanders and crews, secured armaments, and hired experienced civilian river pilots to navigate the tortuously difficult midcontinental waterways. But General George B. McClellan, commander of the army's Department of the Ohio, would decide when and how the gunboats were to be used.[26] To the disappointment of the troops at Cairo, McClellan deployed the flotilla initially as a defensive force, protecting that strategic river junction.

Months before the timberclads arrived at Cairo, the War Department had begun planning operations to reopen the Mississippi River from Cairo to New Orleans, and to use ironclad gunboats, the first in the western hemisphere, to spearhead the reconquest. It was the beginning of a new era in naval warfare.

In May 1861, U.S. General-in-Chief Winfield Scott put forward a plan to win the war by blockading the Confederacy's seaports along the Atlantic and the Gulf of Mexico and sending a tremendous amphibious force down the Mississippi—an army of eighty thousand carried by river steamers and led by "shot-proof" gunboats—to capture and hold the Confederacy's principal river ports and suppress enemy steamboat commerce on the Mississippi. This coordinated economic blockade—

the Anaconda Plan, the press called it—would close off the Confederacy to the rest of the world, slowly strangling it, like a giant snake suffocating its prey in its coils. The war would be won without a single major battle, Scott theorized.[27]

Scott's plan was never formally adopted, but the Union would employ a strategy roughly similar to it: a blue-water blockade by the saltwater fleet and a brown-water blockade by ironclad gunboats.[28]

From the first days of the war, building a gunboat fleet was an urgent priority for political leaders in the western states. The Mississippi was of "transcendent importance" to both the North and the South, wrote Adam Badeau, later in the war Grant's secretary and eventually his military biographer. "Its possession was by far the most magnificent prize for which the nation and the rebels were contending." Without it the Confederacy was "cut in twain"; without it "the North was crippled almost to its ruin."[29] Along with a rapidly expanding railroad network connecting Chicago, Cincinnati, and St. Louis with New York, Boston, and Philadelphia, the river was an outlet for the crops and livestock of northwestern farmers. After Fort Sumter, this "great highway pass," through the port of New Orleans, to overseas markets was in the hands of a "foreign power."[30]

That had become alarmingly clear three months before Sumter, when Mississippi governor John J. Pettus ordered a battery at Vicksburg to fire a warning shot at the steamer *A. O. Tyler* as it approached the town. "The people of the valley of the Mississippi will [never] consent that the great river shall flow for hundreds of miles through a foreign jurisdiction," proclaimed Governor Yates.[31] To Ohio-born William Tecumseh Sherman, the river was the "trunk of the American tree," the "spinal column of America." The side that commanded the Mississippi would win the war.[32]

"That river," proclaimed Missourian Edward Bates, Lincoln's attorney general, "is one and indivisible and *one* power will control it." In the very first weeks of the war, Bates had brought his friend James Eads, a St. Louis boat builder and self-taught engineer, to Washington to convince the government to build a fleet of ironclad gunboats to shield Cairo and mount aggressive operations from it.[33] Eads ran into entrenched opposition from army officials. Iron gunboats, they argued, would be "useless" in the west, where the rebels were constructing river forts capable of "knock[ing] the vessels to pieces."[34] But with Bates's persistent support, Eads won over the president and his cabinet to the idea that the Union would need an entirely new kind of navy to reconquer the Lower Mississippi Valley.[35]

In July, the War Department solicited bids for the construction of seven ironclad gunboats. The following month, Eads was awarded the contract. He would be the sole builder, but would work from the plans and specifications of Samuel Pook, Naval Constructor at the Washington Navy Yard. Pook sent Eads rough sketches of a flat-bottomed sidewheeler that drew only six feet of water, carried thirteen large-caliber guns, and was partially plated with two and a half inches of iron.[36] The "propelling power" was a large steam-driven paddlewheel, placed in a protected opening amidships, in the stern.[37] The hull was covered by casemate of heavy timber, faced with cast-iron plates on the sides and front half of the boat to protect the boilers and forward batteries. The casemate sloped outward and down at an angle of forty-five degrees, an engineering innovation designed to deflect cannon fire.[38] Atop the casemate was an iron-sheathed pilothouse. The long, low-sitting boats would be "creatures of the river itself." Pook's Turtles, they were dubbed, because the enclosing casemate looked like the shell of that aquatic creature.[39]

Eads also entered into a separate agreement with General John C. Frémont, McClellan's replacement as commander of federal forces in the west, to convert a Mississippi "snag boat," *Benton*, into the most powerful gunboat on western waters.[40] Snag boats were large steam-driven vessels designed to recover sunken steamboats and cargo from the bottoms of rivers. This was the business that had made James Buchanan Eads one of the richest men in the west before he was forty years old.

When Eads landed his government contract, he pledged to deliver all seven iron-plated boats at Cairo, ready for service, in sixty-five days. Iron vessels were nothing new. England and France had them, and both the U.S. and the Confederate navy were developing steam-driven ironclad warships in the summer of 1861: the turreted *Monitor*, designed by Swedish-born boat builder John Ericsson; and *Merrimack*, a federal frigate the rebels had raised from the bottom of Norfolk harbor and were turning into the ironclad ram *Virginia*. But no ironclad had yet been built for river warfare, and Eads had never worked with plate iron. Nor had he ever built a boat from scratch.

Within two weeks of securing his government contract, he had four thousand men working around the clock, seven days a week.[41] Eads purchased oak timber for his hulls from eight states, had mills in Ohio, Kentucky, and Missouri roll iron plates, and foundries in Pittsburgh and St. Louis hammer out steam engines and boilers. He then built a shipyard at Carondelet, a river port seven miles south of St. Louis. Carpenters there laid the keels for four of his gunboats. The other three were built at Mound City, Illinois, on the Ohio River just east of Cairo. When government payments for the work were repeatedly delayed, Eads poured in his own money. When that was exhausted, he borrowed from friends.[42]

Commander Rodgers oversaw the project for the government. When the work fell behind schedule, Frémont replaced him in the first week of September with a tougher taskmaster, Captain Andrew Hull Foote.[43] A midshipman and an officer for almost forty years, with service along the African coast suppressing the slave trade he despised, Foote was one of the most aggressive commanders in the United States Navy. "Foote had more of the bulldog than any man I ever knew," recalled a fellow officer. "[W]hen the fighting came . . . he was in his element—he liked it."[44] Foote "feared no one but his God," said a sailor who served under him.[45]

A militant Christian and a temperance crusader—"a naval Savonarola"—he delivered fire-and-brimstone sermons to his crews at obligatory Sabbath services and forbade "profane swearing" on board ship.[46] Foote was "ordinarily, one of the most amiable . . . of men," James Eads described him, ". . . but when angered . . . his face impressed me as being most savage and demoniacal."[47] He was in a permanently foul mood in his first months at Cairo and Mound City, infuriated by bureaucratic delays in Washington that prevented Eads from completing the ironclads on schedule.[48] That November, he persuaded Secretary Welles to promote him to the newly created rank of flag officer, the equivalent of an army major general. This gave him additional authority to move construction along and recruit crews made up of an odd and never sufficient allotment of navy jack-tars from the East, civilian freshwater sailors from the Great Lakes, steamboat hands from western rivers, New Bedford whalers, and foot soldiers reassigned to river service.[49] "We want men," Foote wrote the War Department in December.[50]

The first Mississippi ironclad, *St. Louis*, was completed at Carondelet in early October, but not until the following January were all seven of Eads's gunboats fully armed and commissioned for combat.[51] All were named, like *St. Louis*, after river towns: *Cairo, Carondelet, Mound City, Louisville, Pittsburgh*, and *Cincinnati*.[52] The formidable *Benton*, Foote's command vessel, joined the seven "city-class" boats at Cairo.[53] These eight ironclads became the workhorses of a western river squadron that would number over one hundred vessels by the end of the war. Forced to fight "a slow, dirty, sand bar kind of a war," the menacing looking iron monsters, all painted a dull black, were more dreaded by the rebels than their achievements warranted but were, nonetheless, among the most effective warships afloat in the Civil War.[54]

Tied up near Eads's gunboats at Cairo in January 1862 were thirty-eight partially constructed mortar boats, flat-bottomed rafts with protective wooden bulwarks, each craft designed to carry a 13-inch mortar with a range of 4,300 yards. They were siege guns, designed for use against enemy river fortifications and towns. General Frémont had authorized their construction, and President Lincoln had taken a personal interest in them, pushing hard for their development. They would remain moored at Cairo for a few more months while their mortars were tested and mounted, their magazine chests waterproofed, and river steamers rigged to tow them.[55]

That January, as Foote prepared to take Eads's ironclads into battle, he knew that they were far from invincible. Iron protected only the front two-thirds of the boats, the expectation being that they would fight head-on, showing only their iron faces to the enemy. Pook's Turtles were also dangerously slow, with a top speed of only six knots, making it difficult, sometimes impossible, for them to successfully battle strong currents. They were effective only when attacking downriver.

There were other vulnerabilities. The sloped casemates could only deflect fire traveling in a low arc, as from other gunboats. Fire from high bluffs had a fair chance of penetrating their protective shells. Plunging fire could also cut through the thin wooden decks of the casemates, killing and injuring crew and fatally damaging machinery. One well-aimed shot could knock out a ship's boiler, scalding crewmen with fiercely hot steam.

The thinly plated pilothouse was the most dangerous yet important station on the vessel. "To kill the pilot would be equivalent to disabling the vessel," wrote Henry Walke, a commander in Foote's fleet.[56] Disease would also become a problem, unforeseen by either Pook or Eads. In southern climes, summer temperatures would rise to over one hundred degrees inside the enclosed casemate, and crews would be packed together in foul air while fighting, eating, and sleeping. Under these conditions, one sailor's contagious disease could bring down dozens of his mates. Over the course of the river war, it was not uncommon for up to half of a gunboat's crew to be on sick leave.[57]

The first naval officers sent west hated river service—"resented stepping down from gallant men-of-war with their pitching decks and salt spray to 'tubs' operating in the muddy waters of the Mississippi."[58] They were, moreover, reduced to apprentices in the perilous, ever-changing western rivers, dependent upon seasoned civilian pilots for guidance in waters bristling with hidden snags and sandbars and channels too shallow to navigate. In early 1862, no saltwater officer was fully prepared to command a Mississippi gunboat. But Andrew Foote was a man built to surmount obstacles.

Unlike Rodgers, he was convinced that the navy's war on the western waters could be won only by close cooperation with the army. The rival services had to be "like blades of shears—united, invincible; separated, almost useless."[59]

In November 1861, when Andrew Foote sent *St. Louis* to Cairo to be fitted out with guns, waiting on the levee to greet her was Ulysses S. Grant, the new commander of the army gathered there. Though he and Foote had yet to meet, Grant was an equally ardent advocate of joint operations.[60] James Eads's black boats—long, low, and built for quick-striking warfare—would soon make him the western army's preeminent river warrior.

CHAPTER 2

River Warrior

"The River must *be opened."* [1]

—Ulysses S. Grant

When Ulysses Grant arrived at Cairo on September 2, 1861, not a soul was at the rail station to greet him and no one at headquarters knew anything about him, other than rumors that he had a weakness for whiskey.

Grant had recently been promoted from colonel to brigadier general and had not had time to purchase a uniform befitting his new rank. He presented himself at the headquarters of Colonel Richard J. Oglesby, temporary commander at Cairo, dressed in an ill-fitting business suit, his long chestnut-brown beard uncombed and greatly in need of a trim. He was an unimpressive man, short, slight, and slouch-shouldered— five foot eight inches tall and weighing just over 130 pounds—and was painfully shy in social company.

Oglesby's headquarters was in a bank building on the town's Ohio River levee. The room was crowded and alive with activity when Grant entered unannounced and unnoticed. He quietly introduced himself, but Oglesby apparently did not catch the name and paid no attention to him. Grant waited a few minutes and then picked up a piece of paper from the table where Oglesby was seated and wrote out an order assuming command of the military district of Southeast Missouri, which also included southern Illinois. Oglesby stared at it incredulously, gave the stranger a long look, and "surrendered the office." [2] Thirty-nine-year-old Ulysses Simpson Grant was exactly where he wanted to be: commanding men and war boats on the Mississippi.

Grant arrived with a fierce resolve to carry the war deep into the Confederacy. While stationed at Ironton, Missouri, his first major posting since leaving his home in Galena, Illinois, he would sit for hours at a pine table outside his rustic headquarters, his hat pulled down over his face, studying a map of the midcontinent and marking with a thick red crayon the principal southern rivers—the Tennessee, the Cumberland, and the Mississippi—that he hoped to turn into invasion routes for Union amphibious expeditions. "The rebels *must* be driven out," he would tell John Wesley Emerson, an Ironton lawyer who owned the land on which Grant made his headquarters and would visit him frequently. "The rivers *must* be opened."

Peering over Grant's shoulder, Emerson noticed that strategically important places that the rebels controlled were marked with large red crosses: chief among them, Columbus, Kentucky; Forts Donelson and Henry on the border between Tennessee and Kentucky; Nashville; Memphis; and Vicksburg. "I was amazed at such a sudden plunge into the heart of the Confederacy," Emerson recalled, "when we were every hour fearing the Confederates would be upon us . . . in Missouri!"[3]

In his first week at Cairo, Grant advanced on one of the places he had marked on his map. On September 5, he learned from a Union spy that General Leonidas Polk, stationed in Tennessee, was casting a covetous eye on Columbus, Kentucky, a rail center that sat on high bluffs overlooking the Mississippi, twenty miles south of Cairo. Tall, ramrod-straight Polk, the "Fighting Bishop," had graduated near the top of his West Point class but left the army to enter the ministry, rising to become bishop of the Episcopal diocese of Louisiana. When war broke out, Jefferson Davis, beguiled by his early promise, convinced him to join the Confederate army as a major general.

On September 5, his troops captured Columbus, threw a chain across the river to impede navigation, and installed 140 guns on the river bluffs. The invasion was a brazen violation of Kentucky's neutrality and was one of the great blunders of the war, helping to swing the state legislature "from lukewarm to warlike unionism."[4] But Polk saw it at the time as a masterful strategic move and followed it up by sending a raiding party under Brigadier General Gideon Pillow to seize Paducah, a small Ohio River port in the northwest corner of the state. Paducah was even more important than Columbus, and Grant—raised in the Ohio basin and a master of military maps—understood this.

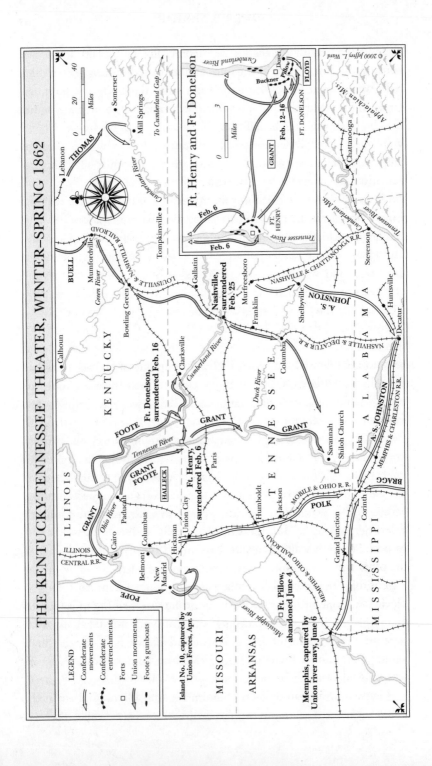

THE KENTUCKY-TENNESSEE THEATER, WINTER–SPRING 1862

Ft. Henry and Ft. Donelson

© 2000 Jeffrey L. Ward

Situated forty-five miles northeast of Cairo, at a point where the northward-flowing Tennessee River emptied into the Ohio and just ten miles below where the Cumberland River reached the Ohio, Paducah, in rebel hands, could block his future access to these rivers. Grant saw the Cumberland as a riverine highway to Nashville, a Confederate rail and industrial center; while the Tennessee, which ran nearly parallel to and only a few miles apart from it, stretched all the way into northern Alabama. If he could take Paducah, both rivers would be open to Union amphibious forces stationed at Cairo under his and Foote's command.[5] "There [is] no time for delay," Grant alerted his staff, no time to wait for orders from Major General John C. Frémont, commander of federal forces in the west.[6] Telegraphing Frémont that he would proceed unless ordered otherwise, Grant loaded two regiments and a battery of artillery onto navy transports and headed for Paducah that evening. In the lead were the timberclads *Tyler* and *Conestoga*, commanded by Andrew Foote.[7]

The Federals reached Paducah early the next morning. The town was crawling with Southern sympathizers and rebel flags were hoisted to welcome Pillow's men, expected that afternoon. Grant had his troops disembark. Battle flags aloft, they marched to the drums of their regimental bands and took possession of the town without firing a shot. "I never saw such consternation depicted on the faces of . . . people," Grant wrote afterward. "Men, women and children came out of their doors looking pale and frightened at the presence of the invader." Grant tried to allay their worst fears. He had come, he assured the rebel-leaning population in a short proclamation, to "protect them from the enemies of our country," and he offered them "the protection" of the federal government. "This was evidently a relief to them," he said in retrospect, "but the majority would have much preferred the presence of the other army."[8]

His mission accomplished in a matter of hours, Grant left troops to block the roads leading into town, positioned one of the gunboats to guard the riverfront, and headed back to Cairo. He arrived at four that afternoon, less than twenty-four hours after he had left.[9] On his desk was a telegram from Frémont authorizing him to seize Paducah "if you feel strong enough."[10]

Grant's occupation of Paducah "didn't look like much" at the time, noted historian E. B. Long, but "it is possible, even probable, that the whole future of the war in the West was altered by this, Grant's first major action." If the Confederates had been permitted to hold the Ohio and Mississippi River line from Columbus to Paducah, the Federals would not have been able to advance to the head of the Cumberland and Tennessee Rivers in 1862, and Northern shipping on the Ohio "would have been severed." The northern boundary of the Confederacy would have been on the Ohio River, not farther south at Columbus.[11]

Pillow's raiders returned to Columbus when word reached them as they neared the town that Paducah was in Union hands. Later that month, the Kentucky state legislature voted to expel the rebel invaders from the state, a move that caused the pro-secessionist governor to resign and help form a provisional government, which the Confederate congress admitted into the Confederacy as its thirteenth state.[12] Kentucky would be divided for the remainder of the war, but Paducah remained a Union-controlled town.

To more tightly secure it, Grant sent reinforcements and assigned Brigadier General Charles Ferguson Smith, the commandant at West Point when he was a cadet, to command the post. Smith then sent a force to occupy the village of Smithland, at the mouth of the Cumberland.[13] If Union forces were to go down that river they could be supplied from this conveniently located post.

C. F. Smith would serve Grant superbly all the way to Shiloh. A veteran of nearly forty years of military service, he found himself in the uncomfortable position of reporting to his former pupil. Considered one of the finest officers in the regular army, Smith was Grant's mentor and model, his beau ideal of a soldier: grim and courageous, poised and professional. The two looked incongruously unlike. At six foot three, Smith towered over Grant, and his regal equipage and crisply pressed uniform made Grant look like "a dumpy and slouchy little subaltern," as Captain Charles Francis Adams Jr. later described him.[14] Smith "had the bearing of a marshal of France," said Brigadier General Lew Wallace, an Indiana officer who would serve under him. "He could ride along a line of volunteers in the regulation uniform of a brigadier-general— plume, chapeau, epaulets and all, without exciting laughter—something nobody else could do in the beginning of the war."[15]

Erect and perfectly proportioned, with a ruddy complexion and a snow-white mustache that hung below his chin, he exuded health, energy, and strength. Grant, by contrast, was tormented by recurring headaches and colds, and he rarely looked completely well. "It does not seem quite right for me to give General Smith orders," Grant confided to his staff.[16] When it was necessary, he did so deferentially, signing the orders: "Very Respectfully, Your Obedient Servant." But Smith's conviviality made it easy for Grant to work with him. "I am now a subordinate," Smith told Grant, "I know a soldier's duty. I hope you will feel no awkwardness about our new relations."[17]

Smith swore often and with virtuosic skill; Grant never swore. Smith drank heavily and with delight and could hold his liquor. Grant struggled not to drink, and when he did, he drank alone or with close friends and became inebriated easily. Surmounting these differences was Smith's instinct for battle, a trait teacher and pupil shared. "Battle is the ultimate to which the whole life's labor of an officer should be directed," Smith once said.[18]

In the summer of 1861 "every eye was looking for the Coming Man," wrote the *New York Tribune*'s Albert Richardson, "every ear listening for his approaching footsteps, which would make the earth tremble. The impression was almost universal throughout the North that the war was to be very brief" and that some great commander would decide its course.[19] Grant's "quiet earnestness, which seemed to 'mean business,' won greatly upon me," Richardson recalled upon their first meeting, "but kindled no suspicion that he was the Coming Man."[20]

No one could have suspected that this untried commander who had yet to overmaster a succession of soul-crushing personal setbacks would become, in a matter of months, the first Union hero of the war—and in less than two years the conqueror of Vicksburg. "Grant's life is, in some ways, the most remarkable one in American history," wrote historian T. Harry Williams. "There is no other quite like it."[21]

He was born in a small one-story cabin in the village of Point Pleasant, Ohio, near Cincinnati on April 27, 1822, the eldest son of Jesse Root Grant and Hannah Simpson, parents with clashing temperaments— Jesse forceful and outspoken, Hanna serene and self-contained. Baptized as Hiram Ulysses Grant, he was called Ulysses, never Hiram, by family and friends. Raised in Georgetown, Ohio, where his Methodist family moved a year after his birth, he attended local schools and worked for a time in his father's tannery, a place he detested because he could not stand the sight or smell of blood.[22] He insisted always that his meat be cooked to a crisp; as a general, visiting field hospitals filled with mangled men would be difficult duty for him.

Never a first-rate student, he did, however, possess a retentive memory, absorbing information "like a sponge," said classmates.[23] He loved horses and rode them expertly, but "was the most unmilitary of boys in a military age," wrote novelist Hamlin Garland, author of an outstanding early biography of Grant. "He had small love for guns, could not bear to see things killed, and was neither a hunter nor a fighter."[24]

He was proud of, but not emotionally close to, his father, an enterprising frontiersman who prospered in business, built a comfortable brick house, and became mayor of Georgetown. A disciple of Henry Clay, the "Great Compromiser," Jesse opposed the expansion of slavery into the western territories; so did his son.

Jesse was tall, strong, and "alive to his finger-tips." Bombastic and hard driving, he was both "disliked and respected" by locals. His slender wife was one of the "best beloved women of the town," admired for her "steadiness of purpose" and "equable temper," characteristics she passed on to her son.[25] When Ulysses turned seventeen, Jesse arranged his appointment to West Point with a local congressman, without his son's knowledge or approval. "I won't go," Grant remembered telling his father. "He said he thought I would, *and I thought so too, if he did.*"[26]

The congressman who nominated him had bungled his name on the appointment document, and the adjutant at the academy refused to correct the error. He would go out into the world as Ulysses Simpson Grant. His fellow cadets turned his initials, U.S., to Uncle Sam, and began calling him Sam. It stuck and became his army name.

An indifferent student with an independent streak, he spent hours in the library devouring books outside the curriculum: the adventure novels of Washington Irving, Walter Scott, and James Fennimore Cooper. He gave his full attention only to the subjects he loved—math and drawing—and graduated a lackluster 21st in a class of 39. His friends described him as "markedly unmilitary," but he possessed two attributes that would serve him superbly in the army: an instinctive feel for topography and peerless horsemanship.[27] The "great student of maps" would become an outstanding military strategist, and his equestrian skill would save his life on the battlefield on at least two occasions.[28] Grant could tame and manage the most fractious animal, and he set a jumping record at West Point that stood for decades. "There was something mysterious in his powers to communicate to a horse his wishes," wrote Garland, who interviewed Grant's friends and family for his biography.[29] In its inimitable wisdom, the army assigned him to the infantry, not the cavalry.

After serving his obligatory term in the military, his great goal was to become an assistant professor of mathematics at "some respectable college."[30] Two circumstances, however, changed the direction of his life: He found a woman, and a war found him. Posted at Jefferson Barracks, just outside St. Louis, Grant would ride out frequently to White Haven, the impressive country home of his West Point classmate Frederick Dent Jr., whose father, Frederick Sr., was a slaveowning planter—a self-proclaimed "Colonel"—and an ardent Confederate sympathizer. On these visits Grant met and soon fell in love with the Colonel's oldest daughter, Julia. She shared his passion for horses and breakneck rides in the open countryside. Before Grant could convince the Colonel to allow a miserably paid lieutenant to marry his favorite daughter, he was ordered to join an army being assembled by General Zachary Taylor in western Louisiana in May 1844. Taylor was there to compel Mexico to accept American annexation of Texas, an independent republic in the process of becoming a U.S. state.

Grant served as a quartermaster in a war he would come to consider "one of the most unjust ever waged by a stronger against a weaker nation." President James K. Polk, a Tennessean, had pulled the country into it to acquire territories from Mexico that could eventually come into the union as slave states.[31] Not content to stay in the rear keeping his regiment supplied, Grant would regularly ride to the front without orders; he distinguished himself under fire, receiving two brevet promotions for gallantry. In house-to-house fighting at Monterrey, his regiment ran low on ammunition and he volunteered to deliver an urgent call for supplies through sniper-infested streets. He got through "without a scratch," riding full out, Comanche-style, hanging on the side of his mount with one foot hooked on the cantle of the saddle and an arm around the horse's neck.[32] "You want to know what my feelings were on the field of battle!" he wrote an Ohio friend. "I do not know that I felt any peculiar sensation. War seems much less horrible to persons engaged in it than to those who read of the battles."[33] He never changed.

After the war, he returned to St. Louis and married Julia, having secured her father's approval while serving in Mexico. Unable to land a professorship, Grant remained in the army and was stationed at Sackets Harbor, New York, on the inhospitable eastern shore of Lake Ontario, where he drank enough to convince himself to take the pledge in 1851 and join a local chapter of the Sons of Temperance. "I have become convinced that there is no safety from ruin by liquor except by abstaining from it altogether."[34] The next year he was posted to the West Coast, winding up eventually, in 1854, at Fort Humboldt, located in a picturesque but isolated corner of northern California. Julia stayed behind with her parents to await the birth of their second child, Ulysses Jr. (The first of their four children, Frederick, was born in 1850.) "You do not know how forsaken I feel here!" he wrote Julia. Desperately lonely, repeatedly sick with the chills and fever, and assaulted by migraine headaches, he began to drink heavily and was caught inebriated while on duty. There is strong but not incontrovertible evidence that his stiff-necked commanding officer, Major Robert C. Buchanan, gave him an ultimatum: face a court-martial or resign.[35] On April 11, 1854, the very day he received notice of his promotion to captain, Grant resigned and later rejoined Julia and the children in St. Louis, "moneyless and disheartened."[36]

Grant failed to mention the alleged drinking incident either in his correspondence or his memoirs, but during the Vicksburg campaign he confessed to army chaplain John Eaton: "The vice of intemperance had not a little to do with my decision to resign."[37] At age thirty-two, Grant set about farming on sixty acres of unimproved land Colonel Dent had given Julia as a wedding present. He facetiously called the modest log house he built on that unpromising land "Hardscrabble"— and that it was. With the help of William Jones, a mulatto slave he purchased from his father-in-law, and a handful of free black men—whom he paid excessively and worked without sufficient "severity," according to disapproving neighbors—he planted potatoes, oats, and corn, and sold firewood from the farm on St. Louis street corners.[38] Neighbors told Hamlin Garland that "Grant was helpless when it came to making slaves work. . . . He couldn't force them to do anything. He wouldn't whip them. . . . He was too gentle and good tempered—and besides, he was not a slavery man."[39]

Peddling wood in St. Louis, dressed in a seedy army overcoat, Grant occasionally ran into old military friends. "Great God, Grant, what are you doing?" asked an officer who had served with him in Mexico. "I am solving the problem of poverty," Grant replied sadly.[40]

He cut back on his drinking and worked furiously, but was forced to quit farming during the Panic of 1857, which disastrously depressed commodity prices. Grant was "a dead cock in a pit"—William Tecumseh Sherman's description of himself in that year.[41] Sherman had left the army to become a banker and lost everything in the economic calamity that took down Grant. After accidentally running into Grant in St. Louis in 1857, the former classmates concurred: "West Point and the Regular Army were not good schools for farmers [and] bankers."[42]

That winter, Grant had to pawn his gold watch to buy Christmas presents for his family.[43] Selling William Jones at auction for the going price of over one thousand dollars would have greatly enhanced his economic circumstances, but Grant freed him before moving his family to St. Louis.[44] Julia may have objected. She saw nothing wrong with slavery. Grant had no settled views on the morality of slavery, but one of Frederick Dent's slaves, Mary Robinson, recalled that he made it clear to the Colonel, within earshot of the house servants, that "he wanted to give his wife's slaves their freedom as soon as possible."[45]

In St. Louis, Grant went into the real estate business with Julia's nephew Harry Boggs. The partnership broke up after nine months. Grant was temperamentally unsuited for either salesmanship or collecting rents. He was too honest to be successful in a "business of that sort," said a local lawyer. "I don't believe that he knows what dishonesty is."[46] Grant next found work as a clerk in the local United States customs house, but the collector died a month later and the new political appointee fired the entire staff. Grant was back on the street without money or prospects. Colonel Dent, who had slaves and land but almost no liquidity, was in no position to help.

"He was a sad man. I never heard him laugh out loud," Boggs's wife described Grant at this time. "I don't think he had any ambition further than to feed and clothe his little family."[47] This became doubly difficult because he continued to be afflicted by high fevers and shivering fits—ague, it was called at the time. In every way, he was a broken man. "The eager, erect, hopeful and ambitious youth of the Mexican War had become a prematurely bent, care-worn, and somber man of thirty-five," Garland wrote.[48]

At Julia's urging, he turned to his father, now a moderately wealthy tanner and merchant in Covington, Kentucky.[49] Jesse owned a leather store in Galena, a thriving lead-mining town in western Illinois, across the Mississippi River from Iowa. Grant's younger brothers, Orvil and Simpson, ran the store, and, at Jesse's instigation, they took Ulysses on as a sales clerk and purchasing agent, one of over fifty employees in a burgeoning business with retail outlets all over the northwest. Simpson was critically ill with tuberculosis, and Jesse, no doubt, hoped Ulysses would replace him as comanager after his death.

On an April morning in 1860, Ulysses, Julia, and their four children boarded a Mississippi steamboat for Galena, not suspecting that the worst times were behind them. Years later, when the family was residing in the White House, Grant would tell an old acquaintance why he had agreed to become a store clerk at age thirty-eight, the only one of his West Point classmates to fall so far. "I was doing the best I could to support my family."[50]

The Grant family took up residence in a two-story brick house they rented not far from the leather store and the large Methodist church they attended, with its imposing conical tower. Slavery had been outlawed in Illinois, so before leaving Missouri, Julia hired out the four young household slaves her father had presented her and did the cooking and housework with the help of a paid servant. Though her husband drew only a meager salary, "it was enough, and we were happy," she wrote later. By all accounts he remained sober in these Galena years.[51] For the first time in years, Grant found contentment—not on the job, which he loathed, but at home with his family. In the evenings he would playfully wrestle on the floor with his young boys. After Julia led the children off to bed, he'd sit with her and read aloud from the newspapers about the approaching secession crisis, puffing on his long-stemmed meerschaum pipe while Julia did her sewing.

Grant had no close friends and had a distant relationship with his brothers. Like his mother, Hannah, "he had a quiet way of keeping people at arm's length," and an aversion to disclosing his emotions to everyone but Julia. He loved his mother but she never opened herself to him, nor did he to her. "We are not a demonstrative family," she told a reporter late in her life. Grant said he never saw his mother shed a tear.[52]

Ulysses Grant was made by war. Galena did not save him; the war did. Had he died in 1860, "he would have been remembered only as a pure, shy, kindly gentleman of moderate abilities," wrote journalist Albert Richardson, one of his first biographers.[53]

Politically, Grant was on the fence when the war broke out, a luke-warm Democrat who had voted in only one presidential election—in 1856, for James Buchanan. He had feared that the election of John C. Frémont, the Republican Party's first presidential candidate, would provoke the South to secede. As a new resident of Illinois, he was not yet eligible to vote in the 1860 elections. Had he cast a ballot, it would have been for the Democrat, Stephen A. Douglas of Illinois, the champion of popular sovereignty—the right of western territories appealing for statehood to determine by free elections whether they would permit or prohibit slavery. But when Fort Sumter was attacked on April 12, 1861, Grant threw his support enthusiastically to Lincoln and the Union. "Now is the time, particularly in the Border slave states, for men to prove their love of country," he wrote his father-in-law, who was leaning strongly toward the Confederacy, "No impartial man can conceal from himself the fact that in all these troubles the South have been the aggressors."[54]

Grant was drawn into the war after attending a Union meeting in Galena. There he met attorney John A. Rawlins, the vehement son of a failed charcoal burner who had died an alcoholic. Rawlins impressed him tremendously. Slender and erect, with jet-black hair, a full dark beard, and flashing eyes, he stood up unannounced at the meeting and gave a stirring forty-five minute peroration to the Union. "The time for compromise ha[s] passed . . . we must appeal to the God of Battles to vindicate our flag." [55]

"I never went into our leather store after that meeting, to put up a package or to do other business," Grant said later. [56]

The war energized Grant. "He dropped a stoop-shouldered way of walking, and set his hat forward on his forehead in a careless fashion," Rawlins recalled. [57] The only man in Galena with professional military experience, Grant organized a local militia company but declined to put himself forward as a candidate for captain, hoping to serve in a larger way. After escorting his unruly recruits to Springfield, the state capital, he stayed on, at the request of Governor Richard Yates, to raise and muster in additional volunteers. All the while, he sought a permanent commission, writing to the adjutant general of the army to offer his services "in such capacity as may be offered." He made it emphatically clear, however, that he was "competent to command a Regiment." [58] Receiving no reply, he traveled to Cincinnati to try to land a position on the staff of Major General George B. McClellan, commander of Ohio volunteers. He had known him "slightly" from West Point and Mexico, but McClellan had him wait for two days, then refused to see him. Grant returned to Springfield, where Yates appointed him colonel of the Twenty-first regiment of Illinois infantry. [59]

After taking out a loan from a Galena bank to purchase a horse and a dress uniform appropriate to his new rank, Grant marched his boys into northeast Missouri to hunt down a band of rebel partisans. [60] In Missouri, he bounced around from command to command, without fighting a single battle, but while in St. Louis visiting his former real estate partner, Grant read in a newspaper that he had been nominated to be a brigadier general by President Lincoln, a surprisingly sudden promotion for a recently appointed colonel with a sullied prewar service record. Frémont, who had met Grant only twice, had recommended the promotion, but Grant's congressman and Galena neighbor, Elihu B. Washburne, whom Grant knew only casually, may have given Lincoln, a close friend of many years, a "gentle nudge." [61] Orders followed to take command of the District of Southeast Missouri, with headquarters in Cairo, southern Illinois being part of his jurisdiction.

Grant asked thirty-year-old John Rawlins to join him as his assistant adjutant general—i.e., chief of staff—with the rank of captain. Grant

hardly knew him—he spelled his name "Rollins" in a letter to Julia—
but since that Galena rally he had felt a strong emotional affinity with
him.[62] Rawlins would be the first to see his fellow townsman as "a man
of destiny."[63]

"From the occupation of Paducah up to the early part of November,
nothing important occurred with the troops under my command,"
Grant would later write in his memoirs.[64] That is not right. During this
very time Grant turned Cairo into a forward base for offensive operations on western waters. By early November, he had twenty thousand
men in his command, all untested volunteers, sons of the west eager for
action, thoroughly sick of the mud and misery at Cairo. This was the
nucleus of the mighty Army of the Tennessee Grant would send against
Fort Donelson and Vicksburg.[65] "Grant came into his own in Cairo,"
writes biographer William S. McFeely.[66] There he developed his style
of command. "Grant at Cairo was not an assertive man; didn't interfere with small affairs," recalled an associate, but he did look for "big
results" and wasted little time on "formalities."[67] He did most things on
his own, rarely consulting staff members and division commanders, or
even his new post commander, General John A. McClernand, a former
Democratic congressman from Illinois whom Grant knew only slightly
at the time, but would play a prominent part in his Mississippi Valley
campaign.[68]

Grant loathed office work, preferring to be in the camps with his
men, supervising their training. Unavoidably, however, much of his
work was done at headquarters: ordering rifles, tents, maps, rations,
and proper uniforms, the things that made up "the spirit of an army."
Having served in Mexico under immensely efficient General Zachary
Taylor, he knew "that a commander had to be an administrator as well
as a fighter."[69] Grant did this obligatory office work silently and deliberately, sometimes alone, well into the night, smoking his clay pipe, the
only noise in the room the scratching his pen made on paper.

Grant would become one of the outstanding prose writers of his
century, and it was at Cairo that he first developed the taut, vigorous
style of his *Personal Memoirs*, which Mark Twain considered the finest
military work since the *Commentaries* of Julius Caesar.[70] "I only knew

what was in my mind, and I wished to express it clearly": That was Grant's entire intention when he picked up pen or pencil.[71] From the beginning of the war he wrote fluidly and with ease, putting to paper exactly what he intended to say without wasting a word. "Grant was a ready writer," recalled Major John H. Brinton, the army surgeon who shared an office with him at Cairo. "He wrote tersely, rapidly, and very rarely struck out or altered." We see Grant's mature style emerging in his earliest dispatches and reports—diamond-hard sentences without a trace of ambiguity.

Unlike most Civil War generals, Grant did not delegate the drafting of orders and dispatches to staff officers. (Rawlins was an abysmal writer.) If someone whom he trusted happened to be in his office, he would read a sentence or two aloud and ask for an opinion. Brinton once suggested that Grant's concluding paragraph of an official report seemed too abrupt. Grant reread it deliberately, putting every sentence on trial for its life. "So it is," he said; and when he added a line or two he looked visibly pleased.[72] But mostly he worked in a cocoon of concentration, so intently focused that he remained hunched in a seating position when he rose from his chair to retrieve a document from across the room.

Grant spoke as he wrote: only when necessary, and then incisively. When Colonel John "Black Jack" Logan, a former congressman from southern Illinois, introduced Grant to Franc B. Wilkie, Grant shook the reporter's hand "heartily, pulled on the stump of a cigar, and said nothing."[73]

But Grant opened up around friends he could trust. "If you could get him talking, he was one of the most entertaining talkers I ever listened to," said a Galena man who served with him.[74] Relaxing with his staff in the evening hours, whittling with his pocketknife, he enjoyed listening to humorous stories, even ones spiced with racy language, though he was never known to tell an off-color joke or utter a profanity himself. "Gen. Grant never swears," said a *New York Times* reporter. "No man in his camp has ever heard him give utterance to profanity."[75] Rawlins's vocabulary was "picturesque and unrighteous," said Samuel H. Beckwith, Grant's telegraph operator. He and Sherman "could outswear any two officers in the army."[76] If Grant disapproved, he never showed it.

Later in the war, Grant explained to General Horace Porter why he never swore, even when things went horribly wrong on the battlefield. "I have always noticed . . . that swearing helps to rouse a man's anger; and when a man flies into passion his adversary who keeps cool always gets the better of him."[77]

He was hard to arouse to either laughter or anger, but he had "a dry way of saying things that oftentimes brought smiles" to those around him, recalled Beckwith.[78] "When he was about to say anything amusing, there was always a perceptible twinkle in his eyes before he began to speak and he often laughed heartily at a witty remark or a humorous incident."[79] He picked up these traits—his reticence, his iron self-control, and his aversion to using foul language—from his mother, Hannah. His vaulting ambition and occasional recklessness came from his father, Jesse, a gambler in frontier enterprises he'd built from scratch.[80]

Ulysses Grant saw his first Civil War combat at Belmont, Missouri, a steamboat landing and rebel encampment directly across the Mississippi from Columbus, Kentucky, at that time a more formidable river garrison than Vicksburg. Frémont had grown cautious after Leonidas Polk fortified Columbus's bluffs with heavy artillery pieces and had ordered Grant not to bring on a battle at or near what was considered "the strongest bastion on the continent."[81] But Grant was spoiling for a fight, eager for a chance to demonstrate his worth and test his untried men. Belmont, located just downriver from Cairo, was a convenient target. Rebel troops from Columbus were gathering there, Grant believed, preparing to move deeper into Missouri. But in striking Belmont, he would be openly disobeying the general to whom he owed his Cairo command. Grant thought it worth the risk.

On November 1, he was freed to go downriver with his troops in the vicinity of Columbus to conduct a series of "demonstrations . . . without, however, attacking the enemy."[82] Frémont was pursuing Confederate forces in southeast Missouri and hoped Grant's threatening movements would prevent Polk from "sending a force to fall in the rear" of his armies. Grant had other ideas; he wanted to "menace" Belmont, he confided to General C. F. Smith, and "drive . . . out of Missouri" enemy reinforcements assembling there.[83]

Grant was operating with undue haste and without reliable intelligence. The rebel column assembling at Belmont comprised only one undersized regiment of infantry. And unknown to Grant, Polk had no intention of sending reinforcements into Missouri.[84]

On November 6, Grant left Cairo with five regiments, two companies of cavalry, and a six-cannon battery. The 3,100 troops were packed into six steamers supported by the timberclads *Tyler* and *Lexington*, under the direction of Commander Henry Walke. The troops had no idea where they were going; neither did Walke.[85] Only C. F. Smith knew that they were about to strike Belmont.[86]

After tying up for the night on the Kentucky shore, out of range of the big guns at Columbus, Grant landed his troops at first light at Hunter's Point, three miles above Belmont. The gunboats engaged Polk's batteries, providing covering fire for the regiments as they marched southward, their 64-pounders roaring like blasts of thunder.

In his memoirs, Grant claimed he left Cairo with no intention of attacking Belmont but had reconsidered while on the river, not wanting to disappoint his men, "who were elated at the opportunity of doing what they had volunteered to do—fight the enemies of their country."[87] The record fails to support him. He had gone downstream looking for a fight.

The autumn morning broke clear and crisp, and when rebel scouts spotted the Yankee flotilla at Hunter's Point around seven o'clock, Polk ferried heavy reinforcements, under Gideon Pillow, to Belmont. They were there in battle lines when Grant arrived with his raw volunteers, most of them Illinois and Iowa farm boys.

The opposing forces were equally matched, five regiments and one battery on each side, but the morning belonged entirely to the Federals, who smashed the rebel center and swept into the Confederate camp, cheering and shouting oaths, "driving the enemy before them, storming their guns, and taking them."[88] When a bullet struck and killed Grant's horse, one of his aides speedily provided a replacement. The rebels escaped to the river in disarray, taking shelter behind its low earthen banks.

At that very moment of triumph, Grant lost control of his troops. His regiments became a rabble and began to loot and pillage the enemy tents in search of "trophies." Other soldiers gathered around their regimental bands and began singing "Yankee Doodle" and "The Star-Spangled Banner" as the Stars and Stripes was "unfurled in the face of the foe, and defiantly supplant[ed] the mongrel colors."[89] General John McClernand, a politician known for his bombastic flights of oratory, stopped to congratulate his men on a stirring victory.[90] "The higher officers were little better than the privates," Grant described the antics of McClernand and other commanders. "They galloped about from one cluster of men to another and at every halt delivered a short eulogy upon the Union cause."[91]

Grant was unable to restore order. "The men had done their day's work and did not care much about further fighting," recalled Major Brinton, the ranking surgeon of the command.[92] Alerted by Brinton, Grant looked toward the river and spotted two steamers "black . . . with soldiers from boiler-deck to roof" approaching from Columbus. Grant sprang into action, ordering his officers to set fire to the rebel tents so as to stop the looting and celebrating.

When the cross-river reinforcements landed, they merged with the instantly emboldened rebels on the riverbank and, supported by crushing fire from guns at Columbus, cut off Grant's forces from their transports at Hunter's Point. Grant's panicked officers were ready to raise the white flag. Grant stopped them. "We . . . cut our way in and [will] cut our way out."[93]

Grant and Black Jack Logan led the fight back to the boats. Brinton followed with the wounded. The gray-clad enemy was in front of them, but the retreating Unionists managed to push through, the rebels being as new to war and as frightened as they were. "It was only through terror that [we] were able to move at all," recalled a Union artillerist.[94]

Grant was the last man to reach the steamers. As he would learn later, General Polk had spotted him with his spyglass from across the river, a solitary horseman in an open field. " 'There is a Yankee; you may try your marksmanship on him if you wish,' " he said to his staff. No one did.[95]

As Grant's sweat-soaked horse drew near the headquarters boat, *Memphis Belle*, Grant shouted to the captain: "Chop your lines and back out."[96] The crew hastily laid a plank from the deck to the shore. Grant's horse instinctively put his forefeet over the steep, slippery riverbank, and, with his hind legs under him, slid down it and trotted up across the gangplank. Grant dismounted, raced to the captain's stateroom on the upper deck, and threw himself on a sofa. Moments later, he left the room to check on his men. When he returned, he noticed that a rebel musketball had ripped through the ship's bulkhead and pierced the sofa exactly where his head had been.[97]

On the voyage upriver the men celebrated a great victory. It was hardly that. The rebels retook and fortified Belmont the morning after the fight. Grant had stormed an enemy position that would have been impossible to hold even if his troops had routed the rebels. The artillerists of Columbus would have made sure of that. "I see that he & his friends call it a victory," one of Grant's commanders wrote his wife, "but if such be victory, God save us from defeat."[98]

Casualties were heavy and roughly equal—some six hundred killed, wounded, and captured on both sides. But it was worse for the outnumbered Union forces; approximately 20 percent of those engaged were casualties.[99] Writing long after the war, Grant thought Belmont worth the cost. "The National troops acquired a confidence in themselves at Belmont that did not desert them through the war."[100] But Grant was apparently not seeing things that way as the *Memphis Belle* steamed toward Cairo. Officers in the main cabin drank wine liberally and talked in excited tones about the Union triumph. Grant sat alone at the head of the table and spoke to no one.[101] "We thought he was hardhearted, cold and indifferent," recalled a veteran who had been in the thick of the fight, "but it was only the difference between a real soldier and amateur soldiers."[102]

The *Chicago Tribune* called Belmont a Union defeat, and Senator James Harlan of Iowa demanded that Grant be relieved of command for making an "egregious and unpardonable military blunder."[103] Two days after the battle, Frémont's adjutant general, Chauncey McKeever, wrote to Frémont: "General Grant did not follow his instructions. No orders were given to attack Belmont or Columbus."[104]

At the time, the war was going badly for the North. In the nation's capital, General George McClellan had raised and trained a mighty host, the seemingly invincible Army of the Potomac, but had failed as yet to move on Richmond. Desperate for some sign of Union progress, the *New York Herald* proclaimed Belmont "as clear a victory as ever warriors gained."[105]

Eager to be promoted over Grant and given an independent command, John McClernand was determined to have the last word on the battle. In both his official report and his dispatch to the general-in-chief, McClernand had his brigade winning the Battle of Belmont almost singlehandedly.[106] The volcanic Rawlins flew into a rage when he learned of McClernand's deceitful self-aggrandizement. "God damn it, it's insubordination! . . . The bastard! The damned slinking, Judas bastard!"[107] It was the beginning of one of the bitterest military rivalries of the war.

Grant's performance at Belmont was mixed. He had fought splendidly in the morning but failed to pursue Pillow's beaten rebels, lost control of his volunteers, was surprised by the enemy's counterthrust, and nearly lost his entire force in an inglorious retreat. It would soon build into a pattern: heroic audacity intermingled with inexcusable underestimation of the enemy. "Grant always thought more about what he was going to do to the enemy than what the enemy might do to him," writes biographer Jean Edward Smith, "and he rarely credited his Confederate opponents with either the capability or the inclination to attack." This would cost his army dearly at Fort Donelson and nearly lead to his replacement at Shiloh. Still later, at Vicksburg and Cold Harbor, Virginia, his impetuosity would lead him to order unnecessary assaults on impregnable enemy positions. But at Belmont, Grant had shown his salient characteristics as a commander: "serenity and self-poise."[108] There and in later engagements, he was best when things went bad. Formed but not controlled by his past, he had confronted failure in his personal life and never forgot how he surmounted it—by unyielding persistence. And for all his mistakes of judgment at Belmont, he would prove to be "something rare" in this or any other war, concluded historian Shelby Foote: "a man who could actually learn from experience."[109] The Grant war story is one of "steady progression."[110] The brigadier who stormed Belmont would have failed at Vicksburg. The commander he became in the year after Belmont was superbly equipped to take Vicksburg.

• • •

After Belmont, Grant pressed headquarters for a slashing advance on rebel strongholds south of it, all the way to Vicksburg. That might mean attacking slavery, something he had not expected to do when assuming command at Cairo. "My inclination is to whip the rebellion into submission, preserving all constitutional rights," he wrote his father shortly after returning from Belmont. "If it cannot be whipped in any other way than through a war against slavery, let it come to that legitimately. If it is necessary that slavery should fall that the Republic may continue its existence, let slavery go."[111] A war for the preservation of the Union could easily evolve into a crusade against slavery. But at the time that Grant took Belmont, his views on slavery and rebellion were close to those of Lincoln: Restoration of the Union was the paramount objective.

Grant was in an emotional slump when he wrote this letter to Jesse, fearing he might "lose" his command. Major General Henry Wager Halleck had recently replaced Frémont as commander of the renamed Department of the Missouri, which included western Kentucky and Arkansas, and Grant believed Halleck was likely to replace him with a more senior commander now that operations far larger than Belmont were apparently in the works.[112]

Three weeks later, Congressman Washburne informed Rawlins that he had heard credible reports that Grant was "drinking very hard."[113] Washburne had known Rawlins in Galena, where this son of an alcoholic was a militant temperance crusader who was heard to say he "would rather see a friend of his take a glass of poison than a glass of whiskey."[114] The congressman knew Rawlins had appointed himself Grant's moral watchdog and had forsworn that the general should never again allow alcohol to interfere with his military duties. But Washburne also knew Cairo's reputation. "It was the era of whiskey," and Cairo was its capital. "This fluid was as plentiful as the yellow flood of the river. . . . It was on tap at the headquarters of every commissioned officer, in the departments of the quartermaster and the commissaries, in the room of every civilian, at a thousand bars in the town, on every steamer, and in the tent or pocket of every private," wrote Franc Wilkie, who rose from a twelve-dollar-a-week city editor of the *Dubuque Herald* (Iowa) to become one of the finest war correspondents in the western theater of war, working for editor Henry J. Raymond's *New York Times*.

Wilkie knew Grant and the town well as a transient resident, with fellow reporters, at the St. Charles Hotel, where he divided his off-hours "between the bar and the billiard tables."[115]

Washburne, a burly, thick-chested man known for his rectitude and personal courage, had been keeping a close eye on Grant at Cairo. He knew Grant had forbidden his officers and men from frequenting local saloons and had posted troops at the doors of the most notorious dives—"The Whiskey Blockage," Cairo reporters called it.[116] But Grant, he suspected, had succumbed to old habits.

"Utterly untrue," Rawlins fired back. The allegations "could have originated only in malice," he wrote Washburne. Known to press his opinions vehemently and in tortured syntax, Rawlins went further, and in his clumsy effort to exculpate Grant unintentionally implicated him. "When I came to Cairo, Genl Grant was as he is today, a strictly total abstinence man." Then, in an unintended volte-face, Rawlins offered evidence that undercut that very assertion. Shortly after arriving at Cairo, he admitted, Grant had been given a box of champagne as a "gift," and "on one or two occasions he drank a glass of this with his friends." About the same time, Grant's physician had suggested he drink two glasses of beer a day to cure his dyspepsia. Then, after the Battle of Belmont, some home-state politicians visited his headquarters and "he was induced out of compliment to them to drink with them on several occasions." Days later, he drank champagne in Rawlins's presence as a dinner guest of the president of the Illinois Central Railroad. Rawlins mentioned Grant's lapses from "his usual total abstinence," he told Washburne, to point out that he was drinking only occasionally and in moderation. "In no instance did he drink enough to any manner affect him . . . and at the end of that period he voluntarily stated he should not during the continuance of the war again taste liquor of any kind."[117]

On the day Rawlins penned his thinly convincing defense of his chief, William Bross, a partner of the *Chicago Tribune* Company, wrote to Secretary of War Simon Cameron. "Evidence entirely satisfactory to myself and Associate Editors of the *Tribune* had become so convincing that Gen. U.S. Grant commanding at Cairo is an inebriate, that I deem it my duty to call your attention to the matter. . . . We think it best to call your attention to this painful matter, rather than to attack Gen. Grant in the *Tribune*," a staunchly Republican paper.[118] Cameron for-

warded the letter to Lincoln, who endorsed it: "Bross would not know-
ingly misrepresent Grant." The president did not take action, but he
did urge Cameron to send Bross's letter to Washburne, whom Lincoln
counted upon to keep a close eye on Grant.[119]

Rawlins's letter undermines the argument advanced by some of
Grant's most sympathetic biographers that he never drank while in the
presence of the enemy. Grant was not actively engaged in a major campaign in late 1861, but rebels were all around him at Cairo and Paducah,
bases that were on perpetual high alert. It was exactly the wrong time
for a commander with a drinking problem to be indulging, albeit moderately, if Rawlins is to be believed.

While Grant kept his drinking under control during most of the
remainder of the war, there were notable lapses. Early in the Vicksburg
campaign, Rawlins confided to a fellow member of Grant's staff that
while the general's occasional binges were "not so bad" as some hostile
reporters "made them out," they were—to his true friends—"cause for
concern."[120]

Grant was a binge drinker. He could go months between drinks, but
when he partook he found it nearly impossible to stop. And he could
not hold his alcohol. "A single glass of liquor visibly affected him," his
army friends confided to Hamlin Garland.[121] What stands out, however, is not Grant's drinking but his unending battle to control it. He
was never forthcoming either about his drinking or his strenuous efforts
to stop, but from early in his military career "he had known his danger,
and had fought against his enemy," wrote Garland.[122]

Beginning at Belmont, he would be accused repeatedly and with
malice of drunkenness on the battlefield, but he never drank when
commanding troops under fire and never needed alcohol for reinforce-
ment. Historian Lyle Dorsett went so far as to claim that Grant's drinking problems early in his army career made him a better commander.
With "no sterling military reputation to protect," Grant was willing
to take the kind of bold risks that McClellan—a commander with an
impressive prewar résumé—avoided, Dorsett agued. "Because he had
absolutely nothing to lose, Grant could brush aside caution."[123] This is
unconvincing.

● ● ●

Action was Grant's antidote for alcohol. When he was driving against the enemy he was tightly focused and Spartan in his habits—eating sparely, sleeping little, living cleanly. In January 1862, he began finalizing the plan he had begun fashioning six months earlier at Ironton, Missouri, to attack two recently constructed enemy garrisons in northernmost Tennessee: Fort Henry, on the east bank of the Tennessee River and Fort Donelson, on the west bank of the Cumberland. The two forts, a dozen miles apart, were highly vulnerable—poorly constructed and unfinished as of January 1862. Fort Henry was sited on low ground subject to winter flooding, and Donelson was more a stockade than a solidly built fortress.

The forts anchored the center of a long Confederate defensive line extending from Kentucky's Appalachian Mountains to Columbus, Tennessee, on the Mississippi River. Major General Albert Sidney Johnston, the rebel commander in the west, had created the line as a bulwark against federal incursions into Tennessee and Mississippi. Johnston, a burly, charismatic Kentuckian who had relocated to Texas, was the highest-ranking officer in the Confederate army to hold a field command and enjoyed the complete confidence of President Jefferson Davis, who considered him the South's "foremost soldier." [124]

The rebel line looked imposing on paper but Johnston knew it was thin at best. He had fewer than twenty-five thousand "badly-armed and equipped" men to hold it against twice as many Federal troops north of the line.[125] In seeking to hold on to the states of the Deep South, the Confederate strategists had made a colossal strategic blunder. Anticipating a direct descent down the Mississippi, they had thrown up powerful batteries at Columbus, Island Number Ten on the Mississippi, and Vicksburg, but had largely neglected the possibilities of an invasion by way of the Cumberland and Tennessee Rivers. These highly navigable streams "threatened catastrophe" for Johnston, wrote Shelby Foote: "Running parallel and piercing as they did the critical center of his line, the two were like a double-barreled shotgun leveled at his heart." [126]

In the winter of 1861–62, Johnston finally began strengthening his earthen forts on the Tennessee and the Cumberland, but the engineer assigned to shore them up, Major Jeremy Gilmer, doubted the enemy would launch an offensive before the late spring.[127] His miscalculation gave Grant an unexpected opportunity. If he attacked vigorously that winter, the entire rebel line would likely collapse, forcing Johnston to pull back as far as northern Mississippi. It would have to be a quick-striking amphibious assault—a shock attack—taking out one river garrison before the other could be sufficiently reinforced. Grant now had what he needed to carry it out: Eads's iron monsters would be completed and armed for action by the end of January. And Grant had just been named head of the new District of Cairo, which encompassed the mouths of the Tennessee and Cumberland Rivers in northwest Kentucky, his passageways to the forts.[128]

On January 23, 1862, Grant left Cairo for St. Louis to get Halleck's permission to move south. He arrived armed with maps and compelling intelligence provided by Flag Officer Foote, but Halleck was frigidly dismissive. "I had not uttered many sentences before I was cut short as if my plan was preposterous," Grant described the meeting. "I returned to Cairo very much crestfallen."[129]

Grant was wrong: Halleck did not think his plan was "preposterous"; he thought Grant was preposterous. The portly, short-tempered western commander, who had reenlisted in the wartime army in 1861 after a highly successful career as a lawyer, engineer, land dealer, and railroad president in California, was planning a similar move on the forts but was procrastinating, unwilling to move until he had larger numbers of men than the War Department was able to provide. But he planned in anticipation of getting this additional manpower; and he was—at least by his own lights—a masterful military strategist. He had authored a definitive treatise on tactics—*Elements of Military Art and Science*—and was at work on a translation of a four-volume biography of Napoleon by the great Swiss military theorist Antoine-Henri Jomini. Meeting Grant in the midst of one of his St. Louis planning conferences, "Old Brains," as he was known, had been in no mood to be lectured on strategy by an "unkempt" former quartermaster who had been cashiered for drinking. He thought Grant had been reckless at Belmont and was convinced he had been drinking at Cairo.[130]

Irritable and aloof, the forty-seven-year-old Henry Halleck was Grant's polar opposite, a balding, bug-eyed desk general who rarely moved his flabby body—or his armies—with energy. He preferred to command from his Planter's House headquarters in St. Louis, where he had near at hand the things he greatly prized: excellent French wines and a library stocked with books.[131] Grant, by contrast, was a brawler who distrusted military theory. At West Point, where Jomini had commanded the curriculum, he had not bothered to read him.[132] Grant subscribed to but one military axiom: Find the enemy and hit him fast and hard. And while he was straightforward and naively trustworthy, Halleck was a plotter and schemer, known to have made—as well as destroyed—military careers.

Seven years older than Grant, Halleck impressed his subordinates with his "immense knowledge of military science," but it wouldn't take long for Grant to locate his fatal flaw: his "timidity in taking responsibilities. . . . He would never take a chance in a battle. A general who will never take a chance in a battle will never fight one," Grant would write later of Halleck.[133] Sherman, who admired both generals, acutely described their differences: "Halleck was a theoretical soldier. Grant was a practical soldier." [134]

Persistence was Grant's core characteristic. "He habitually wears an expression as if he had determined to drive his head through a brick wall, and was about to do it," said a fellow Union officer.[135]

On January 28, Grant telegraphed Halleck: "With permission, I will take and hold Fort Henry on the Tennessee." [136] His request arrived with the endorsement of Andrew Hull Foote, not a man easily brushed aside.[137] It was Lincoln, however, who got the project moving. Impatient with the inaction of all his theater commanders, he issued General Order No. 1, mandating "a general movement of the land and naval [forces] of the United States against the insurgent forces" by the end of February 1862. "The army and flotilla at Cairo," Lincoln made emphatic, must be part of this offensive.[138] Grant's telegram crossed Halleck's desk a day after he received the president's directive. On January 30, Old Brains wired Grant: "Make preparations to take & hold Henry.[139]

When Halleck's message was read aloud at Grant's Cairo headquarters, the staff officers "stopped work at their desks as suddenly as if a one hundred-pound 'bomb' had landed in their midst," recalled Grant's Ironton friend John W. Emerson, who served in the war and afterward wrote a perceptive history of Grant's campaign in the Mississippi Valley. "They all sprang to their feet and cheered." Rawlins kicked over chairs and hammered the wall with his fists. Others threw their hats in the air and then kicked them around the room. Grant sat calmly at his desk. When the excitement died down, he ordered his staff to begin final preparations for the first great Union campaign in the Mississippi Valley.[140]

The river warrior would move south with roughly seventeen thousand men, nearly six times as many as he had brought to Belmont. John McClernand, narrow-faced, dark, and heavily bearded, led one division, C. F. Smith the other. The fleet left Cairo on February 3 and stopped at Paducah to pick up Smith's regiments. As the boats pulled away from the pier, there "arose a hurricane of cheers long continued, and the rivalry of bands playing, flags streaming."[141]

Traveling in the rear boat, Grant paced the deck anxiously, peering behind him with his field glasses, half expecting the irresolute Halleck to send out a wharf boat with orders to call off the operation. As Grant's steamer passed the last telegraph station, he clapped Rawlins on the shoulder, an uncharacteristic gesture. "Now we seem to be safe, beyond recall by either electricity or steam. . . . We *will* succeed, Rawlins. We *must* succeed."[142]

Foote had gone ahead the day before with seven gunboats, four of them ironclads—"black, creeping, menacing." The reporters went with the infantry, a correspondent "attached to the button of every officer."[143] The scribes were as anxious to get out of Cairo as the volunteers. Weeks of idleness had spawned "much mischief." There were dozens of drunken brawls and "some shooting matches." To move to the battlefront by water instead of horseback was a welcome experience for thirty-two-year-old Franc Wilkie and his fellow correspondents, the self-styled Bohemian Brigade. "It was for me the beginning of an aquatic career which was immensely desirable in that it involved no saddle contusions, nor any of the annoyances connected with equestrian expeditions," wrote Wilkie, a lean, intense Union College graduate who had been covering the war on a borrowed horse and looked every bit the road warrior with his wildly unkempt beard and dust-stained pants.[144]

Grant and Foote were flushed with confidence. The rebels holding

Fort Henry would have to fight two battles: one against the enemy, the other against the river, which was cresting dangerously. By the time Foote arrived at the low-sitting fort, the swirling waters of the Tennessee were up to the mouths of the cannon and threatening to inundate the ammunition magazine. The high water also put the fort's cannons at a disadvantage—level with the guns of Foote's ironclads, not above them.

"It was a short and hot contest," wrote Wilkie, won entirely by the navy.[145] After debarking downstream from the fort, Grant's troops were delayed by dense forests and swollen streams. Unable to locate Grant, Foote decided to take the fort without the army. The ironclads advanced assertively, perilously close to the water batteries, and took a terrible pounding, while brittle-skinned wooden boats provided long-range support. The rebels' "heavy shot broke and scattered our iron-plating as if it had been putty and often passed completely through the casemates," wrote Captain Walke, commander of *Carondelet*.[146] A solid shot pierced the port bow of the ironclad *Essex* and penetrated the center boiler, releasing a cloud of hot steam and water that horribly scalded twenty-nine crew members, many of them fatally.[147] The carnage belowdecks was almost "almost indescribable," a crewman recalled.[148]

Essex was lost; otherwise it was a rout, an uneven fight from the start. In seventy-five minutes, Foote's immensely more powerful guns silenced eight of the nine rebel cannon. Brigadier General Lloyd Tilghman, the fort commander, struck his colors, raised a white flag, and asked to be rowed out to Foote's command boat, *Cincinnati*, to surrender.[149]

There was pandemonium on the Union ships. The crew of *Cincinnati* cheered and yelled so obstreperously that Foote "had to run among the men," he reported, "and knock them on the head to restore order." Approaching Foote, Tilghman said graciously, "I am glad to surrender to so gallant an officer." Foote was discourteous. "You do perfectly right, sir, in surrendering, but you should have blown my boat out of the water before I would have surrendered to you."[150]

When Grant arrived at the fort at three that afternoon, the rebel guns had been disabled, their muzzles pointing despairingly skyward. Their carriages were broken and stained with blood, and "masses of human flesh" could be seen "adhering to the broken timbers."[151] The fort was heavily flooded and the river was still rising. Had Foote attacked two days later there would have been no battle; by then, Fort Henry was underwater.

Though expecting determined resistance by the 3,400 infantry under Tilghman's command, Grant's troops had not had to fire a shot. Before the opening of hostilities, Tilghman had put almost all of his ill-disciplined troops in trenches outside the fort, leaving fewer than sixty gunners to battle Foote's black behemoths. The earthshaking force of the naval cannonade had produced panic in the trenches, and the men deserted their positions and headed for Fort Donelson, twelve miles to the east.[152]

"Fort Henry is ours," Grant telegraphed Halleck on the night of the surrender. ". . . I shall take and destroy Fort Donelson on the eighth."[153] This alarmed Halleck. He had not given Grant permission to move on Donelson.[154] His orders, he emphatically reiterated, were to entrench and hold Fort Henry "at all hazards."[155] He had failed to say for how long, however.

Halleck regarded Grant as both underqualified and recklessly ambitious, and had been plotting to place another commander in charge of the Donelson expedition. He first offered the position to Sherman, who had been serving at his St. Louis headquarters before the assault on Fort Henry.[156] When Sherman refused, citing loyalty to Grant, Halleck approached Major General Don Carlos Buell, department commander in Ohio. "Why not come down and take the immediate command of the Cumberland column yourself?" he telegraphed Buell on February 13.[157] Buell did not respond.

While Halleck maneuvered to replace Grant, Grant made plans to take Donelson. Halleck had not answered his petition to resume the offensive, and Grant took his silence as license to move. "I intend to keep the ball rolling as lively as possible," he wrote his sister Mary. ". . . Before receiving this you will hear, by telegraph, of Fort Donelson being attacked."[158]

But Grant had to wait for the heavy rains to stop, and for Foote's ironclads to be repaired at Cairo and Mound City, before he could set out through dense Tennessee wilderness for Donelson. The three ironclads sent north—the entire flotilla except the lightly damaged *Carondelet*—arrived to a tumultuous reception. Whistles blowing, they steamed into port, one of them flying the enormous Fort Henry flag upside down on a nautical rope. The *Chicago Tribune* had reporters in Cairo, and in their excitement they pronounced Fort Henry "one of the most complete and signal victories in the annals of the world's warfare." It was hardly that, but it was the first big Union breakthrough of the war.[159]

Buoyed by the quick conquest of Fort Henry, Grant underestimated the difficulty of taking Donelson. When Albert Richardson stopped at Grant's headquarters before heading back to Cairo to file his story, Grant urged him to "wait a day or two," as he was about to begin the overland drive on Donelson. When Richardson asked if he knew how strong the fort was, Grant replied unhesitatingly: "Not exactly, but I think we can take it; at all events, we can try."[160]

It was the black boats that gave him confidence. Even Albert Sidney Johnston believed Fort Donelson, a half-built bastion of earth and timber, would easily fall to Foote's ironclads. "The slight resistance at Fort Henry," he wrote the Confederate War Department, "indicates that the best open earth works are not reliable to meet successfully a vigorous attack of iron clad boats . . . I think the gunboats of the enemy will probably take Fort Donelson without the necessity of employing their land force in cooperation."[161] No dispatch of the war was ever more mistaken.

CHAPTER 3

Winter Fortress

This stronghold crowns a river-bluff,
A good broad mile of leveled top;
Inland the ground rolls off
Deep-gorged, rocky, and broken up—
A wilderness of trees and brush[1]

—Herman Melville, "Donelson," February 1862

Grant set out for Donelson on the morning of February 12, 1862. It was like "a day of summer," wrote General Lew Wallace. "River, land, and sky fairly shimmered with warmth. Overcoats were encumbrance." Most of the men took them off and threw them beside the rutted forest road—the first great blunder of a campaign replete with them.[2]

Grant wanted his men marching in battle order, ready for action, and had not brought along tents or personal baggage. These were to arrive by boat from Cairo. He himself had no change of clothing, not even a clean shirt. The only toilet article in his possession was a toothbrush he carried in his waistcoat pocket.[3]

Grant rode at the head of one wing of the army, sitting high in the saddle, brimming with confidence and happy, in this wilderness, to be out of touch with Halleck and the temporizing bureaucrats at St. Louis, who could not reach him by boat or telegraph until he arrived at the Cumberland River. Army surgeon Brinton rode beside him on a majestic black stallion. The unruly mount insisted on edging ahead of Grant, who was riding his favorite horse, Jack. Finally, Grant turned to Brinton with a glint in his eye: "Doctor, I believe I command this army, and I think I'll go first."[4]

By late afternoon, Grant's two divisions, under McClernand and Smith, reached the outer perimeter of Fort Donelson, an earthen stockade on the crown of a rugged bluff commanding a bend in the Cumberland River. Here, Foote's ironclads would face guns that were sure to give them trouble.[5] Two water batteries were sunk into the sides of the hundred-foot-high cliff, fifteen guns in all. The fort was more weakly defended on its landward side, but the place looked more imposing to Grant's scouts than it would prove to be.[6] Batteries were placed in commanding spots on a range of steep hills that faced the oncoming Federals, and the fort was rimmed by an entrenched camp: a long, continuous arc of rifle pits protected by mounds of fresh yellow clay.[7] These entrenchments were fronted by a thickly woven abatis—a dense mass of felled trees placed crosswise, one over another, with the sharpened ends pointed menacingly at the enemy.[8] The land around the fort was "the roughest imaginable," said one Union officer. Sharply inclined hills rose to one hundred feet, with narrow ravines separating them, and the ground was blanketed with "an almost impenetrable thicket of oak and vine."[9]

Grant closely surveyed the ground with his new chief engineer, thirty-three-year-old Lieutenant Colonel James Birdseye McPherson, a fellow Ohioan who had graduated first in his West Point class. McPherson had been secretly sent by Halleck to report back to him on Grant's drinking, but he turned the tables and became one of Grant's strongest supporters.[10] One year later, he would become part of the Ohio triumvirate—Grant, Sherman, and McPherson—that conquered Vicksburg.

As Grant and McPherson explored the enemy position, Foote, with six of his gunboats and steamers packed with reinforcements, was moving "as fast as steam would drive him" toward a rendezvous with the army.[11] *Carondelet* had preceded Foote and was in position below the fort on the evening of February 12. That night, Grant and his staff set up headquarters in a log house in the rear of Smith's division. The troops slept on the ground. It remained balmy, and some of them shed their blankets.[12]

The next morning, Grant had his fifteen thousand bluecoats formed into a vast semicircle, investing the fort. McClernand's First Division was on the right, Smith's Second Division on the left. Grant thought his men were on good ground, along a string of ridges, but the terrain disfavored them in many ways. Their lines "stretched away over hills, down hollows, and through thickets, making it impossible for even colonels to see their regiments from flank to flank." Maintaining battlefield coordination would be exceedingly difficult, but balanced against this was Grant's attention to detail. "He appeared to see everything that went on," said Lew Wallace."[13]

Although initially outnumbered by from three to five thousand men, the troops were not ordered to entrench.[14] Grant wanted them ready to attack, not cowering behind earthen breastworks. Having ringed the rebels with firepower, he expected them to remain on the defensive.[15] This was a near-fatal calculation.

Before dawn on the following day, the Union sharpshooters were "astir." They operated alone, never in groups. "All right; hunt your holes, boys," the order went out, and they scattered, hiding wherever they could, some of them in trees within range of the rebel breastworks. The skirmishers went out next, in groups, not alone. They were to the main body of the army what antennae are to insects. Their task: "to unmask the foe."[16] When the sun came up and the enemy positions were located, the batteries opened fire and the rebels answered immediately, filling the gloomy forest with clouds of sulfurous gray smoke. Finally, the regiments advanced, marching route-step behind their colonels, colors flying, drums rolling. But that first morning, most of the units stopped short of the enemy entrenchments. Grant wanted to avoid a general engagement until the fleet had arrived with its murderous firepower and enough infantry to even the odds.

Nor did the rebels engage. Their command structure was unwieldy, creating paralyzing indecisiveness. There were three commanders inside the fort, and they did not see eye-to-eye. Two of them were manifestly incompetent: Brigadier General John B. Floyd, secretary of war under President James Buchanan; and Gideon Pillow, the boastful Tennessee lawyer who had mismanaged the Battle of Belmont. The other commander, Grant's old West Point friend Simon Bolivar Buckner, was battle-tested and able but outranked by both Floyd and Pillow.

Also on hand was forty-year-old cavalry chief Nathan Bedford Forrest with one thousand of his crack troopers. An unschooled Tennessee cotton planter who had risen from "log-cabin privation" to make millions as a slave trader, Colonel Forrest was already known for his ferocity, his skill in the saddle, and his tactical sagacity; but, being outranked, he would have to endure the inept battlefield management of Floyd and Pillow.[17]

Floyd's inactivity on February 13 was "incomprehensible" to some Union commanders, and it infuriated Forrest, who had come to Donelson to kill Yankees.[18] Grant had marched into what could have been a trap, but the irresolute rebels never sprang it. Grant had advanced on Donelson without any idea of the enemy's strength and was operating on unfamiliar terrain. He was not only outnumbered, but his lines were stretched precariously thin.

Grant moved quickly to correct this, calling up General Lew Wallace from Fort Henry, where he had been placed in reserve. Once Foote showed up with reinforcements, Wallace would be put in charge of a fresh division that would bolster the soft center of the Union line. Had Floyd attacked before Foote's reinforcements arrived, the rebels might have thrown Grant's army back toward Fort Henry, putting an end to the expedition. Up to this point in the battle, Grant was surviving on luck and rebel ineptitude.

On the afternoon of February 13, the weather changed violently. A storm blew in, carrying freezing rain, sleet, and snow. The wind picked up tremendously and the temperature plummeted to twenty degrees below freezing, intolerable conditions for the thousands of men who had discarded their blankets and overcoats. Adding to their discomfort, Grant ordered all campfires banked. His troops were within musket-range of the enemy's trenches, and rebel pickets were out in force. Even troops with winter wear suffered intensely. "Our blankets froze stiff around us, and when moved would stand in any position we would put them," wrote an Iowa boy.[19] Men rose in the middle of the night and discovered comrades huddled next to them on the frozen earth, dead from exposure. "Even the horses betrayed the suffering they were enduring."[20]

"Never was morning light more welcome," recalled one soldier.[21] By then, most of the men were "nearly torpid from the intense cold."[22] The mood in the Federal camp brightened when word spread that six gunboats—three ironclads and an equal number of timberclads—had arrived during the night at a dock out of range of Confederate guns. The gunboats had escorted twelve steam-driven transports carrying ten thousand men. Grant assigned most of them to General Wallace.

Thirty-four-year-old Lew Wallace was a native of Indiana, a veteran of the Mexican War, a successful attorney in peacetime, and a former editor of a Free Soil newspaper in Indianapolis. His stepmother, Zerelda Gray Sanders Wallace, was a prominent suffragist, and in 1880 Wallace would write *Ben-Hur: A Tale of the Christ*, a novel which sold over a million copies by 1912. A masterly military writer, he would pen the finest account of the battle about to begin.

Enemy reinforcements arrived that same evening, but neither side expected this to be an infantryman's fight. It would be won or lost by the river forces. Everything depended on Foote and the ironclads, and nearly every Union commander expected a rousing repeat of Fort Henry—but not, surprisingly, Andrew Hull Foote himself. Meeting with Grant the morning he arrived, Foote complained that the topsides of his gunboats were insufficiently armored, unable to withstand plunging fire from the elevated rebel batteries on the banks of the Cumberland. He preferred to wait a day or so for the arrival of his mortar boats from Cairo. Their high-angle, long-range fire was capable of disabling the river batteries without risking the ironclads in close-quarter combat.[23]

But Grant wanted Foote to strike that day—and with vigor. The flag officer sulked but eventually acquiesced. Leaving his meeting with Foote, Grant told bystanders that the heavy guns of the ironclads, with shells as big as corn-fed hogs, would annihilate the wood and earthen fort, allowing his army to quickly overrun it.[24]

Foote positioned the ironclads *St. Louis, Louisville, Pittsburgh*, and *Carondelet* just below the fort. The wooden gunboats would provide long-range support from a thousand yards away. Just before three o'clock, Foote advanced on the rebel water batteries. Grant observed the action from a hidden highpoint. Watching the opening cannonade from a spot a mile or so away was Nathan Bedford Forrest. Shaken by the deafening naval barrage, Forrest shouted to one of his captains, a Methodist minister, "Parson! For God's sake, pray. Nothing but God Almighty can save that fort!"[25]

But the fort stood strong. It was the gunboats that took a beating. At

Fort Henry, the rebel batteries were at water level and hence ineffective; from Donelson's heights they poured plunging fire into the wooden topsides of Eads's ironclads, smashing smokestacks and "tearing off the side armor as lightning tears the bark from a tree," Commander Henry Walke reported.[26] Foote's flagship, *St. Louis*, took fifty-nine hits; the three other boats suffered nearly half that number. Inside the casemate of *St. Louis*, the decks were awash with blood and splattered brains.[27]

It was worse up top. A 32-pound rebel shot struck the pilothouse, and shell fragments mortally wounded one pilot and struck Foote in the ankle. The old sea salt seized the wheel from the dying pilot and tried to take control of the vessel, but the steering mechanism was irreparably damaged and *St. Louis* drifted helplessly downstream along with the three other ironclads. The swift current spun them around like logs as their crews fired wildly, "attempting to hide in the smoke of their own guns."[28] The Union flotilla sustained fifty-four casualties. Not one rebel was killed, not one rebel gun was disabled.[29] Foote had attacked the water batteries at point-blank range, turning his ungainly "turtles" into fat targets for enemy gunners.[30]

While the fight was ongoing, the officers at Lew Wallace's headquarters could hear the distinctive sound of the larger-caliber Union guns echoing across the water and through the forest. When the firing stopped, they looked at one another "like sick men."

"Whipped!" said one of them.[31]

That night Grant wrote Julia: "The taking of Fort Donelson bids fair to be a long job."[32] At this point, both sides were losing. The rebels were buttoned up inside their lines, with all escape roads closed, and Grant now had an army of some forty thousand men, with further reinforcements on the way. "Appearances now indicate that we will have a protracted siege here," Grant wrote despairingly to department headquarters at Cairo. With the rebel abatis "extending far out from the breast works I fear the result of attempting to carry the place by storm with raw troops."[33]

Around four o'clock the next morning, a messenger awakened Grant and handed him a note from Foote: "Will you do me the favor to come on board [*St Louis*] at your earliest convenience, as I am disabled from walking by a contusion and cannot possibly get to see you about the disposition of these vessels, all of which are more or less disabled."[34] Before leaving, Grant instructed his division commanders "to do nothing to bring on an engagement" in his absence. He then set out on horseback, along frozen roads and into a cutting wind.[35]

Eight miles downstream, he found Foote's flagship anchored offshore. A handful of sailors, wrapped in heavy blankets, were waiting to row him out to the ironclad in a skiff. Foote got right to the point: He was taking his battered ironclads to the repair yard at Mound City and would not return with fresh vessels and reinforcements for at least ten days. The army would have to prepare for a longer siege than anticipated. But as Grant noted later: "the enemy relieved me from this necessity."[36]

When Grant returned to shore, one of his staff was there to meet him, his face "white with fear."[37] At five thirty that morning, rebels under the command of Gideon Pillow had slammed into McClernand's division in a desperate effort to break out of the fort. The thick woods and twisting river bends had prevented Grant and Foote from hearing the roar of the battle, which sounded, said Lew Wallace, "as if a million men were beating empty barrels with iron hammers."[38]

The night before, the Confederate commanders had become convinced that the recent infusion of Federal troops made it imperative that they escape before the siege lines were further strengthened.[39] Pillow proposed to cut his way through Union forces holding the Clarkesville Road, which ran southward toward Nashville. If successful, the entire garrison could follow and hook up with Albert Sidney Johnston, believed to be heading to that city with his army.

Pillow's slashing attack took the Federals by surprise and ignited a close-quarters fight as vicious as any small engagement of the war. "Men fell by the score, reddening the snow with their blood."[40] McClernand's troops fought with obstinate courage but ran out of ammunition and were pushed back in a withdrawal that devolved into a stampede. Dismounted cavalry from Forrest's regiment hit the Union flank and rear, and the aroused rebels, many of them carrying shotguns brought from home, had begun "committing great slaughter."[41] The Nashville road was soon open, but having gained it, Pillow abruptly surrendered it in the early afternoon. Over the violent objections of General Buckner, he persuaded General Floyd, the ranking officer, to call off the breakout and have the exhausted men—who had been fighting for seven hours—

return to their entrenchments on the ridge in front of the fort. Having opened the road, Pillow believed it would stay open, allowing the rebel army to retreat the following day, perhaps.[42]

Lew Wallace saw things differently. Floyd's decision to withdraw was a battle-turning mistake. "The road was his," yet he called off the breakout.[43]

"There was then a lull in the battle," wrote Wallace, "and . . . everybody was asking, What next?"[44] Just then, Grant rode up to where Wallace and McClernand were nervously conferring. Visibly irritated but trying to keep his "feelings down," he saluted and said in a level voice, "Gentlemen, the position on the right"—the Nashville road— "must be retaken."[45]

Before galloping off, Grant approached a group of bewildered Union soldiers who were standing around talking excitedly. The men had been searching the bodies of the rebel dead for powder and bullets and noticed their knapsacks and haversacks contained more than one day's rations. This signaled to them the rebels' resolve "to stay out and fight for several days."[46] That had to be wrong, Grant intuited instantly. "They mean to cut their way out; they have no idea of staying here to fight us," Grant told the men.[47] Turning to his chief of staff, Colonel Joseph D. Webster, he said: "Some of our men are pretty badly demoralized, but the enemy must be more so, for he has attempted to force his way out, but has fallen back; the one who attacks first now will be victorious." The rebels had put nearly everything they had into the assault from their left on the Union right. He would hit them on their vulnerable right, where General C. F. Smith was positioned with troops that had not been engaged that morning. And he would hit them instantly. "The enemy will have to be in a hurry if he gets ahead of me," he shouted to Webster.[48]

As Grant sped off to meet with Smith, a cigar clenched in his teeth, he directed Webster to ride with him and call out to McClernand's troops to fill their cartridge boxes quickly and get into line to prevent the enemy from escaping the Donelson stockade. "This acted like a charm," Grant said later. "The men only wanted some one [sic] to give them a command."[49]

It was one of Grant's finest moments of the war. Coolly composed while surrounded by chaos and calamity, he took control of the battle, strengthening the sinking resolve of his men, ordering them to hold, and organizing a counterattack when a less resolute commander would have settled upon a siege.

When Grant reached Smith's quarters, he found the old warrior eager to move. Smith directed five regiments, untested recruits from western farms and shops, to attack through an abatis "too thick for a rabbit to get through."[50] It was to be a bayonet charge; the men were to hold their fire until well inside rebel defenses. Smith led them, sitting high on his horse, his saber held aloft, his six-foot-three frame and intensely white mustache making him a conspicuous target for enemy sharpshooters. He stormed into the field of sharpened timber shouting curses and entreaties to inspire his men. "Come on you . . . damned volunteers! . . . This is your chance. You volunteered to be killed for love of country, and now you can be."[51]

"I was nearly scared to death," said one soldier, "but I saw the old man's white mustache over his shoulder, and went on."[52] Placing his cap on the point of his sword and holding it aloft for his men to see him as he picked his way through the jagged limbs of fallen trees, Smith turned what could have been a rabble into a disciplined assault column.[53]

Smith's two thousand men ascended the steep heights in front of the fort and overran the enemy's outer defenses without firing a shot or letting loose a cheer. Closer to the fort, they ran into a storm of artillery fire and advanced the final yards crawling on their stomachs. They would have taken Donelson had Buckner not called in heavy reinforcements. "It was the most extraordinary feat of arms I ever beheld," said Lew Wallace.[54]

"News [that] our flag . . . waved triumphantly from the rebel entrenchments . . . was borne along our lines, cheering and stimulating the men," reported chief engineer McPherson.[55] An hour later, Lew Wallace regained control of the road to Nashville, sealing the Union victory.

Riding with his staff across a battlefield so thickly covered with the dead and wounded that their horses had to repeatedly shy to avoid them, Grant spotted two mortally wounded soldiers lying side by side in a bed of bloodstained snow. The Union lieutenant was struggling to give the Confederate private a drink from his canteen. One of Grant's officers pulled a flask from his pocket and handed it to Grant, who gave each suffering soldier a swig of brandy. Then he had Rawlins call for stretcher-bearers. As he turned to leave, he noticed that the bearers started first for the Union officer. "Take them both together," Grant said. "The war is now over between them." [56]

That night, February 15, 1862, Grant slept in his cabin headquarters on a mattress that had been thrown on the kitchen floor. Around three in the morning, General Smith came in looking "half frozen." As he headed to the fireplace to warm his feet, Grant slipped out of his covers. "Here's something for you to read," Smith said, handing Grant a letter. It was from General Buckner.

Earlier that evening, Buckner, Pillow, and Floyd had called a council of war. After a stormy debate, the generals unanimously decided their situation was so "desperate" they had to surrender. A full-scale breakout attempt, into the teeth of the "greatly enforced enemy," would cost them three-quarters of their men, Buckner warned. [57] Floyd, however, said he "could not and would not surrender himself." [58] As President Buchanan's secretary of war he had been accused of plotting to move arms from Northern to Southern arsenals on the eve of hostilities. If captured, he could be tried for treason and face the hangman. Floyd then handed over command to Pillow, who cravenly passed it on to Buckner, saying he would rather die than be the first rebel general of the war to surrender. Buckner, the only honorable man among them, pledged to stay with his men and share their fate. [59]

Floyd and Pillow escaped that night on riverboats. Both were later relieved from command for deserting the army in time of peril. Nathan Bedford Forrest fled with his cavalry over a river road his scouts had found open. [60]

Shortly after four in the morning, General Buckner sent a staff officer, under a white flag, through the Union lines. This was the message that reached Grant at his headquarters. [61] Buckner asked Grant to appoint "commissioners to agree upon terms of capitulation of the forces and fort under my command. [62] Grant looked at Smith, who was wiping his lips after taking a long pull from a flask that Dr. Brinton had just offered him to cut the cold. "What answer should I send to this, General Smith?"

"No terms to the damned rebels," Smith barked.[63]

Grant smiled, took out pen and paper, and drafted his reply: "No terms except an unconditional and immediate surrender can be accepted. I propose to move immediately upon your works."[64]

Buckner was aghast, but he had no choice but to accept what he called "ungenerous and unchivalrous terms.[65] He had expected better from Grant: When Grant was drummed out of the service in 1854, Buckner had loaned him money when he passed through New York on his return from the West Coast.

The day Buckner surrendered, Dr. Brinton asked Grant when the defeated enemy would be paraded before the victors and the formalities of surrender executed. There would be no ceremonies, said Grant. "We have the fort, the men, the guns. Why should we go through vain forms, and mortify and injure the spirit of brave men, who after all are our own countrymen and brothers?"[66]

At a cordial post-surrender breakfast with Buckner at a local hotel, Grant agreed to provide Buckner's men rations and allow officers to take their body servants with them to prisons in the North. But the two hundred African American laborers who had been impressed into war service and were working at the stockade would not be returned to their owners. "We want laborers, let the negroes work for us," Grant told Buckner. A local planter who arrived at the fort to reclaim his slaves left "silent and sullen," said a reporter who was present at the meeting between Grant and Buckner.[67]

Before Buckner boarded one of the last transports to Cairo, Grant pulled him aside and asked him discreetly if he needed anything. "My purse is at your disposal." Bucker politely declined.[68] General Smith was less cordial. Buckner had been his pupil at West Point, but Smith refused to shake his hand. "General Smith, I believe I am right," Buckner stiffly defended his cause. "That is for God to decide, not me," said Smith, "for I know I am right."[69]

It was the largest surrender to that point on American soil, surpassing Yorktown. Grant captured an entire army, between twelve and fifteen thousand men. Grant's Army of the Tennessee sustained approximately 2,700 casualties and killed or wounded at least 1,400 rebels.[70] The strategic consequences were far-reaching. The Cumberland, along with the Tennessee, became a Yankee river, secured for the entire war by Union gunboats. This made it impossible for rebel forces to hold Nashville, "the great storehouse and arsenal of the western Confederacy"; it would become the first state capital in the South to fall.[71] Within weeks, much of western and central Tennessee fell to Union forces, and the rebels lost another river bastion. In taking Forts Henry and Donelson, Grant had outflanked and isolated Columbus, Kentucky. It was evacuated and became an important rail and river supply center for the invading army. Albert Sidney Johnston, who had hoped to hold on to Nashville and its fire-breathing mills, retreated to Corinth, Mississippi, a strategically important rail center just south of the Tennessee border. "We lost all," Johnston telegraphed General P. G. T. Beauregard, who had preceded him there.[72]

That February, Jefferson Davis was inaugurated for his six-year presidential term. (Up to then, he had been the "provisional" president.) Davis and his African American footmen wore black suits more appropriate for a funeral. "After a series of successes and victories, we have recently met with serious disasters," he conceded.[73]

Fort Donelson rocketed Grant "into national fame in a day."[74] In towns from Maine to Minnesota, church bells rang, cannon fired salutes, fireworks lit up the night sky, and business was suspended. A state senator from Iowa rose from his seat in the legislature and moved that the body adjourn and "that every member shall get drunk!"[75] "The shame of Bull Run was erased," and overagitated newspaper editors declared the end of the war in sight. "The monster is already clutched in his death struggle," said the *New York Tribune*.[76]

"Grant's victory was most extraordinary and brilliant—he was a plain unostentatious man, and a few years ago was of bad habits, but he certainly has done a brilliant act," William Sherman wrote his brother John, an influential Republican senator from Ohio.[77] Sherman was in Smithland, at the mouth of the Cumberland, during Grant's assault on Donelson, in charge of shuttling troops, medicine, and ammunition to his old West Point classmate. "Every boat that came up with supplies or reinforcements brought a note of encouragement from Sherman, asking me to call upon him for any assistance he could render," Grant wrote later.[78] It was the beginning of an historic partnership.

U. S. Grant now became "Unconditional Surrender" Grant. Having read in the newspapers that the general was clutching a cigar at the culminating moment of the battle, grateful Americans sent him thousands of stogies. A frugal man, Grant switched almost completely from pipes to cigars, and would soon be smoking up to twenty a day.[79]

No congratulations came from Henry Halleck, however. The victory, he told Lincoln, belonged to C. F. Smith. "Promote him and the whole country will applaud," he said.[80] The day Halleck recommended Smith for promotion, the president nominated Grant for elevation to major general of volunteers. The Senate confirmed him enthusiastically, and he was given command of the new District of Western Tennessee, making him second in authority in the western theater.[81] What Washington "could hardly understand," wrote Charles A. Dana of the *New York Sun*, was that "this unknown man and undisciplined army had gained such an advantage over the public enemy, while the Army of the Potomac, with its perfect equipment and organization, its large number of trained officers and its enormous preponderance of force, had not yet begun its forward movement" on the Confederate capital at Richmond.[82]

Reporters who had been covering Grant began to change their minds about him. The navy had conquered Fort Henry, but Donelson was an army victory almost exclusively, and Grant had shown himself to be "our gun of heaviest metal and largest caliber." War correspondent Albert Richardson proclaimed him the "Coming Man" the nation had been awaiting.[83]

Few reporters took close notice of Grant's missteps at Donelson: He had underestimated the enemy he was about to fight and allowed his troops to discard their winter gear on the march to the fort. Once there, he had failed to entrench and left the battlefield without detailed instructions to his division commanders in the event of an attack. He had also improperly distributed his forces; not anticipating a rebel counterassault, he had failed to position sufficient reserves to reinforce the sector that came under heaviest attack. It was a battle he could easily have lost had he faced a competent commander. What the public saw, rather, was "the sweep and slam-bang power of a leader who marched on Wednesday, skirmished on Thursday, imperturbably watched his fleet's repulse on Friday, fought desperately on Saturday, and received the fort's unconditional surrender on Sunday."[84]

Also ignored or underestimated in the conquest of Forts Henry and Donelson was Grant's deployment of a new form of warfare: iron boats against riverfront fortifications, and the use of steamboats to move troops and supplies briskly and in big numbers. "Of all the major commanders in the Civil War," writes historian Allen C. Guelzo, "only Grant and McClellan seem to have had a real grasp of how to use the rivers and inland waterways in conjunction with the army." *[85] McClellan would employ riverine warfare in only one engagement, the Peninsula Campaign, later that year, an effort to capture Richmond by an amphibious landing south of the city at Fort Monroe, in Hampton, Virginia. Grant employed it at Belmont, Forts Henry and Donelson, and later at Shiloh and Vicksburg, the greatest amphibious campaign of the nineteenth century. Western waters, running north and south for hundreds of miles, were uniquely suited for Union offensives, unlike rivers in the eastern Confederacy, which were shorter, ran from west to east, and were not navigable for gunboats except along the Chesapeake Bay and the Atlantic coastline. The principal rivers Grant navigated—the Cumberland, Tennessee, and Mississippi—gave his armies virtually unbreakable supply lines back to Cairo, and from Cairo by rail to Chicago, St. Louis, Cincinnati, and other military-industrial centers.

The majesty and novelty of this mobile warfare impressed the troops. "Up and down as far as the eye could see were steamers crowded with blue coats, and still farther, hidden by the bends of the river, we could hear the puffing and snoring and see the smoke curling upward from still other steamers," recalled a Yankee soldier traveling on the fastest thing in the world on inland waters—a steam-driven Mississippi riverboat. To an Illinois soldier, a continuous line of these big wheels "was a sublime spectacle, far exceeding anything we ever saw."[86]

---

* Shortly after the fall of Donelson, Brigadier General John Pope cooperated with Foote's gunboats and mortar boats to seize Island No. 10, the rebel stronghold located on the tenth island in the Mississippi, below its junction with the Ohio. Pope was then transferred to the Virginia theater.

• • •

Ten days after the fall of Donelson, Grant wrote Halleck's headquarters, "I am growing anxious to know, what the next move is going to be." He wanted to strike farther south into cotton country, all the way to Corinth, Memphis, and Vicksburg.[87] Unless he received orders to the contrary, he informed Halleck, he would send General Smith and the gunboats to occupy Clarkesville and take Nashville on the Cumberland River. Halleck thought this a dangerous overreach and ordered Grant to stop at Clarkesville, sixty miles north of Nashville.[88]

Old Brains was more concerned with advancing his career than advancing his armies.[89] Before he released Grant to move south in pursuit of Johnston and Beauregard, Halleck wanted to be appointed head of all Union troops west of the Appalachians—his just reward, he thought, for Forts Henry and Donelson, victories he considered his, not Grant's. "May I assume command?" he wrote imperiously to George McClellan, the new head of all Federal armies. "Answer quickly."[90] The greatly delayed reply was a resounding "no." Halleck was to "cooperate fully" with the Union's other western commander, Major General Don Carlos Buell, a decorated Mexican War veteran whose Army of the Ohio was cautiously approaching Nashville.[91]

When Grant learned that advanced elements of the Army of the Ohio had captured the Tennessee capital on February 25 he hurried there with his staff, without permission from Halleck, to confer with Buell to learn what he could "of the movements of the enemy."[92] This infuriated Halleck and gave him the opportunity he had been seeking to rein in Grant. On March 3, he telegraphed McClellan saying Grant had "left his command" without his authority and had not been in touch with headquarters for over a week. He "richly deserves" to be "censured," he told McClellan, and suggested General C. F. Smith as "the only officer equal to the emergency."[93] McClellan was aware of Grant's battles with the bottle and may have read a maliciously inaccurate story in the *New York Herald* claiming Grant was so drunk before the Battle of Fort Donelson he had to be helped on to his horse.[94] "Do not hesitate to arrest him at once if the good of the service requires it, and place C. F. Smith in command," McClellan instructed Halleck.[95]

The following day Halleck, who had a more serious drinking problem than Grant, pushed the knife in deeper. "A rumor has just reached me that since the taking of Fort Donelson General Grant has resumed his former bad habits," he wired McClellan. "I do not deem it advisable to arrest him at present, but I have placed General Smith in command of the expedition up the Tennessee." The Tennessee raid was designed to disrupt rail communications to and from Johnston's army at Corinth.[96]

Grant was stunned. Halleck had been slow to respond to his advice and had been rudely dismissive at times, but, amazingly, Grant had never considered him a threat or an enemy. Reading Halleck's telegram ordering him to surrender command of the Tennessee expedition to Smith, Grant had "tears in his eyes" and his voice broke, recalled one of his aides. "I don't know what they mean to do with me. What command have I now?"[97]

Grant was not removed from command of his army, as he intimated in his memoirs. He was instead "suspended" from active command and ordered to remain at Fort Henry on garrison duty. To Grant, this amounted to being "under arrest," and it was widely believed in his army that he had been permanently "removed."[98]

Grant was being punished for failing "to report strength & positions" of his command while he was in Nashville against orders.[99] As it turned out, he *had* been in communication with St. Louis, but, unknown to Halleck or Grant, a telegraph operator in Cairo—a Confederate sympathizer—had failed to transmit messages to and from headquarters and Grant.[100] Grant would not learn of Halleck's earlier efforts to remove him until long after the war. Strangely, he still respected Halleck after being demoted, telling Julia he regarded him "as one of the greatest men of the age."[101] Nonetheless, he put his career on the line rather than supinely submit to Halleck's rebukes. When Halleck continued to harass him with astringently worded complaints about his failure to run his command with proper discipline, he demanded on three occasions to be "relieved from further duty in the Dept."[102] He wanted to "be placed in a separate Department so as to be more independent," he told Julia. But with no suitable commander available to replace Grant, Halleck ignored his requests.[103]

Grant then maneuvered to turn what Halleck had envisioned as a hit-and-run raid against Corinth's rail communications into a major offensive. He had lately been informed, he told Halleck, that Smith's expedition could expect to be met by a force of twenty thousand rebels. "This will take all my available troops," Grant reported, not the smaller number originally allocated.[104] It was a masterful subterfuge and a subtle rebuke for being treated unjustly by a superior jealous of his battlefield accomplishments.

Grant bore no animosity against Smith for accepting command of the upriver campaign. Battle had brought them closer together and had altered the character of their relationship. Watching Grant and Smith walk up and down the deck of Smith's boat on the evening before his expedition sailed, Dr. Brinton detected "an unconscious deference on the part of Smith to Grant as a soldier. It was apart from rank; it seemed indescribable; but it was there, it was the recognition of the master." [105] Grant, however, remained deferential to his former teacher. "Grant is a very modest person," Smith wrote to a friend. "From old awe of me— he was one of my pupils . . . —he dislikes to give me an order and says I ought to be in his place." [106]

The outrage in the army over Grant's supposed dismissal "quieted down," said Lew Wallace, when it was learned that Charles F. Smith would lead the Tennessee "enterprise." The Army of the Tennessee that Grant had fathered at Cairo was on the move again, this time into the heart of Dixie, and morale was sky-high. "I can give a faint idea of the spectacle of the embarkation," wrote Wallace. "One must think of thirty thousand uniformed men in array on the river-bank, drums going, arms glistening, and nearly seventy steamboats with smoking funnels at anchor ready to haul in and take their assignments aboard. He must think, too, of the excitement that prevailed, of the cheering, and braying of bands, and the waving of flags, for this . . . was a victorious army that knew its strength and rejoiced in it." [107]

Gaunt, red-bearded William T. Sherman, the newest and most senior of Grant's commanders, led the movement onto the boats.[108] He had recently arrived from Paducah, where, on Halleck's orders, he had been forming his own division out of fresh recruits from western states. Grant had wanted Sherman by his side, in his army, and he slipped deeper into depression on the day Smith's expedition departed. Days before the embarkation, a group of officers who had loyally served under Grant since Belmont came on board his headquarters boat at

Fort Henry and presented him with a sword of honor for his recent triumphs. Grant was speechless and had to retire to the outer deck to get hold of his emotions. There he ran into Dr. Brinton, who had not witnessed the ceremony. With tears in his eyes, Grant took Brinton by the arm, "without a word," and led him back to the table on which the sword lay in its open case. He pushed it toward Brinton. "Doctor, send it to my wife. I will never wear a sword again." [109]

Then as suddenly as Grant had been degraded, he was restored to full command. Not wanting to lose his most aggressive general, Lincoln instructed Secretary of War Stanton to have the army's adjutant general, Lorenzo Thomas, draft a sternly worded communication to Halleck demanding full documentation of Grant's allegedly insubordinate behavior:

> It has been reported that soon after the battle of Fort Donelson Brigadier-General Grant left his command without leave. By direction of the President the Secretary of War desires you to ascertain and report whether General Grant left his command at any time without proper authority, and, if so, for how long; whether he has made to you proper reports and returns of his force; whether he had committed any acts which were unauthorized or not in accordance with military subordination or propriety, and, if so, what.[110]

It was the first step toward an official inquiry, and Halleck, lacking evidence for his own duplicity and not wanting to alienate the president who had recently given him what McClellan had denied him—full control of Union armies in the west—backed down.*[111] Grant had gone to Nashville with "good intentions," Halleck told Stanton soothingly, and the communication problems between himself and Grant were the unfortunate result of an "interruption of telegraphic communica-

---

* On March 11, 1862, McClellan was removed as general-in-chief. He remained the commander of the Army of the Potomac.

tion."[112] Halleck then wrote directly to Grant: "Instead of relieving you I wish you as soon as your new army is in the field to assume the immediate command & lead it on to new victories."[113]

Flush from his success at Donelson, Grant believed the Confederacy was "on its last legs in Tennessee." One more decisive Union victory might end the war in the west. "I want to push on as rapidly as possible to save hard fighting," he wrote Julia. "These terrible battles are very good things to read about for persons who loose [sic] no friends but I am decidedly in favor of having as little of it as possible. The way to avoid it is to push forward as vigorously as possible."[114]

Finally, and surprisingly, Halleck was in full agreement. Informed that Johnston was being massively reinforced at Corinth, Halleck replied with resolve, ordering Don Carlos Buell, who now came under his authority, to join Grant in a unified effort to smash the rebel army in northern Mississippi.[115] Smith's Tennessee "expedition" was to be turned into a full-scale campaign, with Grant in command. But before Grant could strike he would have to wait for Buell and his thirty-five thousand men, who were moving slowly from Nashville, hindered by washed-out roads and bridges; and for Henry Halleck, who intended to personally lead the overland march of seventy-five thousand bluecoats on Corinth.

On March 16, Grant steamed upriver (southward) to rejoin his army near Savannah, a hamlet on the east bank of the Tennessee River, a hard day's march from the rebel encampment at Corinth. Advanced elements of the army were encamped farther south at Pittsburg Landing, on fields near a tiny log church called Shiloh. Smith had set himself up in a handsome Savannah mansion on a bluff overlooking a bend in the river. It was there, in the living room of the home's owner, William H. Cherry, a rich planter and prominent Union man, that Grant found him.

Smith welcomed Grant fulsomely, but the old soldier was limping noticeably on a leg he had cut badly climbing into a rowboat. But he was in a bright mood, his old martial self. "By God, I ask nothing better than to have the rebels come and attack us! We can whip them to hell."[116]

Smith misspoke. He wanted to hit the rebels before they hit him. So did Grant, but Halleck objected. "We must strike no blow," Halleck warned Grant, "till we are strong enough to admit no doubt of the result." [117] This did not sit easily with Grant. "There is no doubt a large force is being concentrate[d] at Corinth," he wrote Halleck, but "Corinth will fall much more easily than Donelson did, when we do move. All accounts agree in saying that the great mass of the Rank and file are heartily tired." [118]

It was the same miscalculation of enemy strength and resolve Grant had made before moving on Donelson. At Shiloh, the cost would be immeasurably greater.

CHAPTER 4

A Tremendous Murder Mill

"Lick 'em tomorrow." [1]

—U. S. Grant

Before leaving for Savannah, Tennessee, on March 17, Ulysses Grant wrote Julia, saying he expected a "big fight." [2] The battle that erupted three weeks later on a gorgeous Sunday morning was one of the most savagely contested of this or any other war. Its butchery shocked and horrified Americans, North and South. In two days, more men died on the ground near the Shiloh chapel than in all previous American wars combined. It was a battle that would raise Sherman in the estimation of his countrymen and nearly break Grant.

When Grant's steamer *Tigress* docked at Savannah on the morning of March 17, part of his army of thirty-seven thousand was encamped in a maze of fields and forests on high ground above Pittsburg Landing, a steamboat stop nine miles to the south, on the west bank of the Tennessee River. The Union commanders were poised to go on the offensive as soon as Don Carlos Buell arrived. The plan was to deliver a killing blow to the rebel army assembling at Corinth, a bleak, malarial backwater that was the most important rail juncture in the Mississippi Valley. At Corinth, the Memphis and Charleston Railroad, the Confederacy's only complete east-west link, crossed the Mobile and Ohio Railroad, which led south into the heart of the cotton kingdom. [3] If Grant took Corinth, the rebels in the lower Mississippi Valley would have only one major railroad to move troops and supplies, a line running eastward from Vicksburg through central Mississippi. Corinth was "the great strategic position [in] the West between the Tennessee and the

Mississippi rivers and between Nashville and Vicksburg," Grant wrote later.[4] If it fell, the way would be open to Vicksburg. This is why Grant had approved Smith's decision to position the divisions of Sherman and Benjamin M. Prentiss on ground near a tiny Methodist meetinghouse called Shiloh, meaning "place of peace." It sat close to the main road to Corinth, which was only twenty miles to the south.

It was the inexperience of these divisions that concerned Grant. Sherman had fought with distinction at Bull Run, and Prentiss, a scrappy Illinois lawyer, had seen action in the Mexican War, but their troops—plowboys, grocery clerks, and pork packers—were both untested and undisciplined. Great numbers of them had arrived at Pittsburg Landing without knowing how to load their muskets or form a proper firing line. To back them up, Grant moved three experienced units from Savannah to Pittsburg Landing: the divisions of McClernand; Stephen A. Hurlbut, an Illinois politician with close ties to the president; and W. H. L. Wallace, a Donelson veteran who had recently been assigned to take command of the ailing C. F. Smith's troops. The three divisions filed into position directly behind the camps of Sherman and Prentiss. Lew Wallace's division was stationed at Crump's Landing, on the western bank of the river, not far from Savannah. Wallace was to protect the Union flank.

In order to make early contact with Buell, who was marching south from Nashville, Grant remained at the Cherry mansion, directly on the riverfront. Upstairs, in a sunlit bedroom, was C. F. Smith, confined to his bed by a disabling fever. Every morning, Grant would steam south to Pittsburg Landing to meet with his commanders and return that evening.

Smith had put Sherman in charge of organizing the sprawling Union encampment, situated on a broad plateau of woodlands cut by ravines and fast-running streams, with occasional cleared fields—"almost a perfect wilderness," an Illinois soldier described it.[5] The tiny steamboat landing lay at the base of a steep red-clay bluff that separated the narrow dockage area from the plateau above. Confident that the enemy would remain at Corinth and fight behind its stout defenses, Grant chose not to entrench. Most of his troops "needed discipline and drill more than they did experience with the pick, shovel and axe," he reasoned.[6] Expecting to hit rather than be hit, Grant wanted his men in an aggressive posture. Sherman was of the same mind. "We were an invading army . . . our purpose was to move forward in force."[7]* It was the same mistake Grant had made at Donelson: expecting the enemy to behave as he hoped it would.

Sherman believed the army was encamped in an enviably strong position. Two flooded, impassable streams—Lick Creek and Owl Creek—protected its flanks, "narrowing the space over which we could be attacked to about a mile and a half or two miles."[8] But this was a reason to entrench. A dug-in army, fighting behind high earthen parapets, would have made this already formidable position virtually impregnable.[9]

As Grant prepared to strike the rebels, the rebels prepared to strike him. Jefferson Davis was determined to win back—in one lightning counterstroke—all that the Confederacy had lost in the black days of February. Reacting with unusual urgency, he called on nearly every Confederate garrison in the Mississippi Valley to concentrate at Corinth for the first great rebel counteroffensive of the war. By April 1, Albert Sidney Johnston and forty-three-year-old Pierre Gustave Toutant-Beauregard, his second in command, had assembled a resupplied and reanimated army of approximately forty thousand troops. They were led by the "Big Men" of the western confederacy: Leonidas Polk, former defender of Columbus, Kentucky; Braxton Bragg, the Confederacy's sixth-ranking general officer; John C. Breckinridge, a forty-one-year-old Kentuckian who had served as vice president under James Buchanan; and William J. Hardee, a former commandant of cadets at West Point and author of *Rifle and Light Infantry Tactics*, required reading at the academy.[10] Beauregard, the diminutive Louisiana Creole who directed the Confederate victory at Bull Run, was considered by some an astute tactician; and while Albert Sidney Johnston had been chastised in the Southern press for losing Forts Henry and Donelson, President Davis, his West Point

---

* Entrenching would have enabled Grant to "develop his offensive power from a secure base," wrote British historian J. F. C. Fuller, a keen student of Grant's military leadership. J. F. C. Fuller, *The Generalship of Ulysses S. Grant* (1929) (New York: Da Capo Press, 1991), 102.

classmate, had complete confidence in him. Courageous and charismatic, with square-cut, striking features and powerful shoulders, he looked to be everything Davis thought he was. "If he is not a general, we had better give up the war, for we have no general." [11]

The army Johnston aimed to annihilate was enjoying its encampment. "All the camps were beautiful," recalled a Union soldier, "convenient and healthy, with wood, water and parade ground close at hand. The scenery abounded in deep ravines, sparkling waters, rugged bluffs, and beautiful foliage." [12] After a period of rain and light snow in late March, the weather turned pleasantly warm, and peach trees, dogwoods, and wildflowers began to bloom. Soldiers bathed in cold country streams, played cards, pitched horseshoes, and wrote letters. Down by the Tennessee River, a steam calliope, carried on a wagon, played popular songs of the day. The camp had the appearance of "a gigantic picnic," said an Iowa boy. [13]

In early April, Union patrols exchanged fire with enemy skirmishers and cavalry units near the Corinth Road. Grant and Sherman seemed unconcerned. These were probes to assess Union strength, they were convinced, not preparations for a full-out assault. "We are constantly in the presence of the enemy's pickets, but am satisfied that they will await our coming at Corinth," Sherman wrote his wife, Ellen, on April 3. [14] Sherman was determined not to be accused of overestimating the enemy's strength. In Louisville, Kentucky, his first major wartime command, he was ridiculed by the press and forced from office for massively exaggerating the rebel threat in the state. So inflated were his estimates of enemy strength that reporters accused him of being mentally deranged. If he raised the alarm over enemy skirmishers and scouts at Shiloh, "they'd call me crazy again," he feared. [15]

Tall, lanky William T. Sherman had always been anxious and high-strung—and deeply insecure, despite his bravura demeanor. In Kentucky he had fallen into an incapacitating depression, tormented by fears that he was unfit for command, unable to lead in times of trouble. It was a crisis of confidence that had been building for some time.

Sherman's emotional troubles dated back to 1853, the year he resigned from the peacetime army to become manager of a small San Francisco bank. In succeeding years, he failed in every business venture he tried: banking, real estate, law, streetcars, and briefly—like Ulysses Grant—farming. After the collapse of a financial enterprise in which he had invested, he described himself as "the Jonah of banking . . . wherever I go, there is a breakdown."[16]

In 1829, Sherman's father, a successful lawyer and state supreme court justice in Lancaster, Ohio, had died without leaving an inheritance when "Cump"—short for "Tecumseh," the great Shawnee chief in whose memory his father had named him—was nine years old. Various family and friends took in his mother and her eleven children. Cump was taken in by the solidly situated family of Thomas Ewing Sr., a prominent lawyer and future U.S. senator. The Ewings resided in a stately home just up the block from the Shermans. A corpulent, sternly aloof patriarch, Thomas Ewing treated Cump "as his own son" and used his political clout to secure him an appointment to West Point, without the boy's knowledge or consent.[17] He thrived academically, excelling in drawing, chemistry, and natural philosophy, and graduated sixth in his class. The mischievous, high-spirited cadet would have graduated fourth had he not piled up an astonishing number of demerits.

Lieutenant Sherman was stationed in Florida, and saw action in the Second Seminole War. He was later transferred to South Carolina, where he intermingled with Charleston's planter elite. In 1850 he married Ellen Boyle Ewing, Thomas Ewing's bright, headstrong daughter. Nine years later, unemployed and depressed, he feared becoming a permanent ward of his foster father, who was already supporting Ellen and the children. Army friends intervened and helped him secure an appointment as superintendent of the Louisiana State Seminary of Learning and Military Academy in Pineville, which began classes a year before Lincoln's election. (It later became Louisiana State University.) He threw himself into the work of creating a college from scratch: hiring faculty, buying books, and shaping a curriculum modeled on that of West Point. But his modest salary left him financially fragile, and he hated being separated from his growing family. Ellen was immovable. She wanted her children in Lancaster and refused to visit him. "People begin to wonder why you dont [sic] come down," he wrote her.[18] Throughout their long and passionless marriage, Ellen Ewing Sherman never broke from her Ohio home, feeling more secure in the bosom of the Ewing family than she did with her footloose husband.*

Religion further divided them. She was a devout Catholic; he was a secular humanist who ridiculed her efforts to convert him. Back when the Ewing family took in nine-year-old Tecumseh, they had him baptized as a Catholic, a religion he came to regard as a citadel of priestly intolerance. "In sheer pigheaded willfulness, Ellen and William Tecumseh were just about a perfect match," writes biographer Michael Fellman.[19]

When Louisiana split from the Union, Sherman resigned from the academy he had built almost singlehandedly. "On no earthly account will I do any act or think any thought hostile to or in defiance of the old Government of the United States," he wrote the governor of Louisiana.[20] He rejoined the United States Army and was appointed a brigade commander under General Irvin McDowell. Sherman served to save the Union, not to end slavery. "I would not if I could abolish or modify slavery," he told Ellen's brother Thomas Ewing Jr., later a Union general and two-term U.S. congressman. "[Southern] Negroes . . . must of necessity be slaves. . . . All the congresses on earth can't make the negro anything else than he is. He must be subject to the white man, or he must amalgamate or be destroyed."[21]

Sherman had equally strong but opposite opinions about Southern secession, seeing it as high treason.[22] "On the question of secession . . . I am *ultra*—I believe in *coercion* and cannot comprehend how any Government can exist unless it defend[s] its integrity," he told a Southern friend.[23] His exemplary performance in defeat at Bull Run led to his appointment in the new Department of the Cumberland, where he served under Major General Robert Anderson, the Union hero of the siege of Fort Sumter. When Anderson's health declined under "the mental torture of his command," Sherman replaced him.[24]

Headquartered at Louisville, Kentucky, he worked himself into a state of exhaustion and despair over rising rebel strength in his department. When Secretary of War Simon Cameron visited him at the Galt House, his Louisville hotel, Sherman flew into a rage, claiming the rebels in the state were strong enough to storm Louisville and men-

---

* He and Ellen would eventually have eight children.

ace St. Louis. To stamp out the rebellion in Kentucky he would need, he claimed fantastically, two hundred thousand troops. "Great God!" Cameron threw up his hands and exclaimed. "Where are they to come from?"[25]

A correspondent for *New York Tribune* was in the room and published a full account of the meeting in his paper.[26] Sherman's mental condition became national news, but the public embarrassment failed to curb his erratic behavior, which grew worse, his mind veering between fury and despair. Pacing the corridors of the Galt House all night long, chain-smoking over a dozen cigars a day, eating hardly at all and drinking to excess, he imagined "overwhelming" enemy forces entering the state and saw little hope of keeping Kentucky in the Union fold.[27] Hotel guests began whispering about the sunken-faced, unkempt general who never slept and talked incessantly, "a half wild expression" on his face. "The gossip was that he was insane," reported the journalist Henry Villard.[28] "I do think I Should have committed suicide were it not for my children," Sherman later confessed to Ellen.[29]

Sensing he was near the breaking point, Sherman asked to be relieved from command. In mid-November, Don Carlos Buell replaced him, and Sherman was sent to St. Louis to serve under Henry Halleck, a close friend from their time together in California in the 1840s.[30] Halleck defended him publicly against charges of insanity, claiming he was merely exhausted and overworked, although he did confide to his wife that Sherman had "acted insane" in Louisville.[31]

Sherman was a shattered man when he arrived in St. Louis. He had lost confidence in both himself and the Union war effort. The war would bring "ruin to us all . . . I see no hope at all."[32] When he began ordering reprisals against rebel insurrections in Missouri that did not exist, Halleck had the department's medical director evaluate his mental state. He was declared "unfit for command" and Halleck sent him home to recover.[33] On returning to Lancaster, he picked up a copy of the popular *Cincinnati Commercial.* The headline read: "GENERAL Wm. T. SHERMAN INSANE." The accompanying story contained wildly inaccurate charges against a "stark mad" general who needed to be forced out of the service.[34] The next day, Sherman's son Tommy came home from school upset that a friend had said his father was "crazy."[35]

Sherman's condition deteriorated ominously. He would stare out of windows for hours, thoughts of suicide darting through his mind. But with the support of Ellen and the rest of the Ewing clan he slowly recovered. In January 1862, Halleck called him back to service and gave him a safe command, supervising Benton Barracks, an instructional camp for recruits near St. Louis. The reduction of his responsibilities bothered him not at all. "I do not think that I can again be entrusted with a command," he wrote Ellen in one of his recurring bouts of self-contempt. "This is mortifying but true."[36]

The black moods would return periodically, but by early February, Halleck pronounced him fit for command and, after Donelson, as we have seen, assigned him a division. Grant's "most extraordinary and brilliant" victory at Donelson (Sherman's words) also bolstered his faith in the Union cause.[37] "May ecstacy [sic] & glory ever attend you!" Ellen wrote gratefully to Halleck.[38]

So it was Henry Halleck, Grant's nemesis, who inadvertently brought Grant and Sherman together as partners in war; and it was Grant who gave Sherman a glimmer of hope for his country, where there had been only tormented despair. And when Halleck, with Grant's encouragement, gave Sherman command of Grant's newest division and sent Grant's army to Pittsburg Landing, he gave Sherman the opportunity he craved "to redeem" his "good name."[39]

Drilling and training his recruits on the fields near the Shiloh chapel, Sherman was reborn. This is where he most wanted to be, in the Mississippi Valley, the "grand theater" of the war.[40] "All I hope for is a chance to recover from the Past."[41]

With Grant residing at Savannah, Sherman was principally responsible for reporting on enemy activity in the vicinity of the Corinth Road. On April 4, rebel cavalry drove back Union pickets near his lines, capturing eight men. Grant rode out to assess the threat. It had merely been a "strong demonstration," Sherman assured him, "not the prelude to a general advance."[42]

Returning to the steamboat landing that night in a driving rainstorm, Grant's horse lost its footing and toppled over, pinning Grant's leg under its body and injuring his ankle so badly his boot had to be cut off. He was in pain and unable to walk without crutches for an entire week.[43]

The following day he wrote Halleck: "I have scarsely [sic] the faintest idea of an attack . . . being made upon us, but will be prepared should such a thing take place."[44] That evening, Colonel Jessie Appler, commander of the 53rd Ohio Infantry Regiment, sent word to Sherman that he was about to attack rebel skirmishers who had been spotted near their camp. For several days Appler had been sending Sherman alarming reports of rebel activity in the vicinity. Sherman was coldly dismissive. "Take your damned regiment back to Ohio," he rebuked Appler. "There is no enemy nearer than Corinth."[45] Hours later, Union pickets spotted "hundreds of [camp]fires" extending in the distance "as far as the eye could reach."[46]

Sherman and Grant were both guilty of appalling battlefield preparation: Sherman for not taking seriously credible intelligence gathered by his pickets, and Grant for taking Sherman's word that these reports were alarmist. Had Grant ordered a cavalry reconnaissance on the Corinth Road, it would have stumbled upon Johnston's army encamped in the open, less than two miles from the Union camp. "The total absence of cavalry pickets from General Grant's army was a matter of perfect amazement," a rebel officer noted after the battle.[47]

As at Donelson, Grant had also failed to take the precaution of appointing a commander to take charge of the army while he was away from the encampment. The second-ranking officer was John McClernand, who had been reckless at Belmont and surprised and routed at Donelson. This was no reason, however, to leave no one in charge when he was at Savannah.

Years after the battle, Don Carlos Buell, who had always considered Grant overrated as a field commander, penned a devastating, but not unfair, indictment of his battlefield preparation. A vast army lay for weeks, he said:

in isolated camps, with a river in its rear, and a hostile army claimed to be superior in numbers 20 miles distant in its front, while the commander made his headquarters and passed his nights 9 miles on the opposite side of the river. It had no line or order of battle, no defensive works of any sorts, no outposts, properly speaking, to give warning, or check the advance of an enemy, and no recognized head during the absence of the regular commander.[48]

On April 3, Albert Sidney Johnston put his forty thousand men, the largest Confederate army yet assembled in the war, on the road to Pittsburg Landing.[49] Eighty-five percent of the men had never seen combat. It was an army with "more enthusiasm than discipline, more valor than instruction," wrote dour Braxton Bragg, its chief of staff and strictest disciplinarian.[50]

Johnston divided his Army of Mississippi into four corps, and had them march on converging roads. The objective was to crush not one but two Federal armies: Grant's before it united with Buell's, and then Buell's alone. After routing them, Johnston meant to cross the Tennessee, strike north, and regain the territory in Tennessee and Kentucky he had previously lost to Grant.[51]

Johnston wanted to attack on the morning of April 4, but nothing went right on the march. The army left Corinth late and got jammed up on the narrow country roads, forcing him to push back the date. There was an additional postponement after violent storms turned dusty roads into nearly impassable quagmires. The lost time would be crucial. Had Johnston struck when he'd intended, he would have engaged Grant while Buell's army was too far away to help.

Beauregard implored Johnston to call off the assault and fall back to Corinth. Everything depended upon surprise, he said, and that was no longer possible: The night before, ten rebel cavalrymen on a reconnaissance mission had pushed forward without authority and been captured by Union pickets. Surely the Yankees had to know the enemy was near.[52] "Now they will be entrenched to the eyes," Beauregard warned Johnson.[53] Johnston overruled him. "We shall attack at daylight tomorrow," he ordered.[54]

Beauregard had already drawn up the battle plan. It was both audacious and unorthodox, and it would be initially successful. Beauregard stacked three corps of approximately ten thousand men each, one behind the other, and directed them to advance in parallel lines of

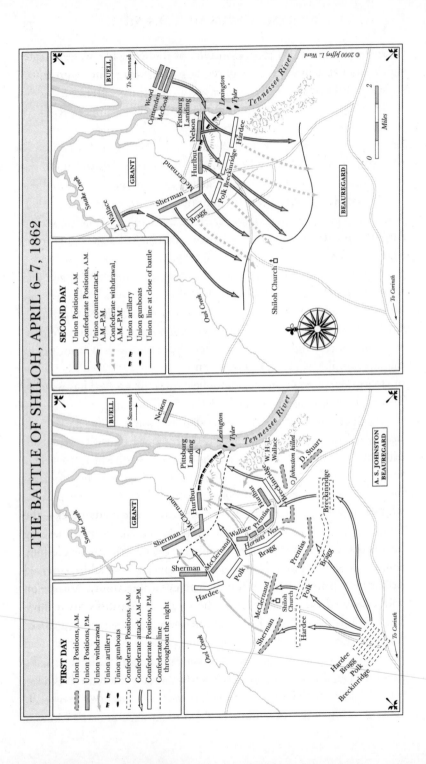

THE BATTLE OF SHILOH, APRIL 6–7, 1862

battle, with a fourth corps held in reserve. The objective was to create shock and panic by hitting every sector of the enemy line "with equal strength."[55] Attacking in successive waves, the thirty thousand troops would create an effect, said Beauregard, like "an Alpine avalanche."[56] As Johnston mounted his Thoroughbred, Fire-eater, to lead the advance, he was exultant. Lately the most disparaged general in the Confederacy, this day he vowed to regain his honor. "Tonight we will water our horses in the Tennessee River," he told his staff.[57]

Although the rebels sprang what Beauregard called "one of the most surprising surprises ever achieved," the Union army was saved from a greater slaughter by the vigilance of several junior officers who had disregarded Sherman's advice and redoubled their reconnaissance patrols on the morning of the rebel surge.[58] Around three o'clock on April 6, Colonel Everett Peabody, a brigade commander in Prentiss's division, sent out a patrol to locate rebel pickets reported to be in front of his camp.[59] Two hours later, Peabody's men spotted and engaged a battalion of General Hardee's corps in a cottonfield a mile from the Union camp. The Battle of Shiloh was on.[60]

The blasts from dozens of muskets were heard back in Prentiss's camp. "At that moment there began the long roll of the Union snare drums, resounding through the oak groves, rousing the men from their sleep and to their guns." Confusion reigned. What was the problem? men asked. And they were promptly answered by their own pickets, who came racing out of the woods shouting "get ready-quick—the Johnnies are here."[61] Moments later, Hardee's infantry was smashing into a battle line Prentiss had hastily assembled. Hardee's mile-long column—nine thousand men marching shoulder-to-shoulder—moved deliberately at first; then, feeling the enemy's vulnerability, it came on with sustained fury. The effect of the shock on Prentiss's Sixth Division was exactly as Beauregard had intended. By nine o'clock Prentiss had lost a fifth of his division, including Peabody, who perished from five bullet wounds sustained in the opening minutes of the attack. By sheer accident Hardee had struck the most vulnerable unit in the Union army, a division that had been in existence less than two weeks. Its more disciplined troops held their ground for nearly an hour but were doomed when some two thousand men panicked, tossed down their weapons, and fled northward toward Pittsburg Landing, "the only safe haven they knew existed in this deadly wilderness."[62]

Sherman's division was hit next. Hearing the muffled sound of gunfire in the distance, Colonel Appler sounded the general alarm—a long roll of drums—and sent word to Sherman, who inexcusably stayed put, believing Appler had "lost his senses."[63] When the cannon fire intensified, Sherman finally rode out with his staff to investigate. As he was peering through his field glasses, one of his officers raced toward him, shouting to him to look to his right. That very second, rebel skirmishers crashed through thick underbrush and opened fire, killing Sherman's orderly, who was riding beside him, and wounding Sherman in the hand.[64] "By God, we are attacked!" Sherman cried, and directed Appler to hold his line.[65] Yet it was not until an hour later, around eight o'clock, when Sherman saw "the glistening bayonets of heavy masses of infantry" in the forest near his camp, that he "became satisfied for the first time," he admitted afterward, "that the enemy designed a determined attack on our whole camp."[66]

"The sound of great guns now came in regular throbbings—the strong, full pulse of the fever of battle," wrote Ambrose Bierce, the noted writer who was then a young lieutenant in Buell's Army of the Ohio. He would not arrive on the battlefield till nightfall, but he later described that first day's action in "What I Saw at Shiloh," one of the finest prose pieces of the war.[67]

For the remainder of their lives, Sherman and Grant would insist that the Union army had not been surprised at Shiloh; it had been "on the alert."[68] But there is a world of difference between being alert for rebel skirmishers and having the army prepared for a full-out attack. If the rebel assault on the morning of April 6 did not "constitute a surprise, then there is no use for such a word in the language," said Confederate general and historian Basil W. Duke.[69]

Sherman's troops had received their muskets for the first time at Paducah only a week earlier, and not a single soldier in the division had seen combat. Still, for nearly three hours, they put up a commendable defense. But the rebel assault columns soon congealed into an unstoppable juggernaut that moved with dread purpose through a "low-lying sulphurous cloud."[70] Sherman's line was pushed back, and thousands of his volunteers joined Prentiss's men in a mad stampede to the steamboat landing.

There were cowards among them, certainly, but most of these men had been psychologically unprepared to fight on the defensive. "For the psychological failure . . . the original blame lies with the command," wrote the British soldier-historian B. H. Liddell Hart. It was not the suddenness of the rebel attack that caused the collapse of the Union front line; it was the inexperience of the regimental officers and men—that and the offensive spirit drilled into them by their commanders. "Filled with the idea of hitting, they had never entertained the idea of guarding."[71]

With his situation hopeless, Sherman ordered his remaining men to fall back and merge with McClernand's division, encamped to their rear. The divisions of Hurlbut and W. H. L. Wallace were soon sucked into the battle, and the fighting became "a grapple and a death struggle."[72]

When the rebels opened their assault on Prentiss's division, Grant was eating breakfast with his staff at the Cherry house, preparing to ride out and meet Buell. Hearing the low rumble of artillery in the vicinity of Pittsburg Landing, he rose from his chair and said calmly, "Gentlemen, the ball is in motion. Let's be off."[73]

Minutes later, he and his staff were aboard *Tigress*, one of the fastest boats on the river. While it was getting up steam, Grant scratched out a hurried dispatch to Brigadier General William "Bull" Nelson, one of Buell's leading commanders, directing him to march his division immediately from Savannah, where they were encamped, to Pittsburg Landing. Nelson, a three-hundred-pound Kentuckian known for his profanity and pugnacity, had arrived at Savannah the day before, ahead of the rest of Buell's army. Buell arrived hours later, on his own, and spent the night in camp without informing Grant.[74] He resented cooperating with him and was in no hurry to meet him. In any event, he could offer no immediate help. The bulk of his army was still a day's ride away.

As *Tigress* struggled upstream against the current of the flood-swollen Tennessee, Grant directed the captain to run in close to Crump's Landing so he could communicate with Lew Wallace. Finding Wallace waiting on the deck of his headquarters boat, Grant leaned over the railing and ordered him "to get his troops in line." He would call on them when he learned where the rebels had struck.[75]

When *Tigress* docked at Pittsburg Landing, Grant was told by Union officers that the rebels had attacked from the Corinth Road. He then sent a dispatch to Wallace to "march immediately" to the battlefield by a road near the river.[76] Spurring his horse, his crutches strapped to the saddle like a carbine, he charged up the slope to the high ground. There he encountered men in blue, without rifles, streaming toward him, down the narrow road to the steamboat landing. "What are you running for?" Grant asked one of them. "Because I can't fly!" came the answer.[77] After setting up a blocking line across the road, Grant headed toward the sound of the guns. Two miles from Pittsburg Landing, the opposing armies were locked in not one battle but dozens of fiercely contested smaller ones, distinct "soldiers' fights," with the onrushing rebels holding the advantage.[78]

Grant realized that the immediate objective was not victory but avoiding annihilation. By ten o'clock, he, Sherman, and McClernand, operating separately, had formed part of the army into a loosely strung-out defensive line, with the men's backs to the river. This was no ordinary accomplishment, for the battle had degenerated into a "frightful melee." Unlike the machine-like European armies with their parade-ground regularity, these were frontier armies unschooled in professional tactics; retreats were "races to the rear, just as charges were rushes forward," Lew Wallace wrote later.[79] "No battle of the war does more to justify Moltke's sneer at the American fighting as a struggle of two armed mobs" than Shiloh, said historian Allan Nevins.[80]

Leadership was required, and Grant, who fought and thought best under pressure, set out to provide it. In the space of nine hours, he would make, by one estimate, eighteen important decisions that saved his army.[81] Grant seemed to be everywhere on the field at once, biting down on a cigar but otherwise betraying no anxiety or excitement, even when a shell fragment struck his scabbard, shattering it. He may have worried about Sherman, however, highly excitable and in the fight of his life. When Grant rode up to him around ten o'clock, he found him commanding, in effect, two divisions, his own and McClernand's, which had been smashed and scattered. He had had two horses shot out from under him and had a blood-soaked handkerchief around his bleeding right hand, where buckshot had hit a bone; a tear in his shoulder strap, where a bullet had grazed his skin; and a bullet hole in his hat. His scraggy red beard was covered with black powder, and there was a feral intensity in his eyes. But the "insane" commander who had been emotionally overwhelmed in Kentucky had about him a commanding confidence. "Erect in his saddle," he "looked a veritable war eagle," said a young soldier in his ranks.[82] Satisfied that Sherman was holding on, Grant rode off to meet Prentiss, who was in deeper trouble.

Driven back a full mile from the ground around the Shiloh church, Prentiss was making an obstinate stand along the shallow ruts of an old wagon trace—misnamed after the war the Sunken Road. Hurlbut and W. H. L. Wallace had their divisions join him there, but he was still badly outnumbered, and Grant had no reinforcements available. All he could do was order Prentiss to maintain his position "at all hazards," in a place where the bullets were flying so freely it was later named the "Hornet's Nest."[83]

As Grant rode off, he must have known that he was sacrificing thousands of these 6,200 men in a desperate effort to blunt the rebel drive. "Unwilling to harm any living thing himself, he had the resolution to send columns of men into battle calmly and without hesitation," wrote Hamlin Garland. "Without this constitution of mind no great commander can succeed."[84]

After leaving Prentiss, Grant sent a message to Buell to rush to the front; reinforcements could "possibly save the day to us."[85] This urgently worded communiqué displays uncharacteristic anxiety—the first sign of nerves Grant had shown that day. His concern was understandable. In the fog of battle, he thought he was facing one hundred thousand rebels, not the forty thousand or so engaged; and he was short an entire division. Lew Wallace was nowhere in sight. Grant had sent scouts to find him, but they had not yet reported back.[86]

Around midafternoon, Grant received word that Don Carlos Buell had arrived at Pittsburg Landing by steamer, ahead of his army. What Buell saw there horrified him. Six to eight thousand terrified stragglers were packed together under the bluff, crying out that the army was "destroyed and beaten." Buell berated them and threatened to have two Union gunboats stationed nearby fire on them if they refused to rejoin the fight—all to no effect.[87] He remained in an ugly mood when he met with Grant on *Tigress*. The commander he encountered showed "none of that confidence" he was reputed to possess, Buell wrote later.[88] Rawlins, who witnessed the meeting, disputed this. When Buell asked Grant "what preparation" he had "made for retreating," Grant reportedly said calmly: "I have not yet despaired of whipping them, General."[89] Buell turned and left, visibly disgusted, believing Grant's optimism delusional.

Late in the afternoon the battle appeared lost when the rebels overwhelmed Prentiss in the Hornet's Nest after his men had repulsed a dozen charges. The coup de grâce was a massed Confederate artillery barrage, the largest yet unleashed on the North American continent. Fifty-three guns opened up simultaneously and at close range, creating a tornado of fire and lead that uprooted trees and tore bodies to pieces. "It was as if the Hornet's Nest exploded."[90] Rebel troops then converged on Prentiss's flanks, mortally wounding General W. H. L. Wallace and forcing Prentiss to surrender his 2,200 survivors, great numbers of them horribly wounded. They had held out through six hours of continuous fighting that allowed Grant to make an organized withdrawal toward the Tennessee River, where Johnston had predicted his men would finish off the Federals.[91]

"We have been falling back all day," wrote a correspondent from the *Cincinnati Gazette* around five thirty that afternoon. "We can do it no more. . . . The hospitals are filled to overflowing. A long ridge bluff is set apart for surgical uses. It is covered with the maimed, the dead and dying. And our men are discouraged by prolonged defeat."[92] The purpose of every Union officer was now to hold on until darkness descended or Buell and Wallace arrived.

Unknown to Grant, Johnston's army was as disorganized as his own. Beauregard's "avalanche," so effective at the opening of hostilities, sowed confusion as the fight wore on. His three corps—deployed a mere five hundred yards apart—became intermingled when the second and third lines advanced to support the first.[93] Men lost touch with their commanders, and thousands broke ranks and began pillaging the Union tents for whiskey, coats and shoes, and most of all fresh food, for they had been subsisting for two days on "sodden biscuits and raw bacon," wrote rebel private, Welsh emigrant, and later famed African explorer Henry Morgan Stanley.[94] Johnston was not there to restore order. He had been killed earlier in the afternoon. A stray minie ball—possibly fired by one of his own men—struck his right leg behind the knee, severing the popliteal artery, and the bleeding could not be stopped.[95] Johnston lost consciousness and expired on the battlefield. A tourniquet would have saved him. Johnston had one in his pocket, but it was not discovered until after he expired.[96] His personal surgeon had been riding close to him in the morning, but he was off, on Johnston's orders, treating wounded Wisconsin soldiers they had passed in the field. "These men were our enemies a moment ago; they are our prisoners now. Take care of them," Johnston had instructed Dr. D. W. Yandell.[97]

The fallen commander was taken in secret from the battlefield, wrapped in a muddy blanket. He was the highest-ranking general officer of either army killed in action in the Civil War.

Beauregard assumed command but was physically unable to direct the battle from the front. Afflicted by a serious throat ailment and a chronic bronchial infection, he was weak and barely able to speak, and remained at headquarters, a mile and a half to the rear.[98]

At this point in the battle it didn't matter who commanded the rebel army. "The spinning wheels on the Confederate war machine had already wasted too much daylight," writes historian Timothy B. Smith.[99] As rebel commanders paused to concentrate their scattered troops for a series of culminating, late-afternoon assaults on the Union position, there was a lull in the battle. This gave Colonel Joseph D. Webster, Grant's chief of staff, time to form a defensive line three hundred yards from the steamboat landing on a ridge overlooking a steep ravine called Dill Branch. Webster positioned seventy cannon wheel to wheel along with a battery of mammoth siege guns originally intended to be used against Corinth's defenses. Dill Branch was flooded by backwater from the fast-rising Tennessee River. The overflow created a moat that slowed the rebel advance, allowing Webster to complete his cannon line.

Formed up near the firing line were nearly twenty thousand infantry. "We had a line of battle over half a mile long . . . as solid as a rock," said a Union gunner.[100] The left side of the line was swept by the monster 32-pound guns of the timberclads *Tyler* and *Lexington*, positioned close to the mouth of Dill Branch. "Everyone seemed to be imbued with the idea that as this was our last stand, so should it be the most desperate," wrote a Chicago artillery officer.[101]

The exhausted Confederates, under Braxton Bragg, made a series of disorganized attacks against this formidable position. "One more charge, my men, and we shall capture them all," Bragg exhorted his troops as they ran into a wall of fire: canister and grape from the field guns, shot and shell from the three-ton siege guns, and thunderous volleys from the timberclads.[102]

As Grant looked on, an aide who happened to be standing next to him had his head blown off by a 6-pound cannon ball. Covered with blood and brain matter, Grant "moved his position a little and sat chewing his cigar as imperturbably as though on dress parade," said one of the gunners.[103] "If [Grant] had studied to be undramatic, he could not have succeeded better," wrote Lew Wallace.[104]

Around this time a reporter asked Grant if he considered the Union situation desperate. "Oh no, they can't break our lines tonight—it is too late. Tomorrow we shall attack them with fresh troops and drive them, of course."[105] Minutes later, Bull Nelson arrived at Pittsburg Landing with advanced elements of Buell's army, and his men began crossing the Tennessee River on steamers. Riding a stately Kentucky stallion, Nelson led his men ashore through the mass of demoralized stragglers and deserters cowering under the riverbank, men "deaf to duty, dead to shame," wrote Ambrose Bierce.[106] Their numbers had grown to upward of ten thousand and they were crying out that the army was "'whipped: cut to pieces,'" said Nelson. "They were insensible to shame or sarcasm—for I tried both on them." He ordered his men to draw their sabers and "trample these bastards in the mud."[107]

The remainder of Buell's army—seventeen thousand veteran troops—had left Savannah and would arrive that night, Nelson informed Grant. Nelson's men had barely gotten into position around six o'clock when Beauregard issued an order to "cease hostilities" and withdraw the troops out of range of the federal gunboats.[108] Braxton Bragg was furious. A final "energetic assault," he protested, would "deal the death stroke."[109] But his men were bone-weary, having fought continuously for eleven hours without rations. Beauregard's order, said a member of Bragg's own staff, was "most timely."[110]

Beauregard's directive provoked one of the hottest controversies of the Civil War. For years afterward, he was subjected to scorching criticism from Bragg, Hardee, and other Southern officers, along with some prominent Southern historians. It became known as the "Lost Opportunity": the Confederate Army's last chance to reverse the course of the war in the west.[111] Few who sided with Bragg, however, mention the depleted condition of the men expected to make that final charge, or the fact that hundreds of them had exhausted their ammunition and would have had to go against the Union cannon with only their bayonets.[112] Grant's guns, not Beauregard's order, ended the battle at Dill Branch.

That night, Beauregard rested in General Sherman's tent, confident he had won a war-changing victory. "After a severe battle of ten hours, thanks be to the Almight [we] gained a complete victory, driving the enemy from every position," he wired Richmond.[113] All that remained was a mop-up operation in the morning. "I thought I had Grant just where I wanted him," he wrote later.[114] Beauregard had no idea Buell's army was preparing to cross the Tennessee and link up with Grant. His scouts had spotted one division of Buell's army in northern Alabama and mistook it for the entire army.[115] It was a stupendous intelligence blunder.

General Prentiss, a prisoner in Beauregard's care, shared a bed that evening with two Confederate staff officers, one of them an old acquaintance. There was some lighthearted banter. "You gentlemen have had your way today, but it will be very different tomorrow," Prentiss said with a laugh. "You'll see! Buell will effect a junction with Grant tonight, and we'll turn the tables on you in the morning."[116]

That evening, Lew Wallace's errant division finally arrived at Pittsburg Landing. Relying upon inaccurate maps, it had taken them ten hours to march six miles. His march also "appeared intolerably slow," said an aide Grant had sent to find him, "resembling more a reconnaissance in the face of an enemy than a forced march to relieve a hard-pressed army."[117] Grant never forgave him.

The army, Wallace could see, had taken a terrible pounding. At least seven thousand men had been lost, and every Union camp on the battlefield was in enemy hands.[118] But they had held. "The steady determination of Grant's troops during that long April Sunday was perhaps unequaled during the war," wrote reporter Albert Richardson.[119] Even veteran troops were physically sickened by the carnage. That night, men carried broken and bloodied comrades to field hospitals, where doctors operated up to their elbows in blood. "These tents," wrote Ambrose Bierce, "were constantly receiving the wounded, yet were never full; they were continually ejecting the dead. . . . It was as if the helpless had been carried in and murdered, that they might not hamper those whose business it was to fall tomorrow."[120]

Out on the darkened and still battlefield could be heard the moans of friends burning to death, roasted by fires that roared across wide areas of undergrowth in the dense woodlands where heavy fighting had raged.[121] There was another sound: feral hogs were chewing apart the corpses of fallen men and "quarreling over their carnival feast."[122]

A heavy rain began to fall, and lightning split the sky. The Federals slept in shallow puddles or on mounds of packed mud, without the warmth of fires. Grant declined the comfort of a steamboat cabin and spent the night with his men. He sought shelter from the pounding rain under an oak tree, but the throbbing pain in his swollen ankle kept him awake. He then hobbled off to a log house that had been his headquarters that day. It had been converted into a field hospital, and the screams of mangled soldiers, blood showering from their amputated arms and legs, drove him off. "The sight was more unendurable than encountering the enemy's fire, and I returned to my tree in the rain."[123]

It was there that Sherman found him. He had come to implore Grant to retreat and "recuperate." Sherman feared Buell's army would not cross the river that night, "lest he should become involved in our general disaster."[124] But as he approached Grant, standing against the tree with a lantern in his hand, a cigar "glowing between his teeth," he was "moved by some wise and sudden instinct" not to bring up the idea of retreat.

"Well Grant, we've had the devil's own day, haven't we?"

"Yes," said Grant. "Lick 'em tomorrow, though."[125]

A short while later, Union troops on the front lines heard the stirring sounds of regimental bands. The Army of the Ohio had arrived.[126] The men were in high spirits, eager to engage, recalled Bierce. "If you had laid your hand in the beard or hair of one of these men it would have crackled and shot sparks." [127]

Nelson's division opened the offensive before first light, completely surprising the enemy. The roar of musketry and field artillery roused General Prentiss, in his tent near the Shiloh church. "There is Buell!" he informed his rebel bunkmates. [128]

The day belonged to the Federals. Their suddenly superior army—Beauregard could muster only twenty thousand or so weary men against forty thousand Federals—pushed back the rebels, who gave way stubbornly but irremediably. They were facing twenty-two thousand of Buell's fresh troops, and every Confederate on the field had fought the previous day. [129] As rebel losses mounted alarmingly, "the fire and animation . . . left our troops," said a Southern officer. [130] By two thirty, Beauregard knew it was over, and pulled his beaten army back onto the Corinth Road, leaving his dead behind. [131]

Grant did not pursue, forfeiting a chance, his critics charged, to destroy Beauregard's demoralized army. The Ohio boys were relatively fresh, and Buell was ready to move, Allan Nevins argued. [132] But Buell's official report tells another story. He was, he said, "without cavalry," his corps had become "scattered," and he "knew practically nothing" about the roads or the country over which the rebels were withdrawing. [133]

Beauregard's retreating troops were, it was true, incapable of repulsing an organized Union pursuit. "Our condition is horrible," Bragg wrote on April 8, halfway back to Corinth. "Troops utterly disorganized and demoralized. Roads almost impassable. No provisions and no forage." But even if Grant had known the piteous condition of the escaping enemy, his troops were in no condition to conduct an effective pursuit. "My force," he wired Halleck, "was too much fatigued from two days' hard fighting and exposure in the open air to a drenching rain during the intervening night to pursue immediately." [134]

Asked about this, years later, Sherman gave historian John Fiske a jocular but dead-on reply: "I assure you, dear fellow, that we had quite enough of their society for two whole days, and were only too glad to be rid of them on any terms!" [135]

• • •

The Battle of Pittsburg Landing ended where it had begun, on the Shiloh chapel ridge. As Sherman rode past his battle-torn regiments, a cheer went "rolling down the line. . . . He rode slowly, his grizzled face beaming with animation, his tall form swaying from side to side, and arms waving. . . . 'Boys,'" he shouted, "you have won a great victory.'"[136] And so had he, over mental demons and public rebuke.

The losses were terrible and nearly equal. Grant and Buell together lost over thirteen thousand men; Johnston and Beauregard suffered 10,699 losses.[137] Roughly a quarter of the hundred thousand soldiers who fought on the broken ground above Pittsburg Landing were casualties. "There has been nothing like it on this continent," Grant wrote after the battle.[138]

The topography had compounded the butcher's bill. With heavily flooded Owl and Lick Creeks forming the right and left flanks of the Union camps, the rebels were compelled to attack head-on, in one direction, and the entire battle was compressed into the narrow area between the creeks—a killing field less than three miles wide. "In places dead men lay so closely that a person could walk over two acres of ground and not step off the bodies," observed one soldier.[139] "Atrocious and sickening smells" rose from the battlefield, where dead men and horses had been tossed into shallow trenches and "barely covered over," wrote a Union officer. The air was so "poisoned" by the "effluvium . . . of decomposition" it could hardly be breathed.[140]

Shiloh, wrote Lew Wallace, was a "tremendous murder-mill."[141]

When the battle ended, the two armies were roughly where they had started. Shiloh "apparently had settled nothing," concluded Shelby Foote.[142] Yet it had: Beauregard and Johnston had failed to drive the Federals from Tennessee and lost the best opportunity of the war to capture or cut to pieces a major Union army, and darken or destroy the careers of Grant and Sherman.

Shiloh changed Grant's mind about the war. "Up to the battle of Shiloh, I . . . believed that the rebellion against the Government would collapse suddenly and soon, if a decisive victory could be gained over any of its armies." But what Grant witnessed on the first day at Shiloh—fighting of incomparable ferocity—convinced him the Union could be saved only by "complete conquest."[143] Henceforth, the war would have to be fought differently, with an intensity "beyond anything that had yet been seen."[144]

When news of the Union victory reached Washington on April 9 there was jubilation. Congress suspended business, and Lincoln set aside a national day of worship. New York newspapers declared Grant a national hero.[145] Then the casualty lists became public. "The desolation of homes was terrible," wrote Hamlin Garland. "Long columns of the dead filled the newspapers. . . . The nation was appalled, and naturally a large part of the bitterness and hate of war fell upon Grant."[146] Reporters and editors pounced on him for being caught by surprise, miles from the battlefield when the fighting commenced. The first report came from twenty-four-year-old Whitelaw Reid of the *Cincinnati Gazette*, who had rushed back to Cincinnati immediately after the battle to file his story. Passing through Cairo, he ran into fellow reporter Franc Wilkie. Reid looked "as if he had just been the witness of some tremendous calamity which he had narrowly escaped," Wilkie related.[147]

Reid's sensationalist account of the battle became the one the nation believed. It was filled with soldier gossip, much of it from men who had fled the field for the safety of the steamboat landing. The army, Reid said, had been surprised in its camps, and men were shot and bayoneted in their cots and left "gasping in their agony" for two days. Grant's army would have been crushed, he concluded, had not Buell's Army of the Ohio arrived on the field.[148]* "I fear [Grant] is played out," Joseph Medill, editor of the *Chicago Tribune*, wrote to Congressman Washburne. "The soldiers are down on him."[149] Grant "was simply another general who had gone up like a rocket and had fallen a charred stick," Garland wrote years later.[150]

Against all evidence, Grant continued to deny he had been surprised at Shiloh. "If the enemy had sent us word when and where they would attack us, we could not have been better prepared," he wrote incredibly to his father.[151] Without Grant's permission or prior knowledge, Jesse

---

* "No self-delusion is more natural, nor so commonly repeated in history, than for an army which arrives on the scene when the enemy has shot his bolt to believe, and proclaim, that this result is solely due to the latest arrivals." W. H. Liddell Hart, *Sherman*, 133.

forwarded the letter to the editor of the *Cincinnati Commercial*, who published it, making Grant the object of further newspaper ridicule.[152]

Yet again, Grant was accused of being drunk on the battlefield, a "fiction [that] showed the tenacity of a bad name," said reporter Albert Richardson.[153] In a letter to the secretary of the treasury, Salmon Chase, Murat Halstead of the *Cincinnati Commercial* called Grant a "drunken imbecile. . . . He is most of the time half drunk, and much of the time idiotically drunk."[154] Congressman James Harlan of Iowa said Grant had blundered badly at Belmont, had been saved at Donelson by Smith and by Buell at Shiloh. "With such a record those who continue General Grant in active command will in my opinion carry on their skirts the blood of thousands of their slaughtered countrymen."[155]

Ohio lieutenant governor Benjamin Stanton visited the Union camps at Pittsburg Landing after the battle and wrote a newspaper account claiming there was "an intense feeling of indignation against Generals Grant and Prentiss. . . . The general feeling amongst the most intelligent men with whom I conversed, is that they ought to be court-martialed and shot."[156] Sherman responded indignantly, but it did nothing to quell the storm. Washburne and John Sherman tried to mobilize support for Grant in Congress, unsuccessfully, but both had the ear of the president. "I can't spare this man; he fights," Lincoln supposedly told Pennsylvania politician Alexander K. McClure, who had been pressing insistently for Grant's removal.[157] Yet if Lincoln was entirely convinced of Grant's capacity it is unlikely he would have had Secretary of War Stanton send a sternly worded note to Halleck inquiring "whether any neglect or misconduct of General Grant or any other officer contributed to the sad casualties that befell our forces on Sunday."[158]

Halleck, surprisingly and honorably, refused to single out Grant for censure.[159] Grant appreciated this support from an unlikely source, but nothing could pull him out of the steep depression into which he fell after Shiloh. "To say that I have not been distressed at these attacks upon me would be false," he wrote Congressman Washburne, still his most steadfast defender, "for I have a father, mother, wife & children who read them and are distressed by them."[160] Then on April 25, General Charles Smith died after a lingering illness. With Smith gone, Grant's only "true friend," he wrote Julia, was Sherman, his "able and gallant defender."[161]

Sherman was as responsible as Grant for being caught by surprise at Shiloh, but the press hailed him as the battle's hero. He was on the field, at his post, when the rebels struck; Grant was having breakfast miles away. And it was Sherman who had formed a defensive line against the initial rebel assault, preventing the army from being pushed into the river. "During eight hours the fate of the army depended on the life of one man," said Bull Nelson. "If General Sherman had fallen, the army would have been captured or destroyed."[162] Halleck proposed that he be made a major general of volunteers, and the promotion was announced on May 1.[163] "I know your father will be pleased that I am once more restored to favor," Sherman wrote Ellen.[164] Sherman said he was in "high feather," and though his mood would continue to shift "like a barometer in a tropic sea," he would not suffer, for the duration of the war, an incapacitating depression.[165]

On April 11, four days after the battle, Henry Halleck arrived at Pittsburg Landing and assumed personal command of all Union forces, superseding Grant, who was assigned the meaningless position of second in command. In preparation for a march on Corinth to finish off Beauregard's army and seize that important rail center, Halleck assembled a gigantic force of 120,000 soldiers and divided them into three corps, under Generals Buell, George H. Thomas, and John Pope. Thomas, one of the rising stars in the western theater, had been a division commander in Buell's Army of the Ohio, and Sherman was assigned to his command. They were friends and former classmates at West Point. Pope and his Army of the Mississippi had just scored one of the most important victories of the Valley campaign. Working in tandem with Andrew Foote's ironclads, they had taken Island No. 10, an enemy stronghold on the Mississippi fifty miles downriver from Columbus.[166] "I was little more than an observer," said Grant of his subordinate role in the reorganized army.[167]

Grant viewed his insignificant position as tantamount to being "relieved entirely from further duty," he told Halleck.[168] Halleck, as devious as ever, claimed to be "surprised" by this; the position of second in command was actually, he claimed, a promotion."[169] Grant was not appeased.[170]

Halleck never revealed his reasons for demoting Grant, but he came as close as he ever would in a letter he wrote later that summer. Never, he said, had he encountered a commander "more deficient in the business of organization. Brave & able in the field, he has no idea of how to regulate & organize his forces before a battle."[171] Were Grant to be put in charge of the march to Corinth, his "undisciplined" army could, Halleck feared, fall victim to yet another surprise attack.[172]

Although the army encountered no serious opposition on its march to Corinth, Halleck fortified every evening encampment, determined "not be attacked unawares."[173] Interminable entrenching duty eroded soldier morale. "My men will never dig another ditch for Halleck except to bury him," John Logan exclaimed after the campaign.[174] A march that should have taken two days would take over four weeks, as men slogged along in woolen uniforms under a blazing Mississippi sun at a rate of a mile per day.

On May 28 Halleck finally reached the outskirts of Corinth and began to entrench, this time in preparation for a siege. The following evening Union soldiers heard "unusual sounds" coming out of the village: "the constant whistling of locomotives."[175] Halleck thought Beauregard was being reinforced, when in fact he was pulling off what one historian has called "the greatest hoax of the war." Empty trains had been ordered to pull into and out of Corinth, blowing their whistles to the welcoming cheers of rebel soldiers. All the while, a regimental band strolled up and down the lines, stopping here and there to play "retreat, tattoo, and taps."[176] Shortly after midnight, John Pope telegraphed Halleck: "The enemy is reinforcing heavily, by trains, in my front and on my left. The cars are running constantly, and the cheering is immense every time they unload in front of me. I have no doubt . . . I shall be attacked in heavy force at daylight."[177]

At dawn, there was "a series of explosions followed by a dense smoke rising high over the town." When Sherman moved ahead to "feel" the enemy, he pushed unimpeded into Corinth and found the village deserted. The night before, Beauregard, his army decimated by disease, had made a "clean retreat" by rail to Tupelo, Mississippi, fifty miles south.[178] Halleck failed to pursue aggressively.[179] At Corinth he forever lost the name "Old Brains," said Richardson.[180]

It was not, however, an empty victory. Beauregard had handed the bewildered Federals a great prize. Henceforth, enemy troop and supply trains heading east to Richmond would have to divert through Mobile and Atlanta, a devastating blow to Confederate logistics. More important, Union troops were now firmly positioned in northern Mississippi, 220 miles from Vicksburg. They had inherited a town, however, that was a squalid disease pit.[181] The day before Beauregard abandoned his camps in the spongy, mosquito-infested ground around Corinth, eighteen thousand of his seventy thousand men were in field hospitals, and more had died of typhoid fever, measles, and dysentery than were killed at Shiloh. The garrison had all but run out of food, and uncontaminated water was nearly impossible to find.[182] Given these conditions, Beauregard had decided his force had no chance of surviving a Union siege. Jefferson Davis disagreed. Deeming Corinth too valuable to have been abandoned, he replaced Beauregard with his gritty Shiloh rival Braxton Bragg.

The loss of Corinth forced the rebels to evacuate Fort Pillow, a Mississippi river bastion the Federal navy had been bombarding since April. This was the last Confederate stronghold north of Memphis. On June 6, two days after Fort Pillow was abandoned, the Mississippi flotilla, now bereft of Foote's resolute leadership, smashed a rebel gunboat fleet at Memphis, opening the Mississippi "from its source to that point."[183] Foote had never recovered from the ankle wound he suffered at Fort Donelson, and the mental strain of the river war had begun to wear on him, making him uncharacteristically cautious. On May 9, when Captain Charles Henry Davis, Foote's friend from their midshipman days, came downriver from Cairo to replace him as commander of the Western Gunboat Flotilla, he found him "reduced in strength, fallen in flesh, and depressed in spirits."[184]*

The Battle of Memphis had produced a new naval hero, Charles Ellet Jr., a diminutive, rail-thin fifty-two-year-old civil engineer from Bucks County, Pennsylvania, designer of some of the nation's first suspension bridges. A student of ancient naval warfare, Ellet had recently built a ram fleet for river fighting: nine small river steamers with their

---

* Foote miraculously recovered but died suddenly one year later on his way to take command of the Southern Atlantic Blockading Squadron.

hulls and bows clad with heavy oak timbers, fastened by iron rods. The vessels mounted no guns and had no iron for protection—"paper rams," skeptics called them.[185] The crews were "daredevils"—army soldiers and river roughnecks whom Ellet and his brother Alfred, an army captain, had personally recruited.[186] Ellet had the rams painted solid black to give them a "fearsome appearance."

Ram warfare, with vessels powered by banks of rowers, was an ancient tactic that had seemingly passed into history with the introduction of gunpowder and sailing ships. Steam power made it practical again, Ellet insisted. A fast and agile steamer with a strong prow "could be far more lethal than any shot or shell then in existence," he told Secretary of War Stanton. "[Ellet] has more ingenuity, more personal courage, and more enterprise than anybody else I have seen," said a convinced Stanton.[187]

Stanton made Ellet an army colonel and sent him to Cairo to build his fleet, which remained for a time independent of the navy.[188] Thirteen other family members joined the Mississippi Ram Fleet, making it very nearly a family-run force. At dawn on June 6, tens of thousands of Memphis citizens gathered at the levee, expecting an easy victory for their country's hastily assembled River Defense Fleet: eight wooden sidewheel paddleboats converted into rams. In early May, the fleet had dealt an unexpected blow to the Mississippi flotilla at Plum Point Bend, thirty miles above Memphis, sinking two of Eads's ironclads. Union gunboats would "never penetrate farther down the Mississippi," Confederate Flag Officer James Montgomery boasted after the victory at Plum Point Bend.[189]*

Montgomery proved to be a poor prophet. In full view of the crowd on the Memphis riverbank, five Union ironclads and four rams annihilated the Confederate fleet in little over an hour. Two Ellet rams, one captained by Charles, the other by Alfred, did most of the damage. Only one rebel vessel escaped. The rest were sunk or captured. "It was the most startling, dramatic, and memorable display of the whole war," wrote Albert Richardson, who observed it firsthand.[190] The Confederate navy would never again appear on the Mississippi as an organized force.[191]

---

* Both Union gunboats, *Cincinnati* and *Mound City*, were later raised and returned to service.

Charles Ellet's nineteen-year-old son, Charles Rivers Ellet, led three crew members to the docks of Memphis in a rowboat. From there they walked unmolested through an angry crowd and raised the Stars and Stripes over the city post office. "Gladness shone from the eyes of all the negroes," Richardson noted.[192]*

Union troops moved in immediately to occupy the lightly defended city. Memphis was the last enemy river obstacle until Vicksburg, some two hundred miles downriver, but Captain Davis, as cautious as Halleck, kept his gunboats in front of the city into the early summer, while the Northern public, by his own admission, became "restless and dissatisfied with our apparent inactivity."[193]

Two days after the occupation of Corinth, Grant—still without an active command—prepared to leave Corinth on a thirty-day leave. After visiting with his family, he would consider seeking a new command, somewhere far from Henry Halleck. Halleck asked him to reconsider. When Sherman learned that his friend was about to leave, he rushed to his tent and found office and camp chests piled up, ready to be moved in the morning.[194] Grant was seated at a camp table, sorting through letters and bundling them with red tape. "I am in the way here . . . ," he said, "and can endure it no longer."

"I then begged him to stay," Sherman recalled, "illustrating his case by my own." Before the Battle of Shiloh, he had been called "crazy" by newspapermen, but "that single battle had given me new life." If Grant departed he would be left out of the war; whereas if he stayed, "some happy accident might restore him to favor." Grant promised that he would "wait a while" and not leave without communicating with his friend.[195]

That night Grant wrote Julia that he would not be coming home.[196] Sherman had been persuasive, but other factors may have played a part.[197] Grant had learned from his staff there was strong "feeling among

---

* Alfred Ellet assumed command of the fleet when his brother Charles died from a pistol wound suffered in the Battle of Memphis, the only Union casualty in that river fight.

the troops . . . against my going," he told his wife.[198] And Halleck had recently asked him to "remain for a few days." Perhaps he had an important assignment for him.[199]

On June 11, the "happy accident" Sherman had anticipated occurred when Halleck restored Grant to his old command.[200] But Halleck, it turned out, would have even greater authority over him, this time from Washington. Fed up with the delaying tactics of George McClellan in the Peninsula Campaign, Lincoln installed Halleck as his new general in chief and directed him to come to the capital immediately. He also asked him to place the western armies under Grant and Buell. On July 16, Grant was put in charge of the new District of West Tennessee, an area bounded by the Mississippi to the west, the Ohio to the north, and the Tennessee to the east. Pope's Army of the Mississippi was folded into Grant's Army of the Tennessee, and Pope was moved east to command the new Army of Virginia. In July Sherman took command of the new District of Memphis, under Grant's authority.[201]

After the war, John Pope wrote "no man living is essential," his way of suggesting that had Grant left the war it might have caused "extremely little injury or embarrassment" to the Union cause. But it is difficult to see Vicksburg falling in 1863, or the Union prevailing by April 1865, without Grant—or, for that matter, without the partnership of Grant and Sherman, formed at Shiloh and solidified at Corinth.[202] On the surface, they were an incongruent pair: Grant serene and stable, Sherman explosive and high-strung—"a splendid piece of machinery with all of the screws a little loose," a fellow officer described him.[203] But they had much in common; former failures with soaring ambition, westerners reaching for significance. And together they viewed the heartland as the pivotal theater of the war. "The man who at the end of this war holds the control of the Valley of the Mississippi will be *the* man," Sherman predicted.[204]

In the summer of 1862, Sherman had thought that man would be Henry Halleck, the friend who had stuck by him at the lowest point in his life. "Buell is our best soldier. Halleck the ablest man—Grant very brave but not brilliant," he wrote that July.[205] Grant lacked Halleck's mastery of "large movements."[206] But Sherman was pleased to serve under the solidly confident victor of Donelson and Shiloh, an ideal superior officer for a subordinate who confessed to having no personal desire "to lead in this war." [207]

Grant also needed Sherman, his most aggressive and dependable division commander and his stoutest defender in the Union army. Grant enjoyed his friend's invigorating company: his blazing energy, his scattered but scintillating intelligence, and his "prophetic realism"— "that the war is ended or even fairly begun I do not believe." [208] Sherman was wildly alive, nervously scratching his scraggly beard and running his hand through his wildly unkempt hair as he remonstrated on nearly every subject in the encyclopedia, showing his bigotry as amply as his brilliance. Direct and fervent, he had raw and ugly views on issues like race and reporters. Rather than protest, Grant silently tolerated him. But he took to heart Sherman's ruminations on logistics, terrain, and strategy, knowing him to be a military mind of the highest order. Grant also understood Sherman's bouts of despair; he was similarly and recurrently afflicted by dark doubts. But while Sherman's melancholia was balanced by an almost manic elation, Grant operated in a more measured manner and was, consequently, impossible to read. [209] Grant understood Sherman; Sherman never figured out Grant.

After taking Corinth at the end of May, Grant and Sherman were eager to move on Vicksburg. The previous month, a federal oceangoing fleet of sloops and gunboats under the command of Flag Officer David Glasgow Farragut, accompanied by a mortar flotilla assembled by his foster brother, Commander David Dixon Porter, had entered the Mississippi at its mouth in the Gulf of Mexico, fought its way past two well-armed stone forts below New Orleans, and captured the Crescent City in the last week of April. Farragut and Porter, joined by an undersized army contingent, moved upriver to Vicksburg, where they would be joined on July 1 by Davis's ironclads.

If Sherman and Grant had had their way they would collaborate with the navy in a joint assault on the city. But instead of marching "directly down the Mississippi," as Sherman and Grant would have done, Halleck broke up and dispersed the tremendous force he had led to Corinth, ignoring Farragut's entreaties for army assistance in subduing Vicksburg, which could not be taken by naval bombardment alone, nor by an infantry force too small and inadequately led to mount a single assault. General Pope, as we have seen, was ordered to Virginia; Buell was sent on a slow march to Chattanooga; and most of the rest of Halleck's Corinth force went on the defensive, protecting Memphis and other Union garrisons in western and central Tennessee.[210] Without Halleck's support, Farragut, Porter, and Davis were forced to pull back to New Orleans and Memphis one month after beginning their ineffective bombardment of Vicksburg.

If Halleck had left a smaller but still effective occupation force in Tennessee and turned the rest of his Corinth column into a "movable force" of eighty thousand, he could have made a "bloodless advance" to Vicksburg, Grant argued years later, and forced the surrender of the city, saving the country from the prolonged and costly campaign he would wage in 1863.[211] Sherman agreed: "By the time we had reached Corinth I believe that army was the best then on this continent, and could have gone where it pleased. . . . Had [Halleck] held his force as a unit, he could have gone to Mobile, or Vicksburg, or anywhere in that region, which would by one move have solved the whole Mississippi problem."[212] It was perhaps the greatest lost opportunity of the war.

The campaign to subdue Vicksburg, we tend to forget, was a sixteen-month-long ordeal begun by the United States Navy in early April 1862, in the waters below New Orleans, and fought for a time with only token army assistance. That's why this first attempt to capture Vicksburg failed and that's why Porter and eventually Grant came to believe that only a joint army and naval offensive—massive and sustained—could take the river citadel and open the entire Mississippi to the sea, capping Farragut's great triumph at New Orleans. This was the lesson taken from what was—in the spring and summer after New Orleans fell—one of the most arduous campaigns in the history of the United States Navy, a river war that culminated in a rebel victory.

— PART TWO —

CHAPTER 5

"The Battle for the Mississippi"

And Farragut sailed up to the town
And anchored—sheathed the blade.[1]
—Herman Melville, "The Battle for the Mississippi," April 1862

Farragut's New Orleans expedition was part of a larger naval campaign to reopen the Mississippi from its mouth to Memphis. The capture and occupation of the city, a commercial and industrial powerhouse and the largest slave market in the Americas, was "a blow at the heart of the Confederacy," said Secretary of the Navy Gideon Welles, "a blow from which [it] never recovered."[2] And it was entirely a naval victory, the greatest naval achievement of the war. It was the work of a proud Virginian who refused to follow his state into the Confederacy and of his fiery foster brother, a commander the equal of Lord Nelson in Grant's overdramatic assessment.[3] Vain, arrogant, and loose with the truth, Porter would boast that he was the first to propose the run up the Mississippi to New Orleans and Vicksburg. The truth is more interesting.

In November 1861, Captain David Dixon Porter had just returned to Washington, D.C., from seventy-six days of blockade duty in the Gulf of Mexico. As commander of the frigate *Powhatan*, he had been charged with sealing off the serpentine water passes that led from the Mississippi River Delta one hundred miles northward to New Orleans. It had been frustrating duty. There were too many outlets to the sea in the capacious New Orleans Delta—inlets, lakes, and bayous—to close down completely. Shallow-draft blockade-runners, guided by seasoned river pilots, slipped in and out of New Orleans with disturbing frequency.[4]

Porter returned to Washington with a bold plan to shut down the seagoing commerce of the Crescent City. Seize New Orleans rather than blockade it. Send an amphibious armada of frigates, gunboats, mortar scows, and troop transports up the narrow passes that led from the Gulf to New Orleans, and have the troops storm the city and place it under Union occupation. While the pacification effort went forward, have the fleet continue up the river to Vicksburg with a phalanx of twenty thousand troops and rendezvous in front of the city with ironclads dispatched from Memphis. Bombard Vicksburg intensively, land the troops, and take its surrender.[5]

Porter expected the plan to meet fierce resistance in the capital. The army considered New Orleans impregnable. It was guarded from attacks from below by two masonry forts located seventy-five miles downriver from the city. Their heavy guns, said army munitions experts, would shred the navy's newest steam-driven, wooden frigates. Fort Jackson, on the west bank of the river, mounted seventy-four guns, among them the most powerful cannon in the rebel arsenal. Upstream approximately half a mile, on the opposite side of the river, Fort St. Philip mounted fifty-two big guns. Each fort had a garrison of nearly seven hundred troops, and the forts were built on a treacherous bend in the river, where ships had to slow to a crawl before proceeding upstream. Although badly in need of repairs, these forts were among the most formidable in the Confederacy. "Nothing afloat could pass the forts; nothing that walked could get through our swamps," the writer George Washington Cable described the confidence the Crescent City deposited in its lower defenses.[6]

But Porter had new intelligence and fort-busting weaponry. While on blockade duty, he had learned from local oyster fishermen that "very little progress had been made in strengthening the forts."[7] Heavily armed wooden warships could pass them, he believed, but only if supported by a flotilla of mortar vessels—Porter proposed twenty-one of them, each carrying a monstrous 13-inch siege gun with a range of nearly two and a half miles. These war machines would bomb the star-shaped rebel forts without cease for forty-eight hours, silencing or irreparably damaging them, opening the water gates to New Orleans for the invasion force.[8] It was an audacious plan from the brain of a seadog known to take long risks and rarely given to self-doubt.

The day Porter arrived in Washington, on leave from blockade duty, he requested an interview with Gideon Welles. But "Father Neptune," as Lincoln called his white-bearded, fifty-nine-year-old naval secretary, refused to see him.[9] Porter was a loose cannon and a notorious troublemaker who was in the habit of publicly ridiculing risk-averse desk officers in the Navy Department—fossils and "old fogies," he brazenly called them at social gatherings.[10]

He had never forgotten the treatment his legendary father—Commodore David Porter, captain of *Essex*, the scourge of British commerce in the War of 1812—received at the hands of stiff-necked navy bureaucrats. After the war, a naval court of inquiry had suspended him from active duty for a diplomatic breach of conduct while suppressing piracy in the West Indies. The commodore resigned his commission and became commander in chief of the Mexican naval forces, taking thirteen-year-old David, the youngest of his four sons, with him on sea duty.[11] The boy served with distinction in Mexico's war for independence before being captured and held for six months in the medieval-like brig of a Spanish ship-of-war in Havana harbor. After his father negotiated his release, he was sent back to the family homestead in Chester, Pennsylvania, and was soon afterward commissioned a midshipman in the U.S. Navy. His first assignment was chasing Barbary pirates in the Mediterranean on the fabled USS *Constellation*.[12]

But promotions came infuriatingly slow in the peacetime navy. Assigned for years to the U.S. Coast Survey, mapping harbors and strategic coastal positions, Porter acquired a practiced eye for terrain that would later serve him wonderfully at New Orleans and Vicksburg. But poring over densely detailed hydrographic surveys was uninspiring duty for a blazingly ambitious officer who had tasted powder before reaching puberty, pursuing pirates with his father when he was eleven years old on the war frigate *John Adams*.[13]

Standing five feet six inches tall, with coal-black hair, flashing eyes, and a spare, muscular frame, Porter looked strikingly like his father; and he had his father's wit and explosive temper, charming one moment, in a royal rage the next. Unlike the commodore, however, he had an appealing blend of briskness and warmth, and he was a legendary storyteller.

In the early winter of 1861, as southern states followed South Caro-

lina out of the Union, Porter became despondent about the slow progress of his career. He was forty-seven years old, his beard was streaked
with gray, and after thirty-one years in service he was still a lieutenant,
a junior officer of inconsequence. He had recently been offered a well-
paying position with a West Coast shipping company and was ready to
leave the navy to take it.* But with war fast approaching, Porter reversed
course. Southern-born officers were betraying their country and joining
the nascent Confederate States Navy by the dozens, opening opportunities for loyal officers who had seen sea duty and been under fire.

Blockade duty in the Gulf had gained Porter a promotion to
captain, but the tedious work failed to coincide with his restless temperament. He yearned to lead an expedition appropriate to his ambition,
but his infuriating propensity for intrigue and adventure led Welles to
distrust him—and for good reason. In late March 1861, Porter and his
friend army captain Montgomery C. Meigs had hatched a plan to save
Fort Pickens—the Federal garrison that commanded the inlet to Florida's Pensacola Bay and was being threatened by the rebels. Porter would
commandeer his old ship, the powerful side-wheel steamer USS *Powhatan*, berthed at Brooklyn Navy Yard, and sail it south to reinforce
Pickens. The secret mission had the support of Secretary of State William Seward, and for a time the president, but not Welles, who was
kept in the dark, for Seward would, in effect, be stealing the ship Welles
had ordered to prepare to escort transports and tugs carrying supplies
and troops to threatened Fort Sumter, in Charleston harbor.[14] When
Welles finally discovered the plot he protested to Lincoln, who did an
about-face and reassigned *Powhatan* to the relief of Fort Sumter. He
then ordered Seward to send a telegram to Andrew Hull Foote, commander of the Brooklyn naval facility, canceling the Fort Pickens mission. Porter, however, was already steaming out of New York harbor,
and he defiantly refused to obey a direct order from Seward, delivered
by a fast-running tug. "I received my orders from the President and shall
proceed and execute them," he wired Seward.[15] Porter made it to Fort

---

* In 1862, the highest rank in the U.S. Navy was captain. Officers commanding squadrons were designated flag officers and were entitled to display a personal flag over their
flagships. Captains, by courtesy, were often called commodores, but this was not an
official rank.

Pickens, but it had already been reinforced. Later, Foote told Porter he "ought to have been tried and shot; no one but yourself would ever have been so impudent." [16]

Porter had been on Welles's blacklist before the *Powhatan* incident. In the months leading up to Fort Sumter, Jefferson Davis and other secessionists had tried to convince him to accept a lucrative offer to become an admiral in the Confederate navy, which Porter declined. [17] But Porter had also convinced Seward to have Lincoln sign a letter appointing his Virginia friend Captain Samuel Barron to an important position in the Navy Department. When Welles informed Lincoln that Barron was "tainted with secession notions," the president canceled the appointment. Weeks later, Barron defected and received a commission in the rebel service. [18]

Porter "[has] dash and energy, [but is] given to intrigues," Welles described him at the time. After the *Powhatan* and Barron affairs, Welles never completely trusted him. Neither did Lincoln, according to Welles. [19]

So when Porter returned to Washington from coastal duty in November 1861 and tried to make an appointment with Welles to present his New Orleans plan, Father Neptune left him standing for hours outside his office. [20] When Welles finally agreed to see him and learned that he was there to talk about New Orleans he listened to him "attentively," Porter recalled. [21] Welles and the navy's assistant secretary, Gustavus Vasa Fox, were putting the final touches on Fox's own plan to take New Orleans, and Porter had information they could use. He was intimately familiar with the lower Mississippi Delta and could provide up-to-date knowledge about its ever-evolving waterways and the current state of rebel defenses.

When Porter described his own plan to capture New Orleans, Welles said it was strikingly similar to Fox's, with two important exceptions. Fox wanted to subdue Forts Jackson and St. Philip by direct naval assault, without the support of mortars, and he insisted it be an all-navy operation. A nighttime surprise attack would not need massive army assistance.

Fox was one of the most respected military minds in Washington. He had made a fortune in merchant shipping after retiring from active military service and was closely familiar with the waters around New

Orleans, having commanded merchant ships that regularly called on the city. He was also a Washington insider. His wife's sister was married to Postmaster General Montgomery Blair, who was keenly interested in the New Orleans expedition. Welles respected Fox's judgment and had formed a close working relationship with him. But while he had tentatively approved his New Orleans plan, he was not yet convinced that the fleet could pass the heavily gunned forts without sustaining disabling damage.[22] Porter's mortar scheme intrigued him. It would immeasurably decrease the risks of what would be, even with the mortars, a supremely dangerous mission.*

If the forts were bombed beforehand, the element of surprise—a sine qua non of Fox's scheme—would be lost; but an around-the-clock shelling for forty-eight hours, would, Porter argued convincingly, reduce Forts Jackson and St. Philip "to a heap of ruins."[23] With that, the meeting closed, and Welles suggested they summon Fox and "go to the President."[24]

Lincoln was taken by surprise. New Orleans was a priority, but every previous plan he had seen proposed capturing it by moving downriver with the ironclads, past Vicksburg's batteries, which were believed to be more imposing than the forts below New Orleans. Porter's plan excited him. "This should have been done sooner," he said.[25] "And while we are about it," Lincoln continued, "we can push on to Vicksburg and open the river all the way along."[26] He then suggested they approach McClellan to see if he could provide the troops.

That night Lincoln and Seward joined Welles, Fox, and Porter at McClellan's Washington home, a place where they could plot in secrecy. McClellan claimed that fifty thousand infantry would be needed to take New Orleans; he could not spare such numbers. When Welles and Porter insisted that ten thousand men could overwhelm the lightly garrisoned city, McClellan's skepticism melted. He would supply 12,500 troops and put them under the command of Major General Benjamin

---

* Writing after the war, both Welles and Montgomery Blair, in works cited in these notes, named Fox, not Porter, as the true author of the New Orleans plan. He had begun working on it after Captain Samuel F. Du Pont's victory at Port Royal on November 7, 1861. This proved to his satisfaction that wooden warships could pass powerful enemy shore batteries without sustaining major damage.

Butler, a Massachusetts Democratic politician with no formal military training. A mortar bombardment, McClellan added—to Porter's delight—would be "absolutely essential for success." [27]

Even Fox was eventually "won over" to the mortar assault "by the forcible arguments of Porter," recalled a senior navy official.[28] Fox was a close friend of the Porter family and he admired David Dixon's appetite for risk. They would forge a brotherly relationship that lasted throughout the war, and they regularly communicated with one another outside regular channels, venting their frustration with Welles and anyone else in government service who opposed their plans. Fox, too, was a canny schemer.

With Fox's backing, Porter was brought into the highly secret planning of the New Orleans operation and given sole command of the mortar flotilla.[29] At one point in the planning process, Lincoln dropped in on Porter and McClellan at the general's headquarters.[30] Striding across the room to McClellan's immense wall map, he pointed to the lower Mississippi region. "See . . . what a lot of land these fellows hold, of which Vicksburg is the key," Porter remembered Lincoln saying. "Here is Red River [south of Vicksburg], which will supply the Confederates with cattle and corn to feed their armies. There are the Arkansas and White Rivers [north of Vicksburg], which can supply cattle and hogs by the thousand. From Vicksburg these supplies can be distributed by rail all over the Confederacy. Then there is the giant depot of supplies on the Yazoo. Let us get Vicksburg and all that country is ours. The war can never be brought to a close until that key is in our pocket."[31]

But who would have overall command of the expedition? Fox would have unhesitatingly chosen Porter, with his combat experience and unequaled knowledge of the lower Mississippi. But Porter lacked the seniority for such an important mission; and all candidates of required rank and capability were presently on active duty and could not be spared. At some point in the deliberations, Porter suggested David Farragut. Fox and Welles were initially skeptical. He was a midlevel officer, thirty-seventh on the list of captains they were considering. The future conqueror of Mobile Bay—"Damn the torpedoes! Full steam ahead!"—had other liabilities.[32]

• • •

Farragut was a southerner to the core. Born in Tennessee in 1801, he had been raised at an early age in New Orleans and moved later in his naval career to Norfolk, Virginia. He had a brother in New Orleans and a sister in Mississippi, and his Norfolk-born wife was a states-rights Virginian, as were most of their friends, who expected him to volunteer for service in the Confederate navy. Two days after Virginia seceded and its militia seized Norfolk harbor, Farragut told his wife he intended to "stick to the flag." He would have to leave Virginia. She agreed to go with him, and they hastily packed and moved, with their sixteen-year-old son, Loyall, to Hastings-on-Hudson, fifteen miles north of New York City. Farragut remained idle for weeks, under scrutiny by the Navy Department as a possible Confederate sympathizer.[33]

He had written to Welles requesting active duty but had not been entrusted with a ship. He served instead on the retirement board at the Brooklyn Navy Yard, a humiliating rebuke for a captain with extensive sea duty.[34] Welles had reason to be cautious in assigning warships to suspected rebels. Three hundred and twenty-two officers in the U.S. Navy—37 percent of the total number of officers in service in 1860—had resigned their commissions to join the Confederate navy.[35] But there was one compelling thing in David Farragut's background that argued strongly in his favor for the New Orleans mission: He was the brother, by adoption, of David Dixon Porter and part of the greatest naval family of the early Republic.

While living in New Orleans, his Spanish-born father, George Farragut, a sailing master in the U.S. Navy, befriended Captain David Porter, David Dixon Porter's grandfather. When the aging captain was stricken by yellow fever, George Farragut took him into his home and put him under the care of his Scotch-Irish wife. Tragically, patient and nurse died on the very same day in the spring of 1808—and of the same scourge. Out of gratitude for the kindness the Farragut family had shown his father, David Porter's son—the future commodore also named David Porter—took seven-year-old George Jr. as his ward, promising to become his lifetime "friend and guardian." In 1814, the boy changed his name to David in honor of the man he had come to revere.[36]

Farragut went to sea at age eleven with Commodore Porter in the War of 1812, and was given responsibility for sailing a prize vessel captured by *Essex* into port. This was, however, the last combat Farragut would see before being considered for the New Orleans command.

Farragut had spent half his career on shore duty and had never commanded a squadron.[37] And he was sixty years old in 1861, one year older than "Grandfather" Gideon. Severely nearsighted, he refused, out of vanity, to wear spectacles, a crippling liability for a commander being considered for a nighttime operation. He had also been weakened by a succession of physical breakdowns—sunstroke, cholera, and yellow fever—he suffered while serving in tropical climes. When Welles told Secretary Seward he was considering Farragut for the New Orleans expedition, Seward was skeptical. Lincoln was consulted but said he had never heard of Farragut.[38] What if newspapers got wind of the expedition and learned its commander was a Virginian?

In Farragut's favor, he had shown deep courage and rectitude by moving his family from their beloved Norfolk, leaving behind friends and family who bitterly resented his disloyalty to his adopted state.[39] Farragut had also passed scrutiny as a loyal officer while serving at the Brooklyn Navy Yard, where no one had thought to question his patriotism. And while he was far down on the list of ideal candidates for the New Orleans command, he had the best record among the senior officers available.[40] "No one in the navy," David Dixon Porter told Welles, "had more personal friends or fewer enemies."[41] Welles decided to give him a look.

But before he made the decision, he sent Porter on a confidential mission to Brooklyn to test his foster brother's loyalty to the Union. Farragut still had family living in New Orleans, and he had told friends before leaving Virginia, "God forbid, that I should raise my hand against the South."[42] Would he fight against his own people? And would he, with his inexperience, accept command of an operation of such magnitude and peril? Welles had to know. He instructed Porter to proceed by indirection, never once mentioning New Orleans.[43]

When Porter met Farragut in the dining room of a Brooklyn hotel in December 1862, he noticed that his foster brother had changed little since they'd last met ten years before. Twelve years apart and never close, they were as different as April and August, the older man calm and self-assured, his younger brother full of fire and force, abrasive and outrageously outspoken, with propulsive energy and intensity. Farragut reposed confidence in an all-mastering Creator, who actively guided earthly affairs; Porter was militantly secular. Unlike Porter, who maintained a "bright shipshape appearance at all times," Farragut dressed plainly, in the manner of Ulysses Grant, his captain's coat held to his chest, informally, by a single button at his throat.[44] Of medium height, square-built, and balding, he had a pleasant manner and was easygoing and talkative—though, when riled, he was to be avoided. Farragut had begun to show the heaviness of increasing age, but still moved with the poise of an athlete. He had been an expert fencer, and remained addicted to physical exercise. Every year on his birthday he turned a handspring, explaining to friends that he would know he was getting old when he could no longer execute it.[45]

After the brothers exchanged pleasantries, Porter came directly to the point. Locking eyes with Farragut, he asked if he would be willing to fight against the South, even if the target were Norfolk. Visibly annoyed, Farragut said he would fight secession wherever it resided, and would accept any command entrusted to him.[46] He was then summoned to Washington, closely questioned by Fox and Welles, and given command of the New Orleans expedition.[47] He had taken a solemn oath to serve his country, he assured Welles, and he would "restore New Orleans to the Government or never return."[48]

On February 2, 1862, Farragut sailed from Hampton Roads on his flagship, *Hartford*, the largest of the most heavily armed sloops-of-war in his fleet—the others being *Richmond, Pensacola*, and *Brooklyn*. They were new ships, part of the navy's recent effort to move from pure sailing vessels to sailing ships with auxiliary steam power.* Three-masted, with a hull of solid oak, *Hartford* carried a complement of twenty-two powerful Dahlgren guns of the latest design, and two long-range Parrott rifled cannon.[49] Formidable on the open seas, *Hartford* and her sister vessels were unsuited, however, for river operations. Their gun decks were too high to be effective against low-lying shore defenses; nor could the

---

* Steam engines were not yet highly efficient, and they required enormous amounts of coal, often unavailable to them on long journeys.

cannon be elevated sufficiently to reach hilltop fortifications.[50] Longer and heavier than any ship that regularly plied the Mississippi, Farragut's sloops-of-war would be entering alien and dangerous waters. They were the command ships of the New Orleans-Vicksburg operation because no other vessels had sufficient mass and firepower to take on the forts below New Orleans. They were also faster than any ironclads afloat.

After a voyage of nearly three weeks, Farragut began assembling his assault force at Ship Island, a mosquito-infested sandbank a dozen miles off Biloxi, Mississippi.[51] He had seventeen war vessels under his command, in addition to Porter's mortar schooners and transports for General Butler's bluecoats. Assistant Secretary Fox, still not completely convinced of Farragut's ability to handle a large-scale operation, asked Porter to keep an eye on him. The "busy schemer," as Lincoln called him, began sending secret, highly critical reports back to Fox.[52] Porter had real cause for concern. Farragut was known as an abysmal planner, and would be saved from mistakes at Ship Island—and later at New Orleans and Vicksburg—by the able flag captain of his squadron, Commander Henry H. Bell, a fellow southerner who had spent nearly forty years at sea in the antebellum navy.[53]

"I never thought Farragut a Nelson," Porter wrote Fox from Ship Island. "I only consider him the best of his rank. . . . Men of his age in a seafaring life are not fit for the command of important enterprises. . . . To be successful we must have young men in command." While "full of zeal" and loved by his men, Farragut "loses too much time in talking" and "has no administrative qualities."

If all else failed, Porter said he had great hopes for the mortars—an unsubtle hint that he was available to take charge of the expedition if his foster brother floundered.[54] Gideon Welles had read Porter perfectly: He "[has] no hesitation in trampling down a brother officer if it would benefit himself."[55]

If Farragut was slow to prepare, the Confederate high command was downright dilatory—undermanned and bewildered. Its land and river forces in the Mississippi Valley were caught between two converging millstones: Grant and the ironclads coming from the north and Farragut's wooden fleet approaching from the south. Grant and Flag Officer Andrew Hull Foote were seen as the greater threat and therefore took precedence in planning the city's defenses.

Major General Mansfield Lovell, a former New Yorker who commanded the land defenses at New Orleans, had been directed to send four thousand troops from his already thinly manned garrison to Beauregard and Johnston at Corinth, where they were poised to attack Grant at Pittsburg Landing. And eight gunboats had been pulled from New Orleans to meet Union ironclads above Memphis—a clear illustration of Jefferson Davis's war-long dilemma of having to meet two enemy threats at the same time and with insufficient forces.[56]

Lovell was also slow to perceive the imminent threat posed by the federal fleet gathering in the Gulf. Not until March, when Farragut was in the final stages of assembling his strike force, in plain view off the beaches at Biloxi, did Lovell anticipate an "impending" attack from below the city. When he finally requested emergency reinforcements, rebel authorities were "wholly incredulous and deaf to his appeals." The immediate threats "were in the opposite direction," he was forcefully reminded. Not a man or a gun could be spared from Albert Sidney Johnston's army at Corinth.[57] Lovell was left with only a small flotilla of gunboats, a single company of regular troops, and a lightly trained militia to defend a city whose population, approximately 168,000, was larger than that of the next four cities in the Confederacy combined.[58] "I have literally stripped the department," he complained to Beauregard, "but never get anything in return that I ask for."[59]

Even if Farragut were to successfully ascend the river, "the forts should destroy . . . his wooden vessels," President Davis assured Louisiana governor Thomas O. Moore, a message that reflected Davis's astounding misreading of the gravity of the situation at New Orleans.[60] To buttress his defenses, Lovell had recently strung across the Mississippi, just below the forts, a barricade of eight hulks, obsolete schooners that were sunk and held in place by fifteen anchors weighing up to four thousand pounds each. The hulks were lashed together, shore-to-shore, by a heavy iron cable. (A part of the barricade could be swung aside for the passage of friendly ships.)[61] The Confederates also had a hastily assembled River Defense Fleet, under the separate command of the Confederate Navy Department. It was an entirely improvised fleet; six of its best fighting vessels were converted river steamboats outfitted with reinforced bows for ramming, and they were manned by civilian steamboat crews. The only real threat was the small ironclad ram *Manassas*.

Two additional iron-sheathed rams—tremendously more powerful—were being pushed to completion in local shipyards. Would they be finished in time?

One of them, *Louisiana*, was nearly ready for service but its engines were not yet in working order. If unable to operate under its own power, *Louisiana* would be towed downstream and positioned along the riverbank as a floating battery.[62]

Lovell, understandably, had no confidence in his defense flotilla or in its commander, Captain John K. Mitchell, the husband of Farragut's wife's cousin.[63] Lovell's ace in the hole was *Mississippi*, a "true river monster," 270 feet long and weighing over four thousand tons.[64] If completed in time, no vessel in Farragut's wooden-hulled fleet would be able to stand up to its twenty guns, while its thick armor would make it virtually impervious to enemy shot and shell.

Reports that the rebel behemoth was nearing completion hastened Farragut's preparations. On March 7 he set sail for the Mississippi Delta. It took nearly a month to get his heaviest ships over the bar at Southwest Pass; some had to be dragged by tow ships through two feet of soft mud.[65] As this work went forward, Farragut took two of his lighter gunboats and sped up to reconnoiter the forts. Accompanying him was the *New York Herald* reporter Bradley S. Osbon, an experienced sailor who had convinced Farragut to take him aboard *Hartford* as fleet signal officer and unofficial historian. "The shots from both forts fell all around us," Osbon remembered. "We realized that to pass between those two well-armed and ably manned works at perfectly point-blank range was going to be a task to try men's souls." In 1815, Fort Jackson alone had stopped the British fleet for nine days. Now there was an additional fort, and "each of them [was] far stronger and better armed than the old works."

The captain of a French vessel that passed Farragut's scouting boat warned him that it was "absolutely impossible for a fleet of wooden vessels to withstand the fire of forts, water-batteries, gunboats, and ironclads that awaited us—that to undertake the passage meant certain annihilation of our fleet." But Farragut, said Osbon, had "an unfaltering faith in a Divine Providence."[66]

Finally, on April 8, all ships were over the bar at Southwest Pass. One week later, Porter's twenty-one mortar boats were in position directly below Fort Jackson, along the river's thickly wooded banks, their spars

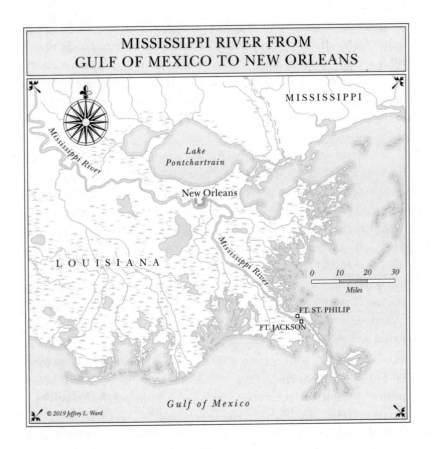

MISSISSIPPI RIVER FROM
GULF OF MEXICO TO NEW ORLEANS

MISSISSIPPI

Mississippi River

Lake Pontchartrain

New Orleans

L O U I S I A N A

Mississippi River

0   10   20   30

Miles

FT. ST. PHILIP

FT. JACKSON

Gulf of Mexico

© 2019 Jeffrey L. Ward

and rigging camouflaged by shrubbery and tree branches.[67] "Americans in the North are on the tiptoe of expectation for news of the fall of New Orleans," reported the London *Times*. "This is the next thrust of the swordfish in the whale."[68]

The mortars delivered the opening blow. Beginning at daybreak on April 18, they battered the forts continuously for six days and nights, far longer than the forty-eight hours Porter had assured Welles would be sufficient to reduce them to rubble and ash.[69] The thunderous explosions of the mortars broke windows thirty miles distant and shook "everything around them like an earthquake."[70] It was "trying work for the poor fellows on the mortar schooners," recalled a Federal sailor, "for when their mortar was fired, all of them were obliged to go aft and stand on tiptoe with open mouths to receive the concussion. The powder blackened everything, and the men looked like Negroes."[71]

The gunners fired three thousand shells, on average, a day, each weighing in excess of 220 pounds. The arched trajectory of their projectiles caused plunging fire to fall directly on top of the brick forts. Porter's "mortar fire was accurate," said the commander of the enemy forts, Brigadier General Johnson K. Duncan. But though the comet-like missiles badly mauled the walls and buildings, casualties were light.[72] Of the 1,100 men in the stone garrisons, only fourteen were killed.[73]

By the sixth day of the bombardment, the gunners were "worn out from want of sleep and rest." Some had lost their hearing from the shock of the concussions, and their ammunition was nearly expended.[74] Porter pleaded for more time—just two more days of bombardment—but Farragut, his patience worn thin by the "uselessness" of the mortar fire, prepared to move upriver. The mortar schooners would be left behind to continue their terror bombing till the forts surrendered.[75] Porter protested, but Farragut was unmovable.[76]

On April 20, Farragut sent out two gunboats on a wildly hazardous mission. The crews were to cut the chain that spanned the river below the forts. It was a stormy night, with lightning forking across the sky. The wind-whipped boats were spotted almost immediately. A signal rocket went up from Fort Jackson and the gunboats came under furious fire for over an hour. On board one of them was an expert with petards—metal boxes loaded with explosive powder. The plan was to blow up one of the hulks and sever the chain, "permitting the rest of the hulks and the raft to swing down against the river banks."[77] While rebel fire shook the waters around the boat, the petard was set in place but failed to ignite, the swirling river current had snapped the connecting wires. Then one of the officers unshackled the cables by hand, setting two of the anchored hulks adrift. The other gunboat revved its engines and smashed through another length of chain, widening the opening. A midshipman on *Brooklyn* called it "one of the most daring feats of the war."[78]

Two days later, at a tense meeting in the flag officer's cabin, a majority of Farragut's leading commanders argued that running past the forts before they were disabled was "suicidal"; the fleet would be "annihilated." At that point Farragut stood up and ended the discussion with a flat declaration. He would run the gauntlet, no matter the risk.[79]* Captain Theodorus Bailey, Farragut's most aggressive officer, would lead the way on *Cayuga*.

The aging flag officer "had a stupendous undertaking before him," recalled his secretary, William T. Meredith. The problems were multitudinous. The thick-walled forts mounted 126 guns; above them was a fleet of rebel gunboats and the sixteen-gun *Louisiana*, moored just above Fort St. Philip. While in the river, above the forts, rafts loaded with kindling "were floating ready to be fired and cut loose on the first sign of an attempt to pass the boom."[80]

Officers and crews prepared by writing final letters to loved ones.[81] Most of the sailors had never seen combat. Not a few believed they would "see the sun again."[82]

Chain armor was draped over the sides of the ships to protect the engines, tubs of water were set in strategic places around the decks, netting was strung above the deck to catch falling debris, and the gun decks were covered with sand and ashes to prevent crewmen from slipping in their own blood and gore.[83] At two o'clock on the morning of April 24, Signal Officer Osbon hoisted two red lanterns to *Hartford's* mizzen peak—the signal to get under way. At this moment, Flag Offi-

---

* In his private journal, Porter wrongly claimed that he had urged Farragut to order the mortars to stop firing on the sixth day and to "commence the attack with the ships" because "the mortar ammunition was growing scarce." Porter, "Journal"; see also Porter to Welles, ORN, I/18/367; and Porter, *Incidents and Anecdotes*, 48.

cer Farragut "stood facing his destiny," Meredith wrote, "imperishable fame or failure."[84]

It was a bright, moonlit night, but somehow the gunners in Fort Jackson failed to sight the fleet—seventeen warships carrying four thousand men—until it was almost under their guns. Then both sides let loose, turning the black river into a sheet of sulfurous fire.[85] This was the signal for Porter to begin throwing shells into Fort Jackson at furiously accelerated intervals. "The . . . shells shot upward from the mortar boats," wrote a Confederate officer inside the fort, "rushed to the apexes of their flight, flashing the lights of their fuses as they revolved, paused an instant, and then descended upon our works like hundreds of meteors or burst in mid-air, hurling their jagged fragments in every direction."[86] It was as if "the artillery of heaven were playing upon the earth," said Farragut.[87] The mind of one of his sailors was running in an opposite direction: "My youthful imagination of hell did not equal the scene about us at this moment."[88]

The rebels sent their blazing rafts downriver, their flames shooting hundreds of feet into the night sky. "The whole extent of the river for a mile above the forts was as light as day," Porter reported from his command steamer, anchored downstream. "[The] fire-rafts . . . illuminated the fleet and the forts as if in a diorama."[89]

Early in the action, the rebel ram *Manassas* pushed a raft piled high with blazing pinecones and pitch toward *Hartford*. Turning violently to avoid it, Farragut ran his ship aground, directly under the guns of Fort St. Philip—so close the spar on the ship's prow hung over a part of the fort's wall. The raft found its target and set *Hartford*'s portside on fire.[90] "My God, is it to end this way?" Farragut lifted his arms and cried out, his heart hammering in his chest. A shell exploded belowdecks, starting another fire. At this moment, Osbon spotted some 20-pound rifle shells lying on the deck. He rolled three of them to an opening just above the blazing scow. Throwing his coat over his head as protection from the flames, he "uncapped" the shells, and rolled them into the raft. They exploded instantly, tearing a gaping hole in the raft and driving away *Manassas*. Midshipmen manning hoses extinguished the fires on *Hartford* before they got out of control. With the engines rumbling so tremendously that few sailors could stay on their feet, Captain Bell maneuvered the charred vessel off the muddy bottom of the river.[91]

As *Hartford* righted and moved upriver, the smoke from the coal-fired fleet was so thick "one could see nothing ten feet from the ship."[92] Farragut climbed high on the port mizzen, above the blinding smoke, for a view of the action. With his feet clinging to the ratlines and "his back against the shrouds, he stood there as cool as if leaning against a mantel in his own home," said Osbon.[93] Osbon shouted to him to come down: His leadership was indispensable at this critical hour. A moment after Farragut's feet hit the deck, a shell exploded and cut away the rigging where he had been standing.[94]

The fleet got past the forts in an hour and ten minutes, with heavy damage but minimal losses: one gunboat sunk, 37 men killed, 147 wounded.[95] Three of the smaller gunboats were forced to turn back: One of them had taken a disabling shot in her boiler; the other two had become entwined in the chain barricade.[96] But rebel losses were catastrophic. Eight CSA gunboats assailed the Federal fleet, but only the ram *Manassas* and three smaller gunboats had attacked with purpose.[97]

Only two boats escaped to the city. *Manassas* pursued the Yankee fleet upriver but was intercepted by the side-wheeler *Mississippi*, the oldest ship in the Federal fleet. "Signal the *Mississippi* to sink that damn thing," Farragut shouted to Osbon.[98] Moments later, *Mississippi* delivered two broadsides straight through the armor of the rebel ship. Sinking rapidly, *Manassas* struggled to shore; the crew "escaped over her roof into a swamp."[99] Looking on with satisfaction from *Mississippi*'s pilot-house was twenty-four-year-old Lieutenant George Dewey, later Admiral Dewey, hero of the Battle of Manila Bay thirty-six years later.

"Thus closed our morning's fight," Farragut telegraphed Welles.[100] On the second anniversary of the battle, Farragut wrote his son, Loyall: "This night two years ago was the [most] anxious night of my life when I felt as if the fate of my country, and my own life and reputation were all on the wheel of fortune, to be turned by the finger of the All-Wise. . . . It was only left to do or die. God was my leader, and we passed through the fiery furnace where none but He could have carried us."[101]

A sweeping Federal victory could have easily been a dismal defeat had the rebel "leviathan" *Louisiana* been mobile and battle ready. Afloat and maneuverable, she could have destroyed the entire Union fleet, whose "fragile wooden vessels . . . could be pierced by any ordinary smooth-bore gun," Porter wrote later. Every vessel under Farragut's command poured shot into her at close quarters, doing "no more harm than so many popguns." [102]

As the Union fleet steamed toward New Orleans, *Louisiana*—commanded by John K. Mitchell—was still tied to the riverbank "where the light from the fire-rafts showed her as plainly as if it had been daylight." [103] Days later, Mitchell ordered the ironclad set afire, lest she fall into enemy hands. The flames burned through the ropes holding her to shore, and she floated downriver and exploded in front of Fort St. Philip.

By the onset of dawn, on April 25, Farragut was steaming upriver to anchor for the night and bury his dead. Captain Thomas T. Craven, of the USS *Brooklyn*, was one of the officers who had implored Farragut not to risk the ships against the forts. He was contrite now—and thankful. "I must confess that I never expected to get through," he wrote his wife. "But the Lord of Hosts was with us. . . . A more desperate, a more magnificent dash was never made. . . . [It was] the most brilliant . . . naval fight ever performed. [104]

Later that morning, after crews had washed the decks of "blood and mangled remains," the fleet started for the great Southern metropolis. [105] On the outskirts of New Orleans, a rebel battery opened up on the gunboats at Chalmette, where in 1815 Andrew Jackson's army, fighting behind a cotton-bale barricade, beat back a numerically superior British force in the first Battle of New Orleans. It was a history-making fight in which Farragut's soldier-of-fortune father had participated. [106]

Farragut's big guns made quick work of the rebel cannon, and the fleet "passed up to the city in fine style," pennants and flags snapping in the breeze—"a march of the victors." [107] Entering the harbor, Farragut's navigators saw bearing down on them a floating object that looked like a flaming furnace.

For days rumors had spread through the city that *Mississippi*, then being rushed to completion at an upriver naval yard, would be launched in time to save the city. It was "the most formidable warship in the world," its builders boasted. [108] Unfortunately for the city it might have saved, its completion was at least two months behind schedule.* "We were too quick for them," said Farragut.[109]

From the levee at New Orleans, George Washington Cable, then a seventeen-year-old store clerk, could see the towering masts of Farragut's ships as they rounded Slaughterhouse Point "into full view, silent grim, and terrible; black with men, heavy with deadly portent." Just then, the ironclad that was to be "the terror of the seas" came into view, "drifting helplessly, a mass of flames."[110] Unable to get her engines and guns ready, her builders had set her on fire. The flames sliced through her moorings and "she floated past us, formidable even in her expiring flames," wrote Farragut.[111]

In the distance, the New Orleans riverfront was a maelstrom of fire and smoke. On the levees, for a distance of seven miles, gigantic piles of cotton bales, millions of dollars of rebel gold, had been set aflame on orders from General Lovell, who was preparing to head to Vicksburg to try to stop the Yankees farther upriver.[112] As the Federal fleet approached Jackson Square, Farragut's crews spotted looters pouring over the decks of half-burned river steamers, breaking into casks of rice and barrels of corn, and emptying molasses into the gutters of Canal Street.[113]

The fleet dropped anchor at one o'clock on the afternoon of April 25, in drenching rain, with lightning streaking the sky. An enraged mob had gathered in the streets leading off from the levee, men, women, and children waving pistols and knives and shouting oaths of defiance. Warehouses and stores were burning uncontrollably, set aflame by the "the riffraff of the wharves, the town, the gutters." The crowds "howled and screamed with rage," wrote Cable. "The swarming decks [of the Union ships] answered never a word; but one old tar on the *Hartford*, standing with lanyard in hand beside a great pivot-gun, so plain to view that you could see him smile, silently patted its big black breech and blandly grinned."[114]

At two o'clock Farragut sent ashore Captain Theodorus Bailey and Lieutenant George Perkins to demand the unconditional surrender of

---

* The builders of *Mississippi* believed they could have had her ready by early May, but Commander Arthur Sinclair, who was to captain her, did not believe the vessel could have been completed before July 1. See Dufour, *Night the War Was Lost*, 296.

the city and the removal of Confederate flags from public buildings.[115] As they made their way to City Hall to confront Mayor John T. Monroe and General Lovell, the crowd pressed in on them, hurling stones and bricks and shouting: "hang them!" Cable and his mother followed the mob. The two naval officers walked abreast, looking straight ahead, "never frowning, never flinching," while the mob pressed in on them, waving cocked pistols in their faces. "It was one of the bravest deeds I ever saw done," Cable would write years later.[116]

Mayor Monroe refused to surrender the city, and sent Farragut's emissaries back to the fleet with armed escorts.[117] Farragut was furious. The city was under his guns yet out of his control. It had to surrender, if only to end the anarchy. If even one of his sailors were harmed, he informed Mayor Monroe, he would "open fire from all the ships and level the town." [118]

To establish his authority, Farragut had his sailors raise the Stars and Stripes over the U.S. mint building. When word reached him that a rebel diehard named William B. Mumford had pulled it down and helped a crowd of citizens tear it to shreds, Farragut exploded. "There is [a] reign of terror in this doomed city," he thundered.[119] After his second demand to surrender was rejected, Farragut gave authorities forty-eight hours to evacuate the women and children. He would then destroy New Orleans. Only at that point did Monroe invite him to take possession of the city. Monroe refused, however, to haul down the Louisiana state flag, flying from the dome of City Hall.[120] Farragut then sent a contingent of officers into the city, accompanied by a battalion of marines pulling two brass howitzers loaded with shrapnel. They marched with grim purpose to City Hall, on Lafayette Square. With an armed and sullen mob held in check by the howitzers, George Russell, a boatswain's mate from *Hartford*, ascended to the roof of the building and pulled down the Louisiana flag.[121] As he did, Mayor Monroe placed himself in front of one of Farragut's howitzers, folded his arms, and "fixed his eyes upon the gunner who stood lanyard in hand ready for action." He remained there until the Federals had marched out of the gated square with the state flag under Russell's arm.[122]

On April 29, General Benjamin Butler arrived with Union troops and officially took control of the city. Farragut yielded authority to him and began preparations to move upriver to Vicksburg.[123] Butler's first order of business was to hunt down William B. Mumford and have him hanged for treason. Mumford dropped to his death on June 6, 1862, from gallows constructed inside the U.S. mint, where he had desecrated the flag.[124] There were no demonstrations. The defiant city was solidly under Union control.

So were the forts. On April 28, they had surrendered to Porter.[125]

The fall of New Orleans was a Confederate calamity. "The extent of the loss is not to be disguised," wrote the *Richmond Examiner*. "It annihilated us in Louisiana . . . led . . . to our virtual abandonment of the great and fruitful Valley of the Mississippi, and cost the Confederacy . . . the commercial capital of the South . . . and . . . the largest *exporting* city in the world."[126] In London, a young Henry Adams returned to the American legation from an afternoon walk to find his tight-buttoned father, Charles Francis Adams, the U.S. ambassador to London, dancing across the floor and shouting, "We've got New Orleans."[127]

New Orleans was just one of a "deluge" of Union victories in the West in 1862: Forts Henry and Donelson, Columbus, Nashville, Island No. Ten, Fort Pillow, Shiloh, Corinth, and Memphis. Between February and May, Federal naval and ground forces had conquered fifty thousand square miles of territory, gained control of one thousand miles of navigable river, captured two state capitals and the South's largest city, and put thirty thousand enemy troops out of action.[128] Of all these Federal conquests, some achieved bloodlessly, New Orleans stands out the strongest.[129]

In Vicksburg, news of the fall of New Orleans arrived by telegraph. "People walked the streets aimlessly," said a local woman, "as one does when troubled, with bowed heads and saddened mien. It was like the slaying of the firstborn child of Egypt. Sorrow was in every house."[130]

Farragut was headed there next.

CHAPTER 6

"These Troublous Times"

"Our only hope is in desperate fighting." [1]

—Kate Stone

"The excitement [here] has reached almost the crazy point," Sarah Morgan wrote in her diary. A twenty-year-old rebel patriot, Sarah lived in solid comfort with her widowed mother and their house slaves on tree-lined Church Street, in one of Baton Rouge's most fashionable neighborhoods. Three of her brothers were serving in the Confederate army. It was April 26, and news had just reached Baton Rouge, the state capital, that Farragut had broken through to New Orleans. "Nothing can be heard positively . . . except that our gunboats were sunk, and theirs were coming up the river," Morgan wrote. [2]

Sarah's deceased father, Judge Thomas Gibbes Morgan, had opposed secession and so had she, but no one in the Morgan family was willing to fight against their own people. In the weeks after Fort Sumter, Sarah had expected a short war. Once the South prevailed and dictated its terms, she prayed it would return to the Union. But she had evolved, hardened by recent Confederate losses in the Mississippi Valley. By the spring of 1862 she was a committed Yankee hater. "Death in the confederacy, rather than bliss in the Union," she declared in her diary. In her purse she carried a pistol and was "ready" to use it, she wrote, against the "vile" invaders. [3]

On May 7, USS *Iroquois*, a sloop-of-war in Farragut's fleet commanded by Captain James S. Palmer, anchored in front of Baton Rouge, a handsome city of 5,400 souls situated on a bluff on the eastern side of the Mississippi River. [4] "A graceful young Federal stepped ashore, carrying a Yankee flag over his shoulder, and asked the way to the Mayor's office," Sarah described the scene. [5] The mayor refused to meet with

Palmer but sent a courier to his vessel. Baton Rouge, he declared, was defenseless but "will not be surrendered voluntarily to any power on earth."[6] Palmer weighed anchor, steamed abreast of the state arsenal, and sent his marines ashore. They seized the arsenal and the militia barracks and hoisted their "Bloody banner . . . over our heads," Sarah wrote with cold fury. "Much as I once loved that flag, I *hate* it now!"[7]

Late that afternoon, Farragut arrived at Baton Rouge with a convoy of transports packed to the gunnels with bluecoats. Their commander was Brigadier General Thomas Williams, a forty-six-year-old veteran of the Mexican War and a martinet known more for his hard discipline than his hard fighting. The troops were raw volunteers assigned to the river expedition by General Benjamin Butler. Part of the brigade took possession of Baton Rouge and remained there on occupation duty. The others, 1,500 of them, remained on the transports with orders to accompany Williams and Farragut to Vicksburg.[8]

David Dixon Porter was no longer with the fleet. Farragut had sent him and his mortar flotilla back to Ship Island to await orders to move on Mobile, Alabama.[9] Welles expected Farragut to make fast work of Vicksburg and then head to Mobile Bay, where his heavy ships were to join the mortar squadron and reduce to rubble the three forts defending the city.[10] For now, Farragut was focused exclusively on Natchez and Vicksburg. While *Hartford* took on coal at Baton Rouge, the flag officer sent a flotilla of gunboats upriver under Captain S. Phillips Lee to take the surrender of Natchez, the capital of slave culture in the Mississippi Valley. Forty of its most prominent citizens, the "nabobs," were among the largest slaveholders in the South.[11] The city surrendered without a fight; only fourteen armed men came forward to defend it.[12] Farragut followed Lee to Natchez and ordered him to take his war boats up to Vicksburg to impel city authorities to surrender. He would remain in front of Natchez with his big sloops-of-war, unsure if they could safely navigate the dangerous shoals above the city without experienced Mississippi pilots.

Farragut didn't expect trouble. He had talked to a traveler in Baton Rouge who had passed through Vicksburg on his way downriver from Memphis. The rebels, reportedly, had only a six-gun battery on a high, sloping hill that ran down to the river. "There are no [big] guns there yet," Farragut assured Captain Lee.[13]

• • •

Farragut had been in a sour mood all the way up to Natchez. A blue-water sailor, he would have preferred to storm Mobile Bay with Porter. He wanted no part of the "Big Muddy," a crooked stream with an endless succession of precipitous turns—"meander loops"—that his long ships found difficult to negotiate. On some razor-sharp bends the current ran at "the fearful rate of 9 and 10 miles," reported Thomas Craven, captain of *Brooklyn*. Twice the "impetuous" current hurled his tremendous ship, one of the largest in the fleet, against the banks of the river.[14]

Farragut's troubles multiplied north of Baton Rouge. Great stretches of the river were nearly blockaded by immense floating trees. These "forest giants," some of them up to one hundred feet tall, had broken free from the river's loose, muddy banks and become entwined, creating swift-running wooden phalanxes capable of fatally damaging the fleet's wooden gunboats. But the greatest danger lay hidden from the naked eye. Great numbers of trees fastened themselves to the river's soft muddy bottom. Their spike-like shafts, known as snags, were fully or partially submerged. "The terror of steamboat pilots," they were the river's "Scylla and Charybdis," wrote a nineteenth-century traveler.[15]

The river was almost a hundred feet deep in places, but the powerful drag of its current along the alluvial bottom created sandbars that reduced the depth of some channels to a few feet. Boats were known to run aground and remain stuck for days, occasionally weeks, until they were either pulled off the bar or released when the river rose. "In seasons of low water these bars made the river essentially impassable," writes historian Lee Sandlin.[16] Going up to Natchez, Farragut had gone aground and very nearly lost *Hartford*. "Fortunately, by taking out some of the guns and coal," he reported to Welles, "I got her off in two days, but my health suffered from anxiety and loss of sleep.[17]

It was a "lawless river," impossible to tame, said former steamboat pilot Mark Twain.[18] On the floodplains between Cairo and the New Orleans Delta, "Old Devil River," as African American slaves called it, remade and reshaped itself endlessly, spilling over its low banks to turn broad flatlands into deep-water lakes.[19] Towns that were sitting on the riverbank one year might be twenty miles inland a year later. There has never been a consistently trustworthy map of the river's eternally changing course. It went east and west, then looped north again, taking twenty to thirty miles to advance one land mile. One moment, the sun was shining in the eyes of Farragut's men, the next minute on their backs.

Anyone navigating a craft larger than an old-fashioned flatboat—the kind Abraham Lincoln took down to New Orleans in his youth—required an experienced pilot who could "read the face of the water." Farragut had been unable to find seasoned pilots in New Orleans who were willing to serve with him. The only guides he had were boatmen he encountered occasionally on the river. "We have to force them, but they know little or nothing of the river's depth or channel for vessels of our draft," he informed the Navy Department.[20] So his veteran captains were largely on their own in alien waters. And they were on a river "whose obstructions must be confronted in all nights and all weathers," wrote Twain, "without the aid of a single lighthouse or a single buoy; for there is neither light nor buoy to be found anywhere in all this three or four thousand miles of villainous river."[21]

It is no wonder Farragut had his big ships sail only in daylight. At night, they rested at anchor, close to shore, where they could purchase wood from local slaves when their supply of coal ran low. Some of the captains hired runaway slaves as coal stokers in their undermanned boiler rooms.

Guiding a massive saltwater ship up the Mississippi required both patience and vigilance. Captain Craven was so fearful of going around that he kept on his feet "from sunrise to sunset," with a flickering candle at his side to fight off clouds of mosquitoes. The only sound in his cabin was the distant beat of the engines.[22] Moving upriver at dusk against the heavy current, some Federals were thrown into despair—almost spooked—by the forbidding "monotony" of the scenery: "the dark, gloomy, impenetrable woods along the banks and the solemn stillness broken only by the noise of the steamers' machinery."[23] It was the most tedious, "ennui-producing" river in the world, wrote a nineteenth-century German traveler—bending, twisting, and crawling "like a snake through the primeval forest."[24] Now and then "a large section of land covered with trees and vines . . . falls with a loud splash into the water and disappears in the depths," wrote a Union soldier on one of General

Williams's transports. "At night when the stars come out the silence and the gloom becomes doubly impressive."[25]

The river was unusually high for this time of year and had overflowed its banks and smashed through or passed over the high earthen levees that cotton and sugar planters had built to protect their homes and crops. Some plantations were "entirely submerged" and abandoned by their owners; slaves could be seen hanging for life on the rooftops of sugarhouses and cotton barns.[26] Locals called the annual overflow "freshets," but the word "floods is more appropriate," wrote naturalist John James Audubon, who had hunted birds on the river before the war.[27]

Behind the levees were tangled networks of bayous, sluggish streams as crooked as the river itself, and long and deep enough during the biannual floods—every spring and fall—to be navigable for miles by double-decker steamboats. On the western bank of the river, far flatter than its eastern counterpart, the bayous merged and became basins of considerable size. A strong eddy threw one of Farragut's smaller gunboats, *Wissahickon*, into what captain and crew thought was the riverbank. But the bank was submerged under twelve feet of water, and they found themselves floating over cottonfields flooded as far as the eye could see. Then, in an instant, a whirlpool shot *Wissahickon* back "into the bosom of Old Mississippi."[28]

"They will keep us in this river until the vessels break down, and all the little reputation we have made has evaporated," Farragut wrote his wife back in New York State. "Fighting is nothing to the evils of the river—getting on shore, running afoul of one another, losing anchors, etc." His greatest fear was that his ships would go aground and remain stuck on a sandbar "till next year; or, what is more likely, be burned to prevent them falling into the enemy's hands. A beautiful prospect for the 'hero' of New Orleans!"[29]

When David Farragut first entered the great river above New Orleans, he joined a struggle begun at Cairo the previous year by Ulysses Grant. But the Mississippi Valley had been a cockpit of war since the first arrival of Europeans. "From the colonization of the valley to the close of the Civil War, control of the Mississippi was the most important single objective in American military strategy," wrote historian Hodding Carter. "In its four hundred recorded years more men have died defending or conquering or exploiting this river than any other in North America."[30]

Though Farragut occasionally took slaves aboard, he did not come into the Valley as a liberator. His was a military mission. A number of his captains, Thomas Craven chief among them, had no argument with slavery and held ugly views of African Americans. In Craven's correspondence with his wife, he alluded to the "monkey traits of the negro character," and he ordered officers serving under him to return to their masters slaves they were protecting or employing.[31] Some refused and were reprimanded; most obeyed. "We are not on a cotton, or nigger, or chicken-stealing expedition," Craven assured a plantation overseer who feared the Yankees had entered his world to steal cotton and slaves.[32]

The Federals *were* there, however, to destroy rebel railroads and steamboats, and any warships they encountered. One rebel vessel occupied their attention. Before Memphis fell, the Confederates had floated the shell of the uncompleted ironclad ram *Arkansas* down the river from Memphis and towed it far up the Yazoo River, the stream that empties into the Mississippi a few miles north of Vicksburg. The mystery ship, as Farragut's sailors called it, was reportedly being readied for battle. Farragut doubted he had a vessel in his fleet that could "resist her."[33]

The Vicksburg, Shreveport & Texas Railroad was another priority target. It stretched eastward seventy-five miles from Monroe, Louisiana—a major supply post in the western Confederacy—to De Soto Peninsula just across the river from Vicksburg. The Confederate government had recently taken control of the line and was working furiously to extend it into northeastern Texas. Even in its uncompleted state, it was delivering to Vicksburg molasses, salt, and cattle. Cars were loaded onto ferries on the Louisiana shore, deposited at the rail depot in Vicksburg, and sent to armies in Tennessee and Alabama.[34] Destroying the railroad was General Thomas Williams's responsibility. Farragut had his eye only on Vicksburg.[35]

He was expected there. At Brokenburn, a sprawling cotton plantation in Madison Parish, Louisiana, thirty miles northwest of Vicksburg,

Kate Stone had been reading reports of Farragut's advance upriver. She was the twenty-one-year-old daughter of Amanda Stone, the widowed mistress of an estate worked by nearly one hundred and fifty slaves. The Yankee fleet that had taken Natchez threatened everything Amanda Stone and her late husband had built for themselves and their children: a white-columned mansion with a lacy Italianate portico; a richly stocked library; a whirlwind European tour Amanda had planned for Kate and her younger brother William; the household slaves who waited on the family's every need; and the field hands who were the foundation of her fortune. Two of Amanda's seven children were in uniform and she had not wanted to put her younger sons at risk. Now her entire family was threatened.

Her daughter's war diary—a sharply observant record of rebel patriotism and intransigence—chronicled, day by day, the encroaching danger: the experience of a "whole country . . . awake and on the watch," thinking and talking "only of war"; the deflating defeats at Forts Henry and Donelson and Pittsburg Landing; the Yankee occupation of Nashville, where Kate had been educated at the Female Academy; and, lately and most shockingly, the fall of New Orleans. On May 22, Kate heard what she had been dreading for weeks: "cannonading at Vicksburg. . . . Oh, if we could only know just what is going on there."[36]

The muffled cannon fire turned out to be insignificant: a sharp exchange between a jittery Union gunboat crew and an equally impatient rebel battery. What was significant—and electrifying news in every part of the Confederacy—was Vicksburg's refusal to bow to Union power.

On Sunday, May 18, Captain S. Phillips Lee's squadron had dropped anchor in front of Vicksburg and launched a small gig with a white flag attached to its bow. It was met midstream by a rebel steamer. A naval officer handed over a dispatch from Lee. It was an ultimatum: Vicksburg was to surrender to "the lawful authorities of the United States." Town officials were given three hours to reply.[37]

The answer came two hours late. There were three letters: one from Lieutenant Colonel James L. Autry, military governor of the Vicksburg district; another from General Martin Luther Smith, a former New Yorker who commanded rebel forces in Vicksburg; and a final one from Mayor Lazarus Lindsay. All said the same thing. But it was Autry's reply that Vicksburg residents would long remember with pride: "Mississippians don't know, and refuse to learn, how to surrender to an enemy. If Commodore Farragut and Brigadier-General Butler can teach them, let them come and try." [38]

General Smith had already called for a civilian evacuation. Most residents had left to join family and friends in the countryside or to camp in the woods outside town; but a sizable number remained. Across the river, in Madison County, slave-owning families began migrating to central Louisiana and Texas, leaving old and infirm slaves behind, abandoning them to whatever fate had in store for them. But Amanda Stone was immovable. "In these troublous times home was the best place," her daughter Kate spoke for her. [39]

With the Yankees nearby, the field hands at Brokenburn grew restless and insubordinate, and Kate and her family felt threatened. They had cause for concern. There were approximately eleven thousand residents in Madison County; 9,800 of them were slaves—nine African Americans to every white person. [40] Not unexpectedly, field hands were watched more closely than ever at Brokenburn and everywhere else in the plantation country astride the river, where the enemy threat was immediate.

President Jefferson Davis and an older brother, Joseph, had adjoining plantations—Brierfield and Hurricane, respectively—at Davis Bend, located on a sweeping curve of the Mississippi fifteen miles south of Vicksburg. It was land Joseph Davis had acquired in 1818, one year after Mississippi achieved statehood. [41] After the fall of New Orleans, Joseph reported to his brother in Richmond that the advancing Yankees, along with the recent rise in the river, had forced him to remove some of their "people" to Vicksburg and to farms in the interior. [42] When a steamboat arrived at Vicksburg's wharf with a load of furniture, provisions, and slaves, a dockhand asked one of the slaves where he came from. "I belongs to Jeff Davis," he replied. [43]

On June 24, sailors and marines from Farragut's fleet landed at Davis Bend under the cover of darkness, carried off slaves and horses, and plundered both mansions, slashing paintings with bayonets and tossing furniture and books into a bonfire. Before leaving, they put the torch to Hurricane, Joseph's estate. "The red glare from rocketing flames" could be seen clearly in Vicksburg. [44]

There, fear of racial reprisals fomented by Yankee invaders had ignited agitation for an eight o'clock "negro" curfew, to be enforced by individual slaveholders. "We apprehend no particular danger from the slaves," wrote Marmaduke Shannon, editor of the *Vicksburg Daily Whig*, "but there are a 'few black sheep in every flock,' and these 'few' might do us and our cause considerable damage."[45] The Warren County board of police went further. Slaves found walking about without passes issued by their masters were to be apprehended and receive thirty-nine lashes. Dogs owned by slaves were to be killed. Slaves were not permitted to carry firearms, or even to hunt with their masters, and licenses granting free blacks permission to reside in the county were revoked.[46] No white person felt safe.

The most serious threat came from the Yankees on the river. Volunteer regiments arrived from local communities to bolster General Smith's small defense force, raising it to around 3,600 men, but most of the defenders, residents noticed, were boys with nothing but hunting knives and shotguns. Not sure he could hold the city, Smith issued orders to "push the *Arkansas* to completion."[47] Farragut would soon be in front of the town with his full fleet.

When Farragut received word of Vicksburg's intransigence, he transferred his flag to the speedy gunboat *Kennebec* and headed upriver. Approaching the city, just out of range of its guns, he called for his spyglass and surveyed its defenses. Vicksburg—he now fully realized—was the strongest place on the river. Its steep bluffs ran directly down to the waterfront. An amphibious force would have no safe place to land and gain lodgment. There was also the threat, to both ships and infantry, of direct as well as plunging fire. Gangs of black workers could be seen digging gun pits and mounting cannon on forested slopes by the river and on "tortuous ridges" along four miles of riverfront.[48] Farragut spotted what he surmised were twelve guns, "ten mounted below Vicksburg, two above." *[49]

---

* Actually, seven batteries had been completed, giving Vicksburg thirteen guns below the city and five up top, including a powerful 18-pounder known as "Whistling Dick." M. L. Smith to M. M. Kimmel, n.d., OR, I/15/7–10; Brown addendum, n.d., *ibid.*

The terrain alone made Vicksburg formidable.[50] Vicksburg "[is] very strong . . . without any of the defensive works," reported a Confederate engineer who had recently inspected its batteries. "Any probable attack the enemy may attempt with his land forces can be repelled."[51]

After completing his reconnaissance, Farragut met with his gunboat commanders. General Williams, who reported directly to the War Department, not the navy, was invited to join them. It was an emotion-charged meeting. "Flag-officer was indignant at the opposition and defiance of the enemy and thought they should be 'chastised,'" Fleet Officer Bell reported in his diary. At this point, Williams, a small, self-important man with a precisely cut mustache, said his infantry force of 1,500 was "too weak to capture the town and the higher forts." His spies estimated—far too generously—that there were eight thousand rebel troops in Vicksburg and another several thousand at Jackson, Mississippi, forty miles to the east.[52] Farragut replied sharply that he didn't need the army to force the city to surrender. All that was required was an intimidating display of naval power. The fleet's gunboats could knock out the town's batteries and destroy two small Confederate gunboats moored at Vicksburg—if, he said pointedly, the gunboat commanders "had the will." Most did not. Three of five considered Farragut's proposal "impractical or madness," and they told him that directly. Captain Lee "carried his objection so far as to say anyone who would undertake it might have his vessel," said Bell.[53]

Indignant over his commanders' failure of nerve, Farragut slipped downriver to his flagship and ordered his sloops-of-war up to Vicksburg. He would bomb it into submission. The river was falling nearly a foot a day, but Farragut was angry enough to take the risk. He wanted to destroy the town, said Bell.[54] But when he called another council of war after a second reconnaissance of Vicksburg's defenses, all but one of his commanders called for caution. Their ships' flat-trajectory guns could not effectively reach the highest batteries, while the rebel guns were capable of delivering pulverizing fire on the fleet.[55] Earlier in the Mississippi campaign, before running past Forts Jackson and St. Philip, Farragut had overruled his officers. This time he sullenly acquiesced in their decision. He was ill with what he called a "nervous fever," his supplies of coal were nearly exhausted, and, with the river falling rapidly, he feared being stranded at Vicksburg for months.[56] It was time to turn back.

The news surprised "all hands" on *Hartford*. The men had expected a fight.[57] Before leaving for New Orleans on the morning of May 16, Farragut transferred command of the gunboats from S. Phillips Lee, who had greatly disappointed him, to James S. Palmer, one of the few officers who voted to "attack and destroy the town."[58] Palmer's *Iroquois* and seven other vessels remained behind to shell Vicksburg intermittently and to conduct a naval siege, sealing off the town from the river upon which it depended for nearly everything.[59]

Williams informed Farragut that he would also be leaving Vicksburg, and he requested that the navy convoy his troop steamers back to Baton Rouge. The Louisiana railroad he had been directed to destroy was underwater, a casualty of widespread flooding in the lowlands. And without the support of Farragut's full fleet, Williams could only annoy Vicksburg's defenders with ineffective hit-and-run raids. Still burning over his officers' rebuff, Farragut told Williams that in "ten days" the dissenters "will be of my opinion, and then the difficulties [of capturing Vicksburg] will be much greater than they are now." He was "very sick" when he yielded to his officers' "advice," he wrote his wife, Susan. "I doubt if I would of taken it had I been well."[60] But in a cooler moment, he admitted he may have been wrong. Even if Vicksburg surrendered, he lacked the troops to hold it.[61]

On May 30, Kate Stone learned from a Vicksburg newspaper that the Yankee shelling "did no harm," and that the rebel defenders were "full of hope," confident that if the Federals sent more ships and troops they would give them the "worst beating they ever had in their lives."[62]

That same day, William Pitt Chambers, a twenty-two-year-old former schoolteacher from the piney woods of Mississippi, was on picket duty near the river, five miles below Vicksburg. He had no idea that the Yankee soldiers—whose numbers he could only guess at—were heading back to Baton Rouge. His great fear was that enemy infantry, supported by fearsome fire from the gunboats still in front of the city, would storm and overrun the weakly defended city. His regiment, the 46th Mississippi Infantry, had not been issued rifles. "Some other companies," he wrote in his diary, "are in the same predicament." When on duty, he and his comrades borrowed muskets from units camped near them.[63] They were hardly ready and eager, as Kate Stone had heard, to take on the enemy.

• • •

At one point during the standoff, Chambers obtained a pass to see for himself the terraced city his regiment had been sent to defend. The houses, he was amazed to see, were built right into the hills, "the sidewalks of one street often being on a level with or above the roofs of the houses on the next street below." There were well-made stone residences with "the most beautiful yards and gardens," and on the highest hill in town was the new Warren County Courthouse, seated in a stately public square and topped by an impressive cupola.[64] Uniformed infantry guarded its iron gates, and troops were billeted in tent cities in and around the town.[65]

Vicksburg "[has been] deserted by all who could leave," wrote Colonel Winchester Hall of Thibodaux, Mississippi, commander of a regiment—the 26th Louisiana Infantry—he had recently raised "to meet the invader."[66] Businesses that remained open "were barren of goods."[67]

Chambers and Hall were among the first reinforcements to reach the city by train after the fall of New Orleans. Some were surprised to find residents "very angry because we came to their town. They said it would cause the Yankees to come," wrote William Y. Dixon, a private in Chambers's regiment.[68] Other citizens were enraged by the behavior of the boys sent to save them. Provisions were scarce and volunteers would "prowl around day and night and purloin fruit, vegetables etc. from our denizens," complained James W. Swords, editor of the *Vicksburg Daily Citizen.* They broke into stores and homes and took what they wanted; backyards were raided for peaches and pigs.[69] One resident wounded a soldier and killed another who tried to steal from him.[70]

But most citizens were relieved to have the troops in town. Older women opened their homes to wounded and hungry soldiers. When men in Dixon's regiment became sick, "the ladies were very attentive to us," he noted, though many of them were in straitened circumstances themselves, with husbands and sons fighting on distant fields.[71] These women had to deal with grasping storekeepers who refused to sell supplies they were hoarding until prices rose sky-high. The commodities being hoarded were necessities, not luxuries. Salt became scarce, but not stoves or silverware.[72] "Could not get sack of salt," a local planter complained in his business diary, "—offered $100—Duff Green and Company . . . have it, but won't sell."[73] These "extortioners [sic] . . . are preying upon the lifeblood of the people," declared the *Vicksburg Daily Whig*.[74] The businessmen "[we] protect . . . extort the last pound of flesh, for the common necessaries of subsistence," Captain Sidney Champion of the 28th Mississippi Cavalry wrote his wife. He had rushed to Vicksburg after New Orleans surrendered, leaving his wife, Matilda, alone with four children and sixty-five slaves on their plantation in the hill country east of Vicksburg. If it were not for his endangered family, "[he] would be glad," he said, "to see [Vicksburg] plundered and burnt to the ground. A day of retaliation is coming; we will not forget them."[75]

Sid Champion also harbored a grudge against the local master class. When military authorities compelled planters from the Yazoo Delta to release their slaves temporarily to build fortifications in Vicksburg, they rebelled. "Men are actually coming down after their Negroes fearing they will get sick." These same planters had sent their sons to fight and die in Virginia. Did they value their field hands more than their own children? God would punish Vicksburg for this, he said.

Hobbled by shortages of food and guns and preyed upon by greedy businessmen, the defenders of Vicksburg had, nonetheless, done the impossible, Sid told his wife, Matilda. They had defied the conqueror of New Orleans.[76]

"We turn the long bend of the river and the bluffs of Vicksburg are lost to sight," wrote Major Harrison Soule of the 6th Michigan Infantry.[77] He and the rest of Thomas Williams's brigade had been living in filthy transports—"cramped and crowded more like livestock than men"— since sailing from Ship Island to join Farragut's invasion fleet in front of Forts Jackson and St. Philip.[78] Sickness had broken out in their ranks and they had received no mail or news from anywhere. They were as much "out of the world" as they would have been "at the North Pole."[79] The steamboats ferrying Soule and his regiment to Baton Rouge followed closely behind Captain Craven's *Brooklyn* and a line of smaller gunboats. As the fleet passed Grand Gulf, a sleepy hamlet on the Mississippi shoreline, a rebel guerrilla band, hiding somewhere in the village, waited until *Brooklyn* had passed and then opened fire on the unarmed transports, killing one soldier and wounding another. In an instant, Craven ordered one of the gunboats to wheel around and fire at will into the village. "Women, children, men and animals . . . were seen hurrying to the hills back of the city, carrying bundles, bales and baggage of all sorts. . . . Shot and shell went plunging and tearing through the town from thirty guns of our fleet," crushing several houses "into kindling," Soule described the fast-breaking scene.[80]

Soule joined a landing party formed to pursue "the vagrants," who were soon lost in the fading light, but not before mortally wounding Williams's aide-de-camp.[81] Craven and Williams ordered their men to "burn the town." At that point residents began hanging white sheets from their windows, and a deputation of leading citizens called on Craven in his cabin on *Brooklyn* and "protested their innocence." The "wandering band of freebooters" had entered Grand Gulf "without their consent" and received no aid or protection from residents, they claimed. Craven relented, and Grand Gulf was spared. Demanding tribute for their losses, the Federals took "a pretty considerable haul of cattle, pigs, and poultry."[82]

The firefight at Grand Gulf was the beginning of a guerrilla war on Federal shipping on the lower Mississippi that would last nearly the entire war, with atrocities committed by both sides. When *Hartford* anchored at Baton Rouge to take on coal, a group of sailors came ashore in a dinghy to have their laundry done and were fired upon by a band of partisan horsemen. Three men were wounded, none seriously. General quarters sounded on *Hartford*, and Farragut directed his big guns, as well as those on *Kennebec*, to open fire on the partisans. "I spared the town as much as possible," Farragut later reported to Welles.[83] Captain Bell told a different story in his diary. "Most of the sailors blazed away right into the houses without regard to the position of the foe."[84] Only "with difficulty" were the men "compelled to cease firing. The excitement on board ship was intense, and each man desired to see the city in ashes," said another member of *Hartford*'s crew.[85]

As Sarah Morgan and her family stood at the door of their home, terror-stricken and about to flee the city on foot, shells from the fleet sailed directly over their heads. "If I was only a man!" Sarah wrote in her diary. "I don't know a woman here who does not groan over her misfortune in being clothed in petticoats; why cant [sic] we fight as well as the men?"[86]

Two representatives from the town rowed out to *Hartford* and denounced the ambush "as a most cowardly act on the part of guerillas." The mayor came on board that afternoon and assured Farragut he would raise a force to control the firebrands. There was no need: General Williams arrived the next day and had his troops take firm possession of the town.[87]

The following morning Farragut started for New Orleans, leaving two gunboats to support Williams's occupying army. On May 30, he arrived in the city, having completed—but for Vicksburg—the most successful campaign in the history of the United States Navy.[88]

That afternoon Farragut retired to his cabin and wrote Gideon Welles. He concluded his report with a hair-raising description of the troubles he had encountered on the Mississippi. "The elements of destruction to the Navy in this river are beyond anything I ever encountered, and if the same destruction continues the whole Navy will be destroyed in twelve months. More anchors have been lost and vessels ruined than I have seen in a lifetime, and those vessels which do not run into others are themselves run into and crushed in such a manner as to render them unseaworthy."[89]

The trip upriver, Farragut wrote his wife from New Orleans, "wore upon my health more than I could imagine. My anxiety was intense."[90] His nerves frayed to the breaking point, his countenance pale and taut, Farragut prepared to sail for Mobile Bay and the deep waters of the Gulf. But sorting through a mail packet just delivered to him, he came upon a telegram from Gustavus V. Fox: "Carry out your instructions of January 20 about ascending the Mississippi River, as it is of the utmost importance."[91] The president, he told him in a following letter, was distressed that he had returned to New Orleans instead of rendezvousing with the ironclads, which were presently bombing Fort Pillow, fifty miles above Memphis, with orders to head on to Memphis and then Vicksburg. Fox pointedly called Farragut's decision to give up on Vicksburg a "retreat" and a potentially "fatal step as regards our western movements"—words that gravely wounded the prideful flag officer. "It is of paramount importance that you go up and clear the river with the utmost expedition. Mobile . . . sinks into insignificance compared with this. . . . There is not a moment to be lost in the Mississippi."[92] A third message in Farragut's mail packet was a communiqué from Welles, framed as a direct order from the chief executive: "The President of the United States requires you to use your utmost exertions (without a moment's delay . . .) to open the river Mississippi, and effect a junction with Flag-Officer Davis, commanding . . . the Western flotilla."[93]

Benjamin Butler redoubled the pressure on Farragut. Offended by the "insulting letters" Vicksburg authorities had delivered to Captain S. Phillips Lee, Butler wanted Vicksburg "reduced to ashes if need be."[94] If Farragut agreed to attach Porter's mortar flotilla to his fleet, Butler pledged to provide sufficient troops to take the city—an offer on which he would later renege.[95]

Farragut fired off a telegram to Porter, directing him to return at once to New Orleans with his mortars. "[If] this work is done at all, it must be done before the end of June, in order to enable the gunboats to get down river." Otherwise the saltwater fleet would be unable to descend the river "until next spring, if at all."[96] Porter, surprisingly, was unenthusiastic. "Mobile is of more value to us now than a dozen Vicksburgs," he told Farragut.[97] And Vicksburg would be harder to take now that it had been given time to bolster its defenses. Porter also feared it was "too late in the season. . . . One fall of the river . . . will destroy the expedition."[98] He wrote Fox in confidence: "I am heartsick and fear sad failure up the River."[99]

The following day, Farragut turned *Hartford* toward Vicksburg. "They cannot deprive me and my officers of the historical fact that we took New Orleans," he wrote his wife back at Hastings-on-Hudson. "Now they expect impossibilities."[100]

CHAPTER 7

Secessionist Citadel

"The Deed is Done—Disunion the Remedy."[1]
—*Jackson Semi-Weekly Mississippian,* November 9, 1860

Farragut was a commander "absolutely insensible to fear," said a fellow officer.[2] Returning to Vicksburg, it was the elements, not the enemy, that most concerned him: the wicked river, the furnace heat, the malarial swamps, and the hill city's forbidding terrain.

Farragut was also concerned about the morale of his officer corps. "Opinions in the fleet unanimously against the feasibility of the undertaking," Captain Bell described a deflating staff meeting on the eve of the fleet's departure. "Captain Porter decidedly opposed to it, though acquiesces like the rest of us." The commanders could find only one sound reason for going back upriver. They had learned from rebel deserters that the Confederate ram on the Yazoo River was nearly ready to be launched. "We must seek this great danger before it haunts us," Bell wrote in his diary.[3]

At Baton Rouge, General Williams rejoined Farragut with a brigade of 3,200 men, nearly triple the size of the force he had taken to Vicksburg the previous month. On reaching the Louisiana capital, Farragut received the first good news he had heard in weeks: On June 6, a naval force that comprised Charles Davis's ironclads and Colonel Charles Ellet's rams had shattered the rebel River Defense Fleet in front of Memphis. "Now I shall hope to see [Davis] this way soon," Farragut wrote his wife.[4] Eager to have a large force in front of Vicksburg as soon as possible, Farragut sent Thomas Craven ahead with the sloops-of-war *Brooklyn* and *Richmond.* He would join them as soon as Porter arrived at Baton Rouge with his mortar flotilla.

On June 20, Farragut set sail for Vicksburg. Williams followed a

day later with the transports, leaving two regiments behind to maintain order in the "fractious city."[5] Part of Williams's force had been
marked by Butler for pick and shovel duty, with the approval of the
president. They were to cut a ditch, or canal, four feet deep and five
feet wide, across the base of De Soto Peninsula, a "neck of land" protruding like a fat thumb into the Mississippi in front of Vicksburg.
When the trench was completed, Butler expected the river to cut a
new channel across the peninsula, allowing Union ships to bypass the
city's water batteries. Shovels and spades innumerable were packed
aboard the eight troop transports, to the dismay of men prepared to
fight, not to dig.[6]

"Yesterday and the day before, boats were constantly arriving, and
troops embarking from here, destined for Vicksburg," Sarah Morgan
noted in her diary. Women from her church were calling on God to
send down famine and yellow fever on the Northern occupiers. She
publicly chastised them. General Williams and his men had been unexpectedly kind to her family, sending them flour and offering protection
from rebel partisans who threatened to burn the homes of "traitors"
who refused to leave enemy-occupied Baton Rouge. Standing on the
wharf as the bluecoats filed onto the transports, Sarah almost hated to
see them leave.[7] "It was a pretty sight," Farragut described his fleet of
sixteen vessels as it turned out of the harbor, "the *Hartford* like an old
hen taking care of her chickens."[8]

Hours later *Hartford* ran aground and remained stuck until the following morning, when mortar tugs equipped with heavy towing cables
pulled her off a sandbar.[9] All the way up to Vicksburg, roving guerrilla
bands harassed the transports with musket and cannon fire, and when
the fleet dropped anchor just below Grand Gulf, the Mississippi riverfront town just south of Vicksburg, Williams's scouts learned from
local farmers that the Confederates were again emplacing guns in the
village.[10] This time the general carried out his threat to burn down the
town. The transports "proceeded up the river by the light of the blazing
houses," recalled a Vermont volunteer.[11]

On June 25, five days out of Baton Rouge, the Union fleet reached
Vicksburg and tied up on the riverbank just below the city, joining the
light gunboats that Farragut had left behind to blockade the town. It
was an impressive display of Union naval might: twenty-seven heav-

ily armed warships, plus Porter's eighteen mortar scows. But Farragut could see at once that the enemy had strengthened its defenses.

The work had been carried out under the command of Samuel H. Lockett, a recent graduate of West Point who would continue to supervise the construction and maintenance of Vicksburg's defenses into the following year. There were now ten land batteries, one of them commanded by David H. Todd of Kentucky, the half brother of Mary Lincoln, the president's wife. Captain Todd had arrived in the last week of June with Major General John C. Breckinridge and four thousand Kentuckians, seasoned fighters who had tangled with Ulysses Grant at Fort Donelson. Six thousand men from General Daniel Ruggles's northern Mississippi command had joined them. These infusions increased the strength of the garrison to nearly fifteen thousand troops.[12]

On June 27, the defenders were placed under the command of Major General Earl Van Dorn, a cavalry officer educated at West Point and raised in a hilltop mansion outside Port Gibson, a picturesque country town thirty miles south of Vicksburg. A personal friend of Jefferson Davis, Van Dorn had arrived two days ahead of Farragut. At age forty-two, he still had "a near perfect physique" and was both strikingly handsome and gracious in social company, the "stereotype of the flamboyant, dashing, and glamorous cavalryman of his day." He was "the most gallant soldier I have ever known," said one of his staff.[13]

Van Dorn professed undying love to his radiant Alabama wife but remained to his early death in 1863—shot by a doctor whose wife he had been pursuing—a brazen womanizer, a "ballroom beau . . . a thing of paint, perfume and feathers," a disapproving Kentucky soldier sized him up.[14] "He was small, curly or kinky headed, exquisitely dressed [and rode] a beautiful bay horse, evidently groomed with as much care as his rider," said another unimpressed volunteer.[15]

An accomplished painter and poet, Van Dorn was a reckless fighter with an outstanding record for bravery in the Mexican War. There was no more passionate secessionist in the rebel army.[16] He would defend Vicksburg to the last bullet, he promised President Davis. "This will be done at all hazards, even though this beautiful and devoted city should be laid in ruins and ashes."[17]

• • •

On June 26, the Federal mortars opened fire on the town. The following day the entire fleet joined in. "The ridge of the bluff was one sheet of fire," reported a sailor on *Hartford*.[18] The mortars, however, failed to quiet a single rebel battery. When Confederate gunners spotted a shell heading toward them, its long fuse burning fiercely, they would "run to their bombproofs, and, as soon as it burst, would fly to their guns again," Porter reported. Bombing a camouflaged chain of earthen forts was tremendously more difficult, Porter discovered, than shelling a prominently situated enemy fort.[19]

The naval fire was initially directed at the enemy guns, but as the river siege wore on the town also became a target. Few Federal gunners objected to firing on civilians. "We feel that our cause is just and holy," said an officer on *Brooklyn*.[20] Hundreds of Vicksburg families sought protection in caves dug into the city's finely grained loess soil.[21] Women, children, and the elderly scurried to these candlelit caverns "when the regular morning and afternoon shelling began," wrote Major John B. Pirtle, one of Vicksburg's defenders. Families with absent fathers, and without slaves, had to brave the fire in their homes, trusting to Lady Fortune to spare them. During a heavy night bombing, an 80-pound shell from a rifled naval Parrott gun tore through a bedroom in which three children were sleeping, passed through a bureau, grazed the bed, and exited through an outer wall. The bed collapsed to the floor but the children were unharmed.[22]

At one point in the siege, Private William Dixon spotted two terror-stricken women racing through his encampment, pulling the hands of three children. "Just as they were passing our tent a shell burst, hurling the canister all around in every direction—one of which entered the side of one of the ladies, who was the mother of the three poor little girls." She lay unconscious for twenty minutes before expiring.[23]

Fire from the fleet, especially from the mortars, was wildly inaccurate and would claim few civilian or soldier lives. By one reliable count, only seven noncombatants were killed and fifteen wounded during the siege. But the bombardment rattled the nerves of Vicksburg families and hardly a house or place of business would not be struck at one time or another. It was the anticipation, the fear, "the shock of the hit, the destruction, and then the waiting again," said one Vicksburg historian, that made the bombing terrible to endure.[24]

Rebel gunners had their own problems inflicting harm on the enemy. Farragut's ships attacked from positions downriver, out of range of Confederate batteries; and while ten of the eighteen mortar vessels were anchored on the Vicksburg side of the river, only 2,200 yards from the enemy's gun positions, they were well concealed by thick vegetation. Those on the opposite side of the river were "fair targets for the enemy," said Porter, "yet none of their hulls were touched, though hundreds of shot and shell whistled over them." [25]

The constant shelling back and forth did little to break the resolve of the people of Vicksburg. "We [will] fight to the last," the *Vicksburg Daily Citizen* caught the prevailing mood.[26] Townspeople prayed for the best and prepared for the worst. "Make a good crop of corn," Sid Champion wrote his wife. "The object of our enemies is to starve us." [27] Fear and loathing of the invader ran stronger in Vicksburg than in any other Mississippi town. Yet this place that refused to bend to Federal might had been a stronghold of Union sentiment until very recently.

Officially incorporated in 1825, Vicksburg was named after Reverend Newitt Vick, a circuit-riding Virginia minister who founded a Methodist mission on the Walnut Hills, a shaded stretch of high ground commanding a picture-perfect panorama of the river. A planter-patriarch who sired thirteen children, Vick died of yellow fever in 1819, at age fifty-five, before he had a chance to sell the lots he had laid out as the site of a pious riverfront community. His descendants, along with a steady influx of newcomers lured by the Mississippi cotton and land boom of the 1830s and 1840s, carried on the work of town building. By 1860, Vicksburg was a flourishing cosmopolitan city of some 4,500 residents. A bustling river port and rail center, it was ideally situated between Memphis and New Orleans and was part of a cotton-producing district spanning most of west-central Mississippi.

Cotton and the river defined the town and set its course. By the 1850s Vicksburg had surpassed Natchez as the state's busiest port and was already a major rail center. But prewar Vicksburg was preeminently a steamboat town. From New Orleans came Parisian scarves and ballroom gowns; from Manchester, England, knives and needles; from Chicago, salted pork and iron stoves. Cotton paid for all of this. Thousands of bales of it reached the city's docks every week in swaying farm wagons pulled by oxen and mules, and in flat-bottomed steamboats that "could work their way into the shallowest bayou landing and return to the city. The richest land in Mississippi was webbed by roads and waterways, and Vicksburg sat at the center of the web."[28]

On any given day the city's waterfront presented a forest of smokestacks. Tall double- and triple-decker boats from St. Louis, Pittsburgh, Louisville, and Memphis—and a smaller Yazoo steamer that went deep into the Delta swamp four days a week—vied for dockage at the city wharf. And every hour a ferry left for De Soto Point, the eastern terminus of the Vicksburg, Shreveport & Texas Railroad.[29] By 1860, Vicksburg had become a place apart from its primitive backcountry. It had handsome hotels and shops, a lively theater, excellent public and private schools, six newspapers, and a bookshop and reading room—Clarke's Literary Depot—where journals from Boston and London were available. The city, the capital of flourishing Warren County, was home to upward-bound immigrants from seventeen foreign countries and was a magnet of opportunity for easterners eager to get in on the cotton boom that had rapidly raised the town to significance. Signs hanging over shop doors on Washington Street, the city's commercial stem, described this ethnic diversity: Bazzinsky, Simons and Company, millinery; Botto and Spengler, coffeehouse; Antonio Genella, variety store; Henry Scheulier, grocer; Francis Hernandez, Havana cigars; Henry Volker, shoemaker; Mooney and Kuner, jewelers; Jacob Gisill, baker.[30] Most of the churches were Protestant, but there was a synagogue and a Catholic church—St. Paul's, with the highest spire in town.

Cotton plantations, some worked by over two hundred slaves, rimmed the city in three directions: to the north, in the jungle-like Yazoo Delta; to the south, in the broad belt of alluvial soil created by the seasonal overflows of the Mississippi River; and to the southeast, a land of fertile hills broken by ravines and gullies. Most substantial planters resided in the country only part of the year, migrating with their families to their Vicksburg townhouses on holidays and social occasions and during the frenetic and festive cotton-selling season. Their country estates were intermixed with the humble holdings of yeoman farmers whose commanding ambition was to one day become a "planter"—sole owner of at least twenty slaves, according to the arbitrary figure of the census bureau. (Approximately 20 percent of Mississippi farmers were considered planters.) [31]

With cotton came slavery. Slaves purchased in the tidewater regions of the southeast, where tobacco farms were struggling, were brought over the mountains on foot and in chains and resold on the city's wharf. But most planters, like Jefferson and Joseph Davis, sent their overseers down to New Orleans to purchase entire families in the busiest flesh market in North America. The unfortunates arrived at Vicksburg disoriented and vacant eyed, their chains jingling as they were led like steers down the gangways of mud-smeared riverboats. Drifters, cardsharps, and blustery river men gathered in seedy saloons and bordellos near the slave market, in a place known as Vicksburg-Under-the-Hills. The city's other catch basin for thieves, gunslingers, and barroom brawlers was located on a stretch of swampland north of the Washington Street business district. Known as the Kangaroo, after its most notorious bawdy house, this riotous shantytown was burned down by outraged citizens in 1830. Yet it had served too many base needs to remain a charred and idle ruin for long. [32]

Respectable townsfolk turned their eyes from this resurrected Gomorrah, pretending it didn't exist. Most residents were churchgoers, people of solid faith. The self-selected elite resided in Greek Revival homes "scattered in picturesque groups on natural terraces along the river." [33] These stately townhouses were shielded from the noisome streets by high hedges and sculpted iron gates. They were preserves of the privileged, whose owners hosted dancing parties and afternoon teas for select women of the town while their husbands traded land and slaves in cigar-scented libraries.

Most Vicksburg streets remained unpaved into the war years. In the dry season the dust was "unbearable"; after heavy rains some streets became nearly impassable. [34] "To walk is to sink into a foot of debris," complained a German visitor. [35] Merchants tossed garbage directly into the streets. Free-roaming pigs and dogs were the city's refuse brigade.

Antebellum Vicksburg was a violent place. Duels were commonplace, as were wild shootouts in saloons and houses of ill fame. Politics was volatile. In the two decades before the Civil War, four city newspaper editors were killed in gunfights. [36]

. . .

Black faces were ubiquitous in antebellum Vicksburg, where there were four slaves for every three white workers. A dozen or so slaves worked in a local iron foundry by the river; others labored on the construction gangs that built the city's impressive civic edifices. But the greatest number were either household servants or manual laborers in their owners' businesses. To look upon a black person in Vicksburg was to look upon a slave; in 1860, there were only twenty-seven free blacks in all of Warren County.[37]

Out in the countryside, most slaveholding farmers owned fewer than a handful of slaves, but most rural slaves resided on large plantations. On the eve of the Civil War, over 55 percent of Mississippi's population—a total of 436,631 African Americans—were slaves. It was one of the largest slave populations of any state. In two Delta counties, slaves outnumbered whites by more than nine to one; in Warren County, slaves comprised 68 percent of the population.[38]

With Farragut's fleet on the river it became paramount to tighten restrictions on the slave population. Slave patrols, organized by local jurisdictions, became more vigilant. Armed horsemen with snarling bloodhounds hunted down with terrible efficiency slaves escaping to Union boats. Members of the patrols were drawn from the local slave-owning population, and all males subject to militia duty.[39] Taken together, the patrols formed a determined army of slave catchers.

Before Mississippi seceded, Vicksburg was a Deep South anomaly: a citadel of slavery that remained loyal to the Union. Most of the town's men of affairs—established planters, prosperous merchants and bankers, and newspaper editors with property—were moderate Whigs: deep-dyed conservatives opposed to the heated agitation for secession whipped up by extremists—"fire-eaters"—in the Democratic Party. Whig planters in the Vicksburg-Natchez area conducted a burgeoning business with bankers and international traders in New York City, a commerce centered upon the financing, selling, and transport of cotton, America's largest item of export. In the 1850s, this Whig aristocracy saw civil war as a looming threat to the trade that formed the foundation of their fortunes.

When the Whig Party disappeared in the mid-1850s, its strongest supporters continued to call themselves Whigs rather than throw their allegiance to the new, anti-slavery Republican Party. Yet they remained resolutely pro-Union. Slavery, in their view, was safer in the Union, under the protection of the Constitution—which declared slavery a state not a national matter—than out of it.[40]

The Whig elite in the Vicksburg-Natchez area was comprised largely of those who had already made their place in the world. They were as much a stable social class as a dynamic political party.[41] Their stronghold was the Delta, the triangular area north of Vicksburg formed by the Mississippi and Yazoo Rivers. In the 1850s, planters with heavy capital had turned this gloomy, immensely fertile swamp into one of the most productive cotton-growing regions in the country.[42] Patrician Whigs there and in Warren and Hinds County, two of the oldest plantation-dominated areas of the state, saw no reason to risk their status as local patriarchs by supporting the reckless political adventures of their younger Democratic opponents. These unbending extremists lobbied for a vast expansion of slave lands, federal protection of slavery in the territories, and the formation, ultimately, of a sovereign slave republic.[43] The Mississippi Democracy was dominated by ambitious planters and lawyer-politicians, men in a hurry, eager to rise further in the world by spreading slavery to lands west of the Mississippi, where new territories were applying for admission to the Union. The Whig idea of the Union as a guarantor of slavery did not register with them. They saw the federal government as "a brake on their own slaveholding ambitions."[44]

Moderate Republicans like Abraham Lincoln opposed the extension of slavery to new territories but not its expulsion where it already existed. This struck Mississippi Democrats as a deceitfully disguised ruse. Lincoln, William Seward, and other party leaders were abolitionists in disguise, they argued. Once in power, they would move rapidly and with rancor to "expel slavery wherever it may be found."[45]

The 1860 presidential election was Armageddon in Mississippi, the final battle between the forces of Union and secession. Lincoln was not on the ticket, and there was scant support for the Democratic candidate, Senator Stephen A. Douglas of Illinois, a proponent of the doctrine of popular sovereignty, which allowed settlers in new territories to decide by popular vote whether slavery would be permitted. Popular sovereignty was anathema to Southern leaders like Senator Jefferson Davis and his friend John Breckinridge, the sitting vice president of the United States. They argued slavery's right to expand anywhere, even to territories that voted not to allow it. When the Democratic National Convention refused to adopt a platform along these lines, 110 Southern Democrats bolted, convened a "rump" convention, and nominated Breckinridge for president on the Southern Democratic ticket.

In Vicksburg, it came down to a choice between Breckinridge and former senator John Bell of Tennessee, the standard-bearer of the new Constitutional Union Party, comprised largely—in Mississippi—of former Whigs who opposed Breckinridge's ultimatum to have Congress protect slavery in the territories. Bell had been one of the few Southern slaveholders in the 1850s to oppose the expansion of slavery, and his party took no stand on slavery. By ignoring the issue they naïvely hoped to defuse it—and prevent a growing movement toward secession. B. L. C. Wailes, one of the richest slaveholders in the Natchez area, made this entry in his diary on Election Day: "Voted for . . . Union ticket," not the "secessionist or disunion ticket. . . . It's partisans very violent and intemperate—and insane." [46]

On November 6, the Whig Unionists carried Vicksburg by a solid majority. Bell received 816 votes, Breckinridge 580, and Douglas 83. This was small consolation for Whigs like Wailes. Breckinridge carried the state easily, receiving 59 percent of the vote to Bell's 36.5 percent. [47]

On November 9, when Abraham Lincoln was officially declared the winner, the Jackson *Mississippian* proclaimed: "The Deed is Done— Disunion the Remedy." [48] When South Carolina seceded the following month, Mississippi governor John J. Pettus—"a disunion man of the most unmitigated order"—called for the election of delegates to a special state convention to decide whether or not Mississippi would remain in the Union. [49]

Vicksburg voters chose two committed Unionists to the special state convention: Thomas A. Marshall and Walter Brooke. [50] Their most vocal supporter, Marmaduke Shannon, editor of the *Vicksburg Daily Whig*, considered secession "treason" and urged his readers not to retreat from reason simply "because an obnoxious man has been made President." [51] While some secessionists believed the South would be permitted to leave the Union in peace, Shannon argued that the formation of a "Cotton Republic" would set off a civil war, "the most prolonged, extensive and horrible ever recorded in Time's bloody volume." [52]

Slaveholding Democrats dominated the convention that assembled in the state capital on January 7, 1861. Walter Brooke called for caution and more time to deliberate the issue but was shouted down. He and Marshall finally succumbed to the overwhelming will and wish of the convention. On January 9, Mississippi became the second state, after South Carolina, to leave the Union. [53] "Our cause is holy, and we fear not the . . . Sword" of our enemies, proclaimed a leader of the secessionist bloc. Mississippi, he said, would welcome the invading host "with bloody hands and hospitable graves." [54]

By the end of January, there was hardly a prominent voice of moderation in the state. Even Marmaduke Shannon did a complete turnabout. It was "the duty of patriots," he wrote on January 23, "to follow the destiny of the State and abide its fate, be it for weal or be it for woe. [55] On February 11, Jefferson Davis came up to Vicksburg on the steamboat *Natchez* to catch a train to Montgomery, Alabama, to be sworn in as the provisional president of the Confederate States of America. Three months earlier, Vicksburg's voters had repudiated him, an ardent Breckinridge supporter. Now they greeted him as "the greatest and noblest man of the age." [56] Vicksburg's political reversal was complete.

The coming together of the rival groups—Whigs and Democrats—was made easier by their shared belief that the "benefits of the Union" were "secondary to the preservation of slavery," wrote a Mississippi historian. When, therefore, their state seceded, and Lincoln called for troops to crush the rebellion, "the slaveholder and the non-slaveholder arose with religious zeal to defend their social heritage, which, like their religion, was not a subject for the detachment of the laboratory." [57]

"In this part of Mississippi," the visiting British journalist William Howard Russell wrote of the Vicksburg region in the first months of the war, "the expression of feeling is now all one way." People "are animated by only sentiment, and they will resist the North as long as they can command a man or a dollar." [58]

There was not a soldier or sailor in Farragut's armada who knew the particulars of Vicksburg's recent politics, although many had heard that the city they were bombarding had once been a Union stronghold in Secessia. Had they followed the elections in Mississippi in 1860 and 1861 and realized the full extent of the town's commitment to secession and slavery, they would have better understood its determined refusal to surrender.

On April 15, 1861, President Lincoln issued a proclamation calling for seventy-five thousand volunteers to serve for ninety days. That turned even the most reluctant Vicksburg secessionists into rebel patriots. When Vicksburg boys were called that summer to the defense of Richmond, the callow volunteers—bearing badges that read "Victory or Death"—were fêted with dinners and dances on the eve of their departure. And on the Courthouse Square there were emotional presentations of company flags, hand-sewn by wives, mothers, and sweethearts.[59] "The trumpet of war is sounding," wrote Kate Stone from her Louisiana plantation, "and . . . men are hurrying by thousands, eager to be led to battle against Lincoln's hordes."[60] When the first boys went off to fight, the war was a thrilling thing to be read about in newspapers and soldiers' letters, not something that was experienced directly. "The first mutterings of war were like a low, rumbling thunder that one hears on a quiet summer day, when there is hardly a cloud to be seen in the sky," wrote Vicksburg resident Annie Harris.[61] Shiloh changed that. On April 11, 1862, the mutilated bodies of Beauregard's boys began arriving at Vicksburg's train station and were moved throughout the day to hospitals and homes. Mahala Roach, a young widow, spent the entire day tending to the wounded. When she returned home that evening, she made a short entry in her diary: "The war is near us indeed."[62] Two months later, Farragut was in front of Vicksburg, and the thunder of artillery echoed up and down the river valley.

CHAPTER 8

Rebel Victory

*"The Yankees have called off their gunboats
and quit the river in disgust."* [1]

—Kate Stone

On the afternoon of June 25, 1862, David Farragut received a surprise visitor on his flagship, *Hartford*, anchored just below Vicksburg. After returning from an inspection tour of his squadron, he was informed that a brazen young stranger who claimed to be Charles Rivers Ellet, son of Colonel Charles Ellet Jr., mortally wounded when his ram fleet smashed the Confederate river force at Memphis, had been taken aboard with three companions. The man claiming to be Ellet said his family-led ram fleet, now commanded by his uncle, Lieutenant Colonel Alfred W. Ellet, had come downriver to reconnoiter the enemy's river defenses between Memphis and Vicksburg and to make contact with Farragut. He was carrying a message for Farragut from Alfred Ellet, whose fleet, he said, was anchored at the mouth of the Yazoo River, north of De Soto Point. Not wanting to risk taking his wooden rams past Vicksburg's river batteries, he had sent Charles Rivers and his fellow sailors across the point on foot.

None of Farragut's officers knew the colonel's handwriting and thought the letter a clever forgery. Officers who had been interrogating the men for three hours suspected they were spies. No one could believe "the rams had come all the way down to Vicksburg without molestation." And the suspected spies were wearing civilian clothing and were soaking wet and covered with mud. They were also carrying pistols and looked rather menacing. Farragut heard them out and believed them. They were dressed as civilians, they said, to avoid detection and had waded through waist-deep bayous and evaded rebel pickets with the help of a local German immigrant, a Union informant who acted as their guide. On reaching the other side of the peninsula, they had hailed a small boat and were rowed out to the fleet.[2]

The message they carried was welcome news. "The Mississippi," Colonel Ellet informed Farragut, "is free from all obstruction down to this point." Flag Officer Charles Davis's ironclads were at Memphis under repair but would soon join Farragut in front of Vicksburg.[3] Farragut put the letter in his pocket, went to his desk, and scratched out a reply. Ellet, a medical cadet who had dropped out of Georgetown University to join the ram fleet, secreted it in one of his boots and said he would personally deliverer it to Davis at Memphis.

Farragut informed Davis that he was planning to pass Vicksburg's batteries in "a day or two." He wanted to get north of the city, where he could be supplied from Memphis and more easily rendezvous with the ironclads. He had come upriver from New Orleans, he added, under heavy pressure from the president and the Navy Department, and he was not pleased. "I must attack [Vicksburg], although I know it is . . . impossible for us to take the place, as their troops lie in the rear of the hills. . . . So long as they have the military force to hold the back country [sic], it will be impossible for me to reduce the place without your assistance and that of the Army."[4] Since the army seemed unwilling to help, his only hope was Davis and the ironclads. But even with Davis's assistance, he could not take and hold the city without additional troops. But he had his orders, and in passing Vicksburg he planned to deliver all the punishment he could. When safely north of the city, he would await Davis and the ironclads.

On the evening of June 28 he set out with his fleet, leaving a remnant of it, along with the mortars, below Vicksburg.[5] There was no enthusiasm among his staff for the effort. His captains feared the fleet would suffer "an ignominious defeat."[6] It would be passing a three-mile-long artillery gauntlet and fighting a current of six knots, along with treacherous eddies created by the river's horseshoe turn around the tip of De Soto Point.[7]

Farragut could be obstreperous, but when given an order he carried it out with vigor. Brushing aside the reservations of his captains, he summarily ordered them to pass the city "at the slowest speed" and within pistol shot of the shoreline to give the gunners every opportunity to deliver lethal damage.[8] Porter, meanwhile, was to fire directly into the town to terrorize the population. Unknown to Farragut, Porter had something else in mind: He wanted to burn the town. The secessionists had brought this on themselves, he told a fellow officer, by warring ignobly for slavery and disunion.[9] "A large portion of the shells fired into Vicksburg were loaded with combustibles," recalled one of the commanders of the mortars, "but they nearly all failed to set fire to anything," saving Vicksburg from a conflagration.[10]

Farragut had a strong appetite for risk. For the second time in the Mississippi campaign, he was putting his wooden ships in a close-quarters gunfight with enemy shore batteries. As his vessels approached the city with their gun ports open and cannon rolled out, the entire garrison opened up on them. "We were so close to the batteries that the men could be seen working the guns, and waving their hats in defiance," recalled a gunner on *Hartford*.[11] "Their shots came crashing through our bulwarks, brains and blood flying all over the decks," Commander James Alden described the ghastly scene on *Richmond*.[12]

Inside the city, there was widespread panic and yet another exodus to the countryside. It was the first full-out bombardment of Vicksburg at close range. "Men, women and children, black and white, went screaming through the streets . . . some dressed and others almost nude," the editor Marmaduke Shannon reported.[13] The bellowing of mortars was like a "continued peal of thunder," said a correspondent covering the naval campaign for the *Chicago Tribune*, "and the huge shells seemed to hover above the doomed city as if pausing to select a place in which to land their deadly missiles."[14] Some of these "destructive engines" created holes seventeen feet deep in the city's soft soil, reported Confederate engineer Samuel Lockett.[15]

Inside of an hour, the hills three or four miles from the city were draped with terror-stricken families. The shelling shattered the nerves of soldiers as well as citizens. "Vertical fire is never very destructive of life," Lockett wrote later. "Yet the howling and bursting shells had a very demoralizing effect on those not accustomed to them."[16]

The fleet was in front of Vicksburg for an hour and a half and took a terrific pounding. *Hartford* was "riddled from stem to stern," but no ships were lost, and casualties were light—fifteen killed and thirty wounded.[17] Enemy losses were minimal. Two women and one man were killed and a handful of townspeople injured.[18] "The forts can be passed," Farragut wrote Gideon Welles. "It will not, however, be an easy matter for us to do more than silence the batteries for a time, as long as the enemy has a large force behind the hills to prevent our landing and holding the place."[19]

"This place can not be taken by ships," he wrote his wife shortly after the battle.[20] Porter had wanted General Williams to mount a commando assault on the city's river batteries but Farragut killed the idea. It would take at least twelve to fifteen thousand troops to overrun Vicksburg; Williams's force of thirty-two hundred was pitifully insufficient.*[21]

Henry Halleck had nearly thirty-seven times that number of troops in Tennessee and northern Mississippi—part of the army of 110,000 he had marched from Shiloh to Corinth in late May. On the evening Farragut passed the Vicksburg batteries, he wrote directly to Halleck: "My orders, general, are to clear the river. This I find impossible without your assistance. Can you aid me in this matter to carry out the peremptory order of the President? . . . I shall wait with great anxiety your reply."[22] Halleck wrote back with predictable evasiveness. He had broken up the large army he had taken to Corinth, and he needed troops to occupy the territory he had taken in Tennessee and northern Mississippi. "The scattered and weakened condition of my forces renders it impossible for me, at the present, to detach any troops to co-operate with you on Vicksburg. Probably I shall be able to do so as soon as I can get my troops more concentrated; this may delay the clearing of the river, but its accomplishment will be certain in a few weeks."[23] The letter was dated July 3, 1862; the river would not be cleared for a year and a day.

When Halleck's reply was relayed to Porter, he exploded. "Ships and mortar vessels . . . cannot crawl up hills 300 feet high, and it is that part of Vicksburg which must be taken by the army."[24] One week later, Farragut learned that he would be losing Porter, who had been ordered to

---

* Craven's *Brooklyn* and two gunboats did not attempt to run the batteries. Craven blamed Porter for failing to provide sufficient covering fire. He also claimed to have misunderstood Farragut's ambiguously worded orders. Farragut was incensed and fired off a stern reprimand. Craven asked to be relieved. Farragut placed Captain Henry Bell in command of *Brooklyn*.

report to Hampton Roads, Virginia, with twelve of his mortars to join General George McClellan's Richmond campaign.[25] Porter was not displeased. Large numbers of troops camped in the Louisiana swamps and sailors on board the ships in the oppressive heat had contracted malaria and were dying at a rate of five or six a day. Vicksburg, he told his friend Gustavus Fox, back at the Navy Department, was "a useless sacrifice of human life."[26]

On July 10, Porter led his mortar flotilla downriver, the gunners dressed proudly in their whites, the officers in full dress, on parade as they passed river towns they hoped never to see again. In the boiler rooms of Porter's flagship were former slaves working as coal handlers for eight to ten dollars a month. They had approached Porter's mortar scows near Vicksburg, and he had taken in as many as he could use. His towing vessels were desperately undermanned. His conscience also tugged at him. "I would not, of my own accord, give up these people (who came to us for protection) to a brutal overseer, or to parties who claim to be Union now," he wrote pointedly to Captain Craven, who was known to return runaway slaves to their former owners.[27]

The Union had lost a great chance at Vicksburg, Porter wrote his foster brother as he steamed down to New Orleans. The finest strategic point on the river had been "neglected" by the general they called fallaciously "Old Brains." Flag Officer Davis had arrived at Vicksburg with the ironclads nine days before Porter departed, but even the combined firepower of the two fleets would be powerless to take the town, Porter believed. But Porter's rancor and frustration had not hardened into despair. Vicksburg, he believed, would be a long-running campaign, and he was determined to return to the river with a better plan and a larger force, perhaps as head of the expedition.[28]

Flag Officer Charles Davis had steamed down from Memphis in a defiant mood: Vicksburg "must either surrender or be destroyed."[29] As his ironclads glided noiselessly past Kate Stone's plantation, "dark, silent, and sinister," the family came out on the gallery to watch them, river machines that were grim reminders of Yankee technological superiority. "Oh, how we hated [them] deep down in our hearts," Kate recorded in her diary, "not the less that we were powerless to do any harm."[30]

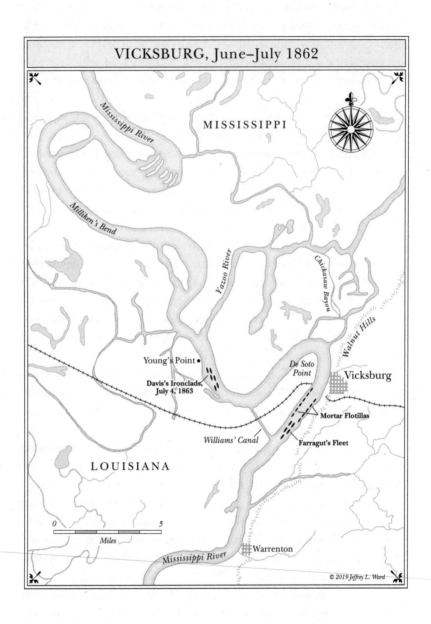

VICKSBURG, June–July 1862

Mississippi River

MISSISSIPPI

Milliken's Bend

Yazoo River

Chickasaw Bayou

Walnut Hills

Young's Point

Davis's Ironclads,
July 4, 1863

De Soto
Point

Vicksburg

Mortar Flotillas

Williams' Canal

Farragut's Fleet

LOUISIANA

0   5
Miles

Mississippi River

Warrenton

© 2019 Jeffrey L. Ward

Davis's flagship, *Benton*, was accompanied by three other ironclads—*Carondelet*, *Cincinnati*, and *Louisville*—along with two towboats, each pulling three mortar scows. *Essex*, the most formidable ironclad in the Mississippi fleet, along with gunboats on duty elsewhere, would join Davis later that month. It was a fearsome display of naval power. The combined river fleets of Davis and Farragut, conquerors of New Orleans, Baton Rouge, Natchez, Forts Henry and Donelson, Island No. 10, and Memphis, comprised the largest navy assembled in American waters during the Civil War.[31]

The union of the blue-water and brown-water navies was cause for celebration. Farragut's sailors stood on the decks and cheered lustily as the ironclads floated abreast of them.[32] Most of them had never seen one of Eads's ungainly looking monsters, boats expressly designed for river warfare, faster and more maneuverable than Farragut's sloops-of-war and drawing only six to eight feet of water. (Farragut's saltwater behemoths drew from ten to sixteen feet.)[33] Nor had most of Davis's men, recruited principally from western farms and shops, ever set eyes on full-masted ships of the line. Tars from the two fleets visited one another, and orders went out to roll out the liquor kegs and splice the main brace. "A memorable day," Henry Bell wrote in his diary. "It rejoiced all hearts. Davis . . . looking well; brought no troops, Bah!"[34]

With their ships riding at anchor, Farragut and Davis began plotting their next move. They were old and close friends, though they could not have been more different. Harvard-educated Davis was tall, solemn-looking, and contemplative, with a drooping mustache that hung over his mouth. Farragut was short, decisive, and explosive, and preferred to go clean-shaven. They would clash repeatedly in coming weeks, Davis struggling unsuccessfully to check Farragut's impetuosity. Initially, however, they agreed on one thing: Vicksburg could not be taken "without a large number of troops," reinforcements Halleck was unlikely to send.[35] This left only one feasible way to open the river: the diversion canal Williams's troops had begun digging across De Soto Point on orders from General Benjamin Butler.

Davis was hopeful about the project. The neck of land "is not a mile across," a navy official who lived near Vicksburg had told them. "This can be done."[36]

General Williams, however, was finding the work more difficult than he estimated. By July 4, the ditch was nearly seven feet deep, but it needed to be four feet deeper to reach the sand that lay below the peninsula's hard clay. Only then could the river be let in to cut through the soft sand, deepening the channel and enticing the capricious river "to take the shortcut" over the narrow neck of land.[37] "The current of the river, however great, will not wash the clay," Williams wrote Butler in New Orleans. And the river was falling fast. It was still above the level of the canal, but if the water surface fell below it, there was no chance of diverting the Mississippi into the ditch. Williams moved stubbornly ahead, however, emotionally tethered to the only task he and his men could possibly accomplish in this dismally unfruitful campaign. The project was, in his sanguine opinion, "a great one and worthy of success. . . . If the cut succeeds . . . the batteries will be made useless, and Vicksburg will fall with the spade."[38] And he would be the victor, the general who had opened the river without firing a shot.

To quicken the pace of the work, Williams rounded up additional African American laborers. "We hear . . . that the Yankees are impressing all the Negro men on the river places," wrote Kate Stone, "and putting them to work on the ditch." The recruiting parties had come within a few miles of the Stone Plantation, and taken slaves from one of her neighbors. Most went "willingly," she admitted, "being promised their freedom by the vandals."[39] When General Williams had enough slaves, he turned over the burden of the digging to these 1,200 unfortunates his raiding parties had pressed into service. They were formed into twenty-man squads, each directed by a uniformed soldier. It was man-killing work. Temperatures hovered near one hundred degrees, clean water was scarce, and the peninsula was a pestilential swamp, with dense copses of cypress, cottonwood, sweet gum, magnolia, and sycamore. The seeming hopelessness of the task caused the troops to christen the trench "Folly Creek."[40] There is no record of how the black workers felt, but Williams treated them, said Captain Edward Bacon of the 6th Michigan Infantry, "no better than dogs."[41] Back at Baton Rouge, Williams had ordered the expulsion of black "fugitives" from his camps, arrested officers who refused to obey, and allowed slave hunters with bloodhounds to retrieve runaways.[42] Now he needed "blackies"—his word—and to get unremitting work out of them, he held out the promise of freedom.[43]

The black workers "flourish and glisten and shine most when the sun's hottest," he wrote his wife.[44] A soldier supervisor told a different story: "The Negroes died off like a disease infected flock of sheep."[45] When sickness broke out among them, the afflicted were placed on the bare floor of abandoned slave huts, fed nothing but hardtack, and left to suffer without medicine or medical attention. And unknown to the workers, the general's promise of freedom was conditional: They would be emancipated only if the canal succeeded. "They work and shout as they work, thinking they're working for their freedom," Williams wrote his wife cynically.[46]

It must have been gratifying to Confederates to see Yankees treating black people this way. It pointed up Northern hypocrisy, the liberators acting worse than the slavers. These Yankees "[have] no sense of honor," or "morality, or even decency," said Samuel Lockett, who had spoken to residents in the area of the Butler canal.[47]

Williams's entire brigade, not just the men who labored on the improbable canal, suffered horribly from heat prostration and disease. The general had inexcusably ordered his men upriver without tents, and he appeared "determined," said one of his officers, "to wage war by means of inspections." His volunteers drilled and paraded in full backpack in heat as high as one hundred and ten degrees. A Connecticut soldier recalled seeing marching "men drop out of the line exhausted, and when we returned many of them would be dead."[48]

The soldiers slept in their horribly congested transports "till the number of sick became so great as to require all the room on board," said a Vermont volunteer. At that point the able-bodied took shelter in lean-tos erected near "large pools of stagnant water covered with a thick green scum"—breeding beds for disease-carrying mosquitoes. These poisonous bayous contained "as much death to the square inch as would be possible for the laboratory of nature to compound," reported a regimental surgeon. Water was gathered in buckets from the river, which served as the sewer and garbage dump for both armies. Nearly every man suffered an attack of dysentery sometime during the siege; scurvy was also prevalent.[49]

The Louisiana swampland that had become home to the Union soldiers was a product of the river. Annual floods inundated the bottomlands of De Soto Peninsula to depths of three to six feet. When the water receded, it created a thick bed of mud that produced but one bumper crop: mosquitoes. "The swamp reeked with malaria," and "the supply of quinine, that panacea for all the soldier's aches and ills, was exhausted; there was little medicine of any sort," complained a Connecticut soldier.[50]

By the second week of the naval siege, the Federal soldiers were dying in appalling numbers.[51] "Malarial diseases pervaded the entire command. . . . Hardly a day passed without a death in the regiment," wrote George G. Benedict of Vermont. His regiment's numbers were so reduced that "none could be spared for funeral escort."[52] Soon Williams didn't have enough healthy men to care for the sick or bury the dead. Some men were so ill they "looked as if they would be glad to die, to get out of their misery."[53] It was almost as bad on the ships: "Nearly every vessel bore the appearance of a hospital, filled with sufferers from swamp fever, ague, dengue, dysentery and general debility."[54]

The city's defenders also suffered, but, unlike the Federals, they kept up hope. Here "in the hills" we are in a better position than the Yankees, Samuel Lockett wrote his wife.[55] But even on high ground, malaria struck "like a plague." By mid-July nearly half the rebel army was on the sick list, and supplies of quinine had been exhausted.[56]

Raised in isolated rural communities, rebel soldiers were also highly susceptible to measles. "We were ill-conditioned to offer resistance to the destroyer," recalled Colonel Winchester Hall. "We had no hospital accommodations; we did not have, nor could we procure, proper medicine and nutriment; nurses were out of the question. Soon the quarters were filled with the sick and the dying; and it seemed we were powerless to succor or to save." The Catholic Sisters of Mercy had a small redbrick convent in Vicksburg, and Hall and his men called on them regularly. "They proved to be Angels of Mercy. They turned their pretty home into a hospital; every room was filled with our sufferers." The "ladies of the town" also began taking sick and hungry soldiers into their homes. Hearing this, hollow-eyed boys began begging door-to-door for blankets and socks.[57]

In the encampment of William Pitt Chambers, pneumonia was the great scourge. In his second week in Vicksburg, Chambers "took the fever," and soon the regiment didn't have enough healthy men to post pickets on the camp perimeter. In some weeks, fewer than 10 percent of the men reported for duty. When Chambers's father arrived in camp, having heard that his son was dead, Chambers was too weak to stand and meet him. He could only weep. "These hills will be my burying place," he wrote in his diary.[58] But neither Chambers nor Hall, nor most of the men whose letters and diaries have come down to us, despaired of the cause. Vicksburg would prevail, even if they didn't.

On the sunbaked morning of July 15, the rebel ram that Farragut had been worried about since leaving New Orleans came out of its Yazoo hiding place and tore into the Union fleet. "In one spectacular dash," wrote historian E. B. Long, "a Confederate gunboat . . . changed the complexion of warfare on the Mississippi."[59]

The Federals had had ample warning. Two days earlier, some rebel deserters had rowed out to the ironclad *Essex* with a message for Captain William "Dirty Bill" Porter, David Dixon Porter's older, snakeskin-tough brother: The partially built iron ram that the rebels had towed down from Memphis to repair yards on the Yazoo, to avoid capture, was finally completed and prepared to strike, they reported.[60] Porter sent the informants to Davis and then Farragut, but both were skeptical. Davis, however, made a precautionary reconnaissance up the river at daybreak. Within an hour, the scouting force ran into something it couldn't handle: an iron-beaked "devil . . . well protected, almost invulnerable, with a heavy battery in casemate."[61]

The story of the CSS *Arkansas* is largely that of one man, Lieutenant Isaac Newton Brown, the explosively temperamental son of a Presbyterian minister. In less than two months, this forty-five-year-old Kentuckian had turned the shell of a ship into an iron-bound steamer whose "armament and propelling force made her equal to any boat of our . . . flotilla," wrote Union war correspondent Thomas W. Knox.[62]

A veteran of twenty-eight years of naval service, Brown had arrived at Greenwood, Mississippi, far up the Yazoo River, on May 28, 1862. *Arkansas* was then a half-sunken hulk. Guns without carriages lay on her deck; engine parts were scattered about her hold; four hundred bars of railroad iron that were to be her armor lay at the bottom of the river, in a sunken barge; and Brown had no workers, machinery, or materials.[63] He had a local boatman fish up the sunken iron and tow the skeleton vessel downriver to Yazoo City, fifty miles north of Vicksburg, where the naval yard had better repair facilities. He then recruited blacksmiths and two hundred carpenters from Delta towns and farms and set up fourteen iron forges on the riverbank. Workers bolted rusty railroad iron to the wooden casemate, installed the engines, mounted ten guns, and painted the vessel rust-red. Within five weeks, "we had a man-of-war (such as she was) from almost nothing," boasted one of Brown's lieutenants.[64]

It was an ungainly looking thing. Its iron-sheathed casemate, or shield, pierced by ten powerful guns, looked like a box with sloping sides. A terrifically high smokestack rose through the top of the box. The wooden-hulled vessel was 165 feet long—small in comparison to Union ironclads—with a ramming beak of solid iron.[65] Brown recruited one hundred seamen from the depleted and defeated Confederate River Defense Force and another hundred or so army volunteers, landlubbers "who knew nothing of handling great guns," recalled Dabney Minor Scales, one of the ram's officers.[66]

The vessel had but one flaw, yet it would prove fatal: The engines and drivetrain were not yet reliable. Brown needed more time to work on them, but, with the level of the Yazoo River falling fast in mid-July, he had to get his heavy vessel downstream quickly. The timing turned out to be exactly right. The Union vessels were lying idle, without their steam up. They had banked their fires to conserve dwindling supplies of coal and give sailors relief from the suffocating heat.[67]

Lieutenant Brown had been given a stupendous task. After attacking an assemblage of thirty-seven warships, he was to land at Vicksburg to refuel, steam downriver to New Orleans, pick up coal somewhere in that Yankee-occupied town, pass the lower forts, and move out to Mobile Bay to raise the blockade there. As he set out on a humid Mississippi morning, "many of the men had stripped off their shirts and were bare to the waists, with handkerchiefs bound round their heads," recalled Lieutenant George W. Gift, the officer in charge of the bow guns.[68] Only Brown remained in full uniform. At around six A.M., he spotted through the morning mist three Federal warships approaching under full steam—the Union scout force: the timberclad *Tyler*, the Ellet ram *Queen of the West*, and the ironclad *Carondelet*, commanded by Henry Walke.[69] Walke had been friends with Brown in the antebellum navy and messmates on a trip around the world. The fast-converging vessels opened fire almost simultaneously.[70] The first casualty was one of Gift's gunners, "an Irishman, with more curiosity than prudence." When *Arkansas* became thickly engaged, he stuck his head out of a gun port and it was sheared off by a Yankee shell. His headless body collapsed onto the deck. Fearing that the sight would "demoralize" the gun crew, an officer "sprang forward" to pitch it into the river and asked the man nearest him to help. "Oh I can't do it, sir. It's my brother." The body was tossed overboard.[71]

In the ensuing close-quarters fight, *Arkansas* pumped a shell directly onto *Tyler's* lightly armored deck, instantly killing six sailors, "piling them up in one sickening heap," wrote a crewman who survived the blast."[72] As *Arkansas* moved in for the kill, intending to ram and disable *Carondelet*, Walke and the captains of the two other Federal vessels turned tail and began steaming downriver. *Queen of the West*, with no armament aside from its ram, raced far ahead, while *Tyler* and *Carondelet* fired their stern guns, engaging in a running battle that lasted half an hour. When *Arkansas* closed within rifle range of *Carondelet*, a piece of shrapnel struck Brown in the head. "This gave me no concern," he related later, "after I had failed to find any brains mixed with the handful of clotted blood which I drew from the wound and examined."[73]

Brown was hit again minutes later while he stood recklessly in the open, near the hatchway of the casemate. Spotting him as *Arkansas* moved to within fifty yards of *Carondelet*, Lieutenant William Gwin, *Tyler's* commander, had his sharpshooters take aim and fire. A low-velocity bullet struck Brown over his left temple and he stumbled senselessly onto the gun deck. He regained consciousness minutes later and directed a broadside that penetrated *Carondelet's* casemate and severed her steering ropes. Another volley caused her to spin out of control into the riverbank, where she became enmeshed in a stew of mud and low-hanging willow trees. Brown pulled his vessel alongside the crippled ironclad and gave her a final portside blast with one of his hundred-pound guns.[74] "Our last view of the *Carondelet*," reported an officer on *Arkansas*, "was through a cloud of enveloping smoke with steam escaping from her ports, and of her men jumping overboard."[75]

Convinced *Carondelet* was doomed, Brown turned his full attention to *Tyler* and resumed the chase. *Tyler's* "decks were literally running with blood, and the killed and wounded lay around in every direction."[76] But *Arkansas* couldn't finish the kill. She had begun to lose power when an enemy shell partially disabled her steam system. That ended the chase. The escaping steam raised the temperature inside the casement to nearly 130 degrees.[77]

It was Brown's great luck that not a single Union vessel had rallied to reinforce the imperiled Yazoo flotilla. The dull boom of the guns had been heard on the Mississippi, but everyone in authority thought it was Walke's reconnaissance party trading shots with a rebel battery on the banks of the river.[78] "Caught with our breeches down!" said *Hartford's* fleet surgeon.[79]

On reaching the Mississippi, Brown saw "a forest of masts and smoke-stacks, ships, rams, iron-clads, and other gun-boats"—a chilling display of enemy might. Aided by the swift river current, he went straight through the fleet, hugging so close to the larger vessels that the fast Federal rams did not have enough room to plow into his ship. Brown, on the other hand, could fire in any direction he chose. His targets were everywhere. Still, he was hit repeatedly. "The shock of missiles striking our sides was literally continuous," he recalled. Brown was knocked off the bridge twice but recovered each time. Federal shot and shell found weak spots in his ship's armor and came screaming through her portholes. One explosion set *Arkansas* on fire, but the blaze was suppressed with hoses and she steamed ahead, with seven of her ten guns still blazing.[80] When the rust-red vessel reached the "outer rim of the volcano," past the last Federal ship, Brown called his officers on deck "to take a look at what we had just come through." The heat-stricken survivors roared lustily, celebrating their unlikely triumph. Minutes later, the battered ironclad reached Vicksburg's wharf with thirty dead and wounded aboard.[81]

Nearly every soldier and civilian in town had witnessed the battle, some of them from the rooftops, and hundreds of them raced to the wharf to welcome Brown and his crew. As the solitary vessel sailed into sight, Brown could be seen on the bow, "waving his cap in one hand and a Confederate flag in the other."[82] General Van Dorn was there to embrace the commander as he climbed from the casemate. His achievement, said Van Dorn, was "the most brilliant ever recorded in naval annals."[83] But the air went out of the celebration when curious spectators peered into the gun deck and saw that "blood and brains [had] bespattered everything, whilst arms, legs and several headless trunks were strewn about." Stretcher-bearers spread ashes on the decks and stairs to keep from slipping in the spreading pools of blood. Onlookers turned away in horror.[84]

Casualties and attrition diminished Brown's crew by half, as many of the men had volunteered only for that single run to Vicksburg. As Brown began recruiting a new crew, Van Dorn wrote to President Davis: "Soon be repaired and then, Ho! for New Orleans."[85] But when reports circulated about the blood and brains in the ship's casemate, Brown found it hard to entice volunteers. His ram would never again have a full crew.[86]

Farragut feared the "rebel monster" would be the ruination of his career.[87] The *Arkansas*'s run through the combined Union fleet was "the most disreputable naval affair of the War," Gideon Welles confided in his diary.[88] The hour that the rebel ironclad reached Vicksburg, Farragut vowed to destroy her "at all hazards."[89] At twilight, he led his big ships once again past Vicksburg's batteries, downstream, closing to within thirty yards of shore, but smoke and descending darkness made it impossible for his artillery officers to spot the dark-colored ram, which was partially hidden behind a wharf boat. Unknown to Farragut, a stray shot had pierced *Arkansas*'s armor, disabling the engines.[90]

Conferring with Captain Bell that evening, Farragut exploded, blaming Davis for refusing to lend full support to the search-and-destroy mission. "The ram will be destroyed . . . or she will destroy us," he told Bell, his voice breaking. He "would have given his commission to have had a crack at her," said Bell.[91] Farragut then proposed to Davis a joint fleet action to destroy *Arkansas*, "regardless of consequences to ourselves."[92] Davis was appalled. He considered "patience as great a virtue as boldness" and was "unwilling," he told Farragut, to put his ironclads in jeopardy "to indulge a momentary spleen."[93] Farragut's "impetuosity" was that of "an excited, hot-headed boy," he complained to his wife.[94]

Unlike Farragut, "Davis feared risk more than he welcomed opportunity," writes historian James McPherson.[95]

After waiting days for Davis to offer his ironclads in a combined attack on *Arkansas*, Farragut called for a barge to take him ashore. He then crossed De Soto Peninsula on foot with a marine guard and met with Davis aboard *Benton*, anchored above Vicksburg. There is no record of the meeting, but Farragut must have been persuasive. Acting in concert, Davis and Farragut agreed to destroy *Arkansas* the following day.[96] Davis assigned two of his most intrepid commanders to the task: Dirty Bill Porter with *Essex*, Davis's largest ironclad; and Alfred Ellet, with *Queen of the West*, the most powerful ram in his fleet.[97]

At daybreak, both fleets opened up on the batteries while Porter and Ellet sped downriver to Vicksburg's wharf. "They could not have taken us at a more unprepared moment," Brown wrote later. "Some of our officers and all but twenty-eight of our crew were in hospitals ashore, and we lay helplessly at anchor, with a disabled engine." Brown had only enough men to fire two of his guns. Porter, dressed iconoclastically in a red jacket, duck trousers, and straw hat, came on "like a mad bull," but Brown smartly swung his bow toward *Essex* and Porter could only deliver a glancing blow. While the two ironclads were nearly entwined, Porter unleashed a lucky shot that went tearing through an opening in *Arkansas*'s casemate. It took down fourteen men and did heavy but not fatal damage to the ship's superstructure.[98]

"Had Porter at the moment of the collision thrown fifty men on our upper deck, he might have made fast to us with a hawser," Brown wrote later, "and with little additional loss might have taken the *Arkansas* and her [reduced] crew of twenty men and officers."[99] But Porter retreated to midriver, under heavy fire from *Arkansas* and Vicksburg's water batteries. As he did so, Ellet moved in and "butted" *Arkansas*, "but did no significant damage."[100] After running aground, the light and quick *Queen of the West* raced back upriver to rejoin the ram fleet, while Porter, in a slower boat, steamed downstream with the current to join Farragut. This left *Arkansas* "still defiant," Brown proudly recalled, "in the presence of a hostile force perhaps exceeding in real strength that which fought under Nelson at Trafalgar"—an understandable exaggeration.[101]

Porter's brave but botched attack was the Vicksburg finale for Farragut. The next morning he received the orders he had been anxiously awaiting. "Go down river at [your] discretion," Welles informed him.[102] At New Orleans, he would be assigned to duty in the Gulf of Mexico blockading Texas. Welles had received final word from Secretary of War Stanton that Halleck could not "at present give Commodore Farragut any aid against Vicksburg." Instead, he had sent troops to Major General Samuel R. Curtis, who was on the offensive in Arkansas; and to Major General Don Carlos Buell, who was protecting railroads in eastern Tennessee and western Kentucky. Grant and Sherman were still eager to move on Vicksburg, but Halleck had them guarding towns and railroads in western Tennessee and northern Mississippi that had recently come under Union control.[103] Attorney General Edward Bates thought that "only 8 to 10,000 men" were needed to capture Vicksburg and that even as late as July, Old Brains had the manpower to do it. "[Halleck] pretended that he had not troops to spare!" Bates told his diary. "Yet at that very time, Curtis, with his 20,000, lay demoralizing and rotting at Helena [Arkansas]," which he had captured in early July.[104]

But it was Welles who had the last word. "Had the army seconded Farragut and the Navy months ago," he wrote on January 9, 1863, "Vicksburg would have been in our possession. Halleck was good for nothing then, nor is he now."[105]

Farragut's fleet departed for New Orleans on July 24, leaving Davis behind to continue the bombardment.[106] Davis expected Williams and his brigade to remain, but the general had had enough of the swamps. Sickness and the falling river had finally killed his canal project, ending his usefulness—such as it was—at Vicksburg.[107]

At the time, he had only eight hundred soldiers fit for duty, out of an original force of 3,200.[108] The other three-fourths, he reported, "have died from exposure and the climate, or are now in the hospital."[109] Davis urged him to stay for a few more weeks but quickly reconsidered and began making his own plans to pull out.[110] Sickness had eaten into his ranks, too. Forty percent of his men were on a hospital ship or confined to their bunks.*[111]

In this prolonged naval siege, both combatants seemed to be los-

---

* Earlier in the war, General Winfield Scott had expressed concern that the disease environment of the Deep South would lay waste to invading Union armies. In his Anaconda Plan for winning the lower Mississippi, he had proposed waiting to send a huge

ing in late July. Davis's spies gave a grim picture of the situation: "[The enemy] suffers a great deal more than we do. He counts seventeen or twenty thousand men on his roll, but can hardly muster five thousand in his ranks." And medicine was even scarcer there than it was in the Union camps.[112] By the third week of July, nearly half of Vicksburg's defenders were on the sick list, principally from malaria.[113] In an ordinary battle, this would have been a rich opportunity for the enemy, but this was an uncommon fight, with disease the common killer. Both sides were distressed, unable to grievously hurt the other.

On July 28, seventy-two days after Captain S. Phillips Lee had presented Vicksburg with an ultimatum to surrender, Flag Officer Charles H. Davis started upriver for recently occupied Helena, Arkansas, one hundred and sixty miles north of Vicksburg. The decision to withdraw—a decision that would eventually cost him his command—was his own, not Washington's. His hospital ship was packed with patients and he was losing ten to fifteen men every day, requiring him to hire escaped slaves to work in his ships' boiler rooms. If he stayed another week he would not have sufficient firemen to bring his vessels upstream.[114]

"The Yankees have entirely and completely 'skedaddled' from these parts," Captain Samuel Lockett wrote his wife, Cornelia. "We are now alone in our glory."[115]

"What will they say [in the] North now about the opening [of] the Mississippi River," Vicksburg-area planter Charles Allen wrote in his log book; "huzzah for Vicksburg."[116] The largest "naval force hitherto assembled at one time in the New World," wrote Arkansas commander Isaac Brown, a river armada, that had been firing ten shots for the rebels' one, had not permanently disabled a single enemy gun or killed more than thirty Vicksburg defenders and civilians.[117] With only one warship and a mere twenty-nine guns, "we have foiled . . . Farragut and Porter, the two best and boldest commanders of the Federal Navy," wrote Captain Lockett. He had reason to be proud. He and Isaac Brown were

---

amphibious force down the river until the autumnal frosts had killed the viruses that lurked in the swamps below Memphis. OR, I/51, part 1/369–70.

the two men most responsible for saving Vicksburg: one the dean of defense, the other the audacious assailant.[118]

It was a humiliating defeat for the Federals. Combat casualties were light, but the ships of the great fleet that went down to Baton Rouge and New Orleans more resembled hospitals than men-of-war. By General Williams's reckoning, only two thousand of his men were fit enough to hold a rifle.[119] In the Vicksburg campaign of 1862, "disease could hardly have been militarily more effective even if it had been deliberately used as a weapon," writes a modern medical historian.[120]

A person standing on the levee at Baton Rouge on the July morning when Williams's "half dead" troops were unloaded from the transports would have thought these men had returned from a battle as murderous as Shiloh. Captain Edward Bacon, a survivor, captured the scene graphically in a book he wrote shortly after the war.

A crowd was gathering at the levee to meet the transports. Locals were smiling and talking freely about "the failure of the Vicksburg ditch." At last General Williams came ashore. He glanced at the crowd and was escorted to his quarters. Behind him came the men of Nims's Massachusetts artillery battery, one of the finest fighting units in the force. Before leaving for Vicksburg it had impressed locals with its starchy discipline and impressive equipage. "Now what a change." The "gaunt, skeleton horses" hung their heads. "Even the worn and cracked harness seem[ed] too much for them to carry."

Then came the regiments. The men appeared "like wretches escaped from the dungeons of the Inquisition; every face and form show[ed] the effect of long continued exercise in tortures." Buildings had been set aside as temporary hospitals, and "long processions of the sick, some in ambulances and wagons, some in litters, and some staggering along on foot, present[ed] scenes of horror in every street." Some men looked "as if they had just been raised from the dead."[121]

And what of the African American canal workers Williams had left behind? Neither Bacon nor anyone else in the Baton Rouge brigade thought to tell their story—then or later. Among them were women and children who had followed their husbands and fathers to De Soto

Point, hoping to be set free when the work was completed. Before leaving Vicksburg, Williams had loaded two steamers with canal workers and their families who had been seized from plantations south of Vicksburg. As the fleet dropped downriver, the transports made stops near their former plantations, where their masters were waiting on the riverbank to reclaim them.

Workers from cotton farms upriver from Vicksburg were given three days' rations and told to return "home" on foot. "They were in terrible distress—fearful of being whipped, if not killed, notwithstanding that they had been taken from home by force," wrote Flag Officer Davis. A desperate few tried to force their way onto the troop transports and were beaten back with rifle butts.[122]

Kate Stone, out for a walk, spotted a group of African Americans moving wearily upriver. They were "returning from their Yankee pleasure trip," she wrote with ironic satisfaction, "weary and footsore and eager to get home. Numbers of them pass here . . . bending their necks to the yoke again, preferring the old allegiance to the new." Then she added, interestingly and incongruously: "Numbers are still running to the gunboats. We would not be surprised to hear that all of ours have left in a body any day."[123]

After the Federals left Vicksburg, a detachment of rebel soldiers went over to the site of the Williams ditch. In a letter to his father, Dabney Scales, the artillery officer on *Arkansas*, described what they witnessed.

They found about 600 Yankee graves, but worst of all they found about 500 negroes, most of them sick, and all left in the woods without anything to eat—or any provision whatever being made for them. They say they were worked hard in the mud and water where their soldiers refused to work—And when they were taken sick, they turned off to hunt a home, probably many miles distant—They were shot down like dogs, because they left the trench when we threw shells among them. This is the way the Yankees treat the race for whose freedom they pretend to fight.[124]

Dabney Scales was from a family of slaveholders.

Digging the Yankee ditch had not been an irreversibly bad experience for some African American workers. It had given a number of them a fresh outlook and attitude, born of the hope for a life after slavery. Samuel Lockett considered their newfound self-confidence insolence. They will have to be "severely dealt with before they will return to their duty," he wrote his wife.[125]

At Baton Rouge, only twenty-one of 140 men in one of General Williams's companies were able to report for duty.[126] That was a fair representation of the strength of the command he brought back from Vicksburg. This horribly depleted force was soon called to fight the kind of pitched battle it had expected to wage upriver.

On July 27, as Flag Officer Davis's fleet prepared to head upriver, Earl Van Dorn sent John Breckinridge with four thousand troops—many of them miserably sick—to Camp Moore, a Louisiana training facility seventy miles north and east of Baton Rouge. After being reinforced by Brigadier General Daniel Ruggles, they were set to retake the city. On Breckinridge's recommendation, Van Dorn ordered the battle-damaged *Arkansas* to cooperate with him.[127] Steaming down to Baton Rouge, Lieutenant Henry Stevens, not Isaac Brown, was at the helm, with a skeletal crew of army volunteers.[128] Brown was violently ill with a fever, and from his sickbed he had ordered his vessel to remain idle until she was fully repaired. Van Dorn overruled him.[129]

Farragut had left four gunboats to protect the state capital and blockade the eastward-flowing Red River, which emptied into the Mississippi forty miles above Baton Rouge. *Arkansas* was to destroy these gunboats and reopen Vicksburg's Red River supply line to western Louisiana, Arkansas, and Texas. "I want Baton Rouge and Port Hudson," Van Dorn declared, "giving me the mouth of the Red River"—located just upstream from Port Hudson.[130] "The importance of the object at which you aim cannot be overestimated," Jefferson Davis endorsed Van Dorn's initiative.[131] Davis's armies on the eastern side of the Mississippi were experiencing severe shortages of cattle, corn, forage, sugar, molasses, and salt. Steamers were ready to bring these Red River supplies to Vicksburg as soon as the Union gunboat blockade was removed.[132]

On August 4, Breckinridge led his disease-depleted army down the dust-covered road to Baton Rouge. Sickness had spread like a scourge through the ranks, and water was scarce along the line of the march.

When Major Pirtle's brigade passed a pool of stagnant water, he watched in disgust as his men cleared off the scum with their hands and "greedily" drank the vile-smelling water.[133]

When the army got to within ten miles of the city there were barely 2,600 men fit for fighting. Of these, hundreds were without shoes or socks and had had nothing to eat except green corn for two days.[134] They were eager to meet the enemy, Breckenridge reported, but gallantry could not overcome scurvy and fever, vomiting, and "bloody evacuations of the bowels."[135]

His army attacked the next day at first light, in a dense fog that reduced visibility to almost zero. Williams's twenty-five hundred men—none of whom had seen battle—were expecting the attack. At sunset the previous day, "a negro came and reported to Williams that a force of the enemy . . . was encamped ten miles from the city and were ready to attack in the morning," recalled an officer from the 9th Connecticut.[136]

Breckinridge's volunteers were vastly more experienced than Williams' men, veterans of Fort Donelson and Shiloh. When the Kentuckian threw his entire force at the Union front line, positioned near the center of town, it buckled and broke, and the Yankees were pushed back into their camps. At that point, however, Breckinridge lost control of his army, which went on a looting spree. And Williams put up an expectedly "determined . . . resistance."[137] As the Union commander was on his steed, ordering an Indiana regiment to fix bayonets for a quick counterstroke, a minie ball pierced his heart, killing him instantly. The shot was part of "a perfect volcano of fire," the sign of another rebel advance. Colonel Thomas W. Cahill, Williams's second in command, led a withdrawal toward the river, where the gunboats were poised to provide fire support.[138] The rebels drove back the panicked Federals "inch by inch," and they could see victory in sight. It might have been their day had *Arkansas* arrived, as expected. "Had she done her part the enemy was ours," Major Pirtle wrote.[139]

Late that afternoon, as the Confederates hunkered down under a storm of fire from the gunboats, a courier informed Breckinridge of the fate of the rebel ram. Persistent engine problems had delayed her and she had broken down four miles above the city and drifted to shore. Indefensible against Dirty Bill Porter's gunboats, her crew set her on fire and pushed her downriver. Breckenridge had no choice but to withdraw.[140]

The rebels lost 453 men in the Battle of Baton Rouge, the Union 383.[141] Nearly a third of the handsome town was destroyed in the fight.

Farragut arrived unexpectedly when the firing stopped. He had been notified at New Orleans the moment *Arkansas* was spotted leaving Vicksburg and had immediately headed upriver with six warships. On landing, he was told the rebel ram had been destroyed. "It is one of the happiest moments of my life," he wrote Welles.[142]

On his return to New Orleans, a band of rebel partisans fired on his fleet from the picturesque village of Donaldsonville, Louisiana. Farragut answered by destroying part of the town. If another Union vessel were attacked in this stretch of the river, Farragut vowed to return and lay waste to all of Donaldsonville.[143] On arriving in New Orleans, before handing out for blockade duty, he learned that Congress had established the new rank of rear admiral and that he was the first recipient.[144]

After Breckinridge withdrew from Baton Rouge, Van Dorn ordered him to send a detachment under General Ruggles to fortify Port Hudson, a tiny settlement on a rugged bluff overlooking a hairpin turn of the Mississippi, twenty-five miles north of the state capital, and also on the eastern side of the river.[145] "Port Hudson is [now] one of the strongest points on the Mississippi . . ." Breckinridge reported back to Van Dorn later that month. "Batteries there will command the river more completely than at Vicksburg."[146] Van Dorn's order to emplace heavy guns at Port Hudson would make it inordinately difficult for the Union navy to blockade the mouth of the Red River. It was a shrewd move by a commander not known as a big-picture strategist.

At the start of the war, there were three steamboat ports along the Mississippi with good rail links to the Confederate states east of the Mississippi: Memphis, New Orleans, and Vicksburg. By the summer of 1862, Vicksburg was the only remaining junction point on the river and hence the main entry point for sugar, salt, and molasses from Confederate states west of the Mississippi. Sugar and molasses were both consumed and used as "commodity-money" to buy meat, which was in short supply in the Confederate states that summer. Molasses, in fact, was one of Richmond's chief means of procuring meat for its armies.[147] At that time, Union officials in Washington had only scattered and incomplete information about the volume of trade between the trans-Mississippi west and Vicksburg.[148] But Gideon Welles believed, on the basis of solid reports from his captains, that Vicksburg had "derived immense supplies" from Texas before Farragut arrived. That's why he planned to station at least three gunboats at Union-occupied Baton Rouge. And that's why he implored Secretary of War Stanton to hold on to Baton Rouge. Without a Mississippi River supply and fuel station, it would be impossible for the navy to maintain an effective blockade of the Red River.[149]

But Benjamin Butler and the army had other plans. Alarmed by reports—all of them erroneous—that a freshly reinforced Breckinridge was preparing to move on New Orleans, Butler began concentrating his forces for the defense of the Crescent City.[150] As part of the plan, he pulled Union forces out of Baton Rouge in late August 1862. Days later Confederate troops walked in and took control. The evacuation of Baton Rouge made the Mississippi from Vicksburg to Baton Rouge—roughly 230 miles—a rebel river once more, with suddenly formidable Port Hudson guarding the mouth of the Red River. "We again have free communication with Texas and Louisiana," wrote a jubilant Captain Samuel Lockett.[151]

Vicksburg's steamboat trade with the trans-Mississippi west was reinstituted in late summer, and "vast quantities of army supplies were brought from Red River and distributed from points on the east side of the Mississippi. . . . Every result hoped for in the battle of Baton Rouge had been accomplished save only the capture of the forces there," wrote Major Pirtle.[152]

The ancient rhythms of the river presented Vicksburg with an additional advantage. When the Big Muddy began its seasonal fall in early September, the formerly submerged rail line from Monroe, Louisiana, to De Soto Point—Vicksburg's iron highway to the west—was reopened.

The departure of the Federal fleets gave Vicksburg an opportunity to bolster its defenses. The job was entrusted to Captain Lockett. More and bigger guns were emplaced on the riverfront. "It was also determined to construct a line of defenses in the rear of Vicksburg, to prepare against an army operating upon the land," Lockett wrote later. The virgin forest of stately magnolia trees and the dense undergrowth of cane that blanketed the hills and hollows just east of the town were cut back or burned to create a continuous defensive system of "redoubts, redans, lunettes and small field works" connected by rifle pits. Slaves hired or impressed from surrounding plantations began work on the new defense system in the first week of September.

Haynes' Bluff, a rocky promontory on the banks of the Yazoo River, and the town of Warrenton, six miles south of Vicksburg, were fortified "as flank protections to the main position."[153] If the Federals "[return] they will find us all the better prepared to meet them," Lockett wrote his wife.[154]

The Farragut campaign—sixty-seven anxious days in front of Vicksburg—was a calamity of errors and misjudgments. But the real authors of the Union's misfortune were disease, service disharmony, and daunting geography. "A year's delay, with much national depression and great loss to the country, was the consequence," Gideon Welles wrote later.[155]

— PART THREE —

CHAPTER 9

Anxiety and Intrigue

"I long to see you in the field" [1]

—Edwin Stanton to John A. McClernand

At a cabinet meeting at the White House on August 3, John P. Usher, assistant secretary of the interior, made a provocative suggestion. Word had just reached Washington that Admiral Farragut had abandoned Vicksburg. The president was perplexed and noticeably disappointed, not knowing what steps to take next to subdue the rebel citadel. Usher urged Lincoln to have newly appointed general in chief Henry Halleck raise a "special force of volunteers" to march down the Mississippi and reopen the river between Vicksburg and Baton Rouge, freeing slaves as it went. Secretary of State William H. Seward and Treasury Secretary Salmon P. Chase "heartily seconded the idea," and it was "a good deal talked over," Chase noted in his diary.

The president then sent for Halleck to get his opinion. Though new to the job as general in chief, Old Brains was known to have forceful opinions on nearly everything. The river had to be reopened at "the earliest possible period," he agreed, but he pronounced Usher's plan impractical. There wasn't enough time to raise a new volunteer force and there were not enough experienced troops available in the lower Mississippi Valley to move successfully on Vicksburg. And while Halleck had recently been pressuring the president to wage unrelenting war on the Confederacy, seizing and destroying property and accepting runaway slaves into Union camps, he did not want to see the national army transformed into an instrument of liberation. On this hotly debated issue, however, he kept his counsel, preferring to dismiss Usher's proposal on strictly military grounds.

Halleck made an impression. When he finished speaking, "it was thought best to drop the idea," Chase recalled.[2]

If Halleck was not yet ready to move on Vicksburg, David Dixon Porter was. He had returned from Vicksburg frightfully ill, suffering from intermittent fever and excruciating pain in his bones—"a souvenir of the Mississippi," he called his affliction.[3] Instead of checking into a hospital, he went directly to the Navy Department to plead for a second Vicksburg campaign, this time with full army cooperation.

In a confidential letter to Gustavus Fox, sent from New Orleans just before he headed back to Washington, he had signaled—indirectly but unmistakably—his desire to replace Flag Officer Davis as commander of the Mississippi gunboat flotilla. "I have just heard of the escape of the *Arkansas*. It is nothing more than I expected; there was one flag officer too many. I saw enough to convince me that Davis should not have been one of them, he deserves to lose his command."[4] He secretly hoped Fox would intercede for him but did not dare ask him directly. This would have been a violation of navy protocol.

When he reported to the Navy Department to make his case for a second Mississippi expedition, Gideon Welles, alarmed by his weakened appearance—he was flushed and shaking from chills—sent him on a two-week leave to Newport, Rhode Island, where his family had gone to escape the oppressive heat in the capital.

He arrived barely able to stand and was put under the immediate care of a physician. He made a quick recovery, however, and was soon shooting billiards and sipping whiskey with old navy cronies at the fashionable Newport Club. Days later, he was ordered back to Washington. No reason was given. He arrived late, and Welles had gone home but Fox was available. He had bad news: Porter's mortar schooners had been transferred to the James River flotilla and assigned to another commander. No new orders had been cut for him. Porter pressed Fox for an explanation and was told that word had reached the department that he had publicly ridiculed the generalship of George McClellan in a heated exchange with members of the Newport Club, many of them senior naval officers. This had "incensed" Welles, who refused to see him and was, Fox said, considering him for an inconsequential posting as assistant inspector of gunboat construction in St. Louis.[5] At that moment, Porter thought his chances "for distinction were at an end." He would return to Newport and await a command commensurate with his experience and élan, he told Fox heatedly. "Treat me in [this] way and I will resign."[6]

Before returning to Newport, Porter dropped in to see the president, who greeted him warmly, eager to hear his opinions about why Vicksburg had not been taken. The navy had done all it could, Porter said, but Halleck had failed to send support. "If I live, you shall see me at the taking of the place," he told Lincoln. The president smiled. Porter would not be sent to St. Louis, he assured him. He would be at Vicksburg when it fell.[7]

Unknown to Porter, Lincoln, Welles, and Fox were at that very time plotting to remove Davis from command of the Mississippi Squadron. He had been irresolute at Vicksburg and had no plausible backup plan for taking the city.[8] Porter's behavior in Newport had upset Welles but not enough to disqualify him for consideration as Davis's replacement. On September 22, Welles wired Porter: "You will be assigned to duty West, and on your way report in person to this Department for further orders."[9] Porter was stunned; he had no idea what this meant.

When he arrived at Welles's office, the secretary greeted him with unexpected warmth, a sly smile crossing his face. After Porter was seated, he was handed a sealed document. He had been selected to command the western gunboats and was to proceed at once to Cairo to relieve Flag Officer Charles H. Davis.[10] The appointment carried with it the rank of acting rear admiral, and, by an act of Congress, the gunboat flotilla would be transferred the next day, October 2, from the War Department to the Navy, and officially designated the Mississippi Squadron. Porter would have complete control of naval operations on western waters—three thousand miles of river—with instructions to cooperate with but not take orders from the army. Farragut would remain in command of the Western Blockading Squadron and assist future operations to disrupt the Vicksburg-Red River supply line. He was still the favored admiral in Washington, but Porter would soon have more officers and men under him than any other commander in the United States Navy.

Porter thought the president had pressed his appointment.[11] Perhaps he had—he signed the appointment letter—but more likely it was Fox who persuaded Welles to choose the battle-hungry commander who knew better than anyone else the challenge Vicksburg presented. It had been a difficult decision for Welles. He liked and admired Davis and disliked and distrusted Porter, yet he considered Davis "more of a scholar than [a] sailor . . . not an energetic, driving, fighting officer, such as is wanted for rough work on the Mississippi." In the coming weeks, Welles would struggle to convince himself that he had not made a damaging mistake. "Porter . . . has . . . excessive . . . ambition, is impressed with and boastful of his powers, [and] given to exaggeration of himself—a Porter infirmity," Welles confided to his diary. "He has, however, stirring and positive qualities . . . has great energy . . . [and] is brave and daring like all his family." And while brutally critical of his superior officers, "he is kind and patronizing to favorites who are juniors. . . . It is a question, with his mixture of good and bad traits, how he will succeed." In the end, Welles decided to consider Porter's appointment an "experiment." [12]

Porter left for Cairo exultant. "How proud my old Father would be if he could see me an Admiral," he wrote his mother." [13]

We need "great energy, great activity," on the Mississippi, Welles had observed in his diary.[14] Porter would not disappoint.

Three new gunships were under construction when he arrived at Cairo, and he placed orders for three more and greatly enhanced the armor of boats shredded by Vicksburg's batteries. New mortar scows were ordered, strict sanitary regulations were set in place, and a hotel at Mound City was leased as a navy hospital. Crews were served fresh meat and vegetables three times a week, and sailors were forbidden to sleep in the "open air" or where "night dews" could affect them. "The comfort and health of the men must be the first thing to be looked after," Porter instructed veteran officers who had seen men die in staggering numbers from malaria and consumption at Vicksburg.[15]

The Mississippi Squadron had a manpower crisis: Nearly four hundred men who had taken sick at Vicksburg had to be discharged. To fill the crews, Porter brought in recently freed slaves as coal heavers and firemen, as he had the previous summer. Gideon Welles went along but ordered that they "are not to be allowed the pay of that grade." They were to be classed as "boys," paid at a lower rate and given only one ration a day.[16] Porter approved, seeing it as a necessary cost-cutting measure. He went further, however. Black seamen were not to be promoted, under any circumstances, to petty officers and were to live and drill separately from their white counterparts.[17]

Porter was given permission to recruit white soldiers from the army to fill his crews, but there were never enough of them. Nonetheless, the eight hundred white soldiers and six hundred African Americans he had enticed into service by early 1863 kept the full fleet afloat.*

Porter had been sent to Cairo to take Vicksburg, but he had other responsibilities as well. Chief among them was defending the Union's river trade in the west from shoreline attacks by rebel guerrilla bands. His ponderous ironclads were not up to the task. They drew too much water to operate effectively in the shallow swamps and bayous into which the bushwhackers escaped after firing on unarmed Federal steamers. Porter sought and gained authority to rush to completion a new breed of river vessels. They were called tinclads, and they drew so little water they could "float on a heavy dew," their builders boasted.[18] They were surprisingly formidable as well. Each vessel could mount ten guns and had bulletproof iron sides to protect the crews from sniper fire. By early December, they began arriving at Cairo.[19]

Porter also pressed for the creation of a combined infantry, cavalry, and artillery force with assault teams small enough to be transported on steamers. Colonel Alfred W. Ellet had first suggested the idea and was promoted to brigadier general and put in charge of assembling and leading the new "Mississippi Marine Brigade," which was attached to his family's ram fleet, now commanded by his nephew, Charles Rivers Ellet. When guerrillas opened fire on Union vessels, Ellet's strike force was to land, pursue, and kill. Officers and men were army personnel, but they were under the direction of Porter and the

* By the end of the war, twenty-three thousand black sailors were serving in the U.S. Navy, at sea and on inland waters, comprising approximately 20 percent of the crews. Only twenty-five "tars" of the 159-man crew of *Cairo*, a typically outfitted ironclad, had sailing experience, their ages ranging from fifteen to sixty-four. A third of the crewmen were not yet American citizens, and many had difficulty understanding orders given in English. See Davis F. Riggs, "Sailors of the U.S.S. *Cairo*: Anatomy of a Gunboat Crew," *Civil War History* 28, no. 3, 271–72.

Navy Department. Volunteers were to be drawn from army convalescent hospitals or "wherever men could be found." Recruits were offered modest bounties to join and were told this would be "soldiering made easy! No long hard marches, camping without tents or food or carrying heavy knapsacks." But recruiting lagged. Infantrymen were better paid than men serving on river vessels, and most young volunteers preferred to join infantry regiments raised in their hometowns. The "Ellet Horse Marines" would not appear downriver at Vicksburg until March of 1863.[20]

At Porter's insistence, Ellet's seven-vessel ram fleet, formerly an independent command under the control of the War Department, was transferred to the Navy.[21] It had been a hard fight. Stanton and Halleck had protested, and Alfred Ellet had refused to hand over his rams. When persuasion failed, Porter had Ellet's rams tied to the Cairo levee. His gunboats would fire on them, he warned Ellet, if they moved from their moorings. It had taken a presidential order, however, to settle the dispute. At a hotly contentious cabinet meeting, Lincoln had agreed with Porter that there must not be "two distinct commands on the river under different orders from different Departments."[22]

"We beat our friend Edwin W. Stanton . . . placing Brigadier-General Ellet under your orders," Fox informed Porter on November 8. "Stanton lost his temper, so we beat him. The cool man always wins."[23]

Consumed with organizing his new Marine Brigade, Alfred Ellet turned over command of the ram fleet to his nephew Charles Rivers Ellet, soon to be the youngest full colonel in the U.S. Army. The rams that had helped open the river to Memphis were now charged with keeping it safe for Union commerce. Each ram carried fifteen sharpshooters equipped with fast-firing, breech-loading carbines and a generous supply of grenades.[24] But the ironclads sent an even stronger message to rebel resisters. Porter ordered them to return fire "with spirit" on enemy artillerymen and "to destroy everything in the neighborhood" from which they fired. A "taste of devastation," Porter believed, was the only way to curb guerrilla warfare.[25]

William Tecumseh Sherman, commander of the Memphis garrison, worked closely with Porter, a kindred spirit. When a band of partisans, operating near Randolph, Tennessee, fired on an unarmed packet vessel, Sherman had the village burned to extinction. "We cannot reach the real actors," he wrote his wife, Ellen, "but cannot overlook these acts of outrage. Therefore, we punish the neighbors for not preventing them."[26] Porter agreed entirely. His gunboats "laid in ashes," houses and farms that harbored guerrillas who fired on Union shipping.[27] "Terror of the Mississippi," Porter came to be called by rebel families along the river.[28]

Working eighteen hours a day and spending federal money fantastically, with or without prior authorization, Porter prepared for yet another go at Vicksburg.[29] By the end of 1862, he would command the most formidable riverine strike force assembled up to that time. After only two weeks at Cairo, he began pressing the Navy Department to authorize him to move downriver to begin preparations for a combined army-navy assault on Vicksburg. Welles and Fox were equally eager for action. "The opening of that river as early as possible is the imperative not to be considered above even the capture of Charleston," Fox wrote Porter.[30] Porter assured Welles he was "ready to move at any moment," but where, he wondered, was the army?[31]

Porter had orders to cooperate with a general he had met only once, in Washington, before leaving for Cairo. And that man was presently in his home state of Illinois, organizing a volunteer army to open the Mississippi. Without consulting or informing Grant, Lincoln and Stanton had secretly appointed his unruly subordinate, Major General John McClernand, to mount the next river assault on Vicksburg.[32] But McClernand had yet to communicate with Porter—not a word. Was the army to ruin, by its inaction, yet another opportunity to take Vicksburg?

McClernand had never been satisfied serving under Grant, whom he considered his inferior in the crush of combat. "Tired," he said, "of . . . furnishing the brains for Grant," he had been pressing Lincoln for an independent command since the Battle of Belmont.[33] As we have seen earlier, his entreaties, along with his official battle reports, were interlaced with barbed criticism of Grant's leadership in the field. McClernand was "ignorant of the meaning of military subordination," Adam Badeau noted later.[34]

Grant knew McClernand was conspiring against him and probably would have removed him had he not been indispensable to the president. He was a strong-voiced Unionist in a Democratic Party with a powerful anti-war wing; Lincoln needed the support of every War Democrat on the Hill. McClernand was also a solid soldier, having served intrepidly at Belmont, Donelson, and Shiloh, although Grant rightly questioned his emotional balance under stress. "He lacked the composure of Grant and the cynical indifference of Sherman," wrote correspondent Franc Wilkie. "I sometimes think that there is a screw loose in his machinery."[35]

In July 1862, McClernand had approached his friend and home-state promoter, Senator Orville H. Browning, requesting command of a corps in the Army of the Potomac.[36] Nothing had come of this, but weeks later, Illinois governor Richard Yates persuaded Halleck to approve the general's petition for a leave of absence to go to Springfield to help raise the additional 26,000 volunteers Lincoln had recently requested from Illinois.[37] McClernand, an inspiring if platitudinous stump speaker, was a capable recruiter, but the real reason he was in Springfield was to persuade Yates to gain him an appointment with the president. He had, he claimed, a sure-fire plan to conquer Vicksburg.

In late September, Yates introduced him to Salmon Chase, who was still lobbying hard for a second Vicksburg campaign after Halleck's cabinet rebuff. Chase was impressed with McClernand's resolve and got him on the President's calendar. When Chase saw Lincoln afterward he asked his opinion of McClernand. "He is [a] brave and capable general," said the president, "but too desirous to be independent of everybody else."[38] That was McClernand exactly.

But Lincoln was drawn to McClernand's plan to carry the war to the core of the Confederacy and to attack Vicksburg from vulnerable spots in its defenses along the Yazoo River, avoiding its Mississippi water batteries. With Porter's gunboats providing cover, his force of sixty thousand volunteers would overrun "the small . . . comparatively insignificant garrison," he assured Lincoln.[39] Port Hudson, isolated and outflanked, would fall days later, and the River of America would be reopened to the sea.

The plan appealed to both Lincoln's political and military instincts. Conquering Vicksburg in one swift stroke would suppress fast-growing opposition to his administration in Illinois, Indiana, Iowa, and Ohio, discontent born of the military's inability to open the Mississippi to New Orleans and the Gulf. With this overseas market denied to western farmers, they had begun shipping their crops by rail to Buffalo and New York City, forced to pay rates they considered "extortionate." The competition of the river trade promised rate relief.*

There was also strong opposition in western states to the Preliminary Emancipation Proclamation Lincoln had issued that September, pledging to free slaves in states still in active rebellion on January 1, 1863, when the final proclamation became law. The proclamation had split the country and the army. Ohio's Thomas Ewing, General Sherman's politically influential father-in-law, "thought it not improbable" that hundreds of army officers would resign "and a 100,000 of our men lay down their arms" when a war to save the Union became, with shocking suddenness, a crusade to abolish slavery.[40]

"Copperheads"—anti-war Democrats who called for a peace conclave to restore the Union with slavery intact—pilloried the proclamation, along with Lincoln's recently instituted military draft and his suspension of habeas corpus. Painting Lincoln as an abolitionist despot, they encouraged military desertion and colluded with rebel spies to form conspiratorial organizations—the Knights of the Golden Cir-

---

* The 1862 congressional elections, held in October and November, went disastrously for Lincoln's party, making it all the more important for him to retain the support of loyal War Democrats like McClernand. Thirty-one Republicans lost their seats in Congress. Republican losses at the state and national level were most devastating in Pennsylvania, Ohio, Indiana, and Illinois. In Illinois, the Democrats took control of the state legislature, and the state sent eleven Democrats and only two Republicans to Washington. The Republican Party retained majorities in both the House and the Senate, but "the results," writes historian Allen C. Guelzo, "were as close to disaster for Lincoln as one could get without actual loss of life." Allen C. Guelzo, *Lincoln's Emancipation Proclamation: The End of Slavery in America* (New York: Simon & Schuster, 2006), 189.

cle, the Sons of Liberty, and the Order of American Knights among them—that plotted the overthrow of state governments in the Old Northwest. The goal of the most strident Copperheads was a Northwestern Confederacy—a rump government that would secede and align with the Southern Confederacy.[41] To counter the growing strength of the Copperheads, Lincoln relied on anti-abolitionist Democrats like McClernand, a racist who was also a resolute Unionist.

Grant hagiographers have made a minor industry of slaying John McClernand for outflanking the military chain of command and taking his Vicksburg proposal straight to the White House. But McClernand's scheme was sound, and there was no reason not to put it in front of the president. McClernand's "vanity" and "grasping ambition . . . made him an unpleasant figure," wrote historian Allan Nevins, but "the idea that his project represented either political intrigue or military insubordination . . . is absurd. On the contrary, it was a thoughtful plan to meet the political exigencies of the period by prompt action to clear the Mississippi under a Democratic leader who had wide influence with his Northwestern party."[42]

Lincoln had further, off-the-record discussions with McClernand, which apparently went well. In early October, McClernand confided to Colonel James H. Wilson, an ambitious young officer who had grown up near his hometown of Shawneetown, Illinois, that he would soon be appointed commander of a war-turning river expedition.[43] That week, at a cabinet meeting, Edwin Stanton made it official. "The President seemed much pleased," Chase observed in his diary. Only Henry Halleck demurred. He thought McClernand "brave and able" but incapable of leading and disciplining a large army.[44] What he meant but didn't say was that he wanted a West Point man in charge.*

---

* David Dixon Porter noted in his memoirs that when Lincoln asked him in September whom he considered best fitted to lead the Vicksburg expedition, he recommended Grant and Sherman. According to Porter, the president said he had in mind "a better general than either of them; that is McClernand, an old and intimate friend of mine . . . He saved the battle of Shiloh, when the case seemed hopeless." (Porter, *Incidents and Anecdotes*, 122.) This is pure fantasy. McClernand was never an "intimate friend" of Lincoln's, and the president did not hold an exalted opinion of his performance at Shiloh. Porter, moreover, would not meet Sherman or Grant until months later.

On October 21, Stanton gave McClernand top-secret orders to proceed to Indiana, Iowa, and Illinois to "organize" troops and forward them to Memphis. When a "sufficient force" was gathered, he was to lead it "against Vicksburg."[45] Lincoln appended a handwritten note to Stanton's order: "I feel deep interest in the success of the expedition, and desire it to be pushed forward with all possible dispatch, *consistently with the other parts of the military service*."[46] That last clause, to which McClernand apparently didn't pay much attention, would come back to haunt him. He thought his appointment came with no strings attached.

The former congressman had little trouble raising regiments. "I long to see you in the field," Stanton wrote him, "striking vigorous blows against the rebellion in its most vital point."[47]

Ulysses Grant would have moved on Vicksburg months before McClernand first met with Lincoln, but Henry Halleck had made that impossible. When Halleck left Tennessee in July to become general in chief, he issued Grant orders that prevented him moving south. He was to remain on the defensive, guarding railroads and garrisons his army had secured in its drive from Forts Henry and Donelson.[48] That summer of 1862 was, for Grant, "the most anxious period of the war," he wrote later. Grant commanded nearly sixty-three thousand troops, but his forces were dispersed across northern Mississippi and western Tennessee, an area rife with rebel obstructionists and spies, and with marauding Confederate cavalry. "We were in a country where nearly all the people, except the negroes, were hostile to us and friend to the cause we were trying to suppress."[49]

His men resented guard duty, and morale plummeted. "I don't consider myself in the war here any more than I would be in Canton [Illinois]," Lieutenant Charles W. Wills wrote his family.[50] Not knowing Halleck had put Grant on a leash, Wills and his comrades could not understand why he remained on the defensive, protecting citizens who claimed to be Unionists while hiding and secretly supplying rebel bushwhackers.[51]

Toward the end of that troublesome summer, Grant was confronted by a new threat: a reinforced and revitalized rebel army. "The progress of our Western armies had aroused the rebel government to the exercise of the most stupendous energy," Sherman described the new situation.[52] Halleck's decision to disperse the enormous force he had marched to Corinth gave Braxton Bragg, Beauregard's replacement as theater commander, the opportunity to mount a counteroffensive to "turn the tide of disaster," recovering all that the Confederacy had lost after Donelson.[53] Bragg intended to "push boldly through Tennessee into Kentucky" and call upon the citizens of those states to join him in driving the enemy "beyond the Ohio."[54]

In late July, he moved his army by rail from northern Mississippi to Chattanooga, Tennessee, and struck northward, straight for Kentucky's Bluegrass country, where Major General Edmund Kirby Smith, with twenty-one thousand men, joined the great invasion. In September, the success of this lightning offensive set off panic in Cincinnati and other Ohio River towns. The two Confederate columns pushed Don Carlos Buell's slow-moving Army of the Ohio all the way to Louisville. If the North lost the populous border state of Kentucky, Lincoln feared it could lose the war.

As Bragg pressed his offensive, Robert E. Lee's Army of Northern Virginia invaded Maryland and advanced toward Pennsylvania. That September, when Bragg entered Kentucky and Lee reached northern Maryland's Catoctin Mountain, the Confederate war effort was reinvigorated. Everywhere in the North, the outlook turned gloomy. New Orleans and Donelson were forgotten; all Federal gains seemed to have been nullified.[55] "Many loyal people despaired in the fall of 1862 of ever saving the Union," Grant wrote years later.[56]

When Bragg began his Kentucky offensive, he left Major General Sterling Price with sixteen thousand troops to anchor his flank in northern Mississippi. Earl Van Dorn, with an equal number of troops, joined him after the Union fleet had sailed away from Vicksburg. Price and Van Dorn were to collaborate to prevent Grant from sending reinforcements to Buell. But hyperaggressive "Buck" Van Dorn had something bigger in mind: a surprise assault on massively fortified Corinth, the headquarters of Grant's Army of the Tennessee. Van Dorn "craved glory beyond everything," said one of his generals, even his own life and the lives of his men.[57]

But "Old Pap," as his men called the grizzled, silver-haired Price, struck first in mid-September, seizing a federal supply depot at Iuka, a tiny spa town twenty-five miles east of Corinth. Grant reacted immediately, organizing a force to surprise and trap him. William Rosecrans approached Iuka from the south with eight thousand men, while Major General Edward Ord, recently arrived from Virginia, moved on Price from the northwest with a slightly smaller army. Grant communicated with the two wings by courier. His objective: to trap Price's army in a pincer or "nutcracker" attack.[58]

Rosecrans was ordered to open the fight, while Ord was to hold back until "the moment he heard the sound of guns." When Rosecrans came blasting into town on September 19, a murderous fight erupted, "a duel to the death," Union infantryman S. H. M. Byers called it. "For hours the blue and gray stood within forty yards of each other and poured in sheets of musketry." But not a sound reached Ord or Grant, positioned close to the town, poised to deliver the deathblow. A phenomenon known as an acoustic shadow, an atmospheric condition that deadens sound waves, prevented them from hearing a single gunshot. "Why Union generals lacked the sense to get off their horses, stretch out, put an ear to the ground, and try to pick up the vibration of artillery fire when they knew a battle was pending is a mystery," writes historian Geoffrey Perrett.[59]

Price's outnumbered army might still have been destroyed had Rosecrans not left an escape road unguarded, allowing him to join Van Dorn, encamped farther west. Grant ordered a pursuit, but Rosecrans called it off after a few miles. "I was disappointed with the result of the battle of Iuka," Grant wrote later, "—but I had so high an opinion of General Rosecrans that I found no fault at the time."[60] The fault, however, was partly Grant's for attempting, on unfamiliar terrain, a complicated double envelopment requiring nearly perfect coordination.

Grant had not been at Iuka during the battle, and this didn't sit well with the men who fought shoulder-to-shoulder with Rosecrans, a burly, excitable commander, and a devout Roman Catholic who carried a rosary into battle yet swore like a stevedore. His men would "storm Hades" for him, Byers said years later, but they "had little confidence in Grant. At Shiloh he was miles away from the battlefield at the critical moment." At Iuka, he "did not even know a battle was going on."[61]

Expecting Van Dorn to attack Corinth, Grant moved Rosecrans's army into that disease-plagued fortress town and transferred his head-quarters to Jackson, Tennessee, sixty miles north of Corinth. From there he would be able to oversee the approaching battle and call in rein-forcements from his widely scattered garrisons.[62] On October 3, Van Dorn and Price smashed into Corinth's defenses with twenty-two thou-sand spirited volunteers. Rosecrans had a slightly larger force. Most of his men were battle-tested, and they fought behind two outer rings of entrenchments. The "air was still and fiercely hot," and Van Dorn's men had made a final, eight-mile march over a "parched country on dusty roads without water."[63] They attacked in hundred-degree heat "with screaming élan and willingness to take high casualties."[64] The first wave broke through the Union's outer defensive line, driving the panicked bluejackets back a full two miles, but the attack stalled when night descended. It was resumed with equal ardency at daybreak, the gray-backs "charging magnificently" and reaching the streets of the town, only to be "mowed down" by sheets of Federal cannon fire.[65] But with desperate courage, the rebels fought their way out and delivered some punishment of their own. The stakes were high. It was a battle "to deter-mine the possession of Northern Mississippi and West Tennessee."[66] If Corinth fell, there would be no Vicksburg campaign that year, and the rebels would have an open road to Union-held Memphis.

Van Dorn should have called off the assault in midmorning, but his blood was up. Early that afternoon, when his scouts reported enemy rein-forcements approaching from the north, his officers finally persuaded him to give way, ending one of the most murderous, momentous, and least known battles of the war. Union losses were heavy—2,500 men—but nothing to compare with Van Dorn's—nearly 35 percent of those engaged.[67] Grant had a directing hand in the battle, but it was Rose-crans's victory.

Grant ordered Rosecrans to "push" Van Dorn's retreating army "with all force possible," but he waited until the next morning, giving his cut-up army an evening to rest and resupply. Grant had no problem with that, but he would later reprimand him for not recovering quickly and aggressively pursuing a badly beaten foe.[68] On October 7, after learn-ing that General Ord had been seriously wounded trying to block Van Dorn's retreat, Grant called off the pursuit. Rosecrans protested, even though he was moving "oppressively slow," said one soldier.[69]

After the war, Rosecrans tore into his commander. "If Grant had not stopped us, we could have gone to Vicksburg" had the pursuing army been strongly reinforced. Cautious Henry Halleck shockingly agreed. "Why order a return of our troops?" he asked Grant. "Why not re-enforce [sic] Rosecrans and pursue the enemy into Mississippi, supporting your army on the country?"[70] To which Grant replied: "An army cannot subsist itself on the country except in forage."[71] Grant had apparently not studied Napoleon's campaigns in Italy and Spain, where the French armies were supported abundantly by the lands they conquered. Rosecrans, however, could never have gotten to Vicksburg. Only a larger, richly supplied force could have carried off a march of that magnitude through the alien terrain of the Mississippi-Yazoo Delta. But by not chasing Van Dorn aggressively after the Battle of Corinth, Rosecrans had lost an opportunity to destroy the only rebel army between Corinth and Vicksburg.

Van Dorn faced a court of inquiry for his reckless attack on Corinth and for allegedly being drunk on the field. He was exonerated but still relieved of command of his department. Jefferson Davis, the friend who removed him, gave him command of a corps in northern Mississippi, where he was reunited with Price. In late October, Rosecrans reaped his reward, replacing Buell as commander of the Army of the Cumberland, the renamed Army of the Ohio. Grant recommended his promotion to major general of volunteers, but was relieved to be rid of him. Grant had enjoyed Rosecrans's lively company, but the thickset defender of Corinth had a wicked temper, a stubborn streak, and what Grant considered a deep-set reluctance to obey the orders of a superior.[72]

Days after the Battle of Corinth, Grant learned that Braxton Bragg's Kentucky invasion had spent its force. After clashing with elements of Buell's army on October 8 in the indecisive Battle of Perryville, forty miles southwest of Lexington, Bragg faced the inevitable. Kentuckians had been unexpectedly loyal to the Union, and news had reached him that Van Dorn and Price had been driven back with great losses at Corinth. Rather than tangling again with Buell's larger army, Bragg slid back into Tennessee. Buell failed to pursue, and for this he gained Lincoln's wrath and the loss of his command.

The previous month the Confederates had suffered an even more devastating setback in the mountains of Maryland. General George

McClellan, restored to command of the Army of the Potomac after Lee had routed Pope in the Second Battle of Manassas, stopped Lee at Antietam Creek. The Confederate summer offensive was spent. Lee would strike again a year later, pushing into Pennsylvania, but Bragg's unsuccessful invasion of Kentucky was the rebels' final offensive in the Mississippi Valley.

For Ulysses Grant, however, the victory of greatest import was Corinth. "The battle relieved me from any further anxiety for the safety of the territory within my jurisdiction, and soon after receiving reinforcements I suggested to the general-in-chief a forward movement against Vicksburg."[73]

Grant's first mention of Vicksburg in his correspondence with Halleck was on October 26, 1862. "You have never suggested to me any plan of operations in this Department," he wrote from his new headquarters in Jackson, Tennessee. "As situated now, with no more troops, I can do nothing but defend my positions." Grant had 48,500 troops. If reinforced, he proposed to concentrate his widely scattered forces at La Grange, Tennessee, a tiny rail center near the Mississippi border. From there he would move southward, following the Mississippi Central Railroad to Jackson, the state capital. At Jackson, he would swing to the west forty miles and "cause the evacuation of Vicksburg."[74]

The plan caught Halleck off guard. It was a young and impatient commander seeking approval from an older and cautious superior, the one "always prepared for defeat," in Badeau's words, the other always expecting "to win."[75] When Halleck failed to reply, Grant moved on his own authority. Halleck telegraphed his approval the following day.[76] Grant was pushing faster than Halleck could think. And he had more authority than before, having just been promoted to command of the Department of the Tennessee, an enormous area encompassing western Tennessee, northern Mississippi, western Kentucky, and southern Illinois.

"The campaign against Vicksburg commenced on the 2nd of November," Grant wrote in his memoirs.[77] On that day, he dispatched orders to James McPherson, with three divisions at Corinth, and Brigadier General Charles S. Hamilton, with two divisions not far from there, to begin converging on the closely linked towns of Grand Junction and La Grange, directly west of Corinth, on the Mississippi Central Railroad.[78] There they would wait for the reinforcements Halleck pledged to provide. Sherman was to move out from Memphis and conduct a "demonstration to the South-east," a feint designed to confuse the enemy.[79]

As Grant rode south on his cream-colored steed, Jack, he relieved the tedium of the road by recalling his time in Mexico, a place he deeply loved. He was confident and composed as he was about to enter the final stage of the campaign he had begun at Cairo. Everything he had accomplished since then was a preparation for this: the climactic moment of his military career.

Facing Grant was the army Rosecrans had shredded at Corinth. After removing Van Dorn, Jefferson Davis had brought in John Clifford Pemberton, a thin, bearded, severe-looking native of Philadelphia, Pennsylvania. Pemberton had sided with the Confederacy at the behest of his Virginia-born spouse, Martha "Pattie" Pemberton—and to the consternation of his socially prominent Quaker parents back in Philadelphia, Unionists to the core, with two younger sons in the U.S. Cavalry.

It had not been an easy decision. Assigned to protect Washington, D.C., after the attack on Fort Sumter, he was torn between his love for his wife and children and his attachment to his Philadelphia family. He had also made Virginia his home, and resented Lincoln's decision to raise a volunteer army to invade the South. But under insistent pressure from his brothers he agreed not to resign his commission unless Virginia seceded.

"My darling husband why are you not with us? Why do you stay?" Pattie wrote him from Norfolk after Virginia left the Union. "John is most dreadfully distressed and worried on our account," his mother wrote a family member, "for his heart and views are that the South is right and we are wrong." His brothers "begged and pleaded with him." He would never be able to return home again, they warned; his friends would shun him as a traitor. In late April he made his decision. "I must accept it," his mother wrote, ". . . we have done all we can."[80]

Pemberton's Northern birth and upbringing, along with his lackluster service record, made him a strange choice to command the only Confederate army protecting Vicksburg. He had solid training and experience, having graduated from West Point and served in the Mexican War, but he had recently been relieved of his only notable assignment: commander of coastal defenses south of Charleston, South Carolina. Governor Francis Pickens had complained repeatedly to Jefferson Davis about Pemberton's performance. He had abandoned critical seacoast defenses erected by his revered predecessor, Robert E. Lee, and seemed "confused and uncertain about everything."[81] Along with other leading Charleston secessionists, Pickens also questioned Pemberton's loyalty to the Confederate cause. "As he is a Pennsylvanian [he] engenders suspicion," wrote Charleston diarist Emma Holmes. "Many even suspect treachery."[82]

The general who would soon face the victor of Donelson and Shiloh had never led an army in combat. This made Davis's decision to appoint him and promote him to lieutenant general all the more puzzling. In Mexico, Pemberton was considered a "solid staff officer," yet one deficient in self-confidence, a mismatched characteristic for a commander with a domineering manner that grated on subordinates.[83] But Davis believed he had been treated unfairly in South Carolina and admired his strength of character. His decision to decline a Union colonelcy and break with his Philadelphia family to defend his adopted state should have put to rest, Davis thought, any doubts about his loyalty to the Confederate cause.[84]

Pemberton arrived at his Jackson, Mississippi, headquarters in the second week of October "in an hour of the greatest gloom and despondency."[85] His small army was short of rations and equipment, and morale had deteriorated alarmingly after the slaughter at Corinth. Pemberton restored discipline and a measure of organization, yet was incapable of providing what was most needed: inspired military leadership.

Mississippians expected this to come from the illustrious Joseph E. Johnston, the newly appointed commander of the Department of the West, with headquarters at Chattanooga. They were to be sorely disappointed.

Johnston's authority extended from the Appalachians to the Mississippi, an area too large, he complained, for a single commander to effectively control. His inaction over the course of the next year would make this a self-fulfilling prophecy.

When the fighting started at First Bull Run, Johnston was widely considered the finest general in the Confederacy and was given command of the defense of Richmond against McClellan's Army of the Potomac. Grievously wounded in one of the campaign's early engagements, he was replaced by Lee. He had not yet fully recovered when Davis appointed him head of the Confederacy's western theater. Vain, pompous, and argumentative—but incontestably brilliant—he accepted the appointment with reluctance, still simmering over Lee's sudden ascension to command of the Army of Northern Virginia. Repeatedly, he petitioned friends in the government to persuade Davis to restore him to his old command and move Lee to the west.[86] He and Davis had been together at West Point, but they were never close and grew farther apart over the years. Davis wanted the prideful and prickly commander—too much like himself for comfort—as far from Richmond as possible. "The president detests Joe Johnston," wrote diarist Mary Chesnut. "And General Joe returns the compliment with compound interest. His hatred of Jeff Davis amounts to a religion."[87] Yet Joseph Johnston's greatest enemy was himself. Though courtly, courageous, and beloved by his men, he would turn out to be an overcautious defeatist, seeing nearly every opportunity as an obstacle.

Yet he *was* a shrewd strategist. On taking command, he pressed Richmond for a concentration of rebel forces in the west: Pemberton's Army of Mississippi, Bragg's Army of Tennessee, and Lieutenant General Theophilus H. Holmes's forces in western Arkansas. Vicksburg could be saved only by concerted action, he was convinced. But headstrong Braxton Bragg insisted on acting independently, and Johnston's authority, by order of the president, stopped at the eastern bank of the Mississippi. The slow-moving, partially deaf Holmes—"Granny" to his troops—reported directly to Davis, not to Johnston. Pemberton was under the same injunction.

Johnston implored Richmond to order Bragg and Holmes to send heavy reinforcements to Pemberton's thirty thousand underfed and ill-equipped men. Davis, however, had invested his commanders with nearly unhindered autonomy, and he advised rather than ordered them to act.[88] He envisioned an arrangement in which Johnston would shuttle troops between Pemberton's and Bragg's commands, whichever area was most directly threatened. Johnston thought this unfeasible given the distances to be overcome and the dismal state of the Confederate railroad system. Davis further compromised Johnston's position by making the Mississippi a departmental dividing line and emplacing on either side of it departmental commanders—Pemberton and Holmes—who were stubborn and indecisive.[89] "Nobody ever assumed a command under more unfavorable circumstances," Johnston wrote sourly to a friend in the government.[90]

Even Davis, a longtime friend, could not move Holmes to the defense of the town closest to Davis's heart. When Holmes claimed he could not spare a single man with Federal forces in Helena threatening Confederate-held Little Rock, Davis countered that if Vicksburg fell, Arkansas would fall with it. Holmes remained obdurate. His resistance was hardened by his feelings about Pemberton, who, he said, "has many ways of making people hate him and none to inspire confidence."[91]

Pemberton did little to help himself. Van Dorn, stationed at Holly Springs, Mississippi, on the Mississippi-Tennessee border, was closely observing Grant's movements. When Pemberton first arrived at Jackson to take command, Van Dorn implored him to "come here as soon as possible" to prevent Grant from occupying La Grange and Grand Junction. "The enemy in West Tennessee is about 45,000 strong, and re-enforcements daily arriving."[92] Inexplicably, Pemberton chose to remain at Jackson. When he finally entrained to Holly Springs on November 7, Grant's army had already secured La Grange and Grand Junction as forward bases for his drive into northeastern Mississippi, and Van Dorn's men were in no mood to receive their new leader. "He is the most insignificant 'puke' I ever saw," a sergeant wrote his wife, "and will be very unpopular as soon as he is known. His head cannot contain sense enough to command a Regt. much less a Corps."[93]

Pemberton's first move was backward. He ordered Van Dorn to withdraw from Holly Springs and position the army on the south bank of the Tallahatchie River, fifteen miles below Holly Springs.[94] There he would make his stand. Chief engineer Samuel Lockett was called from Vicksburg to fortify the position.[95] Pemberton then returned to his Jackson headquarters and asked Davis to order Holmes to send him reinforcements.[96] His army, he said, was outnumbered and "very deficient in clothing, shoes, and blankets. . . . The men suffer greatly."[97]

Then Pemberton did something absolutely incomprehensible. With

Grant's cavalry poised to take lightly held Holly Springs, he left Jackson by train for distant Port Hudson to inspect its defenses. Had he inquired closely, he would have discovered that there was no realistic enemy threat to that river redoubt.[98] Returning several days later, he learned that Holmes had refused a War Department directive to send him ten thousand troops.

There was yet another dose of bad news. Contentious Braxton Bragg was being predictably uncooperative. He would dispatch a cavalry force under Nathan Bedford Forrest to disrupt Grant's communications in west Tennessee, but "to send reinforcements from here to General Pemberton would require the evacuation of Middle Tennessee," he told Richmond. He would instead send three thousand muskets![99] At this point the secretary of war, George W. Randolph *ordered* Holmes to Vicksburg with ten thousand men.[100] When Davis found out, he flew into a rage, countermanded the directive, and rebuked Randolph for not consulting with him. Randolph resigned and was succeeded by James A. Seddon. Davis, who regularly responded to Federal incursions with an incongruous mix of hyperactivity and indecision, then tried unsuccessfully to persuade Holmes to move.[101]

Grant gave Pemberton's army a greatly needed reprieve when he delayed his push south from La Grange to fold into his ranks the twenty thousand reinforcements Halleck had recently sent him.[102] While he reorganized his army, he learned for certain that John McClernand was preparing a separate river raid against Vicksburg. Beginning in November, newspapers began reporting that he was about to mount a "gigantic [expedition] to restore unobstructed navigation of the Mississippi."[103] Then on November 10, Halleck, without mentioning McClernand by name, informed Grant that Memphis "will be made the depot of a joint military and naval expedition on Vicksburg." This confused and upset Grant. Memphis was in his military district, and he had no plans for a "naval expedition."[104]

"Am I to understand that I lie still here while an expedition is fitted out from Memphis or do you want me to push as far south as possible?" he telegraphed Halleck testily that evening.[105] Halleck responded reassuringly. "You have command of all troops sent to your department, and have permission to fight the enemy where you please." [106] The following day, Grant learned from Sherman, who was in communication with Porter, that the president had named McClernand to head the Memphis-based expedition." [107] What Grant did not know was that Halleck, his longtime critic and intermittent adversary, was quietly supporting Grant's overland drive on Vicksburg while undercutting McClernand's effort.

Halleck was doing this by turning to his own purpose language Lincoln and Stanton had embedded in their original orders authorizing McClernand to raise troops and lead them downriver. McClernand had been authorized to outfit his expedition with only a "force not required by the operations of General Grant's command." His Vicksburg army, furthermore, would "remain subject to the designation of the general-in-chief, and be employed according to such exigencies as the service in his judgment may require." [108] This gave McClernand authority to command only those troops Halleck and Grant did not need for other operations. In effect, Halleck was given veto power over McClernand's expedition—the authority to divert to Grant troops that McClernand had been authorized to recruit and send to Memphis. And that is what he had begun to do, not because he completely trusted Grant but because he disliked and distrusted McClernand, a bombastic political general, in his opinion, with no proper military training. All the while, McClernand believed he was operating independently, under the direct authority of the president. Lincoln and Stanton, both of them savvy lawyers, had probably inserted this "escape clause" into McClernand's orders so as not to directly undercut Grant or unduly diminish Halleck's authority over Vicksburg operations. And McClernand had either ignored the clause or failed to see that it restricted his authority to raise a powerful river force.

Halleck kept Grant in the dark about this, never mentioning McClernand by name and leaving Grant with the impression that the troops that began to show up at Memphis were for his use only, when in fact, McClernand had recruited most of these regiments for his expedition. Lincoln and Stanton were the source of this confusion. They had not been forthright with either Grant or McClernand, and they had misgivings about both of them. Though a "volunteer officer of ability," in Lincoln's view, McClernand was a notorious schemer who had never commanded large numbers of men in battle, while Grant "was not a special favorite with either [Lincoln or Stanton]," Gideon Welles reported in his diary. "He had also like General [Joseph] Hooker a reputation of indulging too freely with whiskey to be always safe and reliable." [109] So Lincoln and Stanton clumsily set one general against the other. It was a monumental misstep by America's greatest war president and his highly regarded secretary of war.

Sensing from Halleck's cryptically worded communiqués that a "combined military & naval expedition," probably led by McClernand, would soon leave Memphis for Vicksburg, Grant had to act quickly if he was to be the commander who forced the surrender of the river citadel. On November 14, he ordered Sherman to begin readying his Memphis force to support his plunge into northern Mississippi, where he was to march just to the west of Grant's main army, and rendezvous with it near Oxford, Mississippi, on the railroad Grant would use as his supply line. "I am ready to move from here [La Grange] any day and only await your movements," Grant wrote Sherman. [110]

"The blow will soon be struck," reported the *Chicago Tribune*. [111]

CHAPTER 10

Revolution

"He is looking for the enemy."
—*Chicago Tribune*, November 25, 1862

Grant had more than the enemy on his mind as he made final preparations to move south. Elements of his army had recently become unruly and nearly impossible to control. It had nothing to do with morale, which skyrocketed when the men learned they were "bound for Vicksburg." Rather, some of the troops had taken the war into their own hands, punishing Southerners for the sin of secession. The men who began converging on La Grange from Union outposts all over Tennessee gave the war in the west a new and darker dimension. This was "hard war," a war of recrimination, and it was directed against civilians as well as soldiers. Grant's challenge in the coming months would be to channel indiscriminate attacks on civilian property, which he considered injurious to military discipline, into focused efforts to inflict permanent harm on the enemy. That would take many months, but it would lead eventually to the suppression of the slavocracy in Mississippi, a victory of equal consequence—and coeval with—the capture of Vicksburg.

"A grand movement of the whole army has commenced. Nearly all the troops from Corinth, Bolivar and Jackson, numbering some thirty thousand are now camped in [the vicinity of Grand Junction and La Grange]," wrote Seneca B. Thrall, a young assistant surgeon with the 13th Iowa Infantry Regiment. On the march to these cotton-rich towns on the Tennessee-Mississippi border, the armies of Generals Charles S. Hamilton and James McPherson had begun pillaging and burning, in open disregard of orders to leave civilian property untouched. It started innocently with the destruction of fences to provide firewood for their encampments, but it quickly turned more serious. Plantation houses were broken into, desecrated, and put to the torch, along with barns, stables, and cotton gins. The shelves of country stores were stripped bare and the buildings reduced to ash. "I saw not less than thirty or forty houses burning and one large church," wrote Seneca Thrall. "Such ruthless and wanton destruction and stealing, I entirely condemn."[1]

"We are gradually drifting into a warfare that will lay this country waste," wrote Franc Wilkie, who rode with McPherson's troops. "Our army [is] destroying everything they can, without direction, and in fact are becoming so bold that they care very little if they are detected." Greed and alcohol—confiscated plantation whiskey—were partly to blame, but there was more to it than that. There was a new mood in the army: a desire to extract revenge. And the way to hit the secessionists hardest, the troops had come to believe, was to steal their slaves.[2]

For miles, marching men passed through swirling clouds of crimson and black smoke. Processions of black refugees pulling carts and carrying bundles on their heads followed the armies, rhythmically chanting Old Testament songs of liberation. It had been easy for some of them to escape: Their masters had left Tennessee and northern Mississippi by the thousands when word reached them that Grant's legions were converging on La Grange. They had taken the "best" slaves with them to Alabama, Louisiana, and Texas, leaving behind the very young and the very old, the worn down and the enfeebled—the discards of chattel slavery.

Grant's commanders took in and protected the displaced slaves because they had to: Congressional and presidential action taken the previous summer forbade the army from turning them away. Then, in early September, Lincoln ordered both the army and navy to begin enforcing the emancipation clauses of the Second Confiscation Act. This law of July 17, 1862, declared "forever free of servitude" slaves of disloyal masters who escaped to Union lines, and forbade the army from returning black fugitives to their former owners.[3]

The new law was part of a seismic shift in war policy. In his first annual message to Congress, in December 1861, Lincoln had reaffirmed his commitment to a limited war. "I have been anxious and careful," he said, that the "conflict . . . shall not degenerate into a violent and remorseless revolutionary struggle."[4] But the passage of the Second Confiscation Act spelled full-out war, the beginning of the revolution Lincoln had wanted to avoid.

But the president who reluctantly signed the bill went surprisingly further when he issued the preliminary Emancipation Proclamation, a prelude to the proclamation that would become national law on January 1, 1863. On that day, he warned the Confederacy that slaves held in rebel areas would be "forever free."[5] Lincoln called the proclamation the "central act of my administration, and the great event of the nineteenth century."[6]

The proclamation did not free all slaves, only the roughly three million that resided in Confederate held territory on January 1. Exempted were the nearly half million slaves in the new state of West Virginia and the four border states of Delaware, Maryland, Missouri, and Kentucky, as well as slaves in Union-occupied parts of the South, including the areas of western Tennessee held by the armies of Grant and Sherman. This left untouched by the proclamation approximately eight hundred thousand of the nearly four million slaves who resided in the United States in 1860.[7] Neither the president nor Congress had constitutional authority to abolish slavery in states that remained in the Union. Only a constitutional amendment could affirm the total destruction of slavery.

Critics ridiculed the proclamation as an empty exercise. "Where he has no power Mr. Lincoln will set the negroes free; where he retains power he will consider them as slaves," wrote the London *Times*.[8] Lincoln's "paper threat" had "no power behind it to enforce," said Illinois general William Ward Orme.[9] Confederate leaders confidently agreed. It "will have not the slightest effect upon the slave population," said the *Richmond Dispatch*, "slavery will continue intact and impregnable as the rock of Gibraltar."[10]

But the proclamation did have teeth. It was a war measure, good only in time of war and in states at war with the United States. These renegade states came under the jurisdiction of the president as commander in chief of the armed forces, and he had power to seize their property—including slaves—as an act of war. But declaring this authority did not free a single slave. Lincoln understood this; knew that slavery could only be eradicated in the rebellious states by bayonets and bullets. The *Springfield Republican* got it right: Slaves would become free "as fast as the armies penetrate the Southern section." Henceforth, said the paper, "every victory is a victory of emancipation."[11]

What about those slaves who followed Grant's armies on the way to

La Grange and Grand Junction, a part of Tennessee under Union occupation and hence not covered by the Emancipation Proclamation? They were free by the terms of the Second Confiscation Act. Finding protection behind Union lines, in camps or with men on the march, they became "forever free." The commanders who took them in were merely enforcing the Second Confiscation act.

The final Emancipation Proclamation went further than the Preliminary Emancipation Act, authorizing the enrollment of black troops, a measure that horrified Confederates.* "Up to now," wrote Karl Marx in one of his dispatches to the *New York Tribune*, "we have witnessed only the first act of the Civil War—the constitutional waging of war. The second act, the revolutionary waging of war, is at hand." [12]

The Emancipation Proclamation did not change the purpose of the war: It remained preeminently a war to restore the Union. It was the "character of the war," not its purpose, that "will be changed," Lincoln told a member of his government. "It will be one of subjugation. . . . The [old] South is to be destroyed and replaced by new propositions and ideas." [13] This made a negotiated end to the conflict nearly impossible. Only by waging unyielding war on the Southern plantation system, Lincoln was saying, could the rebellion be extinguished.

To the soldiers of Grant's Army of the Tennessee, remorseless war meant hurting Southerners harder than they had ever been hurt before. At Grand Junction they had the numbers to do it. This "beautiful place," surrounded by "immense" plantations," had been turned into an uproarious army settlement, a city of soldiers, Seneca Thrall wrote his wife. [14] "We covered the fields around the town with our tents," said volunteer Ira Blanchard, "and the camp fires smoked for miles around, lighting up the sky like the lamps of a great city." [15] Troops from these lightly guarded camps "foraged at will" on local plantations, reported the *New*

---

* Congress had already passed—and Lincoln had signed—the Militia Act on July 17, 1862. This authorized the president to enroll men of "African descent" for "any war service [including manual labor] for which they may be found competent," and granted freedom to slave men employed in war service, as well as to their families, if they had been owned by disloyal masters. (U.S. Statutes at Large, xii, 597.)

York Herald's Thomas W. Knox. "There they found in abundance horses, mules, cattle, hogs, sheep, and chickens." Foraging—confiscating food and provisions for the army—quickly evolved into outright theft and destruction. Abandoned houses and plantations became easy targets for Union pillagers, as there was no one to stop them. "When we occupied [La Grange], there were not three men remaining who were of arms-bearing age," reported Knox.[16]

Seneca Thrall blamed the pillaging on "stragglers," soldiers who drifted away from their units to avoid combat or to search for booty, but freshly arrived reinforcements from Cairo joined in with enthusiasm. "The new troops come full of the idea of a more vigorous prosecution of the war, meaning destruction and plunder," Sherman wrote Henry Halleck.[17] Newly recruited Illinois private John G. Given proudly told his family that his regiment had "burned almost everything on the road" to Grand Junction, "stole lots of niggers, killed a cow and five calves for supper."[18]

Veterans of Donelson, Shiloh, and Corinth plundered with equal fervor. Since Shiloh, they had been under constraints to guard the property of civilians, including slaveholders, who professed their loyalty to Washington. Many of these "Unionist" families had fathers, sons, and nephews in the enemy army. "This thing of guarding rebel property when the owner is in the field fighting us is played out," wrote the chaplain of an Ohio regiment. "That is the sentiment of every private soldier in the army."[19] One veteran told his family that pillaging had put a "new zeal into the soldiers . . . They think they have protected rebel property about long enough now."[20] A Confederate officer saw clearly where this war was headed. "Instead conducting the war betwixt two military and political organizations, it is a war against the whole population."[21]

"This is but the commencement," the pro-administration *New York Times* predicted. The feeling was "becoming universal," even among the officers, that the rebels would henceforth "feel . . . [the] full horrors of the war they had so wantonly provoked." The systematic destruction of rebel property "[will spread] until finally it will be recognized as the system of warfare we are prosecuting."[22]

Infuriated by "gross acts of vandalism" against people who claimed to be Union loyalists, or were at least leaning that way, Grant issued Special Field Orders No. 1. Offenders who were apprehended would be imprisoned or dishonorably discharged. If officers failed to enforce "obedience" they would suffer the same consequences.[23] Two days later, Grant issued orders authorizing "stoppage of pay for soldiers in units guilty of such 'depredations.'"[24] Sherman took additional measures, threatening plunderers with execution by firing squad. "No officer or soldier," he ordered, "should enter the house or premises of any peaceable citizen, no matter what his politics, unless on business; and no such officer or soldier can force an entrance unless he have a written order from a commanding officer."[25]

But the pillage continued. It was too widespread, too many officers were caught up in it, and the men were in no mood to obey orders they doubted would be enforced. (No officer or soldier was executed for pillaging.) "Such orders soon got to be a joke with the men," said one veteran.[26] Most soldiers would not abide Grant's idea that growing numbers of Tennesseans were sick of the war and ready to declare their allegiance to the Union. "They are all Secessionists!" wrote an Illinois soldier. "They hate the North, and wish to be divorced from it in every way, politically, socially, religiously, and commercially." Why protect and coddle them?[27] "Hang all officers who won't let us steal from the rebel property," John Given wrote his wife. ". . . I will steal it whenever I get a chance."[28] Federal authorities were wrong to insist that there was a "suppressed Union sentiment" in Tennessee, said brigadier general and future president of the United States James A. Garfield, who served in Tennessee earlier in the year. "The fact can no longer be denied that the white slave interest is inveterately hostile to the Union," he wrote his brother, "and I am most thoroughly persuaded that the Union can never live in these states, except upon the 'broken body and shed blood' of slavery."[29]

Grant's army had been in Tennessee for nearly a year, most of that time on occupation duty, and many of the men had developed a sharp hatred of all things Southern. Boys from well-tended farms in Iowa and Indiana were disgusted by the slovenly appearance of the plantations they encountered. Unlike back home, houses and barns were ill kept, and agricultural machinery was primitive and often rusting in the fields. Pigs and cattle were not fenced in; they roamed the grounds freely with the owner's mangy dogs. Shirtless overseers carried pistols and barked orders in vulgar language, tobacco juice running down the sides of their mouths. Noticed, too, were the high rates of illiteracy, the absence of formal education, and the chasm between rich and poor.

Fueling this hatred of all things Southern was the insolence of local women. "No history of the war is likely to do full justice to the bitterness of the Rebel women," wrote reporter Albert Richardson, who was at La Grange with the army.[30] Unrepentant women "seceshers" spat on the boots of Union soldiers they encountered on the streets and tonguelashed them to their faces.[31]

These were not the perfumed belles Northern boys had expected to encounter. Soldiers "have looked in vain for the . . . fascinating divinities in crinoline they had conjured up to their excited fancy," wrote a *Chicago Tribune* correspondent. ". . . In their stead they have found . . . homely, snuff-dipping females whom no poet's imagination could idealize into loveliness or soften into grace. Nearly all the women I have met in Tennessee . . . [are] attach[ed] to this great social vice. Some of them expectorate like a tobacco-chewing sailor."[32]

Soldiers' letters are replete with detailed descriptions of the local women's addiction to this "disgusting" habit of "dipping" snuff. A stick the size of a pencil was chewed at one end until its fibers were separated, forming a kind of brush. This was moistened with saliva and dipped into the snuff. The fine powder was then rubbed on the gums and teeth, producing "a species of partial intoxication." At after-dinner tea parties "the sticks and snuff are passed round and the dipping commences," wrote Illinois Lieutenant Charles W. Wills. "I asked one [girl] if it didn't interfere with the old-fashioned habit of kissing. She assured me that it did not in the least, and I marveled."[33]

But Wills and other Union officers found a great number of Southern women unavoidably appealing. During the occupation, before the mass pillaging began, they would stop by the homes of women who professed to be Unionists, invited or not, for a glass of buttermilk and some social conversation. The practice made women without men around the house concerned for their personal safety. Yet sexual assault was rare in the occupied South. "Incidents of rape and molestation did occur," writes historian Stephen V. Ash, "perpetrated in nearly every case by deserters, stragglers, or other unsupervised enlisted men who preyed on women they found alone in isolated farmhouses." When the rapists were found, which was rare, army justice was swift. Twenty-two Union soldiers were executed for rape during the war.[34]

When the pillaging and "negro stealing" began in November, the social visits ended. The doors were double locked, and every bluecoat became an implacable enemy. Grant had long been concerned about this, worried that Southerners who claimed to be leaning to the Union cause would think every man in his army an "Abolitionist."[35] Most soldiers who 'stole' slaves were hardly abolitionists." Some did it for purely selfish reasons. Hundreds of officers—Charles Wills among them—gathered up male slaves at random and made them their "private servants" or, as Wills and other officers called them, their "pet negro[s]."[36] Grant, who had his own black body servant, permitted this practice provided officers kept their "servants" at their own expense.[37] A great many Union soldiers had no interest in freeing slaves. Congress and the army "should let the nigger alone," Ohio private John Easton spoke for them.[38] But even racists like Easton were beginning to see that slavery was sustaining the rebellion, whether slaves cultivated cotton and corn or dug military entrenchments for the enemy. Another Ohio boy wrote his anti-abolitionist father to explain his shift to Lincoln and emancipation: "My doctrine has been any thing [sic] to weaken the enemy."[39]

Fighting in the hostile South, however, did change some soldiers' ideas about black people. George E. Stephens, one of the only African American war correspondents in the Civil War, wrote: "When the Union soldier meets the negro in the enemy's country, he knows him as a friend."[*][40] Slaves guided bluecoats to hidden storage cellars stocked with hams and salted bacon, reported the location of rebel cavalry, and

---

* Stephens, a highly educated Philadelphia cabinetmaker active in the Underground Railroad, signed on as the personal servant of an officer in the Army of the Potomac and sent his war reports to the New York–based *Anglo-African*. When the government opened military service to blacks, he joined the 54th Massachusetts Volunteer Infantry and was wounded in the assault on Fort Wagner in Charleston Harbor on July 18, 1863. He survived the war and worked with the Freedmen's Bureau in Virginia. See Donald Yacovone, ed., *A Voice of Thunder: The Civil War Letters of George E. Stephens* (Urbana: University of Illinois Press, 1997).

led Yankee scouting parties through dangerous, unmapped terrain. "The white people are treacherous and unreliable, all lying to deceive us," an Ohio colonel wrote from Jackson, Tennessee. "We can only depend on the statements of negroes."[41]

Exposure to Deep South plantation slavery, where field hands labored longer and were whipped more frequently than slaves in the Upper South, turned one Union general (later awarded the Medal of Honor) into an emancipationist. When reporter Thomas W. Knox first met Brigadier General David S. Stanley in Missouri in the first year of the war, Stanley was opposed "to a warfare that should produce a change in the social status of the south." Riding with Stanley on the march from Corinth to La Grange, Knox saw a changed man, "radical in sentiment and in favor of a thorough destruction of the 'peculiar institution.'" He was determined, he told Knox, "to set free all the slaves . . . that might come in his way."[42]

Seeing commanders like Stanley destroying their masters' whipping posts and killing his bloodhounds gave great numbers of slaves the courage to flee to the Federals. By November approximately 150,000 slaves in the Mississippi Valley were behind Union lines.[43] "The war is evidently growing oppressive to the Southern people," Grant wrote his sister Mary. "Their [slaves] are beginning to have ideas of their own and every time an expedition goes out more or less of them follow in the wake of the army and come into camp. I am using them as teamsters, hospital attendants, company cooks etc. thus saving soldiers to carry the musket. I dont [sic] know what is to become of these poor people in the end but it weak[ens] the enemy to take them from them."[44]

While Grant continued to protect the slaves of Union loyalists, he instructed his commanders to send out "details" under a commissioned officer "to press into service [in Union camps] the slaves of disloyal persons."[45]

By the time Grant's army was ready to move on Vicksburg, his camps were flooded with fugitive slaves. This made it "impossible," he complained, "to advance."[46] The previous September he had sent hundreds of black women and children to Cairo, where they were to be funneled by rail to Chicago to be employed as domestic servants. Lincoln put a stop to this, however, when Illinois political leaders complained that the influx of African Americans from Cairo would "work great harm in the coming Election." This forced Grant to deal with the refugee issue on his own. The Second Confiscation Act forbade him from expelling fugitive slaves—considered "contraband of war" by the government—who came streaming into his camps voluntarily. And "humanity," he said, "forbade allowing them to starve."[47]*

The answer to the refugee problem had been staring him in the face since the hour he arrived at La Grange. The plantations in the area were deserted and the cotton was ripe for picking. Riding from Grand Junction to La Grange on November 10, a *Chicago Tribune* correspondent passed an abandoned plantation where the cotton bolls "were bursting" and the land was "white with the costly staple. Here is an opportunity to replenish the depleted coffers of the government. There are hundreds of women and children . . . whose husbands are in the employment of the government, eating the bread of idleness. Why not," he asked rhe-

---

* Having given belligerent status to the Confederacy, the federal government could confiscate enemy property as a legitimate act of war. In May 1861, an agent of the owner of three slaves who escaped to Union lines at Fortress Monroe, Virginia, approached the commanding officer, Major General Benjamin Butler, and demanded the return of his property, in compliance with the Fugitive Slave Law of 1850, which allowed slaveholders to pursue and retrieve runaway slaves in free states. Butler refused, saying the law "did not affect a foreign country," which the South claimed to be when it seceded. And since the owner of the three slaves, Colonel Charles Mallory, had used them to build fortifications, the rules of war, said Butler, gave him authority to confiscate them as "contrabands of war" and put them to work at Fortress Monroe. Henceforth, slaves who came into Union lines were called contrabands, and soon there would be contraband camps wherever the Union army went in the South.

I have tried to avoid using the term "contraband" to refer to runaway slaves, except when quoting, because of its association of human beings with property. (Butler rejected the idea that the escaped slaves he took in were property.) Taking my cue from historian Chandra Manning, I use a variety of other terms to refer to black people who fled slavery: refugees, escaped slaves, etcetera. I do, however, use the term "contraband camps" to refer to government refugee camps for black people who fled slavery, since this was the official government name for them. (See Manning, *Troubled Refuge,* 24–25.)

torically, "set them at work to secure this crop, which otherwise will be ruined[?]"[48]

This is exactly what Grant decided to do before setting out to meet Pemberton's army. To administer the program, he turned to a young man he had never met: John Eaton, chaplain of the 27th Ohio Volunteer Infantry, a graduate of Dartmouth College, and a former student at Andover Theological Seminary. Eaton would later describe how he was discovered and persuaded to take the position.

On a chilly evening in early November, he was warming himself by a bonfire in a forest encampment at Grand Junction when a messenger approached with a dispatch from General Grant: an order to "take charge of the contrabands that come into camp . . . organizing them into suitable companies for working." For further instructions, he was to "call at headquarters."

Eaton was thunderstruck. Why had he, an inconspicuous chaplain, been ordered to undertake an "enterprise beyond the possibility of human achievement"? The arrival of these "hordes," he wrote later, was "like the oncoming of cities," and "their condition was appalling. There were men, women, and children in every stage of disease or decrepitude, often nearly naked with flesh torn by the terrible experiences of their escapes." Desperate husbands stole army rations for their families, and wives sold their bodies to sex-starved soldiers to feed their children.

On arriving at headquarters, a sentry directed Eaton to a rustic cabin and instructed him to knock on the door. He was wary. Grant, he had been told, was both "incompetent and disagreeable." Entering the room, he saw the general hunched over a table, in conference with some of his commanders. Without looking up, he said, "Oh, you are the man who has all these darkies on his shoulders." After the officers had filed out, Grant invited Eaton to pull up a chair.

Before Grant could speak, Eaton pleaded to have his orders revoked. He had never commanded men, and to take refugees out of the soldiers' camps would put him at odds with officers who were using them as their personal servants and, in some cases, their concubines. Grant listened patiently, his face expressionless. When Eaton finished, he said in a low voice: "Mr. Eaton, I have ordered you to report to me in person, and I will take care of you."[49]

Then he outlined his program. This would not be army charity, he emphasized. The cotton the black refugees picked would be shipped north and sold to support the war effort. A portion of the profits would be allocated to the workers to compensate for the food, clothing, and shelter they received from the army. By supporting themselves, former slaves would be supporting the government that was protecting them from re-enslavement.[50] The experiment, Grant explained, would help "to make the Negro a consciously self-supporting unit . . . and start him on the way to self-respecting citizenship." When it became clear that "the Negro, as an independent laborer . . . could do things well, it would be very easy," he said, "to put a musket in his hands and make a soldier of him, and if he fought well, eventually to put the ballot in his hand and make him a citizen." Eaton was stunned. "Never before" he said later, ". . . had I heard the problem of the future of the Negro attacked so vigorously and with such humanity combined with practical good sense."[51]

In a one-hour conversation with the thirty-three-year-old Presbyterian chaplain, Grant "inaugurated what became the most systematic and continuous effort to organize and care for the freedman conducted during the Civil War," in the opinion of one historian.[52] Grant thought Eaton, the son of a struggling New Hampshire farmer, perfect for the job. He had come highly recommended, a caring but tough-minded chaplain who had worked his way through college. He also had some administrative experience, having served as acting superintendent of schools in Toledo before enlisting.

Grant established the first camp at Grand Junction, where there were abandoned houses for workers and their families. The overflow would be sheltered in large army tents. A regiment of infantry guarded the camp, army surgeons took care of the sick, and Grant ordered his quartermaster to provide farm implements.[53] All this was done without authorization from Washington. That came from Stanton five days after the first workers were transferred to the camp. Years later, Grant remarked to Eaton: "I wonder if you ever realized how easily they could have had our heads!"[54]*

---

* Labor experiments similar to Grant's were already in place both in southern Louisiana and on the Sea Islands off the coast of South Carolina. In Louisiana, General Benjamin Butler had begun hiring out escaped slaves to work for wages on local sugar

The experiment was not without its problems. Grant was forced to exert his full authority to get unwilling soldiers to guard the camp. These disgruntled soldiers stole from the people they were assigned to protect and sexually molested females of all ages. Guerrilla bands attempted to frighten black people from working in the fields. The camp, however, was an unexpected success. The cotton was "gathered, baled and made ready for the market," and Eaton did all in his power to create a self-supporting black community.[55] Common-law marriages were legalized. In one "comprehensive wedding," Eaton's assistant chaplain married over a hundred couples. Cabins were provided for married couples, one per family. "Every man," said Eaton, "took care of his own wife and children."[56] To give Eaton much needed assistance, Grant provided free river transportation to charitable organizations that sent supplies and volunteers to the camp.[57]

That December Grant appointed Chaplain Eaton superintendent of contrabands for the Department of the Tennessee, a position he held until the end of the war. Wherever Grant's army went in the Mississippi Valley in the coming months, Eaton and his subordinates established labor camps as places of refuge for recently liberated slaves. It was a landmark effort, signaling the army's determination to protect all fugitive slaves, not just men able to do military labor. Although black refugees worked under white supervision and guardianship without a voice in camp governance, the contraband camps solved problems of subsistence and survival and established a rudimentary free-labor system for blacks in the Mississippi Valley.[58] Most critical, the people in Eaton's camps were free. Union authorities had determined that slaves who escaped "without solicitation" were emancipated.[59] In voluntarily seeking refuge in the Union army, escaped slaves chose "to own themselves and keep their children from the auction block," wrote *Harper's Weekly* illustrator Alfred Waud.[60]

"General Grant was always up with, or in advance of authority furnished from Washington in regard to the treatment of those of our color

---

estates. On the Carolina Sea Islands, charity workers and reformers had established schools for black children, and Northern land speculators put their parents to work on abandoned plantations. See Foner, *Fiery Trial*, 285. At the time he set up his own labor farm in La Grange, Tennessee, Grant had no knowledge of these other programs.

then slaves," Frederick Douglass wrote after the war.[61] Grant, however, was a military pragmatist, not a humanitarian. Though he continued to show concern for black refugees, his objective was to take Vicksburg, not manage a social upheaval. Military necessity, more than concern for the refugees, had impelled him to set up the camp at Grand Junction; once established, he wanted nothing to do with its management, leaving that entirely in the capable hands of Chaplain Eaton.

On November 15, four days after his first conference with Chaplain Eaton, Grant was ready to move on Vicksburg. That morning he sent word to Sherman to meet him in Columbus, Kentucky, to finalize plans for the campaign. Grant planned to see David Dixon Porter in nearby Cairo the day before he met Sherman. From this point forward, Porter and Grant—in near friction-free cooperation—directed the Vicksburg campaign.

Grant reached Cairo on the evening of November 20. Porter and his staff, decked out in their dress whites, were feasting on roast duck and French champagne when Captain McAllister, the quartermaster at Cairo, ushered in a "travel-worn" man in an old brown suit coat and wrinkled gray pants. "McAllister introduced the gentleman to me as General Grant," Porter recalled, "and placed us at a table by ourselves and left us to talk matters over. While I was looking earnestly at Grant, trying to make out how much of a man there was under the plain exterior, the General was regarding me to see what amount of work there was under all the gilt buttons and gold lace with which the Department had bedizened my coat." *

Grant got straight to the point. He needed Porter to reconnoiter enemy strength on the Yazoo and to knock out any fortifications the

---

* This is virtually the only part of their meeting Porter got right in his memoirs, published in 1891. He even had the date wrong, claiming the meeting took place in December. He wrote: "Soon after my arrival at Cairo I sent a messenger to General Grant informing him that . . . I should be happy to co-operate with him in any enterprise he might think proper to undertake. I also informed him that General McClernand had orders to raise troops at Springfield, Illinois, prior to undertaking the capture of Vicksburg." There is no known record of this communiqué from Porter to Grant. Porter, *Incidents and Anecdotes,* 125; Porter, "Journal," 429–30, LC.

rebels may have erected. Porter explained that his orders were to support
McClernand's expedition when the general arrived at Memphis, probably in early December; inexplicably, however, he had not heard from
McClernand and was willing, in the meantime, to work with Grant. "I
am ready to cooperate with anybody and everybody." [62]

Porter was surprised the meeting went so well. The week before, he
had told Gustavus Fox at the Navy Department that he didn't "trust
the Army. It is evident that Grant is going to try and take Vicksburg
without us, but he can't do it." [63] Halleck's failure to assist Farragut in
front of Vicksburg the previous summer had left Porter with a "particular dislike of West-Pointers." He preferred, he told Welles, to cooperate with McClernand, a political general—probably, Welles suspected,
because he "feared he should be compelled to play a subordinate part
with [Grant], while with a civilian general he would have superiority." [64]
Grant's visit changed this. He had come to Porter asking for help, valu-
ing him as equal partner.

The next day, Grant headed down to Columbus to meet Sherman.
Grant was all business; he had no time for small talk. He ordered Sherman to take seventeen thousand men and move southeastward into
Mississippi, joining his Grand Junction force at Abbeville, just north of
the Tallahatchie River. After smashing Pemberton's outnumbered army,
they would march along the line of the Mississippi Central Railroad and
take Vicksburg from the rear, by way of Jackson, Mississippi, forty-five
miles due east of Vicksburg. Rations, munitions, and medicine would
be sent from Cairo, by steamboat, to Columbus, Kentucky, and from
Columbus, by rail, to Holly Springs, Grant's advance supply base. As
the army moved on Jackson, it would be supplied by rail from Holly
Springs.[65] So Grant's long supply line would lengthen as he moved farther into enemy country. Grant would be the first commander in history to mount a campaign that relied entirely on a single railroad for
logistical support.[66]

Logistics was Grant's métier; he had been a crack quartermaster in
Mexico. But Sherman worried that Grant's supply line was dangerously
vulnerable: two hundred miles of single-track line through country
crawling with rebel cavalry and partisans. He thought it preferable, he
had told Grant back in September, to divide the army into two wings:
one moving overland into northern Mississippi, battering Pemberton,

while the other advanced by transports from Memphis to the mouth of the Yazoo, drawing its supplies from Cairo and Memphis.[67] But he offered no objections or emendations to Grant's plan at their Columbus conference. Grant, he could see, was set on it.[68]

In hindsight, he should not have given way so easily. The conditions of the Vicksburg march were greatly different from those of Grant's earlier campaigns, where he had used western water highways—the Tennessee and Cumberland Rivers—to rapidly move troops and supplies through the interior of the country. A rail line through enemy territory would be far harder to secure than a river patrolled by ironclads. Grant had taken precautions to protect his long supply line through Tennessee, building a series of well-armed garrisons along the tracks; but a strong force of rebel cavalry could feasibly elude or overwhelm Union forces and tear up track and pull down telegraph lines in his rear. In that event, the army would be isolated in forested and hostile country.

Awake to the risks, Grant nevertheless stuck to the plan. It was one of the greatest gambles of his military career. Then again, nearly every risk-filled move he had taken previously—at Paducah, Belmont, Donelson, and, by a razor-thin margin, Shiloh—had paid dividends.

After his meeting with Sherman, Grant headed back to his La Grange headquarters. A day later he wrote his father: "Before you receive this I will again be in motion. I feel every confidence of success but I know that a heavy force is now to my front."[69]

Sherman, too, expected success, but wondered if his countrymen were prepared to endure the fire and slaughter it would take to subdue Mississippi. "The People of the South," he wrote Ellen, "are so much more Zealous in their Cause than our people."[70] The rebellion would take time and bottomless effort to extinguish, and the hardest fighting lay ahead at Vicksburg, which had defied the concentrated might of two federal fleets.

News of Grant's expected march into Mississippi was greeted with jubilation in his home state. Grant "has at last been let loose [by Halleck]," the *Chicago Tribune* reported. "He is looking for the enemy, and when he finds him there will be bloodshed."[71]

CHAPTER 11

Grant's March

"You may calculate on our being at Vicksburg by Christmas."[1]
—William T. Sherman

As Grant made final preparations for his drive to the Tallahatchie his army was astir with anticipation. Chaplains held outdoor services in the camps and in abandoned churches in La Grange. John Campbell, an Iowa volunteer, attended a service in which soldiers were asked to stand, one at a time, and reveal how the Lord had transformed their lives. "The Church was crowded to overflowing," he noted.[2]

"The impression in camp is that we are bound for Vicksburg, away down in the land 'ob cotton,'" Seneca Thrall excitedly wrote to his wife.[3] Thrall's regiment, part of Brigadier General C. S. Hamilton's wing, led the march to Holly Springs on November 28. To prevent pillaging, Grant had ordered Hamilton and James McPherson, commanding the two wings of his La Grange force, to keep all men "in ranks," and to have "at least one field officer . . . march in the rear of his regiments." The day was bright and the roads dry. The regimental bands played "We Are Coming, Father Abra'am."[4]

Grant rode high in the saddle on his cream-colored horse, Jack. The army, minus Sherman's Memphis force of seventeen thousand, numbered thirty-one thousand, "enough to skin Mississippi," wrote Lieutenant Charles Wills. "I never saw men in as good spirits and so confident as this army now appears. We are splendidly equipped and want nothing."[5]

Grant's army was almost entirely western and had its own style. General Joseph Hooker would boast that the Army of the Potomac was "the best on the planet." Watching the Army of the Tennessee march off to Mississippi "one would have declared that Grant commanded the worst," wrote reporter Albert Richardson. "There was little of that order, perfect drill, or pride, pomp, and circumstance, seen . . . in the Army of the Potomac." The men were rough and rugged looking, with scruffy beards and long flowing hair, and they didn't move "with that beautiful symmetry" that Hooker and McClellan demanded.[6] "They seem like a gang of coal-heavers when compared with the trim and snug fellows" in the eastern theater, said another observer. "These westerners came trooping through the streets, roaring out songs and jokes . . . and overflowing with merriment and good-nature."[7] But they fought "wonderfully," wrote Richardson, who had been with them since Cairo, "and were not easily demoralized."[8]

Their leader was as unkempt as they were. His boots and leggings were mud-splattered and he was badly in need of a barber. There was "no glitter or parade about him," said a visitor to his headquarters. "To me he seems but an earnest business man."[9] Nor was he, like McClellan, a student of warfare. Battle, he believed, "was the swiftest of schools."[10] As he once told Dr. John Brinton: "The art of war is simple enough: find out where your enemy is, get at him as soon as you can, and strike him as hard as you can, and keep moving on."[11]

Grant reached Holly Springs, twenty-five miles below Grand Junction, by nightfall and established his field headquarters in a local mansion occupied by the wife of a Confederate officer. Julia Grant and their son Jesse who had arrived earlier in Tennessee for an extended stay, were on their way there, and they planned to join Grant south of the Tallahatchie when it was safe to travel. Grant stopped long enough to leave a letter for her and Jesse.[12]

The small rebel garrison had already fled Holly Springs, and the picturesque town looked deserted. "All were gone but women and children and negroes," wrote bluecoat S. C. Beck.[13] As the army's forward column passed through the main square, the bands struck up "Dixie." From their partially shuddered windows, women of the town watched with "scowling faces." Black people crowded the sidewalks, said Seneca Thrall, "with broad grins on their faces." It took three days for the long line of men to pass through the town. "They must have thought that the whole Yankee nation was coming to tea with [Pemberton]," said Thrall.[14]

GRANT'S INVASION OF NORTHERN MISSISSIPPI
NOVEMBER–DECEMBER 1862

MISSOURI

TENNESSEE

Humboldt

Fort Pillow

Forrest raids Jackson, Dec. 20

MEMPHIS & OHIO R.R.

ARKANSAS

Memphis

• Hatchie

Bolivar

Grant sets out for Vicksburg late Nov.

Sherman departs for the Yazoo, Dec. 20

MEMPHIS & CHARLESTON

R.R.

Mississippi River

Coldwater River

Grand Junction

Corinth

Iuka •

Van Dorn raids Holly Springs, Dec. 20

Ripley •

Van Dorn's Raid

Helena •

Yazoo Pass

Sherman to Memphis

Tallahatchie River

Battle of Arkansas Post, Jan. 11, 1863

College Hill •

Oxford •

Grant retreats, Dec. 21

• Tupelo

MISSISSIPPI CENTRAL R.R.

Yalobusha R.

Mississippi River

MISSISSIPPI & TENNESSEE R.R.

Delta

Granada

MOBILE & OHIO R.R.

Yazoo River

MISSISSIPPI

Sherman reaches the Yazoo, Dec. 26 and is repulsed, Dec. 29

Chickasaw Bayou

to Monroe ←

Vicksburg •

Jackson •

SOUTHERN R.R. OF MISSISSIPPI

LOUISIANA

Grand Gulf •

• Port Gibson

to New Orleans ↓

to Mobile ↓

© 2019 Jeffrey L. Ward

0   100
Miles

As the last of the regiments entered the town, the skies opened up and the roads became a stew of mud. In approving Grant's drive into Mississippi, Halleck had warned him not to go "too far."[15] Grant brushed this off and headed for the Tallahatchie without explicit orders.

"I no longer see burning houses, fences, barns, and churches. . . . No longer is there pillaging," Seneca Thrall wrote home.[16] But the columns behind his regiment treated the country "awfully rough," said Charles Wills.[17] Men foraged for food against orders and went "in pursuit of plunder."[18] An Iowa boy wrote home: "We pressed mules and horses into service to draw our knapsacks, provisions and fresh meat," and "we burned a good many rail fences, buildings and corn [cribs]," and all the "sugar, molasses and cotton we could not use.[19]

There was little respect for personal property, said Charles Wills. Soldiers smashed through the doors of homes with rifle butts and broke open locked trunks in bedrooms while terrified, unresisting women stood by offering them the keys. "The d . . . d [army] thieves even steal from the negroes," wrote Wills, ". . . many of them are learning to hate the Yankees as much as our 'Southern Brethren' do."[20] Apprehending the offenders was nearly impossible. There was a conspiracy of silence in the regiments.

The men of the 7th Kansas Cavalry were the worst offenders. Their announced mission was to "pollute . . . the sacred soil" of Mississippi.[21] "It makes my blood boil to think of the outrages they committed," recalled eighteen-year-old Cordelia Lewis Scales, whose family's sprawling plantation was directly in the path of the Kansas horsemen. "They tore the earrings out of the lady's ears, pulled their rings and breast pins off, took them by the hair, threw them down, and knocked them about," she wrote a friend.[22] They were "entirely unmanageable . . . more bent on plunder than fighting," wrote Lieutenant Major James Wilson, who marched with them.[23] The Jayhawkers had come to Mississippi with a reputation in Tennessee for assaulting and raping women who were home alone, without the protection of husbands and fathers. "Their conduct has been disgraceful to the Army of the United States," reported a Union Colonel. But swift-moving cavalry advancing ahead of the infantry were nearly impossible to rein in.[24]

When a thousand Illinois soldiers camped in the grove of her family's plantation, Cordelia Scales never went anywhere without a holstered six-shooter on her hip. The head of the regiment allowed his men to forage at will in the area, and when rebel partisans hunted down and shot two of them, the regimental surgeon requisitioned her father's bedroom as a hospital. As the mangled men were being carried into the house, Cordelia had to suppress a smile of satisfaction. "I did feel so happy when I looked on the sufferings and heard the groans of those blue devils." [25]

The only remedy for the pillaging was to have the army quicken its pace. Grant's army was able to move on course through unfamiliar countryside because its commander had an extraordinary aptitude for topography. "After looking critically at a map of a locality, it seemed to become photographed indelibly upon his brain, and he could follow its features without referring to it again," said an officer who served with him later in the war. "He was a natural 'bushwhacker,' and was never so much at home as when finding his way by the course of streams, the contour of the hills, and the general features of the country." [26]

On December 2, Grant received an urgent dispatch from Sherman, whose three divisions had reached Wyatt, a village a few miles west of Grant, on the Tallahatchie. "From a hill here at 11 a.m. I saw a high smoke at Oxford. I think the enemy has gone to Grenada, back of the Yalobusha," a stream fifty miles south of the Tallahatchie.[27] They had.

An expedition Grant had requested from Helena, Arkansas—seven thousand men under Generals Alvin P. Hovey and Cadwallader C. Washburn—had crossed the Mississippi on transports and moved on Pemberton's flank, damaging railroad bridges in his rear.* Exaggerated reports about the strength of the expedition had caused Pemberton to panic.[28] Fearing his western flank was too vulnerable to defend, he abandoned the formidable Tallahatchie defensive line. This tactical misjudgment gave Grant a bloodless victory and caused locals to question Pemberton's military capacity.[29] "Our army made a stampede instead of a stand," wrote Cordelia Scales. "Our soldiers were ready and anxious

---

* Cadwallader Washburn was the brother of Congressman Elihu Washburne but they spelled their last names differently.

for a fight, and it was owing to the *bad generalship* of . . . Pemberton that we did not drive the last blue devil from the country."[30]

The Tallahatchie was a highly defensible position. Violent storms had made it "a bold, deep stream," and the rebels had burned the road surface of the railroad bridge to prevent the enemy from crossing.[31] The Confederates had "the strongest fortifications our . . . officers . . . have ever seen," wrote Seneca Thrall.[32] "A crossing," said Grant, "would have been impossible in the presence of an enemy." Relieved to have avoided the "terrible battle" he anticipated at the river, Grant had his engineers repair the rail bridge and pushed on to Oxford, where he halted his pursuit of Pemberton to bring in supplies from Holly Springs.[33]

Sherman's Memphis force, meanwhile, was delayed at Wyatt, where his pioneer detachments were building a second bridge over the Tallahatchie to replace the one the rebels had destroyed. Many of his troops were fresh volunteers eager to plunder and burn. "Our new troops came with the idea of making vigorous war, which means universal destruction," Sherman wrote Admiral Porter, "and it requires hard handling to repress excesses."[34] An Illinois soldier described the onset of Sherman's march: "Just after leaving Memphis our troops commenced setting fire to everything before them and kept it up for about thirty miles. . . . I think [our troops acted] justly as we must win and might just as well destroy now as to wait any longer.[35]

North-central Mississippi was thinly populated and covered with dense forest. The farms and villages were small and most of the settlers scratched out a living as subsistence agriculturists, growing yams for the table and corn both to consume and sell. Only the rich cotton planters of the fertile Tallahatchie and Yazoo bottoms had slaves in large numbers.[36] On arriving at their first substantial plantation, a regiment of Indiana infantry flew out of control, burning nearly every building "as punishment for [the owner's] treasonable conversations with the soldiers." The "desolation," said regimental chaplain M. D. Gage, ". . . continued during the march, the track of our column being distinctly marked by the smoke of burning buildings and fences." A great number of the men were from families with a deep-seated hatred of slavery and were intent, said Gage, on obliterating "a despotism based on oppression."

Scarcity finally curtailed the men's appetite for retribution. On reaching Wyatt, they found "the country, in all directions, . . .

thoroughly impoverished." A number of the farms had been stripped of everything—horses, cattle, mules, hogs, and corn—by Pemberton's foragers. The rebel army was in a deplorable state, struggling to feed itself in this desolate region.[37] Roughly a third of Pemberton's men were barefoot, none had tents, and all were on half rations, having to depend for survival on sweet potatoes and corn confiscated from local farmers. It was unseasonably cold, and the men built crude pine shanties and dugouts to protect themselves from driving rain and sleet and occasional snow showers. Morale, however, was taut but unbroken. The men, said Private W. R. Rorer, cling to but one objective: not to lose. "I cannot think life desirable with such masters as the Yankees will make."[38]

After Sherman's troops crossed the Tallahatchie, heavy rains rendered the roads through the alluvial bottomlands south of the river "practically impassable," recalled engineer William Le Baron Jenney, "and artillery frequently sank almost out of sight in the mud."[39] But Sherman's pioneers, the finest in the Union army, bridged every stream and swamp they encountered, and on December 5 the Memphis army, eighteen thousand strong was on the outskirts of Oxford, ten miles west of where Grant's troops were encamped. "By our movement we have . . . cleaned North Mississippi," Sherman wrote his brother John.[40]

That same day, Henry Halleck suggested a change in the invasion plan. Hold the line in Mississippi with a small force, he telegraphed Grant, and send a larger force "upon Vicksburg with the Gunboats."[41] Halleck wanted Grant to move most of his army to Memphis, and have it there by December 20. A presidentially sanctioned "expedition down the Mississippi now was inevitable," he warned, not saying who would lead it.[42] But Grant knew this meant McClernand—and that Halleck was imploring him to move quickly to beat him to Vicksburg.

Halleck's proposal arrived just as he was growing increasingly concerned about the condition of the roads between Oxford and the Yalobusha, and the vulnerability of his ever-lengthening supply line. Grant took Halleck's advice but altered his plan slightly. He would keep the greater part of his army in its present position, threatening Pemberton, while a smaller force steamed from Memphis to the Yazoo River and attacked Vicksburg from there, avoiding its menacing river batteries.[43]

Halleck approved, and when Grant asked whether he or Sherman should lead the river expedition, he left the decision to him. It would be Sherman, Grant decided.[44]

Three days later, Grant asked Sherman to "come over" to Oxford and stay the night.[45] After meeting together at a quiet spot in Grant's crowded headquarters, Grant wrote out orders authorizing Sherman to proceed to Memphis with one of his three divisions. "Large reinforcements" would reach Memphis "very soon," he told him, "if not already there." They were his for the taking. Grant had also arranged for a full division at Helena to be attached to Sherman's river force, giving him a total of thirty-three thousand men. Still having heard "nothing" from McClernand, Porter agreed to have his gunboat fleet lead the expedition to the Yazoo.[46] Sherman had only to contact the admiral to arrange a meeting to work out the details. Steamers to transport the troops would soon be on their way from St. Louis. Grant's old friend Colonel Robert Allen, chief quartermaster at St. Louis, promised immediate delivery of every riverboat he could spare.[47] Grant executed these lightning-like logistical moves in a matter of days. No major expedition of the war was prepared with greater speed.

Vicksburg was ripe for the taking, Grant assured Sherman; the garrison had been severely depleted to strengthen Pemberton's army at Grenada.[48] And while Sherman was descending the Mississippi, Grant would "hold Pemberton away from Vicksburg."[49] If Pemberton pulled back toward the Yazoo, Grant promised to "follow him even to the gates of Vicksburg."[50] It was a plan that would allow Grant to win the two battles he was fighting simultaneously: the public one against Vicksburg and the personal one against McClernand. And his old nemesis Henry Halleck was smoothing the way.

Grant ordered Sherman to proceed immediately to Memphis.[51] "I feared that delay might bring McClernand," Grant wrote later, "who was his senior, and who had authority from the President and Secretary of War to exercise that particular command—and independently. I doubted McClernand's fitness." He was "unmanageable and incompetent," Grant told Halleck.[52]

Grant kept his correspondence with Halleck from Sherman, who had no idea McClernand was "scheming" for "the honor of capturing Vicksburg." Sherman did know, however, that General Nathaniel

Banks, Benjamin Butler's replacement at New Orleans, was reported to be "working upstream from New Orleans, while we were working down." Sherman assumed Banks was heading for Port Hudson, to seize that imposing river barrier, and after taking it, would move north to Vicksburg.[53]

The morning after meeting with Grant, Sherman selected the troops of Brigadier General Morgan L. Smith, his finest fighting division, and headed for Memphis. Tecumseh was never in better spirits. "My part is exactly what I would have chose," he wrote Ellen at the time. Opening "this Great Artery" of America "is all my ambition."[54]

Sherman arrived at Memphis at noon on December 12. It was then that he began to feel the full weight of his responsibilities. Grant's plan was risky in the extreme. He seemed to have forgotten the lessons of Iuka, where a lack of coordination between elements of his army prevented him from trapping Sterling Price. Once Sherman set out from Memphis he would be cut off from telegraphic communication with Grant. How would they coordinate their movements if something went wrong at either Oxford or on the Yazoo?[55]

While Sherman was at Memphis, Halleck ordered Grant to divide his command into four corps and assign McClernand to head "that part of the army which was to operate down the Mississippi." This "is the wish of the President," he emphatically told Grant.[56] Grant promptly wrote McClernand inviting him to take command of the river expedition, *under his "direction" as theater commander.*[57] The message went out by letter, not telegram, guaranteeing its delayed delivery. Grant must have suppressed a smile when he wrote: "I hope you will find all the preliminary preparations completed on your arrival and the expedition ready to move."[58] This was two days before Sherman was scheduled to sail for Vicksburg with McClernand's recruits.

At the time, McClernand was in Illinois impatiently awaiting orders from Stanton to proceed to Memphis, but not, he hoped, before he completed final preparations for his marriage to the younger sister of his deceased wife. When no word came from Washington, he feared he had been swindled out of an independent command. "I believe I have been superseded. Please advise me," he wrote both Stanton and Lincoln.[59] After consulting Halleck, Stanton telegraphed back a few hours later. "There has been . . . no order superseding you." But the corps he now commanded, Stanton told him, was under Grant's "general supervision."[60]

McClernand had been subverted, and he knew exactly who was responsible. "I am satisfied that the President and the Sec. of War favor me as the commander of the Expedition," he wrote a political friend, "but I am persuaded the Genl in Chief is my enemy—personal enemy and senselessly so."[61] Was this to be his reward, he asked Stanton, for fielding and forwarding to Memphis fifty-seven regiments?[62]*

When Postmaster General Montgomery Blair, a friend of McClernand's, informed Lincoln at a cabinet meeting that the general was being "crowded aside" and that there was "a combination" to prevent him having command of the Mississippi expedition, Lincoln "started from his chair . . . and said it should not be so," Gideon Welles described the scene in his diary. "Stanton declared it was not so, that he and Halleck had arranged the matter that day. The President looked surprised and said he supposed it had been done long ago."[63] But it was the president and Stanton who had initially undermined McClernand by the caveat they had attached to his original orders, placing all troops he recruited under the authority of theater commander Ulysses Grant. There is no evidence that Halleck was responsible for that clause, but he had cunningly used it to undercut McClernand.

With Sherman still in Memphis, Grant began pushing slowly toward Pemberton's army on the Yalobusha, creating the impression of a "continuous" advance in order to keep the rebels from moving back toward Vicksburg.[64] Such caution didn't suit his temperament. When not moving boldly on the enemy he became unsettled, began to worry excessively, and was prone to bouts of self-pity. Oxford was a reprise of the anxious summer in Tennessee on occupation duty. "We are now having wet weather," he wrote glumly to his sister Mary on December 15. "I

---

* This was a gross exaggeration. Richard L. Kiper, McClernand's biographer, has estimated that McClernand personally recruited, at most, fifteen regiments, but that during his time in Illinois in the fall of 1862, forty-four infantry regiments were mustered. Eight of them served with Sherman in the Yazoo campaign, six others in the Vicksburg campaign of 1863. Kiper, *McClernand*, 153.

have a big army in front of me as well as bad roads. . . . I am extended now like a Peninsula into an enemy's country, with a large Army depending for their daily bread upon keeping open a line of rail-road running one hundred & ninety miles through an enemy's country. . . . With all this I suffer the mortification of seeing myself attacked right and left by people at home, professing patriotism, and love of country who never heard the whistle of a hostile bullet." [65]

Shiloh continued to shadow him, and now he was being criticized in the press for relying "upon so slender a thread, a long and single railroad through the enemy's country." [66] Grant was also troubled by rumors still circulating about his unchecked appetite for drink. To reassure Julia, he dutifully reported that he had sent Sherman a bottle of bourbon presented to him by a friend. "Myself nor no one connected with the Staff ever tasted it." [67] He missed Julia, who had stayed behind at Holly Springs, and was tempted to drink when they were separated. In her stead, Rawlins, the son of an alcoholic, "never hesitated to argue [him] off the bottle. [68] Mayor James Wilson, a teetotaler, aligned with him in an ever-going effort to keep Grant from "the clutch of the demon." [69]

At Oxford, Grant again had trouble controlling his troops. It began when the notorious Kansas cavalry entered the town, got stupidly drunk, and began robbing "the people right and left of everything they fancied," wrote correspondent Sylvanus Cadwallader. [70] When the main body of troops arrived, "many of the boys" joined in the pillage, said Ira Blanchard of the 20th Illinois. [71] They raided homes against orders, burned books in roaring bonfires, and stole horses, mules, and corn whiskey." [72]

Blanchard and his Illinois regiment stayed in Oxford for two weeks, "pillaging the town and having a fine time generally . . . when about 12 o'clock one night the 'long roll' was sounded and every man sprang to his arms." Word spread through the ranks that enemy cavalry had raided Holly Springs and "burned all the stores which had been collected there." [73] On that day, December 20, General Earl Van Dorn, defeated and disgraced at Corinth, had returned the favor, plundering and destroying Grant's Holly Springs supply station and nearly capturing Julia and Jesse Grant. Pemberton had ordered the raid on the advice of Texas cavalry officer John S. Griffith, who, unlike his commander, possessed strategic acuity.[74]

On the night of December 19, Van Dorn, known to delight in "desperate ventures," took a crack cavalry force of 3,500 men, rode northward from Grenada, swung around the Union army at Oxford, eluded a cavalry force Grant sent to intercept him, and thundered into the Holly Springs depot at dawn.[75] Before the sleepy-eyed bluecoats could strap on their suspenders, his horsemen captured 1,500 of them, nearly the entire garrison, including the humiliated post commander, Colonel Robert C. Murphy. All were instantly paroled, out of the war until they could be exchanged. (Six hundred Illinois cavalrymen cut their way out of town after refusing to surrender.)[76]

"The work of destruction was pushed with vigor," rebel cavalryman J. D. Deupree described the raid. Every horseman carried a bottle of turpentine and a box of matches. It took Van Dorn's cavalry eight hours to burn the great mountain of supplies. Local women in long nightgowns offered encouragement, "clapping their hands with joy."[77]

By late afternoon, the raiders had completed their work. Swinging their sabers in the air and puffing on confiscated Federal cigars, they let loose a screeching rebel yell and headed out. In a matter of hours they had become, said Deupree, "the best equipped body of cavalry in the Confederate service. Every trooper had from two to six pistols, one or more carbines, one or more sabers, and all the ammunition, rations, blankets, shirts, hats, boots, overcoats, etc., his horse could carry."[78] Moving north, they tore up rail tracks and created general mayhem before returning to Grenada twelve days later, having completed one of the most decisive Confederate raids of the war. Ineffective in commanding large armies, Van Dorn had found a role in the war commensurate with his élan and ability.

Julia and Jesse Grant were fortunate not to have been in Holly Springs when Van Dorn struck. Grant had invited them to come down to Oxford for a visit, and they had left the night before the raid.[79] Julia was surprised that her husband was not at the Oxford depot to meet them. As she and Jesse rode up to his headquarters, he hurried out to their carriage and apologized, saying he was "fully occupied. I have only time to kiss you," he told Julia. He had just learned that hour that

Van Dorn was heading north from Grenada along the railroad toward Holly Springs, and he was frantically telegraphing his garrison commanders to give him "a warm reception."[80]

On the morning Van Dorn struck, Chaplain John Eaton was visiting Grant when a courier handed him the message. Grant read it impassively and turned to Eaton. "People will believe that I was taken unawares and did nothing to protect my supplies . . . [but] I did all that was possible." Grant could see the newspaper headlines in his mind's eye: "Surprised again . . . Donelson! Shiloh! Holly Springs!"[81]

But this was not Shiloh. He had been alive to the danger and had prepared for it, having placed his cavalry on a round-the-clock alert for a surprise attack on his supply line.[82] When cavalry commander T. Lyle Dickey arrived at Grant's headquarters late in the afternoon of December 19 and reported that he had spotted Van Dorn moving northward from Grenada, Grant "was instantly on the alert," said reporter Sylvanus Cadwallader, who accompanied Dickey. "Without waiting for Col. Dickey to finish . . . [Grant] walked out of the house" and to the telegraph office at the railroad depot, a quarter of a mile away, where he "sent off dispatch after dispatch northward, notifying post commandants of Van Dorn's approach." This was twelve hours before Van Dorn struck Holly Springs.[83]

Two of Grant's dispatches had been sent directly to Colonel Murphy, who was having dinner and not a few drinks when word reached him. He failed to leave the table to take precautions. Later, he was dismissed from the service "for his cowardly and disgraceful conduct."[84]

Van Dorn's raid changed everything in Mississippi. To replenish what had been lost at Holly Springs, Grant would need to immediately bring in supplies by rail, but this was now impossible: Nathan Bedford Forrest had been ripping up tracks in Tennessee for five days before Van Dorn's raid. Forrest had been ordered to western Tennessee by Braxton Bragg, at the urging of Pemberton, who feared he would be unable to repel a Federal assault on his position on the Yalobusha.[85] Striking from central Tennessee with two thousand mounted men, half of them armed with only squirrel rifles and flintlocks, the former slave-trader and cotton planter outthought and outfought Union cavalry forces ten times his size. In a furious fifteen-day campaign, riding three hundred miles through pelting rain and sleet, his "critter" cavalry ripped up and twisted rail tracks, burned rail bridges, trestles, wood yards, and depots, and inflicted more than 1,500 casualties on the enemy.

The raid destroyed Grant's rail and telegraphic communications from Jackson, Tennessee, to Columbus, Kentucky, his rear supply base.[86] "This cut me off from all communication with the north for more than a week," Grant wrote later, "and it was more than two weeks before rations or forage could be issued from stores obtained in the regular way."[87] His logistical lifeline severed and forward supply base destroyed, Grant was forced to return to his starting point at the twin towns of La Grange and Grand Junction. "For the first and only time in the Civil War," wrote historian Edwin Bearss, "cavalry and cavalry alone was the decisive factor in a major campaign."[88] With fewer than six thousand mounted men, Forrest and Van Dorn had stopped the seemingly irresistible advance of the mightiest Union army in the west. For the first time in the war, Grant had gambled greatly and lost.

"It has always seemed inexplicable that General Grant retained the confidence of his Government after the failures of this campaign," Confederate general Dabney H. Maury reflected long after the war. "His mistakes were palpable, and their consequences disastrous." He had, Maury said, moved too cautiously throughout the campaign, advancing "leisurely" on Pemberton's shattered army, positioned first at Holly Springs and then on the Tallahatchie, allowing it to refit, reinforce, and reorganize. Then, leaving an incompetent in charge of his main supply station, he allowed Van Dorn to strike his "unguarded" depot and terminate his campaign in northern Mississippi. "What was the mysterious influence of this man over his Government, that he was treated with unabated confidence after such flagrant . . . incapacity?"[89]

The answer was, Forts Henry and Donelson, Shiloh, Iuka, and Corinth. Lincoln had no general near his equal in the west.

The retreat began the morning after Van Dorn hit Holly Springs. That raid, argued Major James Wilson, now Grant's chief topographical officer, "really had but little effect" on Grant's decision. "It had already become apparent that a campaign in midwinter over muddy roads and through poor country was not feasible for the force then in the field."[90] That may be, but Grant had blundered badly in planning his Mississippi invasion. His plan to use a railroad as the sole supply line for forty thousand men was "radically wrong," concluded the nineteenth-century military historian Colonel William R. Livermore; and he and his scouts should have known that the roads in Mississippi were "proverbially bad in winter, and truly so in the eastern part of the state."[91]

On December 23, Grant tried to warn Sherman by courier that he would be unable to cooperate with him.[92] With Pemberton no longer pinned down, the rebels could reinforce Vicksburg. The message never reached Sherman, who was on the river, a day away from his destination. He would be steaming "straight into a trap."[93]

Grant expected a miserable retreat through war-depleted northern Mississippi, with his men stalked by hunger. The weather remained horrid—cold rain and high winds—and he was still convinced, when planning the retreat, that a large army on the move could not be supplied by the countryside. But at Oxford, just before he began his withdrawal, he learned that this thinly populated part of northeastern Mississippi could provide his army food and forage aplenty. All that was required was some hard persuading.

On the advice of his field commanders, he began sending organized foraging parties to bring in provisions from an area fifteen miles east and west of the main roads north of Oxford.[94] Mills for grinding corn were "set to work and kept running night and day," wrote James Wilson, producing fresh cornbread and cornmeal; and "fat stock [were] driven in and slaughtered by thousands."[95] Grant was "amazed" to discover that his army could have "subsisted off the country for two months instead of two weeks." This was a lesson he would draw upon the following spring, in the final stages of his Vicksburg campaign.[96]

Grant took quiet satisfaction from these foraging expeditions. The news of Van Dorn's raid had, he wrote later, caused "much rejoicing among the people remaining in Oxford. They came with broad smiles on their faces . . . to ask what I was going to do now without anything for my soldiers to eat." Grant claimed not to be concerned. He had already, he said, begun to send troops and wagons to collect all they could gather from local farms and homesteads. "What are *we* to do?" the leader of a group of protesters inquired. "I advised them to emigrate east, or west, fifteen miles and assist in eating up what we left."[97]

In his memoirs, Grant described a foraging campaign conducted in a humane and orderly manner, with raiding parties under orders to leave "two months' supplies for the families of those whose stores were taken." [98] His soldiers told a different story. "As soon as our tents were pitched at night," recalled Ira Blanchard, "scores of the boys would strike out with their guns and shoot whatever was eatable." [99] When they had picked the land clean, there was "not enough left to feed fifty chickens," said Charles Wills. [100] The officers "would make some pretense of opposition . . . but their efforts to prevent it were . . . feeble," Blanchard added. [101]

Grant had put his men on half rations for the march back to Tennessee: nothing but hard crackers. "If it was not for the cattle & hogs we kill," Chicago soldier Florison D. Pitts wrote his parents, "we would be in a pretty hard fix, but at every stopping place we immediately start for the plantations and take whatever we can get. Generally find molasses sweet potatoes corn meal and honey. . . . So you see there is no danger of our starving." Foraging was followed by burning. "On our night marches," wrote Pitts, ". . . the country for miles appears to be one mass of fire. [It spreads out] in all directions for miles presenting some of the grandest sights I ever saw." [102]

Sergeant Samuel Byers was assigned to one of Grant's raiding parties. He would later serve with Sherman on his March to the Sea and would afterward describe these Mississippi raids as forerunners of Tecumseh's infamous forage parties in Georgia and South Carolina. Byers and his squad would go out every evening into a Mississippi countryside blasted by war, houses and barns "gone—burned by raiders of both armies . . . The army wagons, in long trains, and the soldiers in great strung-out columns of blue, go over the soft ground across the fields . . . almost in silence." When they came upon a farm that showed signs of life, they loaded their wagons with the aid of slaves, who would quietly appear and then follow them back to their camps. A dozen to twenty men acted as guards on these raids. They were needed. Guerrilla bands prowled the scarred land and killed on sight.

Byers, an observant young lawyer, had spent months on a Mississippi plantation before the war, where he had seen up close "the horrors" of slavery. On the march back to La Grange, he was silently thrilled to see the "procession" of black refugees following the army, some of them, however, with hands and feet, and even tongues, hacked off by fiendish masters, a river of sufferers escaping a life of powerlessness. The women bore their bundles on their heads and their "pickininees under their arms."[103]

Hunger, not freedom, had lured many of them to the Union lines. Last to be fed after a Yankee foraging raid were the slaves. They were "all hungry many a time," they told their liberators.[104] When the leader of a group of refugees was asked if her people had come in pursuit of freedom, she replied sharply: "Freedom! . . . We never hear nothing like it. We's starvn' an' we come to get somefin' to eat."[105]

Some of the slaves who encountered Grant's armies chose to stay on the plantation, preferring the known to the disquieting unknown. "Who could be sure that the brutal uncertainties of life trailing an army on the march were preferable to the meager securities of life on a plantation," writes historian James Oakes.[106] But soldier testimony points to one telling fact: "the negroes believe we came as their deliverers."[107] White Southerners testified to that. "There is no denying the fact that the Union invasion of the south has been a 'John Brown raid' on a grand scale," declared the *Richmond Dispatch*.[108]

By the time the last of Grant's regiments had crossed the border into Tennessee, Mississippi state officials estimated that the majority of slaves in the northern border counties had run away.

The slaves who found it most difficult to escape were those who had to travel great distances to the Union armies, eluding citizen "pickets" that patrolled the roads with snarling bloodhounds.[109] But while the patrols controlled the roads, most slaves were intimately familiar with the backcountry: the swamps, river bottoms, and forests in which they cut timber for their owners, hunted squirrels to supplement their meatless diet, and took shortcuts to carry messages to neighboring plantations. "My friend [was] the forest," recalled the escaped slave John Parker.[110]

These were the perilous routes to freedom for the most audacious slaves, with the forces of the country arrayed against them, white men determined that property remain property.[111] This is how Mississippi slaves were freed in the last months of 1862: not by a president's proclamation but by the strength of his armies—that and their own smoldering resolve to escape the long night of slavery. Once within Federal lines, Lincoln's laws guaranteed their freedom.[112]

The healthiest slaves were put to work as army cooks, male nurses, laundresses, and laborers. All others were eventually shipped to one of Eaton's contraband camps. "When they first came in they had as tough a time as any set of human beings I ever saw, for they were without any shelter or bedding and only half clad," observed Edwin Witherby Brown, an Ohio soldier at Eaton's Corinth camp. ". . . They had to take the winter like cattle" until crude pine cabins could be constructed. "It was pitiful. . . . Hundreds were helpless with acute inflammatory troubles of all sorts, and every day there was a long death list—a dozen funerals in progress all the time." A work gang that Brown supervised "had been so terribly abused, beaten, and branded that they were no better than beasts, and could hardly tell their own names and not half of them had any idea about their own age." They had been branded on their thighs, leaving "deep red scars." Brown thought Harriet Beecher Stowe's Simon Legree "a saint as compared to the owner of these slaves," who, Brown said, he would have happily shot.[113]

Grant left northern Mississippi a "blackened waste," wrote Jane Pickett, the wife of a well-set-up Delta planter. But his army did much more than pillage and burn. It ignited, unwittingly, a social upheaval, the first major threat to the culture of plantation slavery in the cotton empire. And Mississippians knew that the Yankees would be back, and soon.

This was a signal to leave their homes. The Pickett family lived far south of Grant's invasion route, but that December they planned to move to Georgia with their "best negroes." Jane's husband went about packing "as if preparing for his funeral." Jane's letters to her Virginia kin describe the beginning of what would become "a perfect stampede" of masters and their most valued slaves to other states.[114] "I am the only one of my acquaintance who had not . . . attempted to . . . move [my slaves]," wrote a Mississippi planter.[115]

Some slaves refused to move, fleeing at the "first hint of transfer." Hundreds escaped to the woods and returned after their owners had left to run the farms on their own.[116] They were the exception. Most chose accommodation over outright resistance, but this did not equal acquiescence. Slaves who remained with their owners were suddenly more difficult to control. The Yankees were near, and the slaves played upon their owners' fears to extract unprecedented liberties.[117] There is "a disposition on the part of our slaves to do as they please," wrote a concerned Mississippi newspaper editor.[118] A black maid brazenly announced to her mistress: "Answering bells is played out."[119]

Less willing to use the lash for fear their slaves would leave, plantation mistresses, managing farms without men, "resorted to previously unthinkable measures" to get their slaves to work.[120] Emboldened by the Yankee invasion, Elsy, a domestic slave, threatened to flee unless her mistress, Elizabeth Meade Ingraham, paid her wages: $12 a month and provisions for her and her four children. "It seems big wages . . . but I know her ways and she mine, besides she is strictly honest and true, a rare thing in a black," Mrs. Ingraham wrote in her diary.[121] Other masters offered a shorter workweek, exemption from corporal punishment, or enhanced freedom of movement. Some cornered owners promised manumission in return for labor. A Mississippi slave testified after the war that his master "told us we were free to go or stay, as we chose. If we remained at home we were to have half the cotton we raised."[122]

"Our negroes are restless and hard to please," the Reverend Samuel A. Agnew noted in his diary. A Presbyterian minister and cotton farmer in northern Mississippi, Agnew had eleven of his "faithless" slaves "stampede" to the Yankees just before and during Grant's invasion. They were, "ungrateful and hypocritical wretche[s]," he wrote. More galling, those who remained behind no longer hid their feelings of discontent, becoming "insolent and insulting." Agnew was convinced he was witnessing the beginning of the end of slavery in his home state, a revolution brought on by armies as ruthless, he declaimed, as the Vandals and Visigoths.[123]

President Davis fed these fears. In his Emancipation Proclamation, Lincoln enjoined newly freed slaves "to abstain from all violence, unless in necessary self-defence."[124] Davis interpreted that clause—"necessary self-defence"—as a call for "contented laborers" to slay their masters and commence "servile war."[125] Newspaper reactions were equally extreme and rose to high hysteria in Mississippi when a group of slaves near Oxford revolted, drove off their overseers, and divided the plantation property among themselves. There were no more uprisings, but fears of racial reprisals persisted. Laws limiting black people's freedom of movement were tightened and citizen patrols took to the roads day and night.[126]

Agnew's mission as an itinerant preacher took him all over northern Mississippi, and wherever he visited there was excited talk of slave rebellion.[127] Local newspapers assailed Lincoln for "inviting the negroes to the commission of any atrocity which their brutal passions may suggest."[128] Traveling through the South in the spring of 1861, British reporter William Howard Russell noted that plantation masters had "the smallest appreciation of a servile insurrection. They use the universal formula 'Our slaves are the happiest, most contented, and most comfortable people on the face of the earth.'"[129] Less than two years later these "contented" souls were as feared in Mississippi as the Yankee intruders, all the more because they comprised 55 percent of the state's population.*

To calm fears of a "servile" insurrection, the Confederate States Congress had passed that October the so-called "twenty negro law," which exempted from military service one able-bodied male on every plantation with twenty or more slaves. White managers were needed at home, it was argued, to control an alarmingly restless slave population.[130] But men with few or no slaves resented the statute. "Never did a law meet with more universal odium than the exemption of slave-owners," Mississippi senator James Phelan wrote his friend Jefferson Davis. ". . . Its influence upon the poor is most calamitous."[131] The planters' war to preserve slavery had become a poor man's fight. At a time when white Mississippians of all classes needed to cohere to meet the ever-growing Yankee threat, Lincoln by his proclamation, and Grant by his invasion, had created deep divisions.

By pushing, virtually unchallenged, deep into Mississippi, Grant

---

* In 1860, Mississippi had a total population of 791,305; 436,631 were slaves. The state had 30,943 slaveholders. Forty-nine percent of white families owned slaves, the highest percentage in the Confederacy. U.S. Eighth Census, I, 270.

had also shaken public confidence in Pemberton's army; doubts about its capacity lingered even after Van Dorn's spirit-raising raid. Was this army—which seemed to know only defeat and retreat—capable of saving Vicksburg? And did the citizenry have the resolve to fight a war to the last against an enemy of "malignant ferocity," to use Jefferson Davis's phrase? [132]

Senator Phelan, whose mansion Grant had passed on his march to the Tallahatchie, had his doubts, and he expressed them in a letter to Davis on December 9, while Grant was still in Mississippi. It was a glum assessment of the state of his state. Grant's invasion had brought "an Iliad of woes," he told Davis. The army "is in a most deplorable state, as to its morale and organization." Pemberton had not "impressed himself, either upon the people or the Army." His retreat from the Tallahatchie was "a staggering blow." The citizenry, Phelan wrote, were as dispirited as the soldiers. And they were taking the hardest blows. Where was the Vicksburg intransigency of the previous summer? "The spirit of enlistment is thrice dead. Enthusiasm has expired to a cold pile of damp ashes. Defeats—retreats—sufferings . . . are rapidly producing a sense of settled despair . . . I imagine but one event," said Phelan, "that could awaken from its waning spark, the enthusiastic hopes and energy of Mississippians. Plant your own foot upon our soil,—unfurl your banner at the head of the army." [133]

Davis, it turned out, had already decided to go to Mississippi, "the land of my affections." [134] Governor Pettus had pleaded with him on the first of the month to "visit the army of the west. . . . Something must be done to inspire confidence." And Davis had agreed to come. "I propose to go out there immediately . . . to arouse all classes to united and desperate resistance," he wrote Robert E. Lee on December 8. Two days later he left Richmond by train. [135]

When Ulysses Grant's army reached Holly Springs, "the flags were unfurled," wrote Seneca Thrall, "and the band struck, 'De Lincum Gun Boats Come Dis Way.'" It was Christmas Eve. "I would hang up my stockings," Thrall wrote his wife, "only that for the past four or five nights I have not taken them off at night." The next day, McPherson's pioneer corps sent Grant and his staff a Christmas dinner of roast turkeys, meat

pies, baked bread, hominy, and stewed fruits.[136] Grant politely refused
the feast and headed for Memphis to began planning another assault on
Vicksburg. He had yet to hear from Sherman. "I am now feeling great
anxiety about Vicksburg," he wrote Elihu Washburne on January 7.[137]
Later that day, Grant received a telegram from Halleck. The Richmond
papers were reporting a rebel victory at Vicksburg.[138] Two days later the
news came like a knife to the heart: Sherman had been repulsed. It was
confirmed. "His loss was small," Grant telegraphed Halleck. "Will send
you the particulars as soon learned." [139]

CHAPTER 12

The Chickasaw Slaughter Pen

*"No engagement in which I was afterward involved impressed
me with the nightmarish sensations of this one."* [1]
—Private Charles Willison, 76th Ohio

Admiral Porter arrived in Memphis on his flagship, *Black Hawk*, on
December 18, two days before Sherman was scheduled to leave for
Vicksburg. He brought with him the ironclad *Louisville* and two tinclads. The remainder of his squadron was already downriver probing
enemy defenses on the Yazoo. They would return to escort the transports. "General McClernand is not heard of at all," Porter notified
Gideon Welles. "He has never communicated with me in any manner. I
shall be ready also to cooperate with him when he comes; none of them
shall complain of want of assistance." [2]

Porter sent word to Sherman that he would meet him at his headquarters at the Gayoso House, the finest hotel in town. [3] The high-
spirited admiral was pacing the hotel's reception room when Sherman
came bounding in two hours late, apologizing for having kept him waiting. He had been supervising the loading of his transports. "Thinking
it probable that Sherman would be dressed in full feather, I put on my
uniform coat," Porter recalled, "the splendor of which rivaled that of a
drum-major." Sherman wore a plain blue flannel uniform, splattered
with mud and grease. He was hatless and his short-cropped crimson
hair was wildly askew. "Halloo, Porter," he bellowed, his eyes beaming.
"I am glad to see you. . . . Devilish cold, isn't it? Sit down and warm
up," he said, as he stirred the coals in the fireplace with a poker.

This was their first meeting, but Sherman found it hard to give Porter his full attention. A crush of aides began dashing in and out of the
reception room in quick succession, as Sherman barked out orders to

be sent to everyone from his quartermaster to the steamboat captains. When the last aide departed, Sherman collapsed into a chair. He had been up since three in morning making final preparations. "Glad to see you, Porter; how's Grant?" he barked, lighting one of the dozen or so cigars he smoked daily.[4]

Porter liked Sherman immediately. He was plainspoken and furiously energetic; and "he talked to me as if he had known me all his life."[5]

Porter brought good news. He had sent his war boats up the Yazoo and found only one formidable battery, and it was far up the river, beyond where the fleet planned to land the army. There were no other batteries within twenty-three miles of the mouth of the slow-flowing Yazoo. Rebel pickets had fired on the Union boats, but these were quickly scattered by their heavy guns. Vicksburg looked unprepared for trouble.[6]

Nor would Sherman have to worry about the naval mines—called "torpedoes"—the rebels had planted in the river.*[7] A squadron of warships had destroyed or removed the "infernal machines," clearing the way for the invasion fleet. But in dragging the river for torpedoes, the Mississippi Squadron lost *Cairo*, one of Eads's seven original ironclads. Two thunderous explosions almost lifted the boat out of the water, and she sank in twelve minutes. The ram *Queen of the West* rescued the crew before the gunboat went down. Miraculously, not a sailor was lost, and only a half-dozen were injured, Porter informed Sherman.[8]

It was a short conversation. Sherman was scheduled to meet with his division commanders. He had complete confidence in two of them: Morgan Smith, who had been serving under him for some time; and A. J. "Whiskey" Smith, a hard-drinking disciplinarian like himself. He knew little about George Washington Morgan, a headstrong Ohio lawyer sent from Don Carlos Buell's Army of the Ohio. A citizen soldier, he had commanded troops valorously in Kentucky under Buell.

---

* These friction-activated engines of destruction were crudely designed. A common five-gallon glass demijohn was filled with black powder, and an artillery friction primer was inserted into the neck. An anchor with a rope attached to it kept the device in place on the river bottom. A wooden float made the device buoyant, allowing it to float below the surface of the water. A copper wire inside the demijohn provided a spark. A boat hitting the wire exerted sufficient pressure on the friction primer to cause the demijohn to explode.

Sherman's pressing concern was the troop transports. There were only fifteen of them at Memphis, but at least sixty were needed. "I only await the fleet of Transport to be off," he wrote Grant that morning.[9] Grant had things under control. He had already wired Robert Allen, the chief quartermaster at St. Louis, requesting every transport he could rush to Memphis. Allen had only eight boats available in St. Louis, but he dispatched Colonel Lewis B. Parsons to round up the fleet of river steamers Sherman needed. A graduate of Yale College and Harvard Law School, and former president of the Ohio and Mississippi Railroad, the uncommonly efficient Parsons was in charge of Union river and rail transportation in the Mississippi Valley.[10] The unsung hero of Grant's river expeditions in the west, he had provided the steamboats that carried the Army of the Tennessee swiftly and without a hitch to Paducah, Belmont, Forts Henry and Donelson, and Pittsburg Landing. He was the Union's great "mover of armies."[11]

Parsons went out himself on the Ohio and Tennessee Rivers and seized boats from private steamship companies. There was no time to haggle with private operators for their purchase; he simply confiscated them for wartime service, promising compensation if the boats were not returned or were seriously damaged.[12] In five days, Parsons performed a logistical miracle, assembling at Memphis, 450 miles from St. Louis, sixty-seven fully fueled steamers.[13] They arrived the day after Porter dropped anchor, "almost by magic," and by midnight the first group of troops was embarked and heading downriver with colors flying and drums beating—and, by one account, with men and officers "nearly all lively with drink."[14]

At daybreak, Parsons joined Sherman on his headquarters boat, *Queen of the West*. He would personally supervise the transports all the way to Vicksburg.[15] "General Sherman . . . makes things move," Parsons wrote Halleck. "I like his business mode of doing things, his promptness and decision."[16]

Sherman left Memphis with twenty thousand troops, and he would pick up another thirteen thousand, under Brigadier General Frederick Steele, at Helena, Arkansas. It was a strong force, but "dont [sic] expect me to achieve miracles," Sherman wrote his brother John. "Vicksburg is . . . well fortified and is within telegraphic & railroad reach of . . . Grenada," where Pemberton had an army ready to spring to the relief of the fortress city.[17] Sherman hoped to catch the Vicksburg garrison by surprise, but there was no chance of that. The Confederates had cavalry scouts and guerrilla bands on both sides of the river, from Memphis to the Yazoo, and Porter's gunboats had been on the Yazoo for weeks, fully exposed, exploding torpedoes and skirmishing with enemy sharpshooters. Memphis itself was also crawling with rebel spies and informers. To tighten security, Sherman issued orders banning reporters from the boats. If any were found—and plenty had snuck aboard—they were to be arrested and conscripted into the army. A scribe writing anything for publication would be charged with espionage.[18]

When the fleet stopped for the night at Helena to pick up Steele's division, Sherman met with Brigadier General Francis Blair Jr., an old acquaintance from St. Louis. Blair had received orders direct from Lincoln to report to Helena to join McClernand's river expedition. Having heard nothing from McClernand, he hooked up with Sherman, who was eager to have him. His family carried weight with the president and War Democrats in Congress. The younger brother of Postmaster General Montgomery Blair and son of newspaper editor Francis Preston Blair, longtime advisor to presidents going back to Andrew Jackson, he belonged to the most influential political family in the country. The Missouri Blairs were Lincoln loyalists, conservative counterbalances to the growing power of the Radical Republicans. They owned slaves but opposed the spread of slavery to new territories. The patriarch had been one of the founders of the Republican Party and his son and namesake had been instrumental in preventing his home state from seceding in 1861. Tall and thickset, with reddish hair and a long flowing mustache, Frank Jr., was "handsome and commanding," with an "outward calmness" that disguised "tremendous force," wrote reporter Franc Wilkie, one of a number of reporters who had boarded a troop transport in defiance of Sherman's order.[19] The summer before joining Sherman at Helena Blair had resigned his seat as a United States congressman from Missouri and raised a brigade to liberate Vicksburg.[20]

Hours before the expedition set out, Sherman received word that Grant's supply depot at Holly Springs had been laid waste by rebel cavalry. Sherman wired Grant for confirmation, but the message didn't get through; Grant's communications had yet to be restored.[21]

At the break of day on December 22, all vessels assembled at Friars Point, just below Helena. The signal gun was fired and the great fleet—125 transports, gunboats, and supply vessels—set out for the Yazoo, with Porter, on *Black Hawk*, in the lead. "It was a grand and glorious sight to see the whole fleet moving downstream," a Chicago soldier proudly wrote his father. "As far as the eye could see the whole fleet, a sea of boats meets your gaze, and when one boat passes another, a loud hurrah is heard from the boat that goes ahead."[22] Confidence ran strong. "I wish you could see these gunboats," another soldier wrote home. "They are powerful looking monsters and look so they could walk thro' the 'jaws of death.'"[23] How could the rebels hold up against this assemblage of machine age might?

The troops passed around newspaper copies of the Emancipation Proclamation and hotly debated its merits: "It is endorsed in the Army generally," wrote Henry C. Bear of rural Illinois. Soldier talk was animated by alcohol.[24] Some enterprising men had filled their canteens with cheap whiskey back at Memphis, "enough," said a Missouri correspondent on board, "to keep them drunk for two days." Most of their officers drank and gambled "day and night."[25]

The riverbanks were desolate below Friars Point, monotonous, forested flatlands submerged by the river's seasonal overflow. For most of the journey the only signs of life were slaves standing on the levees waving and shouting to the river pilots, pleading to be taken aboard.[26]

On December 23, two days upriver from Vicksburg, Sherman issued each of his four division commanders—George W. Morgan, A. J. Smith, M. L. Smith, and Frederick Steele—a hand-drawn map of the Vicksburg region. It was bundled with a circular letter outlining the plan of operations.

> Our object is to secure the navigation of the Mississippi River and its main branches. . . . The enemy still holds the river from Vicksburg and Baton Rouge, navigating it with his boats, and possession of it enables him to connect his communications and routes of supply, east and west. To deprive him of this will be a severe blow, and, if done effectually, will "probably [be] the most decisive act of the war.

"To accomplish this important result," the letter continued, "we are to act our part, an important one of the great *whole*. General Banks, with a large force . . . is coming northward" intending to take Port Hudson and move upriver to Vicksburg. "General Grant . . . is moving southward. The naval squadron (Admiral Porter) is operating with his gunboat fleet by water, each in perfect harmony with the other." Any breakdown in his symphony of converging forces, Sherman made it clear, would kill any hopes for victory.[27]

The officers had their instructions; the enlisted men had none. Some were completely in the dark. "I have not the least idea where we are going, or what we are to do," an Illinois boy wrote his father.[28] Even the generals had no clear idea of what awaited them in the Yazoo swamps. Although Porter's boats had been operating on the Yazoo River since the early summer of 1862, landing parties had not been sent out to reconnoiter its nearly impenetrable terrain.

The following evening the expedition arrived at Milliken's Bend, Louisiana, twelve miles above the mouth of the Yazoo, "a dreary, unwholesome stream," a reporter from *Harper's Weekly* described it, "its pale-green, sickly-waters having their origin in swamps, and being so fatal to health that it is well named . . . the 'River of Death.'"[29]

It was Christmas Eve. The troops spent the night aboard the brightly lit transports. Regimental bands played holiday music, soldiers sang carols to dampen their fears, and there were impromptu patriotic addresses fueled by alcohol.[30]

That evening Confederate president Jefferson Davis was in Grenada conferring with John Pemberton. He had arrived in Vicksburg five days earlier, via Chattanooga (where he had met with General Bragg), and had spent two days inspecting the hill city defenses with General Joseph Johnston before entraining to Grenada. Pemberton was eager to see him, but had to interrupt their meeting when one of his cavalry commanders rode into camp with news that a Union fleet had passed Friars Point two days earlier.[31] Pemberton had already been receiving reports of heavy Union traffic on the river below Memphis and had sent a brigade to Vicksburg by rail.[32] He immediately sent another, Tennesseans under Brigadier General John Gregg. Later that night, he learned that the enemy's gunboats had arrived at the mouth of the Yazoo and that "his transports [were] not far behind." [33]

The unsuspecting citizens of Vicksburg were notified by wire on Christmas Eve, before Pemberton's reinforcements arrived. The rebels had a telegraph station at De Soto Point, just across the river from the city, manned by Colonel Philip H. Fall. Fall was connected by wire with a station sixty-five miles upriver, near Lake Providence, Louisiana, on the property of a local planter. About 8:45 P.M., a tiny black girl showed up at that station and asked the operator, Major L. L. Daniel, to come outside. She had heard "a boat coming." It was a "monster," Daniel recalled years later, and it was coming around a bend just upriver from the station. Close behind were seven more "black devil[s]" and "fifty-nine transports 'chock full of men." Daniel rushed back to his hut and clicked out a warning to De Soto Point.

The sky was pitch-dark and streaked with lightning, and there were whitecaps on the river, but Philip Fall had to chance it. He untied his small skiff, rowed to the other side, and raced to the Greek Revival mansion of Dr. William Balfour and his wife, Emma. They were hosting a gala ball for the ranking officers serving under General M. L. Smith, still commander of the Vicksburg garrison. "I was muddy and woe begone as . . . I passed through the dancers and they gave . . . me wide berth," Fall wrote later. General Smith eyed the breathless messenger suspiciously and asked what he wanted. "I told him eighty-one gunboats and transports had passed Lake Providence and were still passing." Smith quieted the orchestra and announced: "This ball is at the end. The enemy are coming down the river." [34]

On Christmas morning Smith appointed South Carolinian Stephen Dill Lee to defend the Walnut Hills, a line bluffs that began on the northern edge of the city and faced the Yazoo River. The Federals were believed to be heading there.

Brigadier General Lee was a West Point graduate who had recently arrived in the city from R. E. Lee's Army of Northern Virginia. This would be his first command of an army under fire. He was twenty-nine years old, bland and taciturn, but had a record of resourcefulness in battle. And he didn't lack confidence. Back in November he had written his friend E. Porter Alexander, Robert E. Lee's chief artilleryman:

"The Yankees can never . . . take Vicksburg." The city commanded the heights over both the Yazoo and the Mississippi, and "our batteries are strong."[35] Upon arriving in Vicksburg he inspected the heights and knew he had not misspoken.

The Walnut Hills followed the serpentine course of the Yazoo and terminated at two rugged promontories whose guns commanded the river: Haynes' Bluff and Snyder's Bluff. Lee moved three thousand men and two batteries from their encampments along the Mississippi to marshy, heavily forested land below the hills. This force included two veteran regiments that had rallied to the city's defense against Farragut: William Pitt Chambers's 46th Mississippi Infantry and Colonel Winchester Hall's 26th Louisiana. "At 3 o'clock A. M. on the 25th we were aroused by the 'long roll' and ordered to proceed at once to man the fortifications above the city," Chambers recalled in his postwar memoir.[36] This was not quite right. There were no fortifications on the Yazoo, except for those on Haynes' and Snyder's Bluffs. The rebel defenders would have to dig rifle pits with their bayonets, "being the only implements at hand."[37] As General Lee noted later: "Not a spade of dirt had been thrown up along this entire line and there were no entrenchments nor covered batteries."[38]

Lee erected his main defensive line at the base of the Walnut Hills, not on top of them, as some historians claim. It was an inspired decision: Positioning his big guns on the bluffs would have created a "dead angle"—a place just below the hills that his artillerymen could not reach, giving the enemy an opportunity to carry the rebel position by scaling the heights.[39] Lee emplaced rifle pits and artillery stands on a strip of slightly elevated tableland—a kind of shelf—extending along the bottom of the bluffs and facing an uncultivated cottonfield that provided clear lines of fire.

The Walnut Hills—or Chickasaw Bluffs, as the Yankees called them—"were scarred all the way up with rifle-trenches and the crowns of the principal hills presented heavy batteries," Sherman would write in his after-action report.[40] He was mistaken, imagining fortifications "where none existed," wrote General Lee. There were only a few hurriedly dug rifle pits at the tops of the hills, and there were no cannon.[41]

Lee counted on the tangled terrain between the hills and the river to put his defenders in a strongly advantageous position. Behind the cot-

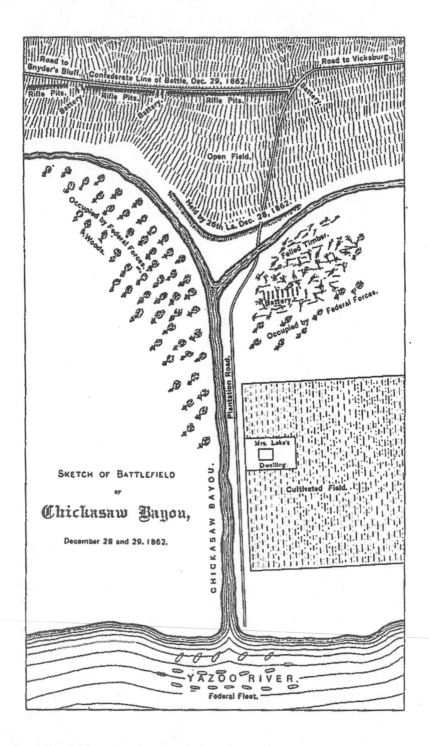

Road to Snyder's Bluff.

Confederate Line of Battle, Dec. 29, 1862.

Road to Vicksburg.

Rifle Pits.   Battery   Rifle Pits.   Battery   Rifle Pits.   Battery

Open Field.

Occupied by Federal Forces.

Woods.

Held by 26th La. Dec. 28, 1862.

Felled Timber.

Battery

Occupied by Federal Forces.

Plantation Road.

CHICKASAW BAYOU.

Mrs. Lake's Dwelling.

Cultivated Field.

SKETCH OF BATTLEFIELD

OF

Chickasaw Bayou,

December 28 and 29, 1862.

YAZOO RIVER.

Federal Fleet.

tonfield was a triangle of low wetland about five miles wide. The base of the triangle was the Walnut Hills and its apex was a labyrinth of bayous, sloughs, and stagnant lakes—a "dismal swamp," Admiral Porter would call it.[42] The largest of the waterways was a sluggish stream called Chickasaw Bayou, deep enough in places "to drown a man on horseback." The heavy timber between the bayous and the open ground in front of the bluffs had been felled and woven into an abatis—sharpened tree limbs stacked in a dense crisscross pattern, with the pointed ends facing the river.[43]

Lee's deployment, however, was as vulnerable as it was formidable. Should the Federals somehow reach the Walnut Hills in force, the rebel defenders would be in an untenable position: The bluff behind them formed an "insuperable barrier" to their escape. But nature gave the defenders compensating advantages. As Chickasaw Bayou flowed toward the bluffs, it split left and right, forming an open Y. This acted like a moat, shielding rebel gunners on the shelf beneath the bluffs.[44] Lee further strengthened his position by placing field guns and sharpshooters on the flanks of the triangle, poised to unleash withering enfilading fire on Yankee assault teams.

The shape of the terrain gave the rebels yet another advantage. The swamp narrowed markedly at the apex of the triangle, near Chickasaw Bayou. The passageways from the bayou to the bluffs were only wide enough to accommodate two soldiers moving side by side. The terrain was thus perfectly architected to funnel the assailants into the sight lines of the defenders at the base of the bluffs. General Lee planned to turn these cramped avenues of advance into slaughter pens.

He shrewdly placed his heaviest concentration of firepower at the center of the line, facing Chickasaw Bayou, hoping to lure the Yankees to this place where the two natural features of the land—the shelf and the moat-like bayou—formed a nearly impenetrable barricade for advancing infantry. In the battle to come, Lee would fight entirely on the defensive, the only way his smaller army could hope to prevail. Finally, Lee placed a signal station on the highest point of the bluffs, with a commanding view of the constricted battlefield. From here, officers with spyglasses could spot every enemy movement and call in crushing fire.

Other parts of the Yazoo bottomland were covered with a heavy growth of tall cypress trees, whose limbs were interlaced and draped with hanging moss, which gave them "a most gloomy appearance," wrote Thomas Knox, one of a handful of Northern reporters who defied Sherman's orders and sailed with the fleet. "The forest floor was covered with tangled undergrowth, and the limbs of the intersecting trees shut out the light, on the few occasions when the sun shone."[45]

The rebels would force Sherman to fight in this impossible place, where he would have to contend with two enemies: the secessionists and the swamp; and where the triangulated battlefield was so constricted he would be able to use only half his army "to good effect."[46] He had no choice. To attack Vicksburg from its Mississippi riverfront would have been to play to the town's greatest strength: its water batteries and precipitous cliffs. Landing farther up the Yazoo and attacking from there presented even greater problems than the swamp or the water batteries. The rebels had erected heavy cannon on Haynes' Bluff and two adjacent ridges, and had placed an enormous submerged raft in the river to prevent Sherman's amphibious force from proceeding farther up the Yazoo to dry ground behind Vicksburg, exactly where he wanted to be.

The Walnut Hills were the softest spot in the Vicksburg defense line. That's how it looked on the map Sherman had distributed to his commanders. But the Yazoo swamp failed to show its menacing face on paper. Nor did Sherman expect the enemy to be furiously preparing for him.

The rebel fortifications were only half completed on Christmas Day, and most of the reinforcements ordered to the town had yet to arrive. Had Sherman steamed into the Yazoo that morning, he would probably have taken the place.[47] "No man ever had so fine an opportunity given to him as Sherman had on this occasion," wrote rebel general Dabney Maury.[48]

Sherman would have liked to have moved directly on the city on Christmas Day but was hamstrung by orders from Halleck. Before assaulting Vicksburg, he was to land a raiding party on De Soto Point and destroy a section of the Vicksburg, Shreveport & Texas Railroad, severing the city's iron artery to Texas longhorns and salt deposits in

Lousiana. A brigade from A. J. Smith's division was given the job.[49] "It was a very nice Christmas spree for us tearing up the track," Private Henry C. Bear wrote home, but floodwaters had already washed out most of the key railroad bridges.[50] The raid had been unnecessary, and the delay allowed General Lee urgently needed time to prepare.

All of Christmas Day the fleet lay anchored at the entrance to the Yazoo, with the troops lounging about listlessly. Late that evening, Sherman issued the order all were awaiting: They would enter the Yazoo at eight the next morning. "Immediately all was life and activity."[51] It was "bitterly cold, dark and raining" when the rebel lookouts spotted Porter's black behemoths leading a procession of transports upriver.[52] Around noon, Sherman's headquarters boat tied up to the banks of the abandoned plantation of Captain W. A. Johnson and found himself in a place "as desolate as the dark side of the moon."[53]

At that exact hour, forty miles away, Jefferson Davis was speaking in the legislative chambers of the golden-domed capital building at Jackson. The galleries were packed, and flanking Davis on the rostrum were Governor Pettus and Senator Phelan, the two men who had implored him to come to Mississippi. Davis spoke first of the enemy: "You have been involved in a war waged for . . . your conquest and your subjugation, with a malignant ferocity and with a disregard and contempt of the usages of civilization entirely unequal in history. Such, I have ever warned you, were the characteristics of the northern people. . . . Were it ever to be proposed again to enter into a Union with such people, I could no more consent to do it than to trust myself in a den of thieves."

He then paused to accept the applause of the galleries, looking up at spectators, his gray eyes luminous, though one was sightless. Tall, bent, and reed thin, he looked frail and careworn, but his words were iron. He was there to rally "his Mother Mississippi" to its patriotic duties. "You in Mississippi have but little experienced as yet the horrors of war. You have seen but little of the savage manner in which it is waged by your barbarous enemies." But now "[your] soil is invaded," your cities "menaced. . . . Immense navies have been constructed, vast armies have been accumulated, for the purpose of crushing out the rebellion. . . .

"The issue before us is one of no ordinary character. . . . Will you be slaves or will you be independent? . . . Will you . . . be content to be robbed of your property; to be reduced to provincial dependence?"

He ended on an upbeat note. With Vicksburg threatened again, he had "perfect confidence" in the Southern patriots defending it. They were a small force, but they would soon be reinforced; he had already ordered Johnston to send brigades from Bragg's army in Tennessee. And, as always in battle, it was spirit not numbers that truly mattered. "I go therefore, anxious but hopeful." [54]

Had William Tecumseh Sherman possessed a copy of Davis's speech he might have used it to impress upon his men that were facing a people who had shown "no symptoms of a relaxation of their fierce energy." [55] And they would fight them in a place where the enemy possessed every advantage except numbers. "They will be hard to whip here," Private Henry C. Bear confided to his diary. [56]

Studying his hand-drawn map, Sherman pinpointed where he was: twelve miles up the Yazoo from the Mississippi and three miles from the Walnut Hills, looming above the swamp. The first troops to go ashore were Frank Blair's brigade. General Lee sent in skirmishers to slow their advance toward the bluffs while his men completed their preparations. The skirmishing carried over into the evening, each side trying to feel the other's strength.

That night, the Federals camped on the spongy floor of the cypress swamp. [57] Just before daylight, a fiery rocket was seen in the sky several miles upriver, near where Grant was expected to meet them. Spirits rose and then fell just as fast, as rebel cannon opened up on them. With shells bursting all around, they began cutting their way with axes across the trackless swamp. [58]

That morning Porter sent a gunboat flotilla up the Yazoo to clear torpedoes near Haynes' Bluff and to search for a clearing that would allow Sherman to outflank the enemy dug in at the base of the Walnut Hills. That would be preferable to hitting them head-on. William Gwin, captain of the ironclad *Benton* and a veteran of all the big Union river battles, was in charge. Sighting the heavy batteries on the bluff, Gwin flew into action. The river at this point was too narrow to support two gunboats abreast, so he anchored and "bore the brunt of the fight," trading fire with the rebel guns for a full two hours. *Benton* was horribly cut up; thirty shots penetrated its ports. Standing exposed on the quarterdeck, Gwin was struck by a solid rifle shell, which nearly tore one of his arms from its socket. His junior officers withdrew with seven other casualties, two of them fatal.[59]

The battery at Haynes' Bluff was too strong to knock out from the river, Porter informed Sherman that afternoon, but a landing party might be able to capture it from the rear.[60]

Hours later the battle-blasted *Benton* hove into view of *Black Hawk*. Porter had his sailors carry Gwin, unconscious and bleeding profusely, to his cabin. His ribs and one of his lungs were exposed, and his shattered arm hung by a thread from his shoulder. "It was the most fearful wound I ever saw," said Porter. Gwin lingered for two hours and died that evening. He was "my favorite in the fleet," Sherman wrote Ellen.[61]

"The "fighting . . . became more earnest on the 28th, as we crowded the bluffs," wrote Thomas Knox.[62] Guided by runaway slaves, the bluecoats moved stealthily to within a few hundred yards of the main rebel position below the bluffs. It appeared to be progress—although General Lee had actually encouraged it. He aimed to draw the invaders to where his massed artillery could do terrible work on them.[63] "All other approaches to the bluff were obstructed," reporter Franc Wilkie described Lee's ploy, "while [one] was left open, and for fear that we should not see it, they stationed sharpshooters to attract our attention." Rebel forces sent to drive them back found roads "leading across the swamp directly toward the bluff. . . . Sherman fell into the trap at once, and thus it was that our attack was made at the point where it was."[64]

Wilkie was with Knox on the extreme Federal left with General Steele's division. Watching Jacob Ritner's regiment lead two futile attempts to storm the bluffs, it occurred to Wilkie that "we had undertaken an utterly hopeless task, and that a retreat was only a question of a very short time."[65]

Pemberton had arrived in Vicksburg on the day Sherman landed and he assumed overall command, although he allowed Lee to manage the battle. Seeing that his forces were vastly outnumbered, Pemberton wired Dabney Maury, at Grenada, to rush his division to the imperiled city.[66] More troops were also on their way from Braxton's Bragg's army.[67] Help arrived in waves, and it wasn't until the final day of the battle that Lee would have a sizable force of nearly six thousand men.[68]

On his second day in the swamp, Sherman lost his best division commander when General Morgan Smith was seriously wounded while trying to turn the enemy's right flank.[69] By evening, the battle had devolved into an ugly standoff. What minimal advances Union forces had made pushed Lee's forward lines backward, closer to the bluffs, where the rebels were strongest.

That night Sherman conceived a plan to break the stalemate. Brigadier General George Washington Morgan was to smash through the center of the rebel's forward-most line, behind Chickasaw Bayou, move through the field of sharpened trees, race across the cottonfield, and carry the Walnut Hills behind an earth-rattling artillery barrage. By nightfall, his army would be in Vicksburg.

Chickasaw Bayou was wide and deep at the place marked out for Morgan's advance. Believing it an "impassable barrier," Lee had not positioned heavy guns there.[70] Morgan would surprise them by building a pontoon bridge across the bayou under cover of darkness, but in Sherman's haste to leave Memphis, he had neglected to bring a complete pontoon train. Working with what materials they had, Morgan's pioneers struggled through the moonless evening to erect a crossing for the assault teams.

When morning broke, the pioneers realized they had bridged the wrong bayou.[71] They recommenced the work, but enemy fire drove them out of the bayou.[72] The cannonading attracted Lee's attention and he redirected forces to blunt the anticipated advance.[73] From his strengthened position behind Chickasaw Bayou, he invited an attack.

At eleven A.M., Sherman ordered Morgan to prepare his assault. Losses, Sherman knew, would be unbearable. Even if Morgan's columns reached the bluffs, they would have to scale them "under fire of an enemy so securely posed that almost every man amounted to an army on his own account," wrote engineer William Le Baron Jenney.[74] But "time was everything to us," Sherman explained later. He had supplies for only a short engagement, and Lee was being reinforced rapidly and heavily. Sherman could hear the whistles of trains bringing in troops to Vicksburg's station. He had also learned that McClernand was on his way to the Yazoo to "take command." Sherman wanted this to be his battle, the first he had ever directed.[75]

The bluffs could be taken only in a lightning strike by a small, desperately brave part of his army. The tangled terrain decided that. There were not enough openings through the swamp, and the openings were too constricted to send an overwhelming force. Sherman ordered Morgan to assemble his finest brigades.[76] Minutes before the "storming columns" were ordered forward, skirmishers crept out to reconnoiter the ground. The bayou directly in front of Colonel John F. De Courcy's brigade was too deep to be forded. The men would have to cross on a dangerously narrow log bridge with a rebel battery enfilading it. Morgan thought the risk too great and sent word to Sherman to ride out from his headquarters and assess the situation.[77]

Sherman appeared in a flash, made a quick reconnoiter on horseback, and, pointing to the bluffs, barked: "That is the route to take!" He then wheeled his horse and rode off. Minutes later, his adjutant arrived on horseback and told Morgan he was there to give him Sherman's orders verbatim: "Tell Morgan to give the signal for the assault; we will lose 5,000 men before we take Vicksburg, and may as well lose them here as anywhere else." To which Morgan later claimed to reply: "We will lose the men, but from this position we will not take Vicksburg."[78]

Sherman later disputed this account. "I pointed out to General Morgan the place where he could pass the bayou, and he answered, 'General, in ten minutes after you give the signal I'll be on those hills.'" Sherman would also accuse Morgan of cowardice. "He was to lead his division in person."[79] Instead, he watched from afar.

Sherman planned a three-brigade assault led by De Courcy and Brigadier General John M. Thayer on one side of Chickasaw Bayou and Frank Blair on the other, where the bayou was shallow enough to ford.[80] As the assault teams fixed bayonets in the heavy timber just behind the bayou, Sergeant Henry A. Kircher of Belleville, Illinois, noticed the men's faces "got paler and paler." Their eyes seemed to retreat into their skulls and they had a death grip on their weapons.[81]

After a "ferocious cannonade," the three brigades—six thousand men—moved forward at the sound of the drums.[82] De Courcy's 1,500 volunteers marched two-by-two across the wooden bridge. Sergeant Kirchner's regiment was left behind to await orders to attack. They never came. "Our guardian angel took [us] under his wings.[83]

Frank Blair rode at the head of his column, the only man in a saddle. When his horse became mired in the soft mud at the bottom of the bayou, he slid down the animal's neck and led the way on foot, "swinging his sword, cheering his men on."[84] Upon reaching the rebel side of the bayou, his brigade struggled to climb a slick, ten-foot-high embankment carpeted with abatis, the razor-sharp limbs tearing flesh and woollen uniforms. De Courcy, meanwhile, got his men over the log bridge only to run into "immense and fearfully-destructive fire." His men took cover, and he ordered them to move no farther. They were out of the fight.[85]

Blair's boys, with Thayer in close support, fought a running battle through the fallen timber and reached the edge of the cleared cottonfield that led to the bluffs. After halting briefly to fix bayonets, they moved at a "double quick" with Blair in the lead.[86]

Waiting for them in shallow holes below the bluffs were rebel riflemen, among them Winchester Hall's 26th Louisiana Infantry. Looking on from the top of the Walnut Hills were "General Lee and his staff . . . and citizens of Vicksburg, including many ladies. . . . They could see . . . our flag . . . defiantly floating over our works," Colonel Hall wrote later. In front of his regiment were two batteries, which covered "the open ground the enemy had to cross in order to reach us." Around ten o'clock "a terrific storm of shot and shell . . . burst upon us, and its fury it seemed as if no living thing about us could escape."[87]

With bullets whistling around their ears, the defenders delivered round after punishing round on the advancing Yankees. Frank Blair made it through a storm of minie balls and into the rebel rifle pits. Some of his men followed and held their position momentarily, but, seeing they were alone and unsupported, they broke and ran. Hundreds were mowed down by a "hurricane of fire, yet Blair survived unscathed."[88]

On another part of the battlefield, Thayer also penetrated the enemy's works, but of his five Iowa regiments only one was still following him. Ordering a subordinate to hold his position, he dashed back to where De Courcy had been stopped and found his men "lying in a ditch," too traumatized to move. Thayer implored De Courcy "to get his men forward," but he would not expose them, he cried out, to "useless destruction." Returning to the bluffs, Thayer found his single regiment withdrawing under raking fire after taking 30 percent casualties in thirty minutes.[89]

"No engagement in which I was afterward involved impressed me with the nightmarish sensations of this one," wrote Ohio private Charles Willison, whose sixteenth birthday fell on this December day.[90] Blair's brigade alone lost 645 men, roughly a third of its strength.[91] Franc Wilkie, a writer not given to exaggeration, called Blair's assault "one of the most desperate and gallant feats recorded in history."[92]

When Thayer returned to his lines he discovered what had happened to his "lost" regiments. While he and Blair were advancing on the bluffs, General Frederick Steele, on Morgan's recommendation, had inexplicably ordered one of Thayer's regiments to move to another part of the battlefield. The other regiments, blindly obeying Thayer's orders to follow the men in front of them, marched off with them. With the loss of these three thousand men, along with De Courcy's brigade, the final assault had been made by only five of the thirteen regiments Sherman had ordered into the fight.*

After the war, Sherman chastised Morgan in print for not giving Blair proper support once he crossed Chickasaw Bayou. "I have ever felt that had General Morgan promptly and skillfully sustained the lead of Frank Blair's brigade on that day, we should have broken the rebel line, and gained lodgment on the hills behind Vicksburg."[93] Morgan "lost me a battle otherwise won."[94]

---

* Thayer would later regret not preferring court-martial charges against Morgan and Steele, "for between them they were responsible for one of the most terrible blunders which has ever occurred in military affairs." Steele blamed Morgan, and Morgan said only that it had been a "mistake." Stanley P. Hirshson, *The White Tecumseh: A Biography of William Tecumseh Sherman* (New York: John Wiley and Sons, 1997), 139–41.

That is questionable. The rebel position that afternoon was virtually unassailable. Even if the assault force had taken the bluffs, it would have found itself "in a worse trap," as Sherman himself conceded in a more measured mood. When Sherman ordered the assault, he was still convinced that Grant was taking care of Pemberton. But with Grant no longer threatening him, Pemberton would have "run his whole [Grenada] force against us" at Vicksburg.[95]

The Battle of Chickasaw Bayou was essentially a one-day affair.* An Ohio soldier summed up the fight in the swamp: "We had bitten off more than we could chaw."[96]

On the evening after Blair's assault, Sherman went to see Porter on *Black Hawk*. His friend could see he was exhausted and demoralized. "He had shared the privations of his men, bivouacking out in the cold with them. No general could long conduct an army that way." It was the only time in the war Porter saw him "unhinged."[97]

That night "the rain came on—and such a rain!" Porter remembered. "The heavens seemed trying to drown our army; the naval vessels were the only arks of safety. The level lands were inundated, and there were three feet of water in the swamps where our army was operating."[98] Sherman had ordered the men to travel light. Coats, tents, and oilcloth ground covers had been discarded back at Memphis. Many of the men camped on the "miry, swampy ground" had no protection other than blankets and rubber shawls.[99] The wounded suffered horribly. All beds on the makeshift hospital steamers were full, and "all that pitiless night and all the next day, the wounded lay in their agony on [an] oozy bed, under a soaking rain, uncared for," wrote a reporter on the scene. "Many who had fallen on their faces and were unable to turn themselves smothered in the mud."[100]

Battle-numbed boys from a Missouri regiment stood leaning against tall cypresses "in silent resignation. . . . Not a word was uttered," said

---

* The only other Federal unit to attack on December 29 was Colonel James H. Blood's Sixth Missouri Infantry, which attempted a diversionary assault from the Union right to draw off fire from Morgan's brigades. They were repulsed attempting to cross Chickasaw Bayou.

Sergeant Major E. Paul Reichhelm. The only sounds were the howling wind, the groans of the wounded, and the rumble of rebel cannon.[101]

The next morning the storm broke and Sherman scrutinized the rebel line. It was stronger than the previous day. "New combinations therefore became necessary."[102] Perhaps, as Porter had suggested earlier, Haynes' Bluff could be taken from the rear. This would allow part of the army to get behind Vicksburg, on good ground, and "open communications with Grant," who, Sherman assumed, was either advancing toward the Yazoo or holding Pemberton's army in place at Grenada.[103]

Haynes' Bluff had unexpectedly become vulnerable. Charles Rivers Ellet, commander of the ram fleet, had assembled that day an ungainly "apparatus" to remove the mines protecting the bluff. It was a giant "rake" attached to the bow of his ram *Lioness*. Its curved claws would either "explode . . . the infernal machines," Ellet assured Porter, or sever their detonating wires. The rake extended out from the bow forty-five feet, a buffer zone that protected his vessel from harm.*[104]

Porter agreed to have Ellet's *Lioness* lead his ironclads upriver—silently and without running lights—on the evening of December 31.[105] The gunboats would engage the batteries at dawn, while Sherman kept General Lee's army in front of him at Chickasaw Bayou, ready to mount a diversionary attack at "the sound of the battle above." After Porter had silenced the guns, troop transports would race upriver with ten thousand "choice troops" from General Steele's division. Landing beyond the range of the rebel guns, they would storm Haynes' Bluff from the rear, disarm the guns, and turn the rebels' right flank.[106]

At midnight, "everything appeared favorable," Sherman assured his men. The attack was scheduled for three thirty that morning, but the river valley remained eerily quiet till well past that time. Where was Porter?

Near daylight, General Steele handed Sherman a note, then watched his face drop as he scanned it. The fog on the river was too dense for Porter's gunboats. The expedition would have to be postponed to

---

* Ellet also agreed to blow up the raft the rebels had moored athwart the Yazoo near Haynes' Bluff. He would have *Lioness*—with the rake on its bow—pull a barge containing fifteen barrels of gunpowder. On reaching the boom, his crew would saturate it with powder, light a fuse, and retreat downstream. ORN, I/23/589.

another night. Sherman would be ready, but at noon it started to rain "heavier than ever, and the land almost disappeared from sight. There was no chance for a successful attack on Haines' [sic] Bluff," Porter grimly informed him.[107]

There would be no more fighting in the swamp. Sherman had lost 1,776 men, 208 killed. Eighty percent of the men fell or were captured in the December 29 assault. The defenders lost only 206 killed, wounded, and missing.[108] Roughly three thousand entrenched defenders had repulsed an army ten times their number. For the first time in the Civil War, dug-in defenders "dominated the tactical battle," writes historian James R. Arnold. "The era of open field battles was rapidly drawing to a close. The path to Cold Harbor, Kennesaw Mountain, and Verdun could be seen in the footsteps of the doomed Midwestern boys who charged at Chickasaw Bayou."[109]

Sherman took full responsibility for the loss, but attributed it to "the strength of the enemy's position, not to his superior fighting ability."[110] On New Year's Day, Sherman's troops took shelter in their heavily flooded camps, where "marks of overflow stained the trees ten to twelve feet above their roots." All were anxious to be released from the "Chickasaw slaughter pen."[111] The next morning, as the fleet steamed back to the Mississippi, a rebel band played "Get Out of the Wilderness."[112]

"Well, we have been to Vicksburg and it was too much for us," Sherman wrote Ellen.[113]

Waiting for Sherman at the mouth of the Yazoo was General McClernand, aboard the steamer *Tigress*. He was simmering. He had arrived at Memphis with his new bride six days after his wedding, and nine days after Sherman had departed for Vicksburg. At Memphis he found an undelivered letter from Grant assigning him command of the XIII Corps in his army.[114] McClernand shot off a message to Lincoln: "Left here by myself." He had been betrayed, he said, but he counted on Lincoln and Stanton to restore him to command of the Mississippi expedition.[115] He left for Vicksburg the next day.

In a tense meeting aboard *Tigress*, McClernand told Sherman that Grant had been forced to withdraw from Mississippi and was "not coming" south—the last an outright lie. He was now in command, and henceforth Sherman's army, which was anchored off Milliken's Bend, Louisiana, just across the Mississippi, slightly north of Vicksburg, would be the Army of the Mississippi. Sherman would be reduced to a corps commander.[116] Infuriated, Sherman found it hard to contain himself. "McClernand . . . will take command," Porter wrote his ailing friend Admiral Andrew Foote. "Sherman, though, will have all the brains."[117]

The next night, Sherman and McClernand visited Porter on his flagship. McClernand wanted Porter to provide gunboats for an expedition Sherman had suggested and McClernand approved. They would move upriver with the army and reduce Fort Hindman, a rebel garrison at a settlement called Arkansas Post, along the lower Arkansas River, a tributary of the Mississippi between Vicksburg and Helena.[118]

While Sherman was engaged at Chickasaw Bayou, a Confederate raider had slipped out of Arkansas Post into the Mississippi and captured *Blue Wing*, an unarmed Union supply steamer. More raids were likely, and it would be "ill-advised" to leave "such a force on our rear," said Sherman.[119] He also worried about the men he had led into the swamp. They were demoralized and needed to "secure a success" to restore their confidence. Most of them had heard the disheartening war news: Robert E. Lee's rout of Ambrose Burnside's army at Fredericksburg, Virginia, on December 13; Grant's retreat from Mississippi; and General Banks's failure to attack Port Hudson after recapturing Baton Rouge.[120]

Because it was Sherman's plan, Porter agreed to provide his battle boats. He would lead them. The expedition arrived at Arkansas Post on the night of January 9. The gunboats disabled the fort's only heavy battery and smashed its earthen walls. Sherman directed a concentrated assault that forced the surrender of the disease-stricken garrison on January 11. Five thousand prisoners were taken, many of them near death from dysentery and typhoid.[121] There was jubilation in the army. "This was our first victory and we had almost become discouraged," one soldier spoke for thousands of others.[122]

The capture of Fort Hindman removed the only remaining threat to Federal communications on the Mississippi between Memphis and

the Yazoo, giving the Union army a secure supply line for future operations against Vicksburg. Hours after the surrender, Sherman found
McClernand aboard *Tigress* toasting a victory in which he had little
part. "Glorious! glorious! my star is ever in the ascendant!"[123]

McClernand wanted to continue up the Arkansas River to Little
Rock, but Grant ordered him to renew operations against Vicksburg.[124]
Heading downriver, the fleet stopped in front of the town of Napoleon,
Arkansas, where Grant was waiting. He had left Memphis to meet with
Porter and Sherman. Grant had originally opposed the Arkansas Post
expedition, calling it a "wild goose chase," but Sherman and Porter had
convinced him otherwise.[125] "Five thousand Confederate troops left in
the rear might have caused us much trouble and loss of property while
navigating the Mississippi," Grant noted later.[126]

Sherman and Porter had been bombarding Grant with messages,
imploring him to come downriver and take personal command of the
army.[127] Grant needed no convincing; he had already made his decision.
On January 12, he had Rawlins write McClernand: "You are hereby
relieved from the command of the Expedition against Vicksburg." The
letter was not sent, but the intent was there; the axe would soon fall.[128]
"I would have been glad to put Sherman in command," Grant said later,
"to give him an opportunity to accomplish what he had failed in the
December before; but there seemed no other way out of the difficulty,
for he was junior to McClernand."[129]

Had Sherman been offered the command, it's unlikely he would
have accepted it. The victory at Arkansas Post was not enough to clear
his mind of the battering his army had taken at Chickasaw Bayou. It
was more than that. The president had sent McClernand to Vicksburg
to supersede him, humbling him in front of his commanders. "Mr. Lincoln intended to insult me . . . by putting McClernand over me," he
wrote his brother John."[130] He would be relieved if Lincoln replaced
him, he told an old friend.[131] And if sent to another theater for his failure at Chickasaw Bayou, he would resign and return to his family in
Ohio.[132] His talk of quitting alarmed Ellen, who feared he was sliding
into the depression that had nearly broken him in Kentucky.[133] Yet this
was different. In Kentucky, he had questioned his own competency.
Now he was being blamed for losing a battle he believed he would have
won had Morgan followed orders.[134]

He would not quit, he finally decided. He would not disappoint Grant and Porter and embarrass his family, but he was clearly relieved to be serving under Grant and not in his place.

Before steaming back to Memphis, Grant ordered Sherman to proceed to De Soto Peninsula and resume work on the "Ditch" General Thomas Williams had begun digging the previous summer. The objective remained the same: to create a safe passage for Federal vessels through the peninsula opposite Vicksburg. The president attached "much importance" to the canal project, Halleck pointedly reminded Grant.[135]

"Grant will be down soon, and already one Division of about 6,000 men have come from Memphis," Sherman informed Ellen from Young's Point, Louisiana, the Union encampment close to where the canal was being constructed.[136] Three days later, Grant left Memphis with his staff on his flagship, *Magnolia*, feeling "pretty blue" when he set sail, still smoldering over the collapse of his overland campaign against Vicksburg. John Rawlins, who was on board, confided to a friend that if he were in Grant's shoes he would resign.[137] His boss, he suspected, did not enjoy the full confidence of the president, who had recently revoked one of his general orders, a reprehensible act that was embarrassing to the army, the president, and the Union cause.

While headquartered in Tennessee in the early winter of 1862, Grant had waged a war of words with Northern speculators who followed his army in order to purchase cotton from reputably loyal planters. Grant suspected the profits were being channeled to the Confederate government to buy arms and ammunition to be used against his own men. "To all the other trials I have to contend against is added that of speculators whose patriotism is measured by dollars & cents," Grant wrote his sister Mary in mid-December.[138] His frustration boiled over two days later when he received in the mail a pile of complaints about Jewish traders in his department. That very hour he drafted General Orders No. 11, expelling "the Jews, as a class" from the Department of the Tennessee and requiring them to leave within twenty-four hours of being notified. Those who disobeyed were to be arrested and sent out of the department as prisoners.[139]

John Rawlins had begged Grant not to issue what Julia later called that "obnoxious order," but found him in no mood for temporizing.[140] "Well, they can countermand this from Washington if they like, but we will issue it anyhow."[141] It was "the most sweeping anti-Jewish regulation in all American history," wrote one historian.[142]

Why Grant singled out Jews will never be known. Some of the most successful cotton traders were Jewish, and Grant had learned that his father was in Tennessee that December buying cotton, working in league with a Jewish-owned clothing manufacturer, Mack & Brothers, who might have been using Jesse to gain favor with Grant. Had this pushed Grant over the edge? All that is certain is that "a frustrated man chose the age-old scapegoat," wrote Grant biographer William McFeely.[143] Years later, Grant claimed the order "never would have been issued if it had not been telegraphed the moment penned, without one moment's reflection."[144]*

Jewish groups descended on the White House and the major Northern dailies excoriated Grant. The steadfastly pro-Grant *New York Times* called the order "a momentary revival of the spirit of the medieval ages."[145] A resolution to censure Grant was introduced in the House of Representatives. Elihu Washburne managed to table it by a thin margin of three votes.[146] Lincoln revoked the order the hour it came across his desk.[147] On January 21, as Grant was headed downriver to Vicksburg, Halleck notified him.[148]

Lincoln did not ask Grant to apologize—nor did Grant offer to— but the president was clearly displeased with him for issuing an order that violated the spirit of the Emancipation Proclamation and could be used by the enemy to discredit the administration. The *Memphis Daily Bulletin*, a pro-administration paper, printed a copy of the Emancipation Proclamation on the same page as the Jewish edict, citing the irony of Lincoln freeing the slaves while Grant expelled the Jews.[149]

---

* Grant does not mention the order in his memoirs. Biographer Ron Chernow says that Grant "was haunted by this terrible action for the rest of his days." Perhaps it influenced his decision, years later, to appoint more Jews to his presidential administration than had any previous chief executive. Ron Chernow, *Grant* (New York: Penguin Press, 2017), 236.

Lincoln was not pleased with Sherman either, whose displeasure with the president for sending McClernand to replace him was an open secret in Washington. And Sherman was currently warring against the press—"the most contemptible race of men that exist"—when he should have been focusing exclusively on Vicksburg.[150] "He hates reporters, foams at the mouth when he sees them," proclaimed the *New York World*.[151] Instead of going after the *World*, however, Sherman directed his fury at the *New York Herald*, "the single most important paper in the nation," and at one reporter in particular.[152]

Thomas W. Knox had written an account of the Battle of Chickasaw Bayou that blasted Sherman for mishandling the army in the final assault—an act of insanity, he called it—and callously disregarding his wounded on the stormy night after the battle. Sherman had issued an order barring reporters from joining the Yazoo River armada. Knox had not only violated it; his articles had gotten into the hands of the enemy, Sherman falsely claimed, providing the rebels with important military information. "I have ordered the arrest of [Knox], shall try him & if possible execute him as a spy," he told Ellen.[153] The death threat was bluster, but Sherman had Knox court-martialed on February 5 for disobeying his directive forbidding civilians from accompanying the Yazoo expedition and for allegedly providing military intelligence to the enemy. Never before in American history had a newspaper reporter been tried by the military in a war zone.[154]

Knox's reporting was inaccurate. No Union commander was more solicitous of his wounded than Sherman, and Knox later admitted he got the particulars of the battle horribly wrong; but charging Knox with spying was patently preposterous. He didn't have access to Sherman's plans, and his dispatches from Chickasaw Bayou were published several weeks *after* the guns had fallen silent. The military court cleared Knox of this baseless charge but, under pressure from Sherman, found him guilty of violating orders barring citizens from accompanying the Vicksburg expedition. He was expelled from Grant's army lines and told he would be arrested and imprisoned should he return.[155]

Sherman was enraged. He wanted Knox convicted as a spy and imprisoned.[156] Then, under pressure from outraged reporters and members of Congress, the president revoked the military court's decision and allowed Knox to return to the Vicksburg front, but only with Grant's express approval.[157] Grant left it up to Sherman.[158] "My answer is Never," Sherman informed Knox.[159]

Sherman had started his fight with Knox at exactly the wrong time, in January 1863, when almost every Northern daily was excoriating his and Grant's "lamentably puny" efforts to take Vicksburg.[160] On the battlefield, Grant and Sherman were, when together, nearly unbeatable, but how long would Lincoln stick with them if they failed to achieve a breakthrough at Vicksburg?

On his way down to Vicksburg to take command of the army, Grant had stopped at Helena and met with Brigadier General Cadwallader C. Washburn, the cavalry officer who had turned Pemberton's flank at the Tallahatchie River in December. "He . . . feels that he has got a heavy job on his hands," Cadwallader confided to his brother Elihu.[161] But being on the river, out of touch with the press, helped Grant relax, and his spirits improved measurably. "The trip with nothing to bother me, makes me feel well," he told Julia. "The living on the boat is very fine, and my appetite good."[162]

On January 29 Grant arrived off Young's Point and sent word to McClernand that he would "take direct command of the Miss. river expedition which necessarily limits your command to the 13th Army Corps."[163] McClernand had known this was coming, but he couldn't contain his anger and disappointment, which he directed at Grant. His incendiary protests "were highly insubordinate," Grant said later, "but I overlooked [them] . . . for the good of the service."[164] Getting nowhere with Grant, McClernand appealed to the president—"Do not let me be . . . destroyed"—and was stunned by the reply.[165] "I have too many family controversies (so to speak) already on my hands to . . . take up another."[166]

With the McClernand issue behind him for the moment, "the real work of the campaign and siege of Vicksburg now began," Grant wrote years later.[167]

CHAPTER 13

Mud and Misery

*"The problem then became, how to secure a landing on high
ground east of the Mississippi without an apparent retreat."* [1]

—Ulysses S. Grant

The great army began arriving in front of Vicksburg in the third week of January, in advance of its commander. The divisions headed by Sherman and McClernand, slaughtered at Chickasaw Bayou and victorious at Arkansas Post, landed just ahead of the invasion columns Grant had led into northern Mississippi the previous December. Augmented by new recruits at Memphis, the reunited Army of the Tennessee had roughly fifty thousand troops to hurl at the hill city, a force roughly equal in size to Pemberton's defenders. [2]

"It is a grand sight," Iowa surgeon Seneca Thrall described the invasion armada lying off the levee at Young's Point, more steamers than he could easily count and Porter's iron monsters riding impressively at anchor at the mouth of the Yazoo. [3] The thick black smoke of the steamboats floated over the Louisiana mudflats, where leading elements of the army were encamped. Peering out at the shoreline from their front porches, the handful of rebel families that remained on Young's Point knew that a supreme Union effort was in the offing.

Porter's gunboats were shielded from Vicksburg's batteries by thick foliage on the Yazoo shoreline, and Grant's camps were hidden from the eyes of rebel gunners by towering trees on De Soto Peninsula. This three-mile-long tongue of Louisiana shoreline ran parallel to and directly across from the hill city and extended northward into the hollow of the horseshoe-shaped bend the great river had carved out of soft soil just north of the city. The old Williams canal ran diagonally across the base of this mile-and-a-quarter-wide peninsula. Its entrance lay just

above Vicksburg, and its silted-over outlet was directly below the city.
Young's Point was eight miles north of De Soto Peninsula. Milliken's
Bend, Louisiana, the second Vicksburg camp, was seven miles farther
upriver, on the site of a busy prewar steamboat landing. Grant would
have preferred to have a single unified encampment close to Vicksburg,
at Young's Point, but dry ground there was scarce.[4] A third and smaller
camp was established seventy miles upriver at Lake Providence, Louisiana. James McPherson, stationed at Memphis, had been directed to
move his corps there, but would be delayed for almost a month by a
shortage of troop transports. Grant sent a brigade from McClernand's
corps to fill the gap.[5]

The army's forward supply base and principal hospital center was at
Memphis. The irretrievably sick and the severely wounded would be sent
to sprawling medical centers at Cairo and St. Louis, but Grant wanted
soldiers who could be patched up or restored to health quickly to be
transported to Memphis, where they could be conveniently returned
to the army when fully recovered. Grant left behind in Memphis an
occupation force under Major General Stephen A. Hurlbut, a corrupt,
hard-drinking Illinois politician to whom Lincoln had unwisely given a
commission, and whom Halleck, impressed with his administrative skills,
had foisted upon Grant.[6] On January 29, 1863, the Department of the
Tennessee had a total of 130,000 men on active duty. They were divided
into four corps: XIII Corps, commanded by McClernand, XV Corps by
Sherman, XVI Corps by Hurlbut, and XVII Corps by McPherson.

Porter's gunboat fleet controlled the river north of Vicksburg, giving Grant what he fatally lacked in his invasion of northeast Mississippi:
an inviolate supply line. And Porter's flotilla, along with Colonel Lewis
Parsons's transports, tugs, and courier craft, allowed Grant to keep in
touch with and wield control over his far-flung forces on a battlefront
that would eventually extend, north and south, from Helena, Arkansas, to Port Hudson, Louisiana, a distance of over 350 miles; and east
and west, from Jackson, Mississippi, to Monroe, Louisiana, roughly 120
air miles. These steamships and gunboats would give Grant's army the
mobility Pemberton's land-bound defenders lacked. From January to
April, every Union effort to take Vicksburg would be waterborne, and
Porter's gunboats allowed Grant to attack at a time and a place of his
choosing. When he eventually got his army into Mississippi, it would

be an amphibious crossing on Parsons's steamboats, covered by Porter's ironclads.

Everything hinged on amicable relations between Grant and Porter. Neither could give orders to the other. "Though he had no control over me whatever . . . I always deferred to his wishes in all matters," Porter explained, "and went so far as to give orders to those under my command that they should obey the orders of Generals Grant and Sherman the same as if they came from myself. Hence we always acted with the most perfect accord."[7] Poisoned army-navy relations had prevented Farragut from taking Vicksburg the previous summer. The Grant-Porter accord would, in time, seal the fate of Vicksburg.

Before Grant arrived in front of Vicksburg on January 28, most of the army was encamped at Young's Point or just south of it, on De Soto Peninsula, where Sherman and McClernand were supervising the construction of the cut-off canal that would, it was hoped, allow transports to pass below Vicksburg, out of reach of its river batteries. The morning Sherman landed at Young's Point, he assembled his staff and rode down to inspect the diversion canal. On reaching it, he "checked his horse on the bank" and roared: "It is no bigger than a plantation ditch." The water was only two feet deep. Sherman spotted the problem immediately. The mouth of the canal was in "slack water." This prevented the river current from scouring a deep and wide channel. He and McClernand would work to correct this, but both thought the canal project preposterous, a waste of time and manpower.[8] They had their orders, however, and soldiers who had come to Vicksburg to fight were forced to dig.

Black Americans were brought in to do some of the most odious work.[9] Most were slaves impressed from local plantations managed by Irish overseers; some arrived by Union barges from as far as Helena, Arkansas. Before long, four thousand soldiers and over five hundred freedmen were toiling—around the clock in shifts—in slime up to their elbows. Many of the freedmen were of "weak constitution," and "a remarkable proportion of them are deformed or mutilated," observed journalist and landscape architect Frederick Law Olmsted, on an extended visit to Grant's camps in his capacity as executive secretary of the United States Sanitary Commission, a private relief organization that supported sick and wounded Union soldiers. Engineer William Le Baron Jenney told Olmsted they were "industrious, disciplinable, grateful and docile."[10]

As the digging progressed, escaped slaves from the area around Young's Point drifted into the Union camp and the men were put to work on the canal in return for army rations and protection from their former masters. "Poor creatures, these contrabands. They fly for their freedom to the Union army and we are not able to do much for them as it is all we can do to take care of ourselves," observed Iowa infantryman Cyrus F. Boyd. "The men in our camp treat them worse than brutes, and when they come into camp cries of 'Kill him' 'drown him' . . . are heard."[11] Boyd and Chicago soldier Will Brown were in the minority in their sympathy for the escaped slaves. "I presume you have often heard it said that even if President Lincoln did declare the slaves should be free, they would not leave home and their masters . . ." Brown wrote his father. "But if any of these men could come down here and see the contrabands flocking in, I rather think they would change their opinions somewhat. . . . More than half of our camps are flooded with them; big and little, great and small. . . . all flocking into our lines and wanting something to do. I tell you Old Abe's proclamation is one of the most severe blows the Confeds have had to undergo."[12]

The soldiers took to their tents in the evenings. The black workers and their families sought what shelter they could find. It was miserable, however, for nearly everyone at Young's Point. "The driest place I could find to sleep last night the mud was four inches deep," Captain Jacob Ritner wrote his wife back in Iowa after being driven from his tent by ripping winds and flooded ground.[13] High water mandated that most of the army stores be "kept aboard steamboats," wrote a correspondent from *Frank Leslie's Illustrated Newspaper*. "The quartermaster, commissary, provost marshal and other officers maintained their offices afloat. Everything went ashore over the narrow strip of land between the river and the levee. . . . Hay, oats, flour, and ammunition" were carried on the backs of mules. Long lines of them were seen "wallowing through the mud, on their way from the boats to the camps."[14] Wagons pulled by mules got mired in the mud, and the animals had to be unhitched and dragged out, along with the wagons, by heavy ropes.[15]

Under pounding January rains "the swamps became lakes, and camps and roads were sloughs of black mire. If one put his foot squarely down anywhere it was questionable, when he raised it again, if the shoe would stay behind," remembered one soldier.[16]

Thousands of troops encamped upon the tops of the ten-foot-high levees. "In our front was the Mississippi River; in the rear, a dreary swamp, covered with water, from one to two feet deep, leaving us but a narrow strip of dry land along the levee on which to set our tents," an Ohio volunteer described his impromptu encampment.[17] But there was never enough room on the levees for all of the men. Most were crowded together in tent cities on the soggy floodplain. Line officers had it better: They confiscated the furnished homes of rebel refugees. Sherman's and McClernand's quarters "are fine buildings, recently occupied as residences by the proprietors of the plantations upon which our army is encamped," reported a *Chicago Tribune* correspondent.[18] When Grant arrived, he would stay on *Magnolia*, his headquarters boat.

"The whole atmosphere of the place was gloomy and depressing, aggravated especially at night by the peeping and creaking and croaking of all sorts of creatures in the woods and swamps," recalled Chickasaw Bayou veteran Charles A. Willison. The Ohio volunteer had begun his military service in two of the most desolate places on the continent: the Yazoo swamps and the mudflats of the swollen Mississippi.[19]

Grant could not have picked a worse time to launch his campaign. In late winter, rainfall is generally heavy and prolonged in the lower Mississippi Valley, averaging over fifteen inches; and it is the time of year when the river gathers momentum from the floodtide of its myriad tributaries.[20] "It has rained almost incessantly since we pitched our tents," Kentucky surgeon B. F. Stevenson wrote home after landing at Young's Point in late January, "and we can't walk from tent to tent without carrying along with us ten pounds of mud."[21]

A heavy fog settled over the camp in the mornings and it was unexpectedly cold, with occasional snow showers mixed with sleet and high winds. The mud froze at night and thin ice formed on the ponds.[22]

African American canal workers warned soldiers that violent electrical storms came tearing up the river valley with regularity in January and February. On some days the lightning was so "terrific it was dangerous to carry a gun," recalled Private Willison, "so we stuck them, bayonet down, in the ground." More than one soldier was killed by a lightning strike.[23]

The weather was capricious. Some days were "beautifully clear and warm," while others were "wet, gloomy, cold, and disagreeable," noted Cyrus Boyd.[24] To fight off the cold, soldiers placed piles of burning logs in front of their tents.[25]

Wherever armies went in this war they carried deadly diseases with them. "Since the disembarkation of the troops on the Yazoo bottom . . . sickness has prevailed among [the men] to an alarming extent," McClernand wrote Grant on January 26, the day before the commander set out from Memphis.[26] Great numbers of the men were severely sick on arrival. They had served with Sherman in the Yazoo Delta, drinking from stagnant bayous filled with animal carcasses, and had been living on filthy, intolerably crowded transports for five weeks, without facilities to wash or cook. "No hog-pen will compare" to these steamers, Cyrus Boyd confided to his diary on his passage to Young's Point.[27] The boats were so densely packed "men, literally and truly, were found asleep standing," wrote B. F. Stevenson. Many of them slept and ate on open decks, in sleet and storm, directly above the rank-smelling stables of horses and mules. "[We] are filthier than the beasts below," Stevenson described his "prison home" to his daughter.[28]

By the time the steamer *City of Alton* dropped anchor off Young's Point on January 23, with a thousand men on board—members of the 48th Ohio and 108th Illinois regiments—sickness had "disabled" nearly half of them.[29] The 108th was a new regiment, not properly trained to take health precautions, and the men "suffered severely" from dysentery and typhoid. "Nearly three-fourths were rendered unable for duty, and death was thinning their ranks at a fearful rate, so that our steamer had the appearance of a hospital boat," wrote the regimental historian of the 48th.[30]

Shortly after *City of Alton* landed, surgeon Seneca Thrall reported "a vast amount of sickness" in the camps, "many of the new regiments having only three to five hundred men fit for duty, when a short time ago they had 1,000. Many are dying and thousands more will if they stay here two months." There were as yet no adequate hospital facilities at Young's Point, so Thrall laid claim to a slave cabin on an abandoned plantation near his encampment. It was filthy when he took possession, but it had an intact roof, a wooden floor, and two fireplaces. The sick "were glad to get in it," Thrall wrote his wife.[31]

Grant had anticipated, and made preparations for, the fast-developing medical crisis in his camps. Before leaving Memphis, he ordered the medical department in that city to provide hospital beds for at least five thousand additional soldiers. He also directed General Hurlbut to forward to the Vicksburg camps, with "all possible dispatch," surgeons who could be spared from regiments left behind in Tennessee.[32] Only five additional surgeons were sent, however, and they didn't arrive until mid-March.[33] Meanwhile at Milliken's Bend and Young's Point, makeshift field hospitals staffed by bone-weary surgeons "were filled with the sick, who died as though stricken by an epidemic."[34]

After the war, Grant would downplay the severity of the medical situation at Young's Point and Milliken's Bend. "Exaggerated rumors of disease" in the Union camps at Vicksburg spread through the northwest that January and February, wrote Adam Badeau, his official historian.[35] The crisis, however, was real and profound.

On the morning of January 29, General Grant left his cabin on *Magnolia* and set foot for the first time on the spongy soil of Louisiana. He was forty years old, but his crow's-feet and grizzled, untended beard made him look older. He wore no insignia of rank except the twin-starred straps of a major general on the shoulders of his coat. "There's General Grant," an Illinois soldier leaned in and whispered to a friend as they stood watching the general amble down the plank of *Magnolia*, reading a newspaper and chewing on the stump of an unlit cigar.

"I guess not," the other man said unbelievingly. "That fellow don't look like he has the ability to command a regiment, much less an army."[36]

That morning Grant and his division commanders rode down to De Soto Peninsula to examine the Williams ditch. Sherman and McClernand had begun widening the canal from ten to sixty feet so that it could handle broad-beamed transports. And they had relocated its entrance farther upstream, where the river struck the shoreline with the "greatest velocity," giving the current sufficient "cutting power," it was hoped, to deepen the channel. Inspecting the work, Grant was visibly disappointed. Engineers had deepened the ditch and the water was now five feet high, but there was "no wash," he reported to Halleck that evening, "and no signs of its enlarging."[37] The river still "refused to run through the ditch" with enough velocity to scour it sufficiently.[38] "The channel was presented," wrote Franc Wilkie of the *New York Times*, "and the waters refused to enter it."[39]

It would get worse. Instead of cutting a channel, the immense volume of river water let into the shallow ditch would, weeks later, spill over its banks and flood the camps of some of the digging crews, forcing them to move their tents farther upriver, close to Milliken's Bend.[40] Grant saw another problem, one that Sherman had already identified and described to his brother John days before Grant arrived at Vicksburg. Even if the canal drew "a volume & depth of water sufficient to cut a new channel [the enemy would] simply shift his guns to Warrenton, a point on the same range of hills [as Vicksburg], below the mouth of our Canal."[41] Unarmed transports leaving the canal would face annihilating fire. This made the ditch unusable. Grant agreed, but directed Sherman to press on. The canal was a "pet idea of Mr. Lincoln."[42]

The project would also keep Grant's troops occupied until he was able to send them against Vicksburg. Grant foresaw that "the army would be in better condition" by working on the canal "than by laying idle in camp," wrote reporter Sylvanus Cadwallader. Public sentiment was running strongly against him in the North, and "intrigues were at work to remove Grant and place McClernand, or someone else, in his place," said Cadwallader. "It was apparent that continued activity was the only condition on which he could hold his position."[43]

There were also sanguine observers in the North who saw the canal as Grant's best chance of taking Vicksburg. The project, accordingly, received considerable coverage in the press, North and South. The entire country "watched its progress anxiously; and, even in Europe, the plan of turning a mighty river from its course attracted attention and comment," wrote Badeau.[44]

Grant could not hold on to his command, however, by giving full attention to an enterprise in which neither he nor his most trusted commander believed. He had to go on the offensive—but where? An angry mile-wide river separated his army from Pemberton's, which was dug in and determined to fight from its entrenched hilltop fortifications. "No greater problem of warfare ever faced an American general," wrote Grant biographer Hamlin Garland.[45]

After inspecting the canal that January morning, Grant's party rode to a clearing that offered an unobstructed view of Vicksburg. It was the first time he set eyes on the city that would decide his destiny. As he scanned the river batteries with his field glasses, he entered into a spirited discussion with Frank Blair and Sherman about how to take Vicksburg, The conversation would spill over into the evening, back at his headquarters boat.[46]

The immediate temptation was to assail the city head-on, in a coup de main, a lightning amphibious assault spearheaded by the gunboats. But the enemy's defenses, extending from Haynes' Bluff to Warrenton, eight miles below the town, were strongest on the Mississippi waterfront and had been greatly strengthened since the navy attacked them the previous summer. Grant could see them clearly from where he was standing, batteries and lines of rifle pits emplaced either directly on the river or on the hills above it. An assaulting army would be "half slaughtered," one of Grant's spies had recently informed him. This man had been inside the city, dressed in a rebel uniform, and said the enemy positively welcomed such an attack. It would be Grant's Chickasaw Bayou.[47]

Every one of the generals ruled out a direct assault. Grant wanted to take the city from its rear, where its defenses were weakest and where he could employ his overwhelming advantage in artillery. But how to get there, now that the canal seemed unworkable and Sherman's attempt to outflank Haynes' Bluff had failed? Perhaps the army could be landed many miles north of the city, in the thick of the Mississippi Delta, a wildly primitive cotton-growing region that extended from Vicksburg north to Memphis? From there it could advance to the Yazoo at a place far upriver from Haynes' Bluff, cross on transports, and threaten Vicksburg from dry ground behind it.

Two days before arriving at Young's Point, Grant had ordered James Wilson, his topographic engineer, to make a quick reconnaissance of the Mississippi Delta. His report was not encouraging. The terrain was

nightmarishly difficult, "all marsh, heavily timbered, cut up with bayous and much overflowed."[48] It would be insuperably difficult to carry
on "military operations through [its] bottoms and swamps, cut up . . .
by a network of bayous, creeks, and tributary streams. Without roads,
or bridges, this country with its un-fordable watercourses, even if unde-
fended, could hardly be traversed by an army with its impedimenta.
None but the larger bayous was navigable, except in times of flood, and
at such times the country was . . . submerged.[49] The Delta, Wilson concluded, was "a perfect barrier."[50] Grant agreed. "Marching across this
country in the face of an enemy was impossible; navigating it proved
equally impracticable."[51]

Another option was to return the army to Memphis and move along
the line of the Mississippi Central Railroad toward Jackson, as Grant
had done back in December. This was the plan Sherman now proposed,
with several salient modifications. The main force, striking by land,
would be vigorously supported by a smaller amphibious force of gunboats and transports, which would land directly in front of Vicksburg
"the moment the guns of the main attack [could] be heard." And the
army would establish a secure forward supply station at Memphis, not
at vulnerable Holly Springs. "I have always believed," Sherman would
say later, "the place we started out with [was] the best & only [plan]."[52]

Never in the habit of openly arguing with his generals, Grant kept
his counsel. Although he agreed that Sherman's plan was strategically
sound—warfare "according to the rule"—he could not support it.[53] He
had always fought by instinct, not by the book; and Halleck and the
president had ordered the army to Vicksburg, and there it would stay. "I
shall not return to Memphis until the close of this campaign," he told
Julia privately.[54] The timing, he thought, was exactly wrong. The Lincoln
administration and the country would see a return to Memphis as a con-
fession of defeat. "At this time the North had become very much discouraged," he wrote later. "Many strong Union men believed that the war
must prove a failure." The elections of 1862 had gone badly for the party
of the president, which lost thirty-two seats to Democrats in the House
of Representatives. "Voluntary enlistments had ceased throughout the
greater part of the North, and the draft had been resorted to [in August]
to fill up our ranks. It was my judgment at the time that to make a backward movement as long as that from Vicksburg to Memphis, would be

interpreted, by many of those yet full of hope for the preservation of the Union, as a defeat, and the draft would be resisted, desertions ensue and the power to capture and punish deserters lost."[55]

Years later, Grant claimed he was developing at the time his own plan to take Vicksburg, but had decided not to reveal it to anyone, not even his staff, until conditions essential for its fulfillment were favorable.[56] He had, however, given Henry Halleck a hint of where his mind was moving in a dispatch written from Memphis before departing for Vicksburg. "What may be necessary to reduce the place I do not yet know, but . . . think our troops must get below the city to be used effectively."[57]*

Grant envisioned marching his army south, through the Louisiana bayou country, to some place below Vicksburg, and have it cross the Mississippi and begin operations against the city along any good roads it could find. To pull this off, the transports would have to be sent downriver, braving the guns of Vicksburg. They could only get by, he believed, with the ironclads as escorts. He would need to talk to Porter about this.[58]

James Wilson—"quick and nervous in temperament, plain and outspoken on all subjects"—proposed virtually the same plan to John Rawlins on the January morning they accompanied Grant and his generals to examine the canal and Vicksburg's defenses.[59] Sitting on the trunk of a fallen cottonwood tree while Grant spoke with Sherman and Blair, the two friends, who had become brothers in all but blood, quietly swapped ideas on how to take Vicksburg. Rawlins found Wilson's plan risky in the extreme. At Fort Donelson, guns greatly less menacing than Vicksburg's had punished Porter's ironclads. Wilson was quick to remind him, however, that he had witnessed the Union capture of Port

---

* Some officers in Grant's command were thinking along the same lines. "Russ" Jones, a cotton trader, was on *Magnolia* with Grant and his staff on their way to Vicksburg when he overheard officers lounging on the deck discussing ways to reduce Vicksburg. "As I understand it," Jones wrote to his friend Elihu Washburne, "the only hope of getting Vicksburg is in being able to get below it and in behind." ("Russ" Jones to Elihu Washburne, January 28, Washburne Papers, LC.) Some reporters in Grant's camps expected him to try to get south of Vicksburg shortly after he arrived at Young's Point. "The running of the water batteries at Vicksburg by some of the gunboats seems to us more and more imminent as the only means of ensuring any attack upon the lower side of the city," the *Chicago Tribune* noted. CT, February 12, 1863.

Royal, South Carolina, the previous year. The enemy's earthen forts had been "made untenable," he said, by the close-range fire of wooden men-of-war, without losing a single vessel or suffering more than "a trifling loss of life." Wilson was "thoroughly convinced," he said, "that our Mississippi fleet, although composed of comparatively light river steamers, could run by the Vicksburg batteries under cover of darkness without serious loss." [60] Rawlins was persuaded, and agreed to present the idea to Grant that evening when he met with his generals on *Magnolia*.

It did not go well. Grant listened attentively but said nothing. Everyone else at the table opposed the idea.[61] There is no record of their deliberations, but at this desperate time in the war the army could not afford to take long risks; and, anyway, the rebels controlled the river south of Vicksburg, all the way to Port Hudson. Porter would need to recapture it before Grant could move his army in that direction. But in Grant's mind, the deciding issue was weather and terrain. Every Louisiana road south of Young's Point was under water, his scouts had informed him, as were the hamlets and plantations the army would require as forward supply bases and staging areas for a decisive move south. And the waters were not expected to recede until late March at the earliest.

"Like Noah," wrote historian J. F. C. Fuller, "[Grant] looked out upon the waters waiting for them to subside." [62] He was not, however, inactive. The day of the strategy session on *Magnolia* he set in motion two projects "Titan-like in their audacity." Grant aimed to defeat geography by opening obscure waterways, hitherto blocked or closed to commerce, and use them to carry the Army of the Tennessee to "high ground on the east bank of the river . . . avoiding the batteries." [63]

On January 30, he ordered two engineering officers to Lake Providence, in northern Louisiana, to assess the feasibility of connecting the large freshwater lake there to the Mississippi by means of a short canal. The lake spilled into two heavily forested, swamp-like bayous. If river water were let into the lake, it might rush southward into these debris-clogged streams, which flowed into a chain of navigable Delta streams—the Tensas, Washita, and Black Rivers. These streams emptied into the Red River, which met the Mississippi a little above and out of reach of the rebel guns at Port Hudson. If it were possible to cut the canal and clear the clotted bayous, a shallow-draft Union war fleet might use the new passageway to reach dry land south of Vicksburg.[64]

It was a plan of breathtaking reach and complexity. The distance from Lake Providence to where the Red River entered the Mississippi is nearly two hundred miles by twisting backcountry waterways and it is another one hundred and fifty miles by the meandering Mississippi to Vicksburg.[65]

Grant's second initiative was equally ambitious, an effort to slice through a network of narrow streams and bayous in some of the toughest terrain in the South. This was the Yazoo wilderness James Wilson had thought impenetrable by an army, on foot or over water. After closely studying maps of the Delta and conferring with Admiral Porter, Grant discovered, two hundred miles north of Vicksburg, an old steamboat cutoff that ran from the Mississippi, through the Delta, to the main stem of the Yazoo River. Light-draft trading boats from Memphis had used this so-called Yazoo Pass to reach cotton plantations along the narrow, serpentine rivers—the Coldwater, Tallahatchie, Yalobusha, and Yazoo—that transected the Delta.[66]

Five years before the war, politically powerful planters had pressured the state to close the pass with a levee, one hundred feet thick, to prevent their low-lying lands from being flooded whenever the river rose. An experienced river pilot who had plied the old Yazoo Pass told Porter it could be made navigable for Union transports and gunboats.[67] Hearing this, Grant moved to reopen the pass and explore its possibilities as an all-water route for his army to the rear of Vicksburg. It would be a joint army-navy expedition, Grant providing the transports and troops, Porter the gunboats.[68]*

"I, myself, never felt great confidence that any of the experiments resorted to would prove successful," Grant would write years later in his *Personal Memoirs*. "Nevertheless I was always prepared to take advantage of them in case they did."[69] Thus was born one of the enduring myths of the Vicksburg campaign. It was a myth advanced most assiduously by Adam Badeau, who wrote, presumably with Grant's consent: "[The

---

* The Yazoo expedition had an intermediate, and unrealized, objective. Halfway downstream, the river fleet was to ascend the Yalobusha River to Grenada and destroy two railroad bridges the Confederates counted upon to move troops and supplies in and out of Vicksburg. If the expedition made it to the Yazoo River, it was to destroy two rebel gunboats believed to be "in the course of construction." OR I/24, part 1, 373.

general] looked on [these projects] as in reality offering little promise, and simply afforded occupation for his men, till the subsidence of
the waters would allow him to move in the ordinary way."[70] Grant *did*
consider inactivity "injurious" to the health and morale of his army.[71]
But in the dismal winter of 1863—the Valley Forge of the Vicksburg
campaign—he pressed both the Yazoo and Lake Providence projects
aggressively and with high hopes for their success.

CHAPTER 14

"Things Fall Apart . . ."

"Things fall apart; the centre cannot hold . . ."[1]
—William Butler Yeats, "The Second Coming"

On January 29, Ulysses Grant sent twenty-five-year-old James Wilson on a swift steamer to Helena, Arkansas, six miles north and across the Mississippi from the old steamboat entrance to Yazoo Pass. He was to take command of a five-hundred-man work party sent to breach the earthen levee that blocked the old entrance. The levee was gigantic, twenty-eight feet high, over 1,100 feet long, and three hundred feet wide at its base.[2]

Five days later, Wilson's pioneers exploded an enormous mine they had buried under it. The explosion shook the earth for miles and the river water thundered through the gap "like nothing else I ever saw, except Niagara Falls," Wilson reported to Grant. The boiling current created a deep, navigable channel into Yazoo Pass. Wilson pronounced the work "a perfect success," and James L. Alcorn, a prominent local planter who had opposed secession, assured him there would be "no difficulty whatever in reaching the Yazoo River with boats of medium size."[3]

When the swirling water settled down a week later, Wilson entered the pass in the wooden gunboat *Forest Rose* and explored it to within several miles of the Coldwater River. There he ran into three cotton traders in a dugout canoe who had just paddled up from the Tallahatchie. They brought unwelcome news: Confederate soldiers were rounding up slaves at gunpoint and directing them to fell giant oaks and cypresses along the riverbanks and topple them into the stream. "While we are engaged in opening the Pass at one end, the rebels [are] closing it at the other," Lieutenant Colonel Wilson notified Grant.[4]

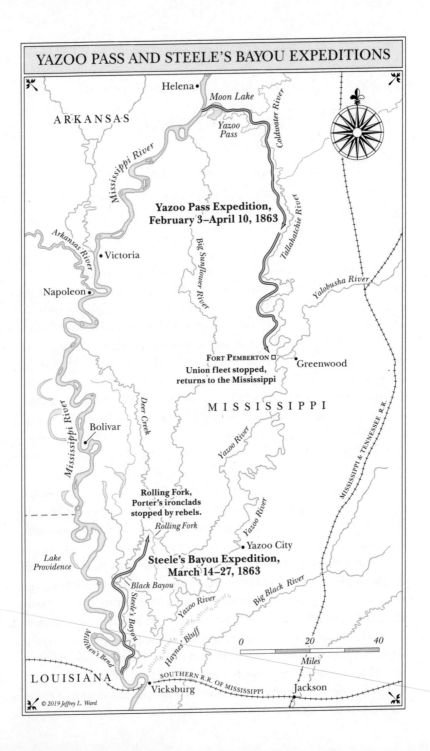

YAZOO PASS AND STEELE'S BAYOU EXPEDITIONS

Helena•

Moon Lake

ARKANSAS

Yazoo Pass

Coldwater River

Mississippi River

**Yazoo Pass Expedition,
February 3–April 10, 1863**

Tallahatchie River

Big Sunflower River

•Victoria

Arkansas River

Yalobusha River

Napoleon•

FORT PEMBERTON □ •Greenwood
**Union fleet stopped,
returns to the Mississippi**

MISSISSIPPI

Deer Creek

Bolivar•

Mississippi River

Yazoo River

**Rolling Fork,
Porter's ironclads
stopped by rebels.**

Yazoo River

Rolling Fork

Lake
Providence

•Yazoo City

**Steele's Bayou Expedition,
March 14–27, 1863**

Black Bayou

Big Black River

Yazoo River

Steele's Bayou

Milliken's Bend

Haynes' Bluff

0   20   40

Miles

LOUISIANA

SOUTHERN R.R. OF MISSISSIPPI

Vicksburg•   Jackson•

MISSISSIPPI & TENNESSEE R.R.

© 2019 Jeffrey L. Ward

There was another problem. Tall forest trees lined both sides of the narrow pass. Their drooping branches intersected at midstream, creating a thick canopy that would prevent the high-sitting transports, with their tall smokestacks, from passing through. Clearing these obstacles would be tedious, time-consuming work. Removing the ancient trees that rebel saboteurs had dropped into the pass would be an even stiffer challenge. Some of them were ninety feet long, had trunks four feet thick, and weighed up to thirty-five tons.

Wilson's work crews, augmented by 1,600 men sent down from Helena, positioned themselves on the narrow, mud-slicked strip of land that lined the banks and began hauling the dead trees out of the stream by brute force, using powerful steamboat cables.[5] Fortunately, Pemberton had ordered no organized effort to impede the expedition. On February 9, Isaac Brown, former captain of the rebel ram *Arkansas* and now naval commander at Yazoo City, notified Pemberton: "The enemy have cut the Yazoo Pass levee; contemplate, perhaps, assailing us down the Yazoo." A movement in that direction was improbable, Pemberton responded.[6]

Wilson's reports to Grant were unrelievedly optimistic. "With all these things against us, there is no doubt of our ability to remove the obstructions and make the Pass navigable for boats that pass through [large canals]," he wrote from Yazoo Pass.[7]

"I expect great results," Grant told Admiral Porter.[8]

Grant was also receiving good news from the exploratory party he had dispatched to Lake Providence. A reinforced brigade from McClernand's corps was cutting through a high levee on the banks of the Mississippi to construct the canal Grant had ordered built to link the river to the lake. It would be completed in less than a week, reported engineering officer George W. Deitzler. Deitzler was equally optimistic about clearing the heavily forested bayous below the lake. "It will only be necessary to cut a few trees so as not to interfere with chimneys. Once in Bayou Macon we shall have a clean coast to Red River." He expected gunboats to be in the cleared channel within three weeks.[9]

It was one of the most misleading engineering assessments of the campaign, but Grant was willfully optimistic. He showed the report to

Sherman, who pronounced the Lake Providence "scheme . . . worthy of determined prosecution."[10] The next day Grant headed upriver to inspect the work. Upon arriving, he contacted James McPherson at Memphis. "A little digging . . . will connect the Mississippi and the Lake, and in all probability will wash a channel in a short time. . . . This bids fair to be the most practicable route for turning Vicksburg. . . . Move one Division of your command to this place with as little delay as practicable, and come with yourself."[11]

Thirty-four-year-old James Birdseye McPherson was one of only a handful of West Point–trained engineers in Grant's army. First in his 1853 class at West Point, and the youngest officer ever to teach engineering at the Point, he had been Grant's chief engineer at Donelson, Shiloh, and Corinth. With McPherson at Lake Providence and Wilson in the Yazoo Pass, Grant would have two feverishly energetic young officers—two of his "best men . . . each worth more than a full Brigade"—directing projects of far greater promise than the cutoff canal at De Soto Peninsula.[12] For the next two months, Grant directed from afar these prodigious projects, "perhaps the most gigantic flanking movement ever attempted in military history," in the opinion of nineteenth-century historian John Fiske.[13]

An impatient Northern public followed the progress of these projects with mounting skepticism, unfamiliar with the obscure rivers and bayous Grant was exploring as possible passageways to victory. Why was Grant not going straight at Vicksburg? Where was the Grant of Donelson and Shiloh, the defiant warrior who refused to entrench? Had the double defeat in Mississippi made him cautious? "We are not much nearer an attack on Vicksburg now apparently than when I first [came] down," Grant confessed to Julia on February 11, but "the attack will be made," perhaps, he surmised, from Lake Providence.[14]

Lake Providence, however, would be a more challenging undertaking than Colonel Deitzler indicated. The canal was nearly completed when Grant arrived there, but William L. Duff, Deitzler's second in command, warned him that the levee would not be cut and the water let into the lake "until the outlet through Bayou Baxter is clear. This cannot be done," he conceded, "with the force now here."[15] McPherson's corps was still stalled at Memphis. The transports he was expecting from St. Louis were being held up by treacherous winter weather up north.[16]

Grant was in no mood to receive this deflating news. He was suffering from hemorrhoids and was laid low by incapacitating migraines.[17]

Union troops at Lake Providence were relieved to be there, miles from the mud and raging disease of their canal camps at De Soto Point. Lake Providence was home to princely cotton plantations, and the splendidly landscaped mansions of the local grandees rimmed the sparkling, blue-green lake and were shaded by stately evergreens. Illinois infantryman Charles B. Allaire thought the country around the lake "as near to . . . Paradise as is possible for mortals ever to witness."[18] When the Yankees arrived, most of the local aristocracy had already fled, leaving nearly everything behind. McClernand's men raided their abundantly provisioned homesteads for poultry, cattle, and sweet potatoes—and slaves to work on the canal. The slaves needed no encouragement. "The negroes are coming in droves everyday," wrote an Illinois soldier.[19]

When Sergeant Cyrus Boyd arrived from Young's Point on February 10, he saw from the bow of his incoming transport a dozen or so "contrabands" digging a "great ditch." The following morning he was in that ditch working alongside them. A few days later he spotted a steamer packed to the gunnels with human beings, "big, little, old and young all shrieking for liberty."[20]

The men were put to work on the canal and the women and children were sent to pick cotton on vacant plantations, where they toiled under the indifferent supervision of soldiers.[21] "We have set the niggers picking cotton and are ginning and bailing it in the gin and press near our camp," wrote Seneca Thrall, who had come up from Young's Point with Cyrus Boyd, his fellow Iowan.[22]

The husbands, sons, and fathers of the pickers did the burden of the labor on the ditch. If the canal was ever to be finished and successful, "it will only be by the work of the darkies," Illinois surgeon Charles Brown Tomkins wrote his wife Mollie, a fellow abolitionist. "They work with a will. The soldiers, who are detailed daily, do nothing but throw mud at the Negroes or at each other."[23]

In late February the weather turned serene, a preview of spring, and soldiers confiscated small boats and sailed and fished on the shimmering lake, entertained on shore by their regimental bands. The health of the army was "excellent," said the *Chicago Tribune*, and so was morale.[24] The men expected to be on the Red River soon, bound for Vicksburg.[25]

Spirits soared when General McPherson arrived with John Logan's division on February 23. Grant steamed up from Young's Point to meet McPherson.[26] The two were close, and Grant treated him like an adopted son. He had risen, as Grant had, "solely on his own merit." McPherson was beloved by his men.[27] He had a "sunny and hopeful disposition," said his friend James Wilson, and was one of the most popular generals in the Union army. Just over six feet tall, with a full brown beard and flashing eyes, he had a commanding presence, without a trace of pomposity. He also got along with reporters; and in an army renowned for its hard-drinking officers, he was a model of moderation.[28]

Lake Providence was an important assignment, and McPherson seemed the man for the job. His engineering expertise would be greatly needed in the tangled swamps and bayous below the lake. Both of those bayous, Macon and Baxter, were covered with a dense cypress forest that hung over a shallow main channel choked by stumps and snags. Grant and McPherson reconnoitered the bayous in a tiny steamboat hauled overland from the river to the lake by an Iowa regiment, using ropes, tackle, and rollers. "I saw then that there was scarcely a chance of this ever becoming a practicable route for moving troops through an enemy's country," Grant recalled in his memoirs. It would take months, he thought, to clear a navigable passageway; and when the water was finally released from the Mississippi it might not scour a channel deep enough for gunboats and light-draft steamers. Even if the project worked to perfection, the enemy might position sharpshooters along the Washita and Tensas Rivers "to obstruct our passage and pick off our troops."[29]

Grant wrote this long after the war, yet he failed to adequately explain why he had not called off the man-draining project that had little chance of succeeding. "I let the work go on, believing employment was better than idleness for the men," was his unconvincing explanation.[30] This is misleading. Grant's enthusiasm for the Lake Providence route, it is true, dimmed considerably after his initial reconnaissance, but he didn't give up on it entirely, as he suggested in his memoirs. "If you think there is a reasonable prospect of the river making a channel through [the bayous] . . ." he told McPherson in early March, "you may prosecute it. . . . At all events clear out the channel of the timber in it, and let the water in to see what it will do."[31]

Work on the Lake Providence canal continued, not because Grant wanted to keep McPherson's men busy but because he feared foreclosing any opportunity, however slim, to get a footing behind Vicksburg.

McPherson assigned the bayou clearing operation to Colonel Josiah Bissell and his western engineering regiment. Working on flatboats and floating rafts, Bissell's pioneers used sharp-toothed underwater saws to cut obstructions in the channel. It was killing work, and many of the men despaired of ever completing the passageway.[32] On March 1, McPherson wrote Grant: "I have just returned from an examination of 'Bayou Baxter' from its source down about seven miles. The work of clearing it out is much greater than I was led to believe from the Engineers Report."[33]

By this time, Grant *had* shifted his interest almost entirely to the Yazoo Pass expedition. James Wilson had been keeping him abreast of his promising progress in Yazoo Pass. Much of the pass had been cleared of felled timber and overhanging vegetation, and it was ready to receive the flotilla already assembled at Helena. "There is little possibility of . . . getting through Lake Providence and Bayou Macon" by way of an "artificial channel," Grant wrote Halleck. "The Yazoo Pass expedition is a much greater success."[34]

The Federal fleet had entered the pass on February 24. It was formidable: two ironclads—the war-tested *Baron De Kalb* and the untried *Chillicothe*—and six lightly armored tinclads, two Ellet rams, a mortar scow, and twenty-two sternwheel steamers carrying roughly six thousand infantry. Lieutenant Commander Watson Smith, a thirty-seven-year-old blue-water veteran with limited experience on Mississippi operations, headed the naval contingent. Porter had wanted to take personal charge, but was preoccupied with operations on the Mississippi.[35] Brigadier General Leonard F. Ross, with long service under Grant, commanded the infantry and artillery brigades.[36]

As his steamer headed into the pass, Iowa sergeant Samuel Byers looked out at a vast inland sea extending for at least "half a hundred miles," the tremendous overflow from the breach in the levee.[37] Then the sky disappeared and it became eerily dark. The fleet was in a luxuriant hardwood forest, where interlocking branches and grapevines shut out the sun, toppled the smokestacks of troopships, ripped off pilothouses, and mashed the paddlewheel of at least one vessel. The forest "almost dismantled the boats," wrote Indiana volunteer Enoch Weiss.[38] And nearly "every hour projecting stumps and trees had to be sawn off under water to allow our craft to get through," said Byers.[39] It was the beginning of "a painful and ever-to-be-remembered expedition."[40]

Before reaching the wide and deep Coldwater River at the end of the month, James Wilson sent Grant a message, carried by courier boat, reaffirming his conviction about "the practicability of this route . . . as a line of military operations."[41] The report had rippling consequences. After reading it, Grant decided to roll the dice and transform what had been an exploratory expedition into a full-scale assault on Vicksburg.[42] On March 5, he directed McPherson to move every man he had available into Yazoo Pass as soon as the transports he had requisitioned arrived at Lake Providence—small steamers capable of navigating the Delta's constricted waterways. "I want your Corps to get in there as rapidly as possible and effect a lodgment at . . . the most eligible point on Yazoo river from which to operate [against Vicksburg]." McPherson was to send into the Delta immediately, "in advance" of his entire corps, a brigade under General Isaac F. Quinby, a brainy veteran of Fort Donelson who had taught math and philosophy at Rochester University. Have him bring "provisions and coal" for a "prolonged campaign," Grant ordered.[43]

Quinby was to overtake Ross and assume command of the expedition until McPherson arrived with the remainder of his corps. The Federals would then have an assault force of twenty-five thousand men. Grant planned to rendezvous with McPherson somewhere on the Yazoo, bringing with him additional infantry from Milliken's Bend and Young's Point. By then he would have a "full plan of attack," he promised a deeply concerned Henry Halleck.[44]

"I will have Vicksburg this month, or fail in the attempt," Grant assured the general in chief the next day.[45]

Halleck did not share his enthusiasm for another roundabout campaign to flank Vicksburg; neither did the president. Grant was dividing his army in front of the enemy, never a sound strategy. All efforts, Halleck cautioned, "should be sacrificed for the sake of concentration," a massive army-navy thrust against Vicksburg. But Grant had already moved in advance of informing Halleck. All Halleck could do was remind him that "the eyes and hopes of the whole country are now directed to your army. In my opinion the opening of the Mississippi River will be to us of more advantage than the capture of forty Richmonds."[46]

It was an unsubtle warning that the Yazoo expedition was being seen by the War Department as a dangerous diversion. He wanted Grant operating, in cooperation with Porter, solely on the Mississippi.

Rather than argue with Halleck, Grant moved ahead with a confidence born of despair. On March 10, he invited his home-state congressman Elihu B. Washburne to come down to Vicksburg to witness "the contest which will take place in the next thirty days from this writing. So far as I now know, and have official reports, the Yazoo Pass expedition is going to prove a perfect success." He would begin operations as soon as transports "adapted to the pass" reached McPherson at Lake Providence.[47]

Grant's optimism was founded upon false information. On March 6, Porter had assured him that Watson Smith's ironclads had reached the Yazoo, above Haynes' Bluff, and had fired a signal gun to alert the rest of the gunboat fleet, berthed at the mouth of the river. Porter was mistaken. The gunboats were nearly a hundred miles away, on the Coldwater River, above the town of Greenwood.[48]

Wilson and Ross pressed naval commander Watson Smith to pick up the pace and get to the Yazoo before the rebels had time to assemble a force to stop them. But Smith had taken sick upon entering Yazoo Pass and moved with unreasonable caution, getting off late in the morning and stopping for the night an hour before dinner, despite disturbing reports from his landing parties that the rebels were seizing cotton bales from riverside plantations to build a fortified blockade downriver.[49]

Pemberton had finally begun to take the Union threat seriously when the "Abolition" fleet entered the Coldwater. Major General William Loring, a contentious, one-armed veteran of the Mexican War, was rushed from Grenada to Greenwood to oversee the construction of a defensive work on a long neck of land between the Tallahatchie and Yazoo Rivers. Light field artillery and a large-caliber rifled cannon were emplaced behind a ten-foot-high line of dirt-covered cotton bales, and two thousand infantry were brought in. Loring sank a raft and an obsolete steamer to block the Tallahatchie. The rifled cannon faced directly upriver, giving its crew an unimpeded line of fire up the Tallahatchie, which flowed in a straight line toward the fort and was only wide enough to allow the passage of one ironclad at a time. The cleared and heavily flooded land around the fort made it impervious to an infantry assault. The defenders called their blockade Fort Pemberton.[50]

On the evening of March 10, the Federal fleet landed about twenty miles above Fort Pemberton. Local slaves warned the Yankees that a big defensive work lay just ahead.[51] The next morning, Watson Smith, accompanied by Wilson and Ross, boarded *Chillicothe* to have a look. "A turn in the stream brought us within view, at about 900 yards distance," Smith wrote later. "The enemy immediately opened fire . . . striking the *Chillicothe* repeated[ly] and seriously damaging the forward face of the casement." Smith withdrew to organize a general attack.[52]

Hours later, *Baron De Kalb* and *Chillicothe* steamed downriver, tied up to the bank, and blasted away. The rebels, fighting with "the courage of despair," got the best of the exchange.[53] Their heavy cannon did terrible damage to *Chillicothe*, killing four of its crew and wounding twelve.[54] The tinclads remained upstream and largely out of the action, the river being too narrow for them to engage. That night landing parties set up a battery seven hundred yards from the fort. The guns scattered cotton and dirt but did no serious damage. "We go at them again . . . until we get possession," Ross ordered.[55] But two more attacks that week failed, and in the final assault *Chillicothe* was struck hard and temporarily disabled.[56] Wilson implored Smith to try again and with greater resolve, running his war boats in close to the fort, at two hundred—not eight hundred—yards, but Smith judged the risk too great. "I've talked to [him] and tried to give [him] backbone," Wilson reported to Grant. Smith was no Lord Nelson, he added.[57]

While *Chillicothe* was being repaired—it had taken over forty direct hits—Wilson sent out reconnaissance parties to scout the deep swamps and bayous around the fort, searching for a "point of attack for infantry." None was found.[58] The situation had become critical. Wilson knew Quinby was on his way with reinforcements, but he had received no word from him; and the two ironclads were nearly out of ammunition.[59] Wilson and Ross feared the rebels were about to box them in and "bag" the "entire force" by setting up a blockade in their rear.[60]

On March 18, Watson Smith's health broke and he was sent back to Helena in "dying condition." Naval command passed to Lt. Commander James P. Foster, captain of *Chillicothe*. That evening he met with Ross and Wilson and they agreed to withdraw.[61] In three furious exchanges their gunboats had killed only one rebel.[62]

"We have thrown away a magnificent chance, to injure the enemy and all because of the culpable and inexcusable slowness of the Naval Commander in the first place, and his timidity and cautiousness in the Second," Wilson conveyed his disappointment to Grant.[63] If Smith had sent the gunboats ahead of the transports, when they were back on the Coldwater, they could have arrived at Fort Pemberton, Wilson was convinced, nine days in advance of the rest of the fleet and destroyed the partially completed, badly outgunned fort.[64] Porter would also blame Smith, claiming he "showed symptoms of aberration of mind."[65] The moment he became sick, he should have surrendered his command to Foster, Porter informed Welles.[66]

As the Yazoo fleet headed back to the Mississippi, Grant had no idea it was withdrawing. He had not heard from Wilson or Ross since early March. Wilson had been communicating with him, but the messages had yet to reach him by maddeningly slow dispatch boats. Grant had, however, received word from his scouts along the Yazoo. The gunboats, they reported, had reached Greenwood and "exchanged a few shots with the fort at that place." Reinforcements and additional guns were being sent from Vicksburg. The Ross expedition was clearly in trouble. Grant consulted with Porter, and Porter began mobilizing a naval relief force to prevent its encirclement.[67]

At exactly this time, some friendly slaves provided Porter's captains with information about the existence of a lazy tributary of the Yazoo hidden from view by thick vegetation.[68] It was called Steele's Bayou, and it became the basis of the rescue plan Porter and Grant would fashion.

• • •

Porter knew from old river charts that Steele's Bayou led northward to a chain of narrow streams and bayous that joined the Sunflower River, which flowed directly south, emptying into the Yazoo not far from the Confederate naval station at Yazoo City, upriver from Haynes' Bluff. The rebels were using Yazoo City to shuttle supplies and soldiers to Fort Pemberton. If Porter's gunboats could threaten Yazoo City, Loring would be forced to abandon Fort Pemberton to avert a possible enemy effort to flank Vicksburg. Grant considered the enterprise "of vast importance." [69]

It would be a risky operation, but there was no other way to get to Yazoo City without running under plunging fire from the bluffs upriver from Chickasaw Bayou. To reach Yazoo City via Steele's Bayou, Porter's boats would have to travel over one hundred miles through an untracked wilderness to arrive at a point only twenty miles from where they had first entered the bayou, going directly north to meet the Sunflower and then turning south down that river to the Yazoo, an operation that looked on the map like an upside-down U.[70] But Porter was keen to go with or without Grant, and he committed five of his prize gunboats, the original City-class series designed by James Eads. Four mortar boats—towed by tugs—accompanied them, with "shells enough to bombard a city." [71]

Porter personally explored the pass on March 13 and found it wider than expected and at least fifteen feet deep. In opening Yazoo Pass, allowing the waters of the Mississippi into the Delta river courses, James Wilson's engineering crews had transformed a shallow bayou into a lake wide enough for the gunboats "to ply about" giant trees, "old monarchs of the woods . . . with perfect impunity." [72] A local river pilot assured Porter that his shallow-draft ironclads could easily navigate the streams above Steele's Bayou.[73] High water, "the curse of the campaign," would now prove an asset.[74]

On March 15, Porter invited Grant to join him on the ram *General Price* on the first leg of his push up Steele's Bayou. "It was a curious sight," Porter wrote later, "to see a line of ironclads and mortar boats, tugs and transports, pushing their way through the long, wide lane in the woods without touching on either side." [75] After several hours, however, the bayou "grew narrower and crooked, till it resembled more the course taken by some erratic meadow brook," wrote reporter Franc

Wilkie, who accompanied the expedition. They had entered a stream called Black Bayou, and its gray-black waters were filled with alligators and enormous snapping turtles. Battalions of insects swarmed around the heads of the sailors as their progress upstream slowed to a crawl.[76]

When night fell, Grant returned to Young's Point aboard *General Price*, and Porter moved to the ironclad *Carondelet* to take charge of the advance. Encouraged by the depth and breadth of most of the waterway they had explored, Grant reformulated his plan and began assembling an infantry force to accompany Porter. It would survey the streams north of Steele's Bayou to see if they might provide him a brown-water highway to dry ground behind Vicksburg.

Taking Yazoo City might save the Ross expedition, but it would also make an excellent base from which to attack Vicksburg. A rescue effort had suddenly become something far larger.[77]

News from Colonel Parsons, the quartermaster in St. Louis, convinced Grant he had no choice but to pursue this new plan to the exclusion of all others. There were not enough small steamers presently available to carry McPherson's corps into Yazoo Pass. This changed everything. Even if Wilson's Yazoo force were saved, the expedition would amount to nothing. There were not enough small boats to carry an invasion army to Vicksburg by way of Yazoo Pass. But perhaps the Steele's Bayou route would prove wide and deep enough for large steamers, boats Grant had in abundance at his Louisiana camps.

"I have just returned from a reconnaissance up Steele's Bayou with the admiral, and five of his gunboats," Grant wrote Sherman at De Soto Point. "With some labor in cutting tree-tops out of the way, it will be navigable *for any class of steamers.*

"I want you to have your pioneer corps, or one regiment of good men for such work, detailed, and at the [Young's Point] landing as soon as possible. . . . The Eighth Missouri (being many of them boatmen) would be excellent men for this purpose."[78]

Relieved to be released from the mud and monotony of canal duty, Sherman sprang into action, shooting a communiqué to Colonel Giles A. Smith, commander of the 8th Missouri, ordering him to have his men board two small steamers, *Diligent* and *Silver Wave.* They were

to head to Black Bayou and begin cutting overhanging trees and clearing underwater obstructions for the passage of troop transports.[79] When
the bayou was opened, a division from Sherman's corps would arrive
at Eagle Bend on the Mississippi, one mile west of Steele's Bayou, and
march inland to the bayou. Transports would be waiting for them there.
The expedition would then head upstream to rendezvous with Porter
and provide protection for his five ironclads.

"You will proceed . . . up Steele's Bayou and through Black Bayou
to Deer Creek, and thence with the gunboats now there, by any route
they may take to get into the Yazoo River, for the purpose of determin-
ing the feasibility of getting an army through that route to the east bank
of that river, and at a point from which they can act advantageously
against Vicksburg."[80] Sherman's orders could not have been clearer. Part
of Grant's genius as a commander was his facility with the English language, his ability to write orders that communicated to his subordinates
exactly his intentions and their responsibilities.

In his memoirs, Grant was as dismissive of this new effort to flank
Vicksburg from the north as he was of the Yazoo Pass initiative, suggesting that neither mission had an influence on the strategic pulse of
the campaign. But with the collapse of the Yazoo Pass offensive, all real-
izable efforts to take Vicksburg in March of 1863 had been reduced to
one: a chancy run into the heart of darkness.

Halleck again disapproved, seeing Steele's Bayou as a dangerous
diversion. "These "excentric [sic] operations may have been very proper,
for the purpose of reconnoitering the country;" he scolded Grant, "but
it is very important that, when you strike any blow, you should have
your troops sufficiently concentrated to make that blow effective."[81]

The Steele's Bayou expedition made the Yazoo Pass offensive "look
simple," wrote historian Bruce Catton. "It met all the problems which
Commander Smith's troops had met, most of them multiplied by
five."[82] But what else could Grant do? "*Not a blow* has been struck at
[Vicksburg] since I assaulted Chickasaw," Sherman wrote despondently
to his brother John, echoing Grant's frustration.[83] Even if the expedition failed, it was better to go ahead, Grant agreed with Porter, than to
"sit . . . down before Vicksburg and simply look . . . at it."[84] Intolerant
of stalemate, inclined always to advance, he and Porter launched "one

of the most remarkable military and naval expeditions that ever set out in any country," Porter wrote later.[85]

The audacious admiral expected to "get into the rear of Vicksburg without loss of life or vessels," but the expedition almost cost him his life, along with the core of the gunboat fleet essential for taking Vicksburg.[86] It very nearly cost Grant his command.

CHAPTER 15

Steele's Bayou

"The darkness drops again . . ."[1]
—William Butler Yeats, "The Second Coming"

Admiral Porter found the Delta waterways more challenging than he anticipated. Entering gloomy Black Bayou, just north of Steele's Bayou, he ran into thick beds of willow saplings embedded in the bottom of the stream, a deadly hindrance for boats powered by big paddle wheels that moved through rather than over the water. His sailors had to wade into the dark waters and yank them out by their roots. As at Yazoo Pass, moss-draped trees lined both banks and their branches interlocked at midstream, closing off sunlight and sweeping away smokestacks and pilothouses.[2] Halfway through the bayou, the flotilla's seasoned pilot confessed he was lost.[3] "Not a plantation or clearing broke [the] dreary solitude for forty miles," wrote *Chicago Times* reporter Sylvanus Cadwallader, an observer on one of the gunboats. "Birds, fish, snakes, turtles and alligators were the only living things we saw while traversing its dark and gloomy labyrinths."[4]

It took a day and a night to get through four-mile-long Black Bayou. On the morning of March 18, the gunboats berthed at a local landmark, Hill's plantation, where the abandoned slaves were "in charge of the place."[5] An hour later, the Union tugboat *Fern* hove into view. Sherman was on board and he wanted to see Porter. Leaving his work parties behind at Black Bayou, Sherman had impulsively rushed ahead to test the depth of the water upstream, alone except for a few staff officers on an unarmed vessel, an easy target for a rebel sharpshooter.[6]

After meeting with Porter to map out a plan of cooperation, he dropped back to Black Bayou to bring forward Giles Smith and his 8th Missouri regiment. They were to hold Hill's plantation as a staging area for additional troops Grant was funneling from Young's Point. Sherman's hazardous run upstream had convinced him that Grant's plan to move an entire army through these perilously narrow bayous and creeks would be defeated by the terrain. The route Porter was taking, he informed Grant by courier boat, was not "practicable" for large troop transports.[7] Only sturdy gunboats, and possibly small sidewheel steamers, could get through. Grant did not reply. It was too early to concede defeat.[8]

The farther north Porter went, the more difficult the terrain became. Deer Creek, connected to and north of Black Bayou, was barely wide enough for his gunboats to pass through. Dead trees hanging over the banks "were full of vermin of all sorts," Porter recounted. ". . . Rats and mice, driven from the fields by the high water, had taken up their abode in the hollow trunks and rotten branches. Snakes of every kind and description had followed the rats and mice to these old arks of safety." When a tank-like ironclad smashed into one of these decaying trees, "a multitude of vermin would be shaken out on the deck . . . and would be swept overboard by the sailors standing ready with their brooms."[9]

Farther upstream, Confederate revenue agents spotted the fleet and began stacking cotton bales on the banks of the creek in advance of the gunboats and setting them on fire to keep them out of enemy hands.[10] Tremendous sheets of flame—a "fiery gauntlet"—scorched the sides of Porter's boats and slowed their progress. "The thick white smoke sent the crews into spasms of coughing, while the heat singed their hair, scorched their faces, and blistered the paint from the vessels' iron flanks."[11]

On March 19, Porter's flotilla was within sight of Rolling Fork, which led directly to the Sunflower River, a wide stream that led south to their ultimate destination, Yazoo City. That morning, rebel cavalry were spotted in the forests by the stream.[12]

Later that afternoon, Porter learned that Confederate soldiers and local planters were forcing slaves to chop trees and drop them into Deer Creek to impede the fleet's progress. And a rebel force was seen a few miles ahead, emplacing artillery.[13] "I beg that you will shove up troops to us at once," Porter wrote Sherman. "I am holding the mouth of Rolling Fork against . . . troops which have attacked our 200 men." The hyperbolic admiral said he needed ten thousand.[14]

The message—carried by a small tug—reached Sherman at midnight. He had already begun loading troops onto small transports, but the boats were experiencing difficulty getting through Black Bayou, he told Porter, "and men can not march, for the whole country is submerged." Sherman would do all in his power "to push the troops through," but it would be impossible, he told Porter, to deliver the number of men he had requested.[15] The admiral would have to survive on his own for a time. Sherman had not heard from Grant, and Grant had no idea where he was. "There is fearful silence in regard to the progress of Sherman's division up the Steele's Bayou," reported a correspondent stationed near Grant's headquarters at Young's Point.[16]

The following day shells from an enemy Parrott gun found the fleet.[17] Isolated and in imminent danger, unable to raise his ships' guns above the high earthen levees that bordered the stream, Porter had to rely on his wildly inaccurate mortars for long-range fire.[18] In desperation, he sent out a landing party of three hundred sailors armed with two boat howitzers. The men threw up a makeshift battery on an ancient Indian burial mound to cover Porter's entrance into Rolling Creek.[19]

The rebels threatening Porter were part of a cavalry-infantry team headed by Lieutenant Col. Samuel W. Ferguson, an impetuous commander known for his iron resolve. Heeding the warnings of local planters, he had rushed his force to Rolling Fork and dispatched a courier to Major General Carter Stevenson, the new commander of the Vicksburg garrison, with a request for reinforcements. The following day, he had Major General Dabney Maury, commander of the Yazoo defenses, send General Winfield Featherston's brigade to Rolling Fork.[20] "Had I been able to give [Ferguson] more troops in time," Maury recalled, "he would have captured the whole fleet."[21]

When Featherston arrived the next day with his Mississippi boys, he and Ferguson determined to rush the gunboats that afternoon, wade through the water, and capture them in hand-to-hand fighting.[22] Field artillery would cover the assault. Around six in the afternoon, the rebel guns began roaring, concentrating their fire initially on the sailor battery on the Indian mound. Within minutes Porter's bluejackets were in panicky retreat back to the gunboats, where they were pinned in their iron-sided caissons by rebel riflemen.[23] But when Ferguson deployed his infantry to launch the assault, Featherston's Mississippians were nowhere in sight. Their leader had lost his nerve and failed to inform Ferguson he was standing down. Later that night, Ferguson found Featherston calmly eating his supper. The attack, he lamely explained, would have been suicidal. The boats were in the middle of the stream and the water, he claimed, was, unexpectedly, "from 10 to 20 feet deep," a gross exaggeration.[24]

Featherston's caution allowed Porter to hold on for another day, but he was prevented from moving to the creek's junction with the Sunflower, just ahead, by the thickest batch of willow snatches he had yet encountered. That night, he ordered the rudders unshipped and began backing the squadron out of Rolling Fork, with enemy sharpshooters, perched on tree limbs, harassing them.[25]

The next morning, local slaves informed Porter that they had spent the night with rebel rifles at their backs, cutting trees and slipping them into the creek in the rear of the fleet.[26] Porter alerted his captains "to prepare for [enemy] boarders." They were to smear the hulls of their five ironclads with mud and slime from the creek bottom, load grape and canister for close-in fire, and block the gunports with hammocks. Men were "to sleep at the guns," and be "ready to repel boarders. . . . Every precaution must be taken to defend the vessels to the last, and when we can do no longer we will blow them up." Gunpowder was spread about the boats. The commanders were to strike a match on a signal from the admiral. Officers and men were to prepare to abandon ship armed with "muskets, pistols or pikes." They were then to reassemble in a patch of woods near the boats and try to escape on foot to Steele's Bayou. Few expected to survive.[27]

Around four o'clock that afternoon, a group of excited freedmen began racing along the sides of the Union boats, shouting "Your folks is coming."[28] It was Giles Smith with eight hundred Missourians. Sherman had sent them forward from Hill's plantation after receiving another message from Porter, this one carried by a slave.[29] It was scrawled on a piece of tissue paper and rolled into a tobacco leaf. It read: "Hurry up, for Heaven's sake."[30] The freedman who delivered the message had guided Smith's brigade through the wilderness to Rolling Fork. Knowing Smith would need heavy reinforcements, Sherman had stayed behind at Hill's plantation to hurry forward troops expected imminently from Black Bayou.

Smith's force was too small to securely cover Porter's escape. The Missourians, however, were able to "scatter the sharpshooters," and the next day, they helped Porter's sailors clear trees and willows from the stream.

Standing in the pilothouse of *Cincinnati*, supervising the operation, Admiral Porter spotted "a large column of gray-uniformed soldiers swooping down on us from the woods . . . determined," he recalled, "to overwhelm us by numbers." A bullet struck the boat's first lieutenant in the head while Porter was giving him an order. He fell at the admiral's feet. Porter called another officer to remove him. He too was hit and collapsed onto the wounded lieutenant's body.[31] An old quartermaster approached Porter, dragging a large, quarter-inch-thick iron plate and told him to stand behind it. As the quartermaster turned to find shelter behind a cotton bale, the man was shot through the head. Peering over the top of his iron shield, Porter saw the advancing rebel column begin to "fall into confusion" and seek cover behind thick trees. "They were retreating before some one," Porter thought. It was Sherman, "steadily driving them back."[32]

Sherman's forced march from Hill's plantation to Rolling Fork was one of the great rescue missions of the war. Had he not arrived that afternoon, Porter likely would have lost his five ironclads and been killed or taken prisoner with his officers and crews.[33] "The Admiral and his boats were at [the enemy's] mercy," wrote Sylvanus Cadwallader. Even if the rebels had not boarded the boats, the sailors "would have been starved into a surrender beyond all question without outside aid!"[34]

Sherman had begun assembling his rescue mission immediately after sending Giles Smith's brigade to Rolling Fork.[35] Too impatient to wait at Hill's plantation for reinforcements, he had jumped into a canoe, alone, and paddled toward Black Bayou to bring forward his pioneer corps, along with troops Grant had sent to Steele's Bayou. Four miles downstream he ran into *Silver Wave*, its decks black with officers and men prepared to move up to Hill's plantation. Sherman then loaded his pioneers into an empty coal barge and hooked it to a navy tug.[36]

When the tiny flotilla found it impossible to force its way through Black Bayou, Sherman had the men debark and press ahead on foot through a driving rainstorm.[37] It was "intensely dark. There was but a narrow strip of land above water, and that was grown up with underbrush or cane," Grant later recounted Sherman's mission. "The troops lighted their way through this with candles carried in their hands for a mile and a half, when they came to . . . [Hill's] plantation. Here the troops rested until morning."[38]

At daybreak, they started along the route Giles Smith had taken the day before. "We could hear Porter's guns, and knew that moments were precious," Sherman recalled. They increased their pace to double quick. In places, the path ended and they had to cross the swamps. "The water came above my hips," said Sherman. "The smaller drummer-boys had to carry their drums on their heads, and most of the men slung their cartridge-boxes around their necks." By noon, they had covered twenty-one miles.[39]

At a plantation near the Indian burial mound they met a detachment of the 8th Missouri. They were acting as pickets to prevent rebels from blocking Porter's withdrawal. The gunboats, they reported, were under intense fire. Sherman ordered his men to sweep forward. Entering a large cottonfield, he spotted the boats just ahead. The rebels were pouring fire into them from a nearby swamp. As Sherman halted momentarily to survey the situation, one of Giles Smith's officers rode up to him on a stolen horse with a rope bridle around its neck and offered it to Sherman. "I got on *bareback* and rode up the levee, the sailors coming out of their ironclads and cheering most vociferously as I rode by, and our men swept forward across the cotton-field in full view." Galloping ahead of his men, Sherman found Porter on the deck of one of the ironclads with a "shield made of the section of a smoke-stack. . . . I doubt if he was ever more glad to meet a friend than he was to see me."[40]

After Sherman's regiments drove off the rebels, working parties cleared the channel, using long-handled axes seized from the enemy.[41] Porter resumed backing downstream, moving at a snail's pace, surrounded by a cordon of Union troops. The enemy pursued halfheartedly, more an annoyance than a lethal threat.[42] So Porter "bumped on homeward," back to the Yazoo River, where he had started picking up great numbers of slaves along the way, all of them in "high glee," wrote one of his officers—"going to freedom . . . they say." [43] The admiral was proud to play the liberator, telling the slaves they were free forever. "More than any place that I have seen do slaves seem determined" to be free, he wrote Welles. "I do not blame them, for slavery exists in the worst form in the valley of the Mississippi." [44]

Porter had other, less morally commendable reasons for liberating slaves. His "squadron," he wrote Gustavus Fox at the Navy Department, "was chock full of niggers. . . . I take all that come—It is the only satisfaction we can take of these [rebels]—It takes the fight out of them. Take away their niggers and you stop the war." [45] There were too many slaves to take on the boats. The overflow walked with Sherman's troops as they sacked and burned plantations along the line of Porter's withdrawal. "One of the richest portions of Mississippi was laid waste and made desolate," said a disconsolate Confederate soldier. [46]

The gunboats entered the Yazoo five days after leaving Rolling Fork. "As we returned down the Yazoo, at every possible point where the river could be reached there were throngs of Negro families waiting to be taken away," wrote Franc Wilkie, who was on the steamer *Silver Wave.* "Many of them had flatboats in which they were already embarked, ready to fasten a line to the returning Federal boats and be towed down the river and to freedom."

Silver Wave stopped to take on wood at an "immense encampment of negroes," where there were families with all their belongings: furniture, farm animals, and small keepsakes. A large flatboat was tied to the shore, near the stern of *Silver Wave*, and Wilkie's eyes were drawn to it. "There were at least twenty colored persons in it, of all ages and both sexes." In the back sat an old blind man with a heavy beard and hair "as white as wool." Wilkie surmised that the folks that surrounded him were his descendants. "They were all chattering [and] laughing. . . . Freedom was before them . . . Only the patriarch was silent."

A line was thrown from the deck of the steamer to the flatboat and tied fast. When the wheel started to revolve, it "threw back waves which enveloped the flatboat, and then, as the speed increased," the bow of the flatboat "was drawn under, and the entire boat with all its human freight . . . disappeared under the greenish waters of the Yazoo."

Wilkie watched in horror for some sign of the family "but not even a rag, or a fragment of any kind, came to the surface. The cruel waters held them fast. . . . Nothing that I saw during the war shocked me as did this occurrence. Rescue was impossible; the boat did not even stop. It steamed swiftly away, and I felt in my heart that another and humbler Moses had died at the moment of anticipated deliverance." [47]

The Steele's Bayou expedition arrived at the mouth of the Yazoo River on March 27, roughly two weeks after Porter had first explored Steele's Bayou. Casualties—army and navy—were light: only three men killed. [48] But this was scant consolation. Steele's Bayou was the fourth failed attempt—the De Soto canal, the Lake Providence cutoff, Yazoo Pass, and now Steele's Bayou—to get to the rear of Vicksburg—to "ground I so much desire," Grant told his aides. [49] The disconsolate general was nearly out of options.

When Sherman's troop transports bumped onto the riverbank at Young's Point, standing there was Frederick Law Olmsted, nearing the end of his inspection tour of the Union camps. "The stern-wheel transports [were] wonderfully knocked to pieces; their smoke-stacks all down, so that the black coal-smoke was thrown directly upon the hurricane decks, which were . . . crowded with men, who must have been nearly suffocated by it." [50] The next morning, one of Sherman's commanders, a gritty veteran of the Mexican War, came to the cabin of William Le Baron Jenney, who had been with him at Black Bayou and Rolling Fork. After carefully closing the door, he "looked around to see that we were alone," recalled Jenney, "and in a manner that indicated that he had a great secret to impart, whispered to me, 'I command a battalion of regulars,—I have been on an expedition,—I must write a report,—I want you to tell me where I have been, how I went there, what I did, and if I came back the same way I went, or not, how I did get back.'" [51]

In mid-April, boats began arriving at Milliken's Bend from the Yazoo Pass expedition. They, too, looked like they had passed through a savage storm. James Wilson and General Ross had expected to return to Milliken's Bend much sooner, but as their expedition was heading back to the Mississippi, it had bumped into Isaac Quinby's brigade, sent to reinforce it. [52] Outranking Ross, Quinby took command of the army contingent and convinced the naval commanders, after furious debate, to return with him to Fort Pemberton to renew the offensive.[53] But Quinby had failed to mount a single assault. After Porter was turned back at Rolling Fork, Pemberton had sent additional men and guns to General Loring, who threw up a second line of defense that neither Quinby nor the gunboat commanders was willing to challenge. While stalemated in front of the fort, the naval captains had informed Quinby that they intended to leave on their own. A little later Quinby received orders from Grant to withdraw. Grant had failed, as we have seen, to get the small steamers he needed to carry McPherson's Lake Providence corps to the rear of Vicksburg, to nearly the same place Porter and Sherman had hoped to reach.

The fleet—ten thousand men and seven warships—backed upriver a full one hundred miles, after being defeated by an outnumbered force fighting behind a fort constructed of cotton. Pemberton failed to send reinforcements and pursue, losing a tremendous opportunity to deal the Federals an unrecoverable loss.[54]

On reaching the Mississippi across from Helena, Arkansas, the troops let loose a thunderous musket salute, a survival, not a victory celebration. The men had been in the swamps nearly six weeks, and the cramped steamers reeked of spoiled meat and excrement; more men than not had raging diarrhea. "The boats passed by here a few days ago," a Union soldier wrote from Lake Providence. "The men were a sorry looking set I can tell you. More than one third of them were sick and the rest so dirty as to be hard[ly] recognizable."[55]

"We know nothing of what the generals thought of this fiasco," wrote Sergeant Samuel Byers. Were they to "hunt some other road to Vicksburg?"[56] Grant would, but not through the Delta. The Steele's Bayou venture ended all efforts to turn the enemy flank from the north.

The morning Porter returned from Steele's Bayou, a dispatch boat pulled alongside *Black Hawk*. Rear Admiral David Farragut's secretary came aboard bearing a message. Farragut's flagship, *Hartford*, was anchored below Vicksburg's batteries and had been there for a week.[57] The conqueror of New Orleans had come upriver from the Gulf to help his foster brother take the city that had defied their bombardment and blockade the previous summer. They had not set eyes on each other since then.

Farragut had intended to bring along the great part of his blockade squadron, but only *Hartford* and the tiny gunboat *Albatross* had made it past the batteries at Port Hudson, twenty-one heavy guns positioned on towering bluffs commanding a sharp bend of the river. "The others were repulsed," and one was seen "in flames," its ultimate fate unknown to Farragut, the messenger informed Porter.[58]

Farragut's appearance at Vicksburg was welcome news for Secretary Welles. Perhaps he could keep Porter's eyes on the main prize— the Mississippi—instead of having him venture again into backwater quagmires. "The accounts from Porter, above Vicksburg, are not satisfactory," Welles wrote in his diary. ". . . Porter has capabilities and I am expecting much of him but he is by no means an Admiral Foote."[59] Porter was also on shaky ground with the president, who considered the Yazoo expeditions dangerous diversions from the Union's main objective: reopening the Mississippi from Vicksburg to Port Hudson, the only part of the river still controlled by the Confederacy. "The occupation of the river below Vicksburg between Vicksburg and Port Hudson is the severest blow that can be struck upon the enemy . . . and, in the opinion of this Department, is of far greater importance than the flanking expeditions which thus far have prevented the consummation of this most desirable object . . ." Welles wrote Porter after his return from Rolling Fork, echoing the president's position.[60]

The way to beat Vicksburg, Lincoln, Halleck, and Wells believed, was to cut off its supply line to the Red River and the trans-Mississippi Confederacy and then land the army somewhere on the Mississippi below the city and take it by a direct infantry assault, in cooperation with troops supplied by General Nathaniel Banks, after he moved out from New Orleans and subdued Port Hudson. The president and Halleck agreed with Welles that military operations should be concentrated on the Mississippi, not in difficult backwaters north of it.

Grant and Porter had no argument with Washington's base strategy. They had launched the Yazoo expeditions for the very purpose of locat-

ing good ground for military operations behind Vicksburg, but Halleck
had failed to press home that point to the president or his cabinet. And
it was actually pressure from Washington—pressure to do something
and soon, that had compelled Grant to try to get behind Vicksburg
through the forbidding delta.

Grant, as we have said, would have preferred to move his army
south, through Louisiana's bayou country, to a place below Vicksburg,
where he could cross the river with Porter's assistance. But that campaign would have to wait for dry weather and a sustained and successful effort by Porter to take command of the Mississippi south of
Vicksburg.

Porter's fleet had actually gained a tenuous hold on the Mississippi
immediately south of Vicksburg the previous February, only to lose it
the following month while he was in the Yazoo swamps with Sherman—
and regain it yet again, with Farragut's assistance, on his return. One of
the most underappreciated chapters of the Vicksburg story, this short,
sharp naval engagement—from February 1 to March 31—opened the
way for Grant's eventual march into Mississippi.

On February 1, 1863, Porter directed Col. Charles Rivers Ellet to run
past Vicksburg batteries in his ram *Queen of the West*. He was to destroy
an enemy steamer docked at Vicksburg's wharf and proceed to the
mouth of the Red River to assault rebel shipping. Porter held Ellet in
high regard. At the Battle of Chickasaw Bayou, he had devised the ingenious device to destroy rebel mines at Haynes' Bluff and had unself-
ishly volunteered to risk his life to lead the mission that was eventually
aborted. "I can not speak too highly of this gallant and daring officer,"
Porter wrote Welles. "The only trouble I have is to hold him in and keep
him out of danger. He will undertake anything I wish him to without
asking questions, and these are the kind of men I like to command."[61]

Porter ordered a night attack, but last-minute repairs delayed Ellet.
Rather than wait until the next evening, he impetuously shoved off
at the break of day. Braving hammering fire, he rammed the cotton
steamer *City of Mississippi*, leaving her in sinking condition, and tied up
near Sherman's canal camps to repair the damage to his wooden vessel.
After being fitted out with additional guns, he sped to the Red River

that afternoon with Porter's injunction to sink and destroy every rebel vessel he encountered.[62]

In three days, Ellet and his marines, accompanied by the small ferry boat *De Soto*, pounced on three enemy supply boats loaded with sugar, pork, molasses, and military supplies, and seized the corn-laden packet *Era No. 5*. Ellet captured her pilot and ordered him to guide *Queen of the West* up the Red River, where, against Porter's orders, Ellet engaged an earthen fort on the riverbank. When the rebels opened fire with their four 32-pounders, *Queen of the West* ran aground on a shoal, where shells tore through her sides and severed an essential steam line, disabling her. With scalding steam spewing from belowdecks, Ellet and his crew, a number of them horribly burned, jumped overboard and floated on cotton bales to *De Soto*. Ellet sent volunteers on a yawl to torch *Queen of the West* and rescue a gravely wounded officer who had been mistakenly left behind. But they dared not strike a match because the dying captain was trapped behind a stack of cotton bales and could not be moved. Ellet wanted to go back on his own but the rebels reached the boat first, and the best ram in the Yankee river fleet passed into the hands of the enemy "with no damage other than a burst steam pipe."[63]

Blinded by heavy fog, *De Soto*'s pilot ran aground and sheered off the boat's rudder. Ellet transferred his men to *Era No. 5* and sent a detail to set fire to *De Soto*. He then headed up a narrow channel for the Mississippi.[64] His career as a commerce raider had lasted all of four days. The next morning, the fast rebel ram *William H. Webb*, mounting a 32-pounder on her bow, went in pursuit of the far slower *Era No. 5*. Struggling against a downriver current, Ellet spotted through the mist a twin-stacked, heavily gunned goliath bearing down on his frail, unarmed boat. It was the USS *Indianola*, a freshly commissioned ironclad that had passed Vicksburg's batteries unscathed, carrying two coal barges lashed to her sides. Not knowing Ellet had run into trouble, Porter had sent *Indianola* to support *Queen of the West*. There were no rebel boats on the river that could stand up to their conjoined might.[65]

Indianola's commander, George Brown, consulted with Ellet and they agreed to go after *William H. Webb*, which had managed to elude them in a dense, low-sitting fog bank. Feeling vulnerable in his gimcrack rebel steamer, Ellet headed back to Vicksburg.[66] *Indianola* remained at the mouth of the Red River and maintained a tight blockade.[67] "This gives us entire control of the Mississippi, except at Vicksburg and Port Hudson, and cuts off the supplies and troops from Texas," Porter informed Welles.[68]

The blockade lasted only five days. The rebels repaired Ellet's lightly damaged *Queen of the West* and, along with *William H. Webb* and two steamers fitted out with armed boarding parties, went in search of *Indianola*. Knowing he was outgunned, Commander Brown headed upriver, burdened by the weight of the heavy coal barges. On the night of February 24, *William H. Webb* and Ellet's captured ram caught *Indianola* twenty-five river miles below Vicksburg and rammed her seven times, creating a gaping hole along her waterline. Brown ran her into shallow water on the Louisiana side of the river and surrendered his partially sunken vessel. The rebels towed her across the river, where she sank in ten feet of water, within sight of the plantations of Joseph and Jefferson Davis. Salvage crews began raising her the next morning.[69]

Incredibly, only one Union sailor was killed in the ninety-minute, close-quarters brawl. Three crewmen escaped and carried news of the disaster to Porter. After hearing them out, Porter decided the inexperienced Brown had given in "too soon."[70] He then wrote Welles, expressing his mortification: "This has . . . been the most humiliating affair that has occurred during this rebellion."[71]

Porter heard rumors that the rebels planned to raise *Indianola*. "She is too formidable to be left at large, and must be destroyed," Welles telegraphed him.[72] Welles wanted Porter to send down two of his gunboats to destroy her. Porter demurred; he didn't have boats available for such a risky mission.[73] Instead, he decided upon a safe and "cheap expedient." He would build a formidable-looking phantom vessel—a ram without captain or crew—and float it downriver to frighten and scatter the salvage party that was attempting to raise *Indianola*.[74]

Porter got hold of an old coal barge and had his carpenters lengthen it with a raft of logs three hundred feet long and turn it into a gigantic dummy gunboat, one without engines or real guns. It had two paddle-wheel boxes, a log casemate with fake guns protruding from its port-holes, a pilothouse that was an intact privy, and two tall smokestacks made of pork barrels piled one upon another and lashed together. They rose impressively from the deck, emitting smoke from iron pots packed with burning tar and oakum. The surface of the vessel was coated with mud and thick tar, and a skull and crossbones flew from the bow. It was built in twelve hours and cost, by Porter's estimate, $8.23. His sailors christened it *Black Terror*.[75]

Two days after *Indianola* was sunk, Porter's mock ram was towed to the head of De Soto Point, its iron pots were fired, and it was set adrift. It made it past the blazing guns of Vicksburg virtually unharmed. Just below the city it drifted to shore near Grant's canal, where Union soldiers towed it back into the stream, and "she drifted rapidly down upon the rebel prize."[76]

It looked fearsome to the captain of *Queen of the West*, who passed it on his way up to Warrenton for salvage equipment for crews working on the half-sunken *Indianola*. Fearing it was a new kind of Yankee war machine, he reversed course and sped downstream to spread the alarm. Word reached General Carter Stevenson at Vicksburg and he sent a courier to the salvagers, ordering them to blow up *Indianola*. The blast could be heard on Porter's flagship off Young's Point.[77]

The next morning, seeing the shattered black monster at rest in midstream, some curious rebel soldiers rowed out to have a look. Nailed to the starboard wheelhouse was a sign: "Deluded Rebels, Cave in!"[78]

An improvised contrivance had kept a rare prize from falling into rebel hands, but this was thin consolation to Union naval commanders. Porter had lost two of his finest warships—*Indianola* and *Queen of the West*—and the rebels were again "masters of the line from Vicksburg to Port Hudson."[79] Writing to Gideon Welles, Porter blamed it all on Charles Rivers Ellet, a brave but "brainless" lad. He had "foolishly engaged" the batteries on the Red River, losing the fastest ram in the fleet. Had he "waited patiently" at the mouth of the Red River, as he had been instructed, he would have been joined in less than twenty-four hours by *Indianola*, and he'd have set in place with her an unbreakable blockade. "My plans were well laid, only badly executed. I can give orders, but I can not give officers good judgment."[80]

Two weeks after sending his Trojan horse downstream, Porter was exploring Steele's Bayou, ready to begin an expedition that was, by Welles's reckoning, more strategically misguided than Ellet's gambit up the Red

River. It was only when Farragut arrived at Vicksburg on March 20 and tried to communicate with Porter that he learned from Grant that his adoptive brother was somewhere deep in the Delta.

Farragut had decided on his own to head to Vicksburg after learning from secessionist newspapers that Porter had lost *Queen of the West* and *Indianola*.[81] He had come upriver from the Gulf to recapture them "or be sunk in the attempt."[82] Although only two of Farragut's seven wooden warships had passed through the Port Hudson gauntlet on the night of March 14–15, Lincoln was elated. "The President . . . is rather disgusted with [Porter and Grant's] flanking expeditions and predicted their failure from the first and he always observed that cutting the rebels in two by our force in the river was of the greater importance," Fox wrote Farragut. "Grant who I judge by his proceedings has not the brains for great work, has kept our Navy [in] the swamps to protect his soldiers when a force between Vicksburg and Port Hudson . . . would have been of greater injury to the enemy." His roundabout swamp expeditions "set us back three months."[83]

Fox counted on Farragut to hold the river south of Vicksburg, but Farragut said he "lacked the vessels" to do it.[84] This is why he had steamed up to Vicksburg to meet with Porter. He needed two ironclads and two rams to reinforce *Hartford* and *Albatross*.[85] When he learned that Porter was somewhere in the Delta, he approached Henry Walke, Porter's second in command, but Walke was unwilling to put in jeopardy another gunboat without Porter's approval. Undeterred, Farragut contacted Brigadier General Alfred W. Ellet, commander of the Mississippi Marine Brigade. Ellet had just arrived at Young's Point from St. Louis, where he had been recruiting and training his special amphibious brigade, formed to suppress guerrilla activity along the river.

When Charles Rivers Ellet informed his uncle that Farragut was anchored below Vicksburg and was asking for rams, Alfred Ellet sent the admiral a note offering his services. A squad of his marines delivered it on foot, led by a local guide across eleven miles of De Soto Peninsula.[86] Farragut sent back word that he would be happy to meet him the next day on *Hartford*. "Nothing would be more gratifying to me than to have two of your rams."[87] The next day, General Ellet, accompanied by a guard, made the trek across the peninsula and assured Farragut, in defiance of his limited authority, that two rams—*Lancaster* and *Switzerland*—would be delivered to him that night. Charles Rivers Ellet would lead the expedition aboard *Switzerland*, accompanied by General Ellet's son, Edward. Another of the general's nephews, Lieutenant Colonel John A. Ellet, would command *Lancaster.*[88]

There had been little time to prepare for a scheduled two o'clock morning launch. Running several hours late, Charles Rivers Ellet, in "an excess of zeal," set out at sunrise on March 25, denying himself the protection of darkness.[89] Vicksburg's gunners, alerted by spies, opened up on the rams.[90] The shoddily constructed *Lancaster* was struck first and lethally.[91] The faster, better-built *Switzerland* got through with only a single shot through her boiler.[92] All three Ellets survived. "In sending his boats past the batteries in broad daylight, [Colonel Ellet] afforded the enemy nothing but target practice," Farragut wrote in disgust.[93]

When Admiral Porter returned from the Steele's Bayou expedition two days later and learned what had happened, he exploded. "Will you please inform me," he wrote General Ellet, "by what authority you sent the rams . . . past the batteries at Vicksburg, in open day, and without taking any precautions to guard their hulls [with cotton bales]?"[94] By law, he, not Ellet, commanded the ram fleet. Farragut, who felt some responsibility for the misunderstanding, intervened. He assured Porter that General Ellet had acted in response to his own urgent request to close the Red River trade.[95]

When Porter settled down, he agreed to have the repaired *Switzerland*, under John Ellet's command, accompany Farragut to the Red River. Porter then banished the other members of the Ellet family, sending Alfred's Mississippi Marine Brigade, along with Charles Rivers Ellet, to the Tennessee River to serve under General William S. Rosecrans. The rams remained at Vicksburg under Porter's close control, to be used primarily as transports.[96] Porter was delighted to be rid of the uncontrollable Ellets and proud to be working again with his foster brother. "Your services at Red River will be a godsend . . ." he wrote Farragut. "It is death to these people; they get all their supplies from there."[97]

On March 31, *Hartford, Switzerland,* and *Albatross* steamed to the mouth of the Red River.

• • •

Farragut's blockade helped turn the Vicksburg campaign in a new geographical direction, southward, where Grant had long wanted to go. Two amphibious operations had failed to take the city from the north. If the river stronghold were to fall, it would have to be by a hammer blow struck from the south by his infantry, in cooperation with naval forces. The Red River blockade finally made this possible. The first Union triumph of the campaign, it severed Vicksburg's trans-Mississippi supply line and cleared rebel shipping from the strategic stretch of river between Port Hudson and Vicksburg.*

But while a single ironclad, two wooden rams, and a "dummy" gunboat had successfully passed the Vicksburg batteries, neither Grant nor Porter was confident that an entire fleet of wooden steamers—providing essential supplies and cross-river transportation for the invasion army—could do it, even if "under the lee of the iron-clads." [98] Should the two commanders be willing to hazard the risk of a great southward movement, there remained two obstacles: Persistent high water in Louisiana bayou country; and an army that had recently suffered through a depressing period of defeats and disease. Would the men be emotionally prepared and in good health for a sustained overland campaign?

---

* Farragut would not have to be concerned about *Queen of the West*. On April 14, she steamed into the Atchafalaya River and was sunk by a single shot, at long range, from the USS *Calhoun*. ORN, I/20/134–38.

CHAPTER 16

Crisis

*"All Grant's schemes have failed. He knows that he
has got to do something or off goes his head."* [1]

—Union General Cadwallader Washburn

While the Union expeditionary troops were in the Delta, the men who remained behind in the camps continued to die in discouraging numbers. That February, Jane Hoge, a director of the Chicago-based Northwestern Sanitary Commission, a branch of the national Sanitary Commission, visited Young's Point and began reporting her findings to Northern newspapers. An estimated twelve thousand soldiers, roughly a third of Grant's army, were on the sick list. Without sufficient hospital beds, men with raging fevers lay on the bare ground, untended by physicians, while soldiers with communicable diseases—mumps, measles, and typhoid—were crowded together on squalid troop steamers serving as emergency field hospitals.

"There is . . . no reason why our men should be packed like hogs in narrow pens, and left to die in filth, darkness and neglect," declared the editors of the *New York Times*. One of the paper's investigative reporters discovered sick soldiers left to die in filthy slave shacks, "dark hovels located deep in the swamps." A physician who set up practice in one of these appalling huts had no medicine, firewood, or food other than "coarse army rations." At least fifteen of his patients died every day, he told a *Times* reporter. [2] "This is a hard place for a sick man," an Iowa soldier Cyrus Boyd wrote in his diary. "He must have plenty of grit or die." [3]

The dead continued to be buried on the levee, the only dry ground available. "For miles along the river bank this narrow strip was all that appeared above the water; furrowed in its whole length with graves."

The troops who camped there "were thus hemmed in by the burial-places of their comrades."[4] When the river water rose to the top of the levee, the wheels of wagons carrying supplies from the transports would sometimes strike the end of a coffin and "heave it clear out of the ground." The dead were then buried "a second time, a little deeper," said a reporter.[5] There was a shortage of wood in the camps, causing hundreds of the dead to be buried in their army blankets; and when river water broke through the levee their decaying bodies were disinterred.[6] Every day, from dawn till dark, soldiers could be seen carrying deceased comrades to the levee, where they would dig a shallow hole, cover it with a thin layer of dirt, and mark the resting place with a humble piece of pine board, giving the man's name and regiment. They would then retrace their steps and "await their turn," wrote Jane Hoge.[7]

One morning, while working in the Sanitary Commission's storehouse near the levee, Hoge looked out the window and saw an "animated and cheerful group of soldiers" standing on the riverbank. A steamer laden with coffins had arrived during the night. Curious, she went outside and overheard the men talking among themselves. "I'm glad my time didn't come till the coffins got here. 'Tis . . . hard to think of being carried on a board and buried in a dirty blanket."

"That's so," said another man, " 'taint human to be buried like a dog. Death don't seem half so bad since I've seen these coffins."[8]

The next day Hoge witnessed a soldier's funeral. One of the newly arrived coffins had been placed on a board and was being carried on the shoulders of four men. Two musicians led the procession, one with a pipe, the other with a drum. A chaplain and eight soldiers from the dead man's regiment followed the bier with bowed heads. The funeral procession "brought out a swarm of admiring soldiers, who felt the elation of men restored to civilization and humanity," wrote Hoge. Their fallen comrade had been "got up in style," an onlooker commented.[9]

Men died of exposure, but most were struck down by disease, "the soldier's worst enemy."[10]

The Civil War produced the greatest biological crisis of the nineteenth century. Disease killed more combatants than combat—roughly two deaths from disease to one from battle wounds.[11] Men died at

Vicksburg from nearly every known disease. The most common were dysentery, measles, smallpox, typhoid fever, pneumonia, tuberculosis, scurvy, and, later in the campaign—when mosquitoes made their seasonal appearance—malaria.* Dysentery alone caused twice as many Union deaths as wounds. The chief causes were believed to be fecal contamination of the food and water supply and a chronic shortage of fresh meat and vegetables. Men in military encampments everywhere in the country considered dysentery their "worst scourge and deadliest enemy," but available evidence suggests it was more prevalent at Vicksburg than in any other campaign of the war.[12] Unlike Union soldiers in the eastern theater, troops at Vicksburg tended to be stationed in one place for prolonged periods of time, often on swampy ground, where the men infected the local water supply with their feces and contracted typhoid fever and diarrhea at alarming rates.[13]

Army surgeons fought a prolonged but losing battle to impress upon the men the importance of personal hygiene and field sanitation, of separating toilet facilities from the food and water supply and having soldiers refrain from relieving themselves outside their tents. At any time in the Vicksburg campaign nearly half of Grant's men suffered from dysentery.[14] Instructed not to drink Mississippi River water, they sank shallow wells in the Louisiana floodplain and hauled the water out with buckets. Regimental surgeons implored them not to drink this dangerously polluted water; it was "death to either man or beast," they warned. But well water was easily available, "clear as crystal," and deceptively "delicious."[15]

A clean camp, with toilet facilities separated from the food and water supply and with a ready supply of pure water, might have kept down

---

* Union medical authorities reported 6.4 million separate medical diagnoses of soldiers, mostly of infections. Some 220,000 men were discharged for reasons of chronic disability; an estimated 164,000 rebel soldiers died among the 750,000 who served in the Confederate army. Pneumonia was the principal killer of Union soldiers, claiming 45,000 victims. Typhoid killed 35,000 men; diarrhea/dysentery, 21,000; malaria, 10,000. Confederate death rates were probably similar. See Sartin, "Infectious Diseases," 580–82. Confederate figures are incomplete because most medical records were destroyed by fire during the fall of Richmond in April 1865. A Confederate medical officer, Dr. Joseph Jones, however, made copies of several reports. They are deposited at the Howard-Tilton Memorial Library of Tulane University in New Orleans, Louisiana.

the spread of typhoid and dysentery, but only minimally, for these preventive measures failed to take into account the microbiological causes of disease.[16] The existence of pathogenic microbes, detectable only by magnification, was unknown at the time, except to a handful of medical researchers in Europe who had yet to refine and publish their research. With the exception of smallpox—preventable by vaccination—the most common infectious diseases were clinically recognized and diagnosed, but doctors were in the dark about their "causation, transmission, and control."[17] Civil War physicians fought an "unfair opponent."[18]

The Civil War took place in the waning years of the medieval era of medicine, and infectious diseases remained "the third army."[19] Not until World War I would more American fighting men die from bullets than bacteria.[20]

Sickness in the rebel camps was as prevalent as it was at Young's Point and Milliken's Bend, but medicine and medical supplies were in lamentably shorter supply. Most rebel soldiers were without "tents or shelter of any kind," recalled General Dabney Maury. "[Their] victuals and clothing . . . was quite insufficient. For many weeks they suffered more than our forefathers did at Valley Forge."[21] But in the winter of 1863, as in the summer of 1862, Confederate morale did not sink to the depths it did in Union camps, and for the same reason: they thought they were winning. The Confederates were holding on successfully into late March, having thwarted four major Union efforts to take the city: Grant's invasion of northern Mississippi, Sherman's assault on the Walnut Hills, Wilson's Yazoo Pass expedition, and Porter's thrust up Steele's Bayou.

"Will we ever be able to conquer this rebellion and return to our homes?" a Union soldier wrote despairingly that winter.[22] Morale was especially bad among regiments assigned to canal detail on De Soto Point. "Knights of the spade," as they caustically called themselves, they worked in shifts, far into the night, in every kind of weather.[23] Rebel shelling made this dangerous as well as degrading duty. Sometimes the projectiles "would knock our staging, wheelbarrows and planks all over the place," wrote Illinois soldier William R. Eddington. "We would sit down under the bank until they got in better humor and then we would get up and go to work again."[24] Many soldiers had become convinced that Vicksburg could not be taken for another year, if at all.[25] "Vicksburg defiant and proud sits upon the hills across the stream and dares us to come over . . . and here we are in this unhealthy place squatting along the levee and looking like geese so far as hostile intentions are concerned," wrote an Iowa soldier.[26]

"These were the dark days of the war," recalled Hoosier Oran Perry.[27] "Completely whipped everywhere, outgeneraled and outwitted in the east and in the west, we are completely disgusted and despair of ultimate success," added a fellow Indiana volunteer.[28] Maybe the South was unbeatable, maybe the Confederate States of America was a "lasting" government, a Chicago soldier wrote his father.[29]

Defeatism spawned defection. "Since the battle of Chickasaw Bluffs . . . from thirty to forty men [from our regiment] have deserted," surgeon B. F. Stevenson informed his wife.[30] Other regiments suffered greater losses. Some men headed home out of concern for their families. Grant's army had not been paid for five months because of administrative ineptitude in the paymaster department of the west. Grant complained vigorously and insistently, but a paymaster would not appear in his camps until early April.[31] Most married soldiers used their army allotment to support wives and children. Besieged by distressed letters from loved ones, a considerable but unknown number of them deserted.*

With the enactment of the Emancipation Proclamation, letters began pouring in to Grant's camps from the southern tiers of Illinois,

---

* Ella Lonn's classic work *Desertion During the Civil War* (New York: The Century Co., 1928) focused on the eastern theater. She argued that the proportion of desertion was greater in the Union than in the Confederate army. There was one desertion to seven enlistments in the Northern army, and one to nine in the Confederate ranks.

Some 80,000 of an estimated 200,000 Union deserters were caught and returned to the army; an estimated 21,000 of 104,000 rebel deserters were caught and returned. *Ibid.*, 226; Gerald F. Lingerman, *Embattled Courage: The Experience of Combat in the American Civil War* (New York: The Free Press, 1989), 176. Lingerman's outstanding account of the conduct and opinions of men under fire, along with two other penetrating works by James M. McPherson, incited my interest in the fullness of the combat experience in the Civil War. See McPherson's *What They Fought For, 1861–1865* (Baton Rouge: Louisiana State University Press, 1994) and *For Cause & Comrades: Why Men Fought in the Civil War* (New York: Oxford University Press, 1997).

Indiana, and Ohio, where the Copperheads, or so-called Peace Democrats, had made deep incursions among lukewarm Unionists." These
"Butternuts," as their enemies called them, pressed for a negotiated end
to the war, with slavery intact, and were militantly opposed to black
emancipation. Many of them received letters from home telling them
to desert.[32] Those who left rarely returned. There was no way of "getting
back" a soldier who had fled to the southern tier of these states, Grant
complained to Julia. "Northern secessionist[s] defend and protect them
in their desertion."[33]

Soldiers loyal to the Union wrote to their families, urging them to
take action against "Democratic Traitors" at home.[34] "Hang [them],"
wrote Private Isaac Jackson, "or confiscate every cent worth of property
they own."[35] Eighteen-year-old George Oliver Boucher told his mother
he would rather blow the brains out of one of these "northern traitors"
than kill two of the enemy.[36] But the vehemence of these young loyalists was an indication of the persuasiveness of the Copperhead message.
"We have plenty of accursed right here in this army," wrote Jackson,
"plenty of them working out their treason right here among us."[37]

The Copperhead *Chicago Times*, along with the anti-administration
New York World, circulated freely in the camps, inciting disillusionment
and dissatisfaction. "The confidence of the army is greatly shaken in
Gen. Grant, who hitherto undoubtedly depended upon good fortune
than upon military ability for success," proclaimed the *World*, adding,
weeks later, that it had good reason to believe Grant neither expected
nor hoped "to take Vicksburg this year."[38] Soldiers' letters were uncen-
sored, and many of the men freely vented their mounting disillusionment with Grant, which, as we have seen, had begun to set in as far
back as Shiloh. "General Grant is hated and despised by all the men and
cursed ever since the 6th of April [1862]," wrote Shiloh survivor Cyrus
Boyd.[39]

Grant was on trial yet again. Major General Charles S. Hamilton, one
of his top commanders in Tennessee and a man cavalryman Benjamin H. Grierson called "the most disagreeable" officer he had served
under—vain, arrogant, and "tyrannical"—accused Grant of making a

public spectacle of himself while under the influence of alcohol the previous November. On February 11, 1863, Hamilton relayed the incident to his friend Senator James R. Doolittle of Wisconsin, who was feeling pressure from constituents to have Grant removed from command.

> You have asked me to write you confidentially. I will now say what I have never breathed. *Grant is a drunkard.* His wife has been with him for months only to use her influence in keeping him sober. He tries to let liquor alone—but he cannot resist the temptation always. When he came to Memphis he left his wife at La Grange & for several days after getting here, was beastly drunk, utterly incapable of doing anything. [Brigadier General Isaac F.] Quinby & I took him in charge, watching him day & night & keeping liquor away from him & we telegraphed to his wife & brought her on to take care of him. . . . Now this is in the *strictest confidence.* Grant is a warm friend of mine.[40]

Some Grant biographers dismiss this letter as the work of a "disaffected general . . . with a timely motive for slander." Hamilton did resent Grant for promoting James McPherson over him as one of his corps commanders, yet none of these scholars have been able to refute Hamilton's story.[41]

Eight days after Hamilton sent his explosive note to Doolittle, Joseph Medill, publisher of the *Chicago Tribune,* wrote to Illinois congressman Elihu B. Washburne, who remained Grant's strongest advocate in Washington. Medill was infuriated with Grant for having revoked General Hurlbut's order suppressing the circulation, in his Memphis-based command, of the *Chicago Times,* "a sheet that is more malignantly rebel than any paper published in rebeldom," said Medill.[42] Grant privately agreed with Medill, but he wanted Congress and the president to assume the lead in the battle against the Copperhead press. "I want to see the administration commence a war upon these people. They should suppress the disloyal press and confine during the war the noisy and most influential of the advocates," he wrote Julia.[43] With Hurlbut, however, he took the sensible position that cracking down on the *Times* "would give the paper a notoriety . . . which probably would increase the sale of it." [44] Medill disagreed. Grant, he charged, was a closet Copperhead who "openly encourages the dissemination of secession and treason in his army." [45]

Medill had previously supported Grant over irresolute commanders like McClellan and Hooker, but now he questioned his capacity to lead. "No man's military career in the army is more open to destructive criticism than Grant's. We have kept off of him on your account," he wrote Washburne.

> We could have made him stink in the nostrils of the public like an old fish had we properly criticized his military blunders. Look at that miserable and costly campaign into northern Mississippi when he sent crazy Sherman to Vicksburg and agreed to meet him there by land. Was there ever a more weak and imbecile campaign. But we forbore exposing him to the excruciation of the people. But I assure you that if he has become the patron saint and protector of the secession [movement] again we shall not be so tender on him in the future. [46]

Medill was not posturing. His reporters began tearing into Grant's conduct of operations at Vicksburg. Grant had to be concerned. He knew Medill had influence with the president, though they didn't always agree on war policy. Fellow Illinoisans, they had worked together to found the Republican Party in the mid-1850s, and the *Tribune* had been instrumental in helping Lincoln become his party's standard-bearer at the nominating convention in Chicago in 1860.

In early March, the public learned that Grant's canal project, which had been receiving ongoing and upbeat coverage in some major newspapers, had suffered an unrecoverable setback. On March 6, Grant informed Halleck that the canal was "near completion." [47] But that very night the Mississippi rose over its banks and smashed through a dam built to keep water out of the ditch until the excavation was completed. "A wave of foaming, angry" water "rushed like an avalanche along the whole length of the canal," creating a lake over a thousand acres in area, wrote a reporter on the scene. [48] Soldiers fled for their lives, horses were drowned, and tents and tools were swept away by the cascading current. Swept away, as well, were "all of our hopes of passing Vicksburg by the Williams cut," wrote a despairing soldier in McClernand's division, whose canal crews were forced to move to higher ground, upriver at Milliken's Bend.[49] Sherman's men moved to levees closer to Young's Point and to steamboats docked along the levee. After the waters had receded, Grant stubbornly resumed the work with two giant dredges dubbed, sanguinely, "Sampson" and "Hercules," but enfilading fire from Vicksburg's batteries drove off the civilian machinists operating the dredges. They had not contracted, they said, "to be shot at."[50]

On March 27, Grant told Halleck the canal project was dead.[51] That same day, Sherman returned despairingly from Steele's Bayou and viewed the ruins of the project he had never believed in.

The Lake Providence cutoff also disappointed Grant's slender hopes for it. The levee holding back the Mississippi was finally cut on March 17, and the water rushed into the lake and the bayous below it with great "vehemence and noise," said one observer.[52] "Ordinary boats can now pass from Lake Providence into Bayou Macon, and thence, by easy navigation, to the mouth of Red River," Grant confidently wrote Halleck.[53] He soon learned from McPherson, however, that overhanging trees and underwater obstacles still blocked the channel through Bayous Baxter and Macon.[54] "It is utterly impossible to pass even a very small boat through," wrote one of the workers.[55]

Even if the channel were eventually cleared, the project was doomed for the same reason Grant had closed down the Yazoo Pass expedition— his failure to secure shallow-draft steamers to carry an assault force.[56] "It is probable that Lake Providence will not be used after all," wrote one of McPherson's soldiers.[57] Grant reached the same conclusion, but allowed the work to continue in order to confuse the enemy.[58]

"Whichever way the national forces turned nature seemed to combine with art to render the rebel fortifications impregnable," Adam Badeau summed up prevailing sentiment in the Union camps that dismal March.[59] The Vicksburg campaign was in crisis, stalled indefinitely, and Grant was in the biggest trouble of his military career. "The [president] . . . seems to be rather impatient about matters on the

Miss.," Halleck wrote Grant on April 2.[60] Grant was clearly under close White House scrutiny. "All eyes are centered on your army," the well-connected Lewis Parsons informed Grant, "and there is no mistaking the fact that the anxiety is intense—Many almost feeling that the fate of the Republic now rests on your success or failure."[61]

Grant's troubles were compounded by John McClernand's continuing intrigues. On March 15, the Illinois general forwarded to the president a letter he had received from Captain William J. Kountz, a government contractor who would later supervise river transportation for him. Kountz had had some history with Grant. He disliked him from their time together at Cairo and, egged on by McClernand, had accused him of being "beastly drunk" after the Battle of Belmont.[62] Now he again claimed Grant had been "gloriously drunk" and provided an exact date: March 13, 1863. "If you are averse to drunken [generals] I can furnish the Name of officers of high standing to substantiate the above," Kountz wrote. Lincoln did not reply, either to Kountz or McClernand, perhaps because Kountz admitted he had not actually seen Grant drunk on the date cited. He had been "informed," he said, but did not name the person or persons who allegedly witnessed the incident.[63]

The most sensational charges came from Murat Halstead of the *Cincinnati Gazette*, one of Grant's persistent critics. After being fed stories of the general's drinking by one of his reporters at Vicksburg, Halstead wrote to his old Ohio friend Secretary of the Treasury Salmon P. Chase. "Our noble army of the Mississippi is being *wasted* by the foolish, drunken, stupid Grant. . . . He is a poor drunken imbecile. He is a poor stick sober, and he is most of the time more than half drunk, and much of the time idiotically drunk. About two weeks ago, he was so miserably drunk for twenty-four hours, that his staff kept him shut up in a stateroom on the steamer where he makes his headquarters—because he was hopelessly foolish." Chase passed the letter to Lincoln, adding: "reports concerning General Grant similar to the statements made by Mr. Halstead are too common to be safely or even prudently disregarded."[64]

Ron Chernow, Grant's astute biographer, makes the same point, noting the "recurring consistency" in the accusations against Grant. "He is always described as being foolishly or idiotically drunk, childish and even jolly in behavior, never angry or abusive. This makes one suspect that the letters contained a germ of truth, since the various authors described the drinking episodes in remarkably similar terms, even though they could not have coordinated their messages with one another."[65]

Around this time, John Rawlins thought it necessary to secure a pledge from Grant not to touch liquor for the remainder of the war. And there is a surviving letter from Grant's medical director, Dr. Edward D. Kittoe, to James Wilson, alluding to a possible lapse the month after Grant took the pledge.[66] But Lincoln stuck with his general. When Iowa senator James W. Grimes went to the White House to demand Grant's removal, the president flatly refused, leaving Grimes "in a rage."[67] About the same time, Chaplain John Eaton was at the White House, reporting on his work with contraband camps in the Mississippi Valley. Lincoln reportedly broke into Eaton's report to spin a story about a delegation of congressmen who had recently urged him to remove Grant for incompetence born out of his taste for alcohol. Eaton, a reliable witness, recalled Lincoln saying: "I then began to ask them if they knew what he drank, what brand of whiskey he used, telling them most seriously that I wished they would find out. They conferred with each other and concluded they could not tell what brand he used. I urged them to ascertain and let me know, for if it made fighting generals like Grant I would like to get some of it for distribution."[68]

Even so, in the early spring of 1863 the president was showing signs of unease about the general who had given him the greatest victories thus far in the war. That March, in an interview with Albert D. Richardson, he questioned Grant's Vicksburg strategy. Grant's "swampland expeditions" were "dangerous," he said. "If the rebels can blockade us on the Mississippi, which is a mile wide," Richardson paraphrased the president in a letter to a friend, "they can certainly stop us on the little streams not much wider than our gunboats and shut us up so we can't get back again."[69]

Grumbling soldiers, scheming enemies, and sensation-seeking editors would not get Grant removed, but in late March searing criticism began to be heard inside Grant's command. "I fear Grant won't do," Major General Cadwallader Washburn told his brother Elihu. "He trusts too much to others, and they [are] incompetent." Washburn had been with Grant at Fort Donelson and had led a cavalry division in his December invasion of northern Mississippi. While acknowledging

Grant's military ability, Washburn thought Vicksburg was proving too much for him. "The truth is Grant has no plan for taking Vicksburg & is frittering away time & strength to no purpose. The truth must be told even when it hurts. You cannot make a silk purse out of a sow's ear." John Rawlins, Cadwallader suggested, would make a far better commander. Shaken by his brother's letter, Elihu shared it with Salmon Chase and permitted Chase to put it before Lincoln. Lincoln "seemed much impressed," Chase told Washburne, and had not missed the important fact that Elihu Washburne, Grant's champion since Galena, had been the one who forwarded it to him.[70]

General Washburn wrote again to Elihu from Vicksburg after Porter and the ironclads returned from Steele's Bayou. "That should have been an overwhelming success, and I am mortified and humiliated at its miscarriage. . . . This campaign is being badly mismanaged. . . . I fear a calamity before Vicksburg. All Grant's schemes have failed. He knows that he has got to do something or off goes his head."[71]

Washburn was right: Grant had no thought-out plan for taking Vicksburg other than to attack it from the rear, on dry ground. This comes clear in a revealing note he sent to Sherman after Sherman reported that there was little chance of getting through to the Yazoo River by Steele's Bayou. "I had made so much calculation upon the expedition down the Yazoo Pass, and now again by the route proposed by Admiral Porter, that I have made really but little calculation u[p]on reaching Vicksburg by any other than Hains [sic] Bluff."[72] The failure of the Porter "experiment" had left him, he believed, with but one option: "to collect all my strength and attack Hains Bluff. This will necessarily be attended with much loss but I think it can be done."[73] As soon as Porter's gunboats were repaired and serviced, he planned to gather together his scattered forces and "make a strike." Two months earlier, he had considered an attack upon Haynes' Bluff suicidal.[74]

Grant was perplexed, and General Washburn detected it. He had heard from sources inside Grant's headquarters that he was considering a direct attack on Vicksburg, either at Haynes' Bluff or on its Mississippi riverfront. "The Army will be slaughtered," he wrote his brother, ending the letter with a plea to come down to Vicksburg. "You are responsible for Grant. You must go to see him and talk with him," if only to learn if he really has, as some said, a secret plan to take the city. "Come down, I pray you."[75]

"Grant was now at a turning-point, not only of this campaign but of his whole career," wrote military historian Francis Vinton Greene in his 1882 masterpiece, *The Mississippi*. After the calamitous Steele's Bayou expedition, Grant "occupied a position in popular estimation similar to that held by Hooker, Rosecrans, and Banks . . . and like them he was on trial," Greene wrote.

It had been a year since Shiloh, and "he had apparently done nothing, the defense of the Memphis and Charleston Railroad and its attendant battles of Iuka and Corinth having made but little impression on the public mind. For the last three months his army had been lost to sight in the overflowed swamps of the Mississippi, whence came rumors of abortive expeditions, camp fever, and dissatisfaction. Many people were beginning to believe that Grant belonged to the same dreary class of failure as McClellan, Burnside, Frémont, and Buell, and they importuned the President to relieve him."[76]

Grant knew he was on the hook but he appeared preternaturally calm to those around him. Frederick Law Olmsted, a frequent visitor to his headquarters boat at Young's Point, was surprised how composed he seemed, writing orders in a steady hand, conversing pleasantly with his staff, or welcoming civilian observers to his camp. There was a sentry at the gangway of *Magnolia*, but Grant "stops no one from going on board. . . . He is more approachable and liable to interruptions than a merchant or lawyer generally allows himself to be in his office," Olmsted wrote his father. Fathers who came downriver to claim the bodies of their dead sons stopped by to introduce themselves to Grant and found him sympathetic and generous with his time.[77] "I am well, better than I have been for years," he tried to assure Julia in early March. "Every body remarks how well I look. I never set down to my meals without an appetite no[r] go to bed without being able to sleep."[78]

But a later letter revealed his dismay at the enormity of the challenge he confronted. "I am very well but much perplexed. Hitherto I have had nothing to do but fight the enemy. This time I have to overcome obstacles to reach him."[79] When Grant revealed to Olmsted his plan to attack Haines' Bluff "by direct assault," Olmsted detected apprehension beneath his placid surface.[80] "Both Grant & Porter looked to me like disappointed and anxious men, at a loss what to do."[81]

Grant needed emotional anchorage, and only Julia could provide it. He expected her to come down to Vicksburg in late March or early April and asked her, in the meantime, to send his oldest son, Fred, to him for an extended visit.[82]

When he defended himself to Halleck, and pledged to mount a decisive plan soon, Halleck was apprehensive, and his communiqués turned sternly instructive. "You are . . . well advised of the anxiety of the Government for your success, and its disappointment at the delay . . . Early action" was imperative.[83]

"Because I would not divulge my ultimate plans to visitors," Grant wrote long after the war, "they pronounced me idle, incompetent and unfit to command men in an emergency, and clamored for my removal. . . . I took no steps to answer these complaints, but continued to do my duty . . . to the best of my ability. . . . I had never met Mr. Lincoln, but his support was constant."[84]

Grant could only have intuited this. Lincoln communicated with him solely through Halleck and Stanton, and, as it turned out, Grant misread Lincoln. His support was beginning to waver. In early March, Secretary of War Stanton, with Lincoln's approval, sent his old friend Charles A. Dana, former editor of the *New York Tribune* and now serving as acting assistant secretary of war, to Young's Point as the "eyes and ears" of the government.[85] He was in every sense of the word a spy, operating under the pretense that he was a special commissioner of the War Department investigating the finances of the paymasters in the Mississippi Valley. Grant had complained that his army wasn't getting paid on time and might, therefore, not suspect Dana's true intention.

"Your real duty," Dana's orders from Stanton read, "will be to report to me every day what you see." Stanton wanted daily reports on operations against the enemy, on Grant's conduct of military policy, and especially on his drinking habits—information that would enable Lincoln and Stanton "to settle their minds as to Grant, about whom . . . there were many doubts," recalled Dana, "and against whom there was some complaint." Dana received his orders on March 10 and left at once for Vicksburg. He was given a special cipher, different from that of Grant and his officers, for communicating with Stanton.[86]

In late March, Stanton sent another government official, Adjutant General Lorenzo Thomas, to investigate Grant's allegedly halfhearted commitment to black emancipation and his officers' opposition to black enlistment in the Union army. Stanton had told Massachusetts senator Charles Sumner, who had been pressing him on black military recruitment, that he hoped to have "200,000 negroes under arms before June—holding the Mississippi River & garrisoning the forts, so that our white soldiers can go elsewhere." [87] General Thomas was to enlist white officers and black volunteers, a policy that several of Grant's leading commanders, most prominently Sherman, openly opposed.

Thomas was also to hasten the implementation of the policy Grant had instituted in western Tennessee the previous December: seizing abandoned plantations and putting black families to work growing and harvesting cotton.

Thomas was a curious choice for the job. He was a ponderous fifty-eight-year-old staff officer with a drinking problem, and there was speculation that Stanton had sent him west because he was unable to handle the volume of paperwork in Washington. [88] And he was from Delaware, a slave state, and had not been enthusiastic about the Emancipation Proclamation. Unlike abolitionists, he told a friend, he did not have the "nigger on the brain." But on his way to Vicksburg, he visited a contraband camp in Cairo and was shocked by the deplorable living conditions of the freedmen. From then on, his aim, he said, was to establish "a system of culture for all blacks who do not enter the military service, to transfer the burden of their support from the government to themselves, and to demonstrate that the freed negro can be paid fair wages and yield a handsome profit to his employer." [89] It was a remarkable turnabout, and he went about his duties with a crusading spirit.

He expected resistance from Grant. Concerned that contrabands flooding his camps would overtax his army's ability to feed and clothe them, Grant had issued an order on February 12, 1863, "positively" forbidding "the enticing of negroes to leave their homes to come within the lines of the army." This was a violation of both congressional and executive policy. Stanton was furious, and Halleck made this known to Grant. Writing the general in chief to defend his policy, Grant claimed that "humanity" dictated it. There was, he said, no work for them in his camps; he already had enough "contrabands" to perform essential manual labor. And when his entire army eventually broke camp and moved on Vicksburg, these unfortunate people, most of them women, children, and the aged, would be left behind, without shelter or means of support.[90]

Grant was not being completely forthright. He had issued his controversial directive for strictly military, not humanitarian, reasons. He was finding it nearly impossible to direct the largest campaign of the war while simultaneously managing the social revolution his army had unleashed the previous December in northern Mississippi, when soldiers, on their own, began freeing and inviting behind their lines tens of thousands of runaway slaves.

General Thomas was in the Mississippi Valley to insure that Grant welcomed into its camps runaway slaves and that he and other Union commanders aggressively enforced the government's new policy of recruiting and training recently freed slaves for military service. When Thomas arrived at Cairo on April 1, he informed Grant cryptically that he had come to the Mississippi Valley "to make inspections" required by Stanton and would soon "visit" him. Rumors flew that he had a second, and secret, charge: to assess Grant's military performance—and that he carried the authority to remove Grant from command.[91]

CHAPTER 17

The Entering Wedge

"Mr. Dana is here I suppose to watch us all."[1]

—William Tecumseh Sherman

Charles Dana's cover did not fool Grant and his staff. Word of the real purpose of his mission had reached the army before he did and caused concern among senior officers. Wilson and Rawlins feared "Grant was in imminent danger of being removed" and that his fate hung on the confidential reports Dana would be sending back to Secretary of War Stanton.[2] Lorenzo Thomas was seen as the lesser threat. From the time he arrived in Grant's camp, his sole concern was raising black regiments. He rarely appeared at headquarters and showed little interest in military affairs. It was Dana who would save or sink Grant.

Dana was a man of consequence, a widely known and respected national figure. He had overcome his hardscrabble New Hampshire upbringing to become managing editor and part owner of the *New York Tribune*, the most influential newspaper in the country. Stanton had taken him on as a War Department troubleshooter after his split with Horace Greeley, the paper's legendary owner and publisher. Although Dana strongly denounced slavery, he saw the war preeminently as a struggle for Union, warning "traitors of their doom." Greeley, an emancipationist, was willing to allow the "errant sisters," as he called the seceding states, to leave the Union in peace.[3] "He was for peace, I was for war," Dana summed up their differences.[4] In April 1862, Greeley asked Dana for his resignation.

An eye impairment and family financial problems had forced Dana to drop out of Harvard, but he remained a lifelong autodidact: a widely traveled art collector, a bestselling poet, and an essayist who was fluent in French and German. Dana had an easy manner and wore his learning lightly, which would help immeasurably in his dealings with the ascetic and informal Grant.[5]

On April 6, the steamboat carrying the forty-three-year-old Charles Dana, trim and athletic, wearing a black slouch hat and high western boots, rounded Milliken's Bend. "The sight was most imposing," he recalled. "Grant's big army was stretched up and down the riverbank over the plantations, its white tents affording a new decoration to the natural magnificence of the broad plains. The plains, which stretch far back from the river, were divided into rich and old plantations by blooming hedges of rose and Osage orange. . . . The Negroes whose work made all this wealth and magnificence were gone, and there was nothing growing in the fields."[6]

Dana found Grant at his headquarters tent and was received "with every mark of respect and consideration."[7] Grant had recently moved up from Young's Point to Milliken's Bend to gather together his army for an impending offensive, and he was absorbed with hammering out the details. The following evening, Rawlins called together Grant's staff and explained the object of Dana's visit. Some Grant loyalists were enraged and wanted Dana shunned, but Rawlins insisted that he be received with respect and "taken into complete confidence." Nothing must be withheld from him; Grant had nothing to hide.[8] The "object" was to gain Dana's confidence.[9]

Dana was welcomed into Grant's military family and became fast friends with Rawlins and Wilson. They placed his tent close to Grant's and reserved a prominent place for him at the officers' mess. "Before [long], I was on friendly terms with all the generals," Dana wrote later. "One or two of them I found were very rare men. Sherman greatly impressed me as a man of genius and of the widest intellectual acquisitions."[10]

Grant's qualities were of a different caliber, Dana reported to Stanton. He was self-effacing and deeply honest, "with a temper that nothing [can] disturb, and a judgment that [is] judicial in its comprehensiveness and wisdom. Not a great man, except morally; not an original or brilliant man, but sincere, thoughtful, deep." Dana was surprised to find him affable and openly friendly, not embittered or discouraged by his recent failures. He enjoyed sitting in front of his tent late into the evening, swapping humorous stories with his staff. Dana was soon invited to join them.[11]

A bottle might be passed around, but if Grant partook, Stanton never heard of it. Later in the campaign, when Grant was outrageously drunk on one occasion, Dana suppressed the incident until after Grant's death. "Dana was . . . a revelation to Grant, as well as to those of us who were younger," James Wilson wrote in his 1907 biography of the man who became his lifelong friend. "He was openly genial . . . but far and away the best educated and most widely informed man that any of us had up to that time ever met. His companionship was therefore most acceptable and beneficial to all." When Grant learned that Dana was a passionate equestrian, he provided him with a splendid mare, and he and Grant would ride together at full sprint in the late afternoons.[12]

"I think Grant was always glad to have me with his army," Dana noted later. "He did not like letter writing, and my daily dispatches to Mr. Stanton relieved him from the necessity of describing every day what was going on in the army."[13] The day Dana arrived in camp, Grant took him aside and described his new plan to take Vicksburg, knowing Dana would relay it to Stanton. It was a shrewd move. The secretary and the president needed to know he would be moving against Vicksburg soon, and with resolve.[14]

The plan had evolved slowly in Grant's mind by a process of elimination. After breakfasting together on the morning of April 1, Grant, Porter, and Sherman had left the dock at Young's Point and made a reconnaissance of Haynes' Bluff. Nearly out of options after the failed Delta campaigns, Grant, as we have seen, had been seriously considering a direct assault on the city from the bluffs that rose imposingly above the Yazoo River. He was reconsidering that plan but wanted another look at the rebel defenses before abandoning it. "After the reconnaissance of yesterday I am satisfied that an attack upon Haines' Bluff would be attended with immense sacrifice of life, if not with defeat," he wrote Porter the next day. "This then closes out the last hope of turning the enemy by the right."[15]

He was not without options, however. Recently, there had been a breakthrough. In the last week of March, Grant had sent scouting parties south of Vicksburg, on the Louisiana side of the river. The floodwaters had begun to recede. A road that ran on top of the levees had emerged and, although in wretched condition, was conceivably passable. Grant thought it was worth a closer look.

On March 29, the day President Lincoln told a naval officer in Washington that "they were doing nothing at Vicksburg," Grant changed the tenor and direction of his campaign. "I have sent troops from Milliken's Bend to New Carthage to garrison and hold the whole route, and make the wagon road good," he informed Porter of his new initiative.[16] New Carthage was an inconspicuous Louisiana hamlet on the Mississippi shoreline, thirty miles below Milliken's Bend. From here, Grant planned to launch a cross-river invasion that would place his army on roads south of Vicksburg, at either Warrenton, or more heavily fortified Grand Gulf, farther downriver, where there was a better road system.[17] After pushing inland, he would follow Halleck's directive and send part of his force south to unite with Major General Nathaniel Banks in an assault on Port Hudson. When that downriver bastion had been taken, the two armies would move on Vicksburg. Grant was quietly displeased with this part of the plan. Banks ranked him, and Grant didn't want to play a secondary role in taking the town.[18]

For the moment, however, Grant concentrated on getting war boats and troop transports to New Carthage—the gunboats to silence the rebel batteries and the steamers to ferry an assault force across the river. After returning from his reconnaissance of Haynes' Bluff, he had asked Porter to prepare to run past Vicksburg's batteries "at as early a day as possible." Grant would be back to him for his answer in two days.[19]

In the meantime, Grant began shaping a plan to get ground forces to New Carthage. As far as he knew, there was only a single wagon road to that obscure river town. Would this partially flooded, badly rutted road hold up under the weight of thirty thousand men, hundreds of artillery pieces, and untold numbers of horse-drawn supply wagons? Only when the water had receded more dramatically, he suspected, and after a few days without rain. This was chancy. So Grant began digging another ditch.

He ordered work begun on the new canal the very day he sent a reconnaissance party toward New Carthage. Pioneers were instructed to dig a two-mile-long canal from Duckport Landing, on the Mississippi, just south of Milliken's Bend, to Walnut Bayou, near Young's Point. Walnut Bayou connected to Roundaway Bayou and entered the Mississippi River near New Carthage. After cutting the levee at Duckport Landing, he hoped that fast-running river water would scour a channel and raise the water level in the interlinked bayous to the south of the canal. Fatigue parties would clear out the cypress and tupelo trees clogging the various watercourses that would form the so-called Duckport Canal. If everything went as planned, Grant would have "good water communication" to New Carthage for barges and tugs carrying supplies. For the ground forces, however, it would be a hard slog into rugged country.[20]

The Duckport Canal would take at least a month to complete, but the force bound for New Carthage would need supplies and transportation before then. Speed was essential. Grant hoped to launch a cross-river assault before the rebels had time to refortify Warrenton and Grand Gulf. "Without the aid of gunboats it will hardly be worth while to send troops to New Carthage or to open the passage from here [to] there," he wrote Porter pleadingly.[21]

In his memoirs, Grant claimed that "Porter fell into the plan at once."[22] He did, but not without reservations. "When these gun-boats . . . go below we give up all hopes of ever getting them up again," he cautioned Grant. Breasting the big river's four-mile-an-hour current, the boats would be slowed down appreciably, giving Vicksburg's gunners ample time to cut them to pieces.[23] In a late-night meeting with Grant, Porter agreed to provide four gunboats, not the two Grant had requested. And they were his "best vessels," he assured Grant.[24] Grant, Porter believed, might not survive another botched operation. "It was perhaps the crucial Federal military decision of the war," wrote Bruce Catton, and Grant made it with "a gambler's daring."[25]

Unknown to Grant, Porter had privately favored a vastly different plan, which, in the interest of intra-service amity, he chose not to divulge to Grant. "There is but one thing now to be done, and that is to start an army of 150,000 men from Memphis, via Grenada, and let them go supplied with everything required to take Vicksburg," he wrote

Gideon Welles on March 26. "Let all minor considerations give way to this and Vicksburg will be ours. Had General Grant not turned back when on the way to Grenada [in December 1862] he would have been in Vicksburg before this."[26]

Two things had persuaded Porter to go along with Grant: his absolute trust in his military judgment and pressure from Welles to go downstream and relieve Admiral Farragut at the mouth of the Red River, so he could return to blockade duty in the Gulf of Mexico.[27] "So confident was I of the ability of General Grant to carry out his plans when he explained them to me," Porter wrote Welles months later, "that I never hesitated to change my position from above to below Vicksburg."[28] He *had* hesitated, but only for a day or two.

After securing Porter's cooperation, Grant presented the plan to Dana, Rawlins, Wilson, and some of his most trusted generals at his new headquarters—an abandoned plantation house set back from the levee at Young's Point. "Every officer present who expressed an opinion opposed the proposition," General Frederick Steele confided to reporter Franc Wilkie, although McClernand, who favored the plan, and McPherson, who opposed it, were on duty and unable to attend.[29] The fragile transports "would not live for a minute under the guns," Sherman protested.[30] Even if the fleet miraculously survived the rebel batteries and the troops successfully slogged their way through flooded country to New Carthage, the entire Federal force would be in what he called a "fatal trap," cut off from communication with Memphis, Cairo, and St. Louis, their main supply centers. Sherman refused to believe Grant could "support his army & the fleet at Carthage or Grand Gulf, with the Vicksburg and Warrenton Batteries behind him."[31]

But Grant had called the informal meeting to present his plan, not debate it. When this became clear, discussion ceased. Sherman, however, persisted. On April 8, after meeting personally and unsuccessfully with Grant, he addressed a formal communication to Rawlins suggesting that Grant call a meeting of his corps commanders to reconsider his own plan, which was similar to Porter's. He would have the army return to Memphis and begin the campaign anew from there, marching the army toward Vicksburg, while the gunboat fleet and a "minor landforce" assaulted the city's riverfront.[32] The letter was deferential in tone and ended on a note of loyalty.[33] "Whatever plan of action [Grant] may adopt will receive from me the same zealous co-operation and energetic support as though conceived by myself." [34] Rawlins presented the letter to Grant, who read it in silence. When he put it down, Rawlins advised him to "lay it away unanswered for the present." Grant never answered it, "and the subject was not subsequently mentioned between Sherman and myself to the end of the war, that I remember of," he wrote later. "I did not regard [it] . . . as protest but simply friendly advice." [35]

Sherman seethed in private, however, voicing his opposition to the plan in a stream of letters to his family in which he denounced the strategy he would be given a large role in executing. "My own opinion is that this whole plan of attack on Vicksburg will fail, must fail," he wrote Ellen on April 29, "and the fault will be on us all of course, but Grant will be the front—his recall leaves McClernand next." If that happened, "I could simply get a leave & Stay away. . . . I will not serve under McClernand." But Sherman soon cooled down and gave his full energy and effort to the campaign. [36]

Grant began executing his plan a week before divulging it to Halleck. "This is the only move I now see as practicable, and I hope it will meet your approval." Halleck could not intercede, even had he desired: The train had left the station. [37] Years later, Grant claimed he had this general plan in mind "the whole winter" but "did not . . . communicate [it], even to an officer of my staff . . . until the waters began to recede" in the New Carthage area. [38]

His memory betrayed him. When he had first arrived in front of Vicksburg, he had expressed a preference for moving south as soon as the bayous drained, but he had not considered running the batteries, fearing the losses would be unsustainable. Instead, he had counted for a time on the Lake Providence Canal to get his army below Vicksburg. But by late March, he was in a whole new world of war and had failed too often to be cautious.

Moving the army through Louisiana's bayou country would be nearly as risky as running the batteries. Conditions were not as ripe for a southern movement as Grant later suggested in his memoirs. The waters *had* begun to recede, but not appreciably. Even as late as the third week of April, the "whole country [was] under water save little [ribbons] of alluvial ground along the Main Mississippi or parallel Bayous," Sherman would note.[39] And these primitive roads were discontinuous—severed in places by rushing river water that had torn through the levees, creating deep gullies that would have to be bridged by Union pioneer detachments.

There was another and larger risk: This was Grant's plan entirely. If it failed, he would likely lose his command. And if Vicksburg prevailed, could the Confederacy be defeated?*

The most curious and controversial part of the plan was Grant's decision to have annoyingly difficult John McClernand lead the way to New Carthage with his corps. Grant's commanders were more strongly opposed to this decision than they were to the plan itself. Porter pressed Grant to appoint Sherman. McClernand, he was convinced, was still intriguing against Grant. Dana also weighed in. "I have remonstrated, so far as I could properly do so, against entrusting so momentous an operation to McClernand," he wrote Stanton in confidence, "and I know that Admiral Porter and prominent members of his staff have done the same, but General Grant will not be changed." Dana suspected Grant had made the appointment to appease Lincoln. McClernand "is believed to be an especial favorite of the President," he told Stanton.[40][†]

This had surely entered Grant's mind, but there were solid military reasons for appointing McClernand. He was the army's senior corps commander, and his Milliken's Bend encampment abutted the road to New Carthage. His corps could be there more quickly than Sherman's,

---

* At least two Union officers claimed to have shaped Grant's decision to go south. James Wilson, who saw himself, erroneously, as the author of some of the pivotal decisions of the campaign, claimed he was the first to suggest running the batteries and marching the army south. He had done this, as we have seen, in a conversation he had with Rawlins on the day Grant arrived in Vicksburg. Rawlins had passed the idea on to Grant, and Wilson said it shaped Grant's thinking. See Wilson, *Under the Old Flag*, vol. 1, 156–58. Admiral Farragut said he raised the idea of running past the guns when he and Grant met in his cabin aboard *Hartford* on March 26. This "instantly changed the whole plan of campaign. He had caught my idea," he told a friend. See Nevins, *War for the Union*, 415. There is no evidence for either man's claim.

† Stanton shot back a curt reply, suggesting Dana "carefully avoid giving any advice in respect to commands that may be assigned." Stanton to Dana, April 16, 1863, OR, I/24/ part 1, 75.

The Union's Mississippi Valley campaign was launched from bleak, strategically located Cairo, Illinois, at the confluence of the Ohio and Mississippi Rivers.

General Ulysses S. Grant at Cold Harbor, Virginia, nearly one year after conquering Vicksburg.

John A. Rawlins, a combative attorney from Illinois, joined Grant's staff in 1861 as his adjutant and remained fiercely loyal to him throughout the war.

General John A. McClernand, an irascible U.S. congressman from Illinois, served ably in the field under Grant but worked secretly to undermine his superior—until Grant removed him from command at Vicksburg.

The ironclad USS *Cairo* was part of the Union's powerful gunboat fleet until it was sunk in the Yazoo River in 1862.

6

General Henry W. Halleck, commander in chief of the Union's western forces early in the war, distrusted the inexperienced Grant and nearly removed him from command before Shiloh.

7

General Charles F. Smith was commandant of West Point when Grant was a cadet there, and he served heroically under him at Fort Donelson.

8

General William Tecumseh Sherman became Grant's closest friend and most competent lieutenant.

General James B. "Birdseye" McPherson, Grant's chief engineering officer at Fort Donelson, rose rapidly to become, with Sherman and McClernand, a corps commander at Vicksburg.

Admiral David G. Farragut captured New Orleans in late April 1862, but disease and inadequate army support prevented him from taking Vicksburg that summer.

Admiral David D. Porter, Farragut's foster brother, worked hand in glove with Grant to subdue Vicksburg, which could not have been taken without his ironclads.

Vicksburg was a thriving cotton port and rail center that initially voted against seces-sion because of its economic ties with the North. In holding out against a Union naval bombardment in 1862, it became a symbol of Confederate defiance.

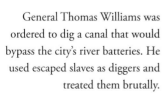

Kate Stone, the young daughter of a widowed plantation mistress, chronicled the Vicksburg campaign in her ardently secessionist diary.

General Thomas Williams was ordered to dig a canal that would bypass the city's river batteries. He used escaped slaves as diggers and treated them brutally.

15

16

John C. Pemberton, a Philadelphian whose Virginian wife convinced him to join the Confederacy, was sent to defend Vicksburg in late 1862.

Joseph E. Johnston, an esteemed Virginian, became head of Confederate forces in the west. He and Pemberton clashed repeatedly and never fashioned a common strategy to save Vicksburg.

17

Union transports take on troops in Memphis before heading south to Vicksburg.

Like these North Carolina slaves, Mississippi slaves flocked to Grant's army and found freedom behind its lines. It was the beginning of a social revolution: the overthrow of plantation slavery by Union military action.

Two proud young African American soldiers. By December 1863, over twenty thousand former slaves in Grant's theater of operations were wearing Union blue.

A rare photograph of the desolate Chickasaw Bayou, after Porter and Sherman were decisively repulsed in December 1862.

A Union steamer navigating in precariously narrow Steele's Bayou: one of several unsuccessful Union efforts to get to dry ground behind Vicksburg through the Yazoo swamps.

Nurse Mary Ann Bickerdyke, known to the troops as "Mother Bickerdyke." She cared for soldiers on nineteen battlefields and improved or established nearly three hundred hospitals as an agent of the U.S. Sanitary Commission.

In the spring of 1863, after failed attempts to take Vicksburg, U.S. Secretary of War Edwin Stanton sent former newspaper editor Charles A. Dana to Vicksburg to secretly spy on Grant. Dana became one of Grant's strongest supporters and part of his inner circle.

On the night of April 16, 1863, Porter's gunboats, with supply vessels lashed to their sides for protection, ran past Vicksburg's batteries.

Grant's march through Louisiana in preparation for his invasion of Mississippi set off a panic migration among area planters.

Lincoln sent Adjutant General Lorenzo Thomas to the Mississippi Valley to raise African American regiments.

When Grant reached the outskirts of Vicksburg on May 18, after crushing Confederate forces in five successive battles, this is what he saw: miles of rugged hills and deep, densely vegetated ravines. Union assault trenches led directly to rebel defenses at the top of the hills. The buildings were constructed after the surrender.

A panorama of the battlefield shortly after it was turned into a national park. Union forces attacked uphill throughout the siege. In this photograph, the steep incline would have been carpeted with felled timber, wire, and other obstacles. The stone markers indicate the farthest penetration by Union regiments.

General John "Black Jack" Logan. The major action in the final days of the siege occurred on his part of the lines.

Arriving at Vicksburg without tents, the men of John Logan's division dug shallow caves into the hills near the Shirley house, the only intact building on the battlefield, to construct two- and four-man dugouts.

Union sharpshooters in their trenches. Bullets claimed many more victims than artillery fire.

4-470 1585

The Vicksburg MINE. Brig Genl Hickenlooper Engr

our men so much loss. That they abandoned The Crater. and started another mine – which being Completed was exploded July 1st destroying The entire Rebel redan. Killing and burying everything within it. and leaving an immense chasm or Crater where it stood – The Union loss in the first mine explosion by holding the Crater. was about 30 – Enemy must have been 100 – no Charge or attempt was made to hold the Crater in the 2nd mine explosion –

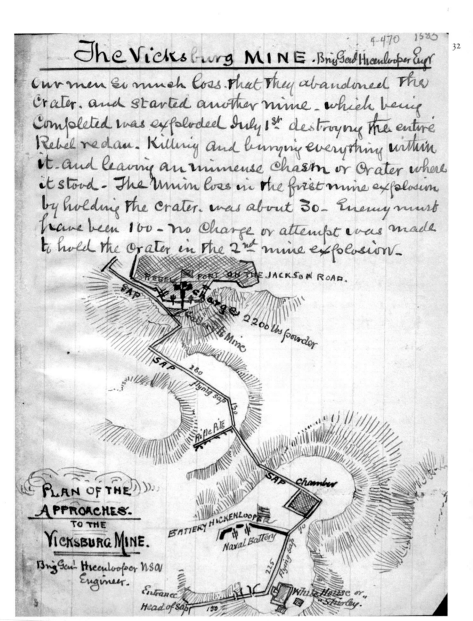

REBEL FORT ON THE JACKSON ROAD.

Charge 2200 lbs powder

Rebel R Mine

SAP 160

Flying sap 130

Rifle Pits

SAP Chamber

BATTERY HICKENLOOPER

Naval Battery 70

Flying sap 215

PLAN OF THE
APPROACHES.
TO THE
VICKSBURG MINE.

Brig Genl Hickenlooper USA
Engineer.

Entrance
Head of Sap 150

White House or Shirley.

Union engineer Andrew Hickenlooper devised a plan, revealed on his hand-drawn map, to breach the rebel line with explosives in the final days of the siege.

The resulting explosion lifted the Confederate earthen fort into the air and created a small, saucer-shaped crater.

The terrible struggle inside the crater, later called the "Death Hole," lasted some twenty hours, but the rebels held. It was the last hard fighting at Vicksburg.

On July 3, Pemberton and Grant met near the spot of the explosion under a flag of truce. Pemberton surrendered the city and his army the next day.

THE OPENING OF THE MISSISSIPPI—ARRIVAL OF THE STEAMER "IMPERIAL" AT NEW ORLEANS FROM ST. LOUIS, JULY 16, 1863.—[FROM A SKETCH BY MR. J. R. HAMILTON.]

On July 9, Port Hudson, the last rebel fort on the Mississippi, surrendered when the commander learned of Vicksburg's fate. Seven days later, the unarmed steamboat *Imperial* tied up at New Orleans, after a nine-hundred-mile run from St. Louis.

and McPherson was still at Lake Providence, far north of the jumping-off point. McClernand was also the only commander to enthusiastically support Grant's plan.[41] The unmanageable commander was likely to stumble on occasion, but Grant would closely monitor his every move.[42]

Even as Grant was moving his army to New Carthage, one corps at a time, he had to deal with the concerns that had brought General Lorenzo Thomas from Washington. The administration had dramatically shifted its war policy, and Thomas had come west to ensure that it had Grant's unqualified support. "It is the policy of the Government to withdraw from the enemy as much productive labor as possible," Halleck alerted Grant days before Thomas arrived. "So long as the rebels retain and employ their slaves in producing grains, etc., they can employ all the whites in the field. Every slave withdrawn from the enemy is equivalent to a white man put *hors de combat.*" With black soldiers defending supply depots behind the main line of advance on Vicksburg, thousands of white soldiers would be freed up for front-line assignments.

Stanton questioned whether Grant's commanders could be counted upon to enforce the new policy. "It has been reported to the Secretary of War," Halleck warned Grant, "that many of the officers of your command not only discourage the negroes from coming under our protection, but by ill-treatment force them to return to their masters. This is not only bad policy in itself, but is directly opposed to the policy adopted by the Government."

There was more. Black families were to be encouraged to flee their masters and seek protection with the Union army. Stanton had learned that Grant had issued orders back in February enjoining his commanders to stop accepting runaway slaves into their lines. Halleck was not admonishing Grant; he was trying to save his skin."[43]

Grant took the advice. That week he instructed his officers to begin aggressively recruiting freed slaves as soldiers and laborers.[44] And he soon came to see this as sound military policy. It would help hammer the slavocracy into submission. "The character of the war has very much changed within the last year," Halleck had explained the reasoning behind the government's new war policy in his letter to Grant. "There is now no possible hope of reconciliation with the rebels. The Union party in the South is virtually destroyed. There can be no peace but that which is forced by the sword. We must conquer the rebels or be conquered by them."[45]

There was no need to preach to Grant on this point. He had reached the same conclusion after the slaughter at Shiloh, and since then his army had been waging the kind of hard war Lincoln was now demanding: "slave-stealing" and sacking cotton-rich plantations. Up to now, the troops had been conducting this kind of warfare without Grant's express approval. Grant now made it official military policy, albeit with strictures against the indiscriminate pillaging of "dwelling houses."[46]

One week after receiving Halleck's directive, Grant sent Major General Frederick Steele, of Sherman's corps, to Greenville, Mississippi, in the heart of the Delta, to wage a campaign of protracted pillage. The Greenville-Deer Creek region, about eighty miles north of Vicksburg, shipped vast quantities of cattle and corn to the armies at Vicksburg. Steele was to plunder this bountiful granary. The raid had another and equally important purpose: to persuade Pemberton that the next Federal offensive would be north, not south, of Vicksburg.[47]

Steele's division landed in twelve steamers and moved inland in search of General Samuel Ferguson's Confederates, the only enemy threat in the area. Steele was a crack commander, "next to Sherman, not in rank, but experience and ability," in the opinion of Franc Wilkie, now the *New York Times*'s top correspondent in the West. "A small and well knit man of [forty-four]," impeccably attired, "with a touch of velvet about the cuffs," his prevailing trait, said Wilkie, "is quietness—a gentlemanly sort of repose." Not a man built for pillaging but, it turned out, excellent at it.[48]

As Steele's division moved along Deer Creek, the men entered a land of broad and bountiful plantations, rich beyond compare in the Vicksburg region. "It is the real 'South' just as we have all read about," one soldier marveled.[49] When General Stephen Lee, the hero of Chickasaw Bayou, arrived at Deer Creek to reinforce Samuel Ferguson, Steele was not displeased.[50] The rebels had taken the bait, sending men who could have been put to better use against McClernand's push south. But Steele was not up for a fight against the combined forces of Ferguson and Lee: That's not why he was at Greenwood. He ordered an about-face and headed back to the boats.

This is when the plundering began in earnest. "We nearly laid the country waste along the road—burned most of the cotton gins, and a large amount of cotton, corn, bacon, etc. intended for the rebels at Vicksburg," wrote Captain Jacob Ritner, a committed abolitionist.[51] Only "the dwelling houses were spared," said fellow Iowan Calvin Ainsworth.[52]

Marching double-file along the banks of Deer Creek, the bluejackets were stalked by runaway slaves.[53] "As soon as our advance column came in sight there was a stampede, probably 2,500 or 3,000 followed us back to the river, the old and young, and babies and all," wrote Ainsworth.[54] The slaves led Steele's men to horses and wagons hidden in the canebrakes and to underground storehouses stocked with honey, eggs, chickens, and sweet potatoes. And they whooped and hollered when the soldiers shot the slavers' bloodhounds and pulled down the whipping posts. There was no one to stop them. "A white man is as hard to find around any of those large plantations as hen's teeth," said one soldier.[55]

"We got more Negroes and mules than you could 'shake a stick at,'" Ritner wrote his wife, Emeline, who shared his views on slavery. "Most of [them] are women and children, miserable, dirty, ragged creatures. I don't know what will become of them."[56] Steele tried, unsuccessfully, to persuade them to remain on their plantations. "What shall be done with these poor creatures?" he asked Grant.[57]

He was stunned by the reply. When Steele had set out for Greenville, he had been under orders to discourage slaves from fleeing to his army. Now Grant was directing him to "encourage all negroes, particularly middle-aged males, to come within our lines." General Lorenzo Thomas "is here," Grant informed Steele by courier, and had begun raising black regiments, a less than subtle suggestion for Steele to follow suit. Remain at Greenville, Grant advised, and "destroy or bring off all the corn and beef cattle you possibly can." This "may serve to keep the enemy from getting provisions from the Deer Creek Country."[58]

At Greenville, the Army of the Tennessee officially became an instru-

ment of "agricultural disorganization and distress as well as of emancipation," James Wilson wrote after the war.[59]

It was Sherman, ironically, who called for restraint. "War at best is
barbarism, but to involve all—children, women, old and helpless—is
more than can be justified. . . . We surely have [a right to take] corn,
cotton, fodder, etc. used to sustain armies in war. Still, I always feel
that the stores necessary for a family should be spared, and I think it
injures our men to allow them to plunder indiscriminately the inhabitants of the country." Steele agreed: "Our men have treated these people too roughly to suit my taste, and they are encouraged in it by many
officers."[60]

Orders went out to avoid molesting families who stayed at home
and remained peaceful. They were widely ignored, and some of the largest plantations in the region were reduced to smoldering piles. "Oh!
What bitter-hatred toward Yankees was in my heart!" wrote seventeen-
year-old Amanda Worthington, daughter of a prominent Greenville
planter. "Rather than go back into a union with such people, I would
have every man, woman, and child in the Confederacy killed."[61]

After his men had stripped the country bare, Steele issued orders
inviting them to apply for leadership positions in the African American regiments he would begin forming instantly. The new Colored regiments were to be led by white officers. Enlisted men who applied and
were accepted were to receive commissions and a generous pay raise.
"There will be no lack of applicants," Captain John N. Bell wrote pro-
phetically.[62] Nor was there a shortage of black volunteers. "It is becoming a perfect mania with the colored population to become yankees; and
most of the men express their willingness to fight for their freedom,"
Steele wrote Sherman.[63] Soon there were five hundred former slaves in
Steele's camps training to be soldiers. There was opposition, but Steele
cut into it, pledging to reduce in rank or drive from the service any soldier who spoke out against arming African Americans.[64]

Many white soldiers went along out of base self-interest. "There are
some fools in our Army who think it would be a disgrace to allow a
colored man to . . . help us fight against his rebellious Master," wrote
Cyrus Boyd. "If any American will stand between me and a rebel bullet
he is welcome to the honor and the bullet too."[65] Soldiers were beginning to see that enlarging the army and freeing white soldiers on camp

duty to fight was "the quickest way to end the war [and] go home," wrote Captain Ritner.[66]

While Steele remained at Greenville, Lorenzo Thomas spoke to the troops at Lake Providence. "General Thomas was a fine, stately looking man, tall, with iron gray hair," wrote Private Seth J. Wells, an Iowan serving with the 8th Illinois Infantry. "He expressed great sympathy for the poor enslaved Africans, and announced the President's settled policy of arming the Negroes. . . . I like the policy." Wells liked it because Thomas was not suggesting blacks be assigned to combat duty. They would be guarding black families, including their own, who labored for the government on abandoned plantations.[67]

After speaking to Wells's outfit, Thomas boarded a steamer and headed a mile or so upriver to address General John "Black Jack" Logan's division. It was the most electrifying of his rallies. Speaking largely to soldiers from southern Illinois, a hotbed of pro-slavery sentiment, he took a hard line. He carried the authority, he warned, to "muster out" any man, "high or low" who opposed or tried to obstruct the new policy, something he had already done and would do again.[68] Soldiers from Logan's old regiment, the 31st Illinois Infantry, hissed and booed. Some of their mates had deserted after the enactment of the Emancipation Proclamation, and Copperhead sentiment ran strong in the ranks.[69]

After Thomas had stepped down, the boys of the 31st called on Logan to speak. He was a presence, standing perfectly erect in the bed of a supply wagon, barrel-chested, with deep-set eyes, jet-black hair, and a flowing mustache. It had not been his intention, he declared, to arm or even free "the black man" when he left Congress in the opening days of the war to raise a regiment. He had told his men at that time that he would march them home if the war became an "abolitionist crusade."[70] But the war had changed him. "I once loved the man who loved slavery, and now I hate the man who loves rebellion." The duty of every Union soldier, he told the men, was to "hurt [the rebels] in every way possible. Shoot them with shot and shells and minie balls, and damn them, shoot them with niggers. Take their corn-raisers and women protectors and fort builders from them, and set them to stopping bullets for us, and the thing is done." The men erupted. Even the 31st was won over.[71]

Three of his four corps commanders favored "arming the negroes and using them against the rebels with a will," Grant assured Halleck.[72] The fourth, it went unsaid, was Sherman. But with a major campaign unfolding, neither he nor Halleck was willing to try to bring him into line. "General Thomas is here raising negro Brigades," Tecumseh wrote Ellen from Milliken's Bend. "I would prefer to have this a white mans [sic] war, & provide for the negro after the Storm had passed. . . . Time may change this, but I cannot bring myself to trust negroes with arms in positions of danger and trust."[73]

He did not, however, object "to the Government taking them from the Enemy & making such use of them as experience may suggest."[74] Unlike Sherman, Grant looked to a day when black soldiers would fight, and commendably. Nonetheless, he assigned the newest African American units to rear duty, guarding the army's supply depot at Milliken's Bend while the main body of the army moved on Vicksburg.

"This army is in very fine shape, unusually healthy, and in good heart," Lorenzo Thomas wrote Stanton in April.[75] Mild and dry weather was a contributor, as was aid from the outside—boatloads of fresh vegetables and medical supplies from the Sanitary Commission in Chicago. Grant had closed down scandalously bad field hospitals and was sending gravely ill men to a complex of Memphis hospitals administered by a corps of volunteer women nurses under the direction of Mary Ann Bickerdyke, or "Mother Bickerdyke," as her grateful patients called her. A Galesburg, Illinois, widow who had been a botanic physician before the war, using herbs and roots to cure, she was formidable and hard-willed, a scourge to drunken and incompetent surgeons—and to army bureaucrats who tried, unsuccessfully, to stop her from using escaped slaves as nurses' aides.[76]

Bickerdyke had begun her war service as a nurse in the amputation ward of a Cairo hospital, where she befriended camp commander William T. Sherman, who had her set up field hospitals at Fort Donelson and Shiloh. After taking a furlough to care for her children, she went down to Memphis after the Battle of Chickasaw Bayou and began establishing her chain of hospitals.[77] Later, Grant named her chief of nursing in his army, and cooperated with her and aid workers from Chicago to improve medical care and sanitation in his Vicksburg camps. Veterans were instructed to teach green volunteers how to keep healthy and clean, and Sherman was seen "going through the camps on foot" to enforce sanitary regulations and visit the sick and wounded. "No one could look after his men more carefully than he does," wrote a representative from the Sanitary Commission. "With the sick he is as delicate and tender as a woman."[78]

While the levee was still honeycombed with graves and the area around the canal remained a miserable mud pond, the camps were cleaner and the men were eating better, their army rations supplemented by boxes of fresh fruit and vegetables collected from western farmers and sent downriver by women volunteers from Iowa and Illinois. On one occasion, Mary Livermore, co-administrator with Jane Hoge of the Chicago branch of the Sanitary Commission and author of a neglected Civil War classic, *My Story of the War*, arrived at Milliken's Bend on a steamer laden with five thousand boxes of hospital supplies and crates of vegetables, eggs, lemons, tea, and butter.[79] "We are living like kings," Jacob Ritner wrote his wife. They had canned fruit, apple butter, honey, cheese, dried fruit, and pound cake.[80] But the greatest gift was the arrival, finally, of a Union paymaster in early April. Morale soared.[81]

Grant made Livermore's friend Annie Wittenmyer part of his army. A wealthy widow residing in Iowa, she had been caring for the wounded and sending medical supplies to the Army of the Tennessee since the opening days of the war. In her midthirties, with prematurely white hair, she was a personal friend of Julia Grant, who would have worked with her had her husband not insisted she give full attention to their children.[82] Along with Livermore, Hoge, and Bickerdyke, she made a number of trips to the Vicksburg front, while Livermore and Hoge mounted huge "sanitary fairs" in the North that raised millions for the medical and humanitarian care of soldiers. When Livermore died in 1905, at age eighty-five, a Boston paper called her "the foremost woman in America."[83]

She and her colleagues helped bring Grant's army back to health just as it was about to mount the deciding drive of the campaign. When

Annie Wittenmyer was in the camps in early February, the firing of salutes over the graves had been discontinued. "The constant noise of funerals was demoralizing."[84] Seven weeks later, Livermore was sending encouraging reports from Milliken's Bend, including the animating news that Grant was sober and steady and had not been demoralized by recent setbacks.[85] As Livermore prepared to board the steamer *Maria Denning* for her voyage back to Chicago, Milliken's Bend was alive with activity. Surgeons were breaking up field hospitals, soldiers were packing their gear, teamsters were loading wagons, and brigade after brigade of Grant's scattered command came flooding into the camp, preparing "for a forward movement of some kind." Even desperately sick men returning on boats from the Delta expeditions "wanted to go forward with the new movement of the forces . . . to Vicksburg," Livermore marveled.[86]

Word spread that advance elements of McClernand's 13th Corps had already pushed into the flooded lands south of Milliken's Bend. The weather had begun to clear, and fair weather was campaigning weather. No one suspected that they were about to march into misery.

"First we pack our knapsacks, which consists of a pair of pants, one woolen shirt, one pair of woolen drawers, 2 pair of socks, one woolen blanket, soap and towel, one rubber poncho . . ." Calvin Ainsworth described his preparation for the march. "Besides the above we have trinkets such as pictures of the loved ones at home and shells we have picked up for souvenirs, brush and comb, stationery, ink, etc. We button up our blue flannel coat with brass buttons, we then put on our cartridge belt, to this belt is attached on the right side a cartridge box which holds 40 rounds." On the left side was a small box filled with rifle "caps, also a bayonet scabbard with the bayonet in, then comes our haversack generally carried on the right, then the canteen generally carried on the left, then the knapsack strapped on our back, thus, we are harnessed with leather and weighted down for a march."[87] They carried only five days' rations. When this was exhausted, they were to live off the land.

The first units to enter Louisiana bayou country were led by German-born brigadier general Peter J. Osterhaus, a competent but

GRANT'S MARCH THROUGH LOUISIANA, APRIL 1863

LOUISIANA

Mississippi River

Steele's Bayou

Yazoo River

Haynes' Bluff

Snyder's Bluff

Sherman

Demonstration at Haynes' Bluff, April 30-May 1

Union Army vanguard leaves Milliken's Bend, March 31

Milliken's Bend

GRANT

Duckport

Brushy Bayou

De Soto Peninsula

Chickasaw Bayou

Vicksburg

Big Black Bridge

Richmond

Walnut Bayou

Young's Point

Porter

VICKSBURG & JACKSON R.R.

Bovina

Roundaway Bayou

McClernand

Holmes

Grant's Canal

Porter's fleet runs the Vicksburg batteries, April 16 & 22

Smith

Pointe Clear

MADISON

Big Black River

Sherman

Dunbar

New Carthage

Mississippi R.

Warrenton

Ione

WARREN

Somerset

Bayou Vidal

Joe Davis

Davis Bend

MISSISSIPPI

Perkins plantation

Jeff Davis

McPherson

Hankinson's Ferry

Union Army arrives at Hard Times, April 28

Lake St. Joseph

Union fleet bombards Grand Gulf, April 29

Hard Times

✕ **Grand Gulf**

Battle of Port Gibson, May 1

Lake Bruin

Disharoon

✕ **Port Gibson**

Union Army crosses Mississippi River at Bruinsburg, April 30-May 1

Windsor

Shaifer House

Bayou Pierre

Bruinsburg

Rodney

0   10

Miles

© 2019 Jeffrey L. Ward

cautious commander. Their mission was to reconnoiter a wagon road that reportedly led along the levees from the hamlet of Richmond to New Carthage. Osterhaus selected Colonel Thomas W. Bennett's 69th Indiana Infantry, a battle-tested outfit, to lead the way. The rest of McClernand's corps would follow the pathfinders.

On the morning of March 31, a bright and beautiful day, Bennett's exploratory force—two companies of cavalry, a horse-drawn mountain howitzer, and wagons loaded with steamboat yawls—filed down the road to Richmond. "We called ourselves the 'Argonauts,' and were about 1,000 strong," wrote Lieutenant Colonel Oran Perry.[88]

The roads were "about as bad as they could possibly be," twisting unpaved tracks scratched out of levees that ran along oxbow lakes and turbid bayous filled with lazy-looking, man-eating alligators.[89] "The heavy artillery wheels cut through the slime and the mud, making the path a perfect mortar bed through which we waded knee deep, and where the hubs of the wheels often disappeared out of sight," wrote one soldier. These roads were repaired in preparation for succeeding waves of troops as the army moved south; and they would have to be repaired continuously, after every rainstorm, by McPherson's and Sherman's men, who would be following McClernand's corps.[90] Soldiers dressed in clinging woolen uniforms grumbled about the unflagging humidity and the insistent mosquitoes, and not a few seasoned officers believed the decision to march south into this inhospitable country "bordered on madness."[91]

It would be one of the hardest marches of the war and the turning point in the Vicksburg campaign. Progress was agonizingly slow. It would take Grant's army a full month to reach a point where it could safely cross the river.

When the Argonauts approached Richmond that first afternoon, the road disappeared under the still, brown-green waters of Roundaway Bayou. And there was a small rebel force, part of Major Isaac F. Harrison's 15th Louisiana Cavalry Battalion, positioned in the town to dispute their crossing. Two companies piled into yawls and, with covering fire from their howitzer, chased the rebel horsemen from the village. The soldiers then laid a log bridge two hundred feet long across wide and deep Roundaway Bayou.[92]

On April 3, Bennett's spearhead reached Smith's plantation, also known as Pointe Clear, situated on a patch of high ground two miles north of New Carthage. Here they ran into trouble.

"To the south, as far as the eye could reach, the country was like a sea," Oran Perry recalled. All of New Carthage was under water; only the rooftops were visible.[93] The levee leading to the town had been broken in places, and the water was too high and swift to be bridged. The initial advance would have to be made on yawls. The objective: a slice of high ground on the banks of the Mississippi. The impromptu swamp fleet was led by a captured flatboat that the Argonauts converted into an assault craft, using wood stripped from local buildings.[94] "We boarded it up as high as a man's head," said Perry, "cut portholes in the sides and ends, arranged the seats and oars like a war galley of old, mounted it with howitzers and ran up [a] pennant. . . . Altogether, she was something wonderful to behold." The Argonauts christened her *Opossum*.[95]

Opossum led a convoy of yawls carrying two infantry companies across the murky bayou the next day. The rest of the Indianans followed on an "intolerably-bad" road. Passing flooded New Carthage and seeing that it was an unsuitable staging area for troops, the crew of *Opossum* cut south and came to Ione, a riverfront plantation set on the only substantial dry ground in the vicinity. A band of Confederate cavalry was holding out in the gin house. They were easily routed by *Opossum's* howitzer.

Perry and his men disembarked and roused the owner, Joshua Jones, a slender, impressively tall man in his midsixties, with long "iron-gray hair brushed behind his ears." Jones pronounced himself an unyielding secessionist. Four of his sons were in active service, and he had been a leading delegate to the convention that pulled Louisiana out of the Union. He warned the Yankees that they had fallen into a trap and would soon be humbled by Harrison's cavalry, which had been recently reinforced by three regiments of Missourians from Grand Gulf, under Colonel Francis M. Cockrell, known to be a tough customer. The rebels were camped at Perkins plantation, just to the south of Ione.[96]

To hold Ione, Osterhaus brought in the entire 69th Indiana. Grant had come down to Pointe Clear, McClernand's forward headquarters, with news that Admiral Porter would run the Vicksburg batteries imminently, bringing badly needed supplies. Ione, with its riverside dock-age, would be an ideal place for the fleet to land, unload, and make repairs. With its eighty acres of cleared land, it could also serve as a staging area for part of McClernand's main assault force.[97] The next day, as Jones had predicted, the enemy attacked the Federals at Ione, cannonading their positions for nearly an hour; but the Confederate force didn't have enough heft to push in and closely engage the fast-firing Indiana infantry.

General John S. Bowen, the hyperalert commander of the Grand Gulf garrison, had sent Cockrell's Missourians across the river. Vastly outnumbered, they were to impede but not attempt to stop the massive Federal advance. Bowen, a volcanic Georgia secessionist, was Pemberton's most astute and aggressive commander. After recovering from wounds sustained at Shiloh, he had been sent to Grand Gulf in March to bolster its defenses. Trained in architecture and topography at the University of Georgia and West Point, he transformed the clifftop river fort into a "little Gibraltar."[98]

Bowen was alarmed by the ever-growing size of the Federal force he had been tracking from his observation tower on Point of Rock, high above his batteries at Grand Gulf. What looked initially like a small raiding party had become, by the second week of April, a looming threat to Vicksburg, he was convinced. This was an invasion army, intent on crossing the river with malice. Bowen reported this to Pemberton on April 9. Pemberton passed on Bowen's report to Richmond, commenting dismissively: "Much doubt it."[99] He was more concerned with Frederick Steele's presence at Greenville and had, as we have seen, sent Stephen Lee to check his anticipated advance toward Vicksburg.

At this same time, Pemberton's commanders spotted steamers heading upriver from Milliken's Bend and Lake Providence.[100] "I think most of Grant's forces are being withdrawn to Memphis," Pemberton wrote Jefferson Davis.[101] It was a calamitous miscalculation.

The steamers were being sent, on orders from Halleck, to William Rosecrans in Tennessee. Feeling secure, Pemberton had bowed to Joseph Johnston's request and sent eight thousand men from his command to

Braxton Bragg in eastern Tennessee, who was convinced that Rosecrans was about to pounce on his army.[102] Of the Confederate commanders, only Bowen had it right, yet all he could do was harass the oncoming Federals.[103]

On April 15, Colonel Cockrell, a devout Christian known to pray aloud as he swung into the enemy, attacked a Union cavalry detachment at Dunbar's plantation, deep in the New Carthage swamps.[104] He had hoped to mount a twin offensive against Dunbar's and Ione, but after failing to dislodge the reinforced Federals at Dunbar's, he called off the main attack at Ione and withdrew to Grand Gulf, mass having trumped audacity.[105] His sole prize was an Illinois chaplain caught in bed with a slave woman at Dunbar's.[106]

On this day John Pemberton finally awoke to what was happening. Stephen Lee reported from Greenville that Union transports packed with troops had been spotted moving downriver from Lake Providence, a prelude, he assumed, to a run past Vicksburg. The movement toward Memphis was "a ruse," Pemberton finally concluded.[107] Yet it had not been intentional. Once more, Pemberton had misread Grant's objective, deepening his predicament.

"An attack expected soon," Pemberton wired Vicksburg on April 15 from his Jackson headquarters.[108] It came the next night. Pemberton thought the city itself was the target. Instead, the Federals were planning to pass it.

On the afternoon of April 16, David Dixon Porter inspected his flotilla: seven ironclads and three army transports, along with a small tug and a wooden ram. Each ironclad had barges laden with coal and supplies lashed to its sides to protect its hull. Cotton bales and sacks of grain were stacked around the boilers of the thin-skinned transports. The only lights were guiding lamps astern. Porter would lead the river fleet in his flagship, *Benton*.[109]* Anticipating heavy losses, Sherman had

---

* The gunboats were Porter's best: *Louisville, Mound City, Pittsburgh, Carondelet, Lafayette, Tuscumbia*, and the flagship, *Benton*.

four yawls hauled across De Soto Peninsula to the Mississippi, just below Vicksburg. He placed soldiers on board to conduct rescue operations.

Only two of the civilian steamboat captains, and one civilian crew, were willing to go. Far more soldiers than were needed stepped forward and volunteered as pilots, masters, engineers, and coal tenders.[110] Many didn't expect to see the morning sun.[111] Farragut's massively armed sloops-of-war had made it past the batteries the previous summer and, lately, so had a single gunboat, *Indianola*, and the Ellet ram *Queen of the West*. But the last time the ironclad fleet had run under elevated enemy guns, at Fort Donelson, it had taken a pounding. The more formidable Vicksburg river defenses "projected an aura of terrible power." The guns were placed to exploit the swirling waters off De Soto Bend, where the river made a ninety-degree turn, causing even highly experienced captains to lose control of their vessels.

The most powerful of the rebel gun stations was positioned at the northern anchor of the defenses, its guns commanding De Soto Point.[112]

There were thirty-seven pieces of anti-ship ordnance in the enemy defense system, and about a dozen smaller fieldpieces. Warrenton, five miles below the city, had a strong water battery. Most of Vicksburg's guns were not, as is commonly believed, on high ground. They were positioned thirty to forty feet above the waterline; only eleven were near the top of the bluffs. Earthen parapets shielded the batteries, but what the gunners gained in protection they lost in potency. The thick parapets made it difficult to depress the guns sufficiently to bear on boats passing close to Vicksburg's shoreline.[113] Porter aimed to exploit this vulnerability by running his ironclads within pistol shot of the lower batteries.[114]

But his greatest advantage was the enemy's unpreparedness. Vicksburg had held out for so long it had grown dangerously overconfident. Three days before Porter struck, a rebel spy warned General Carter Stevenson, still commander of the Vicksburg garrison, that the enemy was "preparing two or three boats to pass our batteries." For unknown reasons, the message was not transmitted to officers commanding the river defenses.[115] "The citizens . . . do not fear an attack," wrote a Missouri soldier stationed in Vicksburg, "and say if they should be attacked, they are not afraid of the result. Everybody goes about their business as if there was not a Yankee in a thousand miles of them."[116] On

April 14, Marmaduke Shannon's *Vicksburg Daily Whig* reported: "Dispatches received . . . indicate that the [assault on] Vicksburg is virtually ended—that the majority of Grant's army and the heaviest of the ironclads will soon be found on the Tennessee River." [117] Two days later, as Porter made his final preparations, Shannon was urging the city government to begin repairing the streets "now that there is no immediate danger here." [118]

All attention was on the gala ball planned for that evening at the handsome townhouse of Major William O. Watts. Artillery officers in charge of the river batteries were expected to attend. That afternoon, while Watts's servants polished the family silver and arranged chairs for the orchestra, Admiral Porter wrote to Gustavus Fox at the Navy Department: "By the grace of God I hope to see us yet with Uncle Abe's foot on Jeff. Davis' neck." [119]

It was a balmy night, with a light breeze coming off the river. Anchored off Young's Point was the steamer *Henry Von Phul*, its decks packed with Union officers and their guests. They were there to see what promised to be one of the grandest spectacles of the war. Thirty other vessels filled with spectators rocked at anchor nearby. It was "a lively party," wrote Franc Wilkie, on board the *Von Phul*. "Champagne corks popped; there were waves of laughter rolling and surging from boat to boat . . . as the vast audience waited for the rise of the curtain." [120] Grant was on the hurricane deck with his eldest son, Fred, puffing on a cigar, "an intensive light" shining in his eyes. [121] Nearby was Julia, and next to her sat James Wilson with five-year-old Jesse Root Grant II, the youngest of the Grant children, on his lap. Another brother and sister—the middle children—clung to their mother. Near ten o'clock, it became suddenly quiet as "a long procession of bulky shadows" glided past, noiseless, "showing neither light nor steam." They slipped out of sight, "Gunboat and transport in Indian file," as Herman Melville would write in his poem "Running the Batteries," and at a quarter to eleven "two fierce sharp lines of flame," looking like "spears of steel," flashed through the starry sky above Vicksburg. Seconds later, the bluffs were "ablaze with crimson fire," and thunderclaps seemed "to tear the sky to pieces above our heads," wrote nurse Annie Wittenmyer, the guest that

evening of her friend Julia Grant.[122] The *Von Phul* swayed with the concussions, and little Jesse Grant grew so frightened he had to be taken
to bed.[123]

Out on the river, in front of the city, it was bright as day. The rebels had set fire to abandoned buildings on the Louisiana shoreline to
give their gunners maximum visibility.[124] The "howling" of their guns
was continuous and earsplitting. Charles Dana would call it "one of the
most terrific . . . scenes . . . ever witnessed in warfare."[125] For an hour
and a quarter, the air was "rent with detonations." Then, suddenly, not
a gun was heard. Turning to Annie Wittenmyer, Julia Grant whispered:
"Our men are all dead men. . . . No one can live in such a rain of fire
and lead."[126] Wittenmyer didn't answer, afraid to admit perhaps that it
was "the most exciting night [she] had ever known, or perhaps will ever
know again, on the earth," she wrote later.[127]

Unknown to the spectators, the damage to the fleet was surprisingly
light.[128] Rebel fire was too inaccurate and infrequent to do lethal damage. Rare well-aimed shots bounced harmlessly off the gunboats' two-
and-a-half-inch-thick iron casemates, reinforced by twenty-four inches
of oak. And Porter's mammoth guns intimidated Vicksburg's artillerists,
who took cover whenever under fire. They were able to fire an average
of only one round per gun every eight minutes.[129] Only twelve of the
two thousand or so soldiers and sailors who ran the gauntlet were casualties, and not a single gunboat was put out of action.[130] "We suffered
most from the musketry fire," said Porter. "The soldiers lined the levee
and fired into our port-holes, wounding our men, for we were not more
than twenty yards from the shore."[131]

After passing the last enemy gun station, Porter was hailed by someone in a small boat: "*Benton* ahoy!" It was Sherman. He checked on
Porter's casualties—one man had a leg blown off, half a dozen others suffered shell and bullet wounds—and rowed off to "find out how
the other fellows fared."[132] An hour or so later, the gunboats found a
temporary landing spot twelve miles above New Carthage. As sweat-
soaked men climbed out of the suffocating iron casemates and saw that
not a single boat had been lost "there were . . . rousing cheers for the
admiral."[133]

"We still live," shouted an officer on *Lafayette*.[134]

The transports had not fared as well. *Forest Queen* took two shattering hits but was repaired in a day; and *Henry Clay* was struck repeatedly, set afire, and abandoned by its panicked crew, left to float downriver, a "great blazing mass." Hours after docking, Porter's flotilla headed down to New Carthage, the admiral having proved himself, in Melville's words, "a brave man's son." [135]

The citizens of Vicksburg had watched the river fight from the bluffs. A number of them had hurried from Watts's party and climbed to the Sky Parlor, one of the highest hills in the city, expecting to witness the annihilation of the intruders' fleet. [136] They saw instead the beginning of their own end. In one stroke, Vicksburg was perilously exposed. Rebel gunner A. Hugh Moss, manning a waterfront battery, read the enemy's intentions exactly. "Their object, I think, in going below," he wrote in his diary, "is to cross troops and try and get in the rear of Vicksburg." [137]

Vicksburg's fate was sealed, Grant told Dana. A campaign that had known nothing but disappointment now "could not fail." [138] The lower Mississippi was a Union river, and Grant could land troops at a place of his choosing. "I regard the navigation of the Mississippi River as shut out from us now," Pemberton wired one of his commanders. "No more supplies can be gotten from the trans-Mississippi department." [139]

Pemberton rushed men south to reinforce Bowen at Grand Gulf, bringing his strength to 4,200 infantry and artillerists. He also wired Joseph Johnston canceling the transfer of the eight thousand men he had sent his way. [140] Yet even in these spasms of resolve, Pemberton remained anxious and confused, unsure where Grant would strike next. In a stunning demonstration of naval power, Porter had put Grant in total command of the situation. Pemberton's every decision from here on would be reactive and insufficient.

Grant had hazarded his career on this night, and he was too impatient to wait until morning for news of the outcome. The instant *Von Phul* landed at Young's Point, he called for his horse and rode through the night to catch up with Porter, accompanied by his son Fred, Charles Dana, and a guard of twenty cavalrymen. When they approached a slough that had been bridged by McClernand's army, Grant made "one of his daring leaps," landing safely on the opposite bank. The rest of his party crossed the narrow bridge and headed for Ione, where Oran Perry and his Indiana boys were holding on.[141]

They had spent an anxious evening on April 16 waiting for news from Vicksburg. To break the tension, the officers had gathered on the second-floor balcony of the manor house and begun singing "Rally 'Round the Flag." Plantation owner Joshua Jones looked on quizzically. Why were they so jubilant, he asked, when their fleet was about to be slaughtered. One of the officers explained: The boats *would* get past Vicksburg, and in a day or so Grant would be on the front lawn of Ione, on his way to Mississippi. Their small force had been "simply the entering wedge."[142]

Around eleven o'clock the men heard cannon fire in the distance. "Then a great light went up and brightened the sky for an hour or two."[143] They waited till three hours past midnight and went to their beds not knowing the fate of the fleet. At daybreak, they saw black plumes of smoke upriver. It was a burnt-out hulk, the remains of a Union steamer. Bales of burning cotton floated in its wake. Then some barges appeared, drifting aimlessly. The troops set out in skiffs and guided them to shore. In one of them was a large American flag. To Joshua Jones's acute distress, they ran it up the pole on which he had been flying the Stars and Bars. Around noon, more smoke appeared over the river. *Pittsburgh* came into view, the rest of the fleet close behind. The Indianans raced to the river, threw their caps in the air, and began "yelling, dancing and drinking."[144] Looking on from the balcony, Jones sank to his knees sobbing.

As the celebration wound down, Grant rode up to where the gunboats were docked, greeted Porter, and was serenaded by the Indianans. The next day the old rebel set fire to his house. He would not have it shelter for another hour his implacable enemy.[145] It was the beginning of the decisive phase of the Vicksburg campaign.

Porter would later explain what lay ahead. "General Grant had turned the enemy's flank with his army, I had turned it with the gun-boats; now Grant needed to cross the river and trust to his brave soldiers."[146]

CHAPTER 18

This One Object

*"All the campaigns, labors, hardships, and exposures from the
month of December previous to this time that had been made and
endured, were for the accomplishment of this one object."*[1]

—Ulysses Grant

Grant's night ride to Ione plantation convinced him he had a problem that could foul the entire campaign. Additional roads had to be found. Marching an entire army down a single, miserably maintained dirt road could take months. He also needed a larger staging area than Ione for his fast-gathering strike force, and one closer to Grand Gulf, its objective. With only three steamboats and a few barges at his disposal, the vessels would have to make frequent shuttle runs to move troops from Ione to Grand Gulf, leaving the first waves of the landing force dangerously vulnerable.[2] He did have Porter's gunboats, but needed them to neutralize enemy defenses and provide cover for the troop transports.

When Grant arrived at Pointe Clear, just north of Ione, he learned from McClernand that scouting parties had located a weather-damaged road that led along the banks of a waterway called Bayou Vidal to Perkins plantation, three miles to the south.[3] It was the former residence of John Perkins Jr., a Harvard-educated lawyer, former U.S. congressman, and passionate secessionist, and had been the headquarters of the rebel units that had been stalking McClernand's ponderously moving army. They had disappeared into the swamps, leaving the farm's 17,500 acres abandoned.[4]

Two days after Porter passed the batteries, Grant ordered McClernand to advance to Perkins. McPherson's corps was not far behind McClernand and was closing rapidly.[5] Grant then returned to Milliken's Bend to round up more wagons. This was crucial: The canal from Duckport to New Carthage was unfinished and unlikely to work, even if completed. All supplies would have to be moved by road.

McClernand's corps could not cross into Mississippi without additional rations. The only way to get them to him quickly was by river. This meant challenging the batteries again. This time it would be an all-army operation—transports only. Porter had two ironclads north of Vicksburg, but they were protecting the army's supply line between Milliken's Bend and Memphis.

The morning Grant returned to Milliken's Bend, he had six stern-wheel steamers fitted out to run past Vicksburg. Each carried one hundred thousand rations and forty days' coal for fuel to be burned once they got below Vicksburg.[6] Twelve barges loaded with supplies were lashed to them, and, as before, double tiers of cotton bales and sacks filled with oats were placed fore and aft of the boilers. The boats had neither armor nor cannon. Each had a crew of twenty-five, nearly all of them soldier volunteers.[7] Five times the number needed had stepped forward to serve.[8] "I confess I never expected to see men or boats again," recalled infantryman Ira Blanchard.[9]

They set out on the night of April 22 with *Tigress*, Grant's command boat at Shiloh, in the lead. The windless night was "black as a bottomless pit" as Grant and other spectators watched from the forward deck of *Von Phul*.[10] With no breeze, smoke from the rebels' guns settled in front of their own batteries, impairing visibility. Hugging the Vicksburg shoreline, every boat was hit repeatedly, but only *Tigress* was lost. The five surviving steamers arrived at New Carthage the next day, damaged but repairable. Six of the twelve barges got through. Only two men were killed and six wounded.[11] It was another night of ignominy for Vicksburg's gunners.

When the steamers reached New Carthage, Grant changed his plans yet again. All the way to Vicksburg it would be like this—a campaign of never-ending improvisation. Advance planning was impossible in Louisiana's tangled bayou country. The army had no reliable maps, and the mighty river transformed the land on its banks ceaselessly and capriciously. Around every bend was a surprise: an impassable stretch of road, a deep bayou to be bridged. When McClernand's corps reached

Perkins plantation it found enough dry ground for only two divisions; the rest of the place was flooded. Grant intervened and moved the staging area farther downstream to Hard Times, a steamboat landing with enough room, it was thought, for all three of his corps. It had the added advantage of being directly across from Grand Gulf.

There was one problem, however. Another road would have to be opened to get part of McPherson's corps to Hard Times before Bowen could strengthen his uncompleted Grand Gulf defenses. With the help of local slaves, the Argonauts found one. It ran discontinuously—because of flooding—around the west bank of Lake St. Joseph, a magnificent sheet of blue-green water. Rebel troops had burned every bridge along the way to the lake, so Osterhaus put his versatile Indiana and Ohio boys to work. In four days, they had built four miles of new roadbed and bridged four swift-flowing bayous.[12] Local houses and barns were torn down to provide planks, and soldiers working in neck-deep water slapped the lumber onto pontoons and secured the bridges to the banks of the bayous.[13] "Those bridges were built by green volunteers, who had never . . . had an hour's drill or instruction in bridge-building," wrote James Wilson.[14]*

While the Lake St. Joseph route was being opened, Union divisions were flooding southward through "one of the most difficult regions that ever tested the resources of an army."[15] Fleas invaded woolen uniforms, and the bayous were populated with insects as "large as turkey gobblers," said Iowa surgeon Seneca Thrall. Soldiers had no tents and no change of clothing; they had been ordered to travel light.[16] With mud up to men's ankles and knees, road building was as pivotal as bridge building. Logs for corduroy roads were cut on the spot by army pioneers working furiously into the night. Without these makeshift roads, enormous supply wagons and heavy guns pulled by twelve to eighteen horses would have been nearly immovable. "I doubt if there ever was any campaign in any war so dependent for success upon engineering skill," wrote Andrew Hickenlooper, an artillery officer who had been transferred, without interest or qualifications, to Grant's engineering

---

* Grant's engineering corps built eight bridges to reach Hard Times and a total of twenty-two to get his army from Richmond to Vicksburg. Phillip M. Thienel, "Bridges in the Vicksburg Campaign," *The Military Engineer* (November–December, 1955): 457.

corps and who would later play a large role in the siege of Vicksburg.[17] With only a handful of West Point–trained engineers in his army, Grant relied upon the Voluntary Engineer Corps, or pioneer corps, as it was more generally known—western farm boys and mechanics whose ingenuity was "equal to any emergency."[18] Recently freed African Americans assisted them, thirty to fifty of them in an average pioneer company.[19]

Speed was the sine qua non. Porter wanted to hit Grand Gulf before it became "impregnable." McClernand was ordered to pick up the pace: "Dispatch is all important."[20] Porter wanted Sherman and Grant at the front, pushing McClernand hard. "I am quite depressed with this [Louisiana] adventure, which as you know never met with my approval . . ." he wrote Gustavus Fox. "Sherman, the moving spirit [of the army], is left behind, where he should have been in the advance."[21] But Sherman was to follow McPherson south from Milliken's Bend, the roads being able to handle only one corps at a time. Porter wrote to Sherman "begging" him to persuade Grant to come to the front and take charge.[22]

Grant was suffering from boils and unable to mount a horse without stabbing pain, but the day after Sherman passed along Porter's message he rode the forty miles to Perkins plantation and established his headquarters there.[23]

When Grant arrived at Perkins in late April he expected most of McClernand's corps to be at Hard Times, "ready for immediate embarkation," but an "irritating delay" had occurred. McClernand was holding up the departure of steamers assigned to carry part of the army to Hard Times.[24] Their captains had been ordered to await the late arrival of McClernand's new bride, who had brought along her servants and all her luggage—a direct rebuke to Grant, who had issued orders to leave personal items behind. Infuriated, Grant called McClernand to his headquarters and demanded he "embark his men without losing a moment."[25] But as of early evening, not a single man or cannon had been moved, and McClernand, incredibly, held a grand review of his Illinois soldiers for the benefit of visiting governor Richard Yates, a favorite with the men. After he and "Uncle Dick," as the Illinois boys called Yates, delivered gassy orations, McClernand ordered an artillery salute, in violation of Grant's directive to save all ammunition for the enemy.[26] When word reached Grant he fired off a stern reprimand, but he filed it the next day when he discovered that McClernand had pushed off during the night and assembled his troops at Hard Times in good order for the amphibious assault.[27]

Two of McPherson's divisions had also arrived over the newly opened Lake St. Joseph road. There had been a slight delay, time wasted on wholesale plunder. Residents of Lake St. Joseph would long remember McPherson's stampede to Hard Times.

"The country through which we are now passing is the most beautiful I have ever seen," wrote Illinois soldier Seth J. Wells. "The plantation mansions are grand, and the grounds and out buildings are fitted up in fine style."[28] Fifteen of the South's most magnificent cotton plantations, with exotic gardens, marble statuary, and deer parks lined the banks of Lake St. Joseph.[29] All but one of them was burned or ravaged beyond repair by the first wave of McPherson's troops, who before setting fire to them set up temporary camp on the lawns, where they chewed on bacon and hardtack while lounging on glass-top tables and rosewood pianos.[30]

Grant had anticipated this and issued strict orders to prevent it. Commanders were authorized to collect beef cattle, corn, and other "necessary supplies" on the line of march but were to prevent the "wanton destruction" or theft of household property. Houses were not to be searched, nor were families to be treated disrespectfully.[31] But officers lost control of their men, who were strung out in columns miles long, and some commanders actively encouraged pillaging.[32] As McPherson's men marched out of Lake St. Joseph they left behind the smoking ruin of a once luxuriant cotton community. Houses not destroyed were ransacked. Articles of clothing and priceless books were strewn about, Parisian mirrors and family portraits smashed and slashed.[33]

Despoiling great libraries and stealing family keepsakes hardly constituted economic warfare, but the destruction of these estates, with their gin houses, tools, animals, and slaves, did irreparable harm to the enemy cause. In 1860, the combined cotton crop of the Lake St. Joseph plantations was greater than the separate totals for thirty Louisiana parishes. And approximately 2,200 slaves gained their freedom when their masters picked up and fled.[34]

Most families in the area headed for backwater towns in western Louisiana or traveled all the way to east Texas. Before leaving, Sarah Ann Dorsey's privileged family hid silverware in sealed barrels at the bottom of a well and placed personal items in leather trunks, hauled on buckboards by their slaves. A family living near the Dorsey farm took five hundred field hands with them, guarded by white overseers with whips, bloodhounds, and deer rifles.[35]

Grant's southern thrust set off one of the great panic migrations of the war. It was unsafe for Confederate supporters to be anywhere within reach of his soldiers, many of whom were driven by a deep desire for vengeance against secessionists who had ignited a war that pulled them from their families and peaceful pursuits. There was no constabulary, no guerrilla bands, nor troops of any consequence to protect secessionist property. "Where we marched, were smoldering ruins," said one Union soldier, "and for miles ahead we could see smoke and flames wrapping roofs and walls that towered high."[36] With Grant's men seizing or slaughtering livestock, invading vegetable gardens, and destroying corn in fields and cribs, food for daily survival became perilously scarce. "The country is been laid waste . . . and what the people is to do for something to eat is more than I can tell," an Iowa soldier wrote his wife. He felt compassion, he said, for families who had lost nearly everything, but he blamed the rebels for bringing this scourge on themselves. They "must reap their reward."[37]

Among the refugees in western Louisiana was twenty-two-year-old Kate Stone. She and her family had gotten out early. The day before Porter ran the batteries they were in Delhi, Louisiana, a small rail center west of Vicksburg, preparing to leave for Texas. They had been driven out not by Yankee depredations—Brokenburn was considerably north of Grant's army—but by their own and their neighbors' slaves. "All the Negroes are running away now, and there are numbers of them," Kate wrote in her diary. A family who lived close to Brokenburn "got up one morning and found every Negro gone, about seventy-five. . . . The ladies actually had to get up and get breakfast. They said it was funny to see their first attempt at milking."

One afternoon, Kate and her sister were visiting friends when they heard loud talking outside the front door. Minutes later, a band of escaped slaves burst into the house and herded the women into a bedroom. They were held at gunpoint by one of the intruders while the others ransacked the house, looking for guns. They left without harming anyone but vowed they'd be back with torches.

When Kate and her sister rode back to Brokenburn, they encountered "strange Negroes standing around. . . . They did not say anything," Kate told her diary, "but they looked at us and grinned and that terrified us." That night, Kate's mother, Amanda, called her family together. It was time to leave. At midnight on a moonless night, they mounted horses and headed into the swamp—Kate, her mother, sister, and two brothers, along with Amanda Stone's sister Laura, riding a pony with her four-year-old daughter. The county was flooded, and they rode through water up to their saddle skirts. At one point, after getting lost, Kate swam across a bayou with her aunt's baby in her arms. Hours later they came to a landing, where they piled into a dugout canoe that Amanda Stone had arranged for in advance. Before they pushed off, one of the slaves escaped with their baggage cart. They were left with nothing but the wet clothing on their backs. Just then, a Union patrol spotted them and pursued "until their horses were nearly swimming."

They landed at the railroad bridge in Delhi. "The scene there," Kate wrote, "beggars description: such crowds of Negroes of all ages and sizes, wagons, mules, horses, dogs, baggage, and furniture of every description, very little of it packed. It was just thrown into promiscuous heaps—pianos, tables, chairs, rosewood sofas, wardrobes, parlor sets, with pots, kettles, stoves, beds and bedding, bowls and pitchers and everything of the kind just thrown pell-mell here and there, with soldiers, drunk and sober, combing over it all, shouting and laughing. While thronging everywhere were refugees—men, women, and children—everybody and everything trying to get on the cars, all fleeing from the Yankees or, worse still, the Negroes."

They reached Monroe the next day. That was as far west as the railroad ran. They stayed for a few weeks in the hope that rebel troops would liberate Brokenburn. While they waited, Kate's sixteen-year-old brother

Jimmy returned home to retrieve the slaves they had left behind. He could not have been more surprised. Webster, their "most trusted servant," had joined the Union army and claimed the plantation "as his own." With the help of half a dozen neighbors, Jimmy Stone entered the house and recaptured every family servant except Webster.[38]

In Monroe, the family boarded with the Wadleys, the wife and five children of William Wadley, whose work as coordinator of Confederate railroad transportation had taken him east. Mrs. Wadley had been reluctant to take in "swamp" people, but the two families got along wonderfully. Kate became attached to Sara, one of the eldest Wadley daughters, and Sara helped her grieve the death of her brother Walter, a private in the 28th Mississippi, who died from fever at age eighteen. Weeks later, when the Stone family left for Texas, "Miss Kate went [a]way in tears," Sara wrote in her diary.[39]

Kate and Sara would keep in touch. They were passionate letter writers and steely Southern patriots. Later, Kate could not contain herself when she learned that Lincoln had been assassinated. She took to her diary: "All honor to J. Wilkes Booth, who has rid the world of a tyrant."[40]

While Kate Stone's family was in Delhi, they heard nothing of the Union assault on Grand Gulf. It was repulsed, but in preparing for it and instantly rebounding from the loss, Grant emerged as one of the most quick-thinking strategists of the war.

His objective had been to take Grand Gulf with minimal casualties. To do this, he needed to pull Pemberton's eyes away from the river. At dawn on April 17, he sent Colonel Benjamin H. Grierson on an audacious raid behind Pemberton's river defenses. Grierson rode out of La Grange, Tennessee, with 1,700 cavalrymen and stormed through the heart of Mississippi with orders to destroy railway tracks and telegraph lines to deflect Pemberton's attention from the Federal buildup in Louisiana.

Thirty-six-year-old Benjamin Grierson was a Jacksonville, Illinois, music teacher with a profound mistrust of horses. As a child he had been kicked in the face by a pony and scarred for life.[41] When war broke out he joined the infantry but was reassigned, under protest, to the 6th Illinois Cavalry, rising to brigade command by 1862.[42] Grant knew him to be one of the finest horse soldiers in his department, and personally approved his selection to lead what Sherman would call "the most brilliant expedition of the war."[43]

Starting west of Jackson, Mississippi, his three regiments slashed through the state, tearing up fifty miles of railroad, burning bridges, freight cars, and depots, and killing or capturing over six hundred rebels before his dust-caked raiders rode into Union-occupied Baton Rouge on May 2 and made a triumphal procession, two miles long, through the streets.[44] They had covered six hundred miles in sixteen days and lost only three men killed and a small number wounded or captured. "Grierson had knocked the heart out of the State," one of Grant's informants told him later.[45]

The confusion he caused was more damaging than the communications he destroyed. Unsure of his intentions, Pemberton personally directed operations against him, focusing on a few cavalry regiments when an entire enemy army was preparing to cross into Mississippi. Then he made his most grievous mistake, sending a cavalry force stationed near Grand Gulf to pursue Grierson. This left Bowen without "eyes and ears." If the Federals were stopped at Grand Gulf they could land anywhere south of it and not be detected or opposed.[46]

Part of Pemberton's problem was his inexplicable refusal to move his headquarters, at this climactic moment in the campaign, from Jackson to Vicksburg. From January to late April, Grant was closer to Vicksburg than he was.[47]

While Grierson was at large in southwestern Mississippi on the final leg of his raid, Grant devised another stratagem to further confuse Pemberton. On April 27, his forty-first birthday, he wrote Sherman, asking him if he thought it "advisable" to mount a diversionary assault on Haynes' Bluff to deflect "the enemy's attention from movements south of Vicksburg." It was a suggestion, not an order. Grant told Sherman he feared "our people at home" might see the faux raid as "a repulse," a second, and equally humiliating Chickasaw Bayou, and he didn't want him pilloried again by his newspaper critics.[48] After reading the letter, Sherman turned to an aide and barked: "Does General Grant think I care what the newspapers say?"[49]

"It shall be done . . ." he told Grant. "I will be all ready at day light."[50]

Porter provided two ironclads, six wooden warships, and three mortar scows.[51] They were to escort transports carrying part of Francis Blair's division. This impressive-looking Union flotilla appeared on the green-blue waters of the Yazoo the next morning. "The gunboats and transports whistled and puffed and made all the noise they could," recalled engineer William Le Baron Jenney. "They showed themselves to the garrison at Haynes' Bluff and then drifted back and landed the men, who were marched through the woods . . . until they were seen by the enemy, marched a mile or so down the river, and taken again on board the transports, to go through the same farce again."[52] The next morning, as the river fleet headed back to Young's Point, an urgent message arrived from Grant: Sherman was to bring his corps to Hard Times. A landing in Mississippi was imminent.[53]

Sherman's demonstration "created great confusion about Vicksburg and doubts about our real design," Grant wrote later.[54] The defenders on the bluffs did not see it that way. A rebel colonel wrote later: "From the strength and manner of . . . [Sherman's] attack, it was manifestly a false one, and designed to cover some other movement."[55] Major General John Forney, commanding a division on the bluffs, agreed.

But Sherman's presence on the Yazoo did create further confusion about Union intentions. If this were not the main attack, where would it come? Carter Stevenson had been ordered to keep five thousand men at Vicksburg, prepared to reinforce Bowen. He was convinced, however, that the Federal army across the river from Grand Gulf was "a feint to withdraw troops from a main attack here." Sherman's raid was the prelude. Do not remove troops from Vicksburg, he urged Pemberton, "until further developments below render it certain that they will cross in force."[56]

By late April Grant had gotten inside Pemberton's head and created a tremendous, buzzing confusion, mastering him decisively before a single shot was fired on Mississippi soil.

• • •

The morning Sherman's flotilla appeared on the Yazoo, Porter was preparing to strike Grand Gulf. Bowen figured he was coming. The day before, he had climbed to his wooden tower atop Point of Rock and seen the Union host assembling impressively at Hard Times. "An immense force opposite me . . ." he wired Pemberton. ". . . I advise that every man and gun that can be spared from other points be sent here."[57] Pemberton wavered and didn't act until the next day.

Bowen was disappointed but confident he could stand up to anything the Federals threw at him. In the short time given him, he had turned Grand Gulf into a "defensive masterpiece," more formidable, because of its concentrated power, than the widely dispersed Vicksburg defenses.[58]

The garrison took its name from the large circular bay, or "gulf," located at the foot of a hundred-foot-high promontory that commanded an unimpeded view for miles up and down the river.[59] Bowen built his defenses above the ruins of the nearly uninhabited hamlet Farragut's fleet had leveled in the summer of 1862. Samuel Lockett, the engineer who supervised the construction of Vicksburg's defenses, had put his signature on the two forts that were the keystones of Bowen's defensive line. They stood, one above the other, a mile apart, connected by a covered trench that served as a protected rifle pit for sharpshooters. The more formidable upper battery, Fort Cobun, was built into the base of Point of Rock, forty feet above the turbulent waters of Grand Gulf. It had four big guns set behind a thick earthen parapet. The other bastion, Fort Wade, was at the foot of the bluff, about 1,500 yards below Cobun. It had a mammoth rifled gun but less total firepower than Cobun.

At seven o'clock on the morning of April 29, Porter's seven gunboats, with his flagship, *Benton*, in the lead, dropped downriver and assembled directly below the rebel forts. At Hard Times, a landing force of over thirty thousand infantry waited anxiously. A third of it—the first wave—was packed together in transports and barges, floating offshore. The men were in good spirits, but the order to go would not be given until the rebel guns were silenced. Fifty minutes later there was a loud exchange of gunfire, and a cauldron of smoke and flame obscured Grand Gulf. Grant looked on from the deck of an army tug, his son Fred and Congressman Elihu Washburne beside him.

Grant had hoped to avoid confronting the batteries. The day before, he had sent James Wilson to locate a landing spot north of Grand Gulf, but Wilson had been unable to find a passable road to the interior.[60] Porter had been pressuring Grant to call off the attack. Bowen had had too much time to prepare. Porter suggested a different plan: either put the army on transports and float them past the guns, with the ironclads providing protective fire; or have the army march south, out of range of the guns, and bring down the transports at night, shielded by the ironclads.

Grant rejected both ideas after making a personal reconnaissance of Grand Gulf on Porter's flagship. "The place," he decided, "would easily fall."[61]

"The Battle of Grand Gulf . . . was as hard a fight as any that occurred during the war," Porter would write later.[62]

"The gunboats went in close, rubb[ing] their noses against the banks . . . and ran down and back with utter disregard of the shower of shot that was poured on them," wrote a Union soldier who watched the battle from across the river.[63] The current was wicked near the bluffs. Boats caught in it were spun round and round, making them easy targets for practiced rebel gunners. From their covered rifle pits, sharpshooters poured lead into the open firing ports of the ironclads. But after a continuous four-hour barrage, the navy's 100-pound shells knocked Fort Wade out of the fight and killed Bowen's chief artillery officer and the fort's namesake, Colonel William Wade.[64] The guns themselves remained intact but were smothered and silenced by immense piles of dirt blown from the parapets.[65]

Fort Cobun held on. Positioned high above the river, it was harder to hit. Late in the morning, its gunners cut up *Tuscumbia*, the most poorly built of the Union gunboats, and she drifted out of range.[66] Around noon, Porter began to run low on ammunition and headed upstream to confer with Grant. With Cobun still delivering lethal fire and the sharpshooters unhindered in their covered trench, it would be too hazardous, they agreed, to attempt a landing. Porter broke off the fight and led his boats back to Hard Times.[67]

The rebels had concentrated their fire on three of them—*Benton*, *Pittsburgh*, and *Tuscumbia*—inflicting heavy damage, yet all except *Tuscumbia* would be in fighting trim within hours. Eighteen men were dead, fifty-seven wounded.[68] Cold numbers fail to give the full story.

When Grant and his son boarded *Benton* they were "sickened" by the carnage.[69] A shell had penetrated its port side and exploded between decks, where sailors had been working the guns. "The sight of the mangled and dying men which met my eye . . . was sickening," Grant wrote later.[70] Porter had been struck in the back of the head by a shell fragment, and "his face showed the agony he was suffering." It was the only time in the war he was wounded.[71]

Rebel casualties were light: three men killed and fifteen wounded.[72] Bowen's defenders were exultant. With only thirteen guns, they had held off a flotilla mounting eighty-one guns.[73] Yet their young commander knew he had won only "a shadow victory."[74] Grant could land his army farther downriver, unopposed, anywhere he wished.[75]

"A landing will be effected [on] the east bank of the river tomorrow," Grant wrote Halleck that night. "I feel that the battle is now more than half won."[76]

He had reason to be confident. Earlier that evening he disembarked the troops and floated the empty transports and barges four miles south to another Louisiana staging area: Disharoon's plantation. Porter's gunboats provided cover and got through unscathed. Later that night, the army marched to Disharoon's, "where the negroes turned out to welcome us with great rejoicing," recalled Fred Grant.[77] The plan Porter had originally suggested had been executed without losing a man. When the soldiers reunited with the fleet at Disharoon's, Pemberton was outflanked, though he did not know it yet.

Grant arrived at Disharoon's plantation on horseback and began assembling his army for the leap into Mississippi. The previous afternoon, he had sent a scouting party to find a landing spot. Eight soldiers crossed in a yawl and ran into a black man who seemed to know every town and terrain feature on the riverfront. He was willing to help but not if it meant meeting face-to-face with the Union commander. He wasn't given a choice. One hour later he was in Grant's tent. The best place to land, he told Grant, was Bruinsburg, five miles downstream. The nearly deserted plantation settlement had a solid embankment for steamboats. A road led from there to Port Gibson, thirty miles south of Vicksburg. Grant had intended to land at Rodney, eleven miles farther downstream, but he took the captured man at his word. It would be Bruinsburg.[78]*

The next morning, April 30, Grant began moving McClernand's XIII Corps and a division of McPherson's command to Bruinsburg.[79] Every vessel available—steamers, gunboats, and barges—was enlisted to ferry the men, in shifts, across the river. The men were traveling light. The order of the day was celerity: get quickly to the interior and in position to move on the enemy. There were no baggage wagons, and only artillerymen and a small number of cavalrymen—scouts and couriers— were permitted horses. This was a beach-storming force. Sherman's corps would bring plenty of supply wagons and horses when he made a separate crossing, days later, after marching eighty-three miles from Milliken's Bend to Disharoon's.

Even the commander was without a horse. Grant also left behind his tents, blankets, and camp chests. He didn't have a clean shirt or a razor. In the coat pocket of his wrinkled private's blouse was his toothbrush.[80]

There were no horse-drawn ambulances or facilities for field hospitals. This was puzzling to men preparing for combat. In the interest of speed, Grant had decided to leave his wounded behind, to be cared for by the enemy. No one, with the exception of his key commanders, knew this.

Grant crossed the river with Porter in *Benton's* pilothouse without Fred, whom he had lost in the confusion of the march to Disharoon's. Unknown to his father, Fred had found space on one of the gunboats.[81]

Halfway across the river Grant nervously surveyed the landing area and the bluffs just beyond, looking for signs of the enemy. "The decks were covered with anxious soldiers, guns were cleared for action, and the crews were at quarters," wrote an Indiana man on one of the gunboats.[82] But the only signs of life were a ramshackle house and a scattering of slave shacks. Grant could thank Grierson for that.†

As *Benton* approached shore, a band struck up "The Red, White,

---

* The settlement was founded by Irish immigrant and Revolutionary War veteran Peter Bryan Bruin, who arrived there with twelve families in 1788, after acquiring the land from Spanish colonial authorities. NYT, May 25, 1863.

† Only one person was found at Bruinsburg, a local farmer, who was held prisoner on a gunboat to prevent him from spreading word of the landing. Shea and Winschel, *Vicksburg Is the Key*, 106.

and Blue." The men cheered lustily and began waving their muskets in the air. "We are nearing the moment of the grand decisive blow," said soldier William H. Jolly.[83] If Grant takes Vicksburg "he will have as big a name as Washington," a bluecoat wrote home after disembarking.[84]

The ferry operation continued into the night, and by morning, twenty-four thousand men and sixty cannon were on Mississippi soil. It was the largest amphibious landing in American history until D-Day, June 6, 1944, and one of the deciding events of the American Civil War.*

In his memoirs Grant famously recorded his first thought on setting foot on dry ground south of Vicksburg:

> When this was effected I felt a degree of relief scarcely ever equaled since. . . . I was now in the enemy's country, with a vast river and the stronghold of Vicksburg between me and my base of supplies. But I was on dry ground on the same side of the river with the enemy. All the campaigns, labors, hardships, and expo-sures from the month of December previous to this time that had been made and endured, were for the accomplishment of *this one object.*[85]

Grant hoped to get his army to Port Gibson in a flash. The enemy, he guessed, would be there, probably Bowen with his Grand Gulf garri-son, but McClernand caused another delay.[86] He had neglected to issue rations to his troops the night before. They had to be brought over the river, putting Grant four hours behind schedule.[87] "Barrels of bread, bacon and coffee were rolled on shore and opened," wrote Ohio veteran Louis Mason, "each man having permission to stuff his haversack and pockets with sufficient food to last five days."[88] General Eugene Carr's lead division was on the bluffs overlooking the landing site an hour before sunset. Port Gibson was twelve miles away.

After a short rest, Carr pushed on, hoping to surprise the enemy and take the place without a fight. At sunrise, Union pickets began "to feel the enemy."[89]

---

* Porter wrote later: "It was in my opinion the most remarkable and most successful military operation of the civil war." Porter, *Incidents and Anecdotes*, 183.

— PART FOUR —

CHAPTER 19

Pursuit

"The road to Vicksburg is open." [1]

—Ulysses S. Grant

Friday, May 1, 1863:

"This has been a glorious day for the Union, and for the despondent hearts in the North," Sergeant Major Charles Edwards Wilcox wrote in his diary. "We have fought a battle and won a complete victory." [2]

Wilcox had seen no heavy combat until his regiment, the 33rd Illinois Infantry, met the enemy on this first day of May. An emancipationist, he had crossed the great river the previous morning determined, he wrote, "to redeem this lovely valley of the Mississippi from fiends and traitors who are desecrating it." [3]

After landing at Bruinsburg on April 30, his regiment, part of Eugene Carr's division, headed down the dust-choked Rodney Road to Port Gibson. Speed was imperative. If the rebels mobilized quickly and in considerable numbers, they might delay or defeat Grant's initial landing force of twenty-two thousand infantry. [4]

Port Gibson had to be taken to secure the Union beachhead. It was strategically located on roads leading to Vicksburg, Grand Gulf, and Jackson, sixty miles to the northeast. Without cavalry to scout ahead, a detail of sixteen Iowans took the lead. Their orders: "go forward . . . until fired on by the enemy." An aged plantation slave named Bob, who had unexpectedly joined them, led the reconnaissance party and would remain with the 21st Iowa throughout the Vicksburg campaign. [5]

The Rodney Road cut unevenly through a thick forest of ancient hickory and oak trees, "abundant and brilliant," wrote Illinois infantryman R. L. Howard. "It was the most rugged [country] we had ever seen, being a continual succession of sharp pitches from fifty to a hundred

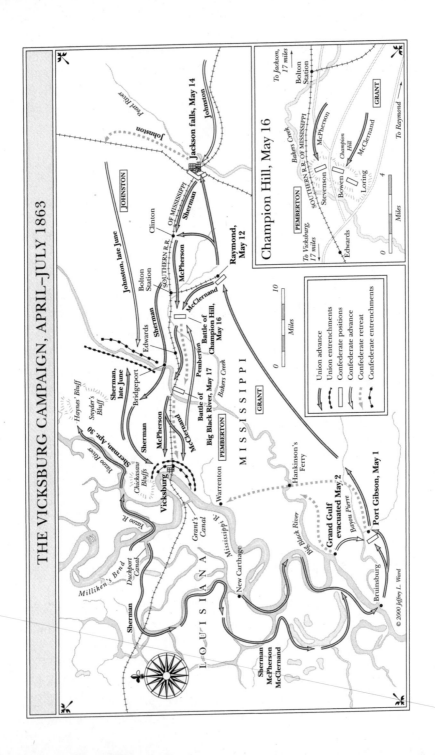

THE VICKSBURG CAMPAIGN, APRIL–JULY 1863

Pearl River

Johnston

Jackson falls, May 14

Johnston

JOHNSTON

Johnston, late June

Clinton

SOUTHERN R.R.

OF MISSISSIPPI

Sherman

McPherson

Raymond, May 12

McClernand

Bolton Station

Edwards

Sherman

Pemberton

Battle of Champion Hill, May 16

Bakers Creek

Battle of Big Black River, May 17

McClernand

PEMBERTON

MISSISSIPPI

GRANT

Hankinson's Ferry

Warrenton

Haynes' Bluff

Snyder's Bluff

Sherman, late June

Bridgeport

Yazoo River

Sherman, Apr. 30

Chickasaw Bluffs

Vicksburg

Grant's Canal

Sherman

McPherson

McClernand

Big Black River

Grand Gulf evacuated May 2

Bayou Pierre

Port Gibson, May 1

New Carthage

Mississippi River

Milliken's Bend

Duckport Canal

L O U I S I A N A

Bruinsburg

Sherman
McPherson
McClernand

© 2000 Jeffrey L. Ward

Union advance
Union entrenchments
Confederate positions
Confederate advance
Confederate retreat
Confederate entrenchments

0   Miles   10

Champion Hill, May 16

To Jackson, 17 miles

Bolton Station

Bakers Creek

McPherson

SOUTHERN R.R. OF MISSISSIPPI

Stevenson

Champion Hill

GRANT

Bowen

McClernand

Loring

To Vicksburg, 17 miles

PEMBERTON

Edwards

To Raymond

0   4
Miles

feet high." The "cuts in the hills . . . were almost defiles, with the stiff clay forming perpendicular walls on either hand." Unable to see more than a few yards ahead of them in the waning hours of the day, disoriented soldiers began to stumble and fall.[6] "Every man was looking into the darkness ahead, with ears alert and nerves strung to the utmost tension. Every man felt that before morning he might be grappling with an overwhelming enemy for his life," wrote Captain George Crooke of the 21st Iowa.[7]

Regimental bands played martial music to quicken the blood but went silent as the Union phalanx crept close to the town. After that, "not a note of music was heard in the whole command till the surrender of Vicksburg," wrote Howard.[8] "We came along slowly, carefully feeling our way . . ." Wilcox noted, "till two o'clock A. M. when we came upon the enemy in force who saluted us with several rounds of grape and canister." Union artillerists returned the favor but the spirited artillery exchange "ceased after an hour or so," never, wrote Grant, "rising to the dignity of a battle."[9] After a dreary winter encampment at Milliken's Bend and a punishing march south to Disharoon's plantation, the men of Carr's division were keen to meet the enemy, even in deep darkness and on ground of his choosing. But Carr would wait till morning to test their resolve.

First light revealed a terrain of bewildering complexity—ground seemingly created to deny the passage of men or beasts. There was a "chaos of ravines and narrow hills" running in every direction. The ridges, some forested, others cultivated, were up to one hundred feet high and were separated by steep-sided ravines thick with fallen timber, tangled vines, and canebrakes six to seven feet tall.[10] It was ground ideal for entrenched defenders, a nightmarish terrain that gave the outnumbered rebels an opportunity "to delay, if not defeat" the superior Federal force.[11]

To advance, the Federals would have to move, completely exposed, along the two plantation roads that led through this maze—the Rodney Road and the Bruinsburg Road, which ran a mile or so north of it, across a sunken creekbed. These rutted trails ran parallel to one another and merged just outside the town. The widely separated roads would make it difficult to carry out a coordinated assault; and they were far too narrow to allow Union generals to deploy all the troops they would have available by the end of the day.[12]

Grant's opponent was John Bowen. The morning the Federals landed at Bruinsburg, he led a small force of twelve hundred men down from Grand Gulf, ten miles north of Port Gibson. Bowen placed Brigadier General Martin E. Green and his brigade of one thousand Arkansans and Mississippians on a wooded ridge on the Rodney Road, just beyond a rustic place of worship, Magnolia Church.[13] As Bowen was forming his defensive line, a relief force of 1,500 Alabamans, commanded by Brigadier General Edward D. Tracy, arrived from Vicksburg. Responding to false reports that Union forces had also been spotted on the Bruinsburg Road, Bowen deployed Tracy's men astride that road.[14] Bowen's objective was to hold off the Federals with his immensely outnumbered force of 2,500 until additional help arrived.

A brigade commanded by Brigadier General William E. Baldwin had left Vicksburg on the morning of April 29 and was expected imminently. Pemberton had also sent Major General William W. Loring from Jackson with a small force. And once Bowen was reasonably sure Admiral Porter would not launch another attack on Grand Gulf, he could call on his finest—the Missouri brigades of Colonel Francis M. Cockrell. That morning they were posted on ridges behind Grand Gulf, ready to march "on a moment's notice."[15] Even when reinforced, however, Bowen knew his chances of holding on were slim. He expected to be outnumbered by more than four to one. The grim arithmetic did not dim his determination.[16]

Pemberton might have stopped Grant had he concentrated at Port Gibson a great part of the widely scattered army of nearly fifty thousand he commanded, about half of them in Vicksburg and the Yazoo Delta. On April 27, Bowen had warned him that the Federals seemed intent on landing a sizable amphibious force somewhere below Grand Gulf, but, thrown off balance by Sherman's diversion along the Yazoo bluffs and Frederick Steele's Greenville expedition, he remained convinced the enemy would strike from above Vicksburg. Not until the evening that Porter's river armada passed Grand Gulf did he awake to the danger.[17] By then it was too late to take strong preventive action.

• • •

The Battle of Port Gibson began at the break of day on May 1, when Eugene Carr's division moved out to meet the enemy on the Rodney Road. When McClernand arrived on the field he ordered Osterhaus's division to challenge Tracy's brigade for control of the Bruinsburg Road, and kept the divisions of Generals Alvin Hovey and A. J. Smith with Carr to confront the more menacing of the two enemy forces. For the entire day the rival armies fought two entirely separate battles on the parallel roads that led to Port Gibson. Grant arrived from Bruinsburg around ten in the morning on a horse borrowed from one of his generals and found McClernand "driving the enemy."[18] He assumed overall command, but this would be largely McClernand's fight, and it would be won by brute force, not tactical agility, never McClernand's strength. Throughout the morning, additional Federal forces from James McPherson's corps poured in from Bruinsburg. Grant and McClernand used them to bludgeon the enemy on both roads, pressing them insistently, willing to take losses for ground gained.

The Federals enjoyed an overpowering advantage in artillery, and McClernand used his field guns to drive Bowen's defenders off one ridge after another. When beleaguered rebel units took cover in the jungle-like ravines, where each soldier's world was "a tiny green-walled room only a few yards across," the boys in blue went after them, and the two sides slugged it out at distances of less than twenty yards.[19]

The battle turned briefly when Confederate reinforcements arrived—Baldwin's Vicksburg brigade and Cockrell's three regiments from Grand Gulf. Bowen formed a new and stronger defensive line closer to Port Gibson and ordered Cockrell's Missourians to mount a fantastically risky counterassault. Surging out of the steep ravines, they charged straight into a fusillade of grape and canister delivered by twenty-four tightly massed Union cannon. They had surprised McClernand, however, and nearly collapsed his right flank, but his implacable veterans held and hurled the rebels back with a storm of lead so thick, soldiers said, it nearly obscured the sun.[20] They then advanced with irresistible momentum, delivering hammer blow after hammer blow to an opponent that was nearly out of ammunition by early afternoon.[21]

McClernand was a resolute if unimaginative commander, and his battle-hardened troops had yet to be beaten. "They were justly regarded as among the best in the army," said Lieutenant Colonel James Wilson, no friend of McClernand's.[22] And they might have finished off the rebels early in the afternoon had not their bombastic commander paused to deliver an impromptu congratulatory address to Hovey's troops after they had rolled over General Green's front line on the Rodney Road. Grant listened impassively to McClernand's encomium, then quietly reminded the general that the enemy was still out in front of him in force.[23]

It never got any better for Bowen's determined defenders. Bowen's battle reports to Pemberton, sent by telegraph, record the unraveling of his doomed defense. At one thirty he reports he has been "engaged in a furious battle ever since daylight; losses very heavy. General Tracy is killed. We are out of ammunition for cannon and small-arms [and] they outnumber us trebly." At three o'clock he asks plaintively: "When can Loring get here?" Loring "[is] on his way," Pemberton replies. "You had better whip them before he reaches you." At five fifteen Bowen says: "I will have to retire under cover of night to other side of Bayou Pierre and await re-enforcements." Fifteen minutes later he telegraphs: "The town will be in possession of the enemy in a few hours and communication cut off."[24] By then he had fallen back and ordered a full retreat across Bayou Pierre, north of town. Logan pursued for two miles, but the last of the retreating rebels set fire to the bridges over Bayou Pierre and a smaller bayou nearby, denying the Federals passage.[25]

That evening the Army of the Tennessee encamped on the soil it had won. "Oh, how thankful we are," wrote Charles Wilcox, "for we have slept but about four hours within the last sixty."[26] The Federals had lost 130 killed to Bowen's 68, and over a thousand men on both sides were wounded.[27] Hundreds had yet to be tended to, and Confederate dead were scattered everywhere. Bowen tried to send a detachment under a white flag to bury his dead, but Grant would not allow it. He never explained why.[28]

Fred Grant, whom his father had not seen since the river crossing at Bruinsburg, reached the battlefield with Charles Dana on two broken-down farm horses and joined a detachment that was gathering the wounded and carrying them to a log house that was serving as a field hospital. "Here the scenes were so terrible that I became faint and ill, and making my way to a tree, sat down, the most woe-begone twelve-year-old lad in America."[29]

"We don't know our whole success," said Wilcox, "but we know this, that we drove the enemy in very close contact."[30] They did more than that: They had broken out of the invasion bridgehead and were free to move against Vicksburg in any direction they chose. Grant wrote Halleck saying he was certain his army would prevail whichever way it marched.[31] "I don't think this army can be whipped," an Iowa soldier declared in his diary.[32]

As Grant rode by his troops early that evening he was cheered lustily, and so was McClernand.[33] It was McClernand's finest hour in the campaign. He had directed a great part of the battle from the front lines, personally positioning some of the guns. "It seemed to Rawlins and myself a suitable occasion for bringing about a *rapprochement* between Grant and him," Wilson noted later. Meeting Grant on the edge of the battlefield, Wilson suggested that he might want to "thank and compliment" McClernand for his performance. "Grant flatly refused, alleging that McClernand had done no more than his duty, and was entitled to no special thanks." The two men "were never reconciled," Wilson wrote, and "the breach between them grew wider and wider."[34]

On Sunday, May 2, McClernand's corps, "refreshed with sleep," marched into Port Gibson. "As we passed through the main street of the city, men, women and children filled the walks or gazed anxiously from the upper story windows, as though a monster show had come to town," recalled veteran Ira Blanchard.[35] While the army rested, the engineers went to work repairing the bridges the rebels had set on fire. James Wilson supervised both operations. By five thirty the next morning the repairs were completed and "the army [was] in full march."[36] With McPherson's fresh brigades in hot pursuit, the Confederates crossed the Big Black River, which had its source in north-central Mississippi and flowed 330 miles in a southwesterly direction until it reached the Mississippi just above Grand Gulf, twenty miles below Vicksburg. Once across the river they merged with Pemberton's main army and were joined, finally, by General Loring, an obstinate, hard-fighting North Carolinian who had lost an arm in the Mexican War and had done solid service north of Vicksburg at Fort Pemberton and against Grant's Steele's Bayou expedition.

Bowen's Port Gibson force had not had time to burn the makeshift bridge over the Big Black after they crossed it, allowing McPherson to cross there and at a nearby ford and head north until he came within earshot of Confederate drums. But Grant stopped McPherson there, not wanting to bring on a major battle until he had time to open a supply line back to Milliken's Bend.[37] Nor did he want to challenge twenty-three thousand entrenched rebels without Sherman's corps, expected to cross the Mississippi in a day or two.[38]

Grant's immediate objective was Grand Gulf. Located farther upriver than Bruinsburg, it would serve as an excellent dockage and storage facility for vessels bringing in supplies from steamboat landings in the New Carthage area, miles south of Vicksburg's batteries. When Grant arrived at Grand Gulf on the evening of May 3 with a small cavalry escort, he found the two rebel forts—Cobun and Wade—already occupied by Admiral Porter's bluejackets. They had taken them after Bowen spiked the guns and retreated across the Big Black.[39] Contrary to most accounts of the battle, Porter was not there to greet Grant. He had gone downriver with some of his ironclads to cooperate with Farragut and Banks against Port Hudson. But his officers were expecting Grant.[40] The first thing on the general's mind was a hot bath and a hearty meal. He had not washed, changed clothing, or eaten anything but hardtack for a week. Porter's captains had a feast and a steaming bath prepared for him, and one of the officers surrendered a pair of his fresh underwear. Grant lit a cigar and waded into the pile of mail waiting for him.[41]

General Nathaniel P. Banks had written inquiring about a joint operation against both Port Hudson and Vicksburg. Before Grant crossed the Mississippi, Henry Halleck had reminded him of their previous understanding that he was not to move on Vicksburg until he detached a corps from his army to cooperate with Banks against Port Hudson, one hundred miles downriver. Once that stronghold was in Union hands, Banks was to partner with Grant in a joint effort to "reduce" Vicksburg.[42] But Banks, it turned out, was nowhere near Port Hudson. He was, he told Grant, on the Red River in western Louisiana and would be unable to move on Port Hudson until at least May 10. Nor could he provide the thirty thousand men Grant had expected him to contribute to the Vicksburg effort. At most, he could release only half that number.

Grant then made one of the pivotal decisions of the Civil War: He would move against Vicksburg without Banks. "To wait for his co-operation would have detained me at least a month . . ." he later explained his decision. "The enemy would have strengthened his position and been reinforced by more men than Banks could have brought. I therefore determined to move independently of Banks, cut loose from my base, destroy the rebel force in [the] rear of Vicksburg and invest or capture the city."[43]

This was "the turning point in Grant's career," wrote one of his early biographers, "—a momentous hour, big with destiny for him, his army, and his country."[44]

Around this time, Grant received information from informers that reinforced his resolve to go it alone. General Joseph E. Johnston, a commander he greatly respected, was on his way from Tennessee to Jackson, Mississippi, to raise an army in support of Pemberton. Jefferson Davis had issued the order to try to save his home state.[45]

Grant did not inform Banks of his new "plan of command" for a full week. He then asked Banks to come north and join him "in the great struggle for opening the Mississippi River."[46] He knew the answer before he sat down to write the letter. "He expects you to cooperate with him," Porter told Grant, confirming the general's suspicions.[47]* Nor did Grant inform Halleck straightaway of his change of plans. It would have taken too long to get Halleck's reply, and Grant didn't want to risk having the general in chief overrule him.[48]

As Bruce Catton has suggested, Grant may have made the decision to go it alone even before hearing from Banks. Halleck wanted a joint operation but had not ordered one.[49] Banks outranked Grant, and had they joined forces Banks would have been the senior commander. It's difficult to imagine Ulysses Grant taking a subordinate position to Banks in the concluding phase of a campaign he had been directing, frustratingly, for nearly seven months—and at the very moment when his army was on dry ground, south of the city, with victory in sight.

---

* After informing Grant on May 12 that it would be impossible to join him in Mississippi, Banks reversed course the next day and notified Grant that it might in fact be possible to join him in ten to twelve days. Grant knew this was an empty gesture, designed perhaps to convince Washington that Banks was fully committed to the original plan for joint operations. Banks to USG, May 12 and 13, 1863, *ibid.*, 191–92.

• • •

Grant's memoirs is a work of matchless clarity. But on one point he created considerable confusion. He did not, as he claimed, "cut loose altogether" from his base and live entirely off the country.[50] Rather, he established one of the war's longest and most heavily used supply lines. And he did not "cut loose" from it until his army began moving too quickly to keep up with it. Later on in his autobiography, Grant corrected himself, saying he had a "base" but "abandoned it" shortly before beginning his final drive on Vicksburg from Jackson.[51] Up to that time, as many as two hundred supply wagons a day reached Grand Gulf from Milliken's Bend. Supplies were brought from Milliken's Bend by wagon and then carried by steamboats that set out, initially, from Perkins plantation, and later from a river port a little north of Perkins, both places out of range of Vicksburg's guns.

Grant had begun building this supply line immediately after he left Grand Gulf. For an entire week he became the quartermaster he had been in the Mexican War, firing off logistical instructions to officers at Milliken's Bend, ordering them to rush forward thousands of wagons loaded with provisions.[52] Every message he sent stressed the importance of speed. He had to move inland quickly and deliver a disabling blow before Johnston had time to assemble a formidable relief force at Jackson and cooperate with Pemberton to trap and destroy his army. "How many teams have been loaded with rations and sent forward?" Grant pressed Colonel William Hillyer, an old friend from St. Louis who was directing his logistics effort at Milliken's Bend. "I want to know as near as possible how we stand in every particular for supplies. How many wagons have you ferried over the river? How many are still ready to bring over? What teams have gone back for rations?" Above all things, Grant wanted bread, coffee, meat, salt, sugar, and ammunition. "Send no other rations until a full supply of these are on hand."[53]

Grant's impatience, bordering on alarm, is understandable. No army in history had begun a major invasion so poorly provisioned. It did not even have horses and wagons to haul its ammunition and meager medical supplies. If the two corps Grant had brought across the river had been met at Bruinsburg or Port Gibson by a large enemy force, they might have been stopped. Crossing the river without knowing the disposition of the enemy was one of the greatest gambles of the war. Even after taking Port Gibson the army looked to be dangerously vulnerable, and it would have been at a great disadvantage had Pemberton anticipated the landing and attacked in force.

Luckily, too, the Army of the Tennessee found itself, days after the battle, in a land of bountiful farms. Before supplies began flowing into Grand Gulf regularly, the men lived off the plenty of the land, supplementing their slim rations with local largesse. But first the army needed horses, mules, and vehicles to haul the forage and food its men collected, and the ammunition and medical supplies that had been carried over the river by steamers. Immediately upon landing at Bruinsburg, Grant had ordered his men to fan out and seize from local farms and homesteads "all vehicles and draft animals, whether horses, mules, or oxen," and load them with ammunition. The army's "motley" land train soon came to include richly upholstered phaetons "drawn by mules with plough-harness [and] straw collars" and farm wagons with racks for carrying cotton bales.[54]

Runaway slaves were hired as teamsters.[55] To supplement the soldiers' diet of hardtack and salted bacon, foraging parties were sent out every day at dusk to scour the land for up to ten miles on both sides of the army's line of advance. They returned with beef and mutton, butter and eggs, molasses and fresh fruit, sacks of grain and jars of honey, along with oats and apples for the animals. Every plantation in the area had a mule-powered stone mill to grind corn. Grant assigned troops to keep them running, day and night, while the army waited for Sherman, and for days thereafter.[56] These measures gave Grant confidence his army could live off the land, as it had the previous December on its retreat from Oxford, Mississippi, after Van Dorn and Forrest had severed its supply line.[57]

Grant's army would soon be moving too quickly to provide time for the full-scale plunder of homesteads.[58] But while it waited for supplies from across the Mississippi, unauthorized pillaging became rampant. When General McPherson made his temporary headquarters at Ashwood, the plantation of Alfred and Elizabeth Ingraham, just north of Port Gibson, his troops vandalized the place. "They had nothing to eat for thirty-six hours and were as ravenous as wolves," Elizabeth Ingraham recalled in her diary. "They opened the dining room closet with a hatchet, stole all the table linen" and tore through the rest of the house, pocketing the silver and "destroying the clothing and keepsakes and little knickknacks of women and children." When McPherson learned that the lady of the house, though an ardent secessionist, was the older sister of General George Gordon Meade, who would soon win an important victory at Gettysburg, he tried to put a halt to the looting. But McPherson's subordinates, said Mrs. Ingraham, "wink and authorize this plundering and thieving."[59]

The eatables these and other foragers confiscated would never be sufficient to support an entire army on the move. The men required salt, sugar, coffee, and hardtack—a baked biscuit—along with ammunition and medicine. These items would have to come from Milliken's Bend, with its excellent steamboat connections to Memphis, Cairo, and St. Louis.

Sherman, a commander as heedful of logistics as Grant, was horrified by his friend's plan to support the army from Milliken's Bend, with Grand Gulf as his forward supply base. "I see in the horizon the first faint clouds that threaten Grants [sic] fair fame and history," he wrote Ellen.[60] A narrow wagon road through flooded swamps and bayous could not possibly support an army of forty thousand men. Sherman feared it would become dangerously congested and would be washed out regularly by spring storms.[61] "Some other way must be found to feed this army," he wrote General Francis Blair, who was guarding the long supply road with only two brigades.[62]

Sherman unburdened himself to Grant on the morning of May 9, after he finally crossed the Mississippi and joined him at a ferry crossing on the Big Black.[63] Grant surprised him, however, with the news that he was shortening his supply line considerably by having engineers build an eight-mile-long corduroy road from Young's Point to Bower's Landing, directly across the river from Warrenton, Mississippi. The rebels still had guns there, but one of Porter's war boats put them out of business. By May 15 the road would be carrying supply wagons to steamboats bound for Grand Gulf.[64] But Grant told Sherman he would not be counting on this shortened supply line to provide his army "with full rations." The steamers would bring down "hard bread, coffee & salt." The army would "make the country furnish the balance."[65] He had found the lands his army was passing through rich enough in beef and forage to support an "active campaign."[66]

The plan's success depended less on its boldness than on "the rapidity of its execution." Napoleon had famously said that he might lose a battle but "shall never lose a minute." And "no man since the great Napoleon . . . understood so fully the value of time as Grant did," wrote British military historian and strategist J. F. C. Fuller.[67]

Viewed at the time, Grant's situation looked desperate. He was in enemy country, between two hostile armies. One had blocked his previous efforts to take Vicksburg; the other was being built up rapidly with reinforcements sent by Richmond. The president and the War Department were becoming impatient with Grant and other Union field commanders. General Joseph Hooker had suffered a humiliating defeat at Chancellorsville, Virginia, that May, opening the way for Robert E. Lee's invasion of Maryland and Pennsylvania. "Were Grant not to act at once," wrote Fuller, "he ran every chance of being recalled and his army of being broken up, for Washington had been thrown into a panic by Lee's bold maneuver."[68]

The supplies Grant needed to begin his march on Vicksburg began arriving at Grand Gulf the day before Sherman joined him: two hundred wagons pulled by one thousand horses and mules and carrying over three hundred thousand rations of hardtack, coffee, sugar, and salt; 250,000 rations of salted meat; and 130,000 bars of soap. On hand at Milliken's Bend were two million additional rations. "There will . . . be no difficulty in supplying your army" with either commissary stores or ammunition, a supply officer telegraphed Grant that same day.[69] Sherman was impressed; and he was surprised, as well, by the bountifulness of the countryside between Port Gibson and the Big Black. "Men who came in advance have drawn but 2 days rations [for ten days] and are fat," Sherman wrote Ellen on May 9. "Tomorrow I march."[70]

Civil War battles are often described in minute detail without attention to how men and animals are fed, or how guns and ammunition reach the front.[71] Had Grant not been acutely attentive to logistics, his army would never have reached Vicksburg.

Grant was relieved to see Sherman, knowing his arrival would have an electrifying effect on the troops. "Here was the general whom everybody knew, and whom everybody loved," wrote Sergeant S. H. M.

Byers, of the 5th Iowa. "If Grant had been the creator of the Western army, Sherman was its idol."[72] Sherman found Grant as confident as he had ever seen him now that he had streamlined his supply line. The enemy north of the Big Black, he assured Sherman, was "badly beaten, greatly demoralized and exhausted of ammunition. The road to Vicksburg is open."[73]

It was not. Pemberton sat astride the Vicksburg-Port Gibson Road with the core of his reorganized army under generals Bowen, Loring, and Carter L. Stevenson, the Virginia native who commanded troops posted in Vicksburg. Stevenson left part of his division inside the city and Pemberton also had troops at Warrenton and Bovina, just east of Vicksburg, on the Southern Railroad of Mississippi, Vicksburg's economic lifeline to Jackson, the most important rail and industrial center in the state. Most of Pemberton's men were emplaced behind imposing earthen breastworks north of the Big Black, in broken terrain akin to the ground at Port Gibson. This greatly pleased Jefferson Davis, who had admonished Pemberton to hold Vicksburg at all costs.[74]

Grant had McPherson and McClernand conduct conspicuous reconnaissance operations on the rebel side of the Big Black to convince Pemberton he intended to cross the river and attack Vicksburg.[75] But he had no intention of hitting Vicksburg from the south. With the rebel army dug in on the southern approaches to the city, that might be too costly. Instead, he planned a campaign of maneuver and deception, its initial objective being to cut Pemberton off from Jackson.[76] "It was my intention . . . to hug the Black River as closely as possible with McClernand & Sherman's Corps and get them on the [Southern] railroad at some place between Edwards Station and Bolton," a depot just east of Edwards.[77] He would then cut the railroad, depriving Pemberton of supplies and troops from Jackson, swing around to the west, and close in on Vicksburg, forcing Pemberton to come out of his fortifications and fight him somewhere east of the city.[78]

The Big Black was deep and could only be crossed at a handful of ferry ports. By posting combat patrols at these crossings, Grant would be able to use the river as a shield to protect his left flank as he moved toward the railroad. It was an ingenious plan, but was risky in the extreme. If he was held up by either supply problems or harassing attacks, he could be caught and crushed between two armies that together would soon outnumber his. Speed was imperative "not only to his success, but his salvation."[79]

On May 9, as Grant prepared to move out, he wrote Julia: "Two days more . . . must bring on the fight which will settle the fate of Vicksburg."[80] When that day arrived, he wrote Halleck: "You may not hear from me again for several days."[81] The message, sent by cipher, did not reach Washington until May 18 and must have caused consternation in the War Department and at the White House.[82]* With the war going badly for the Union, a general with a drinking problem and a propensity to act without orders was heading deep into contested terrain, out of touch with his general in chief and his president.

Grant's three corps of around forty-one thousand men marched on three parallel roads, about eight miles south of the Southern Railroad of Mississippi. McClernand's XIII Corps was in the most precarious position, on the Union left, closest to the Big Black; James McPherson, Grant's most inexperienced commander, covered the right flank; and Sherman was placed in the center, in position to support either of his fellow commanders. Grant rode with Sherman. Beside them was Fred Grant.[83]

The objective was the hamlet of Edwards, about twenty-five miles east of Vicksburg. Here the army would be directly in the rear of Vicksburg and astride the railroad that supplied it. Grant gave his commanders no other orders. This was his standard mode of operation. He rarely gave detailed commands in advance, preferring to await the initial movements of the enemy.[84] To anticipate them, he relied on an informal but extensive intelligence network comprised of cavalry, signal corps scouts, escaped slaves, deserters, civilians sympathetic to the Union, Southern newspapers, and intercepted mail. Occasionally, he used information provided by an extensive intelligence network of paid informers run by General Grenville Dodge, operating out of Corinth.[85]

As the army approached Edwards it entered the rugged Mississippi

---

* Grant's messages were sent by courier to Grand Gulf and by steamer to Memphis—a forty-four-hour trip. There was a telegraph line from there to Columbus, Kentucky. From Columbus, river steamers carried messages twenty miles to Cairo, which had a direct line to Washington.

hill country, where yeoman farmers scratched out a living on thin soil. It remained miserably hot, and water was scarce. "We had few rations, little water, and almost no rest," recalled Sergeant Byers. The dust on the roads came up to men's shoetops. "The atmosphere was yellow with it. The moving of a column far away could be traced by it."[86] Then the sky opened up. "Mud and water, broken bridges, and deep ditches, were all the go," recalled young Ohio volunteer Owen J. Hopkins.[87] The troops had neither parkas nor tents. "Our only shelter from the heavy spring rains were our blankets," wrote Iowa soldier E. B. Soper.[88]

With few well-stocked homesteads to prey upon, men were "pressed by hunger."[89] Lieutenant Soper's Iowa regiment received "one cracker and a half for two days and some of the time not even this."[90] It would get worse later in the march. Some regiments would go for three days without rations, which consisted of bacon, coffee, and hardtack—the biscuits men called crackers. They were unappetizing: "hard as bricks" and often "teeming with worms," wrote one historian. But they became greatly prized on the march. "I have seen the boys offer a dollar for a hard tack but no one had any to sell," wrote Iowa private Calvin Ainsworth.[91]

Occasionally, desperate men broke ranks to pillage thinly provisioned households, but organized foraging ceased. There was no time for it. Instead, patrols were sent out on the fly, as the rest of the men marched. "As we passed farms where there was something to eat the captains would call out to a dozen men of the line to hurry in, carry off all they could, and pass it over to the companies still marching," Byers recollected. "It was a singular looking army. . . . Whole regiments tramped along with sides of bacon or sheaves of oats on the points of their bayonets."[92] These were the fortunate few, however. The bounty the raiding parties brought in went to the troops "nearest by," so that most of the army was deprived "until a new base was established on the Yazoo above Vicksburg."[93]

The sight of an enemy army of forty thousand marching through a state that did not have a city that populous had a chilling effect on locals. Those owning slaves began moving "in droves" to Georgia and eastern Mississippi, a local newspaper reported, "[convinced] that the game is about up."[94] Those who stayed closely guarded their human property. Unlike everywhere else Grant had campaigned in the South, a caravan of slaves did not follow his thundering army.

• • •

On May 11, Grant directed McPherson to push on to the small town of Raymond, sixteen miles southeast of Edwards, to "secure all the subsistence stores that may be there. . . . We must fight the enemy before our rations fail," he instructed him.[95] Rebel cavalry had been shadowing Grant's army, and Pemberton, in a rare aggressive move, sent an infantry force from Jackson under Brigadier General John Gregg to hit part of McPherson's corps. It was to be a spoiling attack, not a general engagement. Gregg commanded only a single brigade, roughly 3,200 men.

The next morning, Gregg smashed into John Logan's leading division in a patch of woods at Fourteen Mile Creek, two and a half miles southwest of Raymond.[96] With two batteries positioned on a knoll that rose above the road and with his infantry hidden in a thick forest and in the vine-choked creekbed, Gregg was confident he could handle the Federals he was ambushing.[97] Acting on false information provided by his scouts, he thought he was tackling a single brigade, not the entire XVII Corps, which was strung out down the road, most of it out of his sight. With Gregg outnumbered by more than three to one, the outcome was never in doubt, but it was a harder fight than it should have been because McPherson mismanaged it.

Gregg's 7th Texas Regiment, undefeated in combat, led the rebel advance. Clawing through thick timber and underbrush, the men tore into the stunned Union line, firing at point-blank range. "All at once the woods rang with the shrill Rebel yell and a deafening din of musketry," recalled Colonel Manning F. Force, whose 20th Ohio would bear the brunt of the battle.[98] The onrushing rebels shattered the Yankee line in several places and drove hundreds of panicked bluecoats to the creekbed, where the fighting became hand-to-hand, "with bayonets, fists, and the butt end[s] of muskets." It was "a worse battle than the Shiloh fight for the time it lasted," an Ohio soldier would later write his family.[99]

Black Jack Logan, wearing an unmarked cloak to conceal his rank from enemy marksmen, tried to rally his troops, riding along the line shouting: "For God's sake men, don't disgrace your country."[100] One regiment was wavering and about to break when Logan rode up "and with shriek of an eagle turned them back to their places."[101] The men

stood firm for two hours until fresh troops from Brigadier General Marcellus Crocker's division arrived and the Federals, led by Logan, began
"driving the rebels like the wind." They chased them through the woods
and into the streets of Raymond, where the local ladies, anticipating
a stirring rebel victory, had put out a picnic feast of fried chicken and
lemonade for their returning heroes.[102] As the men of Force's 20th Ohio
pressed the rebels, dozens of the Union boys broke ranks to devour
the lunch. By evening it was over, and Gregg's shattered brigade was
encamped in a forest enclosure beyond the town graveyard.[103]

McPherson had won his first battle, but he had directed it inde-
cisively, failing to bring up Crocker soon enough. Logan's division
"did the work," James Wilson noted tersely in his journal.[104] He was
"heroic and brilliant," said Charles Dana, saving McPherson great
embarrassment.[105]

The following morning, Gregg's brigade trudged back to Jackson,
fourteen miles to the east, leaving their wounded behind, their moans
filling the air "as they lay uncared for in the field."[106] The rough country, "filled with ravines and dense undergrowth," persuaded McPherson
not to pursue.[107] That, too, was a mistake.

In a three-hour slugfest, part of it fought in a driving rainstorm,
the Federals had lost 446 men killed, wounded, and missing; the rebels had lost slightly more.[108] "Although not a general engagement, and
scarcely mentioned in history . . . seldom in any engagement was the
loss greater in proportion to the numbers engaged than on that bloody
field at Raymond," wrote Ira Blanchard. He too had been at Shiloh and
considered Raymond "the severest fighting we had seen thus far."[109]

"We entered the town of Raymond . . . not with Floating banners
or swelling strains of music," wrote Private Owen Hopkins, ". . . not
as a victorious army generally enters a city of the enemy, but tired and
dejected, hungry and almost disheartened, our boots full of water, our
clothes wet and covered with mud. . . . No wonder Raymond citizens
looked at us with fear and trembling!" The next morning, "a regular pillaging of the town commenced, stores and ware-rooms, kitchen and
dining room, Parlor and Pantry."[110]

After the battle, Sylvanus Cadwallader was lying on a cot in the
tent of Colonel William S. Duff, chief of Grant's artillery, when
Grant entered unannounced around midnight and asked for whiskey.

"Col. Duff drew a canteen from under his pillow and handed it to him," Cadwallader recalled. "The general poured a generous potation into an army tin cup and swallowed it with . . . satisfaction. He complained of extraordinary fatigue and exhaustion as his excuse for needing the stimulant, and took the second, if not the third drink, before retiring." This was the first time Cadwallader had seen Grant drinking. Cadwallader claimed he spoke of the incident to no one, "excepting perhaps to Rawlins," until after the war. But he learned a little later that Duff had catered to Grant's strong need for stimulants long before this, "and continued to do so till his 'muster-out' at City Point, [Virginia]."[111] There is no evidence, however, that Grant took another drink until he reached Vicksburg.

Raymond was a minor engagement with a major impact. The night Grant received McPherson's battle report, he revised his campaign plan yet again. Gregg's brigade was part of the relief army at Jackson, which appeared to be far stronger than Grant had supposed. Grant also had information from scouts that reinforcements were pouring into the city and that Joseph E. Johnston was nearing the city by train from Tennessee.[112] It was a threat he could not ignore. Attacking Edwards would put Johnston in his rear. He needed to take on Johnston first.

Grant sent McPherson and Sherman to Jackson.[113] McClernand's corps was put in a supporting position near Raymond in the event that "resistance at Jackson should prove more obstinate than there seemed to be reason to expect," or in the event Pemberton turned aggressive and attacked Grant's rear.[114] Grant counted on Pemberton's inherent caution and read him perfectly. Given an opportunity to strike a hard blow, Pemberton would remain in place in front of Vicksburg.

The campaign was a psychological mismatch. One commander had a center and a will; the other was conflicted and indecisive. While Grant's columns moved toward Jackson, the editors of the city's leading newspaper wired Jefferson Davis, pleading with him to replace Pemberton, whose "loyalty" and "capacity" they cast in doubt. "Send us a man we can trust [and] confidence will be restored & all will fight to the death for Miss."[115]

It was at this critical juncture in the campaign that Grant cut loose from his Grand Gulf supply line. In moving against Jackson, he had greatly extended his supply line, making it vulnerable to enemy interdiction. "So I finally decided to have none," Grant wrote later "—to cut loose altogether from my base and move my whole force eastward. . . . If I moved quickly enough I could turn upon Pemberton before he could attack me in the rear."[116] From this point forward his army would live off the land. Two more supply trains reached the army as it marched on Jackson, but they were the last ones.[117] Speed, once again, became supremely important. To take Vicksburg, Grant would have to get to Haynes' Bluff on the Yazoo in great haste, capture it, and open communication with Porter's fleet. This would give him the forward supply base he needed to feed and rearm his divisions. Delay could mean defeat.

When General Joseph E. Johnston arrived in Jackson on the evening of May 13, he decided his situation was hopeless. Always a defeatist, he had been sent to Mississippi against his will and was in the final stages of a lingering illness. At a rail station fifty miles east of Jackson, he had been handed a telegram from Pemberton. It was the worst news: Grant was believed to be moving his army toward Edwards, on the Southern Railroad of Mississippi; and Pemberton had decided to stay in front of Vicksburg, protecting the ferry crossings on the Big Black "lest [Grant] cross and take this place."[118]

"I am too late," Johnston wired Richmond hours later. "The enemy's force [is] between this place and General Pemberton, cutting off the communication."[119] Johnston had only six thousand troops on hand, among them Gregg's decimated brigade. Additional men were expected from the eastern Confederacy but had not yet arrived.[120] After ordering Gregg to set up a thin defensive line to cover the army's withdrawal across the Pearl River, east of Jackson, he and his staff left for Canton, a small rail center twenty-five miles to the north. The rest of his army would escape by the Canton Road.

At Canton, Johnston's relief army would await the arrival of the reinforcements the government had promised him. But by abandoning Jackson, with its excellent rail connections, he had made it difficult for these additional troops from the eastern and southern Confederacy to reach him. Throughout the remainder of the campaign, Johnston would not move far from Canton, leaving Pemberton to fight the battle for Vicksburg.

Johnston talked a good fight in his correspondence with Pemberton, knowing his words would remain on the official record—proof that he had never given up on Vicksburg. The only hope of defeating Grant, he told Pemberton, was by acting in unison. Since his small force stood no chance of cutting through Grant's army to reach Vicksburg, he directed Pemberton to abandon his defensive position on the Big Black and strike a Federal force that was assembling at Clinton, ten miles west of Jackson. "If practicable, come up in his rear at once . . ." he had written Pemberton hours before leaving Jackson. "The troops here could cooperate. All the strength you can quickly assemble should be brought. Time is all-important." [121] To be certain his instructions reached Pemberton, Johnston had his staff prepare three copies and send them by three different couriers.

Johnston's communiqué was grossly misleading. Having already determined to flee Jackson that night, he could not possibly carry out his part of the pincer movement he had proposed to Pemberton.

Johnston's order to move on Clinton put John Pemberton in an impossible situation: To obey his superior officer was to disobey his commander in chief.[122] Pemberton hesitated and then did exactly the wrong thing. "He . . . made the capital mistake of trying to harmonize instructions from his superiors [that were] diametrically opposed to each other," wrote his engineering officer, Major Samuel Lockett, who had been promoted the previous December to chief engineer of the Department of Mississippi and Louisiana.[123] "I move at once with whole available force," Pemberton wrote Johnston with apparent resolve. Only it wasn't his entire available force: He left two divisions to hold Vicksburg.[124]

Hours later, Pemberton began to doubt himself. An attack on the Federals at Clinton would be, he thought, "extremely hazardous," as he was convinced, erroneously, he was outnumbered.[125] He was also concerned about McClernand. If he abandoned his Big Black defenses, McClernand, stationed near Raymond, might sweep around his right flank and get into Vicksburg.[126] Uneasy about disobeying a direct order, he put the decision up for discussion. At a council of war of his leading generals he read Johnston's communication. It set the room astir. A majority of his lieutenants strongly favored Johnston's plan of attack, but Loring, the army's senior division commander, asked for the floor and proposed instead a quick strike southward to cut Grant's supply line from Grand Gulf, not knowing he had abandoned it.[127]

Pemberton dug in and argued against both proposals: Johnston's and Loring's. The "leading and great duty of [the] army [is] to defend Vicksburg." This is why Davis had sent him west, he forcefully reminded his commanders. The proper course of action was to fall back to the entrenchments on the Big Black and prevent Grant from breaking through. But realizing he was losing his grip on his army—some commanders accused him of being "averse to a fight with the enemy"—he caved and acceded to Loring's plan.[128]

The following day, May 15, Loring's division led the rebel army toward Dillon's farm, on the main road from Grand Gulf to Raymond. "The object is to cut the enemy's communications and to force him to attack me, as I do not consider my force sufficient to justify an attack on the enemy in position or to attempt to cut my way to Jackson," Pemberton wrote Johnston, explaining the move.[129]*

At this point, Confederate strategy was borderline farcical. Johnston was retreating north to Canton to unite with Pemberton while Pemberton was moving south, away from Johnston, to attack a supply line that no longer existed. And, unknown to Pemberton, Grant had captured Jackson the previous day and was preparing to swing west and hit him with everything he had.

---

* The strategy would have made sense had Pemberton acted quicker. The last two hundred supply wagons from Grand Gulf passed Dillon's farm days before the rebels arrived there. Ballard, *Pemberton*, 156.

CHAPTER 20

The Hill of Death

"It was, after the conflict, literally the hill of death." [1]

—General Alvin P. Hovey

On May 14, Ulysses Grant wrote Henry Halleck: "I will attack the State Capital today." [2] It was his first report to Washington since setting out into the interior of the state. Hours later, McPherson and Sherman met the enemy five miles outside Jackson in a torrential storm. "It rained and thundered fearfully during the battle . . ." wrote Sergeant Byers. "The shocks of thunder intermingled with the shocks from the guns so that we could not tell the one from the other." [3]

Not knowing the strength of the enemy, McPherson proceeded cautiously behind his artillery. Then, feeling the enemy's weakness, he unleashed Marcellus Crocker's division. "Crocker was a fighter in the amplest sense of the word," wrote Franc Wilkie. [4] Thirty-three years old, full-bearded, thin and shallow-chested, he was "dying of consumption but his condition never put him on the sick report when a battle loomed, as long as he could keep on his feet," Grant wrote. [5] Crocker's men drove back rebel pickets to the city's main fortifications, a line of partially abandoned entrenchments that they easily overran. [6]

Two miles to the south, Sherman prepared to assault the enemy's breastworks. Grant intervened, suggesting he send Brigadier General James M. Tuttle's division to reconnoiter the rebel line to his right. It looked to be weaker than the defenses directly in front of him. Tuttle found the parapets thinly manned, and he and Frederick Steele sent their divisions tearing into the city through a disorganized mass of rebel artillerymen and civilian volunteers. [7] Fred Grant galloped ahead of his father and was nearly captured by a band of Confederate troops fleeing the city. [8] Around three in the afternoon, Crocker's Indiana regiments raised their colors above the statehouse, and Jackson became the third Confederate state capital—after Nashville and Baton Rouge—to fall to Union arms.[9] Grant had deprived Johnston of a major transportation center—the finest in Mississippi—a convenient gathering place for reinforcements heading there from points all across the Confederacy.[10]

As at Port Gibson, Grant used speed and strategic acuity to put a force in the field tremendously larger than the enemy's, even though the Confederate army in Mississippi outnumbered his own. "Our movements have been made so rapid and with such determination that the rebels have been perfectly confounded," wrote Illinois soldier James Jessee. "They could not anticipate where we was going to strike nor when & consequently could not reinforce any place."[11]

Hours after taking the city, Grant sent a dispatch to John McClernand. Johnston's retreat to Canton was evidently a design "to get north of us and cross the Black river and beat us into Vicksburg. We must not allow them to do this. Turn all your forces towards Bolton Station and make all dispatch in getting there." McPherson was to meet him at Bolton, located halfway between Jackson and Edwards on the Southern Railroad of Mississippi, to block Johnston's rendezvous with Pemberton on the Big Black.[12] Sherman remained in Jackson to destroy its economic infrastructure; he would join the rest of the army when the job was done.[13]

"He did the work most effectually," Grant would note tersely years later, destroying factories, foundries, and warehouses—and heating and twisting iron rails into what reporters called "Sherman's neckties."[14] The reinforcements Richmond had sent to Johnston eventually hooked up with him near Canton, but Johnston would be without iron rails to move them toward Vicksburg.

Sherman tried to rein in soldier pillaging in Jackson, instructing officers that such purposeless despoliation would "injure the [morale] of the troops and bring disgrace on our cause."[15] His troops flew out of control, however, and the poorest elements of the population joined what became a whirlpool of destruction. "The streets were filled with people, white and black, who were carrying away all the stolen goods they could stagger under, without the slightest attempt at concealment and without let or hindrance from citizens or soldiers," wrote Sylvanus Cadwallader.[16] White families watched in horror from behind window screens as "rejoicing Africans" joined in the pickings, carrying away "French mirrors, boots, shoes, pieces of calico, wash-stands, and towels, hoop-skirts, bags of tobacco, parasols, umbrellas, and fifty other articles equally incongruous."[17] Fires broke out and were fed by brisk winds. Union army soldiers high on stolen whiskey set some of them; rebels leaving the city had set others to keep provisions from falling into enemy hands.[18]

On orders from Grant, Sherman informed families of factory workers whose places of employment had been burned to gather at the Pearl River, "where," in his words, "we could feed them till they could find employment or seek refuge in some more peaceful land."[19] Sherman distributed two hundred thousand rations "to prevent the people from starving."[20] This did little toward reconciliation. When his troops pulled out of the city on May 16 they left behind a citizenry sworn to "bloody revenge." The handful of Unionists who resided in the town of four thousand instantly became "good and earnest rebels," said a British observer.[21]

While Sherman was tearing up Jackson, Grant was trying to pinpoint the location of Johnston's and Pemberton's forces. In his dispatch to McClernand, he had misread Johnston's intention. Later reports indicated he was not headed toward the Big Black. Yet by guessing wrong and sending his army to Bolton, Grant had inadvertently made the right move. That evening he learned that Pemberton, not Johnston, was the immediate threat. Johnston's order to Pemberton to move east to unite with his forces would bring him near Bolton on the Southern Railroad of Mississippi. A Union spy provided this explosive intelligence.

One of the three dispatch bearers assigned to deliver Johnston's orders to Pemberton was an undercover Union agent, who passed along the message to McPherson, who brought it to Grant, giving him what every military captain covets: the enemy's campaign plan.[22] There was more good news: Frank Blair had arrived from Grand Gulf with two hundred wagons weighted down with ammunition and rations. This was the last supply train to reach Grant's army and it could not have come at a more opportune time. Sherman's and McPherson's gunners had run short of ammunition in the preliminary bombardment of Jackson.[23]

On May 15 Grant sped to Clinton, just east of Bolton on the main railroad, to establish his forward headquarters. Meeting with his staff that night, he had no idea that the spy who passed along Johnston's orders had provided outdated information. As we have seen, Pemberton had decided not to strike east to join Johnston but to turn south to sever what he believed was still Grant's Grand Gulf supply line.[24]

On the morning of May 15, as Pemberton's army prepared to move out, officers discovered that a bumbling quartermaster had failed to requisition sufficient rations and ammunition for the march. A train was sent back to Vicksburg to gather the additional supplies, and it took hours more to distribute them to over twenty thousand troops and four hundred wagons. The army did not move until early afternoon, and the going was rough on the mud-caked Rodney Road. Two miles into the march the rebels halted at a rain-swollen stream called Bakers Creek. The bridge had been washed out in a flash flood. It was an intelligence blunder of the first order; the cavalry had not thought to move ahead to reconnoiter the road. When Loring discovered an intact bridge upstream, the exhausted army crossed over and camped near a crossroads east of the creek and by a heavily forested ridge called Champion Hill, part of the plantation of Colonel Sid S. Champion, attached to the Vicksburg-based 28th Mississippi Cavalry, which had been stationed in and around the city, as we have seen, since the spring of 1862, when Farragut first tried to subdue Vicksburg.

As General Loring's scouts patrolled the area around the Champion farm, they learned from captured Yankee skirmishers that the enemy was in the vicinity of Bolton "in large force." Loring notified Pemberton, but Pemberton was not greatly concerned. His cavalry, he insisted, had not yet found the Federals. Before retiring that night, John Bowen spotted the glare of campfires in the black sky off to the east and threw forward "a strong line of pickets."[25] Out there were thirty-two thousand bluecoats. The following morning, the fate of Vicksburg would be decided on Sid Champion's land.

Studying maps of the local countryside at his field headquarters that night, Grant decided to have part of his army take the Jackson Road to Edwards, where he expected to find Pemberton. The road ran past Sid Champion's white-frame plantation house and over a steep incline beside it. On the opposite side of the hill was the sprawling campground of the army of Vicksburg. The bumbling delays Pemberton's army experienced that day had put it directly in the path of Grant's morning march and unprepared to meet it.

For some time, Sid Champion had been expecting trouble for his family and his cause. On the evening the Confederate army pitched its tents on his property, he was with his regiment at Edwards, guarding the western approaches to Vicksburg. He knew Grant's army was somewhere in the vicinity and he worried about his wife, Matilda, and their three young children.

Their farm was a wedding gift from her father, a local plantation grandee who disapproved of Sid's plans to become a professor of literature at a local college. Better, he advised him, to become a gentleman farmer with slaves and social standing.[26] Sid continued to meet regularly with friends at Mississippi College in Clinton, where he had been a student and an assistant instructor, but farming and soldiering—he served in the Mexican War under Jefferson Davis—filled his years. At age thirty-eight, he was one of the first to join the 28th Mississippi Cavalry, formed in Vicksburg at the start of hostilities. Fiery, self-possessed Matilda Champion stayed behind with their children, managing the farm and over sixty slaves with the help of an overseer and Sid's closely detailed instructions about crop management, carried from Vicksburg by his devoted body servant, Jim Clarke.

If it wasn't the crops and the field hands, it was the "villainous" Yankees that Sid dwelled on in his frequent letters to Matilda. He had cause for concern. That spring he had served with Colonel Samuel Ferguson's cavalry at Deer Creek, in the Yazoo Delta, where he was assigned to protect farms and families from General Frederick Steele's scorched-earth raiding parties. "The Yankees . . . are worse than the Goth and Vandals of the middle ages," he wrote Matilda, "stealing negroes," "killing horses and mules," "burning houses," and "ravishing" black women "who would not go with them."[27] Grant had sent these marauders to Deer Creek, and now his entire army was closing in on Edwards, close to Sid Champion's lands and loved ones. "Hard times are in store for us," Sid warned Matilda. "Expect reverses. . . . Nerve yourself for every emergency; trust to God; and you will be prepared for it. . . . Remember me kindly to all the Negroes and Kiss all the children for me." [28]

Early in the morning on May 16, Union soldiers at Clinton stopped an eastbound train from Vicksburg. Two members of the crew were taken to Grant's headquarters, where they reported seeing Pemberton's army, about twenty to twenty-five thousand men, at Edwards, poised, apparently, to strike Grant's rear. (This was just before Pemberton moved south against Grant's supply line.) [29] The enemy had been found. Instantly Grant ordered Sherman to quit Jackson and rush forward his entire command. "The fight may be brought on at any moment—we should have every man on the field." [30]

That morning the Union army pushed westward on three parallel roads, widely separated by difficult terrain that made it hard for the columns to communicate with one another. Frank Blair and A. J. Smith, on the Union left, moved their divisions along the Raymond Road, the same route Pemberton had taken to the Champion farm. To the north, on the Federal right, the divisions of John Logan, Alvin Hovey, and Marcellus Crocker advanced along the Jackson Road, with McPherson commanding. Hovey's brigade was part of McClernand's division, but had been assigned to McPherson for the coming action. McClernand, with Peter Osterhaus and Eugene Carr, marched on the aptly named Middle Road. Sherman had left Jackson and was pushing his troops hard, but they would arrive too late to join the fight.

After interrogating the rail workers, Grant mounted his horse and sped up the Jackson Road with his son beside him. [31] Sergeant Sam Byers spotted Grant. "He rode through the woods and field at the road side on a gallop, his horse leaping logs and whatever obstructions happened in his way." He "was then a perfect picture of fresh strong manhood and he sat his horse like a sportsman behind the hounds." Seeing the commander ride by so resolutely steadied the men, said Byers, "but no one cheered." [32] Farther on, passing his friend John B. Sanborn, one of Crocker's brigade commanders, Grant called out: "Colonel, we shall fight the battle for Vicksburg today." [33]

Grant was eager to keep in touch by courier with John McClernand, commanding nearly twenty thousand troops on the far left of the Union advance. McClernand was notoriously impetuous and might attack before the entire army was in position. He carried orders from Grant to "march so as to feel the force of the enemy, . . . without bringing on an engagement unless you feel entirely able to contend with him." [34]

Incredibly, in this wide-open, lightly populated hill country, with its sweeping vistas, not a single rebel scout detected this tremendous enemy force until it drew near Pemberton's camps. "Those in power knew very little of the movements of the Enemy," wrote Lieutenant William Drennan, a Confederate staff officer. "I saw no evidence of an organized system of information—no couriers passing to and from H'dquarters, and no signal corps in operation—nothing that led me to believe that Gen'l Pemberton knew either the number [and] intentions, either real or probable of the Enemy, and more than that—not even his exact whereabouts." Drennan had been one of the few officers in the Vicksburg army who considered Pemberton a capable commander. From this day forward, he remained "convinced of his incapacity." [35]

Early that oppressively hot morning, Pemberton met with his senior commanders in the parlor of a local family. As they gathered, the generals heard the low rumble of artillery to the east. Around six thirty, cavalry commander Wirt Adams came riding up on a sweat-soaked horse. McClernand's division, he announced, was approaching rapidly and in force on the Middle Road and had exchanged fire with rebel skirmishers. As Adams was conversing with Pemberton, a courier appeared with a dispatch from Joseph Johnston. The telegraph lines had been cut between Edwards and Jackson, and Pemberton only now learned what he feared: Jackson had fallen. This changed everything. Johnston's dispatch directed Pemberton to abandon his plan to hit Grant's supply line and head instantly to Clinton, just west of Jackson, to confront an enemy force Johnston believed to be gathering there. Johnston promised to meet him with nearly six thousand troops. "Do so before he has time to move away." [36]

For reasons still unclear, Pemberton decided to obey a summons he had earlier considered "suicidal." [37] He called for a pen and pad and scratched out an astoundingly ill-advised order, directing his generals to begin a "countermarch," or retrograde movement. The southward-facing army was to make an about-face and head north to Edwards, then east to Clinton. Pemberton's commanders were thunderstruck. Hundreds of wagons had to be turned around on a narrow sunken road, or moved off it into muddy fields to let the infantry proceed to the head of the columns.[38] And the army had to execute this maneuver while being pounded by McClernand's artillery. Unknown to Pemberton, Grant's entire army, including the divisions thought to be at Clinton, was directly in front of him, bent on battle.

General Loring was outraged. A hot-tempered contrarian, he considered Pemberton a "dunce" and a "traitor," and had been feuding with him for some time.[39] The army must form a line of battle, he demanded, "as the enemy [will] very soon be upon us."[40] Pemberton, however, remained mulishly committed to executing the countermarch. Everyone was confused. "No preparations had been made to make or receive an attack," said one soldier, "the artillery was parked, the horses were unharnessed, the general staff officers galloped around furiously delivering orders."[41] Lieutenant Drennan noticed that Pemberton "gave orders in a very uncertain manner that implied to me that he had no *matured* plans for the coming battle."[42]

Around midmorning, Pemberton finally called off the march to Clinton and hastily stationed his army along a three-mile front that blocked the Raymond Road, to the south, and the Middle Road, to the north. It was a superb defensive position, but his heaviest threat, he would soon learn, was an enemy column approaching on the Jackson Road, headed straight for Champion Hill. The road climbed over the hill to a crossroads at the epicenter of the rebel lines. If the enemy got to that point, the game was up.

"The country here is just the reverse of that at Vicksburg, being level," wrote Ohio soldier Isaac Jackson.[43] That's why Champion Hill, only 140 feet high, stood out so prominently in this landscape without any great drama.* On its northern face it melded into cultivated fields that stretched out to the west toward Bakers Creek. A succession of low, featureless hills ran off to the south. Champion Hill itself was layered with

---

* Today, the hill is not as high as it was in 1863. Gravel operations in the 1930s reduced its height.

sharp ledges and declivities and covered with thick timber and rough undergrowth. The crest, facing eastward toward the oncoming Federals, was hard rock and almost devoid of vegetation, giving the defenders unhindered fields of fire.

The far left—and weakest—wing of Pemberton's army was positioned on the summit of Champion Hill. The field commander, General Stephen Dill Lee, knew how to defend an elevated enemy objective: He had repulsed Sherman at the Walnut Hills the preceding December. Pemberton positioned the rest of his army on the wooded hills that ran south from Champion Hill. Carter Stevenson was on the left, or northern end, of the line, his left flank anchored on Champion Hill. John Bowen was in the center and Loring was on the right.

In the early-morning hours there was skirmishing all along the rebel front. Around ten o'clock things erupted on the Jackson Road when Indiana-born Alvin P. Hovey, the "Fighting Hoosier," reached the Champion house. As his cavalry screen approached, Matilda Champion gathered her children and took shelter in the cellar.[44]* Looking into the distance through his field glasses, Hovey spotted gray-clad johnnies scrambling into position on the crest of a ridge less than a thousand yards in front of him.[45] He had caught them napping. Earlier, General Lee had reported seeing a large Union column "determined upon battle," heading straight at him. Pemberton had seemed unconcerned. The principal Union threat, he remained convinced, was McClernand's corps on the Raymond and Middle Roads.[46]

Hovey was a resourceful Shiloh veteran who liked to think he could handle things himself. Raised in an orphanage for a time, he had gone on to become a state supreme court justice at age thirty-four—and, after the war, he would serve as governor of Indiana—but as Charles Dana remarked: Hovey devoted himself to the military "as if he expected to

---

* Historians have long claimed that Matilda Champion, after seeing the Yankees approaching, threw a few belongings into a wagon and escaped with her children to her parents' plantation off to the east, behind Grant's army. But long after the war, an Illinois veteran of the battle, G. B. McDonald, met Mrs. Champion at the dedication of the Illinois monument on the Vicksburg battlefield. She told him she had spent the battle in her cellar with her children. Rebecca Blackwell Drake and Margie Riddle Bearss, eds., *My Dear Wife; Letters to Matilda; The Civil War Letters of Sid and Matilda Champion of Champion Hill* (self-published, 2005), 59.

spend his life in it."[47] Before Grant had gotten to the front, Hovey had Brigadier General George F. McGinnis's brigade in place, facing Champion Hill. John Logan, on his majestic horse, positioned his division to the right of McGinnis. The National army had three of its most aggressive commanders exactly where they were most needed.

When Grant arrived, the Indiana boys were taking a pounding from a rebel battery on the hill, and "Hovey's skirmishing," Grant could see, "amounted almost to a battle."[48] Hovey's men were prepared to die. Hundreds of them had written final letters to loved ones and placed them in their pockets. Grant hesitated, however, not wanting to strike until he heard from McClernand. He wanted both wings of his army moving in unison, bringing maximum firepower to bear.

McClernand's advance guard, under Osterhaus, was moving cautiously, on orders from Grant, on the rebel right flank, about two miles away. McClernand suspected the ground ahead of him was swarming with rebels, when in fact only a thin line of skirmishers lay immediately ahead. "Shall I hold, or bring on an engagement?" he wrote Grant just before ten o'clock.[49] But his courier, unfamiliar with the rugged country, took a roundabout route, and Grant did not set eyes on the message until around noon. He replied at once: "Throw forward skirmishers and feel the enemy and attack him in force if an opportunity occurs."[50] Grant handed the dispatch to the same geographically challenged courier, and it did not reach McClernand until around two in the afternoon. Even then, he failed to press forward with resolve.[51]

Back at the Champion house, Hovey and Logan were itching to move out. Having heard nothing from McClernand, Grant unleashed them at ten thirty.[52] They marched in perfect order up the steep declivity, forming a line a mile and a half long. "When within about 75 yards of the [rebel] battery every gun was opened upon us and every man went to the ground," George McGinnis reported later. The air rocked and trembled with concussions. The men were ordered to lie down until their commanders had time to assess the enemy position and the character of the ground in front of them. Then Hovey's and Logan's brigades moved forward "as one man" and routed the rebels "in a desperate conflict of five minutes, in which bayonets and butts of muskets were freely used." The Federals captured a batch of prisoners and a battery of four guns and sent the rebels "fleeing before us," McGinnis noted.[53]

Just then, John Logan spotted a weak spot in the rebel line and moved to exploit it. Stephen Lee's left flank was vulnerable, unanchored to any physical barrier, giving Logan an opportunity to flank Lee and get in his rear. Logan called for Brigadier General John D. Stevenson's reserve brigade, which bolted forward under terrific fire. "Gen. Logan's charge on the extreme right . . . was one of the finest charges of troops that I witnessed during the war, and I was in nine different battles," wrote Illinois soldier Wilbur F. Crummer.[54] "A man of instinct and not of reflection [Logan] . . . is sometimes unsteady," Dana wrote later. "Inspiring his men with his own enthusiasm on the field of battle, he is splendid in all its crash and commotion."[55] Grant watched the unfolding action from the yard of the Champion house. Turning to one of his aides, he said: "Tell [Logan] he is making history today."[56]

But Grant and Logan were unfamiliar with the terrain. Neither realized that Stevenson was blocking the Jackson Road, the only road over which Pemberton's army could retreat. So when hard-pressed Alvin Hovey pleaded for reinforcements, Grant had Logan send Stevenson to assist him. This saved Hovey but "uncovered the rebel line of retreat."[57]

Within an hour and a half the rebels had been pushed off the crest and down the reverse side of Champion Hill to the strategic crossroads, the three roads the rebels depended upon to shuttle troops and supplies among divisions. Grant appeared to have Pemberton "by the throat."[58] Ten thousand bluejackets pursued until they themselves became exhausted and disorganized and had to stop and regroup. The rebels had lost sixteen cannon, the far left side of their battle line had been shattered, and the Union forces had again closed the rebel line of retreat to Bakers Creek.[59]

Realizing, finally, the immensity of the crisis he faced on the northern end of his line, Pemberton ordered Bowen and Loring to move at once to the left, toward Champion Hill. Both generals despised Pemberton equally, and they refused, claiming, disingenuously, that the enemy was "moving in their front." McClernand was there but wasn't moving on them.[60] Bowen soon relented, however, and started his 4,200 veterans, among the finest troops in the western Confederacy, toward the left of the rebel line. Port Gibson veteran Colonel Francis Cockrell, a massive, grim-faced firebrand, led the way on his powerful mount, swinging his sword in the air. Bowen rode in the rear with General Martin Green, who had also performed splendidly at Port Gibson. As Bowen's two brigades moved at the double-quick, they passed Pemberton and his staff on the side of the road. The starchy commander waved them on with his straw hat. Farther on, Cockrell encountered a group of local women on the front lawn of one of their homes singing "Dixie" to rally his boys.[61]

Led by three hyperaggressive commanders—Bowen, Cockrell, and Green—the wildly cheering rebels slammed into Hovey's division at the crossroads and regained the crest of the hill in murderous close-quarters fighting.[62] They came on "like ten thousand starving and howling wolves," recalled a Yankee soldier.[63] George McGinnis called it "one of the most obstinate and murderous conflicts of the war."[64] For some time, "each side took [its] turn in driving and being driven" until the Union boys began to fall back "in good order, step by step, contesting every inch of ground."[65]

The battle had swung. In less than an hour, the rebels had pierced Grant's center, hurled his best troops back almost a mile, and were in position to break through and split his army on the Jackson Road.[66] But Bowen's men had fired so indiscriminately that they had run out of ammunition. Almost every man had exhausted the forty rounds he carried in his cartridge box. Cockrell sent two staff officers to search for the division's ordnance train, but it could not be found. For reasons unexplained, General Carter Stevenson had sent it over Bakers Creek, far from the battlefield. It was the last of the staff foul-ups that doomed Pemberton's army.

Instead of abandoning Champion Hill, Cockrell's men pilfered bullets, powder, and percussion caps from the fallen, "friend and foe," pawing their bodies frantically.[67] Their lines were then replenished by Georgians who had been driven from the field earlier. Stephen Lee, who had three horses shot from under him that day, rallied his Alabamans, and they helped drive the enemy back.[68]

The prize was in sight. Grant's ammunition train was parked conspicuously in the yard of the Champion house, four to five hundred yards away.[69] If it were captured, the Federals might have to withdraw,

and perhaps Vicksburg would be saved. The rebels were checked temporarily, however, by the cannoneers of a Michigan battery.[70]

It was the climactic moment of the battle. Could the Union hold?
Grant was visibly concerned.[71] Pacing the floor of the Champion house,
he was heard grumbling, "Where can McClernand be?"[72] At this deciding moment, he called on one of Brigadier General Marcellus Crocker's
brigades, waiting in reserve in an open field along the Jackson Road.
Commanded by Colonel George B. Boomer, the men had just arrived
at the front after marching a dozen miles that morning. They were dead
tired, but Grant ordered Boomer to move them "instantly to the support of Hovey's division."[73]

George Boomer was an unlikely warrior, a classically educated thirty-
year-old Massachusetts native who spoke fluent French and played Bach
reasonably on the piano. The son of a Baptist minister, he had raised a
company at the start of the war and was wounded in the Battle of Iuka,
but his only previous action in the Vicksburg campaign was at Jackson,
two days earlier. Now Grant was counting on him to save the Union
line.[74]

Boomer's brigade surged forward at the double-quick. "We were
met in a minute by a storm of bullets from the wood," Sam Byers of
Boomer's 5th Iowa regiment remembered, "but the line in blue kept
steadily on. . . . Now we met almost whole companies of wounded,
defeated men from [Hovey's] division, hurrying by us, and they held
up their mangled hands to show us they had not been cowards. They
had lost twelve hundred men on the spot we were about to occupy."[75]
Hovey's force "was completely routed by the time I got on the ground,"
Boomer wrote later, "and there was terrible danger of panic among my
men for a moment."[76]

Boomer did not have the numbers to stop Cockrell's Missourians,
but he was able to slow them, giving Hovey's men time to retreat and
reform their ranks. For this, his brigade paid a terrible price, losing one
third of its men. Reaching the edge of a narrow ridge, the brigade ran
into "a solid wall of men in gray, their muskets at their shoulders blazing into our faces and their batteries of artillery roaring as if it were the
end of the world." The two colliding lines halted about a hundred yards
apart, said Byers, and for a solid hour stood still and "killed each other
as fast as we could." Men were lifted off their feet by the powerful vol-

leys and fell in heaps. Byers was shot in the hand but was too "excited" to feel pain.

The smoke of battle made it impossible to see. Byers and his Iowans "simply fired at their lines by guess. . . . Biting the ends off my cartridges, my mouth was filled with gunpowder, the thirst was intolerable. Every soldier's face was black as a negro's and, with some, blood from wounds trickled down over the blackness, giving them a horrible look." Moments later, Byers heard one of his men cry out, "By God, they're flanking us." Along with the rest of his brigade, Byers "ran like a racehorse, amid a storm of bullets and yells and curses," with the rebels of Cockrell's brigade in furious pursuit.

Alvin Hovey saved them. He had massed sixteen artillery pieces, "loaded to the muzzle with grapeshot and canister," on a rise near the Champion house. The gunners, Byers wrote, "opened on the howling mob that was pursuing us."[77]

Bowen's rebels were halted, but they held on threateningly in the hope that Loring would arrive.[78] At this point, Grant's only remaining reserve force was a brigade commanded by Colonel Samuel A. Holmes of Crocker's division. It had just arrived on the field after a forced march from Clinton. Grant sent them in to bolster Boomer's line. With support from Colonel Sanborn's brigade, already in the fight, they blunted a rebel effort to turn Boomer's flank.[79]

This gave Hovey time to reorganize his brigades. They summoned their last dregs of strength, and Grant sent them back into the "cauldron." In half an hour the Federals recaptured Champion Hill.[80]

"I never saw fighting like this," said Hovey.[81]

In this final "slugging match," the opposing forces were "about equal," wrote Sanborn, a veteran of Grant's campaigns going back to Iuka and Corinth. Not till Grant committed Holmes's six hundred men was the "knock-out blow" delivered. "It was Grant who won the battle," said Sanborn.[82] But Loring had contributed. His insubordinate refusal to reinforce Bowen—claiming he was fighting sixty to eighty thousand men—had cost the Confederates unimaginably.[83]

Grant prevailed, but he had wanted far more. "Had McClernand come up with reasonable promptness, I cannot see how Pemberton could have escaped with any organized force," he wrote scathingly in his mem-oirs.[84] The destruction or capture of Pemberton's army would have put Vicksburg in Grant's hands. But McClernand's inactivity forced Grant to fight the battle with only 15,500 men, less than half the troops he had available that day.

But Grant must bear some of the blame for McClernand's cau-tion. His battlefield orders were almost always models of concision and clarity. Not in this instance. McClernand was obviously perplexed by Grant's ambiguously worded messages, warning him to "mov[e] for-ward" but "*cautiously.*"[85]

Yet at two thirty in the afternoon, when Grant finally gave McClernand a firm directive to attack in force, McClernand failed to put the whip to his commanders.[86] Osterhaus broke through on the Middle Road but stopped and remained in place only six to eight hun-dred yards from the swirling battle. McClernand did nothing to press him.[87] In Osterhaus's after-action report, he weakly claimed that he feared being flanked by rebels massing on "a commanding elevation" to his left.[88] There is no evidence the rebels were there in a threatening position. McClernand's troops could hear the "continuous roar of bat-tle" and were puzzled by their commanders' inactivity.[89] "For four hours we stood there listening, waiting and wondering why we were not put into the fight," wrote one confused soldier.[90]

Hovey's and Crocker's brigades eventually caught up with Bowen's retreating rebels, scattered them, and secured the crossroads, but if McClernand had aggressively cooperated with his 17,500 troops, Bowen's battered division might have been captured or cut up. "Slowly and reluctantly the brigade fell back, and moved to . . . Bakers Creek," wrote an Arkansas officer, "leaving our dead and wounded on the field."[91] Crossing Bakers Creek with his regiment's ordnance wagons, William Drennan saw "hundreds of men coming wildly along with no regard to order . . . men without hats or guns rushing at full speed." It was "like what I have read of Bull Run," he said later.[92]

Hovey and Crocker were unable to pursue. Their men were done in, great numbers of them suffering from wounds, heat exhaustion, and battle shock. McClernand's fresh divisions were assigned the task. With the Federals controlling the Jackson Road bridge over Bakers Creek, the rebels had to cross at the Rodney Road by a shallow ford and a bridge that had been hastily constructed earlier in the day under the supervision of Samuel Lockett. Loring assigned a brigade under Brigadier General Lloyd Tilghman—the man who had surrendered Fort Henry to Admiral Foote fifteen months earlier—to guard the crossing.[93] While steadfastly defending it he was cut down by a cannon shot that ripped open his chest and nearly cut him in two.[94]

Loring's division did not get across. While Loring held the rear to enable the army to "make good its retreat," the Federals cut in front of him, forcing him to cross the creek farther downstream. As he approached Edwards, he realized he would have to fight his way through McClernand's pursuing army to get to Vicksburg. He swung around and headed east and eventually reached Johnston's army near Jackson.[95] Relieved to be released from Pemberton's command, he had not sent a courier to inform him that he was abandoning the Vicksburg army at the moment of its greatest peril.[96]

With the rebel retreat in full swing, Grant rode along the crest of Champion Hill, slowing down slightly when he passed the 5th Iowa regiment.[97] The men "cheered till they were hoarse," said Sam Byers, "but, speechless, and almost without a bow, he pushed on past, like an embarrassed man hurrying to get away from some defeat. Once he stopped, near the colors, and, without addressing himself to any one in particular, said; 'Well done!' "[98]

Eugene Carr's division tried to catch Pemberton's army before it reached the Big Black, but the rebels had too great a lead. The pursuit ended near Edwards around eight in the evening.[99] By midnight Bowen's troops had reached the railroad bridge over the Big Black and begun setting up a defensive perimeter to allow Loring to cross, Pemberton having determined it would be almost impossible to hold the city without these regiments.

That night most of the Union army bivouacked in and around Edwards, but Hovey's brigade "slept upon the field with the dead and dying around them." It had survived what Hovey called "the hill of death," and the stiff bodies of the fallen "lay scattered in wild confusion."[100] Hideously wounded men begged for deliverance. "Kill me!"

one blinded infantryman screamed. "Will someone kill me?"[101] Hovey recruited slaves from local plantations to shroud the dead in rubber blankets, dig shallow graves in the tough soil, and cut trees to build resting places for the wounded.[102] Soldiers carrying blazing torches wandered through the timber, looking for slain brothers and mates.[103]

Ulysses Grant spent the night on the porch of Pemberton's former headquarters, which had been converted into a rebel field hospital. "While the battle is raging one can see his enemy mowed down by the thousand, or the ten thousand, with great composure," he wrote later, "but after the battle these scenes are distressing, and one is naturally disposed to do as much to alleviate the suffering of an enemy as a friend."[104]

The Champion family home, along with dozens of other homes in the area, became a Union hospital. Most of the furniture was thrown into the yard, and every available table was used to perform amputations. The blood flowed so freely that a hole had to be cut in the floor to drain the main operating room.[105]

Wandering aimlessly around the battlefield in search of his father, Fred Grant stumbled upon a Confederate field hospital. "They were not feeling very friendly toward the Yankees, and they threatened to kill me," he recalled. After fleeing some rebel stragglers who tried to capture him, he found his way to the house where his father was in a dead sleep on the porch.[106] The next day there would be another battle. "I have been riding day and night throughout this campaign," Sylvanus Cadwallader wrote his wife from Champion Hill. "The army is absolutely nomadic. We march and fight alternately."[107]

Both armies had taken a frightful pounding. Of 29,000 men engaged, Grant lost 410 killed, 1,844 wounded, and 187 missing—2,441 total casualties. Confederate records are incomplete, but Pemberton reported 3,840 losses from a field army of roughly 24,000 men: 381 killed, 1,018 wounded, and 2,441 missing, many of them prisoners.[108] Three federal divisions—those of Hovey, Logan, and Crocker—"had all the hot work," as James Wilson put it.[109] Together, they sustained over 92 percent of Union losses. Hovey's Twelfth Division suffered nearly half these losses—a third of his command. The rebels who actually fought on Champion Hill—the divisions of John Bowen and Carter

Stevenson—took 97 percent of total Confederate losses.[110] It was "one of the most obstinate and murderous conflicts of the war," said General McPherson.[111] It was also *the* decisive battle of the Civil War, strategically more consequential than Gettysburg, Antietam, and other great hecatombs in the east.[112]*

At Gettysburg, after a fearsome three-day battle, the Army of the Potomac shattered Lee's Army of Northern Virginia and drove it from Pennsylvania, but Lee's army recovered by the end of that summer and fought with renewed fury around Richmond into April 1865. After the Battle of Champion Hill, Pemberton's army recovered sufficiently to endure a long siege, but it was utterly incapable of taking the field and striking a blow. Champion Hill sealed the fate of Vicksburg. The night the fighting stopped, Grant wrote Sherman: "I am of the opinion that the battle of Vicksburg has been fought."[113]

The night of the Battle of Champion Hill, Grant wrote Sherman, ordering him to move north and cross the Big Black at a place called Bridgeport, where a forest road led straight to Vicksburg. Blair's division would meet him at the river with wagons carrying materials for a pontoon bridge. McPherson and McClernand, meanwhile, were to pursue the rebels to the massive rail bridge across the Big Black, just south and east of Vicksburg. Scouts reported Pemberton was dug in and waiting for them. "Your moving North . . . may enable you to get across [at Bridgeport] . . . whilst the enemy are engaged at the bridge," Grant told Sherman.[114] Once across, Sherman could flank Pemberton's escaping army, forcing it to fall back toward the river city.

Early the next morning, the divisions of Carr and Osterhaus came upon the rebels at the Big Black crossing, six miles west of Edwards. A rear guard was waiting in fortifications designed weeks before by Samuel Lockett. The rest of the army had already crossed the river on wooden flooring Lockett had installed on the big rail bridge and on a small steamboat he had converted into a floating bridge by mooring her "fore and aft across the river" and planking her decks.[115]

---

* For more on this point see chapter 23.

Four thousand men under the command of John Bowen lay in front of the river, dug in behind a mile-long wall of cotton bales that skirted the inner bank of a shallow bayou filled with fallen trees, their sharpened branches pointing outward to form an abatis. Lockett intended the bayou to serve as a protective ditch for the trenches. The river was behind the men, and high bluffs rose from the water's edge on its Vicksburg, or western, side.[116] The position could not be flanked, and to assail it the Federals would have to advance over a farm field and across the stagnant bayou.

The position looked indomitable to McClernand's officers, but they were facing demoralized, bone-tired men, remnants of the army they had cut to ribbons the day before. "I don't think a single man . . . believed we could check the enemy's progress," wrote Chickasaw Bayou defender William Pitt Chambers. Chambers and others in his regiment, one of the first to rally to Vicksburg's defense the previous summer, believed their commanders had blunderingly placed them in unnecessary peril. "We of the rank and file," wrote Mississippi soldier J. H. Jones, "could not understand why a beaten and retreating army, more or less demoralized and facing heavy odds, should have taken position in a level plain, with a deep stream in the rear, and only a pontoon and a trestle bridge as a means of escape in case of further disaster."[117] They should have been positioned, Chambers thought, on the steep bluffs behind them, with a water barrier in front of them. Pemberton had hastily stationed his men here at the Big Black for one reason only: "to enable [Loring] to cross the river should the enemy . . . follow him up closely." Loring had not been spotted, but he was in the habit of reporting late to headquarters.[118]

Pemberton's decision to wait for Loring is understandable, but had it been unwise to retreat to Vicksburg? Joseph Johnston thought so. Pemberton and Johnston had colliding views of campaign strategy. With Porter's gunboats controlling the Mississippi River above and below Vicksburg, the city, Johnston argued, was boxed in and already lost. The objective should have been to save the army, not the city. This is also how Grant saw it in hindsight. "Pemberton might have made a night march to the Big Black," picked up the two divisions he had left in the city, and, "by moving north" toward Canton, "have eluded us and finally returned to Johnston," he wrote in his memoirs. That meant losing Vicksburg, but "it would have been his proper move . . . and one Johnston would have made had he been in Pemberton's place."[119]

Pemberton, however, was under orders from Jefferson Davis to defend the city at all costs, and was, as well, personally committed to this course of action. "The evacuation of Vicksburg . . ." he later explained, "meant . . . the surrender of the Mississippi River, and the severance of the Confederacy." He did not want to go down in history as the general who had allowed that.[120] Duty and honor dictated his decision. He would deploy his remaining forces in fortifications Samuel Lockett had constructed on the landward approaches to the city and rely upon Johnston and the Confederacy to relieve him.[121]

When the Army of the Tennessee arrived in front of the cotton-bale fort on the Big Black, Grant looked on as Osterhaus and Carr finished deploying their troops in a line that mirrored the enemy's. Osterhaus was on the Union left and Carr on the right, with Brigadier General Michael Kelly Lawler's brigade on Carr's extreme flank, well hidden from the enemy in woods and brush that bordered the stream. Lawler was a mountainous man, over six feet tall and weighing nearly three hundred pounds. He "could mount his horse only with difficulty," said a soldier, "and when he was mounted it was pretty hard on the horse."[122] But the corpulent, Irish-born Illinois farmer was quick on his feet, even at age forty-eight, and a born brawler. "His cherished maxim," said Cadwallader, "was the Tipperary one: 'If you see a head, hit it.'"[123]

After a spirited artillery exchange, one of Lawler's scouts spotted a swale in front of the rebel works capable of hiding an attacking force. Lawler leaped at the opportunity, leading his brigade of Iowa and Wisconsin boys, one thousand strong, in a stirring assault, the men advancing "at a run with loud cheers."[124] Never faltering, they stormed across the debris-filled bayou and into the cotton-bale breastworks. Joined by a second blue wave inspired by their thrilling three-minute charge, they captured eighteen cannon, 1,421 stands of small arms, and over 1,700 prisoners—while losing only twenty-seven men killed.[125]

Most of the panicked defenders made it to the bridges behind them. Earlier in the day, Lockett had packed both spans with flammables and barrels of turpentine. After most of the troops were across, he applied the torch.[126] Both bridges went up in flames, trapping men who had reached the river too late. When Lockett looked down from the bluffs, he spotted the limp bodies of rebel soldiers floating facedown just underneath the surface of the water.[127] The water was too deep for the Federals to pursue immediately. Union pioneers built three floating bridges during the night, and McClernand's and McPherson's corps crossed the next day at two separate locations.[128]

Pemberton blamed the calamity at the Big Black on his own men, absolving himself of having deployed them so vulnerably. "A strong position, with an ample force of infantry and artillery to hold it, was shamefully abandoned almost without resistance," he declared in his official report. Riding into Vicksburg on a rail car, he talked quietly with Samuel Lockett. It had been thirty years, he said, since he was appointed a cadet at West Point, and "today—that same date—that career is ended in disaster and disgrace." Lockett tried to offer hope. There were two fresh divisions in Vicksburg that had not been at Champion Hill or the bridges, but Pemberton doubted his troops "could stand the first shock of an attack."[129]

As the broken regiments limped back to the city, the families of planters who resided on the outskirts of Vicksburg joined them, seeking safety from the Yankees. It was a Sunday, and parishioners were returning from services. "I shall never forget the woeful sight of a beaten, demoralized army that came rushing back—humanity in the last throes of endurance," wrote Dora Richards Miller, a Northerner trapped with her husband in the city. "Wan, hollow-eyed, ragged, footsore, bloody, the men limped along unarmed, followed by siege guns, ambulances, gun carriages and wagons in aimless confusion."[130] The women of the town put out coffee, buckets of water, and fresh biscuits on their porches and tried to cheer the men on: "Remember, Mississippians never surrender!" But "we saw no smiling faces as we marched toward the doomed city," recalled William Pitt Chambers.[131]

The family of the Reverend William Lord, rector of Vicksburg's Christ Church, had, months earlier, sought safety from Porter's mortars on his small plantation on the Big Black. Now they and their servants were part of a "stream of stragglers" pouring into Vicksburg.[132] Disgruntled soldiers marching by their carriage were heard murmuring,

"We were sold by [the traitor] Pemberton," still a Yankee at heart.[133] Around ten o'clock, the driver of the carriage halted on Prospect Hill, a ridge overlooking the town. "Below to the right and left, before us and behind us in the valleys were thousands of camp fires . . ." recalled Lida Lord, the rector's daughter. "It was a beautiful . . . sight, but we did not linger to admire it, for behind us on the dark road . . . crept closer and closer the awful shadow of—Grant." [134]

Earlier that day, as Grant was observing his army forming up in front of the rebel rifle pits at the Big Black, a stranger had ridden up to him and introduced himself. He was Brigadier General William Dwight, one of General Nathaniel Banks's staff officers, and he carried a telegram from Halleck to Banks, dated May 11: "It is hoped you will unite with General Grant so as to attack Vicksburg and Port Hudson separately." Dwight, and apparently Banks, took this to mean that Grant was to suspend operations against Vicksburg and send part of his army south to help take Port Hudson.[135]

Grant explained to Dwight that the situation on the ground had changed dramatically since the time Halleck wrote this dispatch. If Halleck knew the army's current position, he would not suggest such a course of action. Dwight was insistent. Halleck's directive was an order, he claimed wrongly, and Dwight demanded that Grant obey it. Just then, Grant heard "cheering" to the right of the Union line and saw Lawler "in his shirt sleeves leading a charge upon the enemy." He mounted his horse "and rode in the direction of the charge," and "saw no more of the officer who delivered the dispatch." [136]

That evening, Grant rode to Bridgeport. Sherman had arrived there in the morning and his troops had already constructed a pontoon bridge. That night, as the men filed across, Grant and Sherman sat on a log and watched. "The whole scene was lit up with fires of pitch-pine . . ." Sherman recalled. "The bridge swayed to and fro under the passing feet, and made a fine war-picture." [137]

By morning all three of Sherman's divisions were on their way to

Vicksburg. McPherson and McClernand took roads farther to the west. Grant and Sherman rode ahead with Sherman's advanced skirmishers and came under fire two miles east of Vicksburg. "The bullets . . . whistled by thick and fast for a short time," Grant wrote later, not mentioning that a soldier was killed within a few feet of him.[138] Grant wanted to get to the Yazoo River, make contact with Porter's fleet, and have it ferry him supplies from Milliken's Bend. He had been operating without a supply line since before the Battle of Jackson. His men were hungry—some had not had rations for days—and he lacked ammunition for a protracted engagement. Sherman sent a cavalry regiment to Haynes' Bluff, which found it abandoned. By outflanking Pemberton, Grant had forced him to move all troops on the outskirts of the city to his main defensive line, a semicircle of earthen forts and rifle pits in the rear of Vicksburg. Sherman's cavalry commander spotted one of Porter's gunboats on the Yazoo and signaled to it. She steamed up and the army turned over the high-sitting fort to the navy.[139] Grant finally had a secure base of supplies, a riverine connection to Milliken's Bend, Memphis, and Cairo protected by a fleet of fearsome ironclads.

As Grant and Sherman drew near the city, they passed the Chickasaw Bluffs. After gazing at the swamp where he had been humiliatingly defeated, Sherman turned to Grant and admitted that he had had no faith in the campaign from its beginning, when the fleet assembled in the night to challenge Vicksburg's batteries. But at this penultimate moment, with Vicksburg in sight, he proclaimed this "one of the greatest campaigns in history." Vicksburg was not yet captured, but "whether captured or not, this was a complete and successful campaign," he told Grant.[140]

"Grant is entitled to all the Credit," he later confessed to his wife, Ellen. He had opposed it because it was "risky and hazardous in the Extreme." But it had succeeded, he said, "because of its hazard."[141]

"Nothing like this campaign has occurred during this war," Cadwallader wrote his wife from the rear of Vicksburg.[142] It was a Civil War blitzkrieg. In eighteen days Grant's army had marched nearly two hundred miles; won five battles—four in six days; inflicted a loss of 5,787 killed, wounded, and missing; compelled the abandonment of two Confederate strongholds—Grand Gulf and Haynes' Bluff; captured the capital of Mississippi; chased Pemberton's army inside Vicksburg; and positioned his own army between the only two rebel forces in the state. Along the way he suffered only 4,379 casualties, among them 695 killed.[143] It was a tactical and strategic masterwork, and the decisions that decided the outcome had to be made in a flash, without consulting staff, other commanders, or his superiors in Washington.

Grant moved so fast he was forced to leave his wounded behind at Port Gibson, Raymond, Jackson, and Champion Hill. Most of them were left in the hands of the enemy, to be cared for by Confederate surgeons, nurses, and women volunteers. Only when Grant reached Vicksburg was he able to send back to them, under a flag of truce, surgeons, medical supplies, and rations. And not until Vicksburg was securely invested did he send ambulances to recover his wounded.[144]

After landing in Mississippi on April 30, 1863, Grant had conquered space and time, hostile terrain and climate, without adequate cavalry and reliable maps. Most of his men had made the march on five days' rations, and none had tents. "The morning we crossed the Big Black," recalled Colonel Manning Force, "I offered five dollars for a small piece of cornbread, and could not get it. The soldier said bread was worth more to him than money."[145] But under Grant's resolute leadership there was little grumbling or complaining, perhaps because the general, said Elihu Washburne, "shared the hardships of the common soldier, living on hardtack and sleeping on the ground" in the first days of the campaign, and often mixing with the men in the encampments." And he was also "always in front and in the midst of danger."[146]

"There is nothing in history since Hannibal invaded Italy to compare with" this campaign, Dana and Wilson wrote in their biography of Grant.[147] Lincoln was equally effusive. "Whether General Grant shall or shall not consummate the capture of Vicksburg, his campaign from the beginning of this month . . . is one of the most brilliant in the world," he wrote his Chicago friend Isaac Arnold in late May.[148] Years later, General Stephen Dill Lee, Grant's opponent at Champion Hill, declared his campaign "bold and masterly," with "but few equals in this or any other war."[149]

· · ·

As General James McPherson reached the Union line outside Vicksburg on May 18, soon to be followed by McClernand's corps, the sun was setting. When he stopped to survey the rebel lines, his brigades, the heroes of Champion Hill, tossed their hats in the air and let out a thunderous cheer. The regimental bands struck up "The Girl I Left Behind," and an officer noticed tears in McPherson's eyes.[150] "The city must fall in a day or two," Porter wrote Grant from his dockage at Young's Point.[151]

Just before midnight, Grant had his three corps in place on two roads and a rail line leading into Vicksburg.[152] Earlier that day, Pemberton received an order from Joseph E. Johnston: He was to abandon Vicksburg and join him at Canton. "If Haynes' Bluff is untenable Vicksburg is of no value and cannot be held. If, therefore, you are invested in Vicksburg, you must ultimately surrender. . . . If it is not too late, evacuate Vicksburg . . . and march to the northeast."[153] After receiving the universal support of his commanders, Pemberton told Johnston he would hold the city "as long as possible, with the firm hope that the Government may yet be able to assist me in keeping this obstruction to the enemy's free navigation of the Mississippi River. I still conceive it to be the most important point in the Confederacy."[154]

The next morning, Grant determined to strike. "The enemy had been much demoralized by his defeats at Champion's Hill and the Big Black," he recalled his mind-set at the time, "and I believed he would not make much effort to hold Vicksburg."[155] It was one of his worst calculations of the war.

CHAPTER 21

A Circle of Fire

"It was now understood that there would be no more charging."[1]

—H. M. Trimble, Union soldier

Grant struck Pemberton's lines on May 19, 1863. To support his assault, he invited Porter to terrorize the town with his mortars.[2]

The day before, Vicksburg citizens had gathered on the bluffs facing the river and watched in silence as Federal tugs rounded the horseshoe bend above the city, pulling six small craft. The tugs were headed straight for De Soto Point, directly across from Vicksburg, where sailors lashed the scows to the shore. Each floating platform carried a massive 13-inch siege mortar weighing over seventeen thousand pounds.

Then the ironclads came into sight, completing the investment of Vicksburg begun that day by the Army of the Tennessee. Confederate soldiers and citizens were now trapped inside "a circle of fire," cut off from the outside world. "What is to become of all the living things in this place once the boats commence shelling—God only knows," wrote diarist Emma Balfour, the forty-four-year-old wife of a socially prominent Vicksburg doctor.[3]

General Pemberton's headquarters was next door to the Balfours' two-story brick home on fashionable Crawford Street, and the commander was a frequent dinner guest, charmed by Emma's patriotic intensity and unabashed candor. When the general returned that day from the calamity at the Big Black River Bridge he asked if Emma and her husband, William, "were provided with a rat-hole"—a cave to provide protection from Porter's bombs. "I told him it seemed to me that we were all caught in a rat-hole."[4]

The previous evening, stately country houses on the eastern flanks of the city, near Grant's lines, were burned to the ground to provide rebel gunners unimpeded avenues of fire, and soldiers patched up Vicksburg's land defenses.[5] The long line of earthen fortifications erected on that side of the city in September 1862 had since then been heavily eroded by the elements. Rebel infantry worked that night and into the next morning to repair them, hacking away at the weather-beaten parapets, using bayonets as picks and crude wooden shovels. Defeated in battle at Champion Hill and the Big Black Bridge, the men went at the work with energy but little hope. "Many of them [have] in their minds already surrendered the place," wrote Private William Lovelace Foster, the chaplain of a Mississippi regiment positioned on the city's eastern defenses.[6]

A little after two o'clock the following afternoon, a servant girl burst into Emma Balfour's bedroom with news that the Yankees were assaulting the Confederate line and "our men are running." Emma raced to the gallery with her spyglass and saw, to her relief, that the Army of Mississippi was actually holding. All that day "the cannonading was terrific and the air was full of conflicting rumors," Lida Lord recalled. A spirited eight-year-old at the time of the siege, she was confined that day to her family home next to her father's Episcopal church, awaiting news from the battlefield. Toward evening, friends brought word to the family that "the enemy had been repulsed with great slaughter." Then began what Lida Lord would later call "the moral reconstruction of our army. . . . Men who had been gloomy, depressed, and distrustful now cheerfully and bravely looked the future in the face. After that day's victory but one spirit seemed to animate the whole army, the determination never to give up."[7]

The greatly defamed Pemberton had once again saved the city, as he had the previous December, when he sent Van Dorn to cut Grant's supply line and mobilized the army that defeated Sherman at Chickasaw Bayou. The following winter his army had also stopped two of Grant's attempts to take Vicksburg from the north, through the Yazoo swamps. And now, on May 19, he had again stopped Grant at the eastern approaches to the city. Unlike at Champion Hill, he had the superior strategy, one forced upon him by Ulysses Grant: Knocked back and hemmed in, Pemberton had no choice but to fight defensively, behind sturdy fortifications.

This time it was Grant who made the mistakes. Like Sherman at

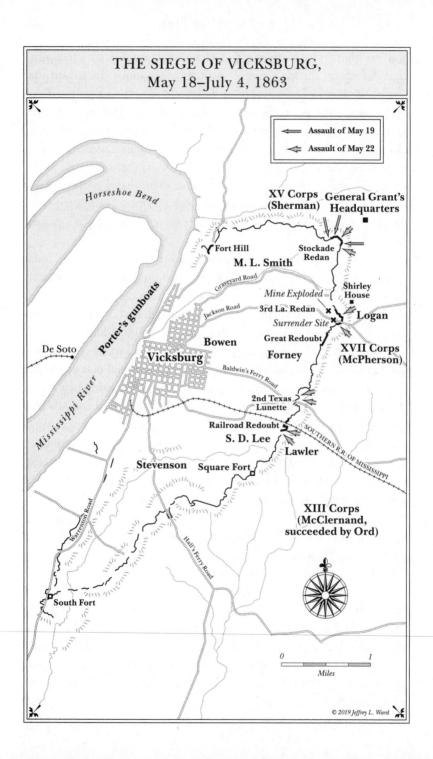

THE SIEGE OF VICKSBURG,
May 18–July 4, 1863

→ Assault of May 19
← Assault of May 22

Horseshoe Bend

XV Corps (Sherman) **General Grant's Headquarters**

Fort Hill
Stockade Redan
M. L. Smith

Graveyard Road

Mine Exploded

Shirley House

Jackson Road

3rd La. Redan
Surrender Site
Logan

Porter's gunboats

Bowen

Great Redoubt

Vicksburg
Forney

XVII Corps (McPherson)

De Soto

Baldwin's Ferry Road

Mississippi River

2nd Texas Lunette

Railroad Redoubt
S. D. Lee

SOUTHERN R.R. OF MISSISSIPPI

Lawler

Stevenson Square Fort

XIII Corps (McClernand, succeeded by Ord)

Warrenton Road

Hall's Ferry Road

South Fort

0   1
Miles

© 2019 Jeffrey L. Ward

the Walnut Hills, he had underestimated the strength of the enemy, believing Pemberton had fewer than twenty thousand troops when he actually had thirty-one thousand.[8] Two of the five divisions opposing Grant, those of Generals Martin Luther Smith and John H. Forney, had not suffered the demoralizing defeats of the previous weeks; Pemberton had cautiously kept these eight thousand men in or near Vicksburg. But Grant's greater error was his failure to account for the psychological impact of fighting behind prepared fortifications. "[Grant] failed to realize that a mob of men entering an entrenched line is automatically reorganized by the actual trench they occupy," wrote military historian J. F. C. Fuller. Behind the high walls of an earthen fort, an army on the run is "no longer a mob." With no chance to maneuver, the tactical options ordinarily open to commanders are radically reduced. Generalship, the supreme attribute of the Grant-led army, is neutralized. As Fuller noted: "All the men [in the fortifications] have to do is to turn about, and open fire on the advancing attacker."[9]

Grant had seen things differently. He was in hot pursuit of a badly weakened army he had crushed at Champion Hill, and he was eager to avoid a long siege by rolling over Pemberton before Joseph Johnston was heavily reinforced and ready to hit him from the rear.[10] But as Grant noted in his memoirs, "the first consideration of all was—the troops believed they could carry the works in their front, and would not have worked so patiently in the trenches if they had not been allowed to try." As Adam Badeau, the general's echo, later explained: "The troops were buoyant with success and eager for an assault."[11]

The evidence does not support this. The men's letters and memoirs reveal a profound and widespread reluctance to mount a go-for-broke assault against Vicksburg's formidable land defenses.

"Some time before daylight on the morning of the 19th we were quietly aroused and instructed to prepare our breakfasts without noise or unnecessary fire or light," wrote Sergeant J. J. Kellogg of the 113th Illinois Volunteer Infantry. Rumors circulated in the camps that the army would tear into the entrenched rebels that morning. "I hadn't had a good view of the Vicksburg fortifications the day before, and now in the first faint light of the morning, while the men were eating and making preparations for the charge, I crept cautiously out on the crest of the hill, and . . . contemplated the defenses against which we had to charge." What Kellogg saw convinced him he would not live another day.[12]

When he returned to his company, he saw men preparing for their deaths—"entrusting their valuables with hasty instructions" to sick and wounded men who would stay behind.[13] Soldiers in other units up and down the Union line did the same. The men "[are] not eager to charge," a Union soldier told his diary.[14]

Vicksburg's land defenses were the most formidable Grant would face in the war. Colonel William E. Strong, McPherson's staff officer, described them. "A long line of high, rugged, irregular bluffs, clearly cut against the sky, crowned with cannon which peered ominously from embrasures to the right and left as far as the eye could see. . . . Rifle-pits, surmounted with head logs, ran along the bluffs, connecting fort with fort, and [were] filled with veteran infantry." In front of the elevated defenses and in the steep-sided ravines that led up to them was a nearly impassable abatis, further strengthened in the hours before the Union assault with telegraph wire placed low to the ground to obstruct attacking troops. Most of these ravines were thick with cane, willow, and rugged underbrush. "The approaches to [the main forts] were frightful—enough to appal [sic] the stoutest heart," wrote Strong.[15]

Strong had been at Port Gibson, yet he had never seen worse ground on which to fight a battle. "There is only one way to account for the hills of Vicksburg," said a rebel soldier. "After the Lord of Creation had made all the big mountains and ranges of hills, He had left on His hands a large lot of scraps. These were all dumped at Vicksburg in a waste heap."[16]

Pemberton's defensive line formed an eight-mile-long semicircle that enclosed the city, with both ends anchored on river bluffs north and south of town. Nine widely spaced earthen forts had thick walls with embrasures for artillery, and all but one was fronted by a seven-foot-deep ditch, or moat, to impede assault forces seeking to surmount the outer walls of the bastions. Some of the forts were redans—triangular-shaped fortifications with their apexes facing the enemy; others were lunettes—two-sided works, crescent-shaped, with an open back; and one of them, the Great Redoubt, was an enclosed square.

The parapets, or protective walls, of most of the forts were ten feet high and fifteen feet thick. The rifle pits connecting the forts were five feet deep, with fire steps for sharpshooters. One hundred and twenty-eight artillery pieces were positioned at prominent points along a ridge facing the enemy. Everywhere along the line the rebels held the high ground. Just to climb up to some of the high-sitting forts with rifle and full military pack, with no one firing at you, would have been arduous duty for healthy young men.

Major Samuel Lockett, the engineer who designed these defenses, placed the main forts on commanding positions guarding the principal roads into Vicksburg. Additionally, two forts guarded the flanks of the deep cut through which trains of the Southern Railroad of Mississippi entered the city.[17] General Bowen's crack division was held in reserve to rally to any part of the line grievously threatened. In addition, seven hundred troops manned the city's two-mile-long river defenses, leaving Pemberton with fewer than twenty-eight thousand men to deal with Grant.[18] To feed this army, cattle, sheep, and hogs on farms in the vicinity of Vicksburg were seized and driven within the lines. Harvested corn was also expropriated. "With proper economy of subsistence and ordnance stores, I knew I could stand a siege," Pemberton wrote later.[19]

He could also withstand a determined assault. On May 18, 1862, when Commodore Farragut sent Captain Samuel Phillips Lee to demand the surrender of Vicksburg, Lee had been scornfully rebuffed. "Having been ordered to hold these defenses, it is my intention to do so as long as in my power," replied Major General Martin Luther Smith, a native New Yorker in command of the city's defense force. "Mississippians don't know, and refuse to learn, how to surrender to an enemy," another officer in gray told Lee.[20] On arriving at Vicksburg on May 18, 1863, Sergeant Kellogg was determined, he said, "to teach them how to surrender."[21] One year and a day after General Smith refused to surrender the city, his brigades were positioned on the northern flank of Pemberton's defensive line, directly in front of Kellogg's unit, and they would have something to say about that.

In the early afternoon of May 19, 1863, Kellogg's regiment, part of Sherman's corps, was among the first to attack.[22] This would be largely Sherman's battle. His XV Corps was the first to reach Vicksburg, and he had positioned his men closer to the enemy than the other two corps, in the northern sector of the city's defenses, across from the Stockade

Redan complex: two forts guarding the Graveyard Road. The Stockade Redan stood south of the road. Directly across the road was the 27th Louisiana Lunette. The mutually supporting forts were about fifty yards apart and connected by a log stockade.

At around two in the afternoon, General Frank Blair unleashed three rapid artillery salvos, the signal for his two lead elements to advance across the steep ridges on both sides of the Graveyard Road, straight into the guns of the Stockade Redan.[23] The timber-littered ground, broken by deep ravines and concealed sinkholes, did early and excellent work for the defenders, scattering the perfectly straight Union lines.[24] When the bluecoats came into view, "the enemy rose behind their parapet and poured a furious fire upon our lines," Sherman described the initial slaughter.[25] "The leaden hell from the enemy was absolutely blinding," Kellogg remembered; wood chips on the ground danced in the air from the percussions.[26] His regiment, and a number of others, found cover behind felled timber and stumps, and the men were pinned down for the remainder of the battle, "lying flat on our backs and loading our pieces in that position."[27] Parts of other regiments made it to the ditch in front of the redan but were unable to surmount the steep walls. They were trapped there till dark, when, one by one, they crawled on their stomachs back to their lines.[28]

"All night long I heard the stretcher bearers bringing in the wounded," wrote Kellogg.[29] A disproportionate number of the casualties were men of the 1st Battalion, 13th U.S. Infantry, led by Captain Edward Washington (grandnephew of George Washington). He was mortally wounded in a crossfire of canister and shell, and seventeen of his color bearers were cut down. Forty-three percent of the battalion became casualties. A fortunate few made it through the bullet-swept battlefield and planted their colors on the exterior slope of the redan.[30]*

A fourteen-year-old drummer boy saved dozens of lives that afternoon by volunteering with three others to race to the rear to implore Sherman to call up ammunition for beleaguered units that had exhausted their supply of cartridges. Orion P. Howe of Waukegan, Illinois, was the

---

* Sherman, who commanded the outfit when it was formed in 1861, would later authorize it to sew on its flag "First at Vicksburg." Soldiers of the 13th U.S. Infantry still wear that inscription on their shoulder patches. Shea and Winschel, *Vicksburg is the Key*, 147.

only one to make it through alive. Gravely wounded, he bcame the youngest soldier to receive the congressional Medal of Honor for service at Vicksburg.[31]

Nearly all of the 942 Federal losses were from Sherman's corps.[32] McPherson's and McClernand's men were positioned too far from the rebel line to fully engage. "We [were] . . . swept [a]way," Sherman said, "as Chaff thrown from the hand on a windy day."[33] He was forthright. Grant, on the other hand, gave only passing mention to the assault— and failed to note the casualties in his official report of the campaign.[34] Although stunned into silence by the setback, he was determined to try again. On May 20, he met with his three corps commanders, and all agreed to mount a much larger and more coordinated assault two days later.[35] This time it would be different. Grant would move McPherson and McClernand closer to the enemy lines and attack every major rebel fort. A prolonged and thunderous artillery barrage would kick off the assault. Commanders were to synchronize their watches (a first in military history) and launch a "simultaneous attack" at precisely 10:00 A.M.[36] Grant asked Porter to have his gunboats shell the rebel entrenchments vehemently and hurl mortar balls into the city the night before the attack to "annoy" the enemy.[37]

Grant aimed to prevail by sheer mass, with unrelenting pressure applied all along the line. The terrain in front of the rebel forts left no other alternative, he believed. The ravines and constricted ridges prevented him from massing his troops and artillery and attacking a precisely targeted objective with speed and focused firepower. There was only one place on the rebel line where such a swift, narrow-front penetration was even remotely possible: on the Graveyard Road that led to the Stockade Redan.

On the first attempt, Sherman had sent his assault force through the ridges and depressions on both sides of that road, a tactic that had allowed the abatis-strewn hollows to break up his columns. This time he would have his men attack straight down the road in a long vertical column, one regiment closely bunched behind the other, the entire assault force forming a hammer-like phalanx strong enough, hopefully, to punch a hole in the enemy line.[38]

The plan was extremely risky. "This is a death struggle & will be terrible" on the men, he confided to Ellen, but the reward would be Vicksburg.[39] Everything depended upon the Forlorn Hope—a suicide squad of one hundred and fifty handpicked volunteers. With their rifles slung over their shoulders, making them absolutely helpless, these men— the tip of the phalanx—would carry planks to build footbridges over the ditches in front of the fort and long ladders to scale the walls of the parapets.[40]* The troops following them would use these bridges to take the fort.

On the evening of May 21, when Kellogg's company began forming up for the assault, an officer from Grant's staff approached with a "proposition." Any unmarried man volunteering for the storming party would be given a sixty-day furlough. The men were at first "speechless," but, after a time, two soldiers stepped forward, then a third. "We looked upon [them] as already dead," said Kellogg.[41] More men in Sherman's corps volunteered than were needed.

Once again, Blair's division took the lead. At daybreak the units of Brigadier General Hugh Ewing, Colonel Giles Smith, and Colonel T. Kilby Smith were strung out in a column along the Graveyard Road, behind the Forlorn Hope, ready to exploit any success the storming force might achieve. The commanders were men of proven ability. West Point–educated Hugh Ewing was Sherman's foster brother and most trusted advisor. Giles Smith had served under Sherman in the Steele's Bayou expedition, where he'd helped rescue Admiral Porter and his gunboats, and T. Kilby Smith had participated conspicuously in nearly every battle fought by the Army of the Tennessee.

A mile or so to the south of Sherman's assault column, James McPherson ordered John Logan to strike both the 3rd Louisiana Redan and the Great Redoubt, the strongest bastion on the rebel line. These forts guarded the place where Jackson Road pierced the rebel defenses and ran into Vicksburg. Farther south, McClernand's corps would take on the 2nd Texas Lunette and the Railroad Redoubt, earthworks that stood guard over the Baldwin Ferry Road and the gap in the lines through which the Southern Railroad of Mississippi ran into and out of Vicksburg.

Union guns on land and water opened up early on the morning of

---

* Grant's headquarters cabin was dismantled for materials to make planks and scaling ladders. He moved to a tent for the remainder of the siege.

May 22 and blazed away continuously for over two hours, blowing huge holes in rebel earthworks and covering the defenders with pulverized brown dust.[42] The "ringing, steady cracking of sharpshooters' rifles . . ." the roar of the big naval guns, "and the shrieking shot and shell from thirty-one batteries of field guns around the city was deafening," recalled Confederate general Stephen Dill Lee, who had commanded part of the rebel force on Champion Hill and was on this day positioned on a ridge behind the Texas Lunette.[43] The air rocked and quivered, but there was "no reply" from either rebel artillery or infantry. "In terrible suspense, the assault was awaited in calmness and decision. . . . No other bombardment by so great an army and fleet occurred during the war," said Lee. "The scene and the occasion was grand, beyond description; 45,000 American troops were ready to spring on nearly 20,000 other American troops lying behind entrenchments."

Near ten o'clock, every Union cannon and rifle went quiet. The unnatural silence was short-lived. "Suddenly, there seemed to spring, almost from the bowels of the earth, dense masses of Federal troops, in numerous columns of attack, and with loud cheers and huzzahs, they rushed forward, at a run, with bayonets fixed, not firing a shot, headed for every salient or advanced position along the Confederate line . . . feeling the flush of their numerous victories, and confident that every thing must go down before them," wrote General Lee, as skilled with the pen as he was in the field.[44] "They never faltered, but came bravely on," wrote another rebel defender.[45] When they approached within 150 yards of the forts, the "troops stood in their trenches and poured volley after volley, into their ranks," and every rebel cannon unleashed "discharges of grape and canister. No troops in the world could stand such a fire."[46]

In Sherman's sector, men came thundering down the road behind the Forlorn Hope. Ewing's Ohioans, eight men abreast, cheered wildly and charged "pointblank for the rebel work." Reaching near it, they were cut down like rows of corn before the harvester. As surviving members of the storming party "vanished into the ditch," the bodies of fallen men "piled up in the road . . . so thick that the living could not advance without stepping on the dead and dying." As the next regiment in line approached the "zone of death," it halted, and men began lying on the road "as if already dead."[47]

Some of Ewing's Ohio boys, including the 47th Ohio, made it into the moat, scrambled up the outer wall, and planted the Stars and Stripes on the ramparts.[48] Ewing, in short sleeves, his sword at his side and a revolver in his right hand, let out a shout, urging on the men pinned to the road.[49] They were immovable. Sherman's assault had ground to a halt twenty minutes after it commenced.[50]

In desperation, Blair ordered two regiments of Ewing's brigade to take up a position in the tangled terrain south of the road.[51] Colonel Augustus Parry of the 47th Ohio "drew his sword" and ordered the men to follow him. "'If you see any officer behind a tree or a stump shoot him on the spot,'" a diarist in the 47th Ohio regiment recorded Parry's battlefield bravado. "Then he said to the officers, 'If you see any privates behind trees or stump, shoot them on the spot.' We were soon going in full run and we went as far as it was possible for men to go." That was a ravine "so close to the enemy," said Private Owen J. Hopkins, "that we could aim at the buttons on the Johnnies' coats." The ground they hugged was like the floor of an oven, and they soon exhausted the water in their canteens. They held their ground till the midday light turned to a deep purple, then moved back to their old line.[52]

Most of the other units, including Kellogg's, didn't make it as far as the 47th and, after burrowing in the earth for cover, were shelled incessantly until they too retreated, forced to abandon their dead and wounded.[53] Kellogg claimed later to be humbled by the courage of the men caught in the ditch in front of the stockade for over twelve hours. One of them lived to tell his story to a Chicago reporter.

Twenty-four-year-old Private John O'Dea was an immigrant from Limerick, Ireland, serving with the 8th Missouri in Giles Smith's brigade. Approaching the Stockade Redan with other members of the Forlorn Hope, he faced fire so intense it felt like "hell was escaping through one great vent and we were rushing into that opening." O'Dea was a tiny, wiry man, and when he reached the ditch, a friend lifted him up on the wall of the fort and together they dug a hole with their hands and planted their standard.

O'Dea then spotted something that looked like a head rolling down the sloping wall of the parapet. "It was a shell with a lighted fuse attached." It exploded, burying O'Dea and at least a dozen other men. Moments later, O'Dea realized he had lost his hearing, and that blood was pouring from his temple and his ears. When another shell came rolling toward him, he impulsively kicked it clear. It went off, killing an unknown number of his comrades. When a third shell tumbled down the embankment, sparks spurting from its shortened fuse, O'Dea "caught the thing" and hurled it over the parapet and into the rebel fort. "It did good execution . . ." he said. "I heard yells of pain and heard commotion." By now the ditch "was a scene of carnage no mortal tongue can describe," O'Dea told the *Chicago Times-Herald* correspondent. "Legs and arms were torn off," and the face of his closest friend was so horribly mangled O'Dea could not recognize him. "I shall never forget his exclamation, 'Jonnie, do you not know me?'"[54]

John O'Dea received the Medal of Honor, one of seventy-eight awarded to survivors of the Forlorn Hope. The other seventy-two members of the storming party did not survive.* On that terrible day, "there was some of the hardest fighting ever witnessed," recalled Union veteran Isaac Jackson, "some of the most daring acts performed during this War."[55] Even the enemy was awed by the resolve of the assailants. "Surely no more desperate courage than this could be displayed by mortal men," wrote a Mississippi soldier.[56]

McPherson's combined assault on the Great Redoubt and 3rd Louisiana Redan was also decisively repulsed. An Irish unit from Missouri, carrying scaling ladders, made it to the walls of the Great Redoubt, only to discover their ladders were too short. Defending the rebel fort was Captain David Todd, brother-in-law of Abraham Lincoln, one of Mary Todd Lincoln's two half brothers serving in the Confederate army during the Vicksburg campaign.[57] Standing on a spur of ground about two

---

* The government awarded a total of 122 Medals of Honor for service at Vicksburg. The Medal of Honor was created by the U.S. Navy in 1861 and called "The Medal of Valor." The following year the U.S. Army began awarding the Medal of Honor for conspicuous gallantry in combat. The Confederate States of America created the Confederate Medal of Honor in October 1862. During the Civil War, it was issued to forty-eight men and one woman, only one of whom served at Vicksburg, Captain Isaac N. Brown of the CSS *Arkansas*. Due to a shortage of wartime metals, recipients were listed in a Roll of Honor in Confederate newspapers and actual medallions were issued posthumously a century later. "Medal of Honor Files," VNMP.

hundred yards from the Great Redoubt, Sherman could see the attack faltering. "At every point we were repulsed," he wrote later.[58]

Around this time, two of McClernand's Iowa regiments—the 21st and the 22nd—led by Michael Lawler, the Union hero at the Battle of the Big Black Bridge, poured into the ditch fronting the Railroad Redoubt, which was being held by a solitary regiment. About a dozen Iowans followed Sergeant Joseph Griffith into the fort through a breach created by Union artillery, and in a hand-to-hand struggle they captured thirteen rebels, killed a handful of others, and drove the rest of the Confederates from one section of the fort. The flag of the 22nd was soon flying from the bastion's highest parapet.[59] A barrage of grape and canister eventually forced the Iowans back into the ditch, where they frantically dug holes in the ground with their bayonets to protect themselves.[60] They were soon joined by an Illinois regiment that had fought its way to the fort and, like the Iowans, held on—but just barely, fighting what one of the men called "an unequal warfare with the rebels on the other side of the breastworks," the opposing forces separated by only a few feet of earth.[61] A handful of Indianans made it to the ditch of the 2nd Texas Lunette, but everywhere else in that sector McClernand's men were "mercilessly torn to pieces by Confederate shot and shell," wrote Sylvanus Cadwallader, who witnessed the action from up close.[62]

What the trapped Union soldiers at the Railroad Redoubt saw as a desperate struggle for survival, John McClernand interpreted as a breakthrough, the only one the Union achieved that day. He needed more men to exploit it, but he had already committed his reserves. In a high state of excitement, he sent two deceptively worded messages to Grant around noon, just after Sherman and McPherson had begun calling back their men. "We have part possession of two Forts, and the stars and stripes are floating over them. A vigorous push ought to be made all along the line."[63] This could well be, he suggested, the turning point in the battle—and, he failed to say, his own career—and he implored Grant to exploit the opportunity by making a "diversion in his favor."[64]

Grant was on high ground a mile and a half north of the Railroad Redoubt, and the smoke obscured his view of the action. Distrusting the source of the report, he immediately questioned its veracity. He then walked over to Sherman's observation post and showed him the message, saying: "I don't believe a word of it."[65] Sherman disagreed. It was official and had to be credited. "A corps commander would not write a misstatement over his own signature at such a time."[66] Grant reversed course and ordered Sherman and McPherson to renew the assault at three o'clock. It failed utterly. "It was a useless sacrifice of life," a Union sharpshooter summed up the day. "We have gained nothing."[67]

"It was now understood that there would be no more charging," said an Illinois sergeant.[68]

"That night there were stirring times at Grant's headquarters," recalled engineer William Le Baron Jenney.[69] Sylvanus Cadwallader told Grant he had been deceived: McClernand's forces had gained partial possession of only one rebel fort, and that success was short-lived. McClernand "never carried any part of his front." Grant and Rawlins questioned Cadwallader closely, and the reporter later recalled the expression on the commander's face when he learned the facts: "a grim glowering look of disappointment and disgust."[70]

Colonel John Sanborn was infuriated. His brigade had suffered staggering losses in the afternoon assault "as a result," he fumed, "of a dispatch which seemed to have no foundation in fact."[71] Egged on by Sanborn and an explosive John Rawlins, Grant considered sacking McClernand. "General McClernand's dispatches misled me as to the real state of facts and caused much of this loss. He is entirely unfit for the position of Corps Commander," he wrote Halleck.[72] The day after the second assault, Grant "determined to relieve General McClernand," Dana informed Secretary of War Edwin Stanton, "but changed his mind, concluding that it would be better of the whole to leave McClernand in his present command till the siege of Vicksburg is concluded, after which he will induce McClernand to ask for a leave of absence."[73] He held back, probably to discourage disunity in McClernand's corps, but also in full knowledge that the former congressman remained a favorite of the president and a clique of powerful Democratic legislators.

The animosity against McClernand spread to his own camps. The men at the Railroad Redoubt knew he had misread the situation and that a major breakthrough was never a prospect. "This may have appeared true to him but he was not near enough to see for himself," wrote an Illinois soldier.[74]

Grant was also assailed by his troops for ordering the May 22 assault. It was "contrary to the dictates of common sence [sic] & the opinion of everyone," said an Indiana soldier.[75] "General Grant sealed the fate of hundreds of his best soldiers," wrote young Owen J. Hopkins, one of Grant's strongest supporters in the ranks. "It was not a charge; it was not a battle, not an assault; but a slaughter of human beings in cold blood."[76]

Union casualties for the day approached 3,200; probably a third of them occurred in the afternoon assaults. The rebels lost no more than five hundred men, a sixth of the Federal total.[77] In two days in front of Vicksburg, Grant had lost nearly as many men as he had in the previous three weeks of continuous fighting.

Grant blamed the afternoon's losses on McClernand, but he should also have blamed himself for heeding Sherman's advice. And in his report to Halleck, he hid the truth: "Today an attempt was made to carry the City by assault but was not entirely successful. . . . Our loss was not severe."[78] This was not unusual behavior. Throughout the campaign he had been reluctant to report discouraging news to his superiors in Washington, fearing, perhaps, that it would pile up the evidence for his removal.

Whatever one may think of Grant's decision to mount two risky assaults on the Vicksburg defenses, he had solid military reasons for proceeding. And he had built his career on running against the odds. What is not debatable is his refusal to request a truce to bury his dead and recover his wounded. This is both inexplicable—Grant never wrote a word about it—and inexcusable.

"In front of our regiment the Federal dead were strewn thickly where they fell . . ." wrote a rebel soldier. "His dead lay . . . decaying under a burning sun. The stench was unbearable. The sight was horrible. The reeking bodies lay all blackened and swollen, and some with arms extended as if pleading to Heaven for the burial that was denied them by man."[79] Many of the fallen were still alive, and their screams of pain unnerved Union soldiers camped within earshot of the carnage. On May 23, McClernand wrote Grant imploring him to request a cessation of hostilities "in order to bury the dead & recover the wounded."[80] Grant did not reply. Two days later, Pemberton sent a message through the lines, asking Grant, "in the name of humanity," to agree to what McClernand had suggested. Grant consented, and at six o'clock that afternoon he sent out stretcher-bearers and burial details.[81] "The dead were buried by simply throwing earth onto the bodies where they had fallen," wrote Kellogg.[82]

While the gruesome work went on, men in both camps slipped out of their fortifications and mingled in the no-man's-land between the lines. "[We met on] friendly terms," said one of them, "shook hands and talked about the war, in good humor."[83] Union soldiers swapped tobacco, plentiful in their camps, for pocketknives and canteens. Brothers and cousins from the same border states found one another and exchanged letters from home. "The rebels . . . say they tried to get our wounded, but they could not as they was exposed to our sharpshooters," wrote diarist Charles Wood, "but they did succeed in getting some away and said they were taking good care of them." At the conclusion of the two-hour truce "each party went into their rifle pits and commenced shooting at each other again as savage as ever," said Wood.[84]

That same day, Grant issued Special Orders No. 140, officially proclaiming the start of siege operations, though they had actually begun hours after the final assault. "Corps Commanders will immediately commence the work of reducing the enemy by regular approaches. . . . Every advantage will be taken . . . to gain positions from which to start mines, trenches, or advance batteries."[85] The "approaches"—or "saps," as they were called—were deep trenches designed to give cover to assault troops. They were dug in a zigzag pattern toward the rebel lines.[86] "We never dug our trench far enough in one direction to make it possible for the enemy to rake it with his deadly fire, but made frequent turns," explained one sapper.[87] The work was urgently pursued, day and night, and no general assaults were planned until the approaches came within a stone's throw of the enemy forts. "It is desirable that no more loss of life shall be sustained in the reduction of Vicksburg," Grant wrote in his special orders.[88] He would "out-camp the enemy," he said.[89]

Grant put Captain Frederick E. Prime, his chief engineer, in charge

of the siege works.* Prime figured he needed at least thirty profession-
ally trained engineers to conduct a successful siege, but at the time there
were only two officers in Grant's army assigned to engineering duty. The
soldiers themselves would do the burden of the work, assisted by men
from the pioneer corps and runaway slaves paid a miserable ten dollars
a month.[90] Officers and men would have "to learn to be engineers while
the siege was going on," said Prime, calling upon "their native good
sense and ingenuity."[91]

Although Grant had taken only a cursory interest in his engineering
courses at West Point, he rode along the siege lines daily, inspecting the
construction of batteries, rifle pits, and trenches. "We see him every day
as [common] as a private soldier," wrote one sapper.[92] Grant was there,
said Sam Byers, to examine every detail of siege work, even the setting
of the sights on the brass cannon.[93]

To conduct a successful siege, the army required a secure supply
line. Porter had already taken care of this by seizing dockage on the
Yazoo River, only ten miles from Grant's camps and safely behind his
lines. In the lull between the two assaults, Grant had directed William
Le Baron Jenney, a graduate—with his classmate Gustav Eiffel—of the
prestigious École Centrale des Arts et Manufactures in Paris, to construct a wagon road from the dockage at Chickasaw Bayou to the
camps of Sherman and McPherson.[94] Steamers running from a landing spot below Milliken's Bend to Warrenton, Mississippi, supplied
McClernand's corps on the southernmost part of the line. Ground was
cleared for the camps, tents and cooking utensils were brought in, and
telegraph lines were strung, putting corps commanders in instantaneous
communication with Grant's headquarters, and Grant in close contact
with Porter at his anchorage at the mouth of the Yazoo. "All was now
ready for the pick and spade," Grant wrote.[95]

But first, the men had to be fed properly. On the army's twenty-day
march from Bruinsburg to Vicksburg, Union soldiers had been issued
only five days' rations. Living on the largesse of Mississippi farms, most
of them had had access to plenty of fresh beef, poultry, and vegetables,
but upon arriving at Vicksburg they had a craving for hardtack—soldier

---

* Prime fell ill in late June and was replaced by Captain Cyrus Comstock.

bread. "I had one last hardtack when I got to Vicksburg that I saved and carried for several days," wrote J. J. Kellogg.[96]

While Jenney's road was under construction, Grant was passing along the line when a soldier, recognizing him, muttered, "hardtack." Soon "the cry was taken all along the line," Grant recalled. When he told the men he was opening a road to provide all the bread they needed, "the cry was instantly changed to cheers."[97] On the night of May 21 the men were "furnished with a good square meal by Uncle Sam—if hard tack, sow bacon, beans and coffee can be called a square meal," said Illinois soldier Wilbur Crummer.[98]

From this point forward, Vicksburg's only chance of prevailing was Joseph E. Johnston. Pemberton could not break Grant's grip or cut out of the city on his own. In the first weeks of the siege, hopes ran high among the hill city's soldiers and citizens that Johnston would soon sweep in from Jackson and lift the siege. Sherman read the mood of the defiant city: "The enemy in Vicksburg must expect aid from that quarter, else they would not fight with such desperation."[99]

Pemberton was in a race against time. He needed to keep Grant at bay in order to give Johnston time to raise a formidable army of relief. The unanswered question was whether Johnston had the resolve to fight a costly battle to regain Vicksburg and save Pemberton's army.

While Pemberton waited for Johnston, Grant's army continued digging toward Vicksburg under the hard summer sun. There were thirteen Union saps, each named after the commander furnishing the guards and working parties.[100] Each was seven feet deep and roughly eight feet wide, deep enough for a soldier to stand in without becoming an easy target for an enemy rifleman and wide enough to accommodate a column of assault troops marching four abreast.[101] The work crews were protected from enemy fire by an improvised contraption called a sap-roller, a large barrel-shaped bundle of cane bound together with cord or vines, packed with cotton, and placed on the ground ahead of the trench. As the excavation moved forward, the digging parties used long poles to push the huge roller—or "bullet stopper," as they called it—to the head of the ditch.[102] Crews entrenching on the steeply pitched incline in front of Union general John Thayer's line used bundles of cane called fascines to serve as a roof over their sap. It proved "impenetrable to musket balls."[103]

Sappers also used gabions to shore up trench walls and provide protection from enemy bullets. These were cylindrical cane baskets, up to ten feet tall, filled with dirt. West Point–trained officers educated in the ancient principles of siege warfare taught soldiers how to make them. While inspecting his lines one afternoon, Sherman spotted some privates gathered around a young corporal holding a piece of paper, all of them looking dumbfounded. They had orders to construct gabions and had no idea how to go about it. Sherman dismounted and asked for an axe. He headed into a canebrake, cut down three trees, shaped the cuttings into stakes, and drove them into the ground. He then knelt down and wove some reeds among the sticks and secured them with grape vines. This took a mere ten minutes, said Colonel Sanborn, who witnessed the scene.[104]

But sappers counted more on hot lead than cotton and cane for protection. Sharpshooters were positioned in the lateral trenches that branched off from the saps, and their persistent fire was a deterrent to rebel riflemen.

The Union sharpshooter was the most dangerous man on the Vicksburg siege line. His minie balls were the deadliest missiles of all, killing and maiming more enemy combatants, by far, than artillery or mortar fire. Federal riflemen were more effective than their rebel counterparts because of the sheer volume of their fire. Grant would be massively reinforced in early June, and from that time he could put nearly twice as many sharpshooters on the line as Pemberton. And Union sharpshooters had unlimited supplies of ammunition. Although the Confederates never ran out of bullets, they had to conserve their irreplaceable supplies and often ran short of percussion caps. "We fire a hundred shots to their one," a Union soldier boasted to his family back home.[105] Union sharpshooters were also fresher and likely more alert than rebel riflemen. They worked in two-hour shifts, while manpower shortages required their Confederate counterparts to remain on the line around the clock. Hot food was brought to them and they slept on their guns.

The high ground gave the rebels a decided advantage against foot soldiers assaulting fixed positions, but it worked against them once the battle settled into a siege. When returning fire from behind parapets, rebel riflemen had to expose their heads and shoulders to get off an accurate shot. And, firing down a steep slope on enemy riflemen hidden behind log and earthen barricades, they regularly overshot their targets.[106] Throughout the forty-seven-day siege, the Confederates lost 3,176 men, while the Federals lost only six hundred. For every Union casualty there were more than five rebels dead or wounded.[107]

Late in the siege, when Union trenches approached within spitting distance of the enemy forts, rebel soldiers would toss down hand grenades, egg-shaped projectiles filled with buckshot. The grenades, however, were unreliable—the plungers on the bottom had to strike the ground properly for the missiles to detonate—so soldiers took to rolling lit artillery shells into the enemy's trenches.[108]

With the lines so close together, sappers were reluctant to call in artillery support. Instead they used small wooden mortars, about four feet long, which they made by boring out tree trunks and reinforcing the wooden barrels with iron bands to prevent them from exploding.[109] The mortars were capable of throwing an eight-pound shell from 100 to 150 yards, and their fire was "exceedingly effective," said Union engineer Andrew Hickenlooper, who, along with many others, claimed credit for inventing the device.[110]

It was never quiet on the battlefield. "The work of slaughter and destruction went on day and night," said Wilbur Crummer.[111] In mid-May the Union had over a hundred cannon firing insistently on the rebel forts, and the exchanges between the two lines were earsplitting, like thunder rolling across mountains.[112] A month later, the Federals had over double that number, giving them total artillery domination.[113] The damage they caused the forts was, at first, repaired at night, but soon parts of Pemberton's line began to look "ragged and dilapidated."[114] Worse for the rebels, they found it almost impossible to fire back. Every time a cannon barrel protruded from a rebel parapet it was met with crushing fire. "We cannot call this fighting, it is merely artillery practice," said a soldier in blue.[115] Toward the end of the siege the rebels were using hardly any of their 101 cannon against the Federal sappers or sharp-shooters. Many of them had already been destroyed by Federal fire, and a number had been withdrawn to places of safety in anticipation of a final Union assault.[116] "We had little besides musketry fire to contend with," reported chief engineer Captain Prime.[117]

All the while, Admiral Porter continued to pound the city with his gunboats and mortars, giving Vicksburg the unenviable distinction of being, with Atlanta in 1864, the most intensely bombed city of the war. (On August 4, 1864, Sherman's army fired five thousand shells into Atlanta, part of a prolonged bombardment.) Porter's mammoth mortar shells were aimed at the center of the city, to terrorize the citizenry and break their will. A siege, wrote Confederate soldier Edward S. Gregory, is a "suspension of civilization," and mortar assaults, "iron storm[s]," were "the most demoralizing agency" of mechanized warfare.[118]

Porter would later claim that he "set the city on fire."[119] He did not. "I am firing incendiary shells and burn a house now and then," he wrote Grant at one point, describing the limit of the damage he was able to inflict in a single raid.[120] But his continuous bombing did destroy or damage hundreds of houses, kill and maim dozens of civilians, anni-hilate rebel livestock in the city, and depress, yet not shatter, civilian morale.

The mortar assault began on May 20, when Porter's crews hurled a 256-pound shell into the city nearly once every five minutes for most of the night.[121] By the end of the siege, twenty-two thousand shells would have rained down on Vicksburg.[122] By that time its citizens had excavated over five hundred caves. "The hills are so honeycombed with [tomb-like] caves that the streets [that run by them] look like avenues in a cemetery," wrote clandestine Union sympathizer Dora Miller.[123] Locals called them "bombproofs," but they were hardly that. Cut out of the city's soft, stone-less soil, they were unable to withstand a direct mortar hit. Amazingly, Porter never achieved a perfectly placed hit on a single Vicksburg cave. Nor is there evidence that his gunners purposely aimed at civilian caves. Their targets were entirely aboveground, though their hit list was quite rich: every habitation, every place of business, everything of military value.

Most cave dwellers were women and children. Romantic stories survived the war of resolute Southern women fitting out their caves with fine rugs, furniture, and wall hangings. Most caves, in fact, were damp, dreary, and dangerous. The Boston writer John T. Trowbridge, who visited the city after the war, called them "gopher holes," the name given them by Union soldiers.[124] Emma Balfour tried for a time to live in a densely crowded communal cave but was overwhelmed by "the sense of suffocation from being underground." Feeling "caged," she preferred to risk danger in the basement of her home rather than in a claustrophobic cave. Her husband had a private cave dug for her in the city's high clay hills but she rarely used it, fearing being buried alive.[125]

In caves like hers, families covered the damp dirt floor with wooden planks, sometimes overlaid with strips of old carpet, and slept on mattresses placed on barrels. Rats were a problem, as were malaria-carrying mosquitoes. When it rained, water seeped through the roof, and blankets and carpets had to be hung out.[126] It is no wonder families with caves preferred to live in them only when the bombs fell.

When Lida Lord and her family returned to Vicksburg with the rebel army defeated at the Big Black, they went straight to their old home, the rectory next to Dr. William Lord's Episcopal church. As the family was about to sit down to dinner, part of a mortar shell blew through the roof and landed in the center of their dining room, "crushing the well-spread table like an eggshell, and making a great yawning hole in the floor." [127] The following day Dr. Lord moved his family to a cave they had to share with eight other families and their slaves, "packed in . . . like sardines in a box."

That night the shelling was tremendous. Families huddled together, and as the ground under their feet began to shake, children screamed uncontrollably. "Candles were forbidden," Lida Lord recalled, "but we could easily see one another's faces by the lurid, lightning-like flashes of the bursting bombs." One of the mortar shells smashed into the roof of the cave, and "a great mass of crumbling earth" fell on a small child. Dr. Lord helped rescue her and then began making preparations to move his family. They relocated outside the city, near the Confederate lines, where they were safer, they believed, than in the city.

Soldiers helped them dig a cave, which was visited occasionally by rattlesnakes.[128]

After the war, Mark Twain talked with a married couple who had survived the siege in a cave. "Sometimes the caves were desperately crowded," the husband recalled, "and always hot and close. Sometimes a cave had twenty or twenty-five people packed into it; no turning-room for anybody; air so foul, sometimes, you couldn't have made a candle burn in it."[129]

A few people stayed out of the caves during an attack so they could track the path of the mortars. "Most shells were set with burning fuses," wrote Emma Balfour. "By day, they left a trail of smoke; by night, a trail of flame. They moved slowly and people could get out of the way."[130] Those intrepid enough to do this faced an additional threat. Porter often timed his bombardments to coincide with Grant's artillery assaults on the city. "We were between two fires," both equally threatening, wrote Balfour.[131]

"The Federals fought the garrison in part," but also "the city. . . . The city was a target in itself," wrote a Confederate soldier. Mortar fire was wildly inaccurate.[132] Every shell Porter's crews sent into the city was a blind shot. Targets were identified, but almost never hit exactly, and when fuses malfunctioned, mortar shells exploded before they hit the ground, throwing off shards of flaming metal that cut through roofs and walls, as happened at the Lord household. This was a consolation. By exploding in the air, the shells failed to achieve full effect. Had a great number of them landed where they were targeted, Vicksburg, a city built largely of wood, would have suffered catastrophic damage. But by landing nearly everywhere the shells served Porter's purpose. Vicksburg had become a city of women, and Porter intended to shake their resolve and undercut their moral and material support for the siege.

Union soldiers commented effusively on the bombing in their letters and diaries, and there was nearly universal support for it. "It may seem to some . . . that it was cruel and inhuman for the Union forces to fire on defenseless women and children, but what could we do; they were in the city and preferred to remain there to cheer on their husbands and brothers in their work of trying to destroy the Union," wrote Wilbur Crummer.[133] Federal soldiers on night duty in the trenches thrilled to the sight of the mortars raining fire on the secessionist citadel, a *splen-*

did sight," some called it, like shooting stars moving across the night sky and then falling suddenly "among the traitors." [134]

"I have heard that many women and children have been killed [in the city]," wrote Illinois general and distinguished jurist William Ward Orme. "It is their fault," he said, for refusing to leave the city when they had the opportunity. [135] Grant, too, had scant concern for the victims of the bombing. "Let me beg that every gunboat & every Mortar boat be brought to bear upon the city," he wrote Porter the evening after his second failed assault. [136] On June 16, he asked Porter to send him incendiary materials—sulfur, potassium nitrate, and powder—"so I can burn such of Vicksburg as may be desirable." Porter did not have a ready supply. [137]

Sherman said he pitied the "women & children . . . living in caves and holes underground whilst our shot & shells tear through their houses overhead." [138] But these same women, he added, "[are] praying that the Almighty or Joe Johnston will come & kill us." They had forgotten that treason had brought this awful fate down on them, he said. "They have sowed the wind & must reap the whirlwind." [139]

Late in the siege, General Alfred Ellet's Mississippi Marine Brigade, an amphibious assault force that had been training upriver, reached the fleet on May 29 and set up a battery of high-velocity Parrott rifled cannon on De Soto Point. Their accurate "missiles of death" punished the city with greater effect than Porter's mortars, knocking out Vicksburg's only iron foundry shortly after the guns were emplaced in late June. [140] They also fired on hospitals that conspicuously flew yellow warning flags. A shell exploded in one small hospital that Emma Balfour visited, and six patients had to have limbs amputated. [141] Both the Washington Hotel, converted into a military hospital easily visible to Federal artillerists, and the equally conspicuous Marine Hospital were hit by both Parrott and mortar fire.

At any time during the siege, there were several thousand sick and wounded soldiers in hospitals and care facilities located all over the city, and nearly all of these hospitals—every one of them flying a yellow flag—suffered damage. No count was kept of the casualties. [142] The gunners were not instructed to fire on hospitals, but they had to know that Porter and Grant considered the entire city a target. [143] "There is no safe place" in Vicksburg, said Confederate physician and diarist Joseph Dill

Alison, who went from hospital to hospital caring for the wounded. "Shot and shell in every direction. . . . Occasionally the wounded are killed in the hospitals" and surgeons "[are] wounded while attending to their duties."[144]

Sherman sent Porter a copy of the *Vicksburg Daily Citizen*, whose editor accused Porter of aiming at hospitals flying a yellow flag. Sherman saw the flags as a ruse. "They stream from nearly every house top" seeking relief from the bombs. "I hope you will keep up the Shelling to the maximum capacity day & night whilst we dig our trenches," he told Porter. We cannot "relax our grip."[145]

Parrott gunners also fired on churches. One Sunday in June, they spotted the congregation of the city's Catholic church filling the street after Mass and opened up on them. "Several persons were struck by fragments," wrote a witness, but no one was killed.[146] By late June, "Vicksburg was in a deplorable condition," wrote Alexander S. Abrams, a former reporter for the now defunct *Vicksburg Daily Whig*, who, as a soldier, had been wounded in the siege. "There was scarcely a building [that] had [not] been struck by the enemy's shells, while many of them were entirely demolished. The city had the appearance of a half-ruined pile of buildings."[147]

Confederate sergeant William H. Tunnard described Vicksburg at that time: "Palatial residences were crumbling into ruins, the walks torn up by mortar shells. . . . Fences were torn down and houses pulled to pieces for firewood. . . . An army of rats, seeking food," roamed the streets.[148]

As the siege wore on into early June, there were signs of mental distress. "Should the siege last a month longer there will have to be built . . . a building . . . for the accommodation . . . of maniacs," William Drennan, Pemberton's supply officer, wrote his wife. "I notice men on the street every day that I am satisfied are more or less becoming deranged. The constant tension of their nerves, the fear of their lives, and the continual roar of cannons and small arms, have made them fit subjects for the asylum."[149]

But civilian morale never broke, perhaps because casualties were lighter than expected. Trowbridge reported after the war that only three civilians were killed by mortar fire, but fragmentary records in Vicksburg archives put the number closer to a dozen.[150] Loyal parishioners continued to attend services at Dr. Lord's Episcopal church, though the church was "considerably injured," said Emma Balfour, "and was so filled with bricks, mortar and glass that it was difficult to find a place to sit." Women braved exploding shells to bring cooked meals to the soldiers on the line; and volunteer nurses tended to the sick and wounded. Once or twice a week the young single women of the city "made up riding-parties to the forts and trenches," recalled Lida Lord, "going in the twilight so that they could see and dodge the fuses of the shells." They brought the men homemade candy, knitted them socks, and patched their clothing. Older, married women invited the sick and wounded into their homes. Emma Balfour took in a soldier amputee suffering from acute battle fatigue. Her courage and equipoise lifted his spirits.[151]

Balfour was convinced that the Federals fired into the city "thinking they will wear out the women and children and sick, and Gen. Pemberton will be [forced] to surrender the place on that account." She "would be content to suffer martyrdom," she wrote, rather than let the Yankees know they were causing suffering in the city. She was not alone. When a petition was circulated asking Pemberton to request a short truce in order "to send the women and children beyond the lines," she joined a movement to kill it. Only three persons signed it.[152] "More than 50,000 shots have gone into that town . . ." General Sherman wrote his brother John late in the siege. "We must give them credit for courage & obstinacy. New York or Cincinnati, or St. Louis would have surrendered to such battering."[153]

The soldiers in the forts were the true heroes of the town. "The hot sun burned and blistered them," wrote Lida Lord, "while the freshly dug earth poisoned them with malaria. They were half starved, shaking with ague, and many of them afflicted with low fevers and dysenteric complaints."[154] On June 17, Hugh Moss, an infantryman who had been in Vicksburg since Farragut's bombardment, wrote, half despairingly, half exultantly, in his diary: "I almost despair of our holding out much longer; but inspired by the love of liberty, if there yet remains one drop of our forefathers' blood coursing through our veins, let us cry like the ancient Gauls—'Victory or death!' Let us not give up this place, for it is the main spring of the Confederacy."[155]

But there was only one more victory after the men in the forts had repulsed Grant's assaults. In late May Vicksburg's water battery sank the ironclad *Cincinnati* when it tried to knock out some big guns on Sherman's northern flank. "The glory of this victory was short-lived," wrote Confederate soldier Edward S. Gregory. A Union rescue party retrieved the ship's 9-inch guns and Porter had them shipped up the Yazoo and remounted on Sherman's line, to be used as siege guns. These "avenging" agents did more damage, and caused more fear, said Gregory, than Porter's monstrous machines.[156]

One name was on the lips of every soldier and citizen in the weeks after the *Cincinnati* episode: Joseph E. Johnston. "A new report [about him] is in circulation every morning," wrote William Drennan. " 'God send him quickly'—is the prayer of thousands." [157]

"Joseph E. Johnston was our angel of deliverance in those days of siege," recalled Lida Lord.[158]

CHAPTER 22

"The Crisis is on Us"

—Lieutenant William Drennan, CSA[1]

"In a week they will cave in." [2]

—William T. Sherman, June 27, 1863

The champion Vicksburg looked to for deliverance had no interest in saving the city. By the first week in June, Joseph Johnston had assembled an army of nearly twenty-three thousand at Canton, Mississippi, sixty-two miles northeast of Vicksburg. From Richmond, an anxiously intent Jefferson Davis pressed him to cut his way into Vicksburg and drive the invaders from his home soil. "Make a junction and carry in munitions," he wired Johnston.[3]*

"I am too weak to save Vicksburg," Johnston wired Pemberton in late May. "Can do no more than attempt to save you and your [army]." That required that he and Pemberton make what Johnston called "mutually supporting movements," with Johnston somehow covering Pemberton's army as it tried to break out of the city.[4] Johnston was asking the impossible. Grant's strangulating siege made it difficult for the two rebel commanders to communicate, let alone cooperate. Most of Johnston's messages were carried into the city by daredevil couriers who floated down the Mississippi at night on boards or in dugout canoes from swamps at the mouth of the Yazoo River. Night riders returned Pemberton's communiqués to him, but Grant's cavalry intercepted dozens of them.[5]

Johnston's proposal to have Pemberton cut his way out of the city

---

* On May 24, Pemberton and Johnston had, between them, 52,000 troops compared to Grant's 51,000. Bearss, *Unvexed to the Sea*, 978; OR, I/24, part 2, 86, 93; *ibid.*, part 3, 901–02.

deeply alarmed Davis and his cabinet. Secretary of War James Seddon warned him pointedly: "Vicksburg must not be lost without a desperate struggle. The interest and honor of the Confederacy forbid it. . . . If better resources do not offer, you must attack."⁶ But, unwilling to take on Grant without thousands of additional reinforcements, Johnston contented himself with sending out patrols to gauge his strength.

Desperate to save Vicksburg, Davis had briefly flirted with the idea of sending General James Longstreet, one of Robert E. Lee's corps commanders at Antietam and Fredericksburg, to the west to relieve pressure on Vicksburg. Longstreet had served under Johnston early in the war and greatly admired him. When Johnston took over command of the western theater in late 1862, Longstreet had wanted to be transferred to him, believing, as he did, that the war would be won or lost in the west. In a casual conversation with Longstreet in early May 1863, a week after Grant had crossed over into Mississippi, James Seddon suggested to him that his corps "might be needed to make the [Vicksburg] army strong enough to handle Grant." Longstreet took the bait, offering to put in for a transfer and take with him two divisions.⁷

But Lee killed the proposal. He was fashioning a plan to invade the North and could not afford to spare a single regiment to reinforce Johnston. It would be useless, in any event, to send troops to Mississippi, Lee warned Davis. They would arrive at the height of the disease season and would be forced "to retire," along with the rest of Grant's army.⁸ Pestilence would enfeeble the Union army as it had the Union navy the previous summer.

Only one member of Davis's cabinet opposed Lee's northern offensive: Postmaster General John Reagan, the only member from west of the Mississippi. This freed Lee to begin the march that would take him to Gettysburg and ended all efforts to massively reinforce Johnston. Davis simply didn't have the numbers.⁹

Grant, of course, knew nothing of this. He expected Johnston to be heavily reinforced and to come at him hard. The Confederate government would surely not cede control of the River of America without an all-out fight. In late May, Grant received reports that Johnston "was using every effort to increase [his strength] to forty thousand."¹⁰ Although Johnston would never have that many men, a division under Major General John Breckinridge did arrive in his camps from Tennessee on June 1, giving him twenty-eight thousand battle-ready troops. At that point, he and Pemberton together had fifty-eight thousand men to Grant's fifty-one thousand. If the two forces were to cooperate, Grant could be caught between them, but Johnston offered no such plan and Grant had Pemberton penned in.[11]

Johnston's cavalry was reportedly making menacing moves near the town of Mechanicsburg, about thirty miles northeast of Vicksburg, and this concerned Grant. When Johnston was ready to move he would "undoubtedly" approach Vicksburg through the Mechanicsburg corridor, a fertile valley running along the Yazoo River and terminating at Haynes' Bluff, Grant's principal supply station. Losing Haynes' Bluff would "compel me to abandon the investment of the City," Grant wrote with concern to General Hurlbut in Memphis. By ripping up rail lines around Jackson, Sherman had stripped Johnston of the iron arteries he needed to move his army quickly toward Vicksburg, but he could easily feed his marching men in the corn- and cattle-rich Yazoo basin.

Grant was never less secure during the entire war. Urgent calls went out to Halleck in Washington and Hurlbut in Tennessee to send every man they could spare.[12] So great was Grant's concern that he implored Nathaniel Banks on May 25 "to come with such force as you are able to spare. . . . All I want now are men."[13] But Banks was under even greater duress. Unknown to Grant, he had begun his investment of Port Hudson on May 22, taken severe losses, and had a letter on the way to Grant asking *him* for troops.[14]

Hurlbut and Halleck, however, would soon send Grant all the men he needed. By late June, he would have seventy-seven thousand troops, nineteen thousand more than Johnston and Pemberton combined. While this buildup was in progress, Grant's attention remained fixed on the Mechanicsburg corridor. He pulled General Osterhaus off the siege line and stationed his division along the Big Black River, east of Vicksburg, ordering him to burn all railroad bridges and tracks in the area and strip the country of livestock, cotton, and foodstuffs Johnston might use to support his army.[15]

Responding to what turned out to be wildly inaccurate reports of a sizable rebel buildup in the Mechanicsburg corridor, he sent General Frank Blair with twelve thousand men to the village of Satartia, a cotton port on the east bank of the Yazoo, near Mechanicsburg. Blair's orders were to "clean out the enemy" and on his return conduct a scorched earth campaign. Anything that could feed Johnston's army was to be destroyed. Roads were to be blocked by fallen timber and bridges burned once he crossed them on his return.[16]

Blair found no enemy force of consequence in the area, and the countryside he marched through on his way to Mechanicsburg "contained," he said, "little or no forage or provisions." He returned, therefore, by a wagon road along the Yazoo, an area believed to be "teeming with agricultural riches."[17]

"[It] is one of the most fertile spots I ever saw," he wrote Grant excitedly after entering the valley. "We found supplies and forage sufficient to supply Joe Johnston's army for a month. . . . I used all that I could and destroyed the rest." His men burned half a million bushels of corn, destroyed every gristmill they passed, and brought back nearly a thousand head of cattle, three hundred horses and mules, and an "army of negroes" equal to the number of men in his command. Our army was "not out of sight of burning buildings and granaries for two entire days," wrote a soldier on the expedition.[18]

The ravaging Grant ordered was "not only necessary in itself, but justified by the laws of war," wrote the *New York Times*, a clear indication of how far public opinion had swung since the limited war fought in the east by McClellan and Hooker. The *Times* called Blair's campaign "justifiable devastation."[19] It was the kind of economic warfare General Steele had waged months earlier in the Greenville area, and it was a prefiguring of Sherman's march of ruin through Georgia and the Carolinas.[20]

Blair ended his report with a warning. While Johnston had not yet moved as far as Mechanicsburg, information gathered from locals indicated that he was massing at Canton for a major strike through the Yazoo Valley. "Every man we picked up was going to Canton to join him." Mechanicsburg, said Blair, was "the great strategic point between the two rivers"—the Yazoo and the Big Black. It was only three miles from Satartia, and Johnston could supply his army from that excellent river port.[21]

When Blair returned to Haynes' Bluff, Grant sent a brigade and twelve hundred cavalry to Mechanicsburg under Brigadier General

Nathan Kimball, an Indiana physician in peacetime. Kimball was to "watch the movements of the enemy" and carry forward Blair's campaign of pillage and expropriation.[22] But even-tempered Nat Kimball was not Frank Blair. When the rebels occupied Yazoo City, thirty miles upriver from Satartia, he retreated in haste to Vicksburg.[23] Grant was furious, and decided to go to Satartia to personally assess rebel strength in the area. On June 6, he and Charles Dana boarded the army steamer *Diligent* and headed upstream. It was the first and only time Grant left the Vicksburg siege lines.

The night before the trip, John Rawlins had written Grant a scolding letter about his drinking. Grant had not been feeling well, bothered perhaps by recurring migraines he suffered throughout the war, and Sherman's doctor had prescribed wine to numb the pain. When Rawlins heard about this, he discovered a box of wine in front of Grant's tent. Grant was keeping it, he told Rawlins lamely, for a future date, to celebrate the fall of Vicksburg with friends. Then, the evening before he left for Satartia, Rawlins found him in the company of officers who were drinking and were known to tempt Grant to do the same.[24] Rawlins strode back to his tent and drafted a letter reminding Grant of the pledge he had made to him the previous March to abstain from alcohol for the remainder of the war.[25] On a copy of this letter, he would add later: "Its admonitions were heeded and all went well."[26] All did not go well.

Shortly after boarding *Diligent*, Grant got "as stupidly drunk as the immortal nature of man would allow," Dana wrote later.[27] He was helped to his stateroom and put to bed. When the steamer approached Satartia, two of Porter's gunboats spotted Grant's personal flag and hailed the captain. The naval officers came aboard and asked to see the general. Informed he was sick and sleeping soundly, they warned Dana that rebels were in the area and Satartia was unsafe.[28] On his own, Dana made the decision to return to Haynes' Bluff. Grant emerged from his cabin the next morning "fresh as a rose" and asked Dana if they were at Satartia.[29]

While they both lived, Grant and Dana never made to each other "the slightest reference" to the Satartia "excursion," James Wilson wrote in his biography of Dana, "nor did Dana report it to Stanton"—a violation of his agreement to inform him "if Grant was drinking to excess."[30]

In the late 1880s, the correspondent Sylvanus Cadwallader, then a sheep farmer in California, began writing an account of his three years with Grant. It was an admiring and balanced portrait, offering penetrating insight into Grant's character, but Cadwallader was never able to find a publisher. Grant, who died in 1885, was at the peak of his fame, revered as the general who had won the war, secured the peace, and authored—in excruciating pain from cancer of the throat and tongue—an autobiography that rises to the level of literature. Cadwallader's book threatened to darken his legacy with what publishers suspected was a highly sensationalized account of a drinking incident on a remote Mississippi stream.

Cadwallader's book, *Three Years with Grant*, was belatedly published in 1955 to great acclaim by eminent Civil War historians, among them Shelby Foote and William McFeely, author of a Pulitzer Prize–winning biography of Grant. It's as controversial today as it was when publishers originally turned it down. A number of historians—not all of them Grant hagiographers—dismiss Cadwallader's account of the general's drinking spree as "a greatly embellished lie."[31]* Some claim Cadwallader was not even on board *Diligent* to witness what he described in lurid detail. As evidence, they point to a letter Dana wrote to Wilson in 1890 stating flatly: "Cadwallader was not along."[32]

They may be wrong. A reporter from the *Chicago Times*, Cadwallader's paper, sent a dispatch from Satartia on the night of June 6, at ten o'clock. Cadwallader was the only *Times* correspondent in the Vicks-

---

* James Wilson, who tried to help Cadwallader find a publisher, found the manuscript pages "so interesting," he told Cadwallader, "that I have read them through from end to end without stopping except to eat and sleep. They are most valuable and interesting, more so historically than any memoirs of the period of the Civil war, that have yet been published." The "details" on Grant's drinking were, he said, "a revelation . . . Your description of Grant's drunkenness during the Satartia trip is most graphic, and more in detail than I have heard before." Wilson to Cadwallader, February 15, March 10, 1905; Cadwallader to Wilson, December 2, 1907; Wilson to Cadwallader, August 29, 1906, Wilson Papers, LC.

burg area, making it likely he was on Grant's steamer, at least on its return to Vicksburg.[33]

Cadwallader's highly colored account of the drinking incident differs markedly from Dana's spare, almost dismissive description of it in his autobiography. Dana and Cadwallader start off perfectly in sync. After Grant had made several trips to the bar he "became," in Cadwallader's words, "stupid in speech and staggering in gait." From this point forward Cadwallader's story devolves into melodrama, with the judicious reporter acting as the sole guardian of Grant's reputation—having the captain refuse Grant any more whiskey, escorting him to his stateroom, locking himself in the room, tossing whiskey bottles out a window, and fanning the general to sleep.[34]

When they returned to Chickasaw Bayou near sundown, Grant, according to Cadwallader, continued to drink aboard a sutler's boat docked beside them, whose captain dispensed free liquor to all officers. When Grant had his fill, he mounted the horse of one of his aides, "gave him the spur," and sped off on a wild ride into the depths of the Yazoo swamp, through several Union camps and past army guards posted at bridges. Cadwallader claims he overtook Grant, seized the reins, and forced him to dismount and lie down on the grass "with the saddle for a pillow." He then persuaded one of Grant's escorts, who had been frantically searching for him, to report to Rawlins and have him send an ambulance so Grant would not be seen riding into camp hideously drunk. Rawlins was supposedly waiting for them when they arrived around midnight. To Cadwallader's amazement, Grant coolly stepped down from the ambulance, straightened his vest, bade him and Rawlins good night, and "started to his tent as steadily as he ever walked in his life."

Cadwallader adds that in the ambulance on the way back to his tent, Grant had told him that henceforth he would consider him a staff officer with power to give orders "in his name"—a story that appears patently preposterous.[35]

The entire story, in fact, looks fishy. Not a single person on record witnessed Grant's alcohol-fueled ride, which had to have been seen by scores of soldiers in the camps through which he tore. And there is nothing in Rawlins's correspondence or papers about encountering

Grant at midnight after his drinking escapade. Perhaps Cadwallader, who was displeased with Grant for undervaluing his friend John Rawlins in his memoirs, had heard the Satartia story from Dana or Rawlins and fantastically embellished it, as Grant biographer Ron Chernow suggests.[36] Or perhaps some, but not all, of this legendary Grant drinking story is in fact true.

In Franc Wilkie's wartime autobiography, *Pen and Powder*, published in 1888, the highly regarded *New York Times* correspondent gives an account of the Satartia inspection trip that is strikingly similar—minus the bottle throwing, the wild ride through the soldiers' camps, and the midnight encounter with Rawlins—to Cadwallader's published account. Wilkie heard of the Satartia incident from a high-ranking Union officer, "one in whom," he says, "General Grant had a wonderful personal interest." As Wilkie tells it, Grant and a group of officers got drunk on a demijohn of whiskey one of them had smuggled aboard *Diligent*. When the little steamer returned from Satartia, horses were waiting for Grant and his staff. Impatient to get back to camp, Grant climbed, with "considerable difficulty," on a spirited mount and rode off, with Cadwallader in hot pursuit. At a sharp turn in the road, he fell from his horse. Cadwallader dragged him from the road, out of sight from his staff, and then rode to camp, secured an ambulance, and took him back to his quarters. Wilkie makes no mention of a Grant-Rawlins encounter.

Cadwallader received repayment in kind, says Wilkie. "Mr. Cadwallader was an excellent correspondent, but he went much higher in the confidence of the commander-in-chief than he would have . . . based on his letters to the newspapers." Cadwallader became the only correspondent Grant permitted at his headquarters, and he had unusual, almost exclusive, access to Grant and Rawlins. "'Cad' was persona grata in camp. . . . Any one who bore the stamp of John A. [Rawlins'] indorsement [sic] was admitted to the comradeship of our official family," recalled Captain Samuel H. Beckwith, Grant's telegraph and cipher officer later in the war.[37]

At Vicksburg, Cadwallader's tent was close to Grant's, "within sight," wrote Cadwallader, "of all Gen. Grant's personal movements." He also had permission to deposit his dispatches in Grant's mail pouch, for expedited delivery to the telegraph station at Cairo, giving him a decided advantage over his "less fortunate competitors."[38] He had gained this position of trust, Wilkie suggests, because of his inside knowledge of Grant's embarrassing episode on the Yazoo expedition, which he kept to himself into advanced old age.[39]

Cadwallader was no sensationalist. Unwilling to jeopardize Grant's public reputation, he never spoke of the Satartia trip during the war to anyone except Rawlins and a "very few friends and relatives of Grant's to whom Rawlins first told the story." By not cutting the Satartia incident from his book, he probably jeopardized his chances to have it published. "The question arises in my mind," he wrote James Wilson in 1907, "whether reference to Grant's drinking habits on that Satartia trip, and others, would come with good grace from me at this late date."[40] He wrote about his relations with Grant honestly and fairly, he assured Wilson, and revealed not half "of what might be truly written . . . about [Grant's] habit of intemperance."[41] Wilson urged him to publish the manuscript as written; and in Wilson's biography of Dana, based closely on his conversations with his friend, he wrote this: "The actual facts" of the Satartia "episode are given in great detail by S. Cadwallader, in an unpublished volume."[42]

Coming from Wilson, this suggests the fundamental truthfulness of Cadwallader's account, its embellishments aside. No one in the Union camp, with the exception of Rawlins, more closely scrutinized Grant's drinking than James Wilson—like Rawlins, a teetotaler. "There are lots of men" in Grant's army "who whenever they get a chance . . . tempt their chief [to drink], and I want you to help me clean them out," Rawlins had told Wilson shortly after the young engineering officer joined Grant's inner circle back in Tennessee. This "sealed our friendship," Wilson wrote, "and united us on a common cause as long as we lived."[43]

None of this makes Cadwallader's account *entirely* convincing. As an old man writing in rich detail about distant events, he undoubtedly made a number of implausible enhancements. But he "was not likely," wrote William McFeely, to have forgotten the "essentials" of the Satartia episode, "and little about the story, including his claim to have been aboard, fails to make sense, unless one is flatly determined to refuse to believe that Ulysses was ever drunk."[44]

The full story of the Satartia trip will never be known. The colliding tales are irreconcilable and none can be verified with certainty. What is certain, and historically significant, is that Grant was falling-down drunk at a pivotal point in the Vicksburg campaign. Dana and Sherman both make the claim, repeated by countless biographers, that Grant never drank when his army was in peril or "any thing was pending." The Satartia trip, Dana wrote, took place during "a dull period in the campaign."[45] It was anything but that. Grant was on edge. He expected Johnston to pounce at any moment, and he would not have gone to Satartia had he not thought the situation critical. Chernow has it right: "The story of the Yazoo bender was an isolated case of Grant's drinking in a dangerous war zone where enemy forces were concentrated."[46]

But the last word on Grant's drinking—and perhaps on Grant the man—is from the pen of William T. Sherman. "We all knew at the time that Genl Grant would occasionally drink too much—" Sherman wrote an old army friend in 1887. "He always encouraged me to talk to him frankly of this & and other things and I always noticed that he could with an hours sleep wake up perfectly sober & bright. . . .

"Grant's whole character was a mystery even to himself—a combination of strength and weakness not paralleled by any of whom I have read in Ancient or Modern History."[47]

The missing voice in the Satartia story is Grant's. This self-enclosed man was not emotionally able to write about his inner struggles. "I always felt that there was an unfathomable depth to Grant," Cadwallader wrote to James Wilson in 1887. Despite "my long and intimate acquaintance with him I was obliged to acknowledge to myself that I did not quite know nor wholly understand his character. There was always something in him withheld or kept back."[48]

On the morning Grant returned from Satartia, he heard alarming news: A rebel raiding party had attacked Milliken's Bend and was turned back after a terrific firefight in which four black regiments fought bravely but might have been slaughtered had not Porter's gunboats arrived.

Urged on by Jefferson Davis, trans-Mississippi commander General Edmund Kirby Smith had ordered the raid to relieve pressure on Pemberton by destroying what he mistakenly thought was the Union army's main supply post, not realizing Grant had moved it to the Yazoo. Smith had put Major General Richard Taylor, a Louisiana sugar planter,

Yale College graduate, and son of former President Zachary Taylor, in charge of the operation. He was given a Texas division under General John G. Walker, "Walker's Greyhounds," and ordered to lead them to Richmond, Louisiana, ten miles south of Milliken's Bend.

Taylor had no enthusiasm for the operation. Even if successful, the raid, he believed, would do nothing to weaken Grant's stranglehold on Vicksburg. But "I was informed that all the Confederate authorities in the east were urgent for some effort on our part in behalf of Vicksburg, and that public opinion would condemn us if we did not *try to do something.*" [49]

At Richmond, Louisiana, Taylor divided his five thousand men into three assault groups, which were to attack simultaneously Grant's former military camps in Louisiana: Milliken's Bend, Young's Point, and, if feasible, Lake Providence. At the time they were auxiliary supply depots and training grounds for newly recruited black soldiers. [50] General Henry E. McCulloch led the strike against Milliken's Bend. His scouts reported seeing "a negro brigade of uncertain strength" holding the Bend, screened by some Illinois cavalry. It looked like it would be a cakewalk. On the evening of June 6, his strike force moved out, the withering heat making a night march desirable. [51]

The African American soldiers at the Bend were former slaves in the initial stages of training. None had handled a firearm until they were outfitted only three weeks earlier. In rifle practice, "when one of them would accidentally hit [the target] he would be as proud as if he had killed his overseer," recalled David Cornwell, a young white officer in charge of training the 9th Louisiana Infantry Regiment (African Descent). [52]

Brigadier General Elias S. Dennis, commander of Union forces in northeast Louisiana, had been expecting an attack on Milliken's Bend. Rebel troops had been spotted streaming into the area. Colonel Hermann Lieb, acting commander at Milliken's Bend, claimed they were headed toward his camp with bad intent, having driven back cavalry he had sent to locate them. Dennis hurried his best combat regiment, the 23rd Iowa, to the Bend on the afternoon of June 6 and asked Porter for naval support. The admiral sent *Choctaw*, one of his mightiest gunboats. It arrived at the Bend that evening. [53]

At three in the morning on June 7, McCulloch's brigade was within a mile or so of the Union camp. Lieb awaited him, his men stacked up behind a ten-foot-high levee crowned with cotton-bale breastworks. (The 23rd Iowa—about 120 men strong—remained in a steamer docked at the levee and would not join the fight until after the opening salvos.) McCulloch had about fifteen hundred troops, the Federals just over eleven hundred, but nearly nine hundred of them were black trainees shouldering badly outdated firearms, some of them issued the day before the battle.[54]

After clawing their way through rows of thick hedges, the rebels fixed bayonets and came on "solid, strong and steady."[55] Hit by a crushing volley, they wavered, but quickly regrouped and let out "yells that would make faint hearts quail," said the chaplain of one of the black regiments.[56] "This charge was resisted by the negro portion of the enemy's force with considerable obstinacy, while the white or true Yankee portion ran like whipped curs almost as soon as the charge was ordered," McCulloch admitted later.[57] After a disorganized close-quarters fight, the Federals were driven back with heavy losses to a second and higher levee, close to the riverbank. "We . . . turned loose our war dogs and . . . they howled!" recalled one of Walker's Greyhounds. "We clubbed guns, bayoneted, cut with the sword, until the enemy fled helter, skelter."[58] At least one of the advancing rebels carried a flag emblazed with a death's head and crossbones, signifying no mercy.[59]

When the Texans reached the top of this levee, they let out a shout—"No quarter"—and lit into the enemy.[60] The fighting was medieval. Few shots rang out. Rifle butts and bayonets were the principal killing instruments.[61] "White and black men were laying side by side, pierced by bayonets, and in some instances, transfixed to the earth," reported a correspondent who arrived after the battle. Two men, one black, the other white, were found dead, "side by side, each having the other's bayonet through his body."[62] The black troops might have preferred this kind of close-in fighting, where their poor marksmanship mattered not at all. "With the bayonet they were equal to the whites," observed historian David H. Slay.[63] It was, said the *Chicago Tribune*, a contest between "enraged men," one side motivated by racial hatred, the other by self-preservation and revenge for past injustices.[64]

When the rebels appeared victorious around four o'clock, the men rashly exposing themselves by firing indiscriminately from the top of the second levee, *Choctaw's* gun crews began sawing them down with shells weighing up to one hundred pounds. The rebels fell back, out of range of the guns, and no amount of encouragement could get them to rush the levee.[65] Around nine o'clock the old timberclad *Lexington* appeared. Seeing he was hopelessly outgunned, McCulloch withdrew after a seven-hour fight in ninety-eight-degree heat.[66] "Unfortunately, I discovered too late that the officers and men of this division were possessed of a dread of gunboats such as pervaded our people at the commencement of the war," Richard Taylor wrote cuttingly in his official report.[67] This was unfair: Walker's Texans would have been decimated had they stayed any longer.

The cost of holding was staggering. The Federals lost 492 men— 43 percent of the 1,148 present for duty that morning. All but 65 of the fallen were African Americans.[68] The 9th Louisiana was the hardest hit of the African American units, losing an astounding 68 percent of its force—195 of its 285 men. The number killed in action, 66, was the highest by any regiment in a single day in the Vicksburg campaign. McCulloch claimed 185 men lost.[69] A white Union officer who had seen plenty of combat said it was the worst fight he was ever in.[70] The other two rebel operations planned for that day against Lake Providence and Young's Point were called off because of overpowering Union strength, the appearance, at Young's Point, of Porter's ironclads, and rebel disorganization.[71]

After the battle, Porter went to Milliken's Bend on his flagship and "saw," he reported, "quite an ugly sight. The dead negroes lined the ditch inside of the . . . levee, and were mostly shot on the top of the head. In front of them, close to the levee, lay an equal number of rebels stinking in the sun."[72]

"This was the first important engagement of the war in which colored troops were under fire," Grant wrote later.[73] If led by good officers, "they will make good troops," he assured Lorenzo Thomas.[74*]

---

* Grant was careful to use the term "important engagement." Black troops had first fought against Confederates in a skirmish at Island Mound, in Bates County in western Missouri, on October 29, 1862. Most of the blacks were escaped slaves. Eight Union combatants were killed: a white man, six blacks, and a Cherokee. NYT, November 19, 1862.

"I never more wish to hear the expression—'The niggers won't fight,'" wrote Lieutenant M. M. Miller, a white officer with the 9th Louisiana. "Come with me 100 yards from where I sit," he wrote his family from near the bloodied levee at Milliken's Bend, "and I can show you the wounds that cover the bodies of [men] as brave, loyal and patriotic . . . as ever drew bead on a rebel. . . . I never saw a better company of men in my life."[75] Word spread rapidly through the Federal camps, and opinions began to change.

"I am happy to report that the sentiment of this army with regard to the employment of negro troops has been revolutionized by the bravery of the blacks in the recent battle of Milliken's Bend," Dana informed Edwin Stanton. "Prominent officers who used in private to sneer at the idea, are now heartily in favor of it."[76] That was overstated: The change was not as complete as Dana indicated, and Grant, although firmly committed to raising black units, refused to use them as front-line infantry; he also allowed wounded blacks to be segregated from whites on hospital ships.[77] But Milliken's Bend did alter opinions at Vicksburg, where men greeted reports from across the river with enthusiasm. Even a number of deeply biased soldiers came around, in their own crude way. "The nigs did very well," Lieutenant George Buck informed his sister back in Illinois. "A fellow from there told me that the nigs fought better than one Regt of the whites."[78]

It was a victory, too, for the emancipationists in the Army of the Tennessee. "Arm the negroes and let them fight for their liberty!" Iowa sergeant Alexander G. Downing declaimed in his diary.[79] That spring and summer, African Americans fought at Port Hudson, Louisiana; and Fort Wagner, South Carolina, where the 54th Massachusetts Infantry Regiment, commanded by Boston abolitionist Robert Gould Shaw, led the assault on the rebel ramparts. But only at Milliken's Bend did African American troops make up the majority of Union soldiers in the fight.[80]

Coverage of Milliken's Bend was either suppressed or badly distorted in Southern papers, but news about the battle spread by word-of-mouth in the Louisiana low country and reached the family of Kate Stone in the town of Monroe, preparing to leave for Texas. "It is hard to believe that Southern soldiers—and Texans at that—have been whipped by a mongrel crew of white and black Yankees," Kate told her diary. "There must be some mistake." Later that night, she returned to her diary: "It is said the Negro regiments fought there like mad demons, but we cannot believe that. We know from long experience they are cowards."[81]

Rumors spread that there had been payback. The day after the battle, General Alfred Ellet's Mississippi Marine Brigade landed near Milliken's Bend and found the bodies of men they believed to be white officers captured at the Bend. "In many cases," said a *Chicago Tribune* correspondent, "these bodies had been nailed to trees and crucified." Fires were built around the trees and the men "suffered a slow death from broiling. The charred and partially burned limbs were still fastened to the stakes." African American prisoners who were recaptured from the rebels "confirmed these facts," said the reporter. The story ran under the headline "Rebel Barbarism."[82]

The report remains unsubstantiated, but there is circumstantial evidence that a white officer captured at the Bend, Captain Corydon Heath, was murdered by Taylor's soldiers. Heath and other officers captured with him never appeared on prisoner of war lists. When Union troops in the Richmond area picked up a Confederate deserter, Thomas Cormal, he claimed to have witnessed Heath's hanging at the hands of rebel soldiers at Richmond. Taylor and his command "were drawn up to witness" Heath's execution, Cormal said, adding that a white sergeant who commanded a company of black troops captured by rebel cavalry was hanged at Perkins plantation.[83]

If these atrocities were, in fact, committed, the Confederate government bears some responsibility. On May 31, the Confederate States Congress authorized the execution of white officers commanding black troops, accusing them of inciting "servile insurrection."[84] Months before this, the legislature, infuriated by the Emancipation Proclamation, had declared that captured "negroes in arms" were to be handed over to state authorities for sentencing.[85]

When Grant learned of the alleged atrocities he wrote Taylor, asking him directly if he was responsible.[86] Taylor was outraged. The stories, he said, were complete fabrications. "My orders at all times have been to treat prisoners with every consideration."[87] Grant took Taylor at his word and dropped the issue. The newspaper reports were "entirely sensational," he told Halleck and Stanton when they pointedly inquired.[88] Alone among Union commanders, Porter demanded brutal closure. "Taylor should be hung himself on the spot if ever taken," he wrote

Grant.[89] It was left to Lincoln to take the proper course of action. On July 30, he declared an eye-for-an-eye policy. If the Confederates executed a Union soldier, one of their soldiers would suffer an equal fate. If a black soldier were enslaved, a Confederate soldier would be placed at hard labor.[90]

The battle at Milliken's Bend interrupted for a day an official army inquiry into the behavior of a white officer stationed there: Colonel Isaac F. Shepard, a Harvard graduate who had been editor of a small Boston newspaper and a member of the Massachusetts legislature. In early May, Lorenzo Thomas had appointed Shepard commander of the yet to be organized 1st Mississippi Regiment (African Descent), to be posted at Milliken's Bend.[91] Shepard, vigilant and decisive, set out to expose and punish white soldiers known to mistreat black recruits and their families, who resided in a nearby contraband camp.[92] When a drunken white soldier, Private John O'Brien, entered the camp with a fellow soldier and tried to rape a ten-year-old girl in front of her mother and then assaulted her hundred-year-old grandmother, along with a boy of fourteen, Shepard ordered him whipped by black soldiers from the 1st Mississippi.[93] Word spread quickly, and outraged officers from O'Brien's regiment demanded that Shepard publicly apologize for disgracing "the service, his country, cause and humanity."[94] General Jeremiah Sullivan, their commander, arrested him.

Shepard wrote Grant requesting a court of inquiry, which convened at Milliken's Bend on June 4, three days before the battle.[95] In his defense, Shepard brought forward explosive, thickly documented charges against other white soldiers who had gone unpunished. Numbers of them had used their fists and knives on black troops who refused to remove their hats when passing them. White soldiers had raped black girls of ten and eleven and sexually assaulted the wives of black soldiers "before their husbands' eyes." Negro quarters had been regularly looted and burned, and black civilians in the area had been murdered. "These outrages have passed with almost utter impunity," Shepard notified Grant.[96]

While the court deliberated, Shepard violated his arrest order by standing with his men at the Battle of Milliken's Bend. Several days later he was exonerated. Grant restored him to command but rejected his request to have the transcript of the inquiry published, seeing "no good purpose to be . . . served" by its dissemination.[97] It might provide ammunition to the enemy.

Grant later recommended Shepard for promotion to brigadier general, but the U.S. Senate, perhaps under pressure from army officials in Washington, failed to act on the request, and Shepard was denied what he deserved.[98]

On June 17, ten days after the Battle of Milliken's Bend, Sherman called Grant's attention to an item in a Memphis newspaper. It was a copy of a congratulatory order, dated May 30, that McClernand had supposedly read to the men in his XIII Corps after the second failed assault on Vicksburg's fortifications. It was bombastic and self-congratulatory, in line with what Cadwallader called McClernand's "uncontrollable itching for newspaper notoriety." Only this time he went too far, assailing Grant for authoring a deeply flawed military plan and Sherman and McPherson for inadequately supporting his own final push to take two rebel forts in his sector. Sherman and McPherson pressed for McClernand's removal. His congratulatory order violated both War Department and Grant's own regulations forbidding officers from publishing official letters and reports without clearance. The congratulatory order was "addressed," Sherman said, "not to an army, but to a constituency in Illinois."[99]

Grant sent the newspaper account to McClernand and asked if it was a "true copy."[100] It was, said McClernand, who blamed his adjutant for not sending Grant a copy "promptly as he ought & I thought had."[101] It was the end of the line for John McClernand. Within the hour, Grant had drafted the order relieving him from command of the XIII Army Corps and appointing in his stead Sherman's roommate at West Point, Major General E. O. C. Ord, a skilled engineer and tactician who had been gravely wounded in Tennessee.[102]

"Though the congratulatory Address . . . is the occasion of Gen McClernand's removal, it is not its cause as McClernand intimates . . ." Dana wired Secretary Stanton. "That cause . . . is his repeated disobedience of important orders—his general insubordinate disposition, and his palpable incompetency for the duties of the position." Above all, he was unable to get along with his other corps commanders. If Grant were disabled McClernand would have taken over, and this would have created "most pernicious consequences to the cause." [103]

This is both true and misleading. Grant was also concerned about the message's potential "to create dissention and ill feeling in the Army." [104] Grant told Halleck he "should have relieved [McClernand] long since for general unfitness for his position." Here he went too far. Although a difficult and often insubordinate commander, he was a bull on the battlefield. Grant had entrusted him, over McPherson and Sherman, to get his army through the flooded Louisiana bayous to a landing site below Grand Gulf, and his corps did the burden of the fighting at Port Gibson and the Big Black Bridge. But now with the Army of the Tennessee poised to deliver the final blow against Vicksburg, Grant had no great need for McClernand. The congratulatory message was a perfect excuse to rid the army of a commander who had been conspiring to have Grant removed since the beginning of the great river campaign. Slow to anger, Grant never forgot—and rarely forgave—disloyalty.

Grant twisted the knife by having James Wilson deliver the career-crushing news to McClernand. Before the war, Wilson had had close ties with McClernand, who had served in his father's company in the Black Hawk War. When Wilson joined Grant's army he had tried to present McClernand in a "favorable light at headquarters," but over time Wilson came to despise him for his choleric temper and underhanded efforts to subvert Grant's authority. Recently, he had nearly come to blows with him when McClernand objected in violent language to an order from Grant that Wilson delivered to him in the field. [105] "I'll be God damned if I'll do it—I am tired of being dictated to," McClernand supposedly shouted. When McClernand turned his ire on Wilson, the young colonel threatened to pull him from his horse and "beat the boots" off him. McClernand apologized, but Wilson was still fuming about the confrontation when he got his chance for cold revenge by delivering to him the last order he would ever receive from Ulysses Grant. [106]

On the afternoon of June 18, Wilson presented a sealed envelope to McClernand, who was seated at a table in his headquarters tent, in full dress uniform, his sword lying across from him. When McClernand finished reading the letter, he turned to Wilson and bellowed, "Well sir! I am relieved!" Then, knowing Wilson's feeling: "My God, sir, we are both relieved!"[107] McClernand was to proceed to Illinois and await orders from the War Department. There he waged a full-scale campaign to retain his command but was unable to convince Lincoln to order a court of inquiry.[108] He served out the war as a corps commander in Banks's Army of the Gulf.

Although a hard campaigner, McClernand had never been an efficient administrator of his corps, nor did he harmonize with his subordinates or his fellow corps commanders. Ord's appointment "materially increased the efficiency of the Thirteenth Corps," William Le Baron Jenney recalled.[109] Grant considered the change "better than 10,000 reinforcements."[110]

Four days after McClernand's removal, Grant received reports that Joseph Johnston had crossed the Big Black River and was massing "to raise the siege."[111] It was false intelligence, but Grant acted on it with alacrity, ordering Sherman to take command of all army forces from Haynes' Bluff to the Big Black. Firmly convinced now that Johnston would attack from the east, across the Big Black—rather than from the north, through the Mechanicsburg corridor—Grant assigned two additional divisions to Sherman. With his thirty-four thousand Union soldiers and cavalry, two thousand more than Grant had brought to Champion Hill, Sherman built a veritable human wall in the rear of the Vicksburg siege lines. "The rear fortifications of Gen. Grant are of stupendous extent and strength," observed the *New York Times*. "Those at Haines' Bluff . . . have been constructed by three hundred escaped slaves, formerly the property of Joseph and Jefferson Davis."[112]

The continuous stream of reinforcements Halleck sent to Mississippi also allowed Grant to close the gap on the southern end of his siege lines, all the way to Warrenton, on the Mississippi River.[113] "A cat could not have crept out of Vicksburg without being discovered," said a rebel soldier.[114] For the first time in the siege, Grant felt at ease. "Have the enemy closely hemmed in all around," he wrote his father on June 15.[115] With things looking "highly favorable," he invited Julia and the children to join him. He and Fred were eager to see them. Grant had bought a pony for his two youngest children and wanted to see how they handled it.[116]

Unknown to Grant, Johnston had delivered to Pemberton, on June 22, a depressing dispatch: escape across the river and join Taylor and his forces in Louisiana. "I will . . . try to make a diversion in your favor."[117] It was an outlandish and irresponsible directive by a commander who had no true understanding of Pemberton's predicament. Pemberton had no shipping; Porter completely commanded the river; and Ellet's marines controlled the riverbank directly across from Vicksburg. When a gossipy rebel picket told his Federal counterpart that Pemberton had begun to tear down houses to obtain wood to build two thousand small boats to carry his army to Louisiana under the cover of darkness, word reached Grant, who passed the report to Porter.[118]* Pemberton never seriously considered a river crossing, but Porter prepared for it nonetheless. He planned to illuminate the river with hundreds of tar barrels, and placed Ellet's sharpshooters and artillerists and nine of his own gunboats on maximum alert, ready to turn to splinters what would have been Pemberton's pathetically vulnerable wooden fleet.[119]

Meanwhile, Grant finally decided to call off the siege and bust through into Vicksburg. By the last week of June, ten of his saps were within ten to two hundred yards of the enemy's forts. The best chance for a breakthrough was at the 3rd Louisiana Redan, which guarded the Jackson Road, the old country trace that led straight to the center of town. The men in McPherson's sap were almost close enough to the rebel fort to shake hands with their adversaries.[120]

Since daybreak on May 26, three hundred troops from John Logan's division of McPherson's corps, working in hundred-man shifts, had been digging a trench toward the Louisiana Redan, under the direction of the corps' self-trained engineer, Captain Andrew Hickenlooper. The trenching operation began near a white-frame structure known as the

---

* "Afterwards this story was verified;" Grant wrote in his memoirs. "On entering the city we found a large number of very rudely constructed boats." (USGM, 373). While his men undoubtedly saw these boats, there is no evidence that Pemberton planned a massive riverine escape. (USGM, 373.)

Shirley house, located some four hundred yards from the redan.* Beginning on June 5, a strange-looking sap-roller began protecting the crews from enemy sharpshooters. Soldiers called it Logan's Gunboat. It was a railroad flatcar stacked high with several dozen bales of cotton, with loopholes in the cotton for riflemen. It had wooden wheels, and sappers pushed it along with bars attached to its wooden axles.[121]

By the first week of June, Logan's sappers had reached a commanding knoll about 130 yards from the redan, where soldiers set up a small artillery emplacement dubbed Battery Hickenlooper. Its two Parrott rifles blew gaping holes in the earthen fort. By the second week of June, the ditch itself was only seventy yards from the rebel fort. This exposed the digging crews to plunging fire from the high parapets of the redan, commanded by General Louis Hébert.

Indiana soldiers led by ace sharpshooter Lieutenant Henry "Coonskin" Foster—named for the distinctive fur hat he wore even in the searing heat—countered by building, under cover of night, an ungainly looking tower of iron rails, about twelve feet high, with steps built on its inside. "Coonskin Tower" overlooked the Louisiana Redan, and Foster hid himself at the top and killed more Confederates in less than a week "than any company of sharpshooters in the army," said a Chicago reporter with more than a hint of hyperbole.[122] Rebel artillerists could have easily destroyed the tower, but they dared not expose the barrels of their guns with Hickenlooper's Parrotts pointed directly at them.

On June 8, with Logan's crews only sixty feet from the redan, "a private soldier," recalled Samuel Lockett, "suggested a novel expedient. He took a piece of 'port-fire' "—a handheld fuse used for firing cannons— "stuffed it with cotton saturated with turpentine and fired it from an old-fashioned large-bore musket into the roller, and thus set it on fire." Within minutes the Union siege machine was a scorched ruin. But the unstoppable Federals built a more conventional sap-roller and continued digging.[123] "After this," said Lockett, "they kept their sap-rollers wet, forcing us to other expedients."[124]

---

* McPherson removed Mrs. Adeline Shirley and her fifteen-year-old son, Quincy, to a cave in the rear of her house. Her husband and daughter were stranded in Clinton, Mississippi, when the Union army cut rail service to Vicksburg.

On June 22, the head of the sap reached the exterior slope of the redan, and the Louisianans began bombarding the crews with hand grenades and 12-pound shells hurled by hand. The next day Hickenlooper recruited thirty-five lead and coal miners and had them dig under the fort, cutting out galleries—or tunnels—to be filled with explosive powder. The work went quickly. The clay soil cut easily and was self-supporting, making bracing, the most difficult part of mining, unnecessary. The rebels inside the fort heard the scraping sound of picks and shovels and began digging a countershaft to try to intercept and destroy the Yankee mine.[125] They got so close they could hear the miners talking but were unable to locate their tunnels.

When Hickenlooper's crews completed the job on June 23, ordnance experts packed the chambers with twenty-two hundred pounds of black powder, enough, they thought, to blow the fort "out of existence."[126] It was a siege tactic as old as organized warfare, but it would be the first mine detonated in warfare in the history of the country. On the morning of June 25, General Mortimer Leggett, in charge of infantry operations, assembled thousands of assault troops in the sap and in trenches branching out from it. Grant joined McPherson at Battery Hickenlooper to watch the explosion, scheduled to go off at three o'clock in the afternoon. The 45th Illinois, the "Lead Mine Regiment," would spearhead the opening assault. As the men waited, their minds a confused mixture of excitement and dread, their bodies shook with fright.[127]

Coonskin Foster and a hundred handpicked sharpshooters were positioned in rifle pits only twenty-five yards from the redan. Just before three o'clock, Union artillery fire subsided and there was a death-like quiet.[128] Colonel William E. Strong of the 12th Wisconsin helped Hickenlooper light the fuse. "We crept forward together on our hands and knees," and after firing the fuse "hurried back to Coon Skin Tower . . . and held our watches and counted the seconds! All was quiet along the entire line."

Three o'clock. Nothing! Three twenty, all quiet! Had they failed? Hickenlooper "was leaning carelessly against the base of Coon Skin Tower, his eyes intently fixed upon the hands of his watch," said Colonel Strong. "His face was white, and there was an anxious expression about his eyes. His reputation with that army was at stake, and I pitied him from the bottom of my heart." Finally, at precisely three thirty, "the huge fort, guns caissons, and Rebel troops . . . were lifted high in the air" and came crashing down "in one great ruin."[129] Billowing clouds of smoke and dust turned day to night, and when the air cleared there was the deafening roar of cannon and musket.

In an act of reckless bravado, Hickenlooper led a party of ten pioneers into the steaming hole created by the blast. Their job was to clear away debris, creating a narrow entry corridor for the Lead Mine Regiment. But the explosion had destroyed only half of the redan, and the saucer-shaped crater was far smaller than Hickenlooper expected—only twelve feet deep and thirty feet wide. Nor had the rebel troops been decimated. The only soldiers in the fort when it exploded were eight doomed Mississippians working in the countermine. Anticipating the explosion, Hébert had moved the rest of his men behind the fort, where an earthen bank, about six feet high, gave them excellent cover. At the head of their barricade they placed a cannon loaded with grape and canister.[130] Within minutes, some of the first Federals into the hole were carried out as corpses.

Then began a terrible struggle of some twenty-six hours. From their higher position, the rebels rolled lit shells and hand grenades onto the Yankees, and the men were soon fighting "bayonet to bayonet."[131] Some men "hurled bayoneted rifles like harpoons."[132] Others had their rifles torn out of their hands. Within an hour, the base of the hole became "slippery with blood."[133]

"Both sides fought with a desperation amounting almost to madness," recalled a Union soldier.[134] The Lead Miners held on until six that evening, when Logan replaced them with men from a fresh regiment.[135] Throughout the night, men were rotated in shifts in a smoke-saturated pit barely large enough to hold eighty men. Two companies at a time were thrown in every hour or so, or until the men's rifles were too hot to fire. Only the bluecoats closest to the rebel traverse had enough room to engage. The men behind them reloaded their rifles for them and passed them forward. The Federals were packed so tightly together "scarcely a [rebel] grenade was thrown without doing damage," recalled one of the first officers into the crater.[136] One Union soldier picked up and threw back over twenty grenades before he was cut in half by canister.

Near daylight, with the battle deadlocked, McPherson pulled his men from the "Death Hole," as the crater would forever be known to them.[137] Casualties were miraculously minimal because so few men could be committed at any one time. The Federals lost 34 killed and 209 wounded; the Confederates lost 94.[138]

It was the last of the hard fighting at Vicksburg.

Union casualties were taken to clean, well-supplied field hospitals, where women volunteers from the Chicago Sanitary Commission helped doctors separate the mortally from the less severely wounded.[139] These large, well-ventilated tent hospitals were located in the ravines between the bluffs, "quiet, cool places . . . comparatively safe from the fire of the enemy," reported Jane Hoge, a fixture on the siege lines.[140]

The men most horribly mangled in the crater were taken, after triage, to Memphis on first-class Mississippi steamboats that had been converted to hospital ships. By the end of the siege, Memphis, with eight army hospitals, had one of the largest medical complexes in the western theater, due in great part to Grant's persistent entreaties that his soldiers receive the same level of care given the wounded in the east.[141] From the time they were pulled from the crater, the grievously wounded could expect to reach an "amply provided" Memphis hospital ward in two days. An officer on Grant's staff, Dr. A. H. Hough, established and equipped these fast-running hospital ships with the assistance of Mary Livermore of the Chicago Sanitary Commission.[142] In Memphis, Annie Wittenmyer met the wounded at the docks and worked tirelessly with her staff to keep the wards antiseptically clean and as comfortable as possible for the patients.

Confederates who were wounded in the crater died in far greater numbers than the Federals. The stricken were conveyed by wagon to either field hospitals located behind the lines or to poorly equipped, understaffed hospitals in Vicksburg. The Confederate boys had been bruised, lacerated, and pierced by shell, shot, and pointed steel, and their faces were "blackened and burned from the effects of the explosion . . ." wrote Private Will Tunnard, one of their own. "Surgeons with sleeves rolled up to their elbows, hands, arms and shirts red," amputated shattered limbs using either ether or chloroform for anesthesia. If supplies ran out men were told to bite the bullet.[143] While doctors worked furiously, aided by the local order of the Sisters of Mercy, enemy shrapnel flew perilously close to men's cots, "unstring[ing] their nerves." Great crashing sounds broke their sleep.[144]

The day after the battle in the crater, Andrew Hickenlooper began sinking another shaft under the Louisiana Redan, and again the rebels countermined, using black laborers. This second Union mine was detonated on July 1 but, on orders from Grant, there was no infantry assault. Hickenlooper wasn't there to witness the blast. Suffering from sleep deprivation and nervous strain, he was confined to his tent from June 29 to July 2.[145] By this time, Federal saps were encroaching so closely upon the rebel trenches and forts "the dirt we cast out with our spades," wrote J. J. Kellogg, "was mingled with that cast out of their pits."[146]

The explosion on July 1 was a pointed warning to John Pemberton. An intensely determined army would soon blast to the heavens every fort on the rebel line and carry the city in a wave-like attack scheduled—unknown to him—for July 6.[147]

By July 1, conditions both inside the stricken city and on the defensive lines were deplorable. Every day was a test of will, civilians and soldiers resigned to whatever would happen next. Few listened anymore for the guns of Joseph Johnston. For over six weeks troops had been in the rifle pits and behind the breastworks without a break, drenched "to the skin" in explosive southern storms, unable to bathe or change clothing. The only relief from the dampness was the blistering Mississippi sun. Masked by dirt and clay, their bodies "were occupied by filthy vermin."[148]

Food was cooked and brought to them by slaves. The standard fare had become pea bread, a "villainous" concoction of bread, ground peas, cornmeal, and water. "Even this was measured out in ounces," said a disgruntled Mississippi soldier.[149] In the fourth week of the siege, General Sherman wrote his wife: "We dig mightily and fire incessantly on the works and the city but the truth is, we trust to the Starvation."[150]

People trapped in the city collected water in cisterns, and there was usually enough of it. Men in the trenches and forts got their water from the river. It was hauled in barrels and was already near poisonous when collected. The river in front of the city had become a depository for horses and mules slaughtered by Porter's gunners. Rats and clouds of flies had fouled the carcasses. Mud and floating human waste worked its way into the decaying remains.[151]

This deplorable liquid would have been half-palatable if the soldiers on the line had had hard spirits to deaden the taste. "We are pretty hungry and dreadfully dry," a rebel picket told some Yankees digging toward him. "Old Pemberton has taken all the whisky for the hospitals. . . . Give our compliments to Gen. Grant [and] ask him if he will send us a few bottles of good whisky."[152]

Exposure and reduced rations began to tell on the rebel soldiery. By July, profoundly more men were dying in the hospitals than at the front.[153] By this time, nearly every man had had unmanageable bowels; now malaria, the summer scourge, began to eat into the army's strength.[154]

Soldiers tried to hold things together by reading their Testaments at night. And there was, in this god-awful place, music to relieve the tedium and terror.[155] The 3rd Louisiana had a choir and "a sort of poet" who knew how to compose songs to fit the moment. "These songs were sometimes humorous, often satirical, but more commonly sad and sung in a minor key," wrote Captain James Henry Jones of the 38th Mississippi. "After nightfall the club would entertain both friends and foes with their music," played in a "living graveyard" to "the boom of artillery."[156]

To pass from one side of the siege lines to the other was to enter another world. Union soldiers had plenty of food, served hot or picked fresh from local farms by foraging parties: plums, peaches, blueberries, apples, and sweet potatoes. Most men did not have tents, but found respite from the clamor of battle in two- and four-man "dog nests" they excavated in the steep hills behind the front lines. A Chicago newspaperman described them: "A place is dug against the hill—and in many cases into it, forming a sort of cave. Poles were put up and covered with oil cloths, blankets or cane rods, of which an abundant supply was near at hand." The cane was also used to make tolerable cots.[157]

Not far from their dugouts men dug shallow wells and drew out fresh water in buckets and barrels.[158] "We live splendid now," a Northern soldier wrote home, which in timeless army language meant they were well fed.[159]

All the while in Vicksburg, the poor roamed the streets in search of food; and those a station or two higher lived "half-hungry continually."[160] On July 2, army chaplain William Lovelace Foster saw a group of men by the city docks cutting up and dressing what appeared to be a steer. Then he spotted the long ears. "It was mule beef."[161]

In another part of the city, Lieutenant William Drennan caught a rat and skinned it, intending to eat it. He abstained at the last minute, disgusted with himself, but wrote his wife saying the mule meat he had seen his men devouring looked "as nice as Texas beef."[162] By this time, Vicksburg looked as if it had been "visited [by] a terrible scourge," recalled Will Tunnard in his wartime memoirs, "houses dilapidated and in ruins, rent and torn by shot and shell; the streets barricaded with earth-works and defended by artillery, over which lonely sentinels kept guard. The avenues were almost deserted, save by hunger-pinched, starving and wounded soldiers, or guards lying on the banquettes, indifferent to the screaming and exploding shells. The stores, the few that were open, looked like the ghost of more prosperous times, with their empty shelves and scant stock of goods, held at ruinous prices."[163]

Vicksburg, one of the most literate cities in the Deep South, had but one newspaper left. That was J. W. Swords's *Daily Citizen*. It was being printed on wallpaper.

"In a week they will cave in," Sherman wrote Ellen on June 27.[164]

At midmorning on July 3, the guns went silent on the siege lines and curious soldiers watched two Confederate officers approach the Union lines bearing a white flag. The men in Chaplain William Lovelace Foster's 35th Mississippi Infantry erupted in righteous anger when they spotted the flag, thinking surrender was imminent. To cool them down, officers suggested Pemberton was merely requesting a truce to remove some of the citizenry.[165] That seemed right, for Porter continued to hammer the city, and rebel gunners in the water batteries were returning "shot for shot." Then, around three o'clock, Chaplain Foster heard for the first time in months "the blast of the bugle." Moments later, white flags flew from the batteries along both sides of the river.[166] That very hour, William Drennan learned that Pemberton and Grant were meeting somewhere between the lines. "The crisis is on us," he wrote his wife.[167]

CHAPTER 23

"It is great, Mr. Welles."

—Abraham Lincoln to Gideon Welles [1]

"You were right, and I was wrong." [2]
—Abraham Lincoln to Ulysses Grant, July 13, 1863

John Pemberton surrendered with great reluctance, knowing that the people whose cause he had taken up would scorn him as the Yankee traitor who lost Vicksburg. But carrying on was not a realistic option. His men were not yet starving, but were running alarmingly short of rations and "not less than ten thousand" of them, he reported, were "ineffective from sickness and wounds." [3] His men had been on the line without relief for forty-seven consecutive days and nights. "A sudden rush at night would have swept them away like chaff," a Mississippi soldier wrote later. [4] And by the last week of June, nearly everyone at Vicksburg had given up on Joseph Johnston. [5] "For an emergency such as then existed a man of Johnston's temperament was peculiarly unsuited," wrote a nineteenth-century historian. [6]

An anonymous letter Pemberton received on June 28, signed "Many Soldiers," may have hastened his decision. "This army is now ripe for mutiny, unless it can be fed. . . . If you can't feed us, you had better surrender us, horrible as the idea is, than suffer this noble army to disgrace themselves by desertion." [7] The letter was found years later in the official papers Pemberton had sent to the Confederate War Department. Pemberton never revealed how much importance, if any, he attached to it, but it must have unsettled him.

On July 1, he sent a circular to his division commanders. The unpalatable choice forced upon the army was this: Surrender, or evacuate and hook up with Johnston's army. Are the men able "to make the marches and undergo the fatigues necessary to accomplish a successful evacuation?" he asked his commanders. Two of them, John Bowen and Martin Luther Smith, proposed making terms with the enemy before the garrison ran out of provisions. The others ruled out an evacuation. The men's spirits were not broken, but they were too "enfeebled" for such a march, said one commander.[8]

At ten o'clock on the morning of July 3, Pemberton sent Bowen, Grant's former neighbor in Missouri, through the Union lines under a flag of truce to ask for an "armistice with a view to arranging terms for the capitulation of Vicksburg." The terms were to be decided by three commissioners on either side.[9] Grant rejected the proposal and demanded "the unconditional surrender of the garrison," the identical terms he had imposed on Simon Bolivar Buckner at Fort Donelson.[10]

When Bowen, who was mortally ill with dysentery and eager to end the siege, reported back to Pemberton, he misled him into believing Grant had requested a "personal conference" with him that afternoon. In fact Bowen had suggested the idea to Grant, who had agreed to the meeting at a place between the opposing lines. At three that afternoon, Pemberton rode out with Bowen and Captain Lewis M. Montgomery, a Pemberton aide, to confer with Grant on a hillside near the Louisiana Redan. Pemberton and Grant had served in the same division in the Mexican War and knew one another "very well."[11] Tall, erect, and hard-faced, Pemberton was flawlessly attired. Grant, a half-chewed cigar in his mouth, wore a mud-splattered field uniform.

To cut the tension, Grant had brought along a demijohn of wine.[12] Expecting to impose his will on Pemberton, he was cordial but contained. Pemberton was edgy and became belligerent when Grant would not revoke his demand for unconditional surrender. That would mean an immediate resumption of hostilities, Pemberton countered.[13] "I can assure you, sir, that you will bury many more of your men before you will enter Vicksburg," he threatened Grant, adding that he had enough provisions to last "an indefinite period." Having learned from rebel deserters that the garrison was perilously low on supplies, Grant took this as a bluff. But as Pemberton prepared to leave, Grant suggested they "step aside" and allow James McPherson and Andrew J. Smith, two of the generals who had accompanied him to the parley, to meet with Bowen and Montgomery to try to hammer out a "satisfactory arrangement." [14] After they had retreated to a spot several hundred yards away, Grant and Pemberton sat under the shelter of a splintered oak tree and had what must have been a most uncomfortable conversation.

When Bowen returned with a proposal to have the Confederate army march out of its fortifications "with the honors of war, carrying their small arms and field artillery," Grant dismissed it with a wave of the hand but agreed to send a letter that evening laying out his final terms. [15] The truce would stay in place until then. Meanwhile in the trenches, anxious Southern soldiers spilled out their distress and concern in their diaries. "The glorious fourth! God grant that we be not surrendered on this day," wrote young Jared Young Sanders. [16]

Back at his headquarters tent, Grant called together his corps and division commanders in what was the closest thing to a "council of war" he had ever convened. It was a sign he was open to alternatives other than unconditional surrender. [17] Heeding the near unanimous opinion of his commanders, Grant allowed the entire rebel garrison to be paroled rather than sent north, at considerable expense, to prisoner of war camps. According to the provisions of the parole system worked out in July 1862, paroled soldiers were to sign a statement agreeing not to take up arms again until exchanged on a one-to-one basis with prisoners from the opposite side. "My own feelings are against this," Grant wrote Porter that night, "but all my officers think the advantage gained by having our forces and transports for immediate purposes more than counterbalances the effect of sending them north." Many of these war-weary rebels would return to their homes for the duration of the war, Grant was convinced. [18]*

With the issue decided, Grant called for a courier. If Pemberton accepted his ultimatum, a single division of Federals would take possession of Vicksburg at eight the next morning. After all surrendered troops had signed their paroles, they would be permitted to march out of Vicksburg to Enterprise, Mississippi, where they would wait out the thirty-day parole period before being moved to western Alabama to be

---

* In his memoirs, Grant said he had favored paroling Pemberton's men "against the general, and almost unanimous judgment of the council [of war]." His correspondence with Halleck indicates he was mistaken. USGM, 376.

exchanged.[19] Officers could take their side arms and clothing, and cavalry and staff officers were allowed one horse each. The rank and file was disarmed.[20] In a shrewd piece of psychological warfare, Grant directed his corps commanders to have their most "discreet" pickets inform their rebel counterparts that Union terms included a proposal to parole all officers and men and "permit them to go home."[21]

When the dispatch containing Grant's final terms arrived at Pemberton's headquarters in Vicksburg, next to the Balfour house, every commander except two—Stephen Dill Lee and William Baldwin—agreed to accept them.[22] Pemberton then stood and, with tears in his eyes, thanked them for saving the army and the city further suffering. Had the odds not been stacked so heavily against them, he would have preferred to put himself at the head of his troops "and make a desperate effort to cut our way through the enemy. That," he said mournfully, "is my only hope of saving myself from shame and disgrace."[23]

When Pemberton informed Grant that his terms were acceptable, he made several requests. The most important to him was a provision allowing his officers to retain their "personal property."[24] Grant saw this for what it was: a transparent attempt to allow rebel commanders to take their black servants with them. He rejected it out of hand, but granted Pemberton one minor concession. His men were permitted a limited surrender ceremony, a point of military honor. They could march out of their fortifications the next morning, stack their colors and arms, and return to their lines as prisoners. The terms were unalterable. If rejected, Grant vowed to "act accordingly."[25]

Pemberton's concession letter reached Grant at dawn on July 4. Hours later the rebel troops were informed. Pemberton "should be stricken from the rolls of our army," wrote Jared Young Sanders.[26]

In the years following the surrender, souvenir seekers ravaged the oak tree, roots and all, under which Pemberton and Grant had met on the steamy afternoon of July 3. "Since then the same tree has furnished as many cords of wood, in the shape of trophies, as 'The True Cross,'" Grant wrote in his memoirs.[27]

At ten o'clock on the morning of July 4, Pemberton's men filed out of their forts, stacked arms, and "marched back in good order. Our whole army witnessed this scene without cheering," Grant recalled.[28]

Some 31,600 rebels surrendered, among them fifteen generals and up to three thousand sick and wounded men in Vicksburg hospitals.*

As John Logan prepared his division to enter the city, the men in butternut and gray "rose out of the long imprisonment of the trenches . . ." wrote a Southern soldier. "Many reeled and staggered like drunken men from emaciation and . . . wept like children that all their long sacrifice was unavailing."[29] Union boys mingled with them, uneasily at first, and offered hardtack and bacon from their haversacks. They were then invited to inspect the rebel defenses, which they found badly battered, in no shape to resist the thunderous Union assault planned for July 6.[30] Most rebels, however, remained with their fortifications, too angry or dispirited to fraternize with Yankees. "How humiliating it is for us to be compelled to submit to such an enemy and that too on the fourth of July," wrote a Mississippi captain.[31]

For William Tecumseh Sherman, it was "the best fourth of July since 1776."[32] He had hoped to march into Vicksburg with Grant, but he had been ordered to set out at once with forty-six thousand men to destroy or drive from the state Joseph Johnston and his Army of Relief. Johnston was at that time on the eastern bank of the Big Black cautiously assessing Grant's strength, and would begin hurrying back to Jackson on July 6, after receiving word of Pemberton's surrender. "I want you to drive Johnston out . . ." Grant told Sherman, "and inflict on the enemy such punishment [as] you can," finishing the work of destruction and despoliation he had begun in the capital in mid-May. Only then, said Grant, would the Vicksburg campaign be complete.[33] "I will push ahead . . ." Sherman vowed. "I did want rest but I ask nothing until the Mississippi River is ours . . . till the river of our greatness is free as God made it."[34]

• • •

---

* The number actually paroled was 28,892. Seven hundred and nine refused to be paroled and were sent north to prison camps. Several hundred died in hospitals before they could be paroled, and over a thousand escaped or hid, some of them disguising themselves as citizens. USG to Halleck, July 6, 1863, USGP, vol. 8, 484–85; Badeau, *Military History*, vol. 1, 386.

As Grant and his staff rode along the Jackson Road into Vicksburg on the morning of July 4, they stopped at a large, high-sitting house where Pemberton and some of his officers were assembled on the porch. When he dismounted and approached with his staff, he was given a glacial reception. No one offered him a chair at first, and when he asked for a glass of water he was told to go inside and get one himself. When he returned, the seat he had been given grudgingly was taken and he remained standing for a few minutes, trying uneasily to make conversation. Then he turned and left.[35]

Residents of Vicksburg looked on sullenly as Logan's columns filed into town, led by the 45th Illinois Infantry, its torn battle flag not yet repaired since its survival fight in the crater. The surrender had come as a shock to many townspeople. The night before, the Reverend William Lord, "pale as death," had arrived at the family's cave and told his wife, Margaret, tearfully, to "take the children home. The town is surrendered, and the Union army will march in at ten o'clock." As they headed to their residence next to the Episcopal church, they ran into groups of officers—"the wreck of our army, pallid, emaciated, and grimy with dust." The men were wandering about town, taking a final look at its cut-up houses and streets. The Lords stopped to shake hands with them. Tears rolled down the men's faces. "Ladies, we would have fought for you forever. Nothing but starvation whipped us."

The Lords' home was an uninhabitable wreck, but "the hardest trial of that bitter Fourth," recalled Lida Lord, "was the triumphant entrance of Grant's army, marching, with banners waving and drums beating, through streets plowed by their cannon-balls and strewn with the ruins of our homes."[36]

"It was a desolate looking place, I tell you," recalled a Union soldier. "I did not notice a house but that was shot through."[37] Most striking were the trees, almost all of them stripped of their branches, with their trunks blasted "as though a thousand bolts of lightning had spent their combined force upon them."[38] Dust was thick in the streets, stores were closed, and houses shuttered. The place looked as if it had been "deserted years ago," said a Union surgeon.[39] "A nasty, sickening stench" arose from decaying horses and mules cut to pieces by Union mortars. A more pronounced odor came from the direction of the city cemetery, where a number of Confederate boys had been "imperfectly buried."[40]

The people "were in a famishing condition," recalled campaign veteran Ira Blanchard.[41] One of his fellow soldiers talked to a man who had been eating mule meat for four days.[42] Later, when Blanchard's regiment opened a bakery and made fresh bread for the men, women "who had been wealthy before, would come out and beg a loaf as we carried it through the streets."[43] This is what rebellion had brought upon them, an Iowa officer told his men.[44]

Emboldened by the display of Yankee power, African American slaves "congregated on the sidewalks . . . with a broad grin of satisfaction on their ebony countenances," Vicksburg reporter Alexander S. Abrams wrote disapprovingly. The "Negroes were already growing arrogant. No white Confederate citizen or soldier dared to speak to them for fear of being called a rebel, or some other abusive epithet."[45]

Reaching the center of town, Grant paused to watch members of McPherson's staff ascend the courthouse steps to its cupola and raise the headquarters flag of their XVII Corps. Then he headed down to the city wharf to meet Porter on his flagship.[46] Every vessel in the fleet was there, with steam whistles blowing and battle flags floating on the morning breeze. Cannon salutes boomed out over the river, and hand-fired rockets carpeted the sky over the armada. Spotting Grant approaching with his generals, their horses raising a tremendous dust cloud, Porter ordered the gangway thrown down and the wine lockers opened. Toasts were offered and swords raised in triumph, while General Grant sat placidly on a chair, a look of "quiet satisfaction on his face." He was, Porter attested, the only one on board who didn't touch the wine, contenting himself instead with an excellent cigar.[47]

Porter's telegram announcing the surrender reached the Navy Department in Washington at 12:40 P.M. on July 7, having been delayed because the closest long-distance telegraph station to Vicksburg was at Cairo, reached by dispatch boat.[48] When Secretary Gideon Welles hastened to the White House to inform the president, he found Lincoln with a map of Vicksburg in his hand, pointing out Grant's progress to Secretary of the Treasury Salmon Chase. At a cabinet meeting that morning Lincoln had been profoundly depressed, his "countenance indicating sadness and despondency," Welles noted in his diary. On July 3, General George Gordon Meade's Army of the Potomac had stopped Lee's invasion of Pennsylvania at Gettysburg, but Meade was not aggressively pursuing Lee as he retreated through mountain passes toward the Potomac and Virginia.

When Welles came bursting into Lincoln's study with a smile on his face and a telegram from Porter in his hand, the president put down the map, leaped to his feet, and announced he would personally telegraph the news to General Meade. As he started for the door, headed for the government telegraph office behind the White House in the War Department building, he "suddenly stopped, his countenance beaming with joy; he caught my hand," Welles recorded the scene, "and, throwing his arm around me, exclaimed: '. . . I cannot, in words tell you my joy over this result. It is great, Mr. Welles, it is great!'"[49]

Grant's telegram to Henry Halleck arrived the next day. It was typical Grant, plain as pie: "The Enemy surrendered this morning."[50] That evening a raucous crowd accompanied by a military band visited the War Department. Secretary Edwin Stanton spoke from the steps, praising Grant's "indomitable energy."[51] Grant's success at Vicksburg "has excited a degree of enthusiasm not excelled in the war," Welles wrote that evening.[52]

The celebration at Cairo, where Grant had launched his Mississippi campaign in September 1861, was more raucous. "The great news of the capture and final occupation of Vicksburg . . . has made nearly every man, woman, and child in Cairo crazy—some of the adult masculines [sic] are certainly crazy drunk," reported the *Chicago Tribune*.[53]

News of Grant's victory was "transmitted over the whole country," said Welles.[54] Emeline Ritner wrote her husband, Jacob, still at Vicksburg, describing the biggest celebration their tiny town of Mt. Pleasant, Iowa, had ever put on. When news of the surrender reached the town, every church bell rang for hours and people pushed into the main square "weeping for joy" and "wild" with excitement. "That night we had . . . the greatest fireworks I ever saw."[55]

On July 13, Lincoln wrote Grant:

> My dear General: I do not remember that you and I ever met personally. I write this now as a grateful acknowledgment for the almost inestimable service you have done the country—I wish to say a word further—When you first reached the vicinity of Vicksburg, I thought you should do what you finally did—

march the troops across the neck, run the batteries with transports, and thus go below; and I never had any faith, except a
general hope that you knew better than I, that the Yazoo Pass
expedition and the like could succeed—When you got below and
took Port Gibson, Grand Gulf and vicinity, I thought you should
go down the river and join Gen. Banks; and when you turned
Northward, East of the Big Black, I feared it was a mistake—I
now wish to make a personal acknowledgment that you were
right, and I was wrong." [56]

Henry Halleck heaped praise on the general he had harassed and nearly
removed earlier in the war but later supported with more enthusiasm
than some historians allow. "In boldness of plan, rapidity of execution,
and brilliancy of results, these operations will compare most favorably
with those of Napoleon about Ulm," he wrote Grant, an apt comparison to the 1805 campaign in which the Corsican enveloped and captured an entire Austrian army at the Bavarian city of Ulm, one of the
great strategic victories of modern warfare that opened the way to the
conquest of Vienna a month later. [57]

Grant "is the greatest Chieftain of the Age: the boys worship him,"
Colonel Marcus M. Spiegel, a German-Jewish immigrant, wrote his
wife on July 4. [58] This was the same general whom Spiegel's "boys"
had denounced as a drunken incompetent during the dismal winter
encampment in Louisiana, the same general correspondents who followed the campaign could not believe had shaped the plan that finally
got the Army of the Tennessee to the gates of Vicksburg. "The brilliant
McPherson," reporters suggested, "must have conceived it"; if not him,
surely Sherman. [59] But Sherman was now telling anyone who would lis-
ten that the plan was entirely Grant's—and that he had strenuously
opposed it: "Grant is now deservedly the hero. He is entitled to all the
Credit." [60]

Sherman worshiped Grant but never considered him a genius, and
rightly so. Genius is a quality inappropriate to leadership in warfare and
can lead to a form of "armchair idolatry" that ignores the role of the
structural underpinnings of victory: factories, railroads, steamships, ordnance, and logistics, along with that elusive quality called luck. "Claims
to genius distance our understanding from war's immense complexity

and contingency, which are its greater truths," wrote historian Cathal J. Nolan. The best generals react more quickly and astutely than others in the fog of battle, but no commander "truly commands or ever controls such a complex and dynamic thing as battle, let alone war. Assertion of genius," says Nolan, "separates us from war's wider and shared character, and from its suffering." It also "obscures the stumbling even of the great generals and the grim endurance of soldiers."[61]

Grant stumbled repeatedly in his ferociously focused campaign against Vicksburg—leaving his supply line dangerously vulnerable in his first plunge into Mississippi; sending Sherman and Porter into a nearly impenetrable swamp infested with enemy cavalry, very nearly losing them and the ironclads he needed to take Vicksburg; and ordering, at Vicksburg, a senseless second charge on fixed fortifications with an army exhausted and bled down at Champion Hill. But in every instance, he bounced back and prevailed through a succession of sure-handed military moves. "Butcher Grant," as he came to be known for the staggering losses he was willing to take later to defeat Lee's Army of Northern Virginia, was at Vicksburg the master of maneuver.

In the climactic period of the Vicksburg campaign, the thirteen-week period between March 29, 1863, when McClernand was instructed to open a road from Milliken's Bend to New Carthage, Louisiana, and the surrender of Vicksburg on July 4, Grant sustained only 10,142 casualties—1,581 killed.[62] The prize was the capture of an entire army—the second time Grant had done this in the war—the surrender and Union occupation of the enemy's last remaining rail and shipping center on the Mississippi, the opening of the river to Union commerce, and the fatal bisection of the Confederacy, conquests, as Sherman notes, that set his legions "free for other purposes."[63]

Grant's reward was instant elevation to major general in the regular army. It was the highest military rank then existing by law, and it gave him "permanent tenure, security for old age, [and] the promise that a starred flag would fly over his grave when things came to an end."[64] The appointment came less than ten years after he had resigned from the army after being caught drinking on duty, his career in apparent ruin.

On Grant's recommendation, Sherman and McPherson were made permanent brigadiers in the regular army.

Nearly lost in the hoopla was the navy's integral role in a struggle that was as much an amphibious operation as America's Pacific campaign in World War II.[65] Singlehandedly the Union navy had reduced New Orleans and Memphis—river redoubts that became, with Cairo, indispensable ports and supply centers for Grant's invasion. Without an all-water supply line secured and protected by Porter's ironclads, Grant could not have broken into Mississippi or prosecuted an effective siege. Porter's brown-water navy also allowed Grant to move his army swiftly to points of opportunity and throw into turmoil and confusion a fortress city whose principal defensive barriers were a dense, only partially navigable swamp and a wide, swift-flowing river. The navy also severed Vicksburg's Red River supply line, over which cattle, salt, and British rifles came into Vicksburg and were trans-shipped by rail to armies all over the South. And when Grant reached Vicksburg, the navy's river blockade became part of a siege line that cut off the city from the rest of the Confederacy and squeezed the life out of it. "The navy under Porter was all it could be, during the entire campaign," Grant gave the Mississippi fleet its due. "Without its assistance the campaign could not have been successfully made with twice the number of men engaged. It could not have been made at all, in the way it was, with any number of men without such assistance."[66] Absent the navy, Vicksburg might have been "Grant's Moscow."[67]

On July 8, Nathaniel Banks informed Major General Franklin Gardner, the rebel commander at Port Hudson, that Vicksburg had fallen. At once, Gardner determined to surrender his river bastion, the last major obstacle to unimpeded Union navigation of the Mississippi. Banks had the fortress invested and was prepared to starve it into submission; and Grant would have reinforced him if the rebels held on much longer.[68] On July 9, after formal ceremonies of surrender, the Mississippi became again a Union river.

On July 16, the unarmed steamboat *Imperial* tied up at New Orleans after completing a trip from St. Louis.[69] "The Father of Waters again goes Unvexed to the sea," Lincoln wrote his friend James C. Conkling.[70] Guerrilla bandits would continue to feast on Union steamboats, and physical communication between the eastern and trans-Mississippi Confederacy was still possible, but only by gimcrack river craft. As Gideon Welles wrote Admiral Porter: "A slave empire divided by this river into equal parts with liberty in possession of its banks and freedom upon its waters cannot exist."[71]

Vicksburg was that rare thing in military history: a decisive battle, one with war-turning strategic consequences. The only Civil War battle remotely like it was Antietam. In stopping Lee's northward thrust at Antietam Creek, Maryland, in September 1862, George McClellan had opened the way for Lincoln to issue the Emancipation Proclamation, which changed a limited war to preserve the Union into a revolutionary struggle to save the Union *and* destroy slavery. Meade's victory at Gettysburg had less of an impact on the course of the war. Importantly, it stopped a second Confederate invasion, and the monumental bloodletting virtually assured that there would be no third attempt, but the battle was decisive only because losing it would have been catastrophic for the Union cause. Gettysburg had nothing to do with emancipation, and Meade's halting pursuit left Lee free to escape to Virginia, replenish his shattered army, and return to his former line defending Richmond, with the army's morale virtually intact.[72]

Vicksburg, by contrast, had immense strategic consequences. It did more than open the river and split the Confederacy. It took the river counties of Mississippi and Louisiana out of the war and left the strongest Federal army in the Deep South, where it could move anywhere at will.

The twin calamities at Gettysburg and Vicksburg, coming a mere day apart, dealt a devastating blow to Southern morale. This is almost orthodoxy among Civil War historians, who invariably illustrate their point with an excerpt from the diary of Colonel Josiah Gorgas, chief of Confederate ordnance. "Events have succeeded one another with disastrous rapidity," Gorgas wrote despairingly on July 28, 1863. "One brief month ago we were apparently at the point of success. Lee was in Pennsylvania threatening Harrisburgh [sic], and even Philadelphia, Vicksburgh [sic] seemed to laugh all Grant's efforts to scorn. . . . All looked bright. Now the picture is just as somber as it was bright then. . . . Yesterday we rode on the pinnacle of success—today absolute ruin seems to be our portion. The Confederacy totters to its destruction."[73]

Evidence unearthed by historian Gary Gallagher gives a different picture, however. A substantial number of Southern opinion makers and diarists, along with soldiers who served with Lee, failed to see Gettysburg as an irrecoverable defeat, equal to Vicksburg. In Pennsylvania Lee had suffered only a "temporary setback" that had no lasting consequences for his army, said his defenders at the time. Trusting in the unequalled Lee and his "invincible army," irreconcilable secessionists like Edwin Ruffin considered Gettysburg "no more than a bloody disappointment." Even Josiah Gorgas did a turnabout. At the end of summer 1863, after hearing reports about the renewed health and spirits of Lee's army, he struck a more positive note in his diary. The army was in "excellent condition," he said, strong enough, perhaps, for another thrust into Maryland.

Vicksburg, on the other hand, was viewed on the Confederate home front in the east as an "unequivocal disaster." It dealt a "terrible blow to our cause," wrote South Carolina diarist Emma Holmes, who, like most other Southerners, had been anxiously following the river city's improbable defense for more than a year. "Vicksburg had fallen! It is all true," Catherine Edmondston, a member of the planter aristocracy of coastal North Carolina, told her diary. She had learned of the capitulation, she wrote, from a "dispatch which freezes the marrow in our bones."[74]

Vicksburg was "the stab to the Confederacy from which it never recovered," Vicksburg veteran and historian Edward Gregory wrote after the war. No reasonable chance of a Southern "triumph remained after the white flag flew on the ramparts of the terraced city. . . . There were desperate battles afterward, and occasional victories, but their light only rendered deeper the advancing and impending shadow of ultimate failure."[75] The military historian J. F. C. Fuller had it right: "Vicksburg, and not Gettysburg, was the crisis of the Confederacy."[76]

• • •

Strangely, the conqueror of Vicksburg failed to mention in his memoirs or battle reports the outstanding strategic accomplishment of his Mississippi campaign. At Vicksburg Grant evolved a war-winning strategy for the North. His triumph led Lincoln to call him east to take on Lee in Virginia, and there he fought as he had in the west. Turning the Army of the Potomac into an agile, improvising force, he used lightning maneuvers, like the crossing of the James; patient siege tactics to bottle up Lee in Richmond; and scorched-earth raids in the Shenandoah Valley—all of which led to Appomattox and the end. All the while, with Grant's approval, Sherman cut a swath of destruction through Georgia and the Carolinas, causing Deep South fathers and sons to desert the trenches around Richmond and return home to protect their families and farms. Even today, Sherman is seen as the North's avenging angel, but it was Grant who had "the real core of iron," said Bruce Catton.[77] It was he who told General Phil Sheridan: "If the war is to last another year, we want the Shenandoah Valley to remain a barren waste."[78]

These culminating campaigns, along with Vicksburg, brought down Dixie. It is campaigns, not battles, that win wars. Civil War armies of sixty and eighty thousand men were too large and powerfully outfitted to be annihilated on the battlefield; and battles between such armies rarely had—contrary to the great Clausewitz—history-altering outcomes. Without ever opening a book on military tactics, Grant broke free from the fixation of Meade, McClellan, and other eastern generals upon Napoleonic battles of maneuver "as the hinge upon which warfare must turn." His Vicksburg campaign, wrote historian Russell F. Weigley, "was a model of persistent long-range planning."[79]

Never, in the long campaign from Cairo to Vicksburg, did he deviate from the river-based strategy he had worked out on a primitive map in a farmer's backyard days before taking command of a small army at flooded-out Cairo. It was all of a piece. His seizure of Paducah, Kentucky, gateway to two great river highways—the Cumberland and the Tennessee—carried his steam-driven army into the beating heart of cotton country, where he took, with naval assistance, Forts Henry and Donelson, opening the way to the capture of Nashville and points farther south. Then it was on to Pittsburg Landing and Corinth, victories that disabled one of the South's most important rail centers and put his armies within striking distance of Vicksburg, the daunting challenge that would demand greater persistence than all the other conquests that preceded it.

Grant did this unwaveringly, sticking intently to the Mississippi Valley, which Sherman called the "strategic directrix" of the North American continent.[80] In the east, Sherman told a friend after Vicksburg had fallen, "they have fought battles and maneuvered fast armies. Here we have achieved a real conclusion."[81]

In losing its hold on the Valley of the Mississippi, the Confederacy would be forced thereafter to fight a desperation battle for survival, a war of attrition—Grant style—that it could win only by an absence of political or moral resolve in the North, not by force of arms.[82] When Grant and Sherman moved east in 1864 they would prevail, as they had at Vicksburg, by protracted campaigns that bore down on the enemy and employed every instrument of the state to crush him. Grant understood that battles of maneuver were "not sufficient in a civil war," wrote Adam Badeau. "The passions were too intense, the stakes too great, the alternatives were too tremendous. It was not victory that either side was playing for, but for existence. If the rebels won, they destroyed a nation, if the government succeeded, it annihilated a rebellion."

In such a struggle, the enemy would not yield if defeated in one or even a succession of fixed battles. "It was indispensable to annihilate armies and resources," to prosecute "a people's war," knowing that "the people as well as the armies of the South must be conquered." And to win that kind of war he had to war on slavery.[83]

When Vicksburg fell, there was little mention in the press of Grant's role as liberator, the enforcing arm of Lincoln's Emancipation Proclamation. This remains the most underappreciated aspect of his Vicksburg campaign. Pressured by his own troops, and later by the Lincoln administration, Grant became, eventually, a committed emancipationist, freeing by military action over one hundred thousand slaves in the lower Mississippi Valley and working with General Lorenzo Thomas to put nearly twenty-one thousand black men in Union blue by the end of 1863. Grant may not have known, as was pointed out at the time by abolitionists, that "the history of the world furnishes no example of an enslaved race which won its freedom without exertions of its own."

But he came around to the idea that black people had to fight for their emancipation if they were to be truly free.* [84]

It is important to note that most of the slaves that Grant's army freed were emancipated before, not after, Vicksburg surrendered. Geography and rebel intransigence prolonged Grant's military campaign, but by holding on inside their fortress city, the rebel army was powerless to keep the Federals from "stealing," as Southerners put it, their slaves. [85] For the defenders of Vicksburg, it was a cruel irony. The longer they held out, the more they lost.

What was lost was a cotton and slave empire that sharp-eyed speculators had begun carving out of a western wilderness since around 1811, when the first steamboat to navigate the Mississippi docked at Natchez. In that year Joseph Emory Davis, a hard-driving country lawyer from western Kentucky, the elder brother and surrogate father of Jefferson Davis, moved to the Mississippi Territory, set up a law practice near Natchez, and purchased land on a pear-shaped peninsula twenty-five miles south of Vicksburg. He called the plantation he built on Davis Bend in the mid-1830s Hurricane, and by 1860 it was one of the largest estates in Mississippi, with 345 slaves and 1,700 acres of improved land.

By the standards of his time and place, Joseph Davis was a benign master. A disciple of the Welsh Utopian socialist Robert Owen, he set out to elevate his slaves morally and mentally. They enjoyed an unusual degree of self-government and ran their own court system, with black judges and juries meting out justice without interference from the Big House. Davis handed over the daily management of his plantation to his trusted slave Benjamin T. Montgomery, a self-taught mechanic, engineer, and architect whom Davis allowed to live with his family in virtual freedom near a dry goods store they managed. He also encouraged him to use his richly stocked library, where Montgomery had learned to read and write.

---

* Nearly 150,000 African Americans from slave states served in the Union army and navy. Northern free blacks provided another fifty thousand. William W. Freehling, *How Anti-Confederate Southerners Shaped the Course of the Civil War* (New York: Oxford University Press, 2001), xiii.

When New Orleans fell to Farragut's fleet on April 25, 1862, Joseph Davis, age seventy-eight, fled with his wife, his household, and seventy of his slaves to a hardscrabble plantation he purchased in Hinds County, not far from Champion Hill.[86] Two months later, as we have already seen, a raiding party from David Farragut's fleet burned Hurricane and looted Brierfield, the adjoining plantation of Davis's brother Jefferson, whom Joseph had lured to Mississippi in 1835, convincing him to abandon his military career and become a plantation grandee. The Montgomery family and most of the other slaves remained to work the land, protected by Admiral Porter's gunboats. Porter hired workers from the Bend to chop wood for his fleet and hired Montgomery's son Isaiah as his chief mate and manservant. He later supported the Montgomerys' move to Cincinnati when Benjamin got into some tangled disputes with families at the Bend.[87]

When Union troops arrived at Hurricane in the fall of 1863 they found roughly a thousand slaves running the Davis estate as if they owned it. The previous summer, in conversations with the army chaplain Colonel John Eaton, Grant had expressed interest in having the Davis lands twenty-five miles below Vicksburg, "occupied by freedmen" and turned into "a Negro paradise," a refuge for slaves flocking to his army. Here they should be permitted to "do and act for themselves," Grant told Eaton.[88] But Eaton had bigger ideas. With Grant's support, he set out to create a new labor system for the postwar South, with black farm families working the land in small groups as independent cultivators.[89]

In November 1863, about the time Grant was called to Chattanooga to rescue General Rosecrans's entrapped army, Eaton received authorization for his experiment from the Department of War. He divided the land and leased plots to independent black farmers. Later, he established a freedman's court modeled on Joseph Davis's justice system.[90]

There were setbacks, but, protected by black soldiers, the independent farmers soon became self-sufficient. When the travel writer J. T. Trowbridge visited the Bend in 1865 he found a prosperous, self-governing community of three thousand souls under the light supervision of twenty-four-year-old Colonel Samuel Thomas, Eaton's chief assistant. Davis Bend bore out Eaton's idea that, when left alone and given land and protection, emancipated slaves could thrive. Trowbridge agreed. He saw the Bend as the possible forerunner of an enlightened "post-war free labor system in the South, and the eventual division of the large plantations into homesteads to be sold or rented to small farmers."[91]

Regrettably, this proved too radical an idea. When the war ended, Davis Bend ceased to be a government-run community. Private ownership was restored, and this brought an end to Eaton's free-labor experiment. President Andrew Johnson's lenient amnesty policy allowed Joseph Davis and other antebellum planters to receive federal pardons and regain ownership of their lands. Fearing that abolitionists in the House of Representatives would revoke the restoration of his lands, Davis sold them to Benjamin Montgomery and his sons in 1866.[92] The Montgomery family returned and reassumed a leadership role in the community, but they and the original homesteaders of Davis Bend steadily lost control of their former lands, which reverted, by a succession of court orders, to the original white owners.[93] By the mid-1870s, the amount of southern land controlled by black people was "minuscule," writes historian Eric Foner.[94]

There was nothing else like Davis Bend in the Mississippi Valley. After Vicksburg surrendered, an exodus of blacks from the vast cotton belt along the river, with a population of nearly a quarter of a million slaves, overwhelmed the original labor camps established by John Eaton in western Tennessee and Mississippi.[95] "The work is too immense for description," Eaton wrote a friend in the North as he tried to feed, house, clothe, and educate freedmen who came pouring into his government settlements around Vicksburg.[96]

Coming downriver from Cairo in July 1863, William D. Butler, an agent of a Christian charity organization, looked out at a scene he could barely believe. Black people by the tens of thousands, wearing tattered clothing that "scarcely covered their nakedness," crouched at the water's edge and "beckoned despairingly to be taken on board." Inside the city of Vicksburg, conditions were even more distressing. All that summer and into the fall, a river of black humanity poured into the city from east of the Big Black and spread over the country around Vicksburg, "the very gate of heaven" to these suffering people. Eager for assistance from private charities, Grant allowed Butler full freedom to roam through his lines and inspect the condition of the refugees. His report was hair-raising. Black refugees filled "vacant houses, churches, sheds and caves" crowded together, most of them sick and without food or medicine. Trembling from fear and fatigue, some longed to be back on their old plantations. Within the city, Butler found black refugees gathered in vacant lots or in the backyards of houses "filled to overflowing with Negroes." Later, at a Vicksburg hospital, doctors told him that grievously sick black men, many of them near death, were crawling up the terraces begging for medicine at open windows. Many of them were still lying dead "in the shrubbery and fence corners."

On the first of August, military authorities, fearing an epidemic that would spread to the army, began moving these powerless people to the mosquito-infested mudflats across the river. On some days Union wagon drivers would find a dozen or more dead bodies in a bombed-out Vicksburg house. Holes were dug on the riverbank and corpses tossed into them. In the chaotic camps on the Louisiana side of the river, people perished in uncountable numbers. "Sometimes they would crawl off in the weeds and die, where their bodies could be found only by the stench which arose from their decay," a Union official told Butler.[97]

It took months for Eaton to bring a measure of order to these camps and begin putting people to work. By November, at least forty-three thousand recently liberated black people were still gathered on the banks of the Mississippi, from Helena, Arkansas, to Natchez, Mississippi, ten thousand within a dozen miles of Vicksburg. But able-bodied freed people had at least been put to work as army cooks, washerwomen, teamsters, and grooms, while thousands more picked cotton on plantations run by Northern leaseholders. Eaton considered this an accomplishment, and it was. But independent inspectors from charity organizations found almost everywhere "the same wretched cabins and half-clothed people; the same dejected look in the old men and women, who have found freedom thus far [an empty promise]."[98]

Grant had unleashed a social upheaval he didn't have the time or the resources to manage. He did, however, look to young black males to assume occupation duty in the areas his army had subdued, to bolster the new defensive fortifications he was building around Vicksburg, and to guard contraband camps, which were regularly and viciously visited by bands of secessionist partisans who were slaughtering or re-enslaving entire families. Preoccupied with war-related responsibilities, he turned this work over to Lorenzo Thomas, who returned to Mississippi that summer and continued the recruiting work he had begun in the spring.[99]

Lincoln pressed the policy on his commanders in the Mississippi Valley and elsewhere in the South. Writing to Grant that August, he saw the raising of additional black regiments as a way to "soon close this contest. It works doubly, weakening the enemy and strengthening us. We were not fully ripe for it, until the river was opened. Now, I think, at least a hundred thousand can, and ought to be organized along its shores, relieving all white troops to serve elsewhere."[100]

Grant replied: "Arming the negro [was] with the emancipation of the negro . . . the heaviest blow yet given the Confederacy." He then assured the president that he was assigning recruiting officers to expeditions he was sending into Louisiana to root out rebel guerrilla units.[101] Yet he was still reluctant—as was the president—to use black volunteers as front-line troops. Writing in confidence to Congressman Elihu Washburne, Grant enunciated his fast-evolving views on slavery and emancipation:

> I never was an Abolitionist, [n]ot even what could be called anti slavery, but I try to judge farely [sic] & honestly and it bec[a]me patent to my mind early in the rebellion that the North & South could never live at peace with each other except as one nation, and that without Slavery. As anxious as I am to see peace reestablished I would not therefore be willing to see any settlemen[t] until this question is forever settled.[102]

Lincoln could not have put it more strongly, and in Vicksburg it was Grant who was seen by black people as their emancipator. After the city surrendered, Grant's friend Annie Wittenmyer, who had come down from Iowa during the siege to help out in the field hospitals and stayed on into the late summer, invited Grant to dine with her at the house she occupied in Vicksburg. The morning of the dinner the black children of the neighborhood "danced a jubilee," Wittenmyer recalled, and excitedly gathered around the house when they learned Grant was coming. "Black faces were peeping from the near houses and the fences were black with colored people. It was perhaps the one chance of their lives to see their deliverer, the great captain who had opened the prison-house of Vicksburg, and given liberty to all the people."[103]

Grant tried to avoid public appearances, but his troops were everywhere, and their mere presence gave black people hitherto unavailable opportunities to challenge the region's oppressive racial order. A single incident is illustrative. On a pleasant Sunday morning in July, a service was held in a small Protestant church in rural Louisiana, across the river from Vicksburg. "When the services were nearly ended a negro man in any but Sunday clothes came boldly up the middle aisle to the pulpit, stopped a little while there, [and] walked to the right hand side of the church," wrote Kate Foster, daughter of a prominent local planter. Mr. Carradine, a pillar of the community, "got up and demanded [to know what he] wanted. The impudent scamp said he came to church and wanted a seat. All of the congregation looked astounded. . . . Mr. Carradine showed him into the gallery where the servants sit. I was so angry," Kate wrote in her diary. "I should not be surprised if some of our enemies had sent him in the church as an insult to us."

The black "intruder" had not accomplished what he had courageously set out to do, but he might not have made the attempt had there not been, as Kate Foster noted, "a great many Yankee [officers] at church." They were in the village, she said, to take "negroes from all the plantations around."[104]

In the second week of July, as Grant focused on subduing guerrilla activity in the countryside around Vicksburg, Pemberton prepared to lead his army to a parole camp at Enterprise, Mississippi, east of Jackson. Before leaving, he persuaded James McPherson, whom Grant had put in charge of governing the city, to allow his officers to keep those African American servants who were willing to accompany them. Grant approved the policy, provided servants were emphatically informed, in the presence of a Union officer, that they were free. John Logan protested. Confederate officers, he charged, were coercing their body servants to leave with them. The issue was set before Grant, who wavered at first, but finally revoked McPherson's dispensation.[105]

On July 11, Pemberton's army of parolees filed out of the city. En route, sixteen hundred of them would slip away and head home.[106] Some of them sat out the rest of the war, as Grant had predicted, but a great many rejoined the army after spending some time with family. One of them was nineteen-year-old Private A. Hugh Moss. When Moss returned to Lake Charles, Louisiana, he found neighbors who claimed to have been "humiliated by their negroes." Recently liberated black men were rumored to be carrying rifles and riding stolen horses, he reported in his diary; and they had, he had heard, broken into plantations managed by white women and stolen clothing and money. Worst of all, they were "putting themselves on an equality with whites. . . . Was this not enough to awake the spirit of '76 and make the blood boil within the veins of those who had stayed at home. . . . Men that will stay back quietly at their firesides after witnessing these outrages upon humanity have lost all principle, all respect," he wrote. That November, at the Battle of Chattanooga, Grant would encounter Vicksburg veterans he had paroled, men without slaves, some of them, like Moss, determined to keep black people in servitude.[107]

John Pemberton rode at the head of his column of prisoners, "silent and sad."[108] It was the last army he would lead. While Jefferson Davis remained a firm supporter, Pemberton was a marked man. Feelings against him were so strong in the army that he had to resign his rank and serve as a lieutenant colonel. Assigned to artillery duty around Richmond, "he was greeted with jeers by the men as he rode down the lines."[109] After the war he moved back to Philadelphia and worked for his solidly established family until his death, in 1881.[110]

He never returned to Vicksburg, although he did run into Joseph E. Johnston on his way to Enterprise with the remnants of his paroled army. Johnston courteously extended his hand. Pemberton saluted and walked away.[111] To his last days, he took comfort in knowing that Jeff Davis blamed Johnston, not him, for losing Vicksburg. A few days after Vicksburg surrendered, Josiah Gorgas suggested to Davis that the garrison had succumbed for want of provisions. "Yes, from want of provisions inside," Davis shot back, "and a general outside who wouldn't fight."[112]

• • •

Sherman marched to Jackson, in pursuit of Joseph Johnston, just ahead of Pemberton's men. It was wickedly hot, and dust lay on the road "like flour, 4 to 5 inches thick," wrote George Washington Whitman of the 51st New York Volunteers, a younger brother of the great American bard.[113] Billowing clouds of it, ten and twenty feet high, blew in men's faces, creating an "intolerable" thirst. With water scarce, men chewed the leaves of trees for nourishment.[114]

Near Champion Hill, they marched through places nearly devoid of life. Deserted, burned-out houses lined the roads, and bloated animal carcasses lay in ditches, their innards exposed. The decaying bodies of dead soldiers, "some of them headless, some armless . . . some mangled by dogs and wolves," were scattered thickly in fields where the worst fighting had taken place. "The countryside was desolate, stripped of food and dwellings, few homes remained standing, no slaves in sight, no livestock of any kind."[115] When signs of civilization were spotted—an intact farm or a smokehouse—the men pillaged, looted, and burned, payback for Johnston's army spoiling what fresh water they had managed to stumble upon. To slow down Sherman's pursuit, Johnston's men had emptied kerosene into wells and cisterns and run cattle, hogs, and sheep into ponds and shot them, leaving their carcasses to spoil the drinking water.[116] "War in this country is a very different thing," wrote a Pennsylvania soldier who had seen action in the east. "This is war in earnest."[117] Marching through enemy lands, these western "[men] will do three times the damage of the army of the Potomac," George Washington Whitman wrote in his diary.[118]

Sherman reached Jackson on July 10 and began shelling the rebels, who were strengthening the trenches he and McPherson had assaulted the previous May.[119] Johnston's army was hopelessly outnumbered, with its back to the Pearl River, but, having had his fill of attacking fixed fortifications, Sherman settled in for a siege—"a miniature Vicksburg," he called it.[120]

He faced an equally cautious commander. After Johnston had failed to capture an ammunition train headed for Sherman's army, he began evacuating the city on the night of July 16, completely surprising Sherman—who then, to Grant's despair, failed to pursue aggressively.

Johnston had slipped across the Pearl River on pontoon bridges and was well on his way to the Mississippi pinelands. Why chase him, Sherman rationalized, and subject his own men to another march in wasting heat? He had accomplished what he had set out to do, ridding the state of the only remaining threat to Vicksburg. And Jackson was his. He could turn now to a task for which he was suited: industrial destruction. He assembled four thousand men and had them finish off the capital as a rail center, dismantling rolling stock, roundhouses, bridges, and trestles inside the city and around it for as far as sixty miles. In town, the men did the work in swirling smoke from fires set by the fleeing rebel army to prevent provisions from falling into enemy hands. "Jackson, the former flourishing capital of the state, is in ashes," wrote a Northern reporter, "and all the region around it is laid waste."[121] Soldiers gazed upon the wreckage and gave the town a new name: "Chimneyville."[122]

Sherman's soldiers had been instructed not to enter private homes or destroy civilian property, but they flew out of control when live shells the enemy had planted in the ground injured a number of them. When Whitman's New York boys entered Jackson, the second Federal force to get inside the capital, most of the houses were "deserted and closed." The New Yorkers put guards at many of the houses, but when Sherman's western troops poured in, they broke through the doors and hauled away heavy furniture, carpets, and entire libraries, untransportable loot they would be forced to leave behind when they headed back to Vicksburg. The vandalism was so extensive Sherman claimed to be "ashamed" of his men.[123] Grant had not authorized it, but he had issued orders to forage, to have the army live off the land.[124] This climaxed the destruction. "For a distance of fifteen miles, on every side, the country was scoured by . . . [our] foragers, and all available supplies for the army were gathered in," wrote an Indiana chaplain.[125]

On July 23, after distributing food and medicine to the suffering people of Jackson, Sherman turned his army back toward Vicksburg.[126] "Nothing is left between Vicksburg & Jackson," he wrote his family.[127] "The inhabitants are Subjugated. They cry aloud for mercy."[128] Sherman had created between Jackson and Vicksburg a no-man's-land, a buffer zone to protect Vicksburg's eastern flank. And he had destroyed the war-making capability of the only city in which an enemy army might assemble. Vicksburg was secure for the duration of the war;

Richmond never seriously considered retaking it. A Northern newspaperman stationed in Mississippi estimated there were fewer than ten thousand rebel troops scattered about the state in late 1863. They were largely man-hunters: tracking deserters and conscripting farm boys who had yet to enlist.[129] That August, there were roughly five thousand Confederate soldiers absent without leave in Mississippi.[130]

On his return from Jackson, Sherman camped near the Big Black River, on the ground he had occupied on July 4. He reached it on July 27, put his four divisions into "handsome, clean camps," and set up headquarters in a pleasant grove on the plantation of a gray-bearded Confederate named Parson Fox.[131] Grant took up quarters in Vicksburg itself, in a house on the heights overlooking the river, and would often visit Sherman in his camp. The generals summoned their families to Vicksburg, and they picnicked together along the banks of the river.[132]

Grant and Sherman talked often and intensely, and they agreed that many despairing Mississippians were resigned to rejoining the Union. Grant detected growing Union sentiment in Vicksburg, where his army was policing with an even hand and using emancipated slaves to clean up the streets and repair houses.[133] While Sherman was at Jackson, Grant had informed him that a number of Vicksburg leaders, former Whigs who had been Unionists as late as 1860, were making plans to establish a new civil government loyal to the Union. Grant saw this as a promising harbinger.[134] "If prominent men in Mississippi admit the fact of being subdued, it will have a powerful effect all over the South," Sherman wrote back encouragingly.[135]

Sherman attributed this apparent softening of secessionist sentiment to the demoralizing impact of his march of ruin. Earlier in the war he had talked often and ardently about waging destructive war, but Jackson was his first opportunity to war unyieldingly on an entire city and region; and for a short time he believed the destruction he had wrought had dimmed hopes among victims for the survival of the Confederacy. His march back to the Big Black had taken Sherman through what he believed to be "the worst whipped communities on the face of the earth." The people had been so thoroughly conquered, he believed, that they would return to the Union on just about any terms.[136]

This didn't wash with Sylvanus Cadwallader. The reporter had accompanied Sherman on the Jackson campaign and witnessed among the conquered only embitterment and a deep desire for revenge. "Gen. Sherman honestly believes that a strong Union sentiment exists. I as honestly disbelieve it," he wrote his family from Sherman's camp on the Big Black. Cadwallader claimed to have talked with hundreds of Mississippians between Vicksburg and Jackson and found only "one citizen who could properly be termed a Union man. . . . All are intensely pro-slavery in feeling, and curse the Yankees for 'stealing their niggers.' " [137]

Cadwallader had a point. Sherman had misunderstood the fruits of his own conquest, mistaking dependency and quiet contempt for resignation. Many of those who were relying upon the Union army for bread were sharing it with guerrilla bands that had become the new rulers of this ruined land. [138] They were a vile lot, wrote another Union reporter. "If they get possession of a negro from our side of the river, and he is sound they sell him; if unsound, they hang or shoot him." [139]

Cadwallader's impressions are borne out by a representative clutch of letters that made their way from Johnston's defeated army to the tiny town of Minden, Louisiana. "I expect to murder every Yankee I ever meet when I can do so with impunity," wrote Sergeant Edwin H. Fay, a Harvard graduate and headmaster of a small boys' school. This was a week after Vicksburg fell. He had no intention of taking prisoners after witnessing the destruction Sherman, Blair, and other Yankee infidels had inflicted on the lands around Vicksburg. "There can be no fellow-ship between us forever . . ." he told his wife, Sara. "I shall never cease to hate them." A "war of extermination" was on the horizon. [140]

By the end of that summer, Sherman and Grant were saying exactly this, their turnabout the result of inflamed guerrilla violence east and west of Vicksburg, in areas far from military posts. "The troops . . . around Vicksburg," Grant would note in his memoirs, "were busily and unpleasantly employed in making expeditions against guerilla bands and small detachments of cavalry which infested the interior." And everywhere there were embittered folks who felt as Private A. Hugh Moss did. "There was quite a peace feeling, for the time being, among the citizens from that part of Mississippi," Grant wrote, "but this feeling soon subsided. [141]

Mississippi and great parts of Louisiana and Tennessee were finished, out of the war, but the great Union victory was also a dark forewarning. What Sherman and Grant were seeing east and west of Vicksburg—conquest accompanied by anarchic violence and venom—meant a longer and crueller war than even they had expected.[142] "If they must have War," Sherman wrote of secessionist diehards, "we must accept the issue, and make War terrific."[143]

Sherman continued to be baffled by secessionist resistance in places his soldiers had ground to powder. "We have ravaged the land, and have sent away half a million . . . negroes so that this country is paralyzed and cannot recover its lost strength in twenty years," he wrote Ellen. What was there to fight for? Instead of making peace with the Union garrison at Vicksburg, which was feeding and protecting thousands of displaced people, rebel families were "flying east into Alabama and Georgia" with the slaves they had managed to keep.[144]

The families of Sid Champion and Joseph Davis had joined this sorrowful parade of secessionist refugees. Their experience indicates the depths of Southern insurgency in the wake of the most crushing setback the Confederacy had yet suffered, a blow that might have finished off a less obstinate people.

EPILOGUE

"Let us leave our land and emigrate to any desert spot of the earth, rather than return to the Union, even as it Was!"[1]

—Sarah Morgan, Diarist

"Nearly every family around . . . are leaving for Georgia," Matilda Champion wrote her husband, Sid, on July 10, 1863.[2] Sid Champion had been captured at Vicksburg and was preparing to march the next day to a parole camp in Enterprise, Mississippi. His wife's letter never caught up with him. She would see him four months later, after he had been exchanged and shown up unexpectedly at her father-in-law's plantation near Clinton, where she and the children had been living since the great battle for Vicksburg was fought on their property.

Sid had returned home through the lands west of Jackson that Sherman had plundered. Wasting no time, he spirited his family and remaining slaves to an isolated spot in the pine woods northwest of Jackson—the "refuge home," he called it. Matilda, lonely and depressed, would struggle to feed their children after he rejoined his regiment and fought under Joseph Johnston in the Atlanta campaign and was later wounded at the Battle of Murfreesboro. After the war, the family returned to Champion Hill and built a modest frame structure a mile or so from the big white house that was probably burned by Sherman's men on their march back from Jackson. Weakened by his battle wounds and burdened by depression brought on by the Confederate defeat, Sid Champion died in 1868, at age forty-five.[3]

The story of Joseph Davis's flight from Mississippi is equally poignant, though more symbolic. Joseph Davis, once one of the ten richest men of the state, represented a way of life that existed among a privileged few in the river counties of Mississippi on the eve of the Civil War. In late June 1863, a week before John Pemberton surrendered Vicksburg, he was liv-

ing with his invalid wife and twenty-one-year-old granddaughter at Fleetwood, the rundown plantation west of Vicksburg he had purchased, sight
unseen, before fleeing Davis Bend a year earlier. He was nearly bankrupt
and in failing health. His life, his entire world, had been broken by a small
quiet man who two years earlier had been loading shelves in a leather
store. His former slaves had taken possession of his prized plantation.

On the evening of July 3, a courier from Joseph Johnston, an old
friend, arrived at Fleetwood with a letter from the general urging the
family to leave. A few days later Joe and his granddaughter, Mary Elizabeth Mitchell—"Lise" to the family—piled a few of their belongings
into an ox-drawn wagon and headed east, toward Alabama. Joe's wife,
Eliza, and other members of their extended family joined them, and
their caravan was soon entwined with Johnston's army as it made its way
back to Jackson after Vicksburg surrendered. Taking up the rear were
slaves Joe Davis had lured back from Hurricane.

They parted with the army at Jackson and "for three weeks we traveled on," Lise wrote in her captivating journal, "occasionally finding an
abandoned cabin where the older members of the party took shelter
while we camped in the wildwoods by the side of some little stream. . . .
We were homeless exiles, uncertain and oh! So hopeless of our future."

The journey proved too much for Eliza. She died in early October
at the home of friends who resided on the Alabama border. Lise and
her grandfather returned to Fleetwood to recover some family property.
Riding from Jackson to Bolton Station, they saw only chimneys "standing amid ashes." Their place had been laid waste, and "nothing could
be found." They left without exchanging a word, and they lived out the
war with friends in Tuscaloosa, Alabama. Two years later Lise received a
post: "Poor, dear Uncle Jeff" was a prisoner of the Yankees.

Joe Davis and Lise returned to Vicksburg after the war and rented
a house called Anchuca, a Choctaw word meaning "happy home." Lise
found it hard to look at the river. "An object of love" had become a
bleak reminder of all she and her family had lost. On its swift current, she wrote in her journal, had come the "devils" who wrecked her
world.[4]*

---

* Lise Mitchell remained by her grandfather's side until his death, in 1870. Anchuca is
now a pleasant bed-and-breakfast.

APPENDIX

Vicksburg Battlefield Casualties: March 29, 1863–July 4, 1863

CONFEDERATE	KILLED	WOUNDED	MISSING/POW	TOTAL
Pre-siege	538	1,709	3,642	5,889
Siege	875	2,169	158	3,202
Total	1,413	3,878	3,800	9,091
UNION				
Pre-siege	1,367	6,785	419	8,571
Siege	214	769	588	1,571
Total	1,581	7,554	1,077	10,142

Grant began his final drive on Vicksburg from Milliken's Bend, Louisiana, on March 29, 1863. The Confederate Army in Vicksburg surrendered on July 4, following a one-day truce.

Bearss, *The Campaign for Vicksburg*, vol. 3, 1311; USG to Halleck, July 6, 1863, USGP, vol. 8, 132. I have relied on my own research and conversations with Terrence Winschel and the late Warren Grabau to come up with a close estimate of battlefield casualties.

ACKNOWLEDGMENTS

I began this book in 1997. Before stepping into an archive, I headed to Vicksburg, rented a room, and started exploring by car, on foot, and in a rented power boat the broken terrain and serpentine waterways that Grant had to surmount to take the town. I needed this exposure in order to give my readers what I expect in an absorbing novel or work of history—what biographer Robert A. Caro calls a "sense of place": a palpable feel for the physical setting in which the characters interact and the story unfolds.

Later in my research, I explored the ground on which every battle of Grant's Mississippi Valley campaign was fought, but for an entire year I was focused entirely on Vicksburg and its antebellum hinterland. On my first visit to the Vicksburg National Military Park I had the good fortune to run into Edwin C. Bearss, the park historian before he became Chief Historian of the National Park Service. Author of a three-volume history of the Vicksburg campaign and a legendary Civil War guide, he invited me to join a small group of historians he was taking on a tour of the battleground. Listening to him lecture from the top of a high-sitting earthen fort along the Confederate defense line, I could almost hear, in the foreground, the rapid reports of the sharpshooters.

The next day Bearss introduced me to military historian Warren E. Grabau. A Vicksburg resident and government geologist, Grabau worked with Bearss to raise the Union ironclad USS *Cairo* from the bottom of the Yazoo River, where it had been sitting since 1862, when it struck a rebel mine and sank in seconds. Bearss and Grabau had also coauthored a succession of scholarly articles on Vicksburg, and Grabau was completing a masterly geographical history of the final months of the Vicksburg campaign.

Warren and I became fast friends, and more than anyone else, he shaped my understanding of Grant's campaign. He invited me into his home and shared with me the exhaustive unpublished research he had done on Grant's Mississippi supply line. And he took me on a two-day-long walking tour of the Vicksburg battlefield. "Battles are not fought on pool tables," he said. "The terrain figures in every decision a commander makes. So you've got to walk the ground and see it as the men who fought here did, as both opportunity and obstacle."

That week I met Terrence Winschel, Bearss's successor as park historian and, like Bearss, author of major works on the Vicksburg campaign. Terry introduced me to the massive collection of soldiers' letters, diaries, and memoirs that the park had accumulated over the past century and a quarter. At the time, most of the manuscripts were stored in file cabinets in his office. He gave me a desk, and I worked in his cramped office for a good part of the next six weeks.

At least once a week I would head to the Old Courthouse Museum in downtown Vicksburg. Gordon A. Cotton, now retired, was the museum's curator and director. He and his associate, Jeff Giambrone, guided me through the museum's unequaled archive of Warren County and Vicksburg history. Down the street from the museum is the Vicksburg City Library, which has copies of every newspaper published in town during the war. The staff was unfailingly helpful as I plowed through the microfilmed collection.

The largest Civil War archive in the state is the Mississippi Department of Archives and History, at Jackson, the state capital. On later visits to Vicksburg I spent most of my days there. Space constraints prevent me from acknowledging by name the librarians and curators who helped me navigate this rich collection and the forty or so others I visited, in every part of the country, over the next several years.

This research would have been impossible without grants and released time from teaching provided by Lafayette College. Special thanks to Neil McElroy, the college's head librarian when I was working on this book, for acquiring for the collection every major resource I requested. The college's extraordinary librarians, chiefly Terese Heidenwolf, Lujuan Xu, Kylie Bailin, and Karen Haduck, head of interlibrary loan, were always there for me. Karen alone rounded up more than 2,700 articles and books on interlibrary loan.

The college's Excel Scholars Program provided me student scholars who were indispensable: Zack Leff, Jason Hill, Elizabeth Lucy, Matthew Ryan, Emily Koenig, and James Onorevole. They ran down citations, prepared bibliographies, fact-checked sources, and proofread chapters.

My principal sources for this book were the Official Records of the Union and Confederate armies and navies; the four thousand or so letters, diaries, and memoirs that I consulted at the archives listed in my bibliography; and the papers of Ulysses S. Grant. Beginning in 1962, John Y. Simon of Southern Illinois University edited thirty-one of the thirty-two volumes of the Grant papers, fifty thousand documents in all. After his death in 2008, the papers moved from Southern Illinois University to Mississippi State University in Starkville. They are housed there in the U.S. Grant Presidential Library, created in 2012 by the Ulysses S. Grant Association under the leadership of the distinguished Grant scholar Chief Justice (Ret.) Frank J. Williams, president of the association. They have been digitized and have long been available in print. John F. Marszalek, author of excellent biographies of William T. Sherman and Henry M. Halleck, is the executive and managing editor. He is also editor, with David S. Nolan and Louie P. Gallo, of a new annotated edition of *The Personal Memoirs of Ulysses S. Grant.*

I traveled to Starkville soon after the papers were archived and researched parts of the collection that are not in the official, published papers. The staff, led by historian Michael Ballard, was superb. Ballard passed away in 2016 after authoring four seminal books on the Vicksburg campaign.

I had met John Simon in 2004 at the Boston studios of WGBH-TV when my friend Margaret Drain, executive producer of *American Experience*, was overseeing the production of a documentary film on the life of Grant. John and I, along with a number of other historians, served as consultants on the project. He and I kept in touch, mostly by phone, and he provided me with fresh perspectives on Grant's private and inner life, which the general chose not to reveal in his memoirs.

I am a late entrant to Civil War studies. Aside from graduate courses I took with John Hope Franklin and Avery Craven, I had no compelling interest in the war until I read the works of Allan Nevins and James McPherson. I never met Nevins, but James McPherson has been a continuing inspiration. He encouraged me to write this book and kept at me to finish.

While colleagues read separate chapters, three persons, aside from my student researchers, read it in its entirety and offered astute criticism: my agent Gina Maccoby; my Lafayette College colleague and friend Jim Tiernan; and my golfing buddy Tom Glyn, an internationally esteemed scientist and inventor and a self-taught authority on Civil War armaments and naval warfare. Tom also did voluntary research on armaments and logistics. We lost Tom last year and I miss him terribly.

Much of the detail work on the book was a family affair. My wife, Rose, accompanied me to half a dozen archives, where she made the research less laborious than it could have been. She is also my principal proofreader. My grandsons, Andrew Miller and Austin Medina, did library work, and with my granddaughter, Alyssa, were my chief consultants on everything pertaining to computers, decidedly not one of my strengths. Alyssa also did major work on the bibliography. Austin and his brother, Devin Medina, helped me choose and organize the illustrations and my son, Greg, spent time with me in Vicksburg researching the battlefield, as did a number of close friends, among them John Elliot, Ed Neugebauer, Bill and Peggy Dermott, Mike Selverian, and Joe Cox. Our guide for two of these excursions was Dr. David Slay, at the time a Vicksburg park historian. He later sent me copies of his extraordinary map collection of the Vicksburg campaign and allowed me to read his soon-to-be-published book on African American soldiers in the Middle Mississippi Valley. I thought I had seen everything of interest at Vicksburg relating to the battle until I met David. He gave me a closer appreciation of the geography, history, and people of the Yazoo River Valley and the hill country around the Champion family farm, where the decisive battle of the campaign was fought. On one visit to

Champion Hill he introduced me to Sid Johnson Champion, great-grandson of Sid and Matilda Champion. I am grateful to Sid Champion for sending me an absorbing history of his family.

This book has had an interrupted life. After completing most of the archival research in 2001, I put it aside and began work on a combat history of World War II, a decision prompted by the death of my father, an Army Air Forces veteran. Not until 2013 did I return to the Vicksburg project, with the blessing of my understanding editor, Bob Bender. We've been a team for twenty-four years and have built a relationship of trust and affection. Backing up Bob is measured, quietly authoritative Johanna Li. Jon Karp, president and publisher of Simon & Schuster, has been encouraging from the time he read my book proposal. Copyeditors Bob Castillo and Lisa Healy worked under pressing time constraints to improve the book. Paul Dippolito worked his magic on the design.

The person I leaned on most heavily when I began the book was my pal Don Meyerson. He lived with our family for a stretch on his return from Singapore and set up living quarters in our finished basement. Piles of Civil War letters and memoirs were spread around the room on tables and shelves. Don read hundreds of these personal accounts, and we would talk about them late into the night. A Marine combat veteran with a Purple Heart, Don helped me understand the innermost feelings of men under fire, far from home, in an incomprehensible place, where nearly everyone but your own outfit looked to be an enemy. He never let me forget about these soldier letters, and eventually prodded me back to Vicksburg.

Lastly, there is Rose. She did a little bit of everything and offered lots of love and clear headed advice. My greatest hope is that little Sophie, the newest addition to the Miller brood, takes inspiration from her.

NOTES

ABBREVIATIONS

BL: Robert Underwood and Clarence Clough Buel, eds. *Battles and Leaders of the
           Civil War*, 4 vols. New York: The Century Company, 1887–88.
CT: *Chicago Daily Tribune*
Duke: William R. Perkins Library, Manuscript Division, Duke University, Durham,
           North Carolina.
EES: Ellen Ewing Sherman
Garland Papers: Hamlin Garland Papers, Huntington Library, San Marino, California
ISHL: State Historical Library, Springfield, Illinois (now part of Abraham Lincoln
           Presidential Library, Springfield, Illinois)
JDG: Julia Dent Grant
LC: Library of Congress, Manuscript Division, Washington, D.C.
LSU: Hill Memorial Library, Louisiana State University, Baton Rouge, Louisiana
MDAH: Mississippi Department of Archives and History, Jackson, Mississippi
NYT: *New York Times*
OR: *The War of the Rebellion: A Compilation of the Official Records of the Union and
           Confederate Armies*, 128 volumes. Washington, D.C.: Government Printing
           Office, 1880–1901. All citations in the book refer to series I. Following OR are
           the volume number and the page number[s].
ORN: *Official Records of the Union and Confederate Navies in the War of the Rebellion*,
           35 volumes. Washington, D.C.: Government Printing Office, 1894–1927.
           All citations refer to series I. Following ORN are volume number and page
           number[s].
Papers of MOLLUS: *Papers of the Military Order of the Loyal Legion of the United States.*
           Reprint, Wilmington, NC: Broadfoot Publishing, 1994.
SCW: *Sherman's Civil War: Selected Correspondence of William T. Sherman*, 1860–1865,
           edited by Brooks D. Simpson and Jean V. Berlin. Chapel Hill: University of
           North Carolina Press, 1999.
SHC: Southern Historical Collection, the Louis Round Wilson Library, Special
           Collections, the University of North Carolina at Chapel Hill
USAMHI: United States Army Military History Institute, Carlisle Barracks, Pennsylvania
USG: Ulysses S. Grant
USGP: *The Papers of Ulysses S. Grant*, edited by John Y. Simon and John Marszalek, 32
           vols. Carbondale: Southern Illinois University Press, 1967–2012.
USGM: Grant, Ulysses S. *Grant: Memoirs and Selected Letters*. New York: Library of

America, 1990. Grant's memoirs were originally published in two volumes in 1885–86 as *Personal Memoirs of U. S. Grant* (New York: Charles L. Webster & Company, 1885–86).

VNMP: Vicksburg National Military Park, Vicksburg, Mississippi

Washburne Mss.:   Elihu B. Washburne Papers, Library of Congress

WTS: Sherman, William Tecumseh.

WTSM: *Sherman, Memoirs of General W. T. Sherman* (1875). New York: The Library of America, 1990. The Library of America edition prints the text of the revised edition of 1886, with maps and Sherman letters written in response to the 1875 edition.

AUTHOR'S NOTE

1. William Faulkner, "William Faulkner, The Art of Fiction," Interviewed by Jean Stein, *The Paris Review*, Issue No. 12 (Spring 1956): 17.

2. All Faulkner quotes in William Faulkner, *Absalom, Absalom!* (New York: Vintage Books, 1986; first published in 1936), 24–34.

PROLOGUE

1. Mark Twain, *Life on the Mississippi* (1875) (New York: Airmont Publishing Company, 1965), 302.

2. Frederick Douglass, "U.S. Grant and the Colored People," *Elevator*, vol. 8, no. 20, 4.

3. Edward T. Eggleston Diary, July 15, 1862, VNMP.

4. Albert Richardson, *A Personal History of Ulysses S. Grant* (Hartford: American Publishing Co., 1868), 300 hereafter, *A Personal History.*

5. Ulysses S. Grant, *Grant: Memoirs and Selected Letters* (New York: Library of America edition, 1990), 735.

6. Gary W. Gallagher, *The Confederate War: How Popular Will, Nationalism, and Military Strategy Could Not Stave Off Defeat* (Cambridge: Harvard University Press, 1997), 29. According to Gallagher's figures, the North mobilized at least 2.2 million men, about half its military-age population. Union armies suffered a death rate of one in six. See also E. B. Long, *The Civil War Day by Day: An Almanac, 1861–1865* (Garden City, NY: Doubleday, 1971), 710–11.

ONE. CAIRO

1. William Tecumseh Sherman to Prof. Boyd, May 13, 1861, SCW, 161.

2. Charles Dickens, *American Notes and Pictures from Italy* (1842) (Oxford: Oxford University Press, 1991), 171, 187. Dickens gives a fuller description of Cairo, thinly described as the fictional town of Eden, in *Martin Chuzzlewit*, the picaresque novel he wrote on his return to London. See Dickens, *Martin Chuzzlewit* (1844) (New York: Alfred A. Knopf, 1994), 381.

3. Anthony Trollope, *North America* (1862), edited by Donald Smalley and Bradford Booth (New York: Alfred A. Knopf, 1951), 402. Trollope was the son of Frances

Trollope, author of *Domestic Manners of the Americans* (1832), a stinging portrait of American life.

4. For Cairo's early history, see John W. Reps, "Great Expectations and Hard Times: The Planning of Cairo, Illinois," *Journal of the Society of Architectural Historians* 16 (December 1957): 18.

5. Bruce Catton, *Grant Moves South* (Boston: Little, Brown and Company, 1960), 44.

6. Trollope, *North America*, 403; John M. Lansden, *A History of the City of Cairo, Illinois* (1910) (Carbondale: Southern Illinois University Press, 1976), 128.

7. John H. Brinton, *Personal Memoirs of John H. Brinton, Civil War Surgeon, 1861–1865* (1883) (Carbondale: Southern Illinois University Press, 1996), 98.

8. Albert D. Richardson, *The Secret Service: The Field, the Dungeon, and the Escape* (Hartford: American Publishing Co., 1866), 141.

9. Quoted in W. A. Pitkin, "When Cairo Was Saved for the Union," *Journal of the Illinois State Historical Society* 51 (1958): 296; see also Robert M. Sutton, "The Illinois Central: Thoroughfare for Freedom," *Civil War History* (September 1961): 276.

10. NYT, May 11, 1861.

11. Adjutant-General's Report for Illinois, Revised (Springfield, Il, 1900), 1, 7.

12. *Ibid.*; *Chicago Daily Tribune*, May 14, 1861 (hereafter cited as CT).

13. Charles B. Kimbell, *History of Battery "A," First Illinois Light Artillery Volunteers* (Chicago: Cushing Printing Company, 1899), 16.

14. NYT, June 12, 1861.

15. Quoted in Pitkin, "Cairo," 296.

16. NYT, May 10, 1861.

17. *Cairo Daily Gazette*, April 25, 1861.

18. Edward Dicey, *Spectator of America* (Chicago: Quadrangle Books, 1971), 208 (first published in 1862 as *Six Months in the Federal States*); Mary Kellogg, ed, *Army Life of an Illinois Soldier: Letters and Diary of Charles W. Wills* (Carbondale: Southern Illinois University Press), 13; CT, June 8, 1861.

19. Aden G. Cavins to Matilda Cavins, February 17, 1862, in Matilda Livingston Cavins, ed., *War Letters of Aden G. Cavins* (Evansville, IN: Rosenthal-Kuebler Printing Co., 1980), n.p.

20. Trollope, *North America*, 405.

21. Hamlin Garland, *Ulysses S. Grant: His Life and Character* (New York: Doubleday-McClure, 1898), 180; Herman R. Lantz, *A Community in Search of Itself: A Case History of Cairo, Illinois* (Carbondale: Southern Illinois University Press, 1972), 25.

22. CT, May 25, 1861.

23. Lt. Commander S. Ledyard Phelps to John Rodgers, August 16, 1861, ORN, 1/22/299.

24. Rodgers to Gideon Welles, June 8, 1862, August 22, 1861, ORN, 1/22/283, 303; A. T. Mahan, *The Gulf and Inland Waters* (Wilmington, NC: Broadfoot Publishing Company, 1989), 12; Kendall D. Gott, *Where the South Lost the War: An Analysis of the Fort Henry-Fort Donelson Campaign, February 1862* (Mechanicsburg, PA: Stackpole Books, 2003), 23.

25. Welles to John Rodgers, June 11, 1861, ORN, 1/22/286; not until October 1862 did Congress put the western river squadrons under navy control.

26. Rodgers to Welles, August 22, 1861, ORN, 1/22/302–03.

27. Scott to George B. McClellan, May 3, 1861, George B. McClellan Papers, LC.

28. James M. McPherson, *War on the Waters: The Union & Confederate Navies, 1861–1865* (Chapel Hill: University of North Carolina Press, 2012), 6.

29. Adam Badeau, *Military History of Ulysses S. Grant, from 1861 to April 1865*, vol. 1 (New York: D. Appleton & Co., 1881), 123–24.

30. Mahan, *Gulf and Inland Waters*, 11.

31. Quoted in John D. Milligan, *Gunboats Down the Mississippi* (Annapolis, MD: United States Naval Institute, 1965), xix.

32. Quoted in Lloyd Lewis, *Sherman: Fighting Prophet* (New York: Harcourt, Brace & Co., 1932), 252.

33. Howard K. Beale, ed., *The Diary of Edward Bates, 1859–1866* (Washington, D.C.: Government Printing Office, 1933), 186.

34. David Dixon Porter, *Naval History of the Civil War* (New York: Sherman Publishing Co., 1886), 134.

35. Porter, *Naval History*, 134; James M. Merrill, *Battle Flags South: The Story of the Civil War Navies on Western Waters* (Rutherford, NJ: Fairleigh Dickinson University Press, 1970), 21.

36. James B. Eads, "Recollections of Foote and the Gun-Boats," in BL, vol. 1, 339.

37. Mahan, *Gulf and Inland Waters*, 13.

38. John D. Milligan, "From Theory to Application: The Emergence of the American Ironclad War Vessel," *Military Affairs* (July 1984): 127. The first ironclad of the Civil War was actually the Confederate ram *Manassas*, but she was only a wooden tug with some iron plates added during the summer of 1861.

39. Florence Dorsey, *Road to the Sea: The Story of James B. Eads and the Mississippi River* (New York: Rinehart & Co., 1947), 60.

40. Eads to Welles, April 29, 1861, ORN, 1/22/278. Eads also converted the ferryboat *New Era* into the ironclad *Essex*.

41. Eads to Montgomery C. Meigs, August 30, 1861, Water Transportation File, Record Group 92, LC; Louis How, *James B. Eads* (Boston: Houghton Mifflin and Co., 1900), 29.

42. How, *Eads*, 31–32.

43. Foote to Gustavus V. Fox, September 13, ORN, I/22/307–08; Spencer C. Tucker, *Andrew Foote: Civil War Admiral on Western Waters* (Annapolis, MD: Naval Institute Press, 2000), 111–16.

44. Quoted in Tucker, *Foote*, 117.

45. Elliot Callender, "What a Boy Saw on the Mississippi," *Military Essays and Recollections*, vol. 1 (Chicago: The Commandery of the State of Illinois, 1891), passim.

46. Ivan Musicant, *Divided Waters: The Naval History of the Civil War* (New York: HarperCollins, 1995), 186; Flag Officer Andrew H. Foote, General Orders, No. 6, December 17, 1861, ORN, 1/22/466–67.

47. Eads, "Recollections," Eads Collection, Missouri History Museum, St. Louis, 346.

48. Foote to Meigs, November 20, 29, 1861, ORN, 1/22/386–438.

49. A. H. Foote to Gustavus V. Fox, Nov. 2, 1861, in Robert Means Thompson and Richard Wainwright, eds., *Gustavus Vasa Fox, Confidential Correspondence of Gustavus Vasa Fox* (Printed for the Naval Society by De Vinne Press, 1918), 8–10 (hereafter *Fox*

Correspondence); Foote to Welles, Nov. 28, 1861, ORN, 1/22/444; Henry Walke, "The Gunboats at Belmont and Fort Henry," in BL, vol. 1, 359–60.

50. Foote to Meigs, December 14, 1861, ORN, 1/22/463.
51. A. W. Pennock to Eads, January 15, 1862, Eads Collection, Missouri History Museum; Foote to Fox, January 27, 1862, Fox, *Fox Correspondence*, 32; Charles B. Boynton, The History of the Navy During the Rebellion, vol. 1 (New York: D. Appleton and Company, 1867), 503.
52. Foote to Welles, January 6, 1862, ORN, 1/22/502. When *St. Louis* was transferred to the Navy Department later in the war, her name was changed to *Baron de Kalb*, the navy already having a ship commissioned *St. Louis*.
53. Foote to Meigs, November 30, 1861, ORN, 1/22/446.
54. John C. Roberts and Richard H. Webber, "Gunboats in the River War, 1861–1865," 9 (Proceedings of the United States Naval Institute, March 1965), 84; Henry Walke, *Naval Scenes and Reminiscences of the Civil War in the United States on the Southern and Western Waters* (New York: F. R. Reed & Co., 1877), 17; Badeau, *Grant*, vol. 1, 24.
55. Fox to Foote, January 27, 1862; Fox, *Fox Correspondence*, 36.
56. Walke, *Naval Scenes*, 20–21.
57. Roberts and Webber, "Gunboats in the River War," 96.
58. Merrill, *Battle Flags*, 28.
59. Quoted in Tucker, *Foote*, 134.
60. Foote to John A. Winslow, November 16, 1861, ORN, 1/22/432–33.

TWO. RIVER WARRIOR

1. John W. Emerson, "Grant's Life in the West and His Mississippi Campaigns," *The Midland Monthly* (February 1898): 116.
2. USGM, 174.
3. Emerson, "Grant's Life in the West," 116.
4. James M. McPherson, *Battle Cry of Freedom; The Civil War Era* (New York: Oxford University Press, 1988), 296.
5. USG to John C. Frémont, September 5, 1861, USGP, v. 2, 193.
6. USGM, 174.
7. USG to John C. Frémont, September 5, 1861, USGP, v. 2, 193. When the gunboats left Cairo, Rodgers was in command; he had not yet been told that Foote had replaced him. Foote overtook him an hour later in a fast boat with orders designating a change in command. Rodgers was crestfallen, as he had built this little flotilla.
8. USGM, 175.
9. USG to Frémont, September 6, 1861, USGP, v. 2, 196–97.
10. Frémont to USG, *ibid.*, 191n.
11. E. B. Long, "Ulysses S. Grant for Today," in David L. Wilson and John W Simon, eds., *Ulysses S. Grant: Essays and Documents* (Carbondale: Southern Illinois University Press, 1981), 14.
12. McPherson, *Battle Cry*, 296–97.
13. USGM, 175; USG to Charles F. Smith, September 7, 1861, USGP, v. 2, 205.
14. Charles Francis Adams Jr. to Charles Francis Adams Sr., May 29, 1864, in

Worthington C. Ford, ed., *A Cycle of Adams Letters, 1861–1865*, vol. 2 (Boston: Houghton Mifflin, 1929), 133–34.

15. Lew Wallace, "The Capture of Fort Donelson," BL, vol. 1, 405.

16. Quoted in Jean Edward Smith, *Grant* (New York: Simon & Schuster, 2001), 181.

17. Quoted in Louis A. Coolidge, *Ulysses S. Grant* (Boston: Houghton Mifflin, 1917), 82.

18. Quoted in Lew Wallace, *An Autobiography*, vol. 1 (New York: Harper and Brothers, 1906), 338–45.

19. Richardson, The Secret Service: 141–42.

20. Richardson, *A Personal History*, vi.

21. T. Harry Williams, *McClellan, Sherman and Grant* (Chicago: Ivan R. Dee, 1991), 79.

22. USGM, 22.

23. Garland, *Grant*, 29.

24. *Ibid.*, 27.

25. *Ibid.*, 2, 12.

26. USGM, 28.

27. Garland, *Grant*, 52.

28. *Ibid.*, 18.

29. *Ibid.*, 13.

30. USGM, 32.

31. USGM, 41.

32. USGM, 78, 81.

33. USG to John W. Lowe, June 26, 1846, USGP, vol. 1, 97.

34. Garland, *Grant*, 111, 114; Lyle W. Dorsett, "The Problem of Ulysses S. Grant's Drinking During the War," *Hayes Historical Journal* 4, no. 2 (Fall 1983): 40.

35. USG to JDG, February 2, 1853 [1854], USGP, vol. 1, 316; Col. Thomas Anderson testimony in Garland, *Grant*, 127. John Y. Simon, former editor of the Grant papers, argued that there is nothing but rumors to support claims that Grant was forced to resign. See Simon, "U.S. Grant: The Man and the Image," in James G. Barber, *U.S. Grant: The Man and the Myth* (Carbondale: Southern Illinois University Press, 1985), 15. But Grant biographer Jean Edward Smith finds the evidence against Grant persuasive, as do I. See Smith, *Grant*, 87.

36. USG to Col. Samuel Cooper, April 11, 1854, USGP, vol. 1, 1854, 328–29.

37. John Eaton and Ethel O. Mason, *Grant, Lincoln, and the Freedmen: Reminiscences of the Civil War with Special Reference for the Work of the Contrabands and Freedmen of the Mississippi Valley* (New York: Longmans, Green, 1907), 100.

38. Richardson, *A Personal History*, 152.

39. Garland, *Grant*, xxv.

40. Quoted in Smith, *Grant*, 91.

41. Quoted in Bruce Catton, *U. S. Grant and the American Military Tradition* (Boston: Little, Brown and Company, 1954), 52.

42. William Conant Church, *Ulysses S. Grant and the Period of National Preservation and Reconstruction* (New York: G. P. Putnam's Sons, 1897), 57.

43. William S. McFeely, *Grant: A Biography* (New York: W. W. Norton, reissue edition, 2002), 62.

44. USGP, vol. 1, 347.

45. Quoted in Brooks D. Simpson, *Ulysses S. Grant: Triumph over Adversity, 1822–1865* (Boston: Houghton Mifflin Company, 2000), 71.

46. Quoted in Lloyd Lewis, *Captain Sam Grant* (Boston: Little, Brown and Company, 1950), 363.

47. Garland, *Grant*, xxiv; Grant's daughter, Ellen—or Nellie, as she was known, was born July 4, 1855; his fourth and youngest child, Jesse Root Jr., was born on February 6, 1858.

48. Garland, *Grant*, 140.

49. Julia Dent Grant, *The Personal Memoirs of Julia Dent Grant*, edited by John Y. Simon (Carbondale: Southern Illinois University Press, 1975), 82. [Hereafter JDG, *Personal Memoirs*.]

50. Quoted in Catton, *Grant and the American Military Tradition*, 53.

51. JDG, *Personal Memoirs*, 84, 86; Interview with Melanethon T. Burke, Hamlin Garland Papers; University of Southern California, Los Angeles, hereafter Garland Papers.

52. *New York Graphic*, September 16, 1879; Garland, *Grant*, 3, 135.

53. Richardson, *A Personal History*, vi.

54. USG to Frederick Dent, April 19, 1861, USGP, vol. 2, 3–4.

55. USGP, vol. 2, 7 note.

56. USGM, 153.

57. "How Grant Got to Know Rawlins," *Army and Navy Journal* (September 12, 1868).

58. USG to Bvt. Brig. Gen. Lorenzo Thomas, May 24, 1861, USGP, vol. 2, 35–36.

59. USGM, 159–60.

60. Sylvanus Cadwallader, *Three Years with Grant* (1955) (Lincoln: University of Nebraska Press, 1996), 347.

61. Ron Chernow, *Grant* (New York: Penguin Press, 2017), 129–30, 145; USGM, 168.

62. USG to JDG, August 10, 1861, USGP, vol. 2, 96.

63. Catton, *Grant Moves South*, 67.

64. USGM, 177.

65. William Tecumseh Sherman, "An Address on Grant," in James Grant Wilson and Titus Munson Coan, eds., *Personal Recollections of the War of the Rebellion* (New York: The Commandery, 1891), 108. Grant's army would not officially be called the Army of the Tennessee until October 1862.

66. McFeely, *Grant*, 89.

67. Interview with John McElroy, Garland Papers.

68. Rawlins to Elihu Washburne, December 30, 1861, Elihu B. Washburne, LC (hereafter Washburne Mss).

69. Williams, *McClellan, Sherman and Grant*, 87.

70. Edmund Wilson, "Northern Soldiers: Ulysses S. Grant," in *Patriotic Gore: Studies in the Literature of the American Civil War* (New York: Oxford University Press, 1962), 132.

71. Quoted in James M. McPherson, "Introduction" to the Penguin Books edition of *The Personal Memoirs of U. S. Grant* (New York: Penguin Books, 1999), xiv.

72. John H. Brinton, *Personal Memoirs of John H. Brinton, Civil War Surgeon, 1861–1865* (Carbondale, IL: Southern Illinois University Press, 1996), 134.

73. Franc B. Wilkie, *Pen and Powder* (Boston: Ticknor and Company, 1888), 98.

74. Quoted in Catton, *Grant Moves South*, 65.

75. NYT, April 30, 1864.

76. John Y. Simon and David L. Wilson, "Samuel H. Beckwith, Grant's Shadow," in Wilson and Simon, eds., *Ulysses S. Grant: Essays and Documents* (Carbondale: Southern Illinois University Press, 1981), 120.

77. Horace Porter, *Campaigning with Grant* (1897) (New York: Bantam Books, 1991), 176.

78. Simon and Wilson, "Beckwith," 91.

79. Porter, *Campaigning*, 13.

80. Garland, *Grant*, 3.

81. Steven E. Woodworth, *Nothing But Victory: The Army of the Tennessee, 1861–1865* (New York: Alfred A, Knopf, 2005), 42.

82. Chauncey McKeever to USG, November 1, 1862, USGP, vol. 3, 143–44.

83. USG to Charles Ferguson Smith, November 5, 1861, USGP, vol. 3, 114–15.

84. Shelby Foote, *Fort Sumter to Perryville* (1958), vol. 1 of *The Civil War: A Narrative* (New York: Vintage Books, 1986), 150.

85. Henry Walke, "The Gunboats at Belmont and Fort Henry," BL, vol. 1, 360.

86. USG to Smith, November 5, USGP, vol. 3, 114; Smith to USG, November 6, 1861, *ibid.*, 114.

87. USG to Smith, November 5, USGP, vol. 3, 114; Smith to Grant, November 6, 1861, *ibid.*, 114.

88. Brinton, *Personal Memoirs*, 76.

89. Richard I. Kiper, *Major General John Alexander McClernand: Politician in Uniform* (Kent, OH: Kent State University Press, 1999), 45.

90. Nathaniel Cheairs Hughes Jr., *The Battle of Belmont: Grant Strikes South* (Chapel Hill: University of North Carolina Press, 1991), 127.

91. USGM, 180.

92. Brinton, *Personal Memoirs*, 78.

93. All quotes in USGM, 180–81. The rebel reinforcements were able to cross the river without harm because the two federal gunboats had withdrawn upstream after being pounded by Polk's artillery.

94. Quoted in Woodworth, *Nothing But Victory*, 53.

95. USGM, 185.

96. Captain John Seaton, "The Battle of Belmont," in *"Sundry Papers" of the Kansas Commandery, Military Order of the Loyal Legion of the United Sates*, vol. 1, passim.

97. USGM, 184.

98. William H. L. Wallace to Ann Wallace, November 14, 1861, Wallace-Dickey Papers, Illinois State Historical Library, Springfield, Illinois (hereafter ISHL).

99. OR, I/3/310; Hughes, *Battle of Belmont*, 184–85.

100. USGM, 185.

101. Hughes, *Battle of Belmont*, 175.

102. Seaton, "Battle of Belmont," passim.

103. CT, November 9, 1861; quoted in Anna Maclay Green, "Civil War Public Opinion of General Grant," *Journal of the Illinois State Historical Society* 22 (April 1929): 23.

104. OR, 1/3/271, 111, 507.

105. *New York Herald*, November 19, 1861; see also NYT, November 11, 1861.

106. McClernand to McClellan, November 8, 1861, John A. McClernand Papers, Abraham

Lincoln Library & Museum, Springfield, Illinois (hereafter McClernand Mss); Kiper, *McClernand*, 48.

107. Quoted in Kiper, *McClernand*, 48.

108. Richardson, *A Personal History*, viii.

109. Foote, *Fort Sumter to Perryville*, 150.

110. Williams, *McClellan, Sherman, and Grant*, 87.

111. USG to Jesse Grant, November 27, 1861, USGP, vol. 3, 227.

112. USG to Jesse Grant, November 27, 1861, USGP, vol. 3, 226–28.

113. USGP, vol. 4, 116n.

114. James Harrison Wilson, *The Life of John A. Rawlins: Lawyer, Assistant Adjutant General. Chief of Staff, Major General of Volunteers, and Secretary of War* (New York: Neale Publishing, 1916), 24–25.

115. Wilkie, *Pen and Powder*, 85–6; Emmet Crozier, *Yankee Reporters, 1861–65* (New York: Oxford University Press, 1956), 69, 77–78.

116. Pitkin, "Cairo," 302; "U.S. Grant in Illinois," file compiled by Roger Bridges, ISHS.

117. John A. Rawlins to Washburne, December 30, 1861, Elihu B. Washburne Papers, LC. [Hereafter Washburne Mss.]

118. William Bross to Simon Cameron, December 30, 1861, USGP, vol. 4, 118.

119. *Ibid.*, 119. Lincoln endorsed the letter on January 4.

120. James H. Wilson, *Under the Old Flag: Recollections of Military Operations in the War for the Union, the Spanish War, the Boer Rebellion etc.*, vol. 1 (New York: D. Appleton and Company, 1912), 137.

121. Garland, *Grant*, 124.

122. *Ibid.*, 128.

123. Dorsett, "Grant's Drinking," 46–47.

124. Lew Wallace, "The Capture of Fort Donelson," BL, vol. 1, 399.

125. P. G. T. Beauregard, "The Campaign of Shiloh," BL, vol. 1, 571.

126. Foote, *Fort Sumter to Perryville*, 173; Wallace, "Fort Donelson," 400; Thomas Lawrence Connelly, *Army of the Heartland: The Army of Tennessee, 1861–1862* (Baton Rouge: Louisiana State University Press, 1967), 79.

127. Connelly, *Army of the Heartland*, 80.

128. USG to Mary Grant, January 23, 1862, USGP, vol. 4, 96.

129. USGM, 190.

130. John F. Marszalek, *Commander of All Lincoln's Armies: A Life of General Henry W. Halleck* (Cambridge, MA: Belknap Press of Harvard University, 2004), 116; Stephen E. Ambrose, *Halleck: Lincoln's Chief of Staff* (Baton Rouge: Louisiana State University Press), 21.

131. Brinton, *Personal Memoirs*, 166.

132. John Russell Young, *Around the World with General Grant* vol. 2 (Subscription News Service, 1879), 213.

133. Young, *Around the World*, vol. 2, 216; see also John Y. Simon, "Grant and Halleck: Contrasts in Command," in *Frank L. Klement Lecture, Marquette University* (Milwaukee: Marquette University Press, 1996).

134. William T. Sherman, "An Unspoken Address to the Loyal Legion" (March 1886), 299.

135. George R. Agassiz, ed., *Meade's Headquarters, 1863–1865: Letters of Colonel Theodore*

Lyman from The Wilderness to Appomattox (Boston: Atlantic Monthly Press, 1922), 80; Williams, *McClellan, Sherman, and Grant*, 82.

136. USG to Halleck, January 28, 1862, USGP, vol. 4, 99.

137. Foote to Halleck, *ibid.*

138. OR, I/5/41.

139. Halleck to USG, January 30, 1862, USGP, vol. 4, 104. At about this time, Halleck received word that General P. G. T. Beauregard, the Louisiana Creole celebrated by the secessionist press as the "hero" of Bull Run, was heading west with fifteen thousand reinforcements. It turned out to be false information, but, along with Lincoln's order, it got Halleck's attention.

140. John W. Emerson, "Grant's Life in the West and His Mississippi Valley Campaigns," *Midland Monthly* (May 1898), 417.

141. Wallace, *Autobiography*, vol. 1, 366.

142. Emerson, "Grant's Life in the West," 419.

143. Wallace, *Autobiography*, vol. 1, 366.

144. Wilkie, *Pen and Powder*, 81, 91–93.

145. *Ibid.*, 81, 90, 91; Crozier, *Yankee Reporters*, 38–9.

146. Walke, "Gunboats at Belmont," 363.

147. Badeau, *Military History*, vol. 1, 30.

148. Quoted in Benjamin Franklin Cooling, *Forts Henry and Donelson: The Key to the Confederate Heartland* (Knoxville: University of Tennessee Press, 1987), 106.

149. Walke, "Gun-Boats at Belmont," 367; Grant to Capt. John C. Kelton, February 6, 1862, USGP, vol. 4, 156.

150. All quotes in Cooling, *Forts Henry and Donelson*, 108.

151. Brinton, *Personal Memoirs*, 114.

152. Frank Moore, *The Rebel Record* (New York: G. P. Putnam, 1862), 4, 69.

153. USG to Halleck, February 6, 1862, USGP, vol. 4, 158.

154. USGP, vol. 6, 160n.

155. Badeau, *Military History*, vol. 1, 34.

156. Smith, *Grant*, 151–52.

157. Halleck to Buell, February 13, 1862, USGP, vol. 4, 196n.

158. USG to Mary Grant, February 9, 1862, *ibid.*, 179.

159. Gail Stephens, *The Shadow of Shiloh: Major General Lew Wallace in the Civil War* (Indianapolis: Indiana Historical Society Press, 2010), 46; Kendall D. Gott, *Where the South Lost the Civil War: An Analysis of the Fort Henry–Fort Donelson Campaign, February 1862* (Mechanicsburg, PA: Stackpole Books, 2003), 105, 117.

160. Richardson, *A Personal History*, 217.

161. Albert Sidney Johnston to Judah P. Benjamin, OR I/7/130–31, 863.

THREE. WINTER FORTRESS

1. Herman Melville, *Battle-Pieces of Herman Melville*, Hennig Cohen, ed. (New York: A. S. Barnes and Company, Inc., 1963), 52.

2. Wallace, *Autobiography*, vol. 1, 378.

3. Brinton, *Personal Memoirs*, 116.

4. *Ibid.*, 149.

5. Badeau, *Military History*, vol. 1, 36. Connelly, *Army of the Heartland*, 118.

6. Henry Walke, "The Western Flotilla at Fort Donelson, Island Number Ten, Port Pillow and Memphis," BL, vol. 1, 430.

7. OR, I/7/162.

8. *Ibid.*, 227.

9. *Ibid.*, 165.

10. Chernow, *Grant*, 170.

11. Lew Wallace, "The Capture of Fort Donelson," BL, vol. 1, 406.

12. Woodworth, *Nothing But Victory*, 86.

13. Wallace, "Fort Donelson," BL, vol. 1, 404.

14. USGM, 198.

15. Brinton, *Personal Memoirs*, 116–17.

16. Wallace, "Fort Donelson," BL, vol. 1, 407.

17. Jack Hurst, *Nathan Bedford Forrest: A Biography* (1993) (New York: Vintage Books edition, 1994), 4.

18. Wallace, "Fort Donelson," BL, vol. 1, 409.

19. F. F. Kiner, *One Years Soldering: Embracing the Battles of Fort Donelson and Shiloh* (1863). (Prior Lake, MN: Morgan Avenue Press, 2000), 13–14.

20. Wallace, "Fort Donelson," BL, vol. 1, 415.

21. Quoted in Woodworth, *Nothing But Victory*, 90.

22. Quoted in Catton, *Grant Moves South*, 157.

23. Walke, "Western Flotilla," BL, 431.

24. Cooling, *Forts Henry and Donelson*, 153.

25. Quoted in Hurst, *Forrest*, 81.

26. Walke, "Western Flotilla," BL, 433.

27. OR, I/7/166–67.

28. Foote to Halleck, February 15, 1862, USGP, v. 4, 215n; Foote, *Fort Sumter to Perryville*, 204.

29. OR, 1/7/166–7.

30. Robert Erwin Johnson, "John Rodgers: The Quintessential Nineteenth Century Naval Officer," in James C. Bradford, ed. *Captains of the Old Steam Navy* (Annapolis, MD: Naval Institute Press, 1986), 167–68; H. L. Bedford, "Fight Between the Batteries and Gunboats at Donelson," Southern Historical Society Papers (January–December 1885): 662–63.

31. Wallace, *Autobiography*, vol. 1, 394.

32. USG to JDG, February 14, 1862, USGP, vol. 4, 211.

33. USG to Gen. G. W. Cullum, February 15, 1862, *ibid.*, 212–13.

34. Foote to USG, February 14, 1862, *ibid.*, 216n; the dispatch was sent on the 14th and received on the 15th.

35. USGM, 203.

36. *Ibid.*, 204.

37. *Ibid.*

38. Wallace, "Fort Donelson," BL, vol. 1, 417.

39. J. F. Gilmer to James A. Seddon, December 2, 1862, OR, I/7/265.

40. Wallace, "Fort Donelson," BL, vol. 1, 417.

41. Hurst, *Forrest*, 82; Wallace, *Autobiography*, vol 1, 402.

42. OR, I/7/265–66, 316–20, 323, 332–33, 365.

43. Wallace, "Fort Donelson," BL, vol. 1, 418.

44. *Ibid.*, 421.

45. Wallace, *Autobiography*, vol 1, 411; Wallace, "Fort Donelson," BL, vol. 1, 422.

46. Badeau, *Military History*, vol. 1, 45.

47. *Ibid.*, 45.

48. USGM, 205.

49. *Ibid.*

50. Wallace, "Fort Donelson," BL, vol. 1, 423.

51. Brinton, *Personal Memoirs*, 121–22.

52. Wallace, "Fort Donelson," BL, vol 1, 423.

53. Brinton, *Personal Memoirs*, 121.

54. Wallace, *Autobiography*, vol 1, 417; the only firing was by the skirmishers in front of Smith's column.

55. OR, I/7/163; V. P. Twombley, *Second Iowa Infantry at Fort Donelson, February 15, 1862* (Des Moines, IA: Pain Talk Printing House, 1901), 27.

56. Emerson, "Grant's Life in the West," 523.

57. OR, I/7/273, 287–88, 295–97, 327, 334–5, 385–86.

58. Statement of Col. N. B. Forrest, March 15, 1862, OR, I/7/295.

59. OR, I/7/297–98.

60. Statement of Col. N. B. Forrest, March 15, 1862, OR, I/7/295–96.

61. Brinton, *Personal Memoirs*, 129.

62. Simon Bolivar Buckner to USG, February 16, 1862, USGP, vol. 4, 218.

63. Brinton, *Personal Memoirs*, 129.

64. USG to Buckner, February 16, 1862, USGP, vol. 4, 218.

65. *Ibid.*, n; USGM, 207–08.

66. Quoted in Brinton, *Personal Memoirs*, 133.

67. *New York Tribune*, February 22, 1862.

68. M. B. Morton interview with General Buckner, *Nashville Banner*, December 11, 1909.

69. Quoted in Arndt M. Stickles, *Simon Bolivar Buckner: Borderland Knight* (Chapel Hill: University of North Carolina Press, 1940), 17, 71.

70. Woodworth, *Nothing But Victory*, 119; see also Badeau, *Military History*, vol. 1, 51, for slightly different figures.

71. Connelly, *Army of the Heartland*, 10.

72. P. G. T. Beauregard, "The Campaign of Shiloh," BL, vol. 1, 572.

73. Quoted in McPherson, *Battle Cry*, 403.

74. Garland, *Grant*, 180.

75. Wilkie, *Pen and Powder*, 119.

76. Foote, *Fort Sumter to Perryville*, 214; *New York Tribune*, February 18, 1862.

77. Sherman to John Sherman, February 23, 1862, in Brooks D. Simpson and Jean V. Berlin, eds. *Sherman's Civil War: Selected Correspondence of William T. Sherman, 1860–1865* (Chapel Hill: University of North Carolina Press, 1999), 193 (hereafter SCW).

78. USGM, 213.

79. Catton, *Grant Moves South*, 181.
80. Halleck letter reproduced in USGM, 214.
81. Badeau, *Military History*, 54; see also Halleck to George B. McClelland, February 17, 1862, GP, vol. 4, 272 n.
82. Charles A. Dana, *New York Sun*, July 24, 1885.
83. Richardson, *Personal History*, vi.
84. Foote, *Fort Sumter to Perryville*, 214–15.
85. Allen C. Guelzo, *Fateful Lightning: A New History of the Civil War and Reconstruction* (New York: Oxford University Press, 2012), 201–02; for joint army-navy operations, see Rowena Reed, *Combined Operations in the Civil War* (Annapolis, MD: Naval Institute Press, 1972).
86. Quoted in Woodworth, *Nothing But Victory*, 134.
87. USG to Cullum, February 25, 1862, USGP, vol. 4, 287.
88. Halleck to USG, February 18, 1862, USGP, vol. 4, 260 n; Foote to USG, February 22, 1862, ORN, I/22/624.
89. Smith, *Grant*, 168.
90. Halleck to McClellan, February 20, 1862, OR I/7/641.
91. Stanton to Halleck, February 22, 1862, OR, I/7/652.
92. USG to JDG, February 26, 1862, USGP, vol. 4, 292.
93. Halleck to McClellan, March 3, 1862, OR, I/7/679–80.
94. J. Cutler Andrews, *The North Reports the Civil War* (Pittsburgh: University of Pittsburgh Press, 1955), 168, 679–80.
95. McClellan to Halleck, March 3, 1862, OR, I/7/680.
96. Halleck to McClellan, March 4, 1862, *ibid.*, 682; Halleck to USG, March 4, *ibid.*, 319.
97. Garland, *Grant*, 198; Halleck to USG, March 4, 1862, USGP, vol. 4, 319.
98. USGM, 221, Wallace, *Autobiography*, vol. 1, 441.
99. Halleck to USG, March 4, USGP, vol. 4, 319.
100. USGM, 219. The rebel sympathizer left his post and fled before he could be arrested.
101. USG to JDG, March 1, 1862, USGP, vol. 4, 306.
102. USG to Halleck, March 7, 1862, *ibid.*, 331; USG to Halleck, March 9, 1862, *ibid.*, 334; USG to Halleck, March 13, 1862, *ibid.*, 353; Halleck to USG, March 9, 1862, *ibid.*, 319.
103. USG to JDG, March 1, 1862, USGP, vol. 4, 306.
104. USG to Halleck, March 5, 1862, USGP, vol. 4, 317–19.
105. Brinton, *Personal Memoirs*, 150.
106. Smith to an unidentified person, March 17, 1862, USGP, vol. 4, 344n.
107. Wallace, *Autobiography*, vol. 1, 442.
108. *Ibid.*, 442.
109. Brinton, *Personal Memoirs*, 149.
110. Lorenzo Thomas to Halleck, March 10, 1862, OR, I/7/683.
111. Smith, *Grant*, 178.
112. Halleck to Thomas, March 15, 1862, *ibid.*, 683–84.
113. Halleck to USG, March 13, 1862, USGP, vol. 4, 354–55.
114. USG to JDG, February 24, 1862, USGP, v., 4, 284.
115. Foote, *Fort Sumter to Perryville*, 318.
116. *Ibid.*, 321.

117. Halleck to USG, March 16, 1862, USGP, vol. 4, 367.

118. USG to Halleck, March 18, 1862, *ibid.*, 386; *ibid.*, March 21, 1862, 400.

FOUR. A TREMENDOUS MURDER MILL

1. Interview with Sherman in the *Washington Post*, quoted in "Grant's Pertinacity," *Army and Navy Journal* 31 (December 30, 1893), 317.

2. USG to JDG, March 15, 1862, USGP, vol. 4, 375.

3. Timothy B. Smith, "'A Siege from the Start': The Spring 1862 Campaign against Corinth, Mississippi," *Journal of Mississippi History* 66 (issue 4, 2004): 405–07.

4. USGM, 222.

5. Lucius W. Barber, *Army Memoirs of Lucius W. Barber, Company "D," 15th Illinois Volunteer Infantry* (Chicago: J. M. W. Jones Stationery & Printing Co., 1894), 46.

6. USGM, 239–40.

7. WTSM, 249.

8. WTSM, 249.

9. Don Carlos Buell, "Shiloh Reviewed," BL, vol. 1, 491.

10. WTS to EES, April 11, 1862, SCW, 202.

11. Davis quoted in Stacey D. Allen, "Shiloh! The Campaign and First Days Battle," in *Blue and Gray* 14 (Winter 1997): 9.

12. Quoted in Woodworth, *Nothing But Victory*, 140.

13. Quoted in Catton, *Grant Moves South*, 220.

14. WTS to EES, April 3, 1862, SCW, 199.

15. Quoted in John F. Marszalek, *Sherman: A Soldier's Passion for Order* (New York: The Free Press, 1993), 176.

16. WTS to John Sherman, September 4, 1857, William T. Sherman Papers, LC (hereafter Sherman Mss).

17. WTSM, 13, 15; Michael Fellman, *Citizen Sherman: A Life of William Tecumseh Sherman* (New York: Random House, 1995), 7.

18. WTS to EES, January 5, 1861, SCW, 31.

19. Fellman, *Citizen Sherman*, 45.

20. WTS to Governor Thomas O. Moore, January 18, 1861, WTSM, 174.

21. SCW, 3.

22. WTS to Thomas Ewing, January 8, 1861, February 3, 1861, SCW, 32, 53.

23. WTS to David F. Boyd, April 4, 1861, SCW, 66.

24. WTSM, 216.

25. WTSM, 220; Lorenzo Thomas to Simon Cameron, October 21, 1861, OR, I/3/548–49, I/4/313–14.

26. *New York Tribune*, October 30, 1861.

27. WTS to EES, November 1, 1861, SCW, 154–55; EES to John Sherman, November 10, 1861, Sherman Mss.

28. Lewis, *Sherman*, 197; Henry Villard, *Memoirs of Henry Villard: Journalist and Financier*, vol. 1 (Boston: Houghton Mifflin, 1904), 206–13; William F. G. Shanks, *Personal Recollections of Distinguished Generals* (New York: Harper & Brothers, 1866), 17–18, 22–26, 52–59.

29. WTS to EES, January 4, 1862, SCW, 174.

30. George McClellan to WTS, November 8, 1861, William T. Sherman Family Papers, University of Notre Dame, South Bend, Indiana (hereafter Sherman Family Papers).

31. Henry W. Halleck to Elizabeth Hamilton Halleck, December 14, 1861, SCW, 171; Halleck to Thomas Ewing, February 15, 1862, WTSM, 235.

32. WTS to EES, December 17 [18 or 19], 1861, SCW, 170.

33. Marszalek, *Sherman*, 164.

34. *Cincinnati Commercial*, December 11, 1861.

35. EES to John Sherman, December 12, 1861, Sherman Family Papers.

36. WTS to EES, January 4, 1862, January 8, 1862, SCW, 174, 176.

37. WTS to EES, February 17, 1862, SCW, 191; WTS to John Sherman, February 23, 1862, SCW, 192.

38. Quoted in Marszalek, *Sherman*, 169.

39. WTSM, 233.

40. WTS to Prof. Boyd, May 13, 1861, SCW, 84.

41. WTS to EES, February 21, 1862, SCW, 192.

42. WTS to USG, April 10, 1862, WTSM, 255.

43. USG, "The Battle of Shiloh," BL, vol. 1, 465–67.

44. USG to Halleck, April 5, USGP, vol. 5, 14.

45. John K. Duke, *History of the 53rd Ohio Volunteer Infantry* (Portsmouth, OH: Blade Printing Company, 1900), 41; Wiley Sword, *Shiloh: Bloody April* (New York: William Morrow & Co., 1974), 127.

46. Woodworth, *Nothing But Victory*, 153.

47. Quoted in Fuller, *Generalship of Grant*, 106.

48. Don Carlos Buell, "Shiloh Reviewed," BL, vol. 1, 487.

49. G. T. Beauregard, "The Campaign of Shiloh," BL, vol. 1, 584; Johnston had 39,830 men and 112 guns, see Allen, *"Shiloh!"* 10, 16, 47.

50. Braxton Bragg, "General Albert Sidney Johnston and the Battle of Pittsburg Landing," Albert Sidney and William Preston Johnston Papers, Tulane University, New Orleans, Louisiana.

51. William Preston Johnston, "Albert Sidney Johnston at Shiloh," BL, vol. 1, 552.

52. Beauregard, "Shiloh," BL, vol. 1, 582.

53. OR, I/10, part 1/407; T. Harry Williams, *P. G. T. Beauregard, Napoleon in Gray* (New York: Collier Books, 1962), 168–69; Thomas Jordan, "Notes of a Confederate Staff-Officer at Shiloh," BL, vol. 1, 597.

54. Williams, *Beauregard*, 168; Charles P. Roland, *Albert Sidney Johnston: Soldier of Three Republics* (Austin: University of Texas Press, 1964), 325.

55. Williams, *Beauregard*, 164.

56. Quoted in Smith, *Grant*, 187.

57. Johnston, "Johnston at Shiloh," BL, vol. 1, 557.

58. Beauregard, "Shiloh," BL, vol. 1, 586.

59. Sword, *Shiloh*, 139.

60. OR, I/10, pt. 1/603; Timothy B. Smith, *Shiloh: Conquer or Perish* (Lawrence: University of Kansas Press, 2014), 84–86; Report of Brig. Gen. B. M. Prentiss, November 17, 1862, OR, I/10, pt/ 1/278–79. Prentiss failed to mention Peabody in his report, leaving the

impression that he had sent out the patrol; Timothy B. Smith, *Rethinking Shiloh; Myth and Memory* (Knoxville: University of Tennessee Press, 2013), 71–72, 84.

61. Lew Wallace, *An Autobiography*, vol. 2 (New York: Harper & Brothers, 1906), 504–05.

62. Allen, "Shiloh!," 21; Badeau, *Military History*, 78.

63. Basil Duke, *A History of the Fifty-Third Ohio Volunteer Infantry, During the War of the Rebellion* (Portsmouth: The Blade Printing Company, 1900), 42–43.

64. WTS to EES, April 11, 1862, in SCW, 201.

65. Duke, *Fifty-Third Ohio*, 44; WTS to USG, April 10, 1862, WTSM, 256; Sword, *Shiloh*, 176.

66. OR, I/10, pt. 1/249.

67. Ambrose Bierce, "What I Saw at Shiloh," in Ambrose Bierce, *A Sole Survivor: Bits of Autobiography*, edited by S. T. Joshi and David E. Schultz (Knoxville: University of Tennessee Press, 1998), 11.

68. Badeau, *Military History*, vol. 1, 96–97; WTS to John Sherman, April 22, 1862, SCW, 206–07.

69. Basil W. Duke, *Personal Recollections of Shiloh, Read Before the Filson Club, April 6, 1914* (Louisville: Filson Club, 1914), 8.

70. Wallace, *Autobiography*, vol. 2, 515.

71. B. H. Liddell Hart, *Sherman: Soldier, Realist, American* (1929) (New York: Da Capo Press, 1993), 126.

72. Johnston, "Johnston at Shiloh," BL, 560.

73. Quoted in Catton, *Grant Moves South*, 193.

74. Rawlins to Brig. Gen. William Nelson, April 6, USGP, vol. 5, 18n; USG to Buell, *ibid.*, 17.

75. USGM, 225.

76. USGM, 226; OR, I/10, pt. 1/185.

77. Fuller, *Generalship of Grant*, 112.

78. Arthur L. Conger, *The Rise of U.S. Grant*, (1931) (New York: Da Capo Press, 1996), 239.

79. Wallace, *Autobiography*, vol. 2, 524.

80. Allan Nevins, *The War for the Union: War Becomes Revolution, 1862–1863* (New York: Macmillan Publishing Co., Collier Books Edition, 1992), 78.

81. Fuller, *Generalship of Grant*, 113.

82. John Cockerill, "A Boy at Shiloh," in *Papers of the Military Order of the Loyal Legion of the United States* (reprint, Wilmington, NC: Broadfoot Publishing, 1994) (hereafter cited as MOLLUS), vol. 6, 17; Lewis, *Sherman*, 222.

83. Report of Brig. Gen. B. M. Prentiss, OR, November 17, 1862, I/10/278.

84. Garland, *Grant*, 207.

85. USG to Buell, April 6, 1862, USGP, vol. 5, 18; William S. Hillyer to Brig. Gen. Thomas J. Wood, Army of the Ohio, *ibid.*

86. Thomas L. Livermore, *Numbers & Losses in the Civil War in America: 1861–65* (1900) (Bloomington: Indiana University Press, 1957), 80. Livermore estimated rebel strength at Shiloh as 40,335.

87. WTSM, 265.

88. Buell, "Shiloh Reviewed," BL, 493; Grant described his meeting with Buell in USGM, 231–32.

89. OR, I/10, pt. 1/186.

90. Foote, *Fort Sumter to Perryville*, 340.

91. OR, I/10, part 1/277–78; Beauregard, "Shiloh," BL, vol. 1, 590.

92. Quoted in Conger, *Grant*, 257.

93. Johnston, "Johnston at Shiloh," BL, vol. 1, 553.

94. Henry Morgan Stanley, *The Autobiography*, edited by Dorothy Stanley (Boston: Houghton Mifflin, 1909), 186, 191; Wallace, *Autobiography*, vol. 2, 515. Stanley, whose birth name was John Rowlands, was taken prisoner at Shiloh and joined the Union army in June 1862. He was discharged three weeks later when he fell ill. After recovering, he served on merchant ships before joining the US Navy in July 1864.

95. Sword, *Shiloh*, 272, 443–45.

96. Roland, *Johnston*, 337–38.

97. Johnston, "Johnston at Shiloh," BL, 565.

98. Fuller, *Generalship of Grant*, 109.

99. Smith, *Shiloh*, 193.

100. Kimbell, *Battery "A,"* 44.

101. Report of Lieut. George L. Nispel, April 11, 1862, OR, I/10, pt. 1/146–4.

102. Larry J. Daniel, *Shiloh: The Battle That Changed the Civil War* (New York: Simon & Schuster, 1997), 255; Smith, *Grant*, 199.

103. Kimbell, *Battery "A,"* 44–45.

104. Wallace, *Autobiography*, vol. 2, 544.

105. CT, November 21, 1880.

106. Bierce, "Shiloh," 15.

107. OR, I/10, pt. 1/323–324, 328; Allen, "Shiloh!" 62.

108. Beauregard, "Shiloh," BL, 590–91.

109. Johnston, "Johnston at Shiloh," 567.

110. Quoted in Smith, *Shiloh*, 232; Alexander Robert Chisholm, "The Shiloh Battle-Order and the Withdrawal Sunday Evening," BL, vol. 1, 606–07.

111. Johnston, "Johnston at Shiloh," 567; Brady McWhiney, "General Beauregard," in Woodworth, ed., *Shiloh Campaign*, 110–12.

112. Allen, "Shiloh!," 62.

113. OR, I/10, pt. 1/384.

114. Quoted in Allen, "Shiloh!," 64.

115. Jordan, "Confederate Staff Officer," 602; Williams, *Beauregard*, 143.

116. Jordan, "Confederate Staff-Officer," 602.

117. Steven E. Woodworth, "Intolerably Slow: Lew Wallace's March to the Battlefield," in Woodworth, ed., *Shiloh Campaign*, 92–93.

118. USGM, 234.

119. Richardson, *Secret Service*, 238.

120. Bierce, "Shiloh," 16.

121. *Ibid.*, 21–22.

122. Winston Groom, *Shiloh, 1862* (Washington, D.C.: National Geographic, 2013), 339.

123. USGM, 235.

124. WTS, "Battle of Pittsburg Landing," 2; WTSM, 267.

125. Interview with Sherman, in *Army and Navy Journal*, 317.

126. Charles A. Morton, "A Boy at Shiloh," in A. Noel Blakeman, ed., *Personal Recollections of the War of the Rebellion: Addresses Delivered before the Commandery of the State of New York, MOLLUS* (New York: G. P. Putnam's Sons, 1907), 65.

127. Bierce, "Shiloh," 17.

128. Jordan, "Confederate Staff-Officer," 603.

129. Badeau, *Military History*, vol. 1, 88.

130. Quoted in Nevins, *War for the Union*, 85.

131. Jordan, "Confederate Staff-Officer," 603.

132. Nevins, *War for the Union*, 86; Buell, "Shiloh Reviewed," BL, vol. 1, 534.

133. OR, I/10, pt. 1/295.

134. OR, I/10, pt/ 1/109.

135. John Fiske, *The Mississippi Valley in the Civil War* (Boston: Houghton Mifflin, 1900), 99.

136. Lyman S. Widney, "Campaigning with 'Uncle Billy,'" *Neales Monthly* 2 (August 1913): 133.

137. Grant's losses were 1,754 killed, 8,408 wounded, and 2,885 missing, for a total of 13,047; of these 2,103 were from Buell's Army of the Ohio. Beauregard reported 1,728 killed, 8,012 wounded, and 959 missing, a total of 10,699. USGM, 245.

138. USG to JDG, June 9, 1862, USGP, vol. 5, 141.

139. Quoted in Sword, *Shiloh*, 429.

140. Peter Cozzens and Robert I. Girardi, eds., *The Military Memoirs of General John Pope* (Chapel Hill: University of North Carolina Press, 1998), 64.

141. Wallace, *Autobiography*, vol. 2, 514.

142. Foote, *Fort Sumter to Perryville*, 350.

143. USGM, 246.

144. Badeau, *Military History*, vol. 1, 95.

145. NYT, April 19, 1862; *New York Herald*, April 9, 1862.

146. Garland, *Grant*, 208.

147. Wilkie, *Pen and Powder*, 154.

148. James G. Smart, ed., *A Radical View: The "Agate" Dispatches of Whitelaw Reid, 1861–65* (Memphis: Memphis State University Press, 1976), 119–71; Catton, *Grant Moves South*, 253–56.

149. Joseph Medill to Washburne, May 24, 1862, Washburne Papers, LC.

150. Garland, *Grant*, 214; see also NYT, April 14, 1862.

151. USG to Jesse Root Grant, April 26, 1862, USGP, vol. 5, 78.

152. *Cincinnati Commercial*, May 2, 1862.

153. Richardson, *Secret Service*, 235.

154. Murat Halstead to Salmon P. Case, April 1, 1863, Abraham Lincoln Papers, LC.

155. Quoted in Lewis, *Sherman*, 234.

156. Stanton quoted in WTS to Benjamin Stanton, June 10, 1862, SCW, 241.

157. Alexander K. McClure, *Abraham Lincoln and Men of War Times* (Philadelphia: Times Publishing Company, 1892), 179–80, 19; Historian Brooks Simpson challenges McClure's account, claiming, correctly, that there is no corroboration for it. Simpson, "After Shiloh: Grant, Sherman, and Survival," in Woodworth, ed., *Shiloh Campaign*, 142–58.

158. Stanton to Halleck, April 23, 1862, OR, I/10 pt. I/98–99.

159. Halleck to Stanton, OR, April 24, I/10, pt. I/99.

160. USG to Elihu B. Washburne, May 14, 1862, USGP, vol. 4, 119.

161. USG to Julia Dent Grant, May 4, 1862, *ibid.*, 110–11.

162. Quoted in Lewis, *Sherman*, 232.

163. Halleck to Stanton, April 13, 1862, OR I/10 pt. I/98.

164. WTS to EES, April 14, 1862, SCW, 204.

165. WTSM, 276; Wilkie quoted in Lewis, *Sherman*, 233.

166. Thomas L. Snead, "With Price East of the Mississippi," BL, vol. 2, 717–18.

167. USGM, 251.

168. USG to Halleck, May 11, 1862, USGP, vol. 5, 114.

169. Halleck to Grant, May 12, 1862, USGP, v. 5, 115.

170. USG to JDG, May 11, 13, 20, 1862, *ibid.*, 117–18.

171. Halleck quoted in John F. Marszalek, *Commander of All of Lincoln's Armies: A Life of General Henry W. Halleck* (Cambridge, MA: Belknap, 2004), 122.

172. After arriving at Pittsburg Landing, Halleck repeatedly rebuked Grant for failing to have his "undisciplined" army "in condition to resist another attack by the enemy." USGP, vol. 5, 48; OR, I/10, pt. 2/105–06.

173. Badeau, *Military History*, vol. 1, 101.

174. Quoted in Nevins, *War for the Union*, 112.

175. WTSM, 273.

176. Foote, *Fort Sumter to Perryville*, 384–85.

177. OR, I/10, pt. 2/225.

178. WTSM, 273–75.

179. OR, I/10 part 2/634.

180. Richardson, *Secret Service*, 25.

181. McPherson, *Battle Cry*, 416.

182. Snead, "With Price," BL, 719; Catton, *Grant Moves South*, 269.

183. USGM, 256.

184. Charles H. Davis, *Life of Charles Henry Davis: Rear Admiral, 1807–1877* (Boston: Houghton Mifflin and Company, 1899), 222–23.

185. Ivan Musicant, *Divided Waters: The Naval History of the Civil War* (New York: HarperCollins, 1995), 214.

186. Charles G. Hearn, *Admiral Davis Dixon Porter* (Annapolis, MD: Naval Institute Press, 1996), 147.

187. Quoted in James M. McPherson, *War on the Waters: The Union and Confederate Navies, 1861–1865* (Chapel Hill: University of North Carolina Press, 2012), 86.

188. Secretary of the Navy Gideon Welles had shown no interest in Ellet's idea.

189. Montgomery to Beauregard, May 12, 1862, ORN, I/23/55–57.

190. Richardson, *Secret Service*, 260–62.

191. William C. Davis, *Jefferson Davis: The Man and His Hour* (Baton Rouge: Louisiana State University Press, 1991), 241.

192. Richardson, *Secret Service*, 263.

193. Davis, *Davis*, 243.

194. There is no solid documentary evidence indicating what Grant planned to do. Catton,

for example, suggested he was merely planning for a routine home leave. Catton, *Grant Moves South*, 274–5.

195. WTSMS, 275.

196. USG to JDG, June 3, 1862, USGP, vol. 5, 137.

197. USGM, 258.

198. USG to JDG, June 9, 1862, USGP vol. 5, 140.

199. USG to Washburne, June 19, 1862, *ibid.*, 145–46.

200. WTSM, 276. Sherman lost Grant's note but kept his reply to him.

201. USGP, vol. 5, 207n.; Chernow, *Grant*, 218–19.

202. Pope, *Military Memoirs*, 65.

203. Quoted in Larry J. Daniel, ed., *Days of Glory: The Army of the Cumberland, 1861–1865* (Baton Rouge: Louisiana State University Press, 2004), 16.

204. Williams, *McClellan, Grant, and Sherman*, 66.

205. WTS to Philemon B. Ewing, July 13, 1852, SCW, 253; WTSM, 274.

206. WTS to EES, August 5, 1862, Sherman Family Papers.

207. WTS to John Sherman, May 12, 1862, SCW, 217.

208. Liddell Hart, *Sherman*, 135; WTS to John Sherman, May 7, 1862, SCW, 216.

209. Edmund Wilson, *Patriotic Gore: Studies in the Literature of the American Civil War* (New York: Oxford University Press, 1962), *passim*.

210. WTSM, 269.

211. USGM, 257.

212. WTSM, 274.

FIVE. "THE BATTLE FOR THE MISSISSIPPI"

1. Melville, *Battle-Pieces of Herman Melville*, ed. Hennig Cohen, 74.

2. Gideon Welles, "Admiral Farragut and New Orleans," *The Galaxy* 12, no. 6 (December 1871): 831.

3. Young, *Around the World with General Grant*, 305.

4. David Dixon Porter, "The Opening of the Lower Mississippi," BL, vol. 2, 22–55.

5. David Dixon Porter, *Incidents and Anecdotes of the Civil War* (New York: D. Appleton and Co., 1891), 63–68.

6. George Washington Cable, "New Orleans Before the Capture," BL, vol. 2, 19.

7. Porter, "Opening of the Lower Mississippi," 22.

8. *Ibid.*, 25.

9. Porter, *Incidents and Anecdotes*, 64.

10. Chester G. Hearn, *Admiral David Glasgow Farragut: The Civil War Years* (Annapolis, MD: Naval Institute Press, 1998), 52.

11. Elmer W. Flaccus, "Commodore David Porter and the Mexican Navy," *Hispanic American Historical Review* 34 (August 1954): 365.

12. Chester G. Hearn, *Admiral David Dixon Porter: The Civil War Years* (Annapolis, MD: Naval Institute Press, 1996), 11–12.

13. *Ibid.*, 1–11.

14. Porter, *Incidents and Anecdotes*, 13–15; Hearn, *Porter*, 36–46.

15. Porter to Seward, April 6, 1861, ORN, I/4/112; Gideon Welles, *The Diary of Gideon*

Welles, Secretary of the Navy under Lincoln and Johnson, vol. 1 (Boston: Houghton Mifflin, 1910), 23–25.

16. Porter, *Incidents and Anecdotes*, 22.

17. *Ibid.*, 7–12.

18. Welles, *Diary*, vol. 1, 16–19, 36.

19. *Ibid.*, 16–19, 36.

20. Porter, *Incidents and Anecdotes*, 64.

21. *Ibid.*

22. Montgomery Blair, "Opening the Mississippi," *The United Service* 4 (January 1881): 34; John Niven, *Gideon Welles: Lincoln's Secretary of the Navy* (New York: Oxford University Press, 1973), 385.

23. William T. Meredith, "Farragut's Capture of New Orleans," BL, vol. 2, 70; Welles, "Farragut," part 1, *The Galaxy* (November 1871), 677, and part 2 (December 1871), 819, 823; Niven, *Welles*, 381.

24. Porter, "Opening the Lower Mississippi," 24; Porter, *Incidents and Anecdotes*, 64.

25. Quoted in Geoffrey Perret, *Lincoln's War: The Untold Story of America's Greatest President as Commander in Chief* (New York: Random House, 2004), 138.

26. Porter, *Incidents and Anecdotes*, 65; Blair, "Opening the Mississippi," 37.

27. Welles, "Farragut," part 1 (November 1871), 677–78.

28. Meredith, "Farragut's Capture," 70.

29. Blair, "Opening of the Mississippi," 38.

30. Porter, *Incidents and Anecdotes*, 96.

31. Quoted in *ibid.*, 95–96.

32. Blair, "Opening of the Mississippi," 38; Welles, "Farragut," part 1, 679–81. Allen H. Gosnell, "Damn the Torpedoes—?," *U.S. Naval Institute Proceedings* no. 517 (March 1946): 442–43.

33. Hearn, *Farragut*, 42.

34. Farragut to Welles, May 1, 1861, *Captains Letters to the Secretary of the Navy*, NA; Hearn, *Farragut*, 43; Charles Lee Lewis, *David Glasgow Farragut: Our First Admiral* (Annapolis: MD: Naval Institute Press, 1943), 3.

35. Office of the Chief of Naval Operations, cited in Clarence Edward Macartney, *Mr. Lincoln's Admirals* (New York: Funk & Wagnalls, 1956), 36.

36. Loyall Farragut, *Life and Letters of Admiral D. G. Farragut: First Admiral of the United States Navy, Embodying his Journal and Letters* (New York: D. Appleton and Company, 1879), 10–11; Hearn, *Farragut*, xviii.

37. Welles, *Diary*, 2: 117; Welles, "Farragut," part 1, 681–82.

38. Nevins, *Welles*, 384.

39. Blair, "Opening of the Mississippi," 38.

40. Farragut's Oath of Allegiance, quoted in Hearn, *Farragut*, 42.

41. Porter, "Opening of the Lower Mississippi," 27.

42. Farragut, *Farragut*, 203.

43. David Dixon Porter, "Private Journal of Occurrences during the Great War of the Rebellion, 1860–1865," David Dixon Porter Papers, LC, 181 (hereafter cited as Porter, "Journal").

44. Richard S. West Jr., *Mr. Lincoln's Navy* (New York: Longmans, Green, 1957), 98–99.

45. John Russell Bartlett, "The Brooklyn in the Passage of the Forts," BL, vol. 2, 56–58.

46. Porter, "Journal," 181.

47. Welles, "Farragut," 822; Farragut met with Fox at the home of Postmaster General Blair.

48. Welles, "Farragut," 683; Farragut to Susan M. Farragut, December 21, 1861, quoted in Lewis, *David Glasgow Farragut* (Annapolis: United States Naval Institute, 1943), 419.

49. Donald L. Canney, *The Old Steam Navy: Frigates, Sloops, and Gunboats, 1815–1885* (Annapolis: Naval Institute Press, 1990), 61–63.

50. Hearn, *Farragut*, 59.

51. B. S. Osbon, ed., *Cruise of the U.S. Flagship Hartford, 1862–1863 . . . From the Private Journal of William C. Holton* (New York: L.W. Paine, 1863), 4, 6.

52. Joseph T. Glatthaar, *Partners in Command: The Relationship Between Leaders in the Civil War* (New York: The Free Press, 1994), 166.

53. Bartlett, "Brooklyn," 58.

54. Porter to Fox, March 28, April 8, 1862, in *Fox Correspondence*, 89, 91, 93, 98; Richard West Jr. "The Relations Between Farragut and Porter," *Proceedings of the United States Naval Institute* (July 1935): 989.

55. Welles, *Diary*, vol. 1, 88, 19, 15.

56. Mansfield Lovell to S. Cooper, May 22, 1862, ORN, I/18/254–505; Steven E. Woodworth, *Jefferson Davis and His Generals: The Failure of Confederate High Command in the West* (Lawrence: University Press of Kansas, 1990), 111.

57. Welles, "Farragut," 825.

58. *Ibid.*, Welles, "Farragut," 825; Macartney, *Mr. Lincoln's Admirals*, 14.

59. Lovell to Beauregard, March 7, 1862, OR, I/6/647.

60. Davis to Thomas O. Moore, April 17, 1862, OR, I/6/878; Report of Mallory to Davis, February 27, 1862, ORN, I/18/830–31; Welles, "Farragut," 825; Raimondo Luraghi, *A History of the Confederate Navy* (Annapolis, MD: Naval Institute Press, 1996), 155–56.

61. Johnston K. Duncan to J. G. Pickett, April 30, 1862, OR, I/6/522.

62. Beverley Kennon, "Fighting Farragut Below New Orleans," BL, vol. 2, 76.

63. Hearn, *Farragut*, 52.

64. Fletcher Pratt, *Civil War on Western Waters* (New York: Henry Holt and Company, 1956), 38–41.

65. Albert Bigelow Paine, *A Sailor of Fortune: Personal Memoirs of Captain B. S. Osbon* (New York: McClure, Phillips, 1906), 174–75.

66. *Ibid.*, 175–77.

67. Porter to Welles, April 30, 1862, ORN, I/18:361. One of Farragut's most powerful men-of-war, *Colorado*, could not be lightened sufficiently to make it over the bar.

68. Reprinted in CT, May 9, 1862.

69. Farragut to Welles, April 20, 1862, ORN, I/18/135.

70. Porter to Welles, April 30, 1862, ORN, I/18/366.

71. Bartlett, "Brooklyn," 59–60.

72. Eugene B. Canfield, "Porter's Mortar Schooners," *Civil War Times Illustrated* 6 (October 1967): 35.

73. OR, I/18/374; Porter suffered one man killed and seven wounded.

74. Bartlett, "Brooklyn," 60; *Harpers Weekly* (August 16, 1862): 523.

75. Paine, *Sailor of Fortune*, 182–84.

76. Proposition of Commander D. D. Porter, ORN, I/18/145–46.

77. Paine, *Sailor of Fortune*, 181.

78. Bartlett, "Brooklyn," 60; Report of Julius H. Kroehl, June 2, 1862, ORN, I/18/429–30.

79. Private Diary of H. H. Bell, April 20, 1862, ORN, I/17/695; Welles, "Farragut," part 2, 826; Blair, "Opening of the Mississippi," 40.

80. Meredith, "Farragut," 72.

81. Francis A. Roe diary, quoted in Charles L. Dufour, *The Night the War Was Lost* (1960) (Lincoln: University of Nebraska Press, 1994), 262.

82. Paine, *Sailor of Fortune*, 187–88.

83. Bartlett, "Brooklyn," 58.

84. Meredith, "Farragut," 71.

85. Craven to Mrs. Craven, May 16, 1862, ORN I/18/197; Paine, *Soldier of Fortune*, 190.

86. Quoted in Dufour, *Night the War Was Lost*, 267.

87. Farragut to Welles, May 6, 1862, ORN, I/18/157; Welles, "Farragut," 826.

88. Quoted in Foote, *Fort Sumter to Perryville*, 366.

89. Porter, *Incidents and Anecdotes*, 48.

90. Farragut to Welles, October 16, 1862, ORN, I/18/170.

91. Osbon, *Hartford*, 11; Paine, *Sailor of Fortune*, 196–7; Bartholomew Diggins, "Recollections of the Cruise of the U.S.S. Hartford," manuscript, New York Public Library, 94–96; Farragut to Porter, April 24, 1862, ORN, I/18/142; Hearn, *Farragut*, 106–7.

92. Bartlett, "Brooklyn," 63; R. B. Lowry, to Craven, April 25, 1862, ORN, I/18/185; Bartlett to Brother Johnny, ORN I/18/193.

93. Paine, *Sailor of Fortune*, 192–95.

94. *Ibid.*; Hearn, *Farragut*, 104–107.

95. ORN, I/18/180.

96. Porter to Wells, April 25, 1862, ORN, 18:357.

97. Luraghi, *Confederate Navy*, 161.

98. Paine, *Sailor of Fortune*, 198.

99. H. H. Bell to Farragut, April 26, 1862, ORN, I/18/175.

100. Farragut to Welles, May 6, 1862, ORN, I/18/157.

101. Farragut, *Farragut*, 395.

102. Porter, *Incidents and Anecdotes*, 50, 55.

103. *Ibid.*, 55.

104. T. T. Craven to Mrs. Craven, May 16, 1862, ORN, I/18/198.

105. Craven to Wife, *Ibid.*, 198.

106. Macartney, *Lincoln's Admirals*, 31.

107. Farragut to Welles, April 25, 1862, ORN, I/18/153; Paine, *Sailor of Fortune*, 199.

108. Boynton, *History*, vol. 2, 211–13; Dufour, *Night the War Was Lost*, 100, 298, 337.

109. Loyall Farragut, Farragut, 261: ORN I/18/162.

110. Farragut Report, May 6, 1862, ORN, I/18/158; George Washington Cable, "New Orleans Before the Capture," BL, vol. 2, 20.

111. Farragut, Farragut, 261.

112. Lovell to Van Dorn, April 30, 1862, OR, I/6/884–5.

113. Harrison Soule, "From the Gulf to Vicksburg with 6th Michigan Infantry" (in War Papers read before the Michigan Commandery of MOLLUSS, vol. 2, 1898): 62; David Dixon Porter, *Naval History of the Civil War* (New York: Sherman Publishing Co., 1886), 247.

114. Cable, "New Orleans," 19–20.

115. John T. Monroe to Farragut, April 25, 1862, ORN, I/18/229.

116. Cable, "New Orleans," 21.

117. Farragut to Welles, May 6, 1862, ORN, I/18/158.

118. Albert Kautz, "Incidents of the Occupation of New Orleans," BL, vol. 2, 91.

119. Farragut, *Farragut*, 262; Kautz, "Occupation of New Orleans," 91–92.

120. John T. Monroe to Farragut, April 26, 1862, ORN, I/18/231–32; Farragut to Monroe, April 28, 1862, *ibid.*, 233; Marion A. Baker, "Farragut's Demands for the Surrender of New Orleans," BL, vol. 2, 98.

121. Kautz, "Occupation of New Orleans," 93; Bell Dairy, ORN, I/18/698.

122. Baker, "Farragut's Demands," 99.

123. Benjamin F. Butler to Edwin Stanton, May 8, 1862, OR, I/6/506–08.

124. *New Orleans Daily Picayune*, June 8, 1862.

125. Brig. Gen. Duncan Report, April 30, 1862, ORN, I/18/272.

126. Quoted in Guelzo, *Fateful Lightning*, 211.

127. Henry Adams to Charles Francis Adams Jr., May 16, 1862, in Worthington Chauncey Ford, ed., *A Cycle of Adams Letters, 1861–1865*, vol. 1 (1920) (New York: Kraus Reprint Co., 1969), 145.

128. McPherson, *Battle Cry*, 422.

129. Blair, "Opening the Mississippi," 34.

130. Annie Laurie Harris, "A Recollection of Thirty Years Ago," p. 12, unpublished mss, SHC.

SIX. "THESE TROUBLOUS TIMES"

1. Kate Stone, *Brokenburn: The Journal of Kate Stone*, 1861–1868 (Baton Rouge: Louisiana State University Press, 1995 edition), 108.

2. Sarah Morgan, *The Civil War Diary of a Southern Woman*, Charles East, ed. (1991) (New York: Simon & Schuster, 1992), 47–48.

3. Morgan, *ibid.*, 51, 59, 74.

4. ORN, I/18/473.

5. Morgan, *Diary*, 63.

6. ORN, I/18/474.

7. Morgan, *Diary*, 63–64, 67.

8. Osbon, *Hartford*, 15.

9. ORN, I/18/462–64.

10. ORN, I/18/8.

11. D. Clayton James, *Antebellum Natchez* (Baton Rouge: Louisiana State University Press, 1993), *passim.*

12. ORN, I/15/737.

13. ORN, I/18/477–78.

14. ORN, I/18/529.

15. Thomas Bangs Thorpe, "Remembrances of the Mississippi," *Harper's New Monthly Magazine* 12, no. 67 (December 1855): 28.

16. Lee Sandlin, *Wicked River: The Mississippi When It Last Ran Wild* (New York: Pantheon Books, 2010), 8.

17. ORN, I/18/519.

18. Twain, *Life on the Mississippi*, 145.

19. A. Miller, *The Mississippi* (London: Orbis Publishing, 1975), 31.

20. Twain, *Life on the Mississippi*, 59; ORN, I/18/519.

21. Twain, *Life on the Mississippi*, 59.

22. ORN, I/18/531.

23. John A. Blackwell, "Personal Recollections of the War of Rebellion," John A. Blackwell Papers, Missouri Historical Society Archives, St. Louis, Missouri.

24. Frederick Trautmann, ed., *Travels on the Lower Mississippi: A Memoir by Ernst Hesse-Wartegg* (Columbia: University of Missouri Press, 1990), 39.

25. Blackwell, "Personal Recollections."

26. ORN, I/18/530.

27. John James Audubon, *Delineations of American Scenery and Character* (New York: G. A. Baker & Company, 1926), 29.

28. ORN, I/18/533.

29. Farragut to Susan M. Farragut, May 2, 1862, in Farragut, *Farragut*, 269.

30. Hodding Carter, *Lower Mississippi* (New York: Rinehart & Co., 1942), 3–4.

31. ORN, I/18/529.

32. *Ibid.*, 531.

33. *Ibid.*, 519.

34. ORN, I/18/519.

35. Private Diary of H. H. Bell, May 13, 1862, ORN, I/18/702.

36. Stone, *Brokenburn*, 90, 93, 108.

37. Diary of Francis A. Roe, ORN, May 20, 1862, I/18/491–93, 783.

38. All messages dated May 18, 1862, ORN, I/18/492.

39. Stone, *Brokenburn*, 104.

40. John Q. Alexander, "Introduction" to Stone, *Brokenburn*, xvii.

41. Frank E. Everett Jr., *Brierfield: Plantation Home of Jefferson Davis* (Hattiesburg: University and College Press of Mississippi, 1971), 7.

42. William J. Cooper, *Jefferson Davis, American* (New York: Knopf, 2000), 405.

43. *Vicksburg Daily Citizen*, May 8, 1862, quoted in CT, June 14, 1862.

44. Everett, *Brierfield*, 18–19.

45. *Vicksburg Daily Whig*, June 3, 1862.

46. Christopher Morris, *Becoming Southern: The Evolution of a Way of Life, Warren County and Vicksburg, Mississippi, 1770–1860* (New York: Oxford University Press, 1995), 176.

47. OR, I/15/7.

48. S. B. Lockett, "The Defense of Vicksburg," BL, vol. 3, 483.

49. Bell Diary, ORN, I/18/704; Farragut to Welles, June 3, 1862, ORN, I/18/578; John B. Pirtle, "Defence of Vicksburg in 1862—the Battle of Baton Rouge," *Southern Historical Society Papers* vol. 8 (1880), 324–32.

50. M. L. Smith Report, August 1862, OR, 1/15/6, Edwin C. Bearss, *Rebel Victory at Vicksburg* (Vicksburg: Vicksburg Centennial Commemoration Commission, 1963), 51.

51. OR, I/52, pt. 2/316–17; Edwin Bearss.

52. Bell Diary, ORN, I/18/704–5; Log of U.S.S. *Kennebec, ibid.*, 810.

53. Bell Diary, *ibid.*, 705.

54. *Ibid.*, 706.

55. Farragut, *Farragut*, 267; Bell Diary, *ibid.*, 706–08.

56. Farragut to Susan M. Farragut, in Farragut, *Farragut*, 267, 272; Bell Diary, *ibid.*, 706.

57. Holton, *Hartford*, 17.

58. Bell Diary, *ibid*, 796; ORN, 18, I/18/509–09.

59. ORN, 18, I/18/519–20; Bell Diary, 705–06, 746.

60. Farragut, *Farragut*, 267.

61. Farragut to Butler, May 22, 1862, in Benjamin F. Butler and Jesse Ames Marshall, *Private and Official Correspondence of Gen. Benjamin F. Butler, During the Period of the Civil War*, vol. 1 (Norwood, MA: Plimpton Press, 1917), 544.

62. Stone, *Brokenburn*, 108, 114.

63. William Pitt Chambers, "My Journal," vol. 5, edited by Ruth Polk (Publications of the Mississippi Historical Society, 1925): 239–41.

64. Chambers, "My Journal," 241.

65. Chambers, "My Journal," 239–41.

66. Winchester Hall, *The Story of the 26th Louisiana Infantry in the Service of the Confederate States* (Gaithersburg, MD, Butternut Press, 1984 edition), xiii.

67. *Ibid.*, 13.

68. William Y. Dixon, "Diary," William Y. Dixon Papers, LSU, Special Collections.

69. Chambers, "My Journal," vol. 5, 243–44.

70. *Vicksburg Daily Citizen*, July 2, 1862.

71. Dixon, "Diary," LSU.

72. Ralph C. Mason, "Military Relief Records, Warren County, 1862–1863," Old Courthouse Museum, Vicksburg, Mississippi; Ella Lonn, *Salt as a Factor in the Confederacy* (Tuscaloosa: University of Alabama Press, 1933), 292–96.

73. Charles B. Allen, Plantation Book, MDAH.

74. Quoted in Samuel Carter III, *The Final Fortress: The Campaign for Vicksburg, 1862–1863* (New York: St. Martin's Press, 1980), 36.

75. Sidney Champion to Matilda Champion, September 26, 1862, Sidney S. Champion Papers, Duke University, Durham, North Carolina (hereafter cited as Champion Mss).

76. Sidney Champion to Matilda Champion, n.d., Champion Mss.

77. Harrison Soule, "From Gulf to Vicksburg," *War Papers Read Before the Michigan Commandery of the Military Order of the Loyal Legion of the United States* (MOLLUS), 2 (Detroit: H. Stone and Co., 1898), 68.

78. OR, I/15/23.

79. Gen. Williams, May 22, 1862 in G. Mott Williams, "The First Vicksburg Expedition, and the Battle of Baton Rouge," *War Papers Read before the Commandery of the State of Wisconsin* 2 (Milwaukee; Burdick, Armitage & Allen, 1896), 53. The author is General Williams's son.

80. Soule, "From Gulf to Vicksburg," 71.

81. Williams, ed., "Letters of General Thomas Williams," May 22, 1862, 319.

82. *Ibid.*, 23–24; ORN, I/18/520, 535.

83. Farragut to Welles, May 30, 1862, ORN, I/18/52.

84. Bell Diary, ORN, I/18/707.

85. Osbon, *Hartford*, 18.

86. Morgan, *Diary*, 77, 89.

87. ORN, I/18/520.

88. Osbon, *Hartford*, 19.

89. Farragut to Welles, May 30, 1862, ORN, I/18/520–21.

90. Quoted in Farragut, *Farragut*, 270–71.

91. Fox to Farragut, May 12, 16, 1862, ORN, I/18/245, 498–99.

92. ORN, I/18/498–99.

93. ORN, I/18/502.

94. Butler and Marshall, *Correspondence of Gen. Butler*, vol. 2, 537.

95. ORN, I/18/576; OR, I/6/673.

96. ORN, 1 I/18/521, 576, 580, 521.

97. ORN, I/18/577.

98. Porter to Farragut, June 3, 1862, ORN, I/18/576–77.

99. *Fox Correspondence*, 112.

100. Farragut to Susan Farragut, June 2, 1862, in Farragut, *Farragut*, 269.

SEVEN. SECESSIONIST CITADEL

1. *Jackson Semi-Weekly Mississippian*, November 9, 1860.

2. S. R. Franklin, *Memoirs of a Rear-Admiral* (New York: Harper Brothers, 1898), 185.

3. Bell Diary, June 6, 1862, ORN, I/18/708.

4. Farragut to Susan M. Farragut, June 15, 1862, in Farragut, *Farragut*, 271–72.

5. Williams, ed., "Letters of General Thomas Williams," 321.

6. Butler to Williams, June 6, 1862, OR, I/15/25–26.

7. Morgan, *Diary*, 112, 123–25.

8. Farragut, *Farragut*, 273.

9. Osbon, *Hartford*, 19.

10. ORN, I/18/727, 790; G. G. Benedict, *Vermont in the Civil War*, vol. 2 (Burlington: The Free Press Association, 1888), 10.

11. Benedict, *Vermont*, vol. 2, 101.

12. Lockett, "The Defense of Vicksburg," 484.

13. Robert G. Hartje, *Van Dorn: The Life and Times of a Confederate General* (Nashville, TN: Vanderbilt University Press, 1967), 9, 77; Dabney H. Maury, "Recollections of General Earl Van Dorn," *Southern Historical Society* 19 (1891): 197–98: for Van Dorn, see also Arthur B. Carter, *The Tarnished Cavalier: Major General Earl Van Dorn, C.S.A.* (Knoxville: The University of Tennessee Press, 1999).

14. John Williams Green, *Johnny Green of the Orphan Brigade: The Journal of a Confederate Soldier*, edited by Albert D. Kirwan (Lexington: University Press of Kentucky, 2002), 118.

15. Quoted in Woodworth, *Jefferson Davis and His Generals*, 115.

16. Hartje, *Van Dorn*, 76.

17. OR, I/15/770.

18. Osbon, *Hartford*, 31–32.

19. Porter, *Incidents and Anecdotes*, 97–98.

20. William B. Brooks Diary, June 27, May 23, 1862, Virginia Historical Society, Richmond, Virginia.

21. Green, *Orphan Brigade*, 115.

22. Pirtle, "Defence of Vicksburg," 326.

23. William Dixon, "Diary," LSU.

24. Pirtle, "Defence of Vicksburg," 326; Gordon A. Cotton and Jeff T. Giambrone, *Vicksburg and the War* (Gretna, LA: Pelican Publishing Company, 2004), 24; there are no available records of military casualties. For the psychological effect of the bombing see Peter F. Walker, *Vicksburg: A People at War, 1860–1865* (Chapel Hill: University of North Carolina Press, 1960), 93.

25. Porter, *Incidents and Anecdotes*, 98.

26. *Vicksburg Daily Citizen*, reprinted in CT, June 20, 1862.

27. Sidney S. Champion to Matilda Champion, May 24, 1862, Champion Mss.

28. Walker, *Vicksburg*, 5.

29. *A General Directory for the City of Vicksburg* (Vicksburg, MS: 1860), 1–30, Old Courthouse Museum, Vicksburg.

30. *Ibid.*, 50, 56.

31. William K. Scarborough, "Heartland of the Cotton Kingdom," in Richard Aubrey McLemore, ed., *A History of Mississippi*, vol. 1 (Jackson: University & College Press of Mississippi, 1963), 334.

32. Morris, *Becoming Southern*, 121; "Vicksburg Gamblers," Mississippi Department of Archives and History, Jackson Mississippi (hereafter cited as MDAH).

33. Anon, *The South-West, by a Yankee*, vol. 2 (New York: Harper & Brothers, 1835), 170; H. C. Clarke, "Vicksburg, Mississippi," *Southern Illustrated News*, November 8, 1862.

34. Alfred R. Waud, "Pictures of the South: Vicksburg," *Harper's Weekly*, in Reps, *Cities of the Mississippi*, 142.

35. Hesse-Wartegg, *Travels*, 77.

36. Morris, *Becoming Southern*, 128.

37. Ibid., 118. In 1860 Warren County had a population of 6,918 free whites and 10,524 black slaves. U.S. Census, Population Schedules for Warren County, 1860; Slave Schedules, 1860, for Warren County, Old Courthouse Museum.

38. John K. Bettersworth, *Confederate Mississippi: The People and Policies of a Cotton State in Wartime* (Baton Rouge: Louisiana State University Press, 1943), 269.

39. Scarborough, "Heartland," 313–25.

40. Percy Lee Rainwater, *Mississippi: Storm Center of Secession, 1856–1861* (1938) (New York: Da Capo Press, 1969), 219.

41. Charles S. Sydnor, *A Gentleman of the Old Natchez Region, Benjamin L. C. Wailes* (Durham, NC: Duke University Press, 1938), 291.

42. William L. Barney, *The Secessionist Impulse: Alabama and Mississippi in 1860* (Princeton, NJ: Princeton University Press, 1974), 77.

43. *Ibid.*, 96.

44. Barney, *Secessionist Impulse*, 100.

45. John F. H. Claiborne, *Life and Correspondence of John A. Quitman*, vol. 2 (New York: Harper Brothers, 1860), 265.

46. Quoted in Rainwater, *Storm Center*, 164.

47. Returns for Presidential Electors, 1860, series F, vol. 85, MDAH.

48. *Jackson Semi-Weekly Mississippian*, November 9, 1860.

49. Glover Moore, "Separation from the Union, 1854–1861," in *A History of Mississippi*, vol. 1, edited by Richard Aubrey McLemore (Oxford: University College Press of Mississippi, 1973), 436.

50. *Vicksburg Daily Citizen*, December 1, 1860.

51. *Vicksburg Daily Whig*, October 17, November 8, 18, 1860.

52. Quoted in Rainwater, *Storm Center*, 184.

53. *Proceedings of the Mississippi State Convention Held January 7th to 26th, A.D. 1861* (Jackson, MS, 1861); Ralph A. Wooster, *The Secession Conventions of the South* (Princeton, NJ: Princeton University Press, 1962), 32–34; Walker, *Vicksburg*, 30.

54. Quoted in Barney, *Secessionist Impulse*, 315.

55. *Vicksburg Weekly Whig*, January 23, 1861.

56. W. Swords quoted in Cotton and Giambrone, *Vicksburg and the War*, 11; *Vicksburg Daily Citizen*, February 12, 1861.

57. Rainwater, *Storm Center*, 218–20.

58. William Howard Russell, *Pictures of Southern Life: Social, Political, and Military* (New York: James G. Gregory, 1861), 13, 74.

59. Cotton and Giambrone, *Vicksburg and the War*, 14, 16.

60. Stone, *Brokenburn*, 15, 20, 36.

61. Harris, "A Recollection," 12, SHC.

62. Roach, "Diary," 92, SHC.

EIGHT. REBEL VICTORY

1. Stone, *Brokenburn*, 135.

2. ORN, I/23/242; ORN, I/18/750; Warren D. Crandall, *History of the Ram Fleet and the Mississippi Marine Brigade on the Mississippi and Its Tributaries* (St. Louis: Society of Survivors, 1907), 57–58.

3. ORN, I/18/583.

4. Farragut to Davis, June 28, 1862, ORN, I/23/231–32; ORN, 1/18/584.

5. Farragut, *Farragut*, 273.

6. ORN, I/18/712.

7. Warren E. Grabau, *Ninety-Eight Days: A Geographer's View of the Vicksburg Campaign* (Knoxville: University of Tennessee Press, 2000), 16–17.

8. Farragut, *Farragut*, 277–79.

9. ORN, I/18/632–39.

10. Henry E. Maynadier to Davis, August 2, 1862, ORN, I/23/279–80; Farragut, Official Report, July 2, 1862 in Farragut, *Farragut*, 277–79; Porter Report, July 3, 1863, ORN, I/18/639.

11. Osbon, *Hartford*, 32.

12. James Alden, "Journal of the Richmond," ORN, I/18/751.

13. *Vicksburg Daily Whig*, July 1, 1862.

14. CT, July 8, 1862.

15. Lockett, "Defense of Vicksburg," BL, 483.

16. *Ibid.*, 483.

17. Osbon, *Hartford*, 32.

18. OR, I/15/12; *Vicksburg Daily Whig*, July 1, 1862; *Vicksburg Daily Citizen*, July 2, 1862.

19. Farragut to Welles, July 1, 1862, in Farragut, *Farragut*, 279.

20. Farragut to Susan Farragut, June 29, 1862, in *ibid.*, 275.

21. Farragut to Halleck, June 28, 1862, ORN, I/18/590.

22. Farragut to Halleck, June 28, 1862, ORN, I/18/590.

23. Halleck to Farragut, July 3, 1862, ORN. I/18/593.

24. Porter to Farragut, July 3, ORN, I/18/641.

25. ORN, I/18/629; Farragut to Porter, July 8, 1862, David Dixon Porter Papers, LC.

26. Porter to Fox, July 3, 1853, *Fox Correspondence*, 122.

27. ORN, I/18/571–72.

28. Porter Report, July 1862, ORN, I/18/679.

29. Davis, *Davis*, 256.

30. Stone, *Brokenburn*, 122.

31. S. L. Phelps to Foote, July 6, ORN, I/23/235.

32. Davis, *Davis*, 257–58.

33. Farragut, *Farragut*, 282–83.

34. ORN, I/18/714.

35. ORN, I/18/714.

36. R. A. Watkinson to C. H. Davis, June 25, 1862, ORN, I/23/226–27.

37. David F. Bastian, *Grant's Canal: The Union's Attempt to Bypass Vicksburg* (Shippensburg, PA: Burd Street Press, 1995), 6.

38. G. Mott Williams, ed., "Letters of General Thomas Williams, 1862," *American Historical Review* 14, no. 2 (January 1909): 322; Williams to Davis, July 4, 1862, OR, I/15/27.

39. Stone, *Brokenburn*, 125, 127.

40. Edward Bacon, *Among the Cotton Thieves* (Detroit: The Free Press Stream Book Center and Job Printing House, 1867), 6. See also William C. Holbrook, *A Narrative of the Services of the Officers and Enlisted Men of the Regiment of Vermont Volunteers from 1862 to 1866* (New York: American Bank Company, 1882), 23.

41. Bacon, *Cotton Thieves*, 1, 13.

42. General Orders, No. 46, reproduced in Bacon, *Cotton Thieves*, 22; William F. Messner, "The Vicksburg Campaign of 1862: A Case Study in the Federal Utilization of Black Labor," *Louisiana History: The Journal of the Louisiana Historical Association* 16, no. 4 (Autumn, 1975): 372.

43. Williams to Mrs. M. A. Baily, July 21, 1862; Williams to Wife, May 22, July 2, 21, 1862, in Williams, ed. "Letters of General Thomas Williams," 318, 323, 327.

44. Williams to Wife, May 22, July 2, 21, in *ibid.*, 318, 323, 327.

45. Quoted in Messner, "Vicksburg Campaign," 377.

46. Williams to Wife, July 2, 1862, in Williams, ed. "Letters of General Thomas Williams," 323.

47. Lockett to Cornelia Lockett, July 26, 1862, Samuel Henry Lockett Papers, SHC.

48. Thomas Hamilton Murray, *History of the Ninth Regiment, Connecticut Volunteer Infantry in the War of the Rebellion, 1861–65* (New Haven, CT: Price, Lee & Co., 1903), 111–12.

49. G. G. Benedict, *Vermont in the Civil War*, vol. 2 (Burlington, VT: Free Press, 1888). 2–13.

50. Murray, *Ninth Regiment*, 109; Andrew McIlwaine Bell, *Mosquito Soldiers: Malaria, Yellow Fever, and the Course of the American Civil War* (Baton Rouge: Louisiana State University Press, 2010), 59–60. On shortages of quinine, see also United States Surgeon-General's Office, *Medical and Surgical History of the War of Rebellion*, vol. 1, part I, Appendix (Washington, D.C.: Government Printing Office, 1861–1865), 335; Paul E. Steiner, *Disease in the Civil War: Natural Biological Warfare in 1861–1865* (Springfield, IL: Charles C. Thomas Publisher, 1968), 193.

51. Murray, *Ninth Regiment*, 59–60.

52. Benedict, *Vermont*, 15.

53. Bacon, *Cotton Thieves*, 7.

54. Benedict, *Vermont*, 15; Holbrook, *Vermont Volunteers*, 23.

55. Lockett to Cornelia Lockett, July 25, 1862, SHC.

56. Pirtle, "Defence of Vicksburg, 325; Steiner, *Disease in the Civil War*, 193.

57. Hall, *26th Louisiana*, 14–15, 30–36.

58. Chambers, "My Journal," 241–45.

59. E. B. Long, with Barbara Long, *The Civil War Day by Day, An Almanac* (New York: Doubleday, 1971), 162.

60. Commander Richard Wainwright, Log of the U.S.S. *Hartford*, ORN, I/18/729.

61. Davis, *Davis*, 263, 292; Thomas W. Knox, *Camp-Fire, and Cotton-Field: Southern Adventure in Time of War* (New York: Jones Brothers and Company, 1865), 202.

62. Knox, *Camp-Fire and Cotton-Field*, 202.

63. ORN, I/18, 647; Isaac N. Brown, "The Confederate Gunboat Arkansas," BL, vol. 3, 572.

64. Quoted in Foote, *Fort Sumter to Perryville*, 552.

65. Brown, "Arkansas," 572–74.

66. Dabney Minor Scales to Father, July 31, 1862, original in Old Court House Museum.

67. Junius Henri Browne, *Four Years in Secessia: Adventures Within and Beyond Union Lines* (Chicago: O. D. Case and Company, 1865), 213.

68. George W. Gift, "The Story of the *Arkansas*," *Southern Historical Society Papers* 12 (1884): 49–50.

69. *Ibid.*, 51.

70. *Ibid.*, 52.

71. *Ibid.*, 52.

72. S. B. Coleman, "A July Morning with the Rebel Ram *Arkansas*" (Michigan Commandery of MOLLUS: Detroit: Winn & Hammond, 1890), 9.

73. Brown, *"Arkansas,"* 574.

74. *Ibid.*, 575–76.

75. Coleman, "July Morning," 5: Walke's badly damaged vessel, with thirty wounded and dead aboard, made it back to the fleet that night.

76. Coleman, "July Morning," 9: *Tyler* lost twenty-five men killed and wounded.

77. Brown, *"Arkansas,"* 575.

78. ORN, I/19/56–58, 672.

79. Quoted in McPherson, *War on the Waters*, 93.

80. Brown, *"Arkansas,"* 575–76.

81. *Ibid.*, 576; ORN, I/19/69.

82. Dixon, "Diary," LSU; Carter, *Final Fortress*, 70–71.

83. OR, I/15/16.

84. ORN, I/19/133; James P. Duffy, *Lincoln's Admiral: The Civil War Campaigns of David Farragut* (New York: John Wiley & Sons, 1997), 146; Philip Katcher, *Great Gambles of the Civil War* (Edison, NJ: Castle Books, 2003), 63.

85. ORN, I/19/132–36; Bearss, *Rebel Victory*, 244.

86. Brown, *"Arkansas,"* 577–80.

87. Williams, ed., "Letters of General Thomas Williams," 324; ORN, I/19/8, 748; Porter, *Naval History*, 260.

88. Welles, *Diary*, vol. 1, August 10, 1862, 72.

89. Farragut to Welles, July 17, 1862, ORN, I/19/4, 8, 748.

90. Brown, *"Arkansas,"* 577.

91. ORN, I/19/8, 712–13, 748; Farragut, *Farragut*, 287; Hearn, *Farragut*, 159.

92. Farragut to Davis, July 16, 1862, ORN, I/23/236.

93. Davis to Farragut, July 17, 1862, ORN, I/23/237; Davis, *Davis*, 264–65; Hearn, *Farragut*, 158.

94. Davis, *Davis*, 264–65.

95. McPherson, *War on the Waters*, 93.

96. ORN, I/19/13, 16; Hearn, *Farragut*, 160–61.

97. Davis to Farragut, July 20, 1862, ORN, I/23/238; Davis to Farragut, July 21, 1862, *ibid.*

98. ORN, I/19/61.

99. Brown, *"Arkansas,"* 578.

100. Ibid.

101. Ibid., 578: At the Battle of Trafalgar in 1805, Lord Nelson had twenty-seven powerful ships-of-the-line and four other smaller ships.

102. Welles to Farragut, July 18, 1862, ORN, I/19/18–19.

103. Halleck to Stanton, July 15, 1862, ORN, I/18/636.

104. Beale, ed., Bates, *Diary*, 283: Curtis's army entered Helena on July 11, 1862.

105. Welles, *Diary*, vol. 1, 218.

106. Welles to Farragut, July 14, 1862, ORN, I/18/595; Farragut to Davis, July 23, 1862, ORN, I/19/18–19.

107. Williams, ed. "Letters of General Thomas Williams, 1862," 323–24.

108. ORN, 1/23/271; Davis to Welles, July 25, ORN, I/23/240.

109. Davis, *Davis*, 267; Williams to M.A. Baily, in Williams, ed., "Letters of General Thomas Williams," 326; ORN, I/19/18.

110. Davis letter, August 1, 1862; Davis, *Davis*, 269.

111. H. Beauchamp to Davis, July 25, 1862, ORN, I/23/240–41; ORN, I/19/18.

112. ORN, I/19/18; Boynton, *History*, 253.

113. Pirtle, *"Defence of Vicksburg,"* 324–332.

114. ORN, I/23/271.

115. Lockett to Cornelia, July 25, 1862, SHC.

116. Charles B. Allen, Plantation Book, 93, MDAH.

117. Brown, *"Arkansas,"* 578; OR, I/15/10.

118. Lockett to Cornelia Lockett, July 25, 1862, SHC.

119. Williams, ed., "Letters of General Thomas Williams," 326–27.

120. Steiner, *Disease in the Civil War*, 186.

121. Bacon, *Cotton Thieves, passim.*

122. Davis, Davis, 271; Williams to wife, July 2, 1862, in Williams, ed., "Letters of General Thomas Williams," 323; NYT, August 2, 1862.

123. Stone, *Brokenburn*, 134–35.

124. Dabney Scales, July 31, 1862, Old Court House Museum.

125. Lockett to Cornelia Lockett, July 26, SHC.

126. Caroline Whitcomb, *The History of the Second Massachusetts Battery (Nims Battery) of Light Artillery, 1861–1865* (Concord, NH: The Rumsford Press, 1912), 33.

127. OR, I/15/76.

128. ORN, I/19/131, 135.

129. Brown, *"Arkansas,"* 578–79.

130. OR, 1/52, part 2, 334.

131. Davis to Van Dorn, August 4, 1862, OR, I/15/794.

132. Pirtle, "Defence of Vicksburg," 330.

133. *Ibid.*, 328; OR, I/16/77.

134. Pirtle, "Defence of Vicksburg," 328.

135. Steiner, *Disease in the Civil War*, 206; OR, I/15/76–79.

136. Quoted in Murray, *Ninth Connecticut*, 114; see also OR, I/15/55.

137. Pirtle, "Defence of Vicksburg," 330.

138. OR, I/15/57, 63.

139. Pirtle, "Defence of Vicksburg," 331.

140. ORN, I/19/135–36; Breckinridge Report, September 30, 1862, OR, I/15/79.

141. Edwin C. Bearss, "The Battle of Baton Rouge," *Louisiana Historical Association* vol. 3, no. 2 (1962), 112.

142. Farragut to Welles, August 7, 10, ORN, I/19/115, 117–18, 120.

143. ORN, I/19/141–43.

144. ORN, I/19/141, 153, 707, 721; Farragut ordered an evacuation before opening fire.

145. OR, I/15/17, 797.

146. OR, I/15/81.

147. Seddon to Pemberton, March 12, OR, I/24, part 3, 664; Michael F. Wright. "Vicksburg and the Trans-Mississippi Supply Line (1861–1863)," *Journal of Mississippi History* vol. 43, no. 3 (1981): 211–12.

148. Historians have long debated the existence of a robust Red River supply line to Vicksburg. Many recent scholars of the Vicksburg campaign side with historian Thomas L. Connelly, who, in a scholarly essay published in 1970, offered speculative evidence that the Red River supply line had been "greatly exaggerated." The main import centers of foreign munitions were, he said, "the Atlantic ports, fed by blockade runners. . . . And it would appear that the main importance for the imports from

Mexico was to supply the trans-Mississippi armies and not the eastern Confederacy."
Nor, Connelly argued, was there enough statistical evidence available to substantiate
the existence of a voluminous flow of cattle across the Mississippi River to Vicksburg.
(Thomas to Connelly, "Vicksburg: Strategic Point or Propaganda Device?" *Military
Affairs*, vol. 34 [April 1970]: 47–53.)

Connelly may have been right on rifles and cattle, but they were not the most
important war resources brought east from the trans-Mississippi Confederacy.
Drawing upon the correspondence of Confederate military officials, historian Michael
Wright presents compelling evidence that in 1862 and 1863 three critically important
commodities—salt, sugar, and molasses—flowed eastward through Vicksburg "in
large quantities" to western Mississippi, Alabama, Tennessee, and a number of other
Confederate states. (Wright, "Vicksburg," 211–12.)

In March 1863, General Joseph E. Johnston wrote from Mobile to General John C.
Pemberton, then commander of the Vicksburg garrison: "The supplies of sugar and
molasses for the troops here and in Tennessee come through Vicksburg. I need not tell
you how important those supplies are to the troops in these times of scarcity of meat."
(Johnston to Pemberton, March 12, 1863, OR, I/23, part 2/685; Wright, "Vicksburg,"
213.) That same day, Confederate secretary of war James A. Seddon requested
Pemberton to send as much sugar and molasses eastward as he could get his hands on.
(OR, I/24, part 3/664) Days later, Johnston again reminded Pemberton: "Sugar and
molasses for the whole army must come through Vicksburg. . . . With these articles
meat can be purchased, which is to be obtained in no other way. You are aware that it
is very scarce in all our armies now." (*Ibid.*, 670.)

In a separate report, Pemberton indicated that most of the riverboats on the Mississippi "were engaged in carrying sugar, molasses and salt either for private parties or for
the government." (OR, I/24, part 1/288). Based on the incomplete shipping records
scholars have available to them, it is likely that "millions of pounds of sugar" were
landed there, Wright argues. (Wright, *ibid.*)

Writing eight years before Connelly, historian Kenneth P. Williams had it right:
"So long as Vicksburg was held, the Confederates could maintain contact with
the three western states west of the river on which they depended extensively for
supplies." Kenneth P. Williams, *Lincoln Finds a General*, vol. 4 (NY: Macmillan,
1952), 430.

149. Welles, *Galaxy*, vol. 12, 830–31.
150. Butler to Halleck, August 27, 1862, OR, I/155–56.
151. Lockett to Cornelia Lockett, July 26, 1862, SHC.
152. Pirtle, "Defence of Vicksburg," 332.
153. Lockett, "Defense of Vicksburg," 484.
154. Lockett to Cornelia Lockett, July 25, 1862, SHC.
155. Welles, *Galaxy*, vol. 12, 829.

NINE. ANXIETY AND INTRIGUE

1. OR, I/17/part 2/302.
2. David Donald, ed., *Inside Lincoln's Cabinet: The Civil War Diaries of Salmon P. Chase*

(New York: Longmans, Green and Co., 1954), 106–09; Stephen E. Ambrose, *Halleck*, 108–09.

3. Porter, *Incidents and Anecdotes*, 115.

4. Porter to Fox, July 26, 1862, *Fox Correspondence*, 124–25.

5. Richard S. West Jr., *The Second Admiral: A Life of David Dixon Porter, 1813–1891* (New York: Coward-McCann, 1937), 137.

6. Porter, *Incidents and Anecdotes*, 118–19.

7. *Ibid.*, 119–121.

8. Hearn, *Porter*, 141.

9. Welles to Porter, September 22, 1862, ORN, I/23/373.

10. ORN, I/23/388.

11. Porter, *Incidents and Anecdotes*, 122.

12. Welles, *Diary*, vol. 1, 157–58, 167–68.

13. Porter to his mother, October 7, 1862, Porter Papers, LC.

14. Welles, *Diary*, vol. 1, 167.

15. ORN, I/23/396, 424–25.

16. ORN, I/23/356.

17. Denis J. Ringle, *Life in Mr. Lincoln's Navy* (Annapolis, MD: Naval Institute Press, 1998), 14.

18. Hearn, *Porter*, 145.

19. George W. Brown, "Service in the Mississippi Squadron, and Its Connection with the Siege and Capture of Vicksburg," in *Personal Recollections of the War of the Rebellion*, James Grant Wilson and Titus Munson Coan, eds. (New York: The Commandery, 1891): 303–04.

20. Norman E. Clarke, *Warfare Along the Mississippi: The Letters of Lieutenant Colonel George E. Currie* (Mount Pleasant, MI: Clarke Historical Collection, 1961), xv, 60, 71.

21. ORN, I/23/418.

22. Welles, *Diary*, vol. 1, 180; ORN, I/23/429; West, *Second Admiral*, 180.

23. ORN, I/23/469.

24. Howard C. Westwood, "War on the River: Running Past Vicksburg," *Civil War Times Illustrated* 2, no. 6 (1982): 14–32.

25. ORN, I/23/421; West, *Second Admiral*, 178.

26. WTS to Ellen Ewing Sherman, September 25, 1862, SCW, 305.

27. ORN, I/23/431.

28. West, *Second Admiral*, 1.

29. Hearn, *Porter*, 151; Fox to Welles, November 11, 1862, Welles Papers, LC.

30. ORN, I/23/443.

31. ORN, I/23/458.

32. Porter, *Incidents and Anecdotes*, 123.

33. Charles A. Dana and James Harrison Wilson, *The Life of Ulysses S. Grant: General of the Armies of the United States* (New York: Gurdon Bill & Co., 1868), 94; McClernand to Lincoln, March 31, 1862, Abraham Lincoln Papers, LC.

34. Badeau, *Military History*, vol. 1, 128.

35. Wilkie, *Pen and Powder*, 213.

36. Theodore M. Pease and James J. Randall, eds., *The Diary of Orville Hickman Browning*, vol. 1 (Springfield: Illinois State Historical Library, 1925), xix, 560.

37. Halleck to McClernand, August 20, 1862, John Alexander McClernand Collection, Illinois State Historical Library, Springfield, Il. (hereafter cited as McClernand Coll).

38. Chase, *Diary*, vol. 1, 97.

39. McClernand to Lincoln, September 28, 1862, McClernand Coll.

40. Quoted in Guelzo, *Emancipation Proclamation*, 211.

41. Christopher Phillips, *The Rivers Ran Backward: The Civil War and the Remaking of the American Middle Border* (New York: Oxford University Press, 2016), 269; Nicole Etcheson, *A Generation at War: The Civil War in a Northern Community* (Lawrence: University Press of Kansas, 2010), 100–17, 148–54.

42. Allan Nevins, *Ordeal of the Union*, v. 3, *The War for the Union; War Becomes Revolution, 1862–1863* (NY: Macmillan Publishing Company, 1992 edition), 379.

43. James Harrison Wilson, *Under the Old Flag: Recollections of Military Operations in the War for the Union . . .* v. 1 (NY: D. Appleton, 1912), 123–127.

44. Donald, ed., *Inside Lincoln's Cabinet*, 98, 162–63, 169–70.

45. OR, I/17, part 2, 282.

46. Roy P. Basler, ed., *The Collected Works of Abraham Lincoln*, vol. 4 (New Brunswick, NJ: Rutgers University Press, 1953), 468–69, italics mine.

47. OR, I/17, part 2, 302.

48. WTSM, 279.

49. USGM, 278.

50. Charles W. Wills, *Army Life of an Illinois Soldier: Letters and Diary of Charles W. Wills*, compiled by Mary E. Kellogg (1906) (Carbondale: Southern Illinois University Press, 1996), 112.

51. NYT, July 30, 1862.

52. WTSM, 277.

53. Joseph Wheeler, "Bragg's Invasion of Kentucky," BL, vol. 3, 2.

54. Thomas L. Snead, "With Price East of the Mississippi," BL, vol. 2, 725.

55. Fiske, *Mississippi Valley*, 151.

56. USGM, 271.

57. Quoted in Peter Cozzens, *The Darkest Days of the War: The Battles of Iuka & Corinth* (Chapel Hill: University of North Carolina Press, 1997), 7.

58. Arthur L. Conger, *The Rise of U. S. Grant* (1931) (New York: Da Capo Press, 1996), 279; USGM, 275.

59. Perrett, *Grant*, 224.

60. USGM, 223–24.

61. Byers, *Fire and Sword*, 37–38.

62. USGM, 225.

63. William S. Rosecrans, "The Battle of Corinth," BL, vol. 2, 740–43, 749.

64. McPherson, *Battle Cry*, 523.

65. Richardson, *Personal History*, 270.

66. Badeau, *Military History*, vol. 1, 116.

67. USGM, 281; Cozzens, *Darkest Days*, 305.

68. USG to William S. Rosecrans, October 4, 5, USGP, vol. 6, 114, 123.

69. Quoted in Woodworth, *Nothing But Victory*, 239.

70. OR, October 8, 1862, OR, I/17, part 1, 156.

71. *Ibid.*

72. Richardson, *Personal History*, 266; Catton, *Grant Moves South*, 319.

73. USGM, 281.

74. Grant to Halleck, October 26, 1862, USGP, vol. 6, 199–200.

75. Badeau, *Military History*, vol. 1, 127.

76. USG to Halleck, November 2, 1862; Halleck to USG, November 3, 1862, USGP, vol. 6, 243.

77. USGM, 283.

78. USG to James B. McPherson, November 2, 1862, USG to Charles S. Hamilton, November 2, 1863, USGP, vol. 6, 244, 249.

79. USG to WTS, November 3, 1862, ibid., 254–55.

80. All quotes from John C. Pemberton, *Pemberton, Defender of Vicksburg* (Chapel Hill: University of North Carolina Press, 1942), 23–24; see also Michael B. Ballard, *Pemberton: A Biography* (Jackson: University Press of Mississippi, 1991), 84.

81. Francis Pickens to Jefferson Davis, June 2, 5, 1862, Samuel Wylie Crawford Papers, LC.

82. John F. Marszalek, ed., *The Diary of Miss Emma Holmes, 1861–1866* (Baton Rouge: Louisiana State University Press, 1979), 174, 177.

83. Michael B. Ballard, "Misused Merit: The Tragedy of John C. Pemberton," in Steven E. Woodworth, ed., *Civil War Generals in Defeat* (Lawrence: University Press of Kansas, 1990), 142; Ballard, *Pemberton*, 63, 112.

84. Foote, *Fort Sumter to Perryville*, 777–78.

85. Quoted in Ballard, *Pemberton*, 116.

86. Craig L. Symonds, *Joseph E. Johnston: A Civil War Biography* (New York: W. W. Norton and Company, paperback edition, 1994), 199; see also Woodworth, *Jefferson Davis and His Generals*, 197.

87. Mary Boykin Chesnut, *Mary Chesnut's Diary* (1905) (New York: Penguin Books, 2011), 249.

88. OR, I/17, part 2, 157–58; Joseph E. Johnston, "Jefferson Davis and the Mississippi Campaign," *North American Review* 143 (December 1886): 473.

89. Woodworth, *Jefferson Davis and His Generals*, 124.

90. Quoted in Symonds, *Johnston*, 187–89.

91. Quoted in Ballard, *Pemberton*, 119; for Holmes's intransigency see OR, I/17, part 2, 754, 767, 786.

92. OR, I/17, part 2, 728.

93. Bell Irvin Wiley and Lucy E. Fay, eds., *"This Infernal War": The Confederate Letters of Sgt. Edwin H. Fay* (Austin: Texas University Press, 1958), 179.

94. OR, I/17, part 2, 742–46.

95. OR, *ibid.*, 745–6.

96. OR, *ibid.*, 737, 742, 754.

97. OR, I/19, part 2, 749.

98. OR, I/17, part 2, 750–51.

99. OR, *ibid.*, 753, 755, 757.

100. OR, I/17, part 2, 753.

101. James M. McPherson, *Embattled Rebel: Jefferson Davis as Commander in Chief* (New York: The Penguin Press, 2014), 109–13.

102. USG to WRS, November 6, 1862, USGP, vol. 6, 262–63.

103. NYT, CT, November 13, 21, 1862.

104. OR, I/17, part 1, 468–69.

105. USG to Halleck, *ibid.*, 469.

106. Halleck to Grant, November 11, 1862, *ibid.*

107. ORN, I/23/479.

108. OR, I/17, part 2, 282; Bruce Catton, *This Hallowed Ground: A History of the Civil War* (New York: Vintage, 2012), 242.

109. Welles, *Diary*, vol. 1, 387.

110. USG-WTS, November 14, 1862, USGP, vol. 6, 310–11.

111. CT, December 1, 1862.

TEN. REVOLUTION

1. Mildred Throne, ed. "An Iowa Doctor in Blue: The Letters of Seneca B. Thrall," *Iowa Journal of History* 85 (April 1960): 103, 113, 186.

2. NYT, November 30, 1862.

3. Eric Foner, *The Fiery Trial: Abraham Lincoln and American Slavery* (New York: W. W. Norton & Company, 2011), 215–16.

4. Abraham Lincoln, annual message to Congress, December 3, 1861, in Roy T. Basler, ed., *The Collected Works of Abraham Lincoln*, vol. 5 (New Brunswick, NJ: Rutgers University Press, 1953–55), 48.

5. *Baltimore Sun*, September 25, 1862; James Oakes, *Freedom National: The Destruction of Slavery in the United States, 1861–1865* (New York: W. W. Norton & Company, 2013), 315–16.

6. Francis B. Carpenter, *Six Months at the White House with Abraham Lincoln: The Story of a Picture* (New York: Hurd and Houghton, 1866), 90.

7. Foner, *Fiery Trial*, 241–2.

8. London *Times*, October 7, 1862.

9. Quoted in Guelzo, *Emancipation Proclamation*, 180.

10. *Richmond Dispatch*, reported in the *New York Tribune*, January 12, 1863.

11. Quoted in Foner, *Fiery Trial*, 215.

12. *Ibid.*, 247.

13. Quoted in McPherson, *Battle Cry*, 558; These sentiments, but not the exact words, were Lincoln's. The author, T. J. Barnett, an official in the Interior Department, paraphrased Lincoln's remarks to him in a letter to a friend.

14. Throne, ed. "Iowa Doctor," 113, 186.

15. Ira Blanchard, *I Marched with Sherman: Civil War Memoirs of the 20th Illinois Volunteer Infantry* (San Francisco: J. D. Huff and Company, 1992), 72.

16. Knox, *Camp-Fire, and Cotton-Field*, 223.

17. WTS to Halleck, November 17, 1862, SCW, 328.

18. John G. Given to wife, November 2, 1862, John G. Given Papers, ISHL.

19. Quoted in Catton, *Grant Moves South*, 296.

20. Joshua R. Barney to his brother, October 24, 1862, John C. Dinsmore Papers, ISHL.

21. R. S. Bevier, *History of the First and Second Missouri Confederate Brigades, 1861–1865* (St. Louis: Bryan, Brand & Company, 1879), 19.

22. NYT, November 30, 1862.

23. Special Field Orders no. 1, USGP, vol. 6, 266–67.

24. Special Field Orders no. 2, *ibid.*, 267.

25. WTSM, 299.

26. Quoted in Catton, *Grant Moves South*, 336.

27. James Dugan, *History of Hurlbut's Fighting Division* (Cincinnati: Morgan & Co., 1863), 136.

28. Given to wife, November 30, 1862, Given Papers, ISHL.

29. Frederick D. Williams, ed., *The Wild Life of the Army: Civil War Letters of James A. Garfield* (East Lansing: Michigan State University Press, 1964), 89.

30. Richardson, *Secret Service*, 258.

31. *Ibid.*; Wills, *Army Life of an Illinois Soldier*, 93.

32. CT, December 1, 1862.

33. Wills, *Army Life*, 99–100.

34. Stephen V. Ash, *When the Yankees Came: Conflict and Chaos in the Occupied South, 1861–1865* (Chapel Hill: University of North Carolina Press, 2006), 61, 197, 200.

35. USG to JDG, June 12, 1862, USGP, vol. 5, 143.

36. Wills, *Army Life*, 103, 123.

37. Order no. 72, USGP, vol. 5, 273.

38. John Easton to family, May 30, 1862, John Easton Papers, Ohio Historical Society, Columbus, Ohio.

39. Chandra Manning, *What This Cruel War Was Over: Soldiers, Slavery, and the Civil War* (New York: Alfred A. Knopf, 2007), 94.

40. *Anglo-African*, April 19, 1862.

41. Quoted in Stephen D. Engle, *Struggle for the Heartland: The Campaigns from Fort Henry to Corinth* (Lincoln: University of Nebraska Press, 2001), 194.

42. Knox, *Camp-Fire and Cotton-Field*, 222.

43. Oakes, *Freedom National*, 224.

44. USG to Mary Grant, August 19, 1862, USGP, vol. 5, 311.

45. General Orders no. 72, *ibid.*, 273.

46. USGM, 284.

47. James M. Tuttle to Edwin M. Stanton, September 18, 1862, USGP, vol. 6, 317n; David Davis to Abraham Lincoln, October 14, 1862, *ibid*; USGM, 230; Chandra Manning, *Troubled Refuge: Struggling for Freedom in the Civil War* (New York: Alfred A. Knopf, 2016), 167, 188.

48. CT, November 17, 1862; USGM, 230.

49. John Eaton, *Grant, Lincoln, and the Freedmen: Reminiscences of the Civil War* (London: Longmans, Green, and Co., 1907), 5–6.

50. *Ibid.*, 27; USGM, 230.

51. Eaton, *Grant, Lincoln, and the Freedmen*, 15, 34.

52. Martha Mitchell Bigelow, "Freedman of the Mississippi Valley, 1862–1865," *Civil War History* 17 (1962): 39.

53. Special Field Order no. 4, November 14, 1862; Special Orders no. 21, November 17, 1862, in Eaton, *Grant, Lincoln, and the Freedmen*, 18, 20–21.

54. Eaton, *Grant, Lincoln, and the Freedmen*, 12, 21–22.

55. Knox, *Camp-Fire and Cotton-Field*, 227.

56. Eaton, *Grant, Lincoln, and the Freedmen*, 34–5.

57. Levi Coffin, *Reminiscences of Levi Coffin: The Reputed President of the Underground Railroad* (1876) (New York: Augustus M. Kelley Reprints of Economic Classics, 1968), 626.

58. Oakes, *Freedom National*, 324–25.

59. *Ibid.*, 100.

60. *Harper's Weekly*, January 31, 1863.

61. Frederick Douglass, "U.S. Grant and the Colored People," *Elevator* 8, no. 20 (August 24, 1872), The Johns Hopkins University Sheridan Library, Baltimore, Maryland, 1.

62. Porter to WTS, November 24, ORN, I/23/500; Porter Journal, LC.

63. Porter to Fox, November 12, 1862, in *Fox Correspondence*, 150.

64. Welles, *Diary*, vol. 1, 220.

65. USGM, 286; Halleck to USG, November 15, 1862, USGP, v. 6, 305.

66. William L. Shea and Terence J. Winschel, *Vicksburg Is the Key: The Struggle for the Mississippi River* (Lincoln: University of Nebraska Press, 2003), 36.

67. WTS-USG, September 30, 1862, OR I/17, part 2/244–45; Lewis, *Sherman*, 256; WTS to Halleck, November 17, 1862, SCW, 328–29; James Lee McDonough, *William Tecumseh Sherman: In the Service of My Country: a Life* (New York: W. W. Norton & Company, 2016), 354.

68. WTSM, 302.

69. USG to Jesse Root Grant, November 23, 1862, USGP, vol. 6, 345.

70. WTS to EES, October 4, 1862, SCW, 313.

71. CT, November 25, 1862.

ELEVEN. GRANT'S MARCH

1. WTS to John Rawlins, December 19, 1862, Sherman mss.

2. John Quincy Adams Campbell, *The Union Must Stand: The Civil War Diary of John Quincy Adams Campbell, Fifth Iowa Volunteer Regiment.* Mark Grimsley and Todd D. Miller, eds. (Knoxville: University of Tennessee Press, 2000), 67.

3. Throne, ed., "Army Doctor in Blue," 114.

4. OR, I/17, part 2, 362–63.

5. Wills, *Army Life*, 132; OR, I/17, part 1, 467.

6. Richardson, *Secret Service*, 245.

7. Quoted in Joseph T. Glatthaar, *The March to the Sea and Beyond: Sherman's Troops in the Savannah and Carolina Campaigns* (Baton Rouge: Louisiana State University Press), 37.

8. Richardson, *Secret Service*, 245.

9. Quoted in John Keegan, *The Mask of Command* (New York: Viking, 1987), 205.

10. *Ibid.*, 194.

11. Brinton, *Personal Memoirs*, 239.

12. JDG, *Personal Memoirs*, 105.

13. S. C. Beck, *A True Sketch of His Army Life* (Edgar, NE: privately printed, 1914), 4.

14. Throne, ed., "Army Doctor in Blue," 118–19.

15. Halleck to Grant, November 25, 1862, USGP, vol. 6, 346.

16. Thorne, ed., "Army Doctor in Blue," 119.

17. Wills, *Army Life*, 134.

18. Lucien B. Crooker, Henry S. Nourse, and John G. Brown, *55th Illinois, 1861–1865* (Huntington, WV: Blue Alcorn Press, 1993), 183.

19. Henry H. Wright, *A History of the Sixth Iowa Infantry* (Iowa City, IA: State Historical Society of Iowa, 1923), 146–47.

20. Wills, *Army Life*, 136.

21. OR, I/17, part 2, 488.

22. Cordelia Lewis Scales to Loulie W. Irby, October 29, 1862; Scales to Irby, January 27, 1863, in Martha Neville Lumpkin, ed., *"Dear Darling Loulie": Letters of Cordelia Lewis Scales to Loulie W. Irby During and After the War Between the States* (Boulder, CO: Ben Gray Lumpkin, 1955), 43, 60 (I have corrected Scales's spelling).

23. Wilson, *Under the Old Flag*, vol. 1, 143.

24. OR, I/17, part 2, 94; USG to Charles S. Hamilton, January 20, 1863, USGP, vol. 7, 237.

25. Scales to Irby, January 27, 1863, Lumpkin, ed., *"Dear Darling Loulie,"* 55–56.

26. Porter, *Campaigning with Grant*, 61–62.

27. WTS to USG, OR, I/17, part 2, 374.

28. OR, I/17, part 2, 531–32; Dabney H. Maury, "A Winter at Vicksburg," BL, vol. 5, 380.

29. Bevier, *Missouri Confederate Brigades*, 165.

30. Cordelia Lewis Scales to Loulie W. Irby, January 27, 1863, in Lumpkin, ed., *"Dear Darling Loulie,"* 51.

31. WTSM, 303.

32. Thorne, ed., "Army Doctor in Blue," 116.

33. USGM, 286.

34. ORN, I/23/488.

35. Richard Brady Williams, *Chicago's Battery Boys: The Chicago Mercantile Battery and the Civil War's Western Theater* (New York: Savas Beatie, 2005), 30–31.

36. Wilson, *Under the Old Flag*, vol. 1, 142.

37. M. D. Gage, *From Vicksburg to Raleigh: A Complete History of the Twelfth Indiana Volunteer Infantry* (Chicago: Clarke & Co., 1805) 32, 35–37.

38. W. R. Rorer Letters, November–December, 1862, undated, USAHI.

39. William Le Baron Jenney, "Personal Recollections of Vicksburg," in *Papers of the Military Order of the Loyal Legion of the United States*, vol. 12 (Wilmington, NC: Broadfoot Publishing Co., 1994, reprint), 248–49.

40. WTS to John Sherman, December 6, 1862, SCW, 339; WTSM, 303.

41. Halleck to Grant, December 5, 1862, USGP, vol. 6, 372.

42. USGM, 287.

43. USG to Halleck, December 3, 1862, vol. 6, 371–72; USG to Halleck, December 5, 1862, USGP, vol. 6, 390.

44. USG to Halleck, December 7, 1862, *ibid.*, 390; USG to Halleck, December 8, 1862, OR, I/17, part 1, 474; USG to Halleck, December 9, 1862, USGP, vol. 7, 40.

45. USG to WTS, December 8, 1862, USGP, vol. 6, 404.

46. Porter to Fox, December 5, 1862, ORN, I/23/535.

47. Halleck to USG, December 7, 1862, in WTSM, 304; Robert Allen to USG, December 12, 1862, USGP, vol. 6, 405.

48. Knox, *Camp-Fire and Cotton Field*, 238–39.

49. WTSM, 304.

50. USGM, 289.

51. USG to WTS, December 8, 1862, in WTSM, 305–06.

52. USGM, 288; USG to Halleck, December 14, 1862, USGP, vol. 7, 29.

53. WTSM, 305.

54. WTS to EES, December 14, 1862, SCW, 343; Marszalek, *Sherman*, 202.

55. Simpson, *Grant*, 166.

56. Halleck to USG, December 18, 1862, USGP, vol. 7, 62–63; USGM, 289.

57. USG to McClernand, December 18, 1862, *ibid.*, 61–62.

58. *Ibid.*

59. McClernand to Lincoln, December 17, 1862, OR, I/17, part 2, 420.

60. Stanton to McClernand, December 17, 1862, OR, I/17, part 2, 420.

61. McClernand to Orville H. Browning, December 16, 1862, McClernand Coll.

62. McClernand to Stanton, December 24, 1863, McClernand Coll.

63. Welles, *Diary*, vol. 1, 217.

64. USG to WTS, December 14, 1862, USGP, vol. 7, 33.

65. USG to Mary Grant, December 15, 1862, USGP, vol. 7, 43–44.

66. NYT, November 25, 1862.

67. USG to JDG, December 14, 1862, USGP, vol. 7, 24.

68. Keegan, *Mask of Command*, 204.

69. Wilson, *Under the Old Flag*, 148; Keegan, *Mask of Command*, 204.

70. Cadwallader, *Three Years with Grant*, 27–28.

71. Blanchard, *I Marched with Sherman*, 74.

72. Wilson, *Under the Old Flag*, 143.

73. Blanchard, *I Marched With Sherman*, 75.

74. Victor M. Rose, *Ross' Texas Brigade* (Louisville: Courier-Journal Book and Job Rooms, 1881), 131–32.

75. Foote, *Fredericksburg to Meridian*, 70.

76. T. M. Eddy, *The Patriotism of Illinois*, vol. 1 (Chicago: Clarke & Company, 1865), 439–41.

77. J. D. Deupree, "The Capture of Holly Springs, Mississippi, Dec. 20, 1862," *Publications of the Mississippi Historical Society* 4 (1901): 57–8.

78. *Ibid.*, 58.

79. JDG, *Personal Memoirs*, 104–07; Jesse R. Grant, *In the Days of My Father General Grant* (New York: Harper & Brothers Publishers, 1925), 15.

80. JDG, *Personal Memoirs*, 107.

81. Eaton, *Grant, Lincoln, and the Freedmen*, 26.

82. OR, I/17, part 2, 353–54.

83. Cadwallader, *Three Years with Grant*, 35–36.

84. OR, I/17, part 1, 516; OR, I/17, part 2, 439; Cadwallader, *Three Years with Grant*, 36.

85. OR, I/17, part 2, 754.

86. OR I/20, part 2, 386; Jack Hurst, *Born to Battle: Grant and Forrest: Shiloh, Vicksburg, and Chattanooga, the Campaigns that Doomed the Confederacy* (New York: Basic Books, 2012), 184.

87. USGM, 289.

88. Bearss, *Campaign for Vicksburg*, vol. 1, 345.

89. Dabney Maury, "Grant's Campaign in North Mississippi in 1862," *Southern Magazine* (July–December 1873): 410–17.

90. Wilson, *Under the Old Flag*, 144.

91. William R. Livermore, "The Vicksburg Campaign," *Papers of the Military Historical Society of Massachusetts*, vol. 9 (Boston: The Society, 1912), 548. Grant could not use Memphis as a supply station because the rebels had wrecked the Memphis & Charleston Railroad between there and Grand Junction on the Mississippi Central Railroad.

92. OR, I/17, part 2, 463.

93. Catton, *Grant Moves South*, 342.

94. USGM, 291.

95. Dana and Wilson, *Life of Ulysses S. Grant*, 98–99; Cadwallader, *Three Years with Grant*, 40.

96. USGM, 291.

97. *Ibid.*, 291.

98. *Ibid.*

99. Blanchard, *I Marched with Sherman*, 76–77.

100. Wills, *Army Life*, 139.

101. Blanchard, *I Marched with Sherman*, 76–77.

102. Pitts letter in Williams, *Chicago's Battery Boys*, 34.

103. Byers, *Fire and Sword*, 43–45.

104. George P. Rawick, ed., *The American Slave: A Composite Autobiography*, supplement, series, 1, vol. 8: Mississippi Narratives, part 3 (Westport, CT: Greenwood Press, 1974), 1155; Noralee Frankel, *Freedom's Women: Black Women and Families in Civil War Era Mississippi* (Bloomington: Indiana University Press, 199), 22–23.

105. Laura S. Haviland, *A Woman's Life Work* (Chicago: privately published, 1887), 264.

106. Oakes, *Freedom National*, 414.

107. General Lew Wallace quoted in Armstead L. Robinson, "Worser dan Jeff Davis: The Coming of Free Labor during the Civil War, 1861–1865," in Thavolia Glymph, et al., eds., *Essays on the Postbellum Southern Economy* (College Station: Texas A & M University Press, 1985), 18.

108. *Richmond Dispatch* quoted in "A Southside View," *Harper's Weekly* (October 25, 1862), 675.

109. Samuel Andrew Agnew Diary, January 2, 1862, SHC.

110. John Parker, *His Promised Land; The Autobiography of John P. Parker, Former Slave and Conductor on the Underground Railroad*, Stuart Seely Sprague, ed. (New York: W. W. Norton, 1996), 59. Parker was an Alabama slave.

111. Walter Johnson, *River of Dark Dreams: Slavery and Empire in the Cotton Kingdom* (Cambridge, MA: Harvard University Press, 2013), 228–33.

112. Ira Berlin, "Who Freed the Slaves? Emancipation and Its Meaning," in *Union & Emancipation: Essays on Politics and Race in the Civil War Era*, David W. Blight and Brooks D. Simpson, eds. (Kent, OH: The Kent State University Press, 1997): 110–12.

113. Philip D. Jordan and Charles M. Thomas, "Reminiscences of an Ohio Volunteer," in *Ohio State Archaeological and Historical Quarterly* 48 (1939): 304–23.

114. Jane E. Pickett to Louise C. Boddie, December 27, 1862, Boddie Family Papers, MDAH. Jane and her husband did not leave the state until the following summer.

115. Quoted in Bercaw, *Gendered Freedom*, 22.

116. Ira Berlin, et al., eds., *Freedom: A Documentary History of Emancipation, 1861–1867*, series 1, vol. 1, *The Destruction of Slavery* (New York: Cambridge University Press, 1986), 11–12; Bettersworth, "The Home Front," 509; Nancy Bercaw, "Politics of Household during the Transition from Slavery to Freedom in the Yazoo-Mississippi Delta," 1861–1876, Ph.D. dissertation, University of Pennsylvania (1996), 101.

117. William Kauffman Scarborough, *Overseer: Plantation Management in the Old South* (Athens: University of Georgia Press, 1984), *passim*.

118. *Southern Republic* of Columbus, Mississippi, quoted in CT, January 30, 1863.

119. Amelia Mandeville to Rebecca Mandeville, January 7, 1864, Mandeville Papers, LSU.

120. Ira Berlin, et al., eds., *Destruction of Slavery*, 412, 677–78.

121. W. Maury Darst, ed. "The Vicksburg Diary of Mrs. Alfred Ingraham (May 2–June 13, 1863)," *Journal of Mississippi History* 44 (May 1982): 174. Over 100,000 Mississippi slaves were freed before the end of the war. Frankel, *Freedom's Women*, 31. Union forces had freed roughly 15 percent of the slaves in the rebellious states by April 1865. Oakes, *Freedom National*, 396–97.

122. Affidavit of Harry Gorman, June 6, 1866, in Ira Berlin, et al, eds., *Freedom: A Documentary History of Emancipation, 1861–1867*, series I, vol. 3, *The Wartime Genesis of Free Labor: The Lower South* (New York: Cambridge University Press, 1990), 671–72.

123. Samuel Agnew Diary, August 16, 18–19, 22, 123–24, October 29–31, November 1, 1862, SHC.

124. "Emancipation Proclamation," January 1, 1863, LC.

125. Haskell M. Monroe Jr. and James T. McIntosh, eds., *The Papers of Jefferson Davis*, vol. 9 (Baton Rouge: Louisiana State University Press, 2016), 21 (hereafter JDP); John Fabian Witt, *Lincoln's Code: The Laws of War in American History* (New York: The Free Press 2012), 216–18.

126. "The Emancipation Proclamation in Secessia," *Harper's Weekly* (October 18, 1862); 659; Bettersworth, *Confederate Mississippi*, 163–64; CT, January 17, 1863.

127. Agnew Diary, November 1, and *passim*.

128. Quoted in Witt, *Lincoln's Code*, 216–17.

129. William Howard Russell, *My Diary North and South* (1863) (Baton Rouge: Louisiana State University Press, 2001), 161–62.

130. OR, 4/2/162, 533.

131. James Phelan to Jefferson Davis, December 8, 1862, JDP, vol. 8, 542.

132. Jefferson Davis, "Speech at Jackson," December 26, 1862, JDP, vol. 8, 566.

133. James Phelan to Jefferson Davis, December 9, 1862, JDP, vol. 8, 539–44.

134. Davis, "Speech at Jackson," JDP, vol. 8, 577.

135. John J. Pettus and Wiley P. Harris to Davis, December 1, 1862, *ibid.*, 525; December 8, 1862, *ibid.*, 533.

136. Throne, "Army Doctor in Blue," 124–25; Dana and Wilson, *Life of Grant*, 99.

137. USG to Washburne, January 7, 1863, USGP, vol. 7, 196.
138. Halleck to Grant, *ibid.*, 197.
139. USG to Halleck, January 9, 1863, USGP, vol. 7, 204.

TWELVE. THE CHICKASAW SLAUGHTER PEN

1. Charles A. Willison, *Reminiscences of a Boy's Service with the 76th Ohio* (1908) (Huntington, WV: Blue Acorn Press, 1955), 35.
2. Porter to Welles, December 12, 1862, ORN I/23/542–43.
3. OR, I/52, part 1, 524; Bearss, *Campaign for Vicksburg*, vol. 1, 121–23.
4. Porter, *Incidents and Anecdotes*, 126.
5. *Ibid.*, 126–27; Porter, *Journal*, 435–38, 467, LC.
6. ORN, I/23/516–17.
7. ORN, I/23/548–49; CT, December 21, 1862.
8. Porter to Welles, December 12, 17, 1862, ORN, I/23/544–45; *ibid.*, 548–49.
9. WTS to John Rawlins, December 18, 1862, USGP, vol. 7, 41.
10. Harry E. Pratt, "Lewis B. Parsons: Mover of Armies and Railroad Builder," Lewis B. Parsons Papers, ISHL, 349.
11. *Ibid.*, 349.
12. Lewis B. Parsons, unpublished autobiographical sketch, n.d., Parsons Papers, ISHL.
13. Parsons to Halleck, December 27, 1862, OR, I/17, part 2, 496.
14. "General Sherman's Expedition," January 3, 1863, *Missouri Democrat*, reprinted in *Rebellion Record, 1862–63*, ed. Frank Moore, vol. 6 (New York; G. P. Putnam, 1863), 311; Stephen D. Lee, "The Campaign of Generals Grant and Sherman Against Vicksburg in December 1862 and January 1st and 2nd, Known as the 'Chickasaw Bayou Campaign,'" *Mississippi Historical Society* 8 (1902): 22.
15. Lewis Parsons to Loyal Legion, n.d., Parsons Papers, ISHL.
16. Parsons to Halleck, December 20, 1862, OR, I/17, part 2, 441.
17. WTS to John Sherman, December 20, 1862, SCW, 348; WTS to Rawlins, December 18, OR, I/17, part 2, 426.
18. OR, I/17, part 1, 618–19; Wilkie, *Pen and Powder*, 237.
19. Wilkie, *Pen and Powder*, 244.
20. William E. Parrish, *Frank Blair: Lincoln's Conservative* (Columbia: University of Missouri Press, 1998), ix–xi, 156–57.
21. WTS to USG, December 21, 1862, OR, I/17, part 1, 604.
22. W. L. Brown to Father, December 25, 1862, Chicago Historical Society (hereafter CHS).
23. Quoted in Williams, *Chicago's Battery Boys*, 37.
24. Henry C. Bear to wife, December 23, 1862, in Wayne C. Temple, ed., *The Civil War Letters of Henry C. Bear: A Soldier in the 116th Illinois Volunteer Infantry* (Harrogate, TN: Lincoln Memorial University Press, 1961), 147.
25. "General Sherman's Expedition," *Missouri Democrat*, 311.
26. *Ibid.*
27. WTSM, 310–11.

28. Quoted in Williams, *Chicago's Battery Boys*, 43.

29. "Our Army in the Southwest," *Harper's Weekly* (April 4, 1863): 215.

30. "General Sherman's Expedition," *Missouri Democrat*, 312.

31. W. Wirt Adams to Pemberton, December 24, 1862, OR, I/17, part 2, 803.

32. OR, I/17, part 2, 803.

33. OR, I/17, part 1, 666.

34. Stephen D. Lee, "Details of Important Work by Two Confederate Telegraph Operators . . ." *Mississippi Historical Society* 4 (1901): 51–55; OR, I/17, part 2, 804.

35. Lee to E. Porter Alexander, November 30, 1862, in E. Porter Alexander Papers, SHC.

36. Chambers, "My Journal," 254.

37. Hall, *26th Louisiana Infantry*, 38.

38. Lee, "Campaigns of Generals Grant and Sherman," 24.

39. Maury, "Grant's Campaign," 417; F. H. Mason, *The Forty-Second Ohio Infantry: A History* (Cleveland: Cobb Andrews & Co., 1876), 152–53.

40. Sherman Report, January 3, 1863, OR, I/17, part 1, 606.

41. S. D. Lee, "General S. D. Lee's Address; Monument to the Defenders of Vicksburg," *Southern Historical Papers*, 194, in VNMP.

42. Porter, *Incidents and Anecdotes*, 128.

43. Simeon R. Martin, "Chickasaw Bayou," 51, VNMP.

44. Marszalek, *Sherman*, 205–06.

45. Knox, *Camp-Fire and Cotton-Field*, 244–45.

46. Francis Vinton Greene, *The Mississippi* (1882) (Wilmington, NC: Broadfoot publishing Co. 1989), 201. Sharply argued and beautifully written, this nineteenth-century volume remains an invaluable account of the Vicksburg campaign.

47. Joseph E. Johnston, *Narrative of Military Operations* (1874), (Bloomington: Indiana University Press, 1959), 151–52.

48. Maury, "Vicksburg," 384.

49. OR, I/17, part 2, 485.

50. Henry Bear to wife, December 26, 1862, Temple, ed. *Letters of Henry Bear*, 19; Bearss, *Campaign for Vicksburg*, vol. 1, 155.

51. "General Sherman's Expedition," *Missouri Democrat*, 312.

52. Chambers, "My Journal," 254; Charles F. Larimer, ed., *Love and Valor: The Intimate Civil War Letters Between Captain Jacob and Emeline Ritner* (Western Springs, IL: Sigourney Press, 2000), 85.

53. Foote, *Fredericksburg to Meridian*, 75.

54. JDP, vol. 8, 566–79.

55. WTS to John Sherman, January 6, 1863, SCW, 352.

56. Temple, ed., *Civil War Letters of Henry C. Baer*, 23.

57. Knox, *Camp-Fire and Cotton-Field*, 245–46.

58. Porter, *Incidents and Anecdotes*, 128.

59. Porter, *Naval History*, 287.

60. Porter to WTS, ORN, I/23/578.

61. ORN, I/23/602; WTS to EES, SCW, 350.

62. Knox, *Camp-Fire and Cotton-Field*, 247.

63. *Ibid.*, 247–48.

64. Quoted in D. Alexander Brown, "Battle at Chickasaw Bluffs," *Civil War Times* 9 (July 1970): 8.

65. Larimer, ed., *Love and Valor*, 90; Wilkie, *Pen and Powder*, 238–39.

66. OR, 23, part 3, 805. They were delayed along the way by rail problems and did not get to Vicksburg until sundown on December 29, when the battle was effectively over. Maury, "Winter at Vicksburg," 384.

67. OR, I/17, part 2, 804–05; OR, I/20, part 2, 449–50.

68. OR, I/17, part 2, 807.

69. "General Sherman's Expedition," *Missouri Democrat*, 314.

70. Bearss, *Campaign for Vicksburg*, vol. 1, 194.

71. OR, I/17, part 1, 637.

72. Morgan, "Chickasaw Bluffs," 465; OR, I/17, part 1, 682.

73. OR, I/17, part 1, 647, 682, 695.

74. Jenney, "Personal Recollections of Vicksburg," 250–55.

75. Parsons to Halleck, December 27, 1862, OR, I/17, part 2, 497.

76. OR I/17, part 1, 606–07, 637.

77. OR, I/17, part 1, 607; Mason, *Forty-Second Ohio*, 160.

78. Morgan, "Chickasaw Bluffs," 466–69; Mason, "Chickasaw Bluffs," 11.

79. WTSM, 314, 318.

80. OR, I/17, part 1, 655.

81. Earl J. Hess, ed., *A German in the Yankee Fatherland: The Civil War Letters of Henry A. Kircher* (Kent, OH: The Kent State University Press, 1993), 47–48.

82. Lee, "Campaigns of Generals Grant and Sherman," 33.

83. Hess, ed., *German in the Yankee Fatherland*, 47–48.

84. OR, I/17, part 1, 652–56; "General Sherman's Expedition," *Missouri Democrat*, 315.

85. OR, I/17, part 1, 649.

86. OR, I/17, part 1, 655; Lee, "Campaigns of Generals Grant and Sherman," 33.

87. Hall, *26th Louisiana Infantry*, 45–46.

88. Morgan, "Chickasaw Bluffs," BL, vol. 3, 468.

89. OR, I/17, part 1, 650, 658–59; John M. Thayer to "My Dear Sir and Comrade," September 18, 1891, in Asa B. Munn, Amos H. Miller, and W. O. Newton, *Military History and Reminiscences of the Thirteenth Regiment of Illinois Volunteer Infantry in the Civil War in the United States, 1861–1865* (Chicago: Women's Temperance Publishing Association, 1872), 264–66.

90. Willison, *Reminiscences*, 35.

91. "General Sherman's Expedition," *Missouri Democrat*, 316; OR, I/17, part 1, 608, 625.

92. Wilkie, *Pen and Powder*, 243.

93. WTSM, 314; William T. Sherman letter to John W. Draper, November 24, 1867, in "'Vicksburg by New Years,'" *Civil War Times Illustrated* 16 (January 1978): 75.

94. WTS to EES, October 26, 1866, Sherman Family Papers, University of Notre Dame Archives, South Bend, Indiana.

95. WTSM, 314, 318; WTS to EES, January 4, 1862, SCW, 351.

96. Quoted in Woodworth, *Nothing But Victory*, 279.

97. Porter, *Journal*, vol. 1, 464–68, LC; Lee Kennett, *Sherman: A Soldier's Life* (New York: HarperCollins Publishers, 2001), 195.

98. Porter, *Incidents and Anecdotes*, 128.

99. OR, I/17, part 1, 608.

100. "General Sherman's Expedition," *Missouri Democrat*, 316.

101. Diary of E. Paul Reichhelm, 3rd Missouri Infantry, n.p., VNMP.

102. OR, I/17, part 1, 609.

103. OR, I/17, part 2, 879.

104. ORN, I/23/582, 593–94.

105. ORN, I/23, 589–90, 605.

106. OR, I/17, part 1, 609; WTSM, 316.

107. Porter, *Naval History*, 287.

108. OR, I/17, part 1, 625; Lee, "Campaigns of Generals Grant and Sherman," 36.

109. James R. Arnold, *Grant Wins the War: Decision at Vicksburg* (New York: John Wiley & Sons, 1997), 37.

110. OR, I/17, part 1, 610.

111. Byers, *Fire and Sword*, 42.

112. Michael B. Ballard, *Vicksburg: The Campaign that Opened the Mississippi* (Chapel Hill: The University of North Carolina Press, 2004), 146.

113. WTS to EES, January 4, 1863, SCW, 349.

114. USG to McClernand, December 28, 1862, USGP, vol. 7, 135–36.

115. McClernand to Lincoln, December 29, 1862, McClernand Coll.

116. WTSM, 316–17.

117. ORN, I/23/602.

118. Porter, *Incidents and Anecdotes*, 130–31.

119. WTS to John Sherman, January 6, 1863, SCW, 352.

120. WTS to Porter, January 3, 1863; ORN, I/23/606; Porter, *Naval History*, 287; OR, I/17, part 1, 612.

121. McClernand to Grant, January 11, 1863, USGP, vol. 7, 217.

122. Quoted in Ballard, *Vicksburg: The Campaign that Opened the Mississippi*, 154.

123. WTSM, 324–25.

124. OR, I/17, part 2, 559.

125. USG to Halleck, January 11, 1863, USGP, vol. 7, 209; USG to McClernand, January 11, 1863, *ibid.*, 210–11.

126. USGM, 293.

127. USGM, 294; Porter, *Incidents and Anecdotes*, 131–32.

128. Halleck to USG, January 12, 1862, USGP, vol. 7, 210; Rawlins to USG, *ibid.*, 210.

129. USGM, 294; OR, I/17, part 2, 570–71.

130. WTS to John Sherman, January 17, 1863, SCW, 362.

131. WTS to Ethan A. Hitchcock, January 25, 1863, SCW, 365; John F. Marszalek, *Sherman's Other War: The General and the Civil War Press* (Kent, OH: Kent State University Press, 1983), 120–21, 124–26.

132. WTS to EES, February 6, 1863, SCW, 393.

133. McDonough, *Sherman*, 374.

134. WTS to Thomas Ewing, January 16, 1863, SCW, 354.

135. Halleck to USG, January 25, 1863, USGP, vol. 7, 252; USG to Halleck, January 20, 1863, USGP, *ibid.*, 233; WTSM, 325.

136. WTTS to EES, January 24, 1863, SCW, 364.

137. Simpson, *Grant*, 169.

138. USG to Mary Grant, December 15, 1862, USGP, vol. 7, 44.

139. General Orders no. 11, Department of the Tennessee, December 17, 1862, USGP, vol. 7, 50; Stephen V. Ash, "Civil War Exodus: The Jews and Grant's General Orders No. 11," *The Historian* 44 (August 1982): 510; John Y. Simon, "That Obnoxious Order," *Civil War Times Illustrated* 26 (1984): 14–15.

140. JDG, *Memoirs*, 107.

141. Quoted in Wilson, *Life of John Rawlins*, 96.

142. Bertram Wallace Korn, *American Jewry and the Civil War* (Philadelphia: Jewish Publication Society of America, 1951), 122.

143. McFeely, *Grant*, 123.

144. USG to I. N. Morris, September 14, 1868, USGP, vol. 19, 37.

145. Quoted in Korn, *American Jewry and the Civil War*, 129.

146. Jonathan D. Sarna, *When Grant Expelled the Jews* (New York: Nextbook/Schocken, 2012), 25. The Senate defeated a censure movement by a vote of thirty to seven.

147. Korn, *American Jewry and the Civil War*, 125.

148. Halleck to USG, January 21, 1863, USGP, vol. 7, 54.

149. Ronald C. White, *American Ulysses: A Life of Ulysses S. Grant* (New York: Random House, 2016), 252.

150. WTS to Thomas Ewing, April 27, 1863, SCW, 212.

151. *New York World*, January 14–15, 20, 26, 1863.

152. McDonough, *Sherman*, 380.

153. WTS to EES, January 28, 1863, SCW, 378.

154. Marszalek, *Sherman's Other War*, 129.

155. Thomas W. Knox to WTS, February 1, 1863, in SCW, 390.

156. WTS to John Sherman, February 12, 1863, SCW, 396.

157. Fellman, *Citizen Sherman*, 129.

158. USG to Thomas Knox, April 6, 1863, USGP, vol. 8, 30–31.

159. WTS to Knox, April 7, 1863, SCW, 440; John F. Marszalek Jr., "The Knox Court-Martial: W. T. Sherman Puts the Press on Trial (1863)," *Military Law Review* 59 (Winter, 1973): 197–214. The Knox affair is documented in OR, I/17, part 2, 580–91; 882–97, and in Marszalek, *Sherman's Other War*, 126–47.

160. NYT, January 12, 1863.

161. J. Russell Jones to Washburne, January 17, Washburne Papers, LC; Simpson, *Grant*, 54; Cadwallader C. Washburn to Elihu B. Washburne, January 28, 1863, Washburne Papers, LC.

162. USG to JDG, January 28, 1863, USGP, vol. 7, 253.

163. USG to McClernand, January 31, 1863, USGP, 265.

164. McClernand to USG, January 30, February 1, 1863, USGP, vol. 7, 265–68; USGM, 294–95.

165. OR, I/17, part 2, 567.

166. Lincoln to McClernand, January 22, 1863, in Basler, *Collected Works of Abraham Lincoln*, vol. 6, 70.

167. USGM, 295.

THIRTEEN. MUD AND MISERY

1. USGM, 297.

2. Badeau, *Military History*, vol. 1, 161.

3. Thorne, ed., "Doctor in Blue," 125. The remainder of the Mississippi River Fleet, numbering sixty vessels carrying 280 guns and eight hundred men, was on patrol.

4. Joseph A. Saunier, ed., *A History of the 47th Regiment Ohio Veteran Volunteer Infantry* (Hillsboro, OH: The Lyle Printing Co., 1903), 122–23; Grabau, *Ninety-Eight Days*, 16.

5. USGP, vol. 7, 257–58, 261, 284–85, 312–13.

6. Woodworth, *Nothing But Victory*, 123–24.

7. Porter, *Incidents and Anecdotes*, 143.

8. Jenney, "Personal Recollections of Vicksburg," *passim*.

9. OR, I/24, part 1, 119; *ibid.*, part 3, 40.

10. Frederick Law Olmsted to John Olmsted, April 1, 1863, in *The Papers of Frederick Law Olmsted*, vol. 4, *Defending the Union: The Civil War and the U.S. Sanitary Commission, 1861–1863*, Jane Turner Censer, ed. (Baltimore, MD: The Johns Hopkins University Press, 1986), 573 (hereafter FLO Papers).

11. Mildred Throne, ed., *Civil War Diary of Cyrus F. Boyd, Fifteenth Iowa Infantry* (1952) (Millwood, NY: Kraus Reprint Co., 1977), 110, 119.

12. Will Brown to father, March 21, 1863, in Williams, *Chicago's Battery Boys*, 87–88.

13. Jacob Ritner to Emeline Ritner, January 24, 1863, in Larimer, ed., *Love and Valor*, 108.

14. *Frank Leslie's Illustrated Weekly*, March 28, 1863, 14.

15. W. R. Eddington, "Memoirs," USAMHI.

16. Quoted in Bearss, *Campaign for Vicksburg*, vol. 1, 439.

17. John A. Bering and Thomas Montgomery, *History of the Forty-Eighth Ohio. Vet. Vo. Inf.* (Hillsboro, OH: Highland News Office, 1880), 71.

18. CT, February 12, 1863.

19. Willison, *Reminiscences*, 44.

20. Robert L. Brandfon, *Cotton Kingdom: A History of the Yazoo Mississippi Delta from Reconstruction to the Twentieth Century* (Cambridge, MA: Harvard University Press, 1967), 32.

21. B. F. Stevenson to Wife, January 26, 1863, in B. F. Stevenson, *Letters from the Army* (Cincinnati: W. E. Dibble & Co., 1884), 178.

22. Throne, ed., "Doctor in Blue," 12.

23. Willison, *Reminiscences*, 47.

24. Throne, ed., *Diary of Cyrus F. Boyd*, 117.

25. Stevenson, *Letters*, 181.

26. McClernand to USG, January 26, 1863, USGP, vol. 7, 241–42.

27. Throne, ed., *Diary of Cyrus F. Boyd*, 114.

28. Stevenson, *Letters*, 175–76.

29. Bering and Montgomery, *History of the Forty-Eighth Ohio*, 69–70.

30. *Ibid.*, 69–70; see also J. T. Woods, *Services of the Ninety-Sixth Ohio* (Toledo, OH: Blade Printing and Paper Co., 1874), 19.

31. Throne, ed., "Doctor in Blue," 128–29.

32. Rawlins to Stephen A. Hurlbut, February 5, 1863, USGP, vol. 7, 394.

33. Robert C. Wood to USG, February 21, 1863, USGP, vol. 7, 394.

34. F. H. Mason, *The Forty-Second Ohio Infantry* (Cleveland: Cobb, Andrews & Co., 1876), 183.

35. Badeau, *Military History*, vol. 1, 162.

36. Foote, *Fredericksburg to Meridian*, 187.

37. OR, 1/24, part 1/8; USG to Halleck, January 29, 1863, USGP, vol. 7, 253–54.

38. OR I/24, part 1, 8; USG to Halleck, January 20, 1863; Porter, *Incidents and Anecdotes*, 139; McClernand to USG, January 26, 1863, USGP, vol. 7, 241–42.

39. Wilkie, *Pen and Powder*, 282.

40. WTS to John Sherman, January 25, 1863, SCW, 372.

41. *Ibid.*

42. Jenney, "Personal Recollections of Vicksburg," 252; USGM, 298.

43. Cadwallader, *Three Years with Grant*, 50.

44. Badeau, *Military History*, vol. 1, 164.

45. Garland, *Grant*, 222.

46. Wilson, *Rawlins*, 108.

47. S. Woolworth, *The Mississippi Scout* (Chicago: self-published, 1868), 11.

48. Wilson, *Rawlins*, 108; Wilson, *Under the Old Flag*, vol. 1, 155; USGM, 297.

49. Wilson, *Rawlins*, 108.

50. Dana and Wilson, *Grant*, 104.

51. USGM, 295.

52. WTS to Stephen A. Hurlbut, March 16, 1863, SCW, 423.

53. USGM, 295.

54. USG to JDG, January 31, 1863, USGP, vol. 7, 270.

55. USGM, 296. For the military draft, see Robert W. Coakley, *The Role of Federal Military Forces in Domestic Disorders, 1789–1878* (Washington, D.C.: Center of Military History, 1988), 230.

56. USGM, 305–06.

57. USG to Halleck, January 18, 1863, USGP, vol. 7, 231.

58. USGM, 305–06.

59. Cadwallader, *Three Years with Grant*, 48.

60. Wilson, *Rawlins*, 108–09; Wilson, *Under the Old Flag*, vol. 1, 156–57.

61. Wilson, *Rawlins*, 108–10; Wilson, *Under the Old Flag*, vol. 1, 158–59.

62. Fuller, *Generalship of Grant*, 135–36.

63. Fiske, *Mississippi Valley*, 211; USGM, 298.

64. USG to Porter, January 30, 1863, USGP, vol. 7, 257; USG to McClernand, *ibid.*, 257–58.

65. USGM, 298.

66. Dana and Wilson, *Grant*, 106.

67. ORN, I/23/405.

68. Wilson, *Rawlins*, 110.

69. USGM, 297.

70. Badeau, *Military History*, vol. 1, 168; J. F. C. Fuller wrote in his otherwise astute study

of Grant's generalship: "All this bayou warfare . . . was a gigantic bluff to deceive the enemy, to deceive the politicians, and to deceive his own troops, so that when he moved [south, through Louisiana] the enemy might be surprised." Fuller, *Generalship of Grant*, 135. This is patently wrong.

71. USGM, 296.

FOURTEEN. "THINGS FALL APART . . ."

1. William Butler Yeats, *The Collected Works of W. B. Yeats*, vol. 1, *The Poems*, Richard J. Finneran and George Mills Harper, eds. (New York: Macmillan, 1989), 187.

2. Wilson, *Rawlins*, 110; Robert W. Harrison, "Levee Building in Mississippi before the Civil War," *Journal of Mississippi History* 12 (1950): 69.

3. James Wilson Reports, February 2 and 4, 1863, USGP, vol. 7, 286–87; ORN, I/24/249.

4. Wilson to Rawlins, February 9, 1863, USGP, vol. 7, 334–35.

5. Wilson, *Under the Old Flag*, vol. 1, 152; OR, I/24, part 1, 374–75, 378, 388; Dana and Wilson, *Grant*, 107.

6. ORN, I/24/294.

7. Wilson to Rawlins, February 12, USGP, vol. 7, 334; USG to Porter, February 14, 1863, *ibid.*, 323; Wilson to Rawlins, February 12, 1863, *ibid.*, 332.

8. USG to Porter, February 14, 1863, *ibid.*, 323.

9. George W. Deitzler to Rawlins, February 3, 1863, *ibid.*, 282; William L. Duff to Rawlins, February 3, 1863, *ibid.*, 282–83.

10. OR, I/24, part 3, 32; WTS to John Sherman, February 12, 1863, SCW, 397.

11. USG to McPherson, February 5, 1863, USGP, vol. 7, 284–85.

12. USG to Elihu B. Washburne, March 10, 1863, *ibid.*, 409.

13. Fiske, *Mississippi Valley*, 216.

14. USG to JDG, February 11, 1863, USGP, vol. 7, 311.

15. William L. Duff to Rawlins, February 9, 1863, *ibid.*, 284.

16. McPherson to USG, February 11, 1863, *ibid.*, 313; USG to McPherson, February 12, 1863, *ibid.*, 312–13.

17. USG to JDG, February 11, 1863, *ibid.*, 311.

18. Charles B. Allaire to his professor, March 4, 1863, LSU.

19. Quoted in Woodworth, *Nothing But Victory*, 299.

20. Thorne, ed., *Diary of Cyrus F. Boyd*, 122.

21. Seth Wells, *The Siege of Vicksburg: From the Diary of Seth J. Wells* (Detroit: Wm. H. Rowe, 1915), 40.

22. Throne, ed., "Doctor in Blue," 135.

23. Charles Brown Tompkins to Mollie Tompkins, February 16, 1863, Duke University.

24. CT, March 24, 1863.

25. OR, I/24, part 1, 15–16.

26. USGP, vol. 7, 351.

27. CT, March 15.

28. Wilson, *Under the Old Flag*, vol. 1, 50.

29. USGM, 299.

30. *Ibid.*
31. USG to McPherson, March 5, 1863, USGP, vol. 7, 389.
32. Charles B. Allaire to his professor, March 4, 1863, LSU.
33. McPherson to USG, March 1, 1863, USGP, vol. 7, 389.
34. USG to Halleck, March 7, 1863, USGP, vol. 7, 399–400.
35. ORN, I/24/265.
36. OR, I/24, part 3, 35–36; USG to Halleck, March 7, 1863, USGP, vol. 7, 1863, 400.
37. Byers, *Fire and Sword*, 50.
38. Enoch Weiss Reminiscences, 19–20, USAMHI.
39. Byers, *Fire and Sword*, 51.
40. Porter, *Incidents and Anecdotes*, 140.
41. Wilson to Rawlins, February 24, 1863, OR, I/24, part 1, 376.
42. Badeau, *Military History*, vol. 1, 171.
43. USG to McPherson, March 5, 1863, USGP, vol. 7, 388–89.
44. USG to Halleck, March 7, 1863, *ibid.*, 400.
45. OR, I/24, part 1, 19.
46. Halleck to USG, March 20, 1863, USGP, vol. 7, 401.
47. USG to Washburne, March 10, 1863, USGP, vol. 7, 409–10; USG to McPherson, March 11, 1863, *ibid.*, 411; USG to Lewis B. Parsons, March 4, 1863, *ibid.*, 384.
48. USG to Halleck, March 7, 1863, *ibid*; OR, I/24, part 1, 394.
49. OR, I/24, part 1, 399; Dana and Wilson, *Grant*, 107; Wilson to USG, June 18, 1863, USGP, vol. 17, 464–65; "Yazoo Pass Expedition," *New York Herald*; ORN, I/24/252.
50. OR I/24, part 3, 622, 626, 629–39; *ibid.*, part 1, 415; ORN, I/24/294, 296; Larry Allen McCluney Jr., *The Yazoo Pass Expedition: A Union Thrust into the Delta* (Charleston, SC: The History Press, 2017), 15–33, 69; Myron J. Smith Jr., *The Fight for the Yazoo, August 1862–July 1864; Swamps, Forts and Fleets on Vicksburg's Northern Flank* (London: McFarland, 2012), *passim.*
51. ORN, I/24/246, 264, 266; OR, I/24, part 1, 20, 393–95; "Yazoo Pass Expedition," *New York Herald.*
52. ORN, I/24/246.
53. Porter, *Incidents and Anecdotes*, 142.
54. OR, I/24, part 1, 395; ORN, I/24/283.
55. OR, I/24, part 1, 395, 397, 401, 412; *ibid.*, part 3, 21.
56. ORN, I/24/281.
57. Wilson to Rawlins, March 15, OR, I/24, part 1, 380.
58. *Ibid.*, 380–81; ORN, I/24/247, 273–74.
59. Wilson, *Under the Old Flag*, vol. 1, 152–53.
60. Wilson to Rawlins, March 18, 1863, USGP, vol. 7, 437.
61. ORN, 1/24, 282–83, 272, 281, 285; OR, I/24, part 1, 397–98, 412. Smith died of a lingering illness on December 19, 1864.
62. OR, I/24, part 1, 416.
63. Wilson to Rawlins, March 18, 1863, USGP, vol. 7, 438.
64. Wilson to Grant, June 18, 1863, OR, I/24, part 2, 390–91.

65. Porter, *Incidents and Anecdotes*, 140.

66. Porter to Welles, March 26, April 13, 1863, ORN, I/24/281–83.

67. USG to McPherson, March 16, 1863, USGP, vol. 7, 422.

68. ORN, I/24/474; USGP, vol. 7, 420.

69. USG to J. C. Kelton, July 6, 1863, USGP, vol. 8, 488.

70. Porter, *Naval History*, 303; Smith, "Gunboats in a Ditch," 176.

71. Porter, *Incidents and Anecdotes*, 145; Porter, *Naval History*, 303.

72. Porter, *Incidents and Anecdotes*, 145–46.

73. ORN, I/24/474.

74. Foote, *Fredericksburg to Meridian*, 207.

75. Porter, *Incidents and Anecdotes*, 145.

76. NYT, April 4, 1863.

77. USGM, 301–02.

78. USG to WTS in WTSM, 329–30 (italics are mine).

79. *Ibid.*, 330.

80. OR, I/24, part 3, 112.

81. Halleck to USG, April 2, 1863, USGP, vol. 7, 428–29.

82. Catton, *Grant Moves South*, 385; Catton, *Hallowed Ground*, 265.

83. WTS to John Sherman, March 14, 1863, SCW, 420.

84. Porter, *Incidents and Anecdotes*, 138.

85. *Ibid.*, 145.

86. ORN, I/24/474.

FIFTEEN. STEELE'S BAYOU

1. Yeats, *The Collected Works of W. B. Yeats*, 181.

2. Porter to Welles, March 26, 1863, ORN, I/24/474; ORN, I/24/493.

3. Porter, *Naval History*, 304; Foote, *Fredericksburg to Meridian*, 200.

4. Cadwallader, *Three Years with Grant*, 51.

5. WTSM, 331.

6. OR, I/24, part 1, 438–39.

7. WTS to USG, March 16, 1863, ORN, I/24/483.

8. WTS to USG, March 16, 1863, USGP, vol. 7, 425.

9. Porter, *Incidents and Anecdotes*, 157.

10. NYT, April 16, 1863.

11. Foote, *Fredericksburg to Meridian*, 208.

12. NYT, April 6, 1863.

13. OR, I/24, part 1, 465.

14. Porter to WTS, March 19, 1863, ORN, I/24/486–87.

15. WTS to Porter, March 20, 1863, *ibid.*, 487.

16. CT, April 3, 1863, dispatched March 25.

17. Porter to Welles, March 26, 1863, ORN, I/24/476; "Private Journal of an Officer of the *Cincinnati*," March 20, 1863, ORN, I/24/494; OR, I/24, part 3, 166.

18. Porter, *Incidents and Anecdotes*, 160.

19. Porter to Welles, March 26, 1863, ORN, I/24/476, 479.

20. OR, I/24, part 1, 455–56, 461, 465–66.

21. Maury, "A Winter at Vicksburg," 391.

22. OR, I/24, part 1, 458, 466.

23. Porter, *Incidents and Anecdotes*, 160–61; OR, I/24, part 1, 459.

24. OR, I/24, part 1, 455–56, 458–59, 466–67.

25. *Ibid.*, 476.

26. ORN, I/24/494, 698; OR, I/24, part 1, 476–77.

27. ORN, I/24/488–89.

28. ORN, I/24/495.

29. WTSM, 332; OR I/24, part 1, 439.

30. Porter, *Incidents and Anecdotes*, 161.

31. Porter, *Incidents and Anecdotes*, 167. Two of the men recovered.

32. *Ibid.*

33. Dana and Wilson, *Grant*, 108.

34. Cadwallader, *Three Years with Grant*, 52.

35. OR, I/24, part 1, 442; Porter, *Incidents and Anecdotes*, 168.

36. WTSM, 332.

37. Porter, *Incidents and Anecdotes*, 168.

38. USGM, 302.

39. WTSM, 333.

40. WTSM, 333–34.

41. ORN, I/24/495.

42. Jenney, "Personal Recollections of Vicksburg," 256.

43. ORN, I/24/495.

44. *Ibid.*, 479–80.

45. Porter to Fox, January 16, 1863, *Fox Correspondence*, 155.

46. Quoted in Ballard, *Vicksburg*, 188; ORN, I/24/477–78.

47. Wilkie, *Pen and Powder*, 309–10.

48. Bearss, *Campaign for Vicksburg*, vol. 1, 589. Eight additional Union men were wounded. The rebels lost two killed and eight wounded.

49. Badeau, *Military History*, vol. 1, 174.

50. Frederick Law Olmsted to John Olmsted, April 1, 1863, FLO Papers, vol. 4, 571.

51. Jenney, "Personal Recollections of Vicksburg," 256.

52. USG to Gen. Isaac F. Quinby, March 22, 1863, USGP, vol. 7, 462–64.

53. OR, I/24, part 1, 407.

54. USG to Benjamin M. Prentiss, March 28, 1863, USGP, vol. 7, 482; OR, I/24, part 1, 407–08; Ballard, *Vicksburg*, 186; McCluney, *Yazoo Pass Expedition*, 96.

55. James K. Newton to parents, April 10, 1864, in Ambrose, ed., *A Wisconsin Boy*, 64.

56. Byers, *Fire and Sword*, 52–53.

57. Pennock to Welles, March 24, 1863, ORN, I/24/512.

58. ORN, I/24/512; Hearn, *Farragut*, 193. The only ship lost was *Mississippi*.

59. Welles, *Diary*, vol. 1, March 17, 1863, 249.

60. Welles to Porter, April 2, 1863, ORN, I/24/522.

61. Porter to Welles, February 2, 1863, ORN, I/24/217–18.

62. ORN, I/24/218–22.

63. ORN I/24/217–24, 374, 382–87; Hearn, *Porter*, 196; Virgil Carrington Jones, *The River War* (New York: Holt, Rinehart, and Winston, 1961), 385.

64. Chester G. Hearn, *Ellet's Brigade: The Strangest Outfit of All* (Baton Rouge: Louisiana State University Press, 2000), 103–07.

65. CT, February 18, 1863.

66. Hearn, *Ellet's Brigade*, 113.

67. ORN, I/24/375–76.

68. Porter to Welles, *ibid.*, 376.

69. OR, I/24, part 1, 380–81, 394–95.

70. ORN, I/24/378–81, 390–91; Mahan, *Gulf and Inland Waters*, 128–29.

71. Porter to Welles, February 27, 1863, ORN, I/24/390.

72. ORN, I/24/391–96.

73. Welles to Porter, March 2, 1863, *ibid.*, 388.

74. Porter, *Incidents and Anecdotes*, 134.

75. *Ibid.*, 134; Marshal Scott Legan, "The Confederate Career of a Union Ram," *Louisiana History* 41, no. 3 (2000): 294–95; Musicant, *Divided Waters*, 276.

76. Porter, *Incidents and Anecdotes*, 135; NYT, March 16, 1863; ORN, I/24/395–96; Jack Polk, "The Union's Trojan Horse," *Proceedings of the United States Naval Institute* 113, no. 6 (1987): 77–78.

77. ORN, I/24/408–10.

78. Porter, *Incidents and Anecdotes*, 134.

79. Mahan, *Gulf and Inland Waters*, 132.

80. ORN, I/24, 382–83; Legan, "Confederate Career," 297; *Fox Correspondence*, vol. 2, 166–68.

81. Farragut to Porter, March 20, 1863, ORN, I/20/6.

82. Quoted in McPherson, *War on the Waters*, 160.

83. Fox to Farragut, April 2, 1863, *Fox Correspondence*, vol. 1, 331.

84. Farragut to Fox, March 27, 1863, *ibid.*, 329.

85. ORN, I/20/9, 12, 34; Farragut to Fox, March 27, 1863, *Fox Correspondence*, vol. 1, 329.

86. Hearn, *Ellet's Brigade*, 133.

87. Farragut to A. W. Ellet, March 23, 1863, ORN, I/20/14; Howard C. Westwood, "The Ellet Family Fleet," *Civil War Times Illustrated* 22, no. 6 (1982): 33.

88. Hearn, *Ellet's Brigade*, 134; ORN, I/20/13, 52–53.

89. ORN, I/20/35.

90. Jones, *River War*, 409.

91. ORN, I/23/407.

92. ORN, I/20/12, 16–20, 35.

93. Farragut to Porter, March 25, 1863, ORN, I/20/25.

94. Porter to A. W. Ellet, March 25, 1863, ORN, I/20/23.

95. Farragut to Porter, March 25, 1863, *ibid.*, 24.

96. Crandall, *History of the Ram Fleet*, 219; Westwood, "Ellet Family Fleet," 35.

97. Porter to Farragut, March 22, 1863, ORN, I/20/11.

98. Porter, *Naval History*, 309.

SIXTEEN. CRISIS

1. Gaillard Hunt, ed., *Israel, Elihu, and Cadwallader Washburn: A Chapter in American Biography* (New York: Macmillan, 1925), 341.
2. NYT, February 23, 1863.
3. Throne, ed., *Diary of Cyrus F. Boyd*, 114.
4. Badeau, *Military History*, vol. 1, 161.
5. Cadwallader, *Three Years with Grant*, 54.
6. Mary A. Livermore, *My Story of the War: A Woman's Narrative* (1887) (New York: Da Capo Press, 1995), 328.
7. A. H. Hoge, *The Boys in Blue, Or Heroes of the "Rank and File"* (New York: E. B. Treat and Co.), 221. Mary Hoge wrote under her married name.
8. *Ibid.*, 224–25.
9. *Ibid.*, 225.
10. Robert C. Myers, "Mortality in the Twelfth Michigan Volunteer Infantry, 1861–1866," *Michigan Historical Review* 20 (Spring, 1994): 47.
11. Jeffrey S. Sartin, "Infectious Diseases during the Civil War: The Triumph of the 'Third Army,'" *Clinical Infectious Diseases* 16 (April 1993): 580; Jim Downs, *Sick from Freedom: African-American Illnesses and Suffering during the Civil War and Reconstruction* (New York: Oxford University Press, 2012), 4. For a demographic analysis of disease and mortality among Union soldiers, see Chulhee Lee, "Socioeconomic Backgrounds, Disease, and Mortality among Union Army Recruits: Implications for Economic and Demographic History," *Explorations in Economic History* 34 (1997): 28–35.
12. Steiner, *Disease in the Civil War*, 168, 170. Solid data on diarrhea and dysentery in the rebel army is not available, but "such information as exists shows that it was at least as common." See Steiner, *Disease in the Civil War*, 19; Frank R. Freemon, "Medical Care at the Siege of Vicksburg, 1863," *Bulletin of the New York Academy of Medicine* 67 (September–October, 1991): 437; and Alfred Jay Bollet, "Scurvy and Chronic Diarrhea in Civil War Troops: Were They both Nutritional Deficiency Syndromes?" *Journal of the History of Medicine and Allied Sciences* 47 (1992): 49.
13. Myers, "Mortality," 33–34.
14. Sartin, "Infectious Diseases," 581.
15. Livermore letter in Hoge, *Boys in Blue*, 253.
16. Steiner, *Disease in the Civil War*, 4–5.
17. *Ibid.*, 2, 179.
18. Sartin, "Infectious Diseases," 582.
19. *Ibid.*, 580, 484.
20. George Worthington Adams, *Doctors in Blue: The Medical History of the Union Army in the Civil War* (New York: Henry Schuman, 1952), 194.
21. Maury, "Winter at Vicksburg," 390.
22. Woolworth, *Mississippi Scout*, 4.
23. Saunier, ed., *History of the Forty-Seventh Regiment Ohio*, 121.
24. William R. Eddington, "Reminiscences of a Boy's Service," William R. Eddington Papers, ISHL.

25. Henry Kuck to Metta, February 17, 1863, Henry Kuck Letters, Historical Manuscript Collection, Columbia, Missouri.

26. Throne, ed., *Diary of Cyrus F. Boyd*, 117.

27. Oran Perry, "The Entering Wedge," in MOLLUS, vol. 24, 359–61.

28. Quoted in Woodworth, *Nothing But Victory*, 295.

29. William L. Brown to Father, January 24, 1863, William Liston Brown Letters, CHS.

30. Stevenson, *Letters from the Army*, 176–77.

31. USG to Paymaster Edwin D. Judd, February 19, 1863, USGP, vol. 7, 343, 344n.

32. Quoted in Woodworth, *Nothing But Victory*, 296.

33. USG to JDG, February 14, 1863, USGP, vol. 7, 324–25.

34. Letters of Lt. Col. Joseph Leslie, 4th Indiana Cavalry, n.d., VNMP.

35. Joseph Orville Jackson, ed., *"Some of the Boys": The Civil War Letters of Isaac Jackson, 1862–1865* (Carbondale: Southern Illinois University Press, 1960), 78.

36. Boucher to Mother, February 15, 1863, Private George Oliver Boucher Papers, USAMHI.

37. Isaac Jackson to Ethan A. Jackson, March 19, 1863, Jackson, ed., *"Some of the Boys,"* 73.

38. Simpson, *Grant*, 174; *New York World*, March 12, April 10, 1863.

39. Throne, ed., *Diary of Cyrus F. Boyd*, 110.

40. Charles S. Hamilton to James R. Doolittle, February 11, 1863, USGP, vol. 7, 308. Grierson quotation in Bruce J. Dinges and Shirley A. Leckie, eds., *A Just and Righteous Cause: Benjamin H. Grierson's Civil War Memoir* (Carbondale: University of Southern Illinois Press, 2008), 139.

41. Chernow, *Grant*, 244. When Grant ordered the disaffected Hamilton to Vicksburg to serve under McClernand, Hamilton offered his resignation from the army. Grant accepted it, reminding General in Chief Halleck of Hamilton's persistent efforts "to get Gen. McPherson removed from the command of his Army Corps, and to get the command himself." USG to Halleck, March 24, 1863, *ibid.*, 467; see also *ibid.*, 469, 480–81.

42. Joseph Medill to Elihu Washburne, February 19, 1863, USGP, vol. 7, 318.

43. USG to JDG, February 14, 1863, USGP, vol. 7, 325.

44. USG to Hurlbut, February 13, 1863, USGP, *ibid.*, 316.

45. Joseph Medill to Elihu Washburne, January 16, 1863, Washburne Papers, LC.

46. *Ibid.*

47. USG to Halleck, March 6, 1863, OR, I/24, part 1, 19.

48. CT, March 24, 1863.

49. Badeau, *Military History*, vol. 1, 161; Perry, "The Entering Wedge," 24, 361–64; "Our Army in the Southwest," *Harper's Weekly*, April 4, 1863, 215; OR, I/24, part 3, 89–90.

50. Frederick Law Olmsted Journal, March 24, 1863, FLO Papers, 565; WTSM, 329.

51. USG to Halleck, March 27, OR, I/24, part 1, 23.

52. Quoted in Bearss, *Campaign for Vicksburg*, vol. 1, 477.

53. OR, I/24, part 1, 21; McPherson to USG, March 18, 1863, USGP, vol. 7, 423.

54. OR, I/24, part 3, 159.

55. Seneca Thrall to Mollie Thrall, March 12, 1863, in Throne, ed., "Doctor in Blue," 140.

56. OR, I/24, part 3, 102–03, 115–17, 131; CT, March 21, 1863; McPherson to USG, March 18, 1863, USGP, vol. 7, 423.

57. Edward Newsome, *Experience in the War of Great Rebellion by a Soldier of the Eighty First Regiment Illinois Voluntary Infantry* (Carbondale, IL: Edward Newsome, 1880), 36.

58. USGM, 299.

59. Badeau, *Military History*, vol. 1, 181.

60. Halleck to USG, April 2, 1863, USGP, vol. 7, 429.

61. Lewis B. Parsons to USG, March 9, 1863, USGP, vol. 7, 386.

62. USGP, vol. 2, 194; Chernow, *Grant*, 237.

63. McClernand to Lincoln, March 15, 1863, USGP, vol. 7, 275.

64. Chase to Lincoln, April 4, which encloses Halstead's letter to Chase of April 1, Lincoln Papers, LC; Catton, *Grant Moves South*, 395. On September 28, 1885, the *Chicago Tribune* printed a letter from Halstead to Chase, dated February 19, 1863.

65. Chernow, *Grant*, 251.

66. Edward D. Kittoe to James H. Wilson, July 15, 1885, James H. Wilson Papers, LC.

67. Nevins, *War for the Union*, 388.

68. Eaton, *Grant, Lincoln, and the Freedmen*, 64, 89–90. Widely believed to be apocryphal, Eaton's account seems credible.

69. Albert D. Richardson to Sydney Howard Gay, March 20, 1863, in Don E. Fehrenbacher and Virginia Fehrenbacher, eds., *Recollected Works of Abraham Lincoln* (Stanford, CA: Stanford University Press, 1996), 381.

70. Cadwallader Washburn to Elihu Washburne, March 16, 24, 28, 1863, Washburne to Chase, April 4, 1863, Chase to Washburne, April 13, 1863, Elihu B. Washburne Papers, Manuscript Division, LC. "Even Washburn had deserted Grant," Lincoln told an interviewer. Quoted in Garland, *Grant*, 223; Simpson, *Grant*, 178.

71. Hunt, ed., *Israel, Elihu and Cadwallader Washburn*, 341; Simpson, *Grant*, 181.

72. USG to WTS, March 22, 1863, USGP, vol. 7, 455–56.

73. USG to Banks, March 23, 1863, USGP, vol. 7, 446.

74. USG to WTS, March 22, 1863, USGP, vol. 7, 455–56.

75. Cadwallader Washburn to Elihu Washburne, April 11, 1863, in Hunt, ed., *Israel, Elihu and Cadwallader Washburn*, 341–42.

76. Greene, *The Mississippi*, 107–08.

77. Olmsted to John Olmsted, April 1, 1863, FLO Papers, 574–75.

78. USG to JDG, March 6, 1863, USGP, vol. 7, 396.

79. USG to JDG, March 27, 1863, *ibid.*, 479–80.

80. Olmsted to John Olmsted, April 1, 1863, FLO Papers, 574.

81. Frederick Law Olmsted to Edwin Lawrence Godkin, April 4, 1863, *ibid.*, 581.

82. USG to JDG, March 6, 1863, USGP, vol. 7, 386.

83. Grant to Halleck, March 6, 1863, *ibid.*, 401; Halleck to Grant, April 9, 1863, OR, I/24, part 1, 28.

84. USGM, 304–05.

85. Simpson, *Grant*, 179.

86. Charles A. Dana, *Recollections of the Civil War: With the Leaders at Washington and in the Field in the Sixties* (1898) (D. Appleton and Company, 1913), 20–21; H. W. Brands, *The Man Who Saved the Union; Ulysses Grant in War and Peace* (New York: Doubleday, 2012), 228–29.

87. Quoted in Walter Stahr, *Stanton: Lincoln's War Secretary* (New York: Simon & Schuster, 2017), 281.

88. Joseph T. Glatthaar, *Forged in Battle: The Civil War Alliance of Black Soldiers and White Officers* (New York: The Free Press, 1990), 37.

89. Quotes in Stahr, *Stanton*, 282.

90. USG to Halleck, February 18, USGP, vol. 7, 338; Special Field Orders no. 2, February 12, 1863, USGP, vol. 7, 339.

91. Lorenzo Thomas to USG, April 1, 1863, USGP, vol. 8, 51.

SEVENTEEN. THE ENTERING WEDGE

1. WTS to John Sherman, April 10, 1863, SCW, 449–51.

2. James Harrison Wilson, *The Life of Charles A. Dana* (New York: Harper & Brothers Publishers, 1907), 201.

3. Quoted in Henry J. Maihafter, "Mr. Grant and Mr. Dana," *American History* 35, no. 5 (December, 2000): 25.

4. Dana, *Recollections*, 1–2.

5. Wilson, *Dana*, 150, 117, 169.

6. Dana, *Recollections*, 28.

7. Wilson, *Dana*, 202; Dana, *Recollections*, 30.

8. Wilson, *Dana*, 22.

9. Cadwallader, *Three Years with Grant*, 61.

10. Dana, *Recollections*, 26–27.

11. *Ibid.*, 61–62.

12. Wilson, *Dana*, 202.

13. Dana, *Recollections*, 30.

14. *Ibid.*, 26–27.

15. USG to Porter, April 2, 1863, USGP, vol. 8, 3–5.

16. USG to Porter, April 2, 1863, USGP, vol. 8, 4; Lincoln quoted in Michael Burlingame, *Abraham Lincoln: A Life*, vol. 2 (Baltimore, MD: Johns Hopkins University Press, 2009), 516.

17. USG to Porter, March 29, 1863, USGP, vol. 7, 486.

18. Livermore, *My Story*, 313.

19. USG to Porter, April 2, 1863, USGP, vol. 8, 4. Grant first asked Porter for the use of his gunboats on March 29. Grant to Porter, March 29, 1863, USGP, vol. 7, 486.

20. USGM, 303–04; Grabau, *Ninety-Eight Days*, 53.

21. USG to Porter, March 29, 1863, USGP, vol. 7, 486.

22. USGM, 306.

23. Porter to USG, March 29, 1863, USGP, vol. 7, 486.

24. *Ibid.*

25. Catton, *Hallowed Ground*, 279.

26. ORN, I/24/479.

27. OR, I/24, part 3, 186; Porter to Fox, April 25, 1863, in *Fox Correspondence*, vol. 2, 172.

28. Porter to Welles, July 13, 1863, ORN I/25/279–80.

29. Wilkie, *Pen and Powder*, 311.

30. Garland, *Grant*, 225.

31. WTS to John Sherman, April 26, 1863, SCW, 462.

32. WTSM, 338.

33. Badeau, *Military History*, vol. 1, 183–85.

34. WTS to Rawlins, April 8, 1863, USGP, vol. 8, 13–14.

35. Wilson, *Under the Old Flag*, vol. 1, 161; Ulysses S. Grant, *The Annotated Memoirs of Ulysses S. Grant*, "Appendix 1: Notes to the First Edition," edited with commentary by Elizabeth D. Samet (New York: Liveright Publishing Corporation, 2019), 938–39.

36. WTS to EES, April 29, 1863, SCW, 465; see also WTS to John Sherman, April 16, 1863, SCW, 461.

37. USG to Halleck, April 4, 1863, USGP, vol. 8, 10–12.

38. USGM, 305–06.

39. WTS to John Sherman, *ibid.*, 460–61.

40. Dana to Stanton, April 12, 1863, OR, I/24, part 1, 74.

41. Dana to Stanton, April 12, 1863, OR, I/24, part 1, 74.

42. Porter, "Journal," vol. 1, 557, Porter Papers, LC.

43. Halleck to USG, March 31, 1863, OR I/24, part 3, 156–57.

44. Grant's General Orders no. 25, April 22, 1863, OR, I/24, part 3, 220.

45. Halleck to Grant, March 31, 1863, OR, I/24, part 3, 157.

46. OR, I/24, part 3, 167–68.

47. USG to Halleck, April 4, 1863, USGP, vol. 8, 10–12.

48. NYT, June 12, 1863.

49. Jacob Ritner to Emeline Ritner, April 12, 1863, Larimer, ed., *Love and Valor*, 150.

50. OR, I/24, part 1, 502–03.

51. Jacob Ritner to Emeline Ritner, April 12, 1863, Larimer, ed., *Love and Valor*, 150–51.

52. Calvin Ainsworth Diary, April 7, 1863, Bentley Historical Library, University of Michigan.

53. Henry Seaman Diary, April 8, 1863, USAMHI.

54. Ainsworth Diary, April 7, 1863.

55. Seaman Diary, April 8, 1863, 4; *History and Reminiscences of the Thirteenth Regiment of Illinois Volunteer Infantry*, 302.

56. April 12, 1863, Larimer, ed., *Love and Valor*, 150–51.

57. OR, I/24, part 1, 502.

58. USG to Frederick Steele, April 11, 1863, USGP, vol. 8, 49.

59. Wilson, *Under the Old Flag*, vol. 1, 190.

60. OR, I/24, part 3, 209. WTS to Rawlins, April 19, 1863, USGP, vol. 8, 50–51. Steele's letter to Sherman, dated April 18, 1863, was enclosed.

61. "Diary of Amanda Worthington, of 'Willoughby,' Washington County, Mississippi, January 1, 1862–October 21, 1865," April 28, June 9–10, 1863, MDAH.

62. Edwin Bearss, ed., "Diary of Captain John N. Bell at Vicksburg," *Iowa Journal of History* 59 (April 1961): 190–91.

63. WTS to Rawlins, April 19, 1863, USGP, vol. 8, 51. Steele's letter to Sherman, dated April 18, 1863, was enclosed.

64. April 29, 1863, Larimer, ed., *Love and Valor*, 159.

65. Throne, ed., *Diary of Cyrus F. Boyd*, 118–19.

66. April 17, April 22, 1863, Larimer, ed., *Love and Valor*, 154, 157.

67. Wells, *Siege of Vicksburg*, 53–54.

68. Wilson, *Under the Old Flag*, vol. 1, 165.

69. For Logan, see James P. Jones, *"Black Jack": John A. Logan and Southern Illinois in the Civil War Era* (Carbondale: Southern Illinois University Press, 1995).

70. Albert Castel, " 'Black Jack' Logan," in *Civil War Times Illustrated* (November, 1876): 8.

71. R. L. Howard, *History of the 124th Regiment, Illinois* (Springfield, IL: H. W. Rokker, 1880), 65–66; Newsome, *Experience in the War of Great Rebellion*, 38.

72. USG to Halleck, April 19, 1863, USGP, vol. 8, 91–92.

73. WTS to EES, April 17, 1863, SCW, 454.

74. *Ibid.*, April 26, 1863, SCW, 461.

75. Quoted in Simpson, *Grant*, 187.

76. Marjorie Barstow Greenbie, *Lincoln's Daughters of Mercy* (New York: G. P. Putnam's Sons, 1944), 119.

77. Hoge, *Boys in Blue*, 121–25, 262, 277.

78. Letter from James E. Yeatman, published in NYT, March 13, 1863.

79. J. Christopher Schnell, "Mary Livermore and the Great Northwestern Fair," *Chicago History* (Spring 1975): 37.

80. Jacob Ritner to Emeline Ritner, April 1, 1863, Larimer, ed., *Love and Valor*, 144.

81. Williams, *Chicago's Battery Boys*, 83–86; CT, March 21, 1863; Elizabeth Stuart Phelps, et al., *Our Famous Women* (Hartford, CT: The Hartford Publishing Company, 1884), 402–03; Hoge, *Boys in Blue*, 272.

82. Elizabeth Leonard, *Yankee Women: Gender Battles in the Civil War* (New York: W. W. Norton, 1994), 69–72; Annie Wittenmyer, *Under the Guns: A Woman's Reminiscences of the Civil War* (Boston: E. B. Stillings & Co., 1895), *passim*; Tom Sillanpa, *Annie Wittenmyer: God's Angel* (Hamilton, IL: Hamilton Press, 1972), 16.

83. Quoted in Schnell, "Mary Livermore," 43.

84. Wittenmyer, *Under the Guns*, 23.

85. Livermore in Hoge, *Boys in Blue*, 213.

86. Livermore, *My Story*, 341.

87. Ainsworth Diary, May 11, 1863.

88. Oran Perry, "The Entering Wedge," a Paper Read Before the Indiana Commandery of MOLLUS, April 19, 1898, 361–64; OR, I/24, part 1, 139, 491.

89. Dana, *Grant*, 110–11.

90. Otto F. Bond, ed., *Under the Flag of the Nation: Diaries and Letters of Owen Johnston Hopkins, a Yankee Volunteer in the Civil War* (Columbus: Ohio State University Press, 1998), 51; OR, I/24, part 1, 46, 495–96.

91. Grabau, *Ninety-Eight Days*, 53.

92. Perry, "Entering Wedge," 364–65; OR I/24, part 1, 139, 491.

93. Perry, "Entering Wedge," 365; OR, 24, part 1, 139–40, 491–93. Pointe Clear belonged to a planter named Pliney Smith.

94. OR, I/24, part 1, 492.

95. Perry, "Entering Wedge," 365.

96. *Ibid.*, 140, 365–69, 373; OR, I/24, part 1, 140, 490–93.

97. OR, I/24, part 1, 140–41, 490; OR, I/24, part 3, 188–89.

98. Phillip Thomas Tucker, *The Forgotten "Stonewall of the West," Major General John Stevens*

Bowen (Macon, GA: Mercer University Press, 1997), 105; Phillip Thomas Tucker, *The South's Finest; The First Missouri Confederate Brigade from Pea Ridge to Vicksburg* (Shippensburg, PA: White Mane Publishing Company, 1993), *passim*.

99. OR, I/24, part 3, 730.

100. *Ibid.*, part 1, 24.

101. *Ibid.*, part 3, 733.

102. OR, I/24, part 1, 734–5.

103. *Ibid.*, part 3, 713–14.

104. Tucker, *Forgotten "Stonewall,"* 200.

105. OR, I/24, part 1, 140, 494, 496–97.

106. Tucker, *Forgotten "Stonewall,"* 116.

107. OR, I/24, part 3, 744–45.

108. *Ibid.*

109. Porter to Welles, April 6, 18, 19, 1863, ORN, I/24/553–55; Porter to Fox, April 25, 1863, *Fox Correspondence*, vol. 2, 172–73.

110. ORN, I/24/545.

111. Blanchard, *I Marched with Sherman*, 83.

112. Grabau, *Ninety-Eight Days*, 40, 43.

113. OR, I/24, part 2, 336–37; Bearss, *Campaign for Vicksburg*, vol. 2, *Grant Strikes a Fatal Blow* (Dayton, OH: Morningside Press, 1986), 64–66.

114. ORN, I/24/544.

115. OR, I/24, part 3, 740.

116. Quoted in Walker, *Vicksburg*, 143.

117. *Vicksburg Daily Whig*, April 14, 1863.

118. *Ibid.*, April 16, 1863.

119. Porter to Fox, April 16, 1863, *Fox Correspondence*, vol. 2, 168.

120. Wilkie, *Pen and Powder*, 313.

121. Frederick D. Grant, "A Boy's Experience at Vicksburg," *The Outlook* (July 2, 1898): 87.

122. Wilkie, *Pen and Powder*, 313, 315–16; Wittenmyer, *Under the Guns*, 94; Dana, *Recollections*, 37; Herman Melville, "Running the Batteries, As Observed from the Anchorage above Vicksburg," in Melville, *Battle-Pieces and Aspects of the War* (1866), edited by Henning Cohen (New York: Thomas Youseloff Publishers, 1963), 78.

123. Wilson, *Under the Old Flag*, vol. 1, 164.

124. Henry Walke, *Naval Scenes and Reminiscences of the Civil War in the United States on the Southern and Western Waters* (New York: F. R. Reed & Company, 1877), 354.

125. Dana, *Grant*, 112.

126. Wittenmyer, *Under the Guns*, 96.

127. *Ibid.*, 97.

128. Porter, *Naval History*, 311.

129. Report of Capt. H. T. Norman, Company C, 1st Tennessee Heavy Artillery, VNMP.

130. OR, I/24, part 1, 517. The rebels fired over five hundred rounds and scored perhaps seventy hits. Shea and Winschel, *Vicksburg Is the Key*, 99.

131. Porter, *Incidents and Anecdotes*, 177.

132. *Ibid.*, 177; OR, I/24, part 3, 201, 207–08.

133. Walke, *Naval Scenes*, 356.

134. *Ibid.*, 253.

135. CT, April 28, 1863; Melville, "Running the Batteries," in Melville, *Battle-Pieces*, 78.

136. Mary Loughborough, *My Cave Life in Vicksburg* (Reprinted from the original by the Vicksburg and Warren County Historical Society: Vicksburg, MS, 1990), 86.

137. A. Hugh Moss, *The Diary of A. Hugh Moss* (New York: Scribner Press, 1948), 21.

138. Dana, *Grant*, 112.

139. ORN, I/24/717.

140. OR, I/24, part 3, 747, 751–53, 760–61, 773–75.

141. Frederick Grant, "A Boy's Experience," 88.

142. Perry, "Entering Wedge," 373.

143. *Ibid.*

144. Paul H. Hess, ed., "The Vicksburg Diary of Henry Clay Warmoth: Part 1 (April 3, 1863–April 27, 1863)," *Journal of Mississippi History* 32, no. 1 (1969): 242–44.

145. Badeau, *Military History*, vol. 1, 193.

146. Porter, *Incidents and Anecdotes*, 178.

EIGHTEEN. THIS ONE OBJECT

1. USGM, 321.

2. OR, I/24, part 1, 79; Grabau, *Ninety-Eight Days*, 83.

3. Perry, "Entering the Wedge," 140, 365–69, 373.

4. OR, I/24, part 1, 47. For more on Perkins and his Somerset Plantation, see the John Perkins Papers, 1822–1885, Wilson Library, University of North Carolina at Chapel Hill.

5. OR, I/24, part 3, 205.

6. OR, I/24, part 1, 77.

7. William E. Strong, "The Campaign Against Vicksburg," in MOLLUS, vol. 11 (Wilmington, NC: Broadfoot Publishing Co., 1994 reprint edition), 322; "How the Steamboats Run the Batteries," *Harper's Weekly*, May 30, 1863.

8. CT, April 29, 1863; USGM, 314; Wilbur F. Crummer, *With Grant at Fort Donelson, Shiloh and Vicksburg* (Oak Park, IL: E. C. Crummer & Co., 1915), 94.

9. Blanchard, *I Marched with Sherman*, 82–83.

10. Strong, "Campaign Against Vicksburg," 316.

11. OR, I/24, part 1, 79; OR, I/24, part 1, 570.

12. OR, I/24, part 1, 571–72.

13. OR, 24, part 1, 601.

14. Wilson, *Under the Old Flag*, vol. 1, 168–69; Charles E. Affeld, "From Milliken's Bend to Vicksburg with Private Affeld," Edwin C. Bearss, ed., *Louisiana Studies 6* (1967): 235.

15. Wilson, *Under the Old Flag*, vol. 1, 169.

16. Throne, ed., "Iowa Doctor in Blue," 146.

17. Andrew Hickenlooper, "Our Volunteer Engineers," Papers Prepared for the Ohio Commandery of MOLLUS, November, 1889 (Cincinnati, OH: Robert Clarke and Co.): 303–05.

18. USGM, 309.

19. CT, April 14, 1863.

20. OR, I/24, part 3, 222; Paul H. Hess, ed., "The Vicksburg Diary of Henry Clay Warmouth," *Journal of Mississippi History* 31 (December 1969), 344–46.

21. Porter to Fox, April 25, 1863, in *Fox Correspondence*, vol. 2, 172.

22. Porter, *Naval History*, 313.

23. Badeau, *Military History*, vol. 1, 197.

24. Dana, *Recollections*, 40–41.

25. USG to McClernand, April 27, 1863, OR, I/24, part 3, 80, 237–38; OR, I/24, part 1, 80; *New York World*, February 20, 1863.

26. Albert O. Marshall, *Army Life: From a Soldier's Journal* (Joliet, IL; privately printed, 1884), 197; OR, I/24, part 1, 81.

27. OR, I/24, part 1, 81; USG to McClernand, April 27, 1863, USGP, vol. 8, 126–27.

28. Wells, *Diary of Seth Wells*, 60.

29. "Winter Quarters," Rush Nutt Collection, Huntington Library, San Marino, CA. For a history of Lake St. Joseph, see Marie T. Logan, *Mississippi-Louisiana: A History of Rodney, Miss., St. Joseph, La., and Environs* (Baton Rouge, LA: Claitors Publishing Division, 1980).

30. Lucien B. Crooker, Henry S. Nourse, and John G. Brown, *The Story of the Fifty-Fifth Regiment Illinois Volunteer Infantry in the Civil War, 1861–1865* (Clinton, IL: W. J. Coulter, 1887), 23.

31. Special Orders no. 110, April 21, USGP, vol. 8, 98.

32. Haller Nutt to Reverdy Johnson, n.d., Winter Quarters Museum, Newellton, LA; original in Rush Nutt Collection, "Winter Quarters," Huntington Library, San Marino, CA.

33. WTSM, 346.

34. Jeffery Alan Owens, "The Burning of Lake St. Joseph," *Louisiana History* 32, no. 4 (Fall 1991): 393; Haller Nutt to Reverdy Johnson, n.d.; Hamilton Smith to Haller Nutt, April 6, 1863, Winter Quarters State Historic Site, Tensas Parish, LA.

35. Sarah Anne Dorsey, *Recollections of Henry Watkins Allen, Brigadier-General Confederate States Army, Ex-Governor of Louisiana* (New York: Thompson Gale, 1866), 171, 319, 322–23, 405.

36. Quoted in Owens, "Burning of Lake St. Joseph," 410.

37. Richard L. Kiper, ed., *"Dear Catherine, Dear Taylor: The Civil War Letters of a Union Soldier and His Wife* (Lawrence; University Press of Kansas, 2002), 89, 99.

38. Stone, *Brokenburn*, 171–73, 188, 191–99, 208, 217.

39. Private Journal of Sarah L. Wadley, May 16–21, 1863, SHC.

40. Stone, *Brokenburn*, 333.

41. For Grierson's life, see William H. Leckie and Shirley A. Leckie, *Unlikely Warriors: General Benjamin H. Grierson and His Family* (Norman: University of Oklahoma Press, 1984). The Hollywood film *The Horse Soldiers*, starring John Wayne, was inspired by Grierson's raid.

42. CT, May 7, 1863.

43. Quoted in D. Alexander Brown, *Grierson's Raid* (Champaign: University of Illinois Press, 1954), 223.

44. NYT, May 18, 1863.

45. OR, I/24, part 1, 34.

46. Grabau, *Ninety-Eight Days*, 122, 139; Stephen Lee, "The Campaign of Vicksburg, Mississippi, in 1863—From April 15 to and Including the Battle of Champion Hills, or Baker's Creek, May 16, 1863," *Publications of the Mississippi Historical Society* 3 (1900): 26–28.

47. Shea and Winschel, *Vicksburg Is the Key*, 94.

48. USG to WTS, April 27, 1863, USGP, vol. 8, 130.

49. Jenney, "Personal Recollections of Vicksburg," 258.

50. WTS to USG, April 28, 1863, USGP, vol. 8, 131.

51. Porter, *Naval History*, 316.

52. Jenney, "Personal Recollections of Vicksburg," 258–59.

53. USG to WTS, April 29, 1863, USGP, vol. 8, 135.

54. USGM, 318.

55. OR, I/24, part 2, 384.

56. OR, I/24, part 1, 574–75.

57. OR, I/24, part 3, 797.

58. Tucker, *Forgotten "Stonewall,"* 146.

59. Porter, *Naval History*, 313.

60. Wilson, *Under the Old Flag*, vol. 2, 169.

61. OR, I/24, part 3, 225–26, 231; *ibid.*, part 1, 79–81; ORN, I/24/606.

62. Porter, *Incidents and Anecdotes*, 180–81.

63. George Smith to Hattie Smith, May 6, 1863, Old Courthouse Museum, Vicksburg, Mississippi.

64. Bevier, *Missouri Confederate Brigades*, 173.

65. Grabau, *Ninety-Eight Days*, 141.

66. Bowen to Pemberton, OR, I/24, part 1, 575; Porter, *Naval History*, 314.

67. ORN, I/24/611; Porter, *Naval History*, 317; Grabau, *Ninety-Eight Days*, 142.

68. ORN, I/24/611–12.

69. Frederick Grant, "A Boy's Experience," 88.

70. USGM, 317.

71. Frederick Grant, "A Boy's Experience," 88; Porter, *Journal*, 591; Hearn, *Porter*, 224–25.

72. OR, I/24, part 1, 575.

73. ORN, I/24/608–28.

74. Grabau *Ninety-Eight Days*, 142.

75. ORN, I/24/627.

76. USG to Halleck, April 29, 1863, USGP, vol. 8, 133.

77. Frederick Grant, "A Boy's Experience," 88; USGM, 318.

78. OR, I/24, part 1, 48; Elliot, *History of the Thirty-third Regiment Illinois*, 236–37; USGM, 318.

79. USGM, 321.

80. NYT, May 17, 1863; Dana, *Grant*, 116.

81. Frederick Grant, "A Boy's Experience," 88–89.

82. *History of the Forty-Sixth Indiana Volunteer Infantry, September 1861–September 1865* (Logansport, IN, 1886, compiled by order of the regimental association), 56.

83. William H. Jolly Letter, April 24, 1863, VNMP.

84. Samuel C. Kirkpatrick to James G. K., April 18, 1863, Samuel Cotter Kirkpatrick Papers, Western Historical Manuscript Collection, St. Louis Historical Society.

85. USGM, 321 (italics mine).
86. USGM, 322.
87. Bearss, *Campaign for Vicksburg*, vol. 2, 318–19.
88. Mason, *Forty-Second Ohio*, 189.
89. Dana, *Grant*, 116.

NINETEEN. PURSUIT

1. USG to WTS, May 3, 1863, USGP, vol. 8, 152.
2. Edgar L. Erickson, ed., "With Grant at Vicksburg: From the Civil War Diary of Captain Charles E. Wilcox," *Illinois State Historical Society* 30 (1938): 446, 467–69; later in the war Wilcox was promoted to captain.
3. *Ibid.*
4. OR, I/24, part 1, 664.
5. George Crooke, *The Twenty-first Regiment of Iowa Volunteer Infantry: A Narrative of Its Experience in Active Service* (Milwaukee, WI: King, Fowle & Co., 1891), 54–55.
6. R. L. Howard, *History of the 124th Regiment: Illinois Infantry Volunteers* (Springfield, IL: H. W. Rokker, 1880), 81.
7. Crooke, *Twenty-first Iowa*, 55–59.
8. Howard, *History of the 124th Regiment*, 85.
9. Erickson, ed., "With Grant at Vicksburg," 469; USGM, 322.
10. Crooke, *Twenty-first Iowa*, 64–65.
11. USGM, 322.
12. USG to Halleck, May 3, 1863, USGP, vol. 8, 146.
13. *Vicksburg Sunday Post*, April 11, 1993.
14. OR, I/24, part 1, 661–67.
15. Bearss, *Campaign for Vicksburg*, vol. 2, 350, 359; OR, I/24, part 3, 812–13.
16. OR, I/24, part 1, 663.
17. OR, I/24, part 3, 792–93.
18. James H. Wilson, "A Staff Officer's Journal of the Vicksburg Campaign, April 30 to July 4, 1863," James Harrison Wilson Papers, LC; USGM, 325.
19. Bearss, *Campaign for Vicksburg*, vol. 2, 257, 392.
20. *Ibid.*, 393n; Shea and Winschel, *Vicksburg Is the Key*, 514.
21. OR, I/24, part 1, 661–62.
22. James Wilson, "Draft of John Rawlins Biography," 124, LC.
23. OR, I/24, part 1, 145, 603, 661; Hess, ed., "The Vicksburg Diary of Henry Clay Warmouth: Part II (March 1970)," 65; Bearss, *Campaign for Vicksburg*, vol. 2, 385–86.
24. OR, I/24, part 1, 659–60.
25. USG to Halleck, May 3, 1863, USGP, vol. 8, 146.
26. Erickson, ed., "With Grant at Vicksburg," 472.
27. OR, I/24, part 1, 582–85, 668. The Federals lost 719 wounded, 25 missing; Bowen reported 380 wounded and 384 missing.
28. OR, I/24, part 1, 662.
29. Frederick Grant, "A Boy's Experience," 89–90; USGM, 325.
30. Erickson, ed., "With Grant at Vicksburg," 472.

31. USG to Halleck, May 3, 1863, USGP, vol. 8, 147.

32. John B. Hancock Diary, May 5, 1863, VNMP.

33. Kiper, ed., *Dear Catherine, Dear Taylor*, 90, 107.

34. Wilson, *Life of Dana*, 211.

35. Blanchard, *I Marched with Sherman*, 86.

36. OR I/24, part 1, 129.

37. USGM, 326–27.

38. Badeau, *Military History*, vol. 1, 215; USGM, 326–28. Sherman crossed his command on May 6–7.

39. Grabau, *Ninety-Eight Days*, 168–69.

40. In his memoirs, Grant claimed, mistakenly, that Porter was there with his flagship. USGM, 327.

41. USGM, 327; USG to Halleck, May 3, 1863, USGP, vol. 8, 147–48.

42. USGM, 327.

43. USGM, 327–28.

44. Hanly, *Vicksburg*, 30.

45. Symonds, *Johnston*, 205. On May 9, Johnston received the order to proceed to Mississippi.

46. USGM, 326–28; USG to Nathaniel P. Banks, May 10, 1863, USGP, vol. 8, 190; USG to Lt. Herman A. Ulffers, *ibid.*, 195–96.

47. Porter to USG, May 14, 1863, USGP, vol. 8, 192.

48. USGM, 328.

49. Catton, *Grant Moves South*, 433–34.

50. USGM, 332.

51. USGM, 340.

52. Smith, *Grant*, 243.

53. USG to William S. Hillyer, May 7, 1863, USGP, vol. 8, 174–75.

54. USGM, 325–26.

55. Badeau, *Military History*, vol. 1, 233.

56. USGM, 328–29.

57. Cadwallader, *Three Years with Grant*, 72.

58. Bond, ed., *Under the Flag of the Nation*, 57.

59. W. Maury Darst, ed., "The Vicksburg Diary of Mrs. Alfred Ingraham, May 2–June 13, 1863," *Journal of Mississippi History* 44, no. 2 (1982): 148–53.

60. WTS to EES, April 29, 1863, SCW, 464.

61. WTS to USG, May 9, 1863, USGP, vol. 8, 178–79.

62. WTS to Frank Blair, Sherman Papers, LC.

63. WTS to USG, May 9, 1863, USGP, vol. 8, 178.

64. USG to Theodore S. Bowers, May 9, 1863, *ibid.*, 187–88; OR, I/24, part 3, 273–75; Grabau, *Ninety-Eight Days*, 181–82.

65. USG to WTS, May 9, 1863, USGP, vol. 8, 183.

66. USG to Halleck, May 3, 1863, USGP, vol. 8, 147.

67. Fuller, *Generalship of Grant*, 145.

68. J. F. C. Fuller, *Decisive Battles of the U.S.A.* (New York: Thomas Yoseloff, Inc., 1942), 262.

69. Robert Macfeely to USG, May 8, 1863, USGP, vol. 8, 179–80.

70. WTS to EES, May 9, 1863, SCW, 470.

71. Warren E. Grabau, "The Logistics of the Army of the Tennessee at Vicksburg," unpublished paper in the possession of the Grabau family.

72. S. H. M. Byers, "Some Recollections of Grant," *Annals of the War* (Philadelphia Weekly Times, 1879): 353.

73. USG to WTS, May 3, 1863, USGP, vol. 8, 152.

74. OR, I/24, part 3, 821, 823, 828, 835–36; Grabau, *Ninety-Eight Days*, 198, 208.

75. USGM, 329.

76. Shea and Winschel, *Vicksburg Is the Key*, 117.

77. USG to J. C. Kelton, July 6, 1863, USGP, vol. 8, 495.

78. USGM, 330.

79. Badeau, *Military History*, vol. 1, 221.

80. USG to JDG, May 9, 1863, USGP, vol. 8, 189.

81. USG to Halleck, May 11, 1863, USGP, vol. 8, 196.

82. USG to Halleck, May 11, 1863, USGP, vol. 8, 196.

83. Bearss, *Campaign for Vicksburg*, vol. 2, 470–71.

84. Badeau, *Military History*, vol. 1, 230.

85. William B. Feis, *Grant's Secret Service: The Intelligence War from Belmont to Appomattox* (Lincoln: University of Nebraska Press, 2002), 160.

86. Byers, *With Fire and Sword*, 67.

87. Bond, ed., *Under the Flag of the Nation*, 59.

88. E. B. Soper to Cousin Em, May 28, 1863, VNMP.

89. William H. Raynor Diary, VNMP.

90. E. B. Soper to Cousin Em, May 28, 1863, VNMP.

91. Calvin Answorth Diary, VNMP; William C. Davis, *A Taste for War: The Culinary History of the Blue and the Gray* (Mechanicsburg, PA: Stackpole, 2003), 43–44.

92. Byers, *With Fire and Sword*, 68.

93. *Ibid.*

94. Wilson, "Vicksburg Journal," LC.

95. USG to McPherson, May 11, 1863, USGP, vol. 8, 200.

96. OR, I/24, part 1, 736–37.

97. *Ibid.*, 37.

98. Quoted in Rebecca Blackwell Drake, *In Their Own Words: Soldiers Tell the Story of the Battle of Raymond* (Raymond, MS; Friends of Raymond, 2001), 45.

99. Anonymous to wife, May 21, 1863, USAMHI.

100. Blanchard, *I Marched with Sherman*, 88.

101. Quoted in Drake, *In Their Own Words*, 118.

102. Letter of Anonymous Yankee of the 68th Ohio Infantry, May 26, 1863, USAMHI; Dana, *Recollections*, 54.

103. Henry Dwight quoted in Drake, *In Their Own Words*, 61; Frank Moore, ed., *The Rebellion Record* (New York: D. Van Nostrand, 1862–68), vol. 6, 613.

104. Wilson, "Staff Officer's Journal," LC.

105. Dana, *Recollections*, 54.

106. Blanchard, *I Marched with Sherman*, 89.

107. McPherson to Grant, May 12, 1863, USGP, vol. 8, 206–07.

108. OR, I/24, part 1, 59. Aggregate rebel losses were 514. OR, I/24, part 1, 739.

109. Blanchard, *I Marched with Sherman*, 89.

110. Bond, ed., *Under the Flag of the Nation*, 59–60.

111. Cadwallader, *Three Years with Grant*, 70–71.

112. USGM, 333.

113. *Ibid.*, 332.

114. USG to Kelton, July 6, 1863, USGP, vol. 8, 496; USG to McClernand, May 13, 1863, 208.

115. Editors of the [Jackson] *Mississippian*, to Jefferson Davis, May 8, 1863, Jefferson Davis Papers, Louisiana Historical Collection, Howard-Tilton Memorial Library, Tulane University, New Orleans, Louisiana.

116. USGM, 332.

117. USG to McClernand, May 12, 1863, USGP, vol. 8, 202–05; USG to WTS, May 11, 1863, *ibid.*, 202–03.

118. OR, I/24, part 1, 260–61.

119. *Ibid.*, 215.

120. *Ibid.*

121. OR, I/24, part 1, 261.

122. Davis to Pemberton, May 7, 1863, OR, I/24, part 3, 842.

123. Lockett, "Defense of Vicksburg," 487; Lauren C. Post, "Samuel Henry Lockett (1837–1891)—A Sketch of His Life and Work," *Louisiana History* vol. 5, no. 4 (Autumn, 1964): 437.

124. OR, I/24, part 3, 877.

125. OR, I/24, part 1, 261.

126. Ballard, *Grant at Vicksburg*, 283.

127. OR, I/24, part 2, 74, 125; *ibid.*, part 1, 261.

128. OR, I/24, part 2, 125.

129. OR, I/24, part 1, 261–62.

TWENTY. THE HILL OF DEATH

1. OR I/24, part 2, 44.

2. USG to Halleck, May 14, 1863, USGP, vol. 8, 213.

3. Byers, *With Fire and Sword*, 69.

4. Wilkie, *Pen and Powder*, 330.

5. USGM, 331. Crocker died on August 26, 1865.

6. OR, I/24, part 1, 783.

7. USGM, 337; OR, I/24, part 1, 754; Badeau, *Military History*, vol. 1, 248.

8. Frederick Grant, "General Grant: His Son's Memories of Him in the Field," *National Tribune*, January 27, 1887.

9. *Harper's Weekly*, June 20, 1863. Union losses were 42 killed, 251 wounded, and 7 missing. Most Confederate regiments did not report losses. OR, I/24, part 1, 751.

10. Bearss, *Campaign for Vicksburg*, vol. 2, 554; NYT, August 1, 1863; Grabau, *Ninety-Eight Days*, 256.

11. William P. LaBounty, ed., *Civil War Diaries of James W. Jessee, 1861–1865, Company K, 8th Regiment of Illinois Volunteer Infantry* (Normal, IL: McLean County Genealogical Society, 1997), 19–20.

12. Grant to McClernand, May 14, 1863, USGP, vol. 8, 215.

13. USG to WTS, May 15, 1863, USGP, vol. 8, 218.

14. OR, I/24, part 1, 754.

15. *Ibid.*, part 3, 315.

16. Cadwallader, *Three Years with Grant*, 75.

17. Quoted in William McCain, *The Story of Jackson: A History of the Capital of Mississippi, 1821–1951*, vol. 1 (Jackson, MI: J. Hyer Publishing Company, 1953), 198.

18. Cadwallader, *Three Years with Grant*, 75.

19. OR, I/24, part 1, 754.

20. Young, *Around the World*, vol. 2, 312.

21. Quoted in McCain, *Story of Jackson*, 199.

22. Feis, *Grant's Secret Service*, 161–62.

23. NYT, August 1, 1863; USGM, 338.

24. OR, I/24, part 2, 125.

25. Bearss, *Campaign for Vicksburg*, vol. 2, 576; OR, I/24, part 2, 110.

26. Anonymous, n.d., Old Courthouse Museum, Vicksburg, Mississippi.

27. Sid Champion to Matilda Champion, March 31, "early 1863," April 4, 1863, Sidney S. Champion Papers, William R. Perkins Library, Duke University.

28. Sidney Champion to Matilda Champion, "Spring, 1863," April 15, 30, 1863, Champion Papers, Duke.

29. OR, I/24, part 1, 51–52; Wilson, "Staff Officer's Journal," Wilson Papers, LC; USGM, 341.

30. USG to WTS, May 16, USGP, vol. 8, 227.

31. Frederick Grant, "A Boy's Experience," 94.

32. S. H. M. Byers, "How Men Feel in Battle," *Annals of Iowa* 2 (July 1896): 440.

33. John B. Sanborn, *The Crisis at Champion's Hill: The Decisive Battle of the Civil War* (St. Paul, MN: n.p., 1903), 10.

34. Grant to McClernand, May 15, 1863, McClernand Collection; OR, I/24, part 1, 51.

35. William Drennan to wife, May 30, 1863, William Drennan Papers, MDAH.

36. OR, I/24, part 1, 263; *ibid.*, part 2, 14, 22–25, 28–29.

37. Bearss, *Campaign for Vicksburg*, vol. 2, 566.

38. OR, I/24, part 1, 263; Lee, "Campaign of Vicksburg," 36.

39. Grabau, *Ninety-Eight Days*, 273; Drennan to wife, May 30, 1863, Drennan Papers, MDAH.

40. OR, I/24, part 2, 75.

41. Quoted in Shea and Winschel, *Vicksburg Is the Key*, 132.

42. Drennan to wife, May 30, 1863, Drennan Papers, MDAH.

43. Jackson, ed., "Some of the Boys," 116.

44. The Champion house burned down in the summer of 1863, cause unknown. The family returned and built another house on a different part of the property. "Descendant Clarifies Champion Hill History," *Jackson Daily News*, May 24, 1984.

45. OR, I/24, part 2, 41.

46. OR, I/24, part 1, 52; *ibid.*, part 2, 101, 104; Lee, "Campaign of Vicksburg," 40.

47. Quoted in Catton, *Grant Moves South*, 443.

48. USGM, 342.

49. McClernand to USG, May 16, 1863, USGP, vol. 8, 225.

50. USG to McClernand, *ibid.*, 226.

51. OR, I/24, part 1, 52; Grabau, *Ninety-Eight Days*, 279–80.

52. OR, I/24, part 2, 94.

53. OR, I/24, part 2, 48–49.

54. Wilbur Crummer, *With Grant at Fort Donelson, Shiloh and Vicksburg* (Oak Park, IL: E. C. Crummer & Co., 1915), 103; OR, I/24, part 2, 42, 49, 53–54.

55. Dana, *Recollections*, 54.

56. Ulysses S. Grant, "The Vicksburg Campaign," BL, vol. 3, 511; OR, I/24, part 2, 100.

57. USGM, 345–46.

58. Woodworth, *Nothing But Victory*, 379.

59. OR, I/24, part 1, 718.

60. OR, I/24, part 2, 121.

61. Ephraim McDowell Anderson, *Memoirs: Historical and Personal Including the Campaigns of the First Missouri Confederate Brigade* (St. Louis: Times Publishing Co., 1868), 311–12; Bevier, *Missouri Confederate Brigades*, 188.

62. OR, I/24, part 2, 111.

63. Quoted in L. B. Northrup, "A Hill of Death," *Civil War Times Illustrated* (May–June, 1991): 32.

64. OR, I/24, part 2, 49.

65. OR, I/24, part 2, 50.

66. OR, I/24, part 2, 110–11; Anderson, *Memoirs*, 313.

67. OR, I/24, part 2, 111.

68. W. T. Moore to W. T. Ratliff, October 5, 1902, VNMP.

69. Anderson, *Memoirs*, 313.

70. Osborn H. Oldroyd, *A Soldier's Story of the Siege of Vicksburg* (Springfield, IL: privately published, 1885), 23.

71. OR, I/24, part 2, 117.

72. Sanborn, *Crisis at Champion's Hill*, 13.

73. OR, I/24, part 2, 66.

74. Timothy B. Smith, *Champion Hill: Decisive Battle for Vicksburg* (New York: Savas Beatie, 2004), 266–67.

75. Byers, "Some Recollections of Grant," 343–44.

76. Mary Amelia (Boomer) Stone, *Memoir of George Boardman Boomer* (Boston: Press of Geo. C. Rand & Avery, 1864), 252–53.

77. Byers, *With Fire and Sword*, 73; Byers, "How Men Feel in Battle," 441–44; OR, I/24, part 2, 66, 315; *ibid.*, part 1, 783.

78. OR, I/24, part 2, 44, 46, 50, 110–11, 117.

79. Sanborn, *Crisis at Champion's Hill*, 13; OR, I/24, part 1, 776.

80. OR, I/24, part 2, 50.

81. OR, I/24, part 2, 44.

82. Sanborn, *Crisis at Champion's Hill*, 24.

83. OR, I/24, part 1, 264; OR, I/24, part 2, 70, 226.

84. USGM, 347.

85. USG to McClernand, May 16, 1863, USGM, vol. 8, 225, 225n, 226n, 226 (italics mine).

86. OR, I/24, part 1, 52; *ibid.*, part 3, 318.

87. OR, I/24, part 2, 15.

88. *Ibid.*

89. Quoted in Woodworth, *Nothing But Victory*, 387.

90. Quoted in Smith, *Champion Hill*, 290.

91. OR, I/24, part 2, 117.

92. Drennan to wife, May 30, 1863, Drennan Papers, MDAH.

93. OR, I/24, part 2, 77.

94. OR, I/24, part 2, 77.

95. *Ibid.*, 73–79.

96. *Ibid.*, 78.

97. Wilson, "Staff Officer's Journal," LC.

98. S. H. M. Byers, "Some Recollections of Grant," 346.

99. Grant to Kelton, July 6, 1863, USGP, vol. 8, 1863, 500.

100. OR, I/24, part 2, 44.

101. Dana, *Recollections*, 54–55.

102. Bearss, *Campaign for Vicksburg*, vol. 2, 632–33.

103. Byers, "How Men Feel in Battle," 447.

104. USGM, 348.

105. Rebecca Blackwell Drake, "Matilda Champion: 'A Sorrow's Crown of Sorrow,'" Vicksburg Courthouse Museum and Archive.

106. Frederick Grant, "A Boy's Experience," 94; Smith, *Champion Hill*, 369.

107. Cadwallader, *Three Years with Grant*, 80.

108. Thomas L. Livermore, *Numbers & Losses in the Civil War in America: 1861–65* (1900) (Bloomington, IN: 1957), 99–100; OR, I/24, part 2, 7–10.

109. Wilson, "A Staff Officer's Journal," LC.

110. Livermore, *Numbers & Losses*, 99–100; Smith, *Champion Hill*, 372; Bearss, *Campaign for Vicksburg*, vol. 2, 642–52.

111. Quoted in Foote, *Fort Sumter to Perryville*, 375.

112. Sanborn, *Crisis at Champion Hill*, 1; Comte De Paris, *History of the Civil War in America*, vol. 3 (Philadelphia: Jos. H. Coates, 1883), 327.

113. USG to WTS, May 16, 1863, USGP, vol. 8, 228.

114. USG to WTS, May 16, 1863, USGP, vol. 8, 228; USG to Blair, May 17, 1863, *ibid.*, 231.

115. OR, I/24, part 1, 266–67.

116. Crooke, *Twenty-first Iowa*, 70.

117. J. H. Jones, "The Rank and File at Vicksburg," *Publications of the Mississippi Historical Society* (1903): 19; Chambers, "My Journal," 279.

118. OR, I/24, part 1, 266.

119. USGM, 349.

120. OR, I/24, part 1, 272–73.

121. Grabau, *Ninety-Eight Days*, 325.

122. Quoted in Woodward, *Nothing But Victory*, 392.

123. Cadwallader, *Three Years with Grant*, 83–84.

124. OR, I/24, part 1, 266.

125. OR, I/24, part 2, 130; Dana and Wilson, *Grant*, 125; J. T. Dorris, "Michael Kelly Lawler: Mexican and Civil War Officer," *Journal of the Illinois State Historical Society* 48 (Winter 1955): 366–94.

126. OR, I/24, part 2, 73.

127. OR, I/24, part 2, 119.

128. USG to Kelton, July 6, 1863, USGP, vol. 8, 501; OR, I/24, part 1, 268. Federal casualties were light: 39 killed, 237 wounded, and 3 missing. Union soldiers captured 1,751 prisoners. The number of Confederate casualties is unknown but small. OR, I/24, part 2, 130.

129. Samuel H. Lockett, "The Defense of Vicksburg," in BL, vol. 3, 488.

130. Dora Richards Miller, "A Woman's Diary of the Siege of Vicksburg," *Century Magazine* 30 (September 1885): 771.

131. Chambers, "My Journal," 270.

132. Hall, *26th Louisiana Infantry*, 66.

133. Lida Lord Reed, "A Woman's Experience During the Siege of Vicksburg," *Century Magazine* 61 (April 1901): 922.

134. *Ibid.*, 923.

135. Halleck to Banks, May 11, 1863, USGP, vol. 8, 221.

136. USGM, 350.

137. WTSM, 349.

138. USGM, 354; WTSM, 350.

139. WTSM, 350; Porter to USG, May 2, 1863, USGP, vol. 8, 240.

140. USGM, 354.

141. WTS to EES, June 2, 1863, SCW, 477.

142. Cadwallader, *Three Years with Grant*, 88.

143. 695 killed, 3,425 wounded, and 259 missing, Badeau, *Military History*, vol. 1, 357–58; Dana and Wilson, *Grant*, 126; "Vicksburg Civil War Casualties," http://thomaslegion.net/Vicksburg_campaign_battle_siege.

144. USG to Lt. Col. Grantham I. Taggart, May 17, 1863, USGP, vol. 8, 234–35; CT, June 23, 1863; Badeau, *Military History*, vol. 1, 274.

145. Manning F. Force, *Personal Recollections of the Vicksburg Campaign: A Paper Read Before the Ohio Commandery of the Military Order of the Loyal Legion of the United States* (Cincinnati: Henry C. Sherick, 1885), 9–11.

146. Elihu B. Washburne to Cadwallader Washburn from Grand Gulf, May 5, 1863, Elihu Washburne Papers, Duke University.

147. Dana and Wilson, *Grant*, 126; Badeau, *Military History*, vol. 1, 357.

148. Lincoln to Arnold, May 26, 1863, Basler, ed., *Collected Works of Abraham Lincoln*, 270.

149. Lee, "Campaign of Vicksburg," 53.

150. William E. Strong, "The Campaign Against Vicksburg," in MOLLUS, 11:329–30.

151. Porter to Grant, May 20, 1863, USGP, vol. 8, 240.

152. WTSM, 351.

153. Johnston to Pemberton, May 17, 1863, OR, I/24, part 1, 272.

154. *Ibid.*, 273.
155. USGM, 354.

TWENTY-ONE. A CIRCLE OF FIRE

1. H. M. Trimble Diary, VNMP.
2. USG to Porter, May 19, 1863, USGP, vol. 8, 239; Porter to USG, May 20, 1863, *ibid.*, 240.
3. "circle of fire" quoted in Walker, *Vicksburg*, 169; Emma Balfour Diary, n.p., MDAH; there is no pagination in this manuscript copy of Balfour's diary.
4. Balfour Diary, n.p., MDAH.
5. *Ibid.*, 4.
6. William Lovelace Foster, *Vicksburg: Southern City under Siege*, Kenneth T. Urquhart, ed. (New Orleans: Historic New Orleans Collection, 1980), 7.
7. Lida Lord Reed, "A Woman's Experience," 923.
8. WTS to EES, May 19, 1863, SCW, 471.
9. Fuller, *Generalship of Grant*, 203.
10. USGM, 355.
11. Badeau, *Military History*, vol. 1, 301.
12. J. J. Kellogg, *Story of the Vicksburg Campaign*, 26–27.
13. *Ibid.*, 27.
14. William Murray Diary, VNMP.
15. Strong, "Campaign Against Vicksburg," 328.
16. Quoted in Foote, *Fredericksburg to Meridian*, 409.
17. Lockett, "Defense of Vicksburg," 484, 490.
18. Lee, "Siege of Vicksburg," 56.
19. Quoted in Badeau, *Military History*, vol. 1, 300.
20. ORN, I/18/491–92, 533, 782–83, 810.
21. Kellogg, *Story of the Vicksburg Campaign*, 18.
22. *Ibid.*, 28.
23. *Ibid.*, 12; Special Order No. 134, USGP, vol. 8, 237.
24. W. W. Gardner to Dr. Levi Fuller, May 25, 1863, VNMP.
25. WTSM, 352.
26. Kellogg, *Story of the Vicksburg Campaign*, 28.
27. *Ibid.*, 28, 30.
28. OR, I/24, part 2, 266–67.
29. Kellogg, *Story of the Vicksburg Campaign*, 32.
30. W. W. Gardner to Dr. Levi Fuller, May 25, 1863, VNMP; Frank Muhlenberg to William T. Rigby, June 6, 1902, VNMP; Terrence J. Winschel, "First Honor at Vicksburg: The 1st Battalion, 13th U.S. Infantry," *Civil War Regiments: A Journal of the American Civil War* 2, no. 1 (1998), *passim*.
31. WTSM, 352.
32. The Union lost 942; the Confederate lost an estimated seventy men: OR, I/24, part 2, 159–60; *ibid.*, part 1, 273–74.

33. WTS to EES, May 19, 1863, SCW, 472.

34. USGP, vol. 8, 502.

35. WTSM, 351; General Field Orders, May 21, 1863, USGP, vol. 8, 145–46.

36. General Field Orders, May 21, 1863, USGP, vol. 8, 245–46.

37. USG to Porter, May 21, 1863, USGP, vol. 8, 247.

38. Grabau, *Ninety-Eight Days*, 370.

39. WTS to EES, May 19, 1863, SCW, 471. McClernand also favored attacking on a narrow front, but Grant overruled him, recognizing that the rugged ground in front of his corps was the toughest to penetrate of all the terrain at Vicksburg.

40. Wayne Jacobs Diary, LSU, 58.

41. Kellogg, *Story of the Vicksburg Campaign*, 15.

42. OR, I/24, part 2, 361, 407.

43. Lee, "Siege of Vicksburg," 59.

44. *Ibid.*, 59–60.

45. J. H. Jones, "The Rank and File at Vicksburg," *Publications of the Mississippi Historical Society* vol. 7, 21.

46. Lee, "Siege of Vicksburg," 60.

47. Grabau, *Ninety-Eight Days*, 371.

48. Saunier, ed., *History of the Forty-Seventh Regiment Ohio*, 147.

49. Wayne Jacobs Diary, 58–59, LSU.

50. George H. Hildt to W. T. Rigby, February 8, 1902, VNMP.

51. OR I/24, part 2, 257–58.

52. Diarist quoted in Edwin Cole Bearss, *The Vicksburg Campaign: Unvexed to the Sea*, (Dayton, OH: Morningside, 1986), 817; Bond, ed., *Under the Old Flag*, vol. 1, 65.

53. Kellogg, *Story of the Vicksburg Campaign*, 16.

54. John O'Dea, "Reminiscences of the War," *Chicago Times-Herald*, May 30, 1897.

55. Jackson, ed., "Some of the Boys," 97.

56. Jones, "Rank and File at Vicksburg," 21.

57. The other brother is Samuel Brown, who was killed at Shiloh. Mary's half brothers were the children of her stepmother.

58. WTSM, 352.

59. OR, I/24, part 2, 140–41, 238; J. D. Pearson to S. D. Lee, May 17, 1902, VNMP.

60. S. C. Jones, *Reminiscences of the Twenty-Second Iowa* (1907) (Iowa City, IA, 1993), 38.

61. Crooke, *Twenty-First Iowa*, 82.

62. Cadwallader, *Three Years with Grant*, 90.

63. McClernand to USG, May 22, 1863, OR I/24, part 1, 172.

64. OR, I/24, part 1, 55.

65. WTSM, 352.

66. OR, I/24, part 1, 55–56.

67. William Murray Diary, VNMP.

68. H. M. Trimble Diary, VNMP.

69. Jenney, "Personal Recollections of Vicksburg," 261.

70. Cadwallader, *Three Years with Grant*, 92.

71. Sanborn, "Campaign Against Vicksburg," 134.

72. USG to Halleck, May 24, 1863, USGP, vol. 8, 260–61.

73. Dana to Stanton, *ibid.*, 255.
74. Quoted in Woodworth, *Nothing But Victory*, 428.
75. *Ibid.*, 427.
76. Bond, ed., *Under the Old Flag*, vol. 1, 65; see also Jacob Ritner to Emeline Ritner, May 23, 1863, in Larimer, ed., *Love and Valor*, 168–69.
77. Union losses were 502 killed, 2,550 wounded, and 147 missing. OR, I/24, part 3, 370–71.
78. USG to Halleck, May 22, USGP, vol. 8, 249.
79. Jones, "Rank and File at Vicksburg," 22.
80. McClernand to USG, May 23, 1863, USGP, vol. 8, 255.
81. Pemberton to USG, May 25, 1863, *ibid.*, 266.
82. Kellogg, *Story of the Vicksburg Campaign*, 48.
83. William Murray Diary, VNMP.
84. Charles Wood Diary, VNMP.
85. USGP, vol. 8, 267–68.
86. OR, I/24, part 2, 177.
87. M. B. Loop, "Campaigning with the Buckeyes," *National Tribune*, November 15, 1900.
88. USGP, vol. 8, 267.
89. USGM, 357.
90. OR, I/24, part 2, 177.
91. OR, I/24, part 2, 170–77.
92. Quoted in Justin S. Solonick, *Engineering Victory: The Union Siege of Vicksburg* (Carbondale: Southern Illinois University Press, 2015), 44.
93. Byers, "Some Recollections of Grant," 350.
94. OR, I/24, part 2, 188.
95. USGM, 359.
96. Kellogg, *Story of the Vicksburg Campaign*, 34.
97. USGM, 355.
98. Crummer, *With Grant*, 110.
99. WTS to EES, May 25, 1863, SCW, 472.
100. OR, I/24, part 2, 171.
101. Loop, "Campaigning with the Buckeyes"; OR, I/24, part 2, 155–56.
102. Crummer, *With Grant*, 118.
103. OR, I/24, part 2, 172.
104. John B. Sanborn, "Remarks on a Motion to Extend a Vote of Thanks to General Marshall for Above Paper," in MOLLUS, 29, 617–18 (Wilmington, NC: Broadfoot Press, 1994), 199.
105. Samuel C. Kirkpatrick to James G. Kirkpatrick, July 1, 1863, James G. Kirkpatrick Collection, WHMC, 103.
106. Bearss, *Campaign for Vicksburg*, vol. 3, 954.
107. Grabau, *Ninety-Eight Days*, 410.
108. OR, I/24, part 2, 294.
109. Stansbury F. Haydon, "Grant's Wooden Mortars and Some Incidents of the Siege of Vicksburg," *Journal of the American Military Institute* 4, no. 1 (Spring 1940): 31, 33–35.

110. Hickenlooper, "The Vicksburg Mine," BL, vol. 3, 540; Hickenlooper, "Personal Reminiscences," folder 3, 145, Cincinnati Museum Center (hereafter CMC).

111. Crummer, *With Grant*, 143.

112. WTS to EES, May 25, 1863, SCW, 472.

113. OR, I/24, part 2, 176. Porter loaned Grant a battery of big naval guns, which fired on both the rebel lines and the city.

114. CT, June 20, 1863.

115. Quoted in Solonick, *Engineering Victory*, 65.

116. A. S. Abrams, *A Full and Detailed History of the Siege of Vicksburg* (Atlanta: Intelligencer Steam Powers Press, 1863), 41.

117. OR, I/24, part 2, 175.

118. Edward S. Gregory, "Vicksburg during the Siege," *The Annals of the War: Written by Leading Participants, North and South* (Philadelphia: The Times Publishing Company, 1879), 116–17, 120; NYT, June 12, 1863; An estimated twenty civilians were killed in the Union bombardment of Atlanta in the late spring and summer of 1864. See Wendy Hamand Venet, *A Changing Wind: Commerce and Conflict in Civil War Atlanta* (New Haven, CT: Yale University Press, 2014), 156–66 and Elizabeth R. Varon, *Armies of Deliverance: A New History of the Civil War* (New York: Oxford University Press, 2019), 348–51.

119. Porter, *Naval History*, 329.

120. USG to Porter, June 16, 1863, USGP, vol. 8, 384.

121. Abrams, *History of the Siege*, 32.

122. Mortar Files, VNMP.

123. Dora (Miller) Richards, "A Woman's Diary of the Siege of Vicksburg," *The Century Illustrated Monthly Magazine* 30 (September 1885): 76.

124. John T. Trowbridge, *The Desolate South: A Picture of the Battlefields of the Devastated Confederacy*, Gordon Carroll, ed. (New York: Duell, Sloan and Pearce, 1956), 190–91.

125. Balfour Diary, n.p.; see also Loughborough, *My Cave Life*, 55.

126. Theodosia F. McKinstry, "My Days of Danger in Vicksburg," VNMP.

127. William W. Lord, "A Child at the Siege of Vicksburg," *Harper's Monthly Magazine*, 118 (December 1908): 44.

128. Lida Lord, "A Child," 23; Lida L. Reed, "A Woman's Experiences during the Siege of Vicksburg," *Century Magazine* 61 (April 1901): 924.

129. Twain, *Life on the Mississippi*, 299–301.

130. Balfour Diary, n.p.

131. Balfour Diary, n.p.

132. Gregory, "Vicksburg during the Siege," 116–17, 120.

133. Crummer, *With Grant*, 144–45.

134. Clarence Hubbard to Brother A. S., June 25, 1863, in Leo M. Kaiser, ed., "Beleaguered City: The Vicksburg Campaign as Seen in Published Letters," *Southern Studies* (Spring, 1978): 82; W. L. Brown to father, June 7, 1863, in *ibid.*, 81; Willison, "76th Ohio," 61.

135. "Civil War Letters of Brigadier General William Ward Orme—1862–1866," *Journal of the Illinois State Historical Society* 23 (July 1930), 277.

136. USG to Porter, May 22, 1863, USGP, vol. 8, 250.

137. USG to Porter, June 16, 1863, USGP, vol. 8, 384; Porter to USG, *ibid.*

138. WTS to EES, June 2, 1863, SCW, 476–77.

139. WTS to EES, June 27, 1863, SCW, 492–93.

140. Drennan to Wife, June 2, 1863, Drennan Papers; Edwin C. Bearss, "Pvt. Charles E. Affeld Reports Action West of the Mississippi." *Journal of the Illinois State Historical Society* 60 (Autumn 1967): 286–87; Grabau, *Ninety-Eight Days,* 436–37.

141. Balfour Diary, n.p.

142. Abrams, *History of the Siege,* 55.

143. Gregory, "Vicksburg during the Siege," 120, 125.

144. Joseph Dill Alison, Diary, MDAH.

145. WTS to Porter, June 14, 1863, SCW, 484–85.

146. Tunnard, *Third Regiment Louisiana Infantry,* 262.

147. Abrams, *History of the Siege,* 47. Lovicy Eberhart Remis, the wife of an army chaplain, moved to Vicksburg after the surrender and found only two buildings, a church and a house, that had not been "struck or partially destroyed by our siege guns." Lovicy Ann Eberhart Papers, Illinois State Historical Library.

148. Tunnard, *Third Regiment Louisiana Infantry,* 260.

149. Drennan to Wife, June 4, 1963, Drennan Papers, MDAH.

150. Funeral Records, May–July, 1863, Old Courthouse Museum; Trowbridge, *Desolate South,* 191.

151. Balfour Diary, n.p.

152. *Ibid.*

153. WTS to John Sherman, June 27, 1863, SCW, 495.

154. Reed, "A Woman's Experience," 925.

155. Moss, *Diary,* 38.

156. Gregory, "Vicksburg during the Siege," 122; Porter, *Naval History,* 323.

157. Drennan to Wife, June 4, 1863, Drennan Papers, MDAH.

158. Reed, "A Woman's Experience," 926.

TWENTY-TWO. "THE CRISIS IS ON US"

1. William Drennan to Wife, July 3, 1863, Drennan Papers, MDAH.

2. WTS to EES, June 27, 1863, SCW, 491.

3. OR, I/24, part 1, 193.

4. Johnston to Pemberton, May 29, 1863, OR, I/24, part 1, 279.

5. Balfour Diary, n.p.

6. OR, I/24, part 1, 227.

7. James Longstreet, "Lee in Pennsylvania," *Annals of the War* (Philadelphia, 1879): 415–16. Guelzo, *Gettysburg,* 34–35.

8. Quoted in Archer Jones, "The Gettysburg Decision," *Virginia Magazine of History and Biography* 68, no. 3 (1960): 331–42.

9. Cooper, *Davis,* 435–36; Symonds, *Johnston,* 210–11.

10. USG to Hurlbut, May 31, 1863, USGP, vol. 8, 298.

11. OR, I/24, part 3, 370, 942–43, 978.

12. USG to Hurlbut, May 31, 1863, USGP, vol. 8, 298; USG to Halleck, May 25, 29, 1863, *ibid.,* 267, 283.

13. USG to Banks, May 25, 1863, *ibid.*, 269.

14. Banks to USG, May 28, 1863, *ibid.*, 270.

15. OR, I/24, part 2, 211–12.

16. USGP, vol. 8, 286; USG to Francis P. Blair Jr., May 29, 1863, USGP, vol. 8, 289.

17. *Harper's Weekly*, June 20, 1863.

18. W. B. Britton to Janesville, *Wisconsin Gazette*, June 1, 1863, Old Courthouse Museum.

19. NYT, June 25, 1863.

20. McPherson, *Battle Cry*, 778.

21. Blair to Grant, May 31, 1863, OR, I/24, part 2, 435–36.

22. USG to Nathan Kimball, June 3, 1863, USGP, vol. 8, 308–9.

23. Kimball to USG, June 5, 6, 1863, *ibid.*, 316–17.

24. Wilson, *Under the Old Flag*, vol. 1, 137.

25. Rawlins to USG, June 6, 1863, USGP, vol. 8, 322–23.

26. *Ibid.*, 323.

27. Dana wrote this in a *New York Sun* editorial of January 28, 1887. A copy is in the Grant Papers, vol. 8, 324–25.

28. OR, I/24, part 1, 94; Dana, *Recollections*, 82–84.

29. Dana, *Recollections*, 84.

30. James Harrison Wilson, *The Life of Charles A. Dana* (New York: Harper & Brothers, 1907), 200, 232.

31. Ballard, *Grant at Vicksburg*, 46. For the historiographical controversy that still swirls around the Cadwallader book, see Bruce D. Simpson's introduction to the Bison Books edition of *Three Years with Grant*, v–xv; Ballard, *Grant at Vicksburg*, chapter 3; and Brian J. Murphy, "Truth Behind U. S. Grant's Yazoo River Bender," Weider History Group, 2012, http://www.historynet.com/truth-behind-us-rants-yazoo-river-bender.htm.

32. Dana to Wilson, January 18, 1890, USGP, vol. 8, 324. Cadwallader's book is replete with inaccurate information about the trip; he fails even to mention Dana's presence on *Diligence*. Chernow, *Grant*, 275.

33. Received and published in the *Chicago Times* on June 15, 1863. Cadwallader also wrote for the *New York Herald*.

34. Cadwallader, *Three Years with Grant*, 103–04.

35. *Ibid.*, 106–09.

36. Chernow, *Grant*, 276.

37. Simon and Wilson, "Beckwith," in Wilson and Simon, eds., *Grant*, 121–23.

38. Cadwallader, *Three Years with Grant*, 100–01.

39. Wilkie, *Pen and Powder*, 206–08.

40. Cadwallader, *Three Years with Grant*, 113; Cadwallader to Wilson, December 2, 1907, Wilson Papers, LC.

41. Cadwallader to Wilson, June 21, 1890, Wilson Papers, LC.

42. Wilson, *Life of Dana*, 21–32.

43. Wilson, *Under the Old Flag*, vol. 1, 137.

44. McFeely, *Grant*, 133.

45. Dana, *Recollections*, 90–91. "When any thing was pending he was invariably abstinent of drink," Sherman wrote long after the war. USGP, vol. 8, 323–24.

46. Chernow, *Grant*, 277. For judicious accounts of the Satartia story that differ in places

from my own, see Simpson, *Grant*, vol. 1, 206–08, and especially Simpson's introduction to the paperback edition of *Three Years with Grant*, v–xix.

47. USGP, vol. 8, 323–24; see also Ronald L. Fingerson, "A William Tecumseh Sherman Letter," *Books at Iowa* 3 (November 1965), 34–38.

48. Cadwallader to Wilson, February 18, 1887, Wilson Papers, LC.

49. Richard Taylor, *Destruction and Reconstruction: Personal Experiences of the Late War* (New York: D. Appleton and Company, 1879), 138.

50. Ira Berlin et al., ed., *Wartime Genesis of Free Labor*, 700–701.

51. OR, I/24, part 2, 458.

52. David Cornwell, "Memoir," 129, USAMHI. Cornwell's report was published just after I began work on this book: John Wearmouth, ed., *The Cornwell Chronicles: Tales of an American Life* (Bowie, MD: Heritage Books, 1998). For other scholarly works on the Battle of Milliken's Bend see Linda Barnickel, *Milliken's Bend: A Civil War Battle in History and Memory* (Baton Rouge: Louisiana State University Press, 2013); Glatthaar, *Forged in Battle*; Richard Lowe, *Walker's Texas Division C.S.A.: Greyhounds of the Trans-Mississippi* (Baton Rouge: Louisiana State University Press, 2004); Lowe, "Battle on the Levee: The Fight at Milliken's Bend," in *Black Soldiers in Blue: African American Troops in the Civil War Era*, edited by John David Smith (Chapel Hill: University of North Carolina Press, 2002); Terrance J. Winschel, "To Rescue Gibraltar: John Walker's Texas Division and Its Expedition to Relieve Fortress Vicksburg," *Civil War Regiments* 3, no. 3 (1993): 33–58; George S. Burkhardt, *Confederate Rage, Yankee Wrath: No Quarter in the Civil War* (Carbondale: Southern Illinois University Press, 2007); and Ann J. Bailey, "A Texas Cavalry Raid: Reaction to Black Soldiers and Contrabands," *Civil War History* 35, no. 2 (June 1989): 138–52.

53. Grabau, *Ninety-Eight Days*, 400–01; OR, I/24, part 2, 447, 458.

54. CT, July 3, 1863; Isaac F. Shepard to Lorenzo Thomas, June 23, 1863, in Barnickel, *Milliken's Bend*, 207–10.

55. Shepard to Thomas, in *ibid.*, 209.

56. *Ibid.*, 90.

57. OR, I/24, part 2, 467. The Iowans were not cowards, they were simply outnumbered and overwhelmed.

58. Peter W. Gravis, *Twenty-Five Years on the Outside Road of the Northwest Texas Annual Conference: Autobiography of Rev. Peter W. Gravis* (Brownwood, TX: Cross Timbers Press, 1966), 28.

59. OR, I/24, part 1, 102.

60. M. M. Miller to Aunt, June 10, 1863, published in CT, July 3, 1863.

61. OR, I/24, part 2, 447.

62. CT, June 18, 1863.

63. David H. Slay, "New Masters on the Mississippi; The United States Colored Troops of the Middle Mississippi Valley," Ph.D. Dissertation, Texas Christian University, 2009, 97.

64. CT, June 18, 1863.

65. OR, I/24, part 2, 459.

66. Porter to USG, June 7, 1863, USGP, vol. 8, 327.

67. OR, I/24, part 2, 460.

68. Total losses were 119 killed, 241 wounded, and 132 missing. The 23rd Iowa lost 23 killed and 42 wounded out of 120 present. These tabulations of losses are the most recent, corrected figures compiled by Linda Barnickel, largely from the 1998 *Supplement to the Official Records*, part 2, vol. 78, 115. See Barnickel, *Milliken's Bend*, 103, 200–06; she has corrected the figures of General Elias Dennis and historians Warren Grabau and Edwin Bearss. See Dennis to Rawlins, July 8, 1863, USGP, vol. 8, 327; Grabau, *Ninety-Eight Days*, 402; Bearss, *Campaign for Vicksburg*, vol. 3, 1183.

69. OR, I/24, part 2, 470, 469.

70. CT, July 3, 1863.

71. OR, I/24, part 2, 448–49.

72. Porter to Grant, June 7, 1863, OR, I/24, part 2, 454.

73. USGM, 366.

74. USG to Lorenzo Thomas, June 16, 1863, OR, I/24, part 2, 446.

75. M. M. Miller to Aunt, June 10, 1863, published in CT, July 3, 1863. Miller was mistakenly referred to as a captain in widely circulated newspaper reports.

76. Dana to Stanton, June 18, 1863, OR, I/24, part 1, 106.

77. Ballard, *Grant at Vicksburg*, 68.

78. George R. Buck to Dolly, June 9, 1863, Old Courthouse Museum.

79. Alexander G. Downing, *Downing's Civil War*, edited by Olynthus B. Clark (Des Moines: The Historical Department of Iowa, 1916), 120.

80. Noah Andre Trudeau, *Like Men of War: Blacks in the Civil War, 1862–1865* (Boston: Little, Brown and Company, 1998).

81. Stone, *Brokenburn*, 218–19.

82. CT, August 6, 1863. Historian Linda Barnickel believes the story, while vastly exaggerated, "might be true," and, if true, probably occurred north of Milliken's Bend, not south of it, as the author of the piece claimed. (Barnickel, *Milliken's Bend*, 127). The *Tribune* story had been taken, without attribution, from the pages of the *Missouri Democrat*.

83. Elias K. Owen to Porter, June 16, 1863, *ibid.*, 401; OR, I/23, part 3, 425; *New York Herald*, August 3, 1863. In his essay "The Execution of White Officers from Black Units by Confederate Forces during the Civil War," *Louisiana History* 35 (Fall 1994): 475–89, historian James G. Hollandsworth Jr. does not mention any hangings in the area of Perkins plantation.

84. Confederate States of America, Congress, House, Joint Resolutions in Reference to the Treatment of Colored Troops, February 15, 1864. In *Confederate Imprints, 1861–1865* (New Haven, CT: Research Publications, 1974), 387.

85. OR/2, vol. 5, 940–41.

86. Grant to Taylor, June 22, 1863, USGP, vol. 8, 400–01; Bearss, *Campaign for Vicksburg*, vol. 3, 1183, 1196–97.

87. Taylor to Grant, June 27, 1863; USGP, vol. 8, 469.

88. USG to Taylor, July 4, 1863, USGP, vol. 8, 468; USG to Halleck, August 29, 1863, USGP, vol. 9, 210. Reliable information about black prisoners in Confederate hands in Louisiana is almost impossible to find. The records of the 9th Louisiana Infantry were lost in the Battle of Milliken's Bend.

89. Porter to USG, June 19, 1863, USGP, vol. 8, 401.

90. Lincoln, Basler, ed., *Works*, vol. 4, 357.

91. Isaac F. Shepard, Court of Inquiry Papers, TS, Wyles MS 74, Isaac F. Shepard Papers, Department of Special Collections, Davidson Library, University of California, Santa Barbara, 3–4. David H. Slay generously provided me a copy of the transcript.

92. Shepard, Court of Inquiry, 4–5.

93. Isaac F. Shepard to Lorenzo Thomas, June 23, 1863, National Archives, reprinted in Barnickel, *Milliken's Bend*, 208.

94. Quoted in *ibid.*, 77.

95. USG to Lorenzo Thomas, July 11, 1863, USGP, vol. 9, 23–24; USGP, vol. 9, 26.

96. Barnickel, *Milliken's Bend*, 75–76.

97. USGP, vol. 9, 26; General Orders 107, June 14, 1863, and General Orders 108, June 17, 1863, Record Group 393, Department of the Tennessee, National Archives; for a summary of the inquiry, see Ballard, *Grant at Vicksburg*, 70–73.

98. USGP, vol. 9, 27.

99. Cadwallader, *Three Years with Grant*, 92–93; OR, I/24, part 1, 162–64.

100. USG to McClernand, June 17, 1863, USGP, vol. 8, 384–85.

101. OR, I/24, part 1, 162.

102. USGP, vol. 8, 385.

103. Dana to Stanton, June 19, 1863, USGP, vol. 8, 386.

104. USGM, 367; Grant to Halleck, June 19, 1863, USGP, vol. 8, 385.

105. James Wilson, "Draft of John Rawlins Biography," 93–94, LC.

106. Wilson, *Under the Old Flag*, vol. 1, 182–83.

107. *Ibid.*, 185–86; OR, I/24, part 1, 103.

108. McClernand to Lincoln, June 30, 1863, OR, I/35, part 1, 167–69.

109. Quoted in Kiper, *McClernand*, 273.

110. Grant letter to Dana quoted in Bernarr Cresap, *Appomattox Commander: The Story of General E. O. C. Ord* (San Diego; A.S. Barnes, 1981), 100.

111. USGM, 368.

112. NYT, June 21, 1863. I have tried but failed to ascertain with certainty if the black laborers were former slaves from Davis Bend.

113. Grant had Brigadier General Jacob Lauman place his recently arrived division on the Halls Ferry Road, along the river, cutting off all approaches to Vicksburg in that direction. USG to Jacob Lauman, May 28, 1863, USGP, vol. 8, 282.

114. Quoted in Catton, *Grant Moves South*, 457.

115. USG to Jesse Root Grant, June 15, 1863, USGP, vol. 8, 375–76.

116. USG to JDG, June 15, 1863, *ibid.*, 376–77.

117. Johnston to Pemberton, June 22, 1863, OR, I/24, part 3, 971–72.

118. USG to Porter, June 21, 1863, USGP, vol. 8, 398–99.

119. Porter to Grant, May 21, 1863, USGP, vol. 8, 399.

120. OR, I/24, part 1, 104; *ibid.*, part 2, 179. Union soldiers confusingly called the Third Louisiana Redan Fort Hill because of the commanding bluff upon which it stood. The actual Fort Hill anchored the northern end of the rebel defensive line.

121. William A. Lorimer, "Memoir," June 1914, VNMP.

122. CT, June 27, 1863.

123. OR, I/24, part 2, 371; Hickenlooper, "Personal Reminiscences," Hickenlooper Papers,

folder 3, 142–43, Cincinnati Museum Center. On the night of June 18, when the sappers were within forty yards of the redan, the second sap-roller was set afire and replaced by a third roller. Hickenlooper, "Vicksburg Mine," 540.

124. Lockett, "The Defense of Vicksburg," BL, vol. 3, 491; Hickenlooper, "Personal Reminiscences," folder 3, 146, Cincinnati Museum Center.

125. OR, I/24, part 2, 201–02, 207, 333, 368; Hickenlooper, "Personal Reminiscences," folder 3, 146, Cincinnati Museum Center; OR, I/24, part 2, 202.

126. Quoted in Solonick, *Engineering Victory*, 179.

127. Hickenlooper, "Vicksburg Mine," 542.

128. OR, I/24, part 3, 440.

129. Strong, "Campaign Against Vicksburg," 339–41; Blanchard, *I Marched with Sherman*, 10.

130. Crummer, *With Grant*, 138–39.

131. OR, I/24, part 2, 207.

132. Woodworth, *Nothing But Victory*, 443.

133. Logan, *31st Regiment Illinois Volunteers*, 734.

134. Quoted in Woodworth, *Nothing But Victory*, 443.

135. OR, I/24, part 2, 207–09.

136. *Ibid.*, 294.

137. Strong, "Campaign Against Vicksburg," 324, 342; USGP, vol. 8, 421.

138. OR, I/24, part 2, 294–95, 373; Bearss, *Campaign for Vicksburg*, vol. 3, 925.

139. Hoge, *Boys in Blue*, 295. For a Union nurse's experience on the siege line, see Kathleen S. Hanson, "Down to Vicksburg; The Nurses' Experience," *Journal of the Illinois State Historical Society* 97, no. 4 (May 2005): 289. Hanson focuses on the experiences of Louisa Maetz, a Quincy, Illinois, volunteer who worked two months, beginning at Chickasaw Bayou, in one of Sherman's field hospitals.

140. Hoge, *Boys in Blue*, 295.

141. CT, June 25, 1863.

142. NYT, June 22, 1863.

143. Tunnard, *Third Louisiana Infantry*, 266–67; Dr. John L. Margreiter, "Anesthesia in the Civil War," *Civil War Times Illustrated* 6, no. 2 (May 1967): 2.

144. Alison Diary, SHC; "nerves" in Foster, *Vicksburg*, 33.

145. Hickenlooper, "Personal Reminiscences," folder 2, 150–51.

146. Kellogg, *Story of the Vicksburg Campaign*, 50.

147. OR, I/24, part 1, 175.

148. Foster, *Vicksburg*, 48–49.

149. Jones, "The Rank and File at Vicksburg," 25.

150. WTS to EES, June 11, 1863, SCW, 478.

151. Gregory, "Vicksburg during the Siege," 120.

152. CT, July 7, 1863.

153. Abrams, *History of the Siege*, 41.

154. Foster, *Vicksburg*, 35.

155. *Ibid.*, 35.

156. Jones, "The Rank and File at Vicksburg," 26.

157. CT, June 25, 1863.

158. Newsome, *Experience in the War of the Great Rebellion*, 53.

159. Samuel C. Kirkpatrick to James Kirkpatrick, Kirkpatrick Collection, WHMC, 104.

160. Foster, *Vicksburg*, 50.

161. *Ibid.*, 55.

162. Drennan to Wife, July 3, 1863, Drennan Papers, MDAH.

163. Tunnard, *Third Louisiana Infantry*, 260.

164. WTS to EES, June 27, 1863, SCW, 491.

165. Foster, *Vicksburg*, 55–56.

166. *Ibid.*, 57.

167. Drennan to Wife, July 3, 1863, Drennan Papers, MDAH.

TWENTY-THREE. "IT IS GREAT, MR. WELLES."

1. Abraham Lincoln quoted in Welles, *Diary*, vol. 1, 364.

2. Lincoln to USG, July 13, 1863, USGP, vol. 9, 197.

3. OR, I/24, part 3, 1000; *ibid.*, part 1, 285–88; *ibid.*, part 2, 424.

4. Jones, "Rank and File at Vicksburg," 29.

5. OR, I/24, part 1, 286.

6. Greene, *Mississippi*, 171.

7. OR, I/24, part 3, 982–83.

8. *Ibid.*, 283–88; OR, I/24, part 2, 347–49, 374.

9. Pemberton to USG, July 3, 1863, USGP, vol. 8, 455.

10. USG to Pemberton, July 3, 1863, *ibid.*

11. USGM, 172.

12. A. M. Brinkerhoff Diary, VNMP.

13. OR I/24, part 1, 284.

14. John C. Pemberton, "The Terms of Surrender," in BL, vol. 3, 544.

15. USGM, 376.

16. Jared Young Sanders II Diary, VNMP.

17. USGM, 376.

18. USG to Porter, July 3, 1863, OR, I/24, part 3, 460; USG to Halleck, July 4, 1863, USGP, vol. 8, 469.

19. Ballard, *Vicksburg*, 403.

20. USGM, 376–77.

21. OR, I/24, part 3, 460.

22. OR, I/24, part 1, 330–31.

23. Quoted in Lockett, "Defense of Vicksburg," 492.

24. OR, I/24, part 1, 284–85.

25. *Ibid.*

26. Jared Young Sanders Diary, VNMP.

27. USGM, 375.

28. *Ibid.*, 379.

29. Gregory, "Vicksburg during the Siege," 13.

30. Newsome, *Experience in the War of the Great Rebellion*, 77.

31. W. L. Faulk Diary, VNMP.

32. WTS to USG, July 3, 1863, USGP, vol. 8, 461.

33. USG to WTS, July 4, 1863, USGP, vol. 8, 479.

34. WTS to USG, July 4, 1863, USGP, vol. 8, 478.

35. Wilson, *Under the Old Flag*, vol. 1, 222–23; Frederick Grant, "A Boy's Experience at Vicksburg," 99.

36. Lord, "Woman's Experience," 927.

37. Jackson, ed., "Some of the Boys," 112.

38. M. D. Gage, *From Vicksburg to Raleigh* (Chicago: Clarke & Co., 1865), 88.

39. Quoted in Walker, *Vicksburg*, 203.

40. William Winters to Wife, July 6, 1863, William Winters, *The Musick of the Mockingbirds, the Roar of the Cannon: The Diary and Letters of William Winters*, Steven E. Woodworth, ed. (Lincoln: University of Nebraska Press, 1998), 64; CT, August 10, 1863.

41. Blanchard, *I Marched with Sherman*, 106.

42. Jackson, ed., "Some of the Boys," 112.

43. Blanchard, *I Marched with Sherman*, 106.

44. Benjamin Franklin McIntyre Diaries, 1862–1864, Duke.

45. Abrams, *History of the Siege*, 63–64.

46. W. T. Clark to Sanborn, January 1, 1886, VNMP.

47. Porter, *Incidents and Anecdotes*, 201.

48. ORN, I/25, 103, 238.

49. Welles, *Diary*, vol. 1, 364.

50. USG to Halleck, July 4, 1863, USGP, vol. 8, 469.

51. *National Republican*, July 8, 1863.

52. Welles, *Diary*, vol. 1, 365.

53. CT, July 11, 1863.

54. Welles, *Diary*, vol. 1, 365.

55. Emeline Ritner to Jacob F. Ritner, July 10, 1863, in Larimer, ed., *Love and Valor*, 198–99.

56. Lincoln to USG, July 13, 1863, USGP, vol. 9, 197.

57. Halleck to USG, August 1, 1863, USGP, vol. 8, 523.

58. Frank L. Byrne and Jean Powers Soman, eds., *Your True Marcus: The Civil War Letters of a Jewish Colonel* (Kent, OH: The Kent State University Press, 1985), 300.

59. James Wilson, "Draft of John Rawlins Biography," 103, LC.

60. WTS to EES, June 2, 1863, SCW, 477.

61. Cathal J. Nolan, *The Allure of Battle: A History of How Wars Have Been Won and Lost* (New York: Oxford University Press, 2017), 579.

62. See Appendix.

63. WTSM, 359; Bearss, *Campaign for Vicksburg*, vol. 3, 1321.

64. Catton, *Grant Moves South*, 487; he had previously been major general of volunteers.

65. Bearss, *Unvexed to the Sea*, 1273.

66. USGM, 385–86.

67. Bearss, *Campaign for Vicksburg*, vol. 3, 1273.

68. Lawrence Lee Hewitt, *Port Hudson, Confederate Bastion on the Mississippi* (Baton Rouge, Louisiana State University Press, 1987), 173–79; Edward Cunningham, *The Port*

Hudson Campaign, 1862–1863 (Baton Rouge: Louisiana State University Press, 1963), 117–18.

69. Bearss, *Campaign for Vicksburg*, vol. 3, 1313.

70. Lincoln to Conkling, August 26, 1863, Papers of Abraham Lincoln, LC.

71. ORN, I/25, 109–10.

72. Guelzo, *Gettysburg*, 465.

73. Frank E. Vandiver, ed., *The Civil War Diary of General Josiah Gorgas* (Tuscaloosa: University of Alabama Press, 1947), 55.

74. All quotes in Gary W. Gallagher, "Lee's Army Has Not Lost Any of Its Prestige," in Gary Gallagher, ed., *Third Day at Gettysburg and Beyond* (Chapel Hill: University of North Carolina Press, 1998), 1–24.

75. Edward S. Gregory, "Vicksburg during the Siege," 133.

76. Fuller, *Generalship of Grant*, 158.

77. Catton, *Grant Moves South*, 462.

78. Quoted in Russell F. Weigley, *The American Way of War: A History of United States Military Strategy and Policy* (New York: Macmillan Publishing Co., 1973), 148.

79. *Ibid.*, 139.

80. WTS to Henry Halleck, September 17, 1863, SCW, 544.

81. WTS to David Stuart, August 1, 1863, SCW, 512.

82. Weigley, *American Way of War*, 128.

83. Adam Badeau, *Military History of Ulysses S. Grant*, vol. 3 (New York: Appleton and Co., 1885), 643.

84. *Preliminary Report Touching the Condition and Management of Emancipated Refugees; Made to the Secretary of War by the African Freedman's Inquiry Commission, June 30, 1863* (New York: John F. Trow, 1863), 36–38; Berlin, et. al, eds., *Destruction of Slavery*, 647. Col. John Eaton, head of contraband camps in Grant's military district, estimated nearly 114,000 freed people were under his jurisdiction by July 1864. Most of them had been freed in 1863 by military operations. Of that number, 41,000 were employed by the Union army as soldiers or laborers. Eaton, *Lincoln and the Freedmen*, 133–34; Berlin, et al., eds., *Wartime Genesis of Free Labor*, 647.

85. WTS to EES, July 5, 1863, SCW, 500.

86. Mary Elizabeth Mitchell Journal, SHC.

87. Janet Sharp Hermann, *Joseph E. Davis: Pioneer Patriarch* (Jackson: University Press of Mississippi, 2007), 1–133; James T. Currie, *Enclave Vicksburg and Her Plantations, 1863–1870* (Jackson: University Press of Mississippi, 1980), 118; see also Janet Sharp Hermann, *The Pursuit of a Dream* (New York: Oxford University Press, 1981); Louis S. Gerteis, *From Contraband to Freedman; Federal Policy Toward Southern Blacks, 1861–1865* (Westport, CT: Greenwood Press, 1973).

88. John Eaton, *Report of the General Superintendent of Freedmen, Department of the Tennessee and State of Arkansas for 1864* (Memphis: U.S. Government, 1865), 39; NYT, April 15, 1865; Frederick Douglass, "U.S. Grant and the Colored People," *Elevator*, vol. 8, no. 20 (August 28, 1872), 1–4.

89. Stephen J. Ross, "Freed Soil, Freed Labor, Freed Men: John Eaton and the Davis Bend Experiment, *Journal of Southern History* 44 (May 1978): 216.

90. *Ibid.*, 219, 224.

91. Trowbridge, *Desolate South*, 384.

92. Ross, "Freed Soil, Freed Labor," 227; LaWanda Cox, "The Promise of Land for the Freedmen," *Mississippi Valley Historical Review* 45 (December 1958): 413–40.

93. Ross, "Freed Soil, Freed Men," 229.

94. Eric Foner, *Reconstruction: America's Unfinished Revolution, 1863–1877* (New York: Harper & Row, 1989 edition), 58. By the end of the Andrew Johnson administration, half the land in the South controlled by the Freedmen's Bureau had been returned to its former owners, Foner points out, "and more was returned in later years." *Ibid.*

95. Foner, *Reconstruction*, 58.

96. Quoted in Walker, *Vicksburg*, 213.

97. William D. Butler, Report to W. G. Eliot, U.S. Christian Commission, "Conditions of Negroes at Vicksburg," September 1, 1863, William D. Butler Papers, Missouri Historical Society.

98. *Statistics of the Operation of the Executive Board of the Friends Association of Philadelphia . . . For the Relief of Colored Freedmen* (Philadelphia: Inquirer Printing Office, 864), 1; CT, November 6, 1863.

99. USG to Lorenzo Thomas, July 11, 1863, USGP, vol. 9, 23.

100. Lincoln to USG, August 9, 1863, USGP, vol. 9, 197.

101. USG to Lincoln, August 23, 1863, USGP, vol. 9, 196.

102. USG to Elihu B. Washburne, August 30, 1863, USGP, vol. 9, 218.

103. Wittenmyer, *Under the Guns*, 176, 178–79.

104. Kate D. Foster Diary, July 28, 30, 1863, Duke.

105. OR, I/24, part 3, 479, 483–84, 502; Logan to Rawlins, July 7, USGP, vol. 9, 3–4; USG to McPherson, July 7, 1863, *ibid.*, 3.

106. OR, I/24, part 3, 484; Ballard, *Pemberton*, 181–82.

107. Moss, *Diary*, 55.

108. Byers, "Some Recollections of Grant," 351.

109. Gregory, "Vicksburg during the Siege," 15.

110. Ballard, *Vicksburg*, 412–13. Pemberton is buried in Philadelphia's Laurel Hill Cemetery; his voluminous papers reside at the Southern Historical Collection, the Library of the University of North Carolina at Chapel Hill.

111. Quoted in Ballard, *Pemberton*, 181.

112. Gorgas, *Civil War Diary*, 50. In July 1863, Davis removed Johnston as commander of the Department of the West and reduced his area of responsibility to Mississippi, southern Alabama, and a thin slice of western Tennessee.

113. Jerome M. Loving, ed., *Civil War Letters of George Washington Whitman* (Durham: Duke University Press, 1975), 97. Whitman's regiment arrived at Milliken's Bend on June 13, 1863.

114. Seth A. Ranlett, "The Capture of Jackson," *Civil War Papers Read Before the Commandery of the State of Massachusetts*, MOLLUS, vol. 1 (Boston: The Commandery, 1900), 253.

115. Quoted in Ballard, *Vicksburg*, 406.

116. WTSM, 356.

117. William Taylor to Jane, July 11, 18, 1863, 100th Pennsylvania file, VNMP.

118. Loving, ed., *Civil War Letters of George Washington Whitman*, 99.

119. WTS to Rawlins, July 11, 1863, USGP, vol. 9, 36.

120. WTS to Porter, July 19, 1863, SCW, 504.

121. CT, August 10, 1863.

122. Catton, *Grant Moves South*, 483.

123. Diary of George Washington Whitman, September 1861 to September 6, 1863, Charles E. Feinberg Collection of the Papers of Walt Whitman, 1839–1919, LC; Gage, *From Vicksburg to Raleigh*, 93–94; WTS to Rawlins, August 4, 1863, SCW, 518–19.

124. USGM, 388.

125. Gage, *From Vicksburg to Raleigh*, 94.

126. OR, I/24, part 3, 531. The army suffered a little over eleven hundred casualties.

127. WTS to Philemon B. Ewing, July 28, 1863, SCW, 508.

128. WTS to USG, July 18, 1863, USGP, vol. 9, 72.

129. CT, October 22, 1863.

130. Butterworth, *Confederate Mississippi*, 205.

131. WTSM, 357.

132. August began the sickness season in Mississippi, and early that October the Shermans lost their nine-year-old son, Willie, to typhoid fever. He was his father's favorite, and Sherman blamed himself for bringing him into that "fatal climate." WTSM, 374–75.

133. CT, September 10, 1863.

134. *Chicago Times*, July 27, 1863.

135. OR, I/24, part 2, 531; USG to Stephen A. Hurlbut, August 4, 1863, USGP, vol. 9, 130.

136. Sherman quoted in Cadwallader, *Three Years with Grant*, 124.

137. Cadwallader, *Three Years with Grant*, 126–27.

138. *Ibid.*, 128.

139. CT, September 22, 1863; see also Bradley R. Clampitt, *Occupied Vicksburg* (Baton Rouge: Louisiana State University Press, 2016), 199–209.

140. Edwin H. Fay, *"This Infernal War": The Confederate Letters of Sgt. Edwin H. Fay*, Bell Irvin Wiley, ed. (Austin: University of Texas Press, 1958), 290–92.

141. USGM, 389–90.

142. WTS to James W. Tuttle, August 20, 1863, SCW, 525; WTS to Henry Halleck, September 17, 1863, SCW, 544–45; SCW, 499.

143. WTS to Frederick A. P. Bernard, September 4, 1863, SCW, 533.

144. WTS to EES, July 5, 15, 1863, SCW, 499, 503.

EPILOGUE

1. Morgan, *Diary*, 606.

2. Matilda Champion to Sid Champion, July 10, 1863, Duke.

3. Drake and Bearss, eds., *My Dear Wife*, 2, 106; Drake, "Five Generations of Sid Champions," http://battleofchampionhill.org/history/five-champions.htm.

4. All preceding quotes in Mary Elizabeth Mitchell Journal, SHC, 49–52, 69.

BIBLIOGRAPHY

MANUSCRIPT COLLECTIONS

Abraham Lincoln Presidential Library, Springfield, Illinois (formerly known as the Illinois State Historical Library, Springfield, Illinois)
John W. Boyd Papers
Sylvanus Cadwallader, unpublished mss.
David Cornwell Papers
John C. Dinsmore Papers
George Ditto Diary
Lovicy Ann Eberhart Papers
William R. Eddington Papers
Engelmann-Kircher Family Papers
Joseph Forrest Papers
John G. Given Papers
Ulysses S. Grant Papers
Benjamin Henry Grierson Papers
John A. Griffin Papers
E. H. Ingraham Letters
Joshua E. Jackson Diary
Robert T. Lincoln Manuscripts
John Alexander McClernand Collection
Lewis B. Parsons Papers
John Rawlins Papers
Wallace-Dickey Papers

Bentley Library, University of Michigan, Ann Arbor, Michigan
Calvin Ainsworth Diary
Ferry Family Papers

Briscoe Center for American History, the University of Texas at Austin
Joseph Emory Davis Papers

Chicago History Museum, Chicago, Illinois (formerly known as the Chicago Historical Society)
Albert Holmes Boardman Diary

William L. Brown Letters
Chicago Board of Trade Collection
Chicago Daily Journal File
Chicago Tribune File
Chicago Times File
Civil War Round Table of Chicago File
Jesse Root Grant Papers
Ulysses S. Grant Papers
John A. Rawlins Papers
William E. Strong Papers

Cincinnati Museum, Cincinnati, Ohio
Andrew Hickenlooper Collection, including his "Personal Reminiscences"

Davidson Library, the University of California, Santa Barbara, California
Isaac F. Shepard Papers

Doheny Memorial Library, University of Southern California, Los Angeles, California
Hamlin Garland Papers

Hill Memorial Library, Louisiana State University, Baton Rouge, Louisiana
Thomas Affleck Papers
Charles B. Allaire Papers
Henry Watkins Allen Papers
Albert A. Batchelor Papers
Gustave Toutant Beauregard Papers
James B. Cable Papers
Rowland Chambers Diaries
William Y. Dixon Diary
Stephen Duncan Papers
Eggleston-Roach Papers
G. W. Giles Papers
Wayne Jacobs Diary
Henry D. Mandeville and Family Papers
Honore P. Morancy Family Papers
Jared Sanders Diary
William T. Sherman Papers
William H. Smith Letters
Micajah Wilkinson Papers

Historic New Orleans Collection, New Orleans, Louisiana
William Lovelace Foster Letters

Historical Manuscript Collection, Columbia, Missouri
Henry Kuck Letters

Historical Society of Pennsylvania, Philadelphia, Pennsylvania
John B. Pemberton Papers

Historical Society of Richmond, Virginia
William B. Brooks Diary

Howard-Tilton Memorial Library, Tulane University, New Orleans, Louisiana
Braxton Bragg, "General Albert Sidney Johnston and the Battle of Pittsburg Landing"
Jefferson Davis Papers
Albert Sidney and William Preston Johnston Papers
Medical Records, Civil War
Wade Family Papers

Huntington Library, San Marino, California
Ulysses S. Grant Collection
Henry Wager Halleck Papers
Rush Nutt Collection
David Dixon Porter Papers
William T. Sherman Papers

Indiana Historical Society, Indianapolis, Indiana
John H. Ferree Papers
John F. Lester Papers
Asa E. Sample Papers
Joseph Willis Young Papers

Library of Congress, Manuscript Division, Washington, D.C.
Sylvanus Cadwallader Papers
Samuel Wylie Crawford Papers
Ulysses S. Grant, "Headquarters Records" and manuscript of "Personal Memoirs"
Abraham Lincoln Collection
John A. Logan Papers
George B. McClellan Papers
David Dixon Porter Papers
John Sherman Papers
William Tecumseh Sherman Papers
Elihu B. Washburne Papers
Water Transportation File
Gideon Welles Papers
James Harrison Wilson Papers
Annie Wittenmyer Papers, 1862–1866

Mississippi Department of Archives and History, Jackson, Mississippi
Joseph Dill Alison Diary
Charles B. Allen Plantation Book
Emma Balfour Diary
Bisland/Shields Family Papers
Boddie Family Papers
William Pitt Chambers Collection
Sidney S. Champion Collection
Crutcher-Shannon Family Papers
Jefferson Davis and Family Papers
William A. Drennan Papers
John J. Pettus Papers
Returns for Presidential Electors, 1860, series F, vol. 85
William Rigby Papers
Ida Barlow Trotter Papers
Vicksburg Gambler File
Amanda Worthington Diary

Missouri Historical Society Archives, St. Louis, Missouri
John T. Appler Diary
John A. Blackwell Papers
Frank and Montgomery Blair Papers
William D. Butler Papers
E. L. Corthell File
Warren D. Crandall Papers
James Buchanan Eads Papers
William Eliot Papers
Thomas Ewing Jr. Papers
Marcus Faust Papers
Gustavus Vasa Fox Collection
John C. Frémont Collection
Joseph E. Johnston File
James G. Kirkpatrick Collection
Samuel Cotter Kirkpatrick Papers
Henry Kuck Letters
Emilie McKinley Diary
David Dixon Porter Papers
Saint Louis Sanitation Collection

National Archives, College Park, Maryland
Confederate Record Series, John C. Pemberton Official Civil War Papers and
    Correspondence
Record Group 393, Department of the Army of the Tennessee

New York Public Library, New York, New York
Bartholomew Diggins, "Recollections of the Cruise of the U.S.S. Hartford."

Ohio Historical Society, Columbus, Ohio
John Easton Papers
Townsend Heaton Papers
William Murphy Letters

Old Courthouse Museum, Vicksburg, Mississippi
George R. Buck Papers
Andrew Bush Letters
C.S.S. *Arkansas* File
Cemetery Association—Confederate File
Civil War Incidents in Vicksburg, Clippings Scrapbook
Deaths in the Court House During the Siege File
Funeral Records, May–July, 1863
A General Directory for the City of Vicksburg, 1860
Edward Gregory Clippings
118th Illinois File
R. R. Hall Diary
Ralph C. Mason, "Military Relief Records, Warren County, 1862–1863"
Dora Miller Diary
Dabney Maury Scales Papers
Jared Sanders Diary
Slave Schedules, 1860, for Warren County
George Smith Papers
Silas Trowbridge Autobiography
United States Census, *Population Schedules for Warren County, 1860*
Vicksburg Cemetery File

Princeton University, Princeton, New Jersey
Mary A. Livermore Collection

Southern Historical Collection, the Louis Round Wilson Library, Special Collections, the University of North Carolina at Chapel Hill
Samuel Agnew Diary
James Lusk Alcorn Papers
Edward Porter Alexander Papers
Joseph Dill Alison Diary
Margret E. Blackwell Papers
George Hovey Cadman Papers
John Henry Comstock Papers
Annie Laurie Harris, "A Recollection of Thirty Years Ago"
Hughes Family Papers
Louis Hebert Autobiography

Stephen Dill Lee Papers
Samuel Henry Lockett Papers
Matthew N. Love Papers
Letitia D. Miller Collection
Mary Elizabeth Mitchell Journal
John Clifford Pemberton Papers
John Perkins Papers
Quitman Family Papers
Mahala P. H. Roach Diary
Roach and Eggleston Family Papers
Andrew J. Sproul Papers
Private Journal of Sarah L. Wadley
Samuel Addison Whyte Papers
Adoniram Judson Withrow Papers
Amanda Worthington Diary

**Ulysses S. Grant Presidential Library at Mississippi
State University, Starkville, Mississippi**
Ulysses S. Grant Papers
Julia Grant Scrapbook

United States Army Military History Institute, Carlisle Barracks, Pennsylvania
John Bates Diary
George Oliver Boucher Papers
George H. Chatfield Papers
Thomas B. Douglas Papers
W. R. Eddington Papers
Harrisburg Civil War Round Table Collection
Richard M. Hunt Papers
William McGlothlin Papers
Miscellaneous Collection
Henry T. Morgan Papers
Israel M. Ritter Diary
W. R. Rorer Letters
Joseph W. Westbrook Papers
William Woodward Papers

University of Iowa Libraries, Special Collections, Iowa City, Iowa
Charles Cady Papers
Robert W. Henry Papers
William T. Rigby Papers
Seneca Thrall Papers

The University of Notre Dame Archives, South Bend, Indiana
William T. Sherman Family Papers

Vicksburg National Military Park, Vicksburg, Mississippi

George Oliver Boucher Papers
A. M. Brinkerhoff Diary
W. T. Clark File
F. W. Curtenius Diary
W. L. Faulk Diary
William Lovelace Foster File
W. W. Gardner File
Charles A. Hobbs Diary and Letters
William H. Jolly File
Stephen D. Lee File
Joseph Leslie Letters
William W. Lord Papers
William A. Lorimer, "Memoir"
Simeon R. Martin, "Chickasaw Bayou"
Theodosia F. McKinstry, "My Days of Danger in Vicksburg"
Mortar Files
William Murray Diary
H. T. Norman, Report
J. D. Pearson File
W. T. Ratliff Letters
Regimental files from the following states:
Alabama, Arkansas, Georgia, Illinois, Indiana, Iowa, Louisiana, Michigan, Minnesota, Mississippi, Missouri, Ohio, Pennsylvania, Tennessee, Texas, U.S. Infantry, 13th, Virginia, and Wisconsin
E. Paul Reichhelm Diary
William T. Rigby Files
Jared Young Sanders II Diary
Henry Seaman Diary
William Taylor File
H. M. Trimble Diary
Charles Wood Diary

Virginia Historical Society, Richmond, Virginia

William B. Brooks Diary

William R. Perkins Library, Manuscript Division, Duke University, Durham, North Carolina

Sidney S. Champion Papers
Jefferson Davis Papers
Kate Foster Diary
Duff Green Papers
Theophilus Hunter Holmes Papers
James Mason Papers
Benjamin Franklin McIntyre Diaries, 1862–1864

James Birdseye McPherson Papers, 1863
Thomas Sewell Papers
Charles Brown Tompkins Papers
Elihu Benjamin Washburne Papers
James M. Willcox Papers

J. D. Williams Library, University of Mississippi, Oxford, Mississippi
Joseph E. Davis Collection

Wisconsin Historical Society Archives, Madison, Wisconsin
Henry Clemons Letters
David G. James Papers
Henry P. Strong Papers

Winter Quarters State Historic Site, Tensas Parish, Louisiana
Haller Nutt Papers
Rush Nutt Collection

Newspapers and Journals
Army and Navy Journal
Baltimore Sun
Cairo Daily Gazette
Chicago Tribune (CT)
Chicago Times Herald
Cincinnati Commercial
Cincinnati Gazette
Frank Leslie's Illustrated Weekly
Harper's Magazine
Harper's Weekly
Jackson Semi-Weekly Mississippian
Jackson Daily News
McClure's Magazine
Midland Monthly Magazine
Mississippi State Journal
Nashville Banner
National Intelligencer
New Orleans Daily Picayune
New York Herald
New York Ledger
New York Post
New York Sun
New York Times (NYT)
New York Tribune
New York World
North American Review

Richmond Dispatch
Springfield Republican
St. Louis Daily Globe Democat
Southern Illustrated News
Times (London)
Vicksburg Daily Citizen
Vicksburg Daily Courier
Vicksburg Daily Times
Vicksburg Daily Whig
Vicksburg Evening Citizen
Vicksburg Weekly Whig

BOOKS, PUBLISHED MEMOIRS, DIARIES, AND LETTERS

Abrams, Alexander S. *A Full and Detailed History of the Siege of Vicksburg.* Atlanta: Intelligencer Steam Power Press, 1863.

Adams, George Worthington. *Doctors in Blue: The Medical History of the Union Army in the Civil War.* New York: Henry Schuman, 1952.

Agassiz. George R., ed. *Meade's Headquarters, 1863–1865: Letters of Colonel Theodore Lyman from the Wilderness to Appomattox.* Boston: Atlantic Monthly Press, 1922.

Ambrose, Daniel Leib. *History of the Seventh Regiment Illinois Volunteer Infantry.* Springfield: Illinois Journal Co., 1868.

Ambrose, Stephen E. *Halleck: Lincoln's Chief of Staff.* Baton Rouge: Louisiana State University Press, 1962.

Anderson, Ephraim McDowell. *Memoirs: Historical and Personal Including the Campaigns of the First Missouri Confederate Brigade.* St. Louis: Times Publishing Co., 1868.

Andrews, J. Cutler. *The North Reports the Civil War.* Pittsburgh: University of Pittsburgh Press, 1955.

Ankeny, Henry G. *Kiss Josey for Me,* edited by Florence Marie Ankeny Cox. Santa Ana, CA: Friis-Pioneer Press, 1974.

Arnold, James R. *Grant Wins the War: Decision at Vicksburg.* New York: John Wiley & Sons, 1997.

Ash, Stephen V. *When the Yankees Came: Conflict and Chaos in the Occupied South, 1861–1865.* Chapel Hill: University of North Carolina Press, 2006.

Audubon, John James. *Delineations of American Scenery and Character.* New York: G.A. Baker & Company, 1926.

Bacon, Edward. *Among the Cotton Thieves.* Detroit: The Free Press Stream Book Center and Job Printing House, 1867.

Badeau, Adam. *Military History of Ulysses S. Grant, from April 1861 to April 1865,* 3 vols. New York: D. Appleton, 1868–81.

Baily, Francis. *Journal of a Tour in Unsettled Parts of North America, in 1796 & 1797.* London: Baily Bros., 1856.

Ballard, Michael B. *Grant at Vicksburg: The General and the Siege.* Carbondale: Southern Illinois University Press, 2013.

————. *Pemberton: A Biography.* Jackson: University Press of Mississippi, 1991.

————. *Vicksburg: The Campaign that Opened the Mississippi.* Chapel Hill: The University of North Carolina Press, 2004.

Baptist, Edward E. *The Half Has Never Been Told: Slavery and the Making of American Capitalism.* New York: Basic Books, 2014.

Barber, James. *U. S. Grant: The Man and the Image, with an Essay by John Y. Simon.* Washington, D.C.: National Portrait Gallery, Smithsonian Institution; Carbondale: in association with Southern Illinois University Press, 1985.

Barber, Lucius W. *Army Memoirs of Lucius W. Barber, Company "D," 15th Illinois Volunteer Infantry.* Chicago: J. M. W. Jones Stationery & Printing Co., 1894.

Barney, William L. *The Secessionist Impulse: Alabama and Mississippi in 1860.* Princeton, NJ: Princeton University Press, 1974.

Barnickel, Linda. *Milliken's Bend: A Civil War Battle in History and Memory.* Baton Rouge: Louisiana State University Press, 2013.

Barton, Michael, and Larry M. Logue. *The Civil War Soldier: A Historical Reader.* New York: New York University Press, 2002.

Basler, Roy P., ed. *The Collected Works of Abraham Lincoln,* vols. 4–6. New Brunswick, NJ: Rutgers University Press, 1953.

Bastian, David F. *Grant's Canal: The Union's Attempt to Bypass Vicksburg.* Shippensburg, PA: Burd Street Press, 1995.

Bates, Edward. *The Diary of Edward Bates, 1859–1866,* vol. 4. Edited by Howard K. Beale. Washington, D.C.: U.S. Printing Office, 1933.

Bearss, Edwin Cole. *The Campaign for Vicksburg,* vol. 1, *Vicksburg Is the Key.* Dayton, OH: Morningside Press, 1985.

————. *The Campaign for Vicksburg,* vol. 2, *Grant Strikes a Fatal Blow.* Dayton, OH: Morningside Press, 1986.

————. *The Campaign for Vicksburg,* vol. 3, *Unvexed to the Sea.*

————. *Rebel Victory at Vicksburg.* Vicksburg: Vicksburg Centennial Commemoration Commission, 1963.

Beck, Stephen C. *A True Sketch of His Army Life.* Edgar, NE: n.p., 1914.

Beckert, Sven. *Empire of Cotton: A Global History.* New York: Alfred A. Knopf, 2014.

Belknap, William W. *History of the Fifteenth Regiment, Iowa Veteran Infantry.* Keokuk, IA: R.B. Ogden & Son, 1887.

Bell, Andrew McIlwaine. *Mosquito Soldiers: Malaria, Yellow Fever, and the Course of the American Civil War.* Baton Rouge: Louisiana State University Press, 2010.

Benedict, G. G. *Vermont in the Civil War,* vol. 2. Burlington, VT: The Free Press Association, 1888.

Bercaw, Nancy. *Gendered Freedoms: Race, Rights, and the Politics of Household in the Delta, 1861–1875.* Gainesville: University of Florida Press, 2003.

Bering, John A., and Thomas Montgomery. *History of the Forty-Eighth Ohio Vet. Vol. Inf.* Hillsboro, OH: Highland News Office, 1880.

Beringer, Richard E., Herman Hattaway, Archer Jones, and William N. Still Jr. *Why the South Lost the Civil War.* Athens: University of Georgia Press, 1986.

Berkin, Carol. *Civil War Wives: The Lives and Times of Angelina Grimke Weld, Varina Howell Davis and Julia Dent Grant.* New York: Alfred A. Knopf, 2009.

Berlin, Ira, et al., eds. *Freedom: A Documentary History of Emancipation, 1861–1867*, series 1, vol. 1, *The Destruction of Slavery*. New York: Cambridge University Press, 1986.

———. *Freedom: A Documentary History of Emancipation, 1861–1867*, series 1, vol. 3, *The Wartime Genesis of Free Labor: The Lower South*. New York: Cambridge University Press, 1990.

———, Joseph P. Reidy, and Leslie S. Rowland, eds. *The Black Military Experience*. New York: Cambridge University Press, 1982.

Berlin, Ira, et al. *Slaves No More: Three Essays on Emancipation and the Civil War*. New York: Cambridge University Press, 1992.

Bettersworth, John K. *Confederate Mississippi: The People and Policies of a Cotton State in Wartime*. Baton Rouge: Louisiana State University Press, 1943.

———, ed. *Mississippi in the Confederacy*. New York: Kraus Reprint Co., 1970.

Bevier, R.S. *History of the First and Second Missouri Confederate Brigades, 1861–1865*. St. Louis: Bryan, Brand & Company, 1879.

Blanchard, Ira. *With Sherman: Civil War Memoirs of the 20th Illinois Volunteer Infantry*. San Francisco: J. D. Huff and Company, 1992.

Boritt, Gabor S., ed. *Lincoln's Generals*. New York: Oxford University Press, 1995.

———, ed. *Why the Confederacy Lost*. New York: Oxford University Press, 1992.

Boyd, Cyrus F. *The Civil War Diary of Cyrus F. Boyd, Fifteenth Iowa Infantry, 1861–1863*, edited by Mildred Throne. Millwood, NY: Kraus Reprint Co., 1977.

Boynton, Charles B. *The History of the Navy during the Rebellion*, vol. 1. New York: D. Appleton and Company, 1867.

Brady, Lisa M. *War upon the Land: Military Strategy and the Transformation of Southern Landscapes during the American Civil War*. Athens: University of Georgia Press, 2012.

Brandfon, Robert L. *Cotton Kingdom: A History of the Yazoo Mississippi Delta from Reconstruction to the Twentieth Century*. Cambridge, MA: Harvard University Press, 1967.

Brands, H. W. *The Man Who Saved the Union: Ulysses Grant in War and Peace*. New York: Doubleday, 2012.

Brinton, John H. *Personal Memoirs of John H. Brinton, Civil War Surgeon, 1861–1865* (1883). Carbondale: Southern Illinois University Press, 1996.

Brown, D. Alexander. *Grierson's Raid*. Champaign: University of Illinois Press, 1954.

Browne, Junius Henri. *Four Years in Secessia: Adventures within and beyond Union Lines*. Chicago: O. D. Case and Company, 1865.

Bunting, Josiah III. *Ulysses S. Grant*. New York: Times Books/Henry Holt, 2004.

Burkhardt, George S. *Confederate Rage, Yankee Wrath: No Quarter in the Civil War*. Carbondale: Southern Illinois University Press, 2007.

Burlingame, Michael. *Abraham Lincoln: A Life*, vol. 2. Baltimore, MD: Johns Hopkins University Press, 2008.

Butler, Benjamin F., and Jesse Ames Marshall. *Private and Official Correspondence of Gen. Benjamin F. Butler, during the Period of the Civil War*, vol. 1. Norwood, MA: Plimpton Press, 1917.

Byers, S. H. M. *With Fire and Sword*. Bethesda, MD: University Publications of America, 1993.

Byrne, Frank L., and Jean Powers Soman, eds. *Your True Marcus: The Civil War Letters of a Jewish Colonel*. Kent, OH: Kent State University Press, 1985.

Cadwallader, Sylvanus. *Three Years with Grant*, edited by Benjamin Thomas. Lincoln: University of Nebraska Press, 1996.

Campbell, John Quincy Adams. *The Union Must Stand: The Civil War Diary of John Quincy Adams Campbell: Fifth Iowa Volunteer Infantry*, edited by Mark Grimsley and Todd D. Miller. Knoxville: University of Tennessee Press, 2000.

Canney, Donald L. *The Old Steam Navy: Frigates, Sloops, and Gunboats, 1815–1885*. Annapolis, MD: Naval Institute Press, 1990.

Carlson, Peter. *Junius and Albert's Adventures in the Confederacy: A Civil War Odyssey*. New York: Public Affairs, 2013.

Carpenter, Francis B. *Six Months at the White House with Abraham Lincoln: The Story of a Picture*. New York: Hurd and Houghton, 1866.

Carter, Arthur B. *The Tarnished Cavalier: Major General Earl Van Dorn, C.S.A.* Knoxville: University of Tennessee Press, 1999.

Carter, Hodding. *Lower Mississippi*. New York: Rinehart & Co., 1942.

Carter, Samuel III. *The Final Fortress: The Campaign for Vicksburg, 1862–1863*. New York: St. Martin's Press, 1980.

Catton, Bruce. *Grant Moves South*. Boston: Little, Brown and Company, 1960.

———. *This Hallowed Ground: A History of the Civil War*. New York: Vintage, 2012.

———. *U. S. Grant and the American Military Tradition*. Boston: Little, Brown and Company, 1954.

Cavins, Matilda Livingston Cavins, ed. *War Letters of Aden G. Cavins*. Evansville, IN: Rosenthal-Kuebler Printing Co., 1980.

Censer, Jane Turner, ed. *The Papers of Frederick Law Olmsted*, vol. 4, *Defending the Union: The Civil War and the U.S. Sanitary Commission, 1861–1863*. Baltimore, MD: The Johns Hopkins University Press, 1986.

Chance, Joseph E. *The Second Texas Infantry: From Shiloh to Vicksburg*. Fort Worth, TX: Eakin Press, 1984.

Chase, Salmon P. *The Salmon P. Chase Papers*, vol. 1, *Journals, 1829–1872*, edited by John Niven. Kent, OH: Kent State University Press, 1993.

Chernow, Ron. *Grant*. New York: Penguin Press, 2017.

Chesnut, Mary Boykin. *Mary Chesnut's Diary* (1905). New York: Penguin Books, 2011.

Church, William Conant. *Ulysses S. Grant and the Period of National Preservation and Reconstruction*. New York: G. P. Putnam's Sons, 1897.

Claiborne, John F. H. *Life and Correspondence of John A. Quitman*, vol. 2. New York: Harper & Brothers, 1860.

Clampitt, Bradley R. *Occupied Vicksburg*. Baton Rouge: Louisiana State University Press, 2016.

Clarke, Norman E. *Warfare along the Mississippi: The Letters of Lieutenant Colonel George E. Currie*. Mount Pleasant, MI: Clarke Historical Collection, 1961.

Clinton, Catherine. *The Plantation Mistress: Woman's World in the Old South*. New York: Pantheon Books, 1982.

Coakley, Robert W. *The Role of Federal Military Forces in Domestic Disorders, 1789–1878*. Washington, D.C.: Center of Military History, 1988.

Coffin, Levi. *Reminiscences of Levi Coffin: The Reputed President of the Underground Railroad* (1876). New York: Augustus M. Kelley Reprints of Economic Classics, 1968.

Committee of the Regiment, ed. *Military History and Reminiscences of the Thirteenth Regiment of Illinois Volunteer Infantry.* Chicago: Woman's Temperance Publishing Association, 1892.

Conger, Arthur L. *The Rise of U. S. Grant* (1931). New York: Da Capo Press, 1996.

Connelly, Thomas Lawrence. *Army of the Heartland: The Army of Tennessee, 1861–1862.* Baton Rouge: Louisiana State University Press, 1967.

Coolidge, Louis A. *Ulysses S. Grant.* Boston: Houghton Mifflin, 1917.

Cooling, Benjamin Franklin. *Forts Henry and Donelson: The Key to the Confederate Heartland.* Knoxville: University of Tennessee Press, 1987.

Cooper, William J. *Jefferson Davis, American.* New York: Alfred A. Knopf, 2000.

Cornish, Dudley Taylor. *The Sable Arm: Black Troops in the Union Army, 1861–1865* (1956). Lawrence: University Press of Kansas, 1987.

Cotton, Gordon A., ed. *Vicksburg: Southern Stories of the Siege.* Vicksburg, MS: Gordon A. Cotton, 1988.

———, and Jeff T. Giambrone. *Vicksburg and the War.* Gretna, LA: Pelican Publishing Company, 2004.

Cozzens, Peter. *The Darkest Days of the War: The Battles of Iuka & Corinth.* Chapel Hill: University of North Carolina Press, 1997.

———, and Robert I. Girardi, eds. *The Military Memoirs of General John Pope.* Chapel Hill: University of North Carolina Press, 1998.

Crandall, Warren D. *History of the Ram Fleet and the Mississippi Marine Brigade on the Mississippi and Its Tributaries.* St. Louis: Buschart Brothers, 1903.

Cramer, Michael John. *Ulysses S. Grant: Conversations and Unpublished Letters.* New York: Eaton & Mains, 1897.

Cresap, Bernarr. *Appomattox Commander: The Story of General E. O. C. Ord.* San Diego: A. S. Barnes, 1981.

Crooke, George. *The Twenty-First Regiment of Iowa Volunteer Infantry: A Narrative of Its Experience in Active Service.* Milwaukee, WI: King, Fowle & Co., 1891.

Crooker, Lucien B., Henry S. Nourse, and John G. Brown. *The Story of the Fifty-Fifth Regiment Illinois Volunteer Infantry in the Civil War, 1861–1865.* Clinton, IL: W.J. Coulter, 1887.

Crozier, Emmet. *Yankee Reporters, 1861–65.* New York: Oxford University Press, 1956.

Crummer, Wilbur F. *With Grant at Fort Donelson, Shiloh and Vicksburg.* Oak Park, IL: E.C. Crummer & Co., 1915.

Cunningham, Edward. *Port Hudson Campaign, 1862–1863.* Baton Rouge: Louisiana State University Press, 1963.

Currie, James T. *Enclave: Vicksburg and Her Plantations, 1863–1870.* Jackson: University Press of Mississippi, 1980.

Dana, Charles A. *Recollections of the Civil War.* New York: Appleton, 1898.

———, and James Harrison Wilson. *The Life of Ulysses S. Grant: General of the Armies of the United States.* New York: Gurdon Bill & Co., 1868.

Daniel, Larry J. *Days of Glory: The Army of the Cumberland, 1861–1865.* Baton Rouge: Louisiana State University Press, 2004.

———. *Shiloh: The Battle that Changed the Civil War.* New York: Simon & Schuster, 1997.

Davis, Charles H. *Life of Charles Henry Davis: Rear Admiral, 1807–1877.* Boston: Houghton Mifflin, 1899.

Davis, William C. *Crucible of Command: Ulysses S. Grant and Robert E. Lee—The War They Fought, the Peace They Forged.* New York: Da Capo Press, 2014.

———. *Jefferson Davis: The Man and His Hour.* Baton Rouge: Louisiana State University Press, 1991.

———. *A Taste for War: The Culinary History of the Blue and the Gray.* Mechanicsburg, PA: Stackpole, 2003.

De Paris, Comte. *History of the Civil War in America*, vol. 3. Philadelphia: Jos. H. Coates, 1883.

DeWolfe, M.A., ed. *Home Letters of General Sherman.* New York: Charles Scribner's Sons, 1909.

Dicey, Edward. *Edward Dicey's Spectator of America*, edited by Herbert Mitgand. Chicago: Quadrangle Books, 1971. (Originally published in 1862 as *Six Months in the Federal States.*)

Dickens, Charles. *American Notes and Pictures from Italy* (1842). Oxford: Oxford University Press, 1991.

———. *Martin Chuzzlewit* (1844). New York: Alfred A. Knopf, 1994.

Dinges, Bruce J., and Shirley A. Leckie, eds. *A Just and Righteous Cause: Benjamin H. Grierson's Civil War Memoir.* Carbondale: University of Southern Illinois Press, 2008.

Dodge, Grenville. *Personal Recollections of President Abraham Lincoln, General U. S. Grant, and William T. Sherman.* Council Bluffs, IA: Monarch, 1902.

Donald, David, ed. *Inside Lincoln's Cabinet: The Civil War Diaries of Salmon P. Chase.* New York: Longmans, Green and Co., 1954.

Dorsey, Florence. *Road to the Sea: The Story of James B. Eads and the Mississippi River.* New York: Rinehart & Co., 1947.

Dorsey, Sarah Anne. *Recollections of Henry Watkins Allen, Brigadier-General Confederate States Army, Ex-Governor of Louisiana.* New York: Thompson Gale, 1866.

Downing, Alexander G. *Downing's Civil War Diary*, edited by Olynthus B. Clark. Des Moines: Iowa State Department of History and Archives, 1916.

Downs, Jim. *Sick from Freedom: African-American Illnesses and Suffering during the Civil War and Reconstruction.* New York: Oxford University Press, 2012.

Drake, Rebecca Blackwell. *In Their Own Words: Soldiers Tell the Story of the Battle of Raymond, Mississippi.* Raymond, MS: Friends of Raymond, 2001.

———, and Margie Riddle Bearss. *My Dear Wife: Letters to Matilda: The Civil War Letters of Sid and Matilda Champion of Champion Hill.* Raymond, Mississippi: privately published, 2005.

Duffy, James P. *Lincoln's Admiral: The Civil War Campaigns of David Farragut.* New York: John Wiley & Sons, 1997.

Dufour, Charles L. *The Night the War Was Lost* (1960). Lincoln: University of Nebraska Press, 1994.

Dugan, James. *History of Hurlbut's Fighting Division.* Cincinnati: Morgan & Co., 1863.

Duke, Basil W. *Personal Recollections of Shiloh, Read before the Filson Club, April 6 1914.* Louisville: Filson Club, 1914.

Duke, John K. *A History of the Fifty-Third Ohio Volunteer Infantry, during the War of the Rebellion.* Portsmouth: Blade Printing Company, 1900.

Eaton, John, and Ethel O. Mason. *Grant, Lincoln, and the Freedmen: Reminiscences of the Civil War with Special Reference for the Work of the Contrabands and Freedmen of the Mississippi Valley.* New York: Longmans, Green, 1907.

Eddy, T. M. *The Patriotism of Illinois*, vol. 1. Chicago: Clarke & Company, 1865.

Elliott, Isaac. *History of the Thirty-Third Regiment Illinois Veteran Volunteer Infantry in the Civil War.* Gibson City, IL: Regimental Association of the Thirty-Third Illinois, 1902.

Engle, Stephen D. *Struggle for the Heartland: The Campaigns from Fort Henry to Corinth.* Lincoln: University of Nebraska Press, 2001.

Etcheson, Nicole. *A Generation at War: The Civil War in a Northern Community.* Lawrence: University Press of Kansas, 2010.

Everett, Frank E. Jr. *Brierfield: Plantation Home of Jefferson Davis.* Hattiesburg, MS: University and College Press of Mississippi, 1971.

Farragut, Loyall. *Life and Letters of Admiral D. G. Farragut.* New York: D. Appleton, 1879.

Faulkner, William. *Absalom, Absalom!* (1936) New York: Vintage, 1990.

Faust, Drew Gilpin. *Mothers of Invention: Women of the Slaveholding South in the American Civil War.* Chapel Hill: University of North Carolina Press, 1996.

———. *This Republic of Suffering: Death and the American Civil War.* New York: Alfred A. Knopf, 2012.

Fay, Edwin H. *"This Infernal War": The Confederate Letters of Sgt. Edwin H. Fay,* edited by Bell Irvin Wiley. Austin: University of Texas Press, 1958.

Fehrenbacher, Don E., and Virginia Fehrenbacher, eds. *Recollected Words of Abraham Lincoln.* Stanford, CA: Stanford University Press, 1996.

Feis, William B. *Grant's Secret Service: The Intelligence War from Belmont to Appomattox.* Lincoln: University of Nebraska Press, 2002.

Fellman, Michael. *Citizen Sherman: A Life of William Tecumseh Sherman.* New York: Random House, 1995.

Fiske, John. *The Mississippi Valley in the Civil War.* Boston: Houghton Mifflin, 1900.

Flood, Charles Bracelen. *Grant and Sherman: The Friendship that Won the Civil War.* New York: Farrar, Straus and Giroux, 2005.

Foltz, Charles S. *Surgeon of the Seas: The Adventurous Life of Surgeon General Jonathan M. Foltz in the Days of Wooden Ships.* Indianapolis, IN: Bobbs-Merrill, 1931.

Foner, Eric. *The Fiery Trial: Abraham Lincoln and American Slavery.* New York: W. W. Norton & Company, 2011.

———. *Reconstruction: America's Unfinished Revolution, 1863–1877.* New York: Harper-Perennial, 2014.

Foote, Shelby. *The Civil War: A Narrative*, vol. 1, *Fort Sumter to Perryville* (1958). New York: Vintage Books, 1986.

———. *The Civil War: A Narrative*, vol. 2, *Fredericksburg to Meridian* (1963). New York: Vintage Books, 1986.

Force, Manning F. *Personal Recollections of the Vicksburg Campaign: A Paper Read before the Ohio Commandery of the Military Order of the Loyal Legion of the United States.* Cincinnati: Henry C. Sherick, 1885.

Ford, Worthington Chauncey, ed. *A Cycle of Adams Letters, 1861–1865*, vol. 1 (1920). New York: Kraus Reprint Co., 1969.

———, ed. *A Cycle of Adams Letters, 1861–1865*, vol. 2. Boston: Houghton Mifflin, 1929.

Foster, William Lovelace. *Vicksburg: Southern City under Siege*, edited by Kenneth T. Urquhart. New Orleans: Historic New Orleans Collection, 1980.

Fowler, James A., and Miles M. Miller. *History of the Thirtieth Iowa Infantry Volunteers.* Mediapolis, IA: T.A. Merrill, 1908.

Frankel, Noralee. *Freedom's Women: Black Women and Families in Civil War Era Mississippi.* Bloomington: Indiana University Press, 1999.

Franklin, S. R. *Memoirs of a Rear-Admiral.* New York: Harper & Brothers, 1898.

Freehling, William W. *The South vs. The South: How Anti-Confederate Southerners Shaped the Course of the Civil War.* New York: Oxford University Press, 2001.

Fullenkamp, Leonard, Stephen Bowman, and Jay Luvaas, eds. *Guide to the Vicksburg Campaign.* Lawrence: University Press of Kansas, 1998.

Fuller, J. F. C. *Decisive Battles of the U.S.A.* New York: Thomas Yoseloff, Inc., 1942.

———. *The Generalship of Ulysses S. Grant* (1929). New York: Da Capo Press, 1991.

———. *Grant and Lee: A Study in Personality and Generalship.* Bloomington: Indiana University Press, 1957.

Gage, M. D. *From Vicksburg to Raleigh: A Complete History of the Twelfth Regiment Indiana Volunteer Infantry, and the Campaigns of Grant and Sherman with an Outline of the Great Rebellion.* Chicago: Clarke & Co., 1865.

Gallagher, Gary W. *The Confederate War: How Popular Will, Nationalism, and Military Strategy Could Not Stave Off Defeat.* Cambridge, MA: Harvard University Press, 1999.

Garfield, James A. *The Diary of James A. Garfield*, edited by Harry J. Brown and Frederick D. Williams. East Lansing: Michigan State University Press, 1973.

Garland, Hamlin. *Ulysses S. Grant: His Life and Character.* New York: Doubleday-McClure, 1898.

Geer, Allen Morgan. *The Civil War Diary of Allen Morgan Geer, Twentieth Regiment, Illinois Volunteers*, edited by Mary Ann Anderson. Denver: Robert C. Appleman, 1977.

Gerteis, Louis S. *From Contraband to Freedman: Federal Policy toward Southern Blacks, 1861–1865.* Westport, CT: Greenwood Press, 1973.

Giambrone, Jeff. *An Illustrated Guide to the Vicksburg Campaign and National Military Park.* Jackson, MS: Communication Arts, 2001.

Glatthaar, Joseph T. *Forged in Battle: The Civil War Alliance of Black Soldiers and White Officers.* New York: Free Press, 1990.

———. *The March to the Sea and Beyond: Sherman's Troops in the Savannah and Carolinas Campaigns.* Baton Rouge: Louisiana State University Press, 1995.

———. *Partners in Command: The Relationship Between Leaders in the Civil War.* New York: Free Press, 1994.

Glazier, Willard. *Down the Great River.* Philadelphia: Hubbard Brothers, 1888.

Goodwin, Doris Kearns. *Team of Rivals: The Political Genius of Abraham Lincoln.* New York: Simon & Schuster, 2005.

Gorgas, Josiah. *The Civil War Diary of General Josiah Gorgas*, edited by Frank E. Vandiver. Tuscaloosa: University of Alabama Press, 1947.

Gott, Kendall D. *Where the South Lost the Civil War: An Analysis of the Fort Henry-Fort Donelson Campaign, February 1862.* Mechanicsburg, PA: Stackpole Books, 2003.

Grabau, Warren E. *Ninety-Eight Days: A Geographer's View of the Vicksburg Campaign.* Knoxville: University of Tennessee Press, 2000.

Grant, Jesse R. *In the Days of My Father General Grant.* New York: Harper & Brothers Publishers, 1925.

Grant, Julia Dent. *The Personal Memoirs of Julia Dent Grant,* edited by John Y. Simon. Carbondale: Southern Illinois University Press, 1975.

Grant, Ulysses S. *The Annotated Memoirs of Ulysses S. Grant,* edited by Elizabeth D. Samet. New York: Liveright Publishing Corporation, 2019.

———. *The Best Writings of Ulysses S. Grant,* edited by John F. Marszalek. Carbondale: Southern Illinois University Press, 2015.

———. *Grant: Memoirs and Selected Letters.* New York: Library of America, 1990. Grant's memoirs were originally published in two volumes in 1885–86 as *Personal Memoirs of U.S. Grant* (New York: Charles L. Webster & Company, 1885–86).

———. *Official Report of Lieut.-Gen. Ulysses S. Grant: Embracing a History of Operations of the Armies of the Union from March 1862 to the Closing Scene of the Rebellion.* New York: Beadle, 1865.

———. *The Papers of Ulysses S. Grant,* 32 vols., edited by John Y. Simon and John Marszalek. Carbondale: Southern Illinois University Press, 1967–2012.

———. *The Personal Memoirs of Ulysses S. Grant: The Complete Edition,* edited by John F. Marszalek. Cambridge, MA: Belknap Press of Harvard University Press, 2017.

———. *Ulysses S. Grant: Essays and Documents,* edited by David L. Wilson and John Y. Simon. Carbondale: Southern Illinois University Press, 1981.

Gravis, Peter W. *Twenty-Five Years on the Outside Row: Autobiography of Rev. Peter W. Gravis.* Brownwood, TX: Cross Timbers Press, 1966.

Green, John Williams. *Johnny Green of the Orphan Brigade: The Journal of a Confederate Soldier,* edited by Albert D. Kirwan. Lexington: University Press of Kentucky, 2002.

Greenbie, Marjorie Barstow. *Lincoln's Daughters of Mercy.* New York: G. P. Putnam's Sons, 1944.

Greene, Francis Vinton. *The Mississippi* (1882). Wilmington, NC: The Wilmington Publishing Company, 1989.

Griffith, Paddy. *Battle Tactics of the Civil War.* New Haven, CT: Yale University Press, 1989.

Grimsley, Mark. *The Hard Hand of War: Union Military Policy toward Southern Civilians, 1861–1865.* New York: Cambridge University Press, 1995.

———, and Steven E. Woodworth. *Shiloh: A Battlefield Guide.* Lincoln: University of Nebraska Presss, 2006.

Groom, Winston. *Shiloh, 1862.* Washington, D.C.: National Geographic, 2013.

———. *Vicksburg, 1863.* New York: Alfred A. Knopf, 2009.

Guelzo, Allen C. *Fateful Lightning: A New History of the Civil War and Reconstruction.* New York: Oxford University Press, 2012.

———. *Gettysburg: The Last Invasion.* New York: Alfred A. Knopf, 2013.

———. *Lincoln's Emancipation Proclamation: The End of Slavery in America.* New York: Simon & Schuster, reissue edition, 2006.

Hagerman, Edward. *The American Civil War and the Origins of Modern Warfare: Ideas, Organization, and Field Command.* Bloomington: Indiana University Press, 1988.

Hall, Winchester. *The Story of the 26th Louisiana Infantry in the Service of the Confederate States* (1890). Gaithersburg, MD: Butternut Press, 1984.

Halleck, Henry Wager. *Elements of Military Art and Science.* New York: D. Appleton, 1846.

Hanly, J. Frank. *Vicksburg.* Cincinnati: Jennings and Graham, 1912.

Hartje, Robert G. *Van Dorn: The Life and Times of a Confederate General.* Nashville, TN: Vanderbilt University Press, 1967.

Hattaway, Herman L. *General Stephen D. Lee.* Jackson, MS: University Press of Mississippi, 1976.

Hattaway, Herman, and Archer Jones. *How the North Won: A Military History of the Civil War.* Urbana: University of Illinois Press, 1991.

Haviland, Laura S. *A Woman's Life Work.* Chicago: privately published, 1887.

Hearn, Chester G. *Admiral David Dixon Porter: The Civil War Years.* Annapolis, MD: Naval Institute Press, 1996.

———. *Admiral David Glasgow Farragut: The Civil War Years.* Annapolis, MD: Naval Institute Press, 1998.

———. *Ellet's Brigade: The Strangest Outfit of All.* Baton Rouge: Louisiana State University Press, 2000.

Henshaw, Sarah Edwards. *Our Branch and Its Tributaries: Being a History of the Work of the Northwestern Sanitary Commission.* Chicago: Alfred L. Sewell, 1868.

Hermann, Janet Sharp. *Joseph E. Davis: Pioneer Patriarch.* Jackson: University Press of Mississippi, 2007.

———. *The Pursuit of a Dream.* New York: Oxford University Press, 1981.

Hess, Earl J. *The Union Soldier in Battle: Enduring the Ordeal of Combat.* Lawrence: University Press of Kansas, 1997.

Hesse-Wartegg, Ernst. *Travels on the Lower Mississippi: A Memoir by Ernst Hesse-Wartegg,* edited by Frederick Trautmann. Columbia: University of Missouri Press, 1990.

Hewitt, Lawrence Lee. *Port Hudson, Confederate Bastion on the Mississippi.* Baton Rouge: Louisiana State University Press, 1987.

Hicken, Victor. *Illinois in the Civil War.* Urbana: University of Illinois Press, 1991.

Hirshson, Stanley P. *The White Tecumseh: A Biography of William Tecumseh Sherman.* New York: John Wiley & Sons, 1997.

History of the Forty-Sixth Indiana Volunteer Infantry, September 1861–September 1865. Logansport, IN: 1886, compiled by order of the Regimental Association.

Hoehling, A. A. *Vicksburg: 47 Days of Siege.* Mechanicsburg, PA: Stackpole Books, 1969.

Hoge, Mrs. A. G. *The Boys in Blue:* or, *Heroes of the "Rank and File"—Comprising Incidents and Reminiscences from Camp, Battle-Field, and Hospital.* New York: E. B. Treat. 1867.

Holbrook, William C. *A Narrative of the Services of the Officers and Enlisted Men of the Regiment of Vermont Volunteers from 1862 to 1866.* New York: American Bank Company, 1882.

Holmes, Emma. *The Diary of Miss Emma Holmes, 1861–1866,* edited by John F. Marszalek. Baton Rouge: Louisiana State University Press, 1979.

Hopkins, Owen Johnston. *Under the Flag of the Nation: Diaries and Letters of Owen Johnston Hopkins, a Yankee Volunteer in the Civil War,* edited by Otto F. Bond. Columbus: Ohio State University Press, 1998.

How, Louis. *James B. Eads.* Boston: Houghton Mifflin, 1900.

Howard, R. L. *History of the 124th Regiment: Illinois Infantry Volunteers.* Springfield, IL: H. W. Rokker, 1880.

Hughes, Nathaniel Cheairs Jr. *The Battle of Belmont: Grant Strikes South.* Chapel Hill: University of North Carolina Press, 1991.

Hunt, Gaillard, ed. *Israel, Elihu, and Cadwallader Washburn: A Chapter in American Biography.* New York: Macmillan, 1925.

Hurst, Jack. *Born to Battle: Grant and Forrest: Shiloh, Vicksburg, and Chattanooga, the Campaigns that Doomed the Confederacy.* New York: Basic Books, 2012.

———. *Nathan Bedford Forrest: A Biography.* New York: Vintage Books, 1994.

Ingraham, Joseph Holt. *The South-West, by a Yankee*, vol. 2. New York: Harper & Brothers, 1835.

Jackson, Isaac. *"Some of the Boys . . .": The Civil War Letters of Isaac Jackson, 1862–1865,* edited by Joseph Orville Jackson. Carbondale: Southern Illinois University Press, 1960.

James, Clayton D. *Antebellum Natchez.* Baton Rouge: Louisiana State University Press, 1993.

Jessee, William W. *Civil War Diaries of James W. Jessee, 1861–1865, Company K, 8th Regiment of Illinois Volunteer Infantry,* edited by William P. LaBounty. Normal, IL: McLean County Genealogical Society, 1997.

Johnson, Robert Underwood, and Clarence Clough Buel, eds. *Battles and Leaders of the Civil War*, 4 vols. New York: The Century Company, 1887–88.

Johnson, Walter. *River of Dark Dreams: Slavery and Empire in the Cotton Kingdom.* Cambridge: Harvard University Press, 2013.

Johnston, Joseph E. *Narrative of Military Operations, Directed during the Last War Between the States by Joseph E. Johnston, General, C.S.A.* New York: D. Appleton, 1874.

Jomini, Antoine-Henri. *The Art of War,* translated by G. H. Mendell and W. P. Craighill. Novato, CA: Presidio Press, 1992.

Jones, Archer. *Civil War Command & Strategy: The Process of Victory and Defeat.* New York: The Free Press, 1992.

———. *Confederate Strategy from Shiloh to Vicksburg.* Baton Rouge: Louisiana State University Press, 1961.

Jones, James P. *"Black Jack": John A. Logan and Southern Illinois in the Civil War Era.* Carbondale: Southern Illinois University Press, 1995.

Jones, Jenkin Lloyd. *An Artilleryman's Diary.* Madison: Wisconsin Historical Commission, 1914.

Jones, S. C. *Reminiscences of the Twenty-Second Iowa* (1907). Iowa City, IA, 1993.

Jones, Virgil Carrington. *The Civil War at Sea*, vol. 2, *The River War.* New York: Holt, Rinehart, and Winston, 1961.

Keegan, John. *The Mask of Command.* New York: Penguin, 1988.

Kellogg, J. J. *War Experiences and the Story of the Vicksburg Campaign and Reminiscences: From "Milliken's Bend" to July 4, 1863.* Copyrighted by Capt. J. J. Kellogg, 1913.

Kennett, Lee. *Sherman, A Soldier's Life.* New York: HarperCollins, 2001.

Kimbell, Charles B. *History of Battery "A," First Illinois Light Artillery Volunteers.* Chicago: Cushing Printing Company, 1899.

Kiner, F. F. *One Year's Soldiering: Embracing the Battles of Fort Donelson and Shiloh* (1863). Prior Lake, MN: Morgan Avenue Press, 2000.

Kiper, Richard L. *Major General John Alexander McClernand: Politician in Uniform*. Kent, OH: Kent State University Press, 1999.

———, ed. *"Dear Catherine, Dear Taylor": The Civil War Letters of a Union Soldier and His Wife*. Lawrence: University Press of Kansas, 2002.

Kircher, Henry A. *A German in the Yankee Fatherland: The Civil War Letters of Henry A. Kircher*, edited by Earl J. Hess. Kent, OH: The Kent State University Press, 1983.

Knox, Thomas W. *Camp-Fire and Cotton-Field: Southern Adventure in Time of War*. New York: Jones Brothers and Company, 1865.

Korn, Bertram Wallace. *American Jewry and the Civil War*. Philadelphia: Jewish Publication Society of America, 1951.

Lansden, John M. *A History of the City of Cairo, Illinois* (1910). Carbondale: Southern Illinois University Press, 1976.

Lantz, Herman R. *A Community in Search of Itself: A Case History of Cairo, Illinois*. Carbondale: Southern Illinois University Press, 1972.

Leckie, William H., and Shirley A. Leckie. *Unlikely Warriors: General Benjamin H. Grierson and His Family*. Norman: University of Oklahoma Press, 1984.

Leonard, Elizabeth. *Yankee Women: Gender Battles in the Civil War*. New York: W. W. Norton, 1994.

Levine, Bruce. *The Fall of the House of Dixie: The Civil War and the Social Revolution that Transformed the South*. New York: Random House, 2013.

Lewis, Charles Lee. *David Glasgow Farragut: Our First Admiral*. Annapolis, MD: Naval Institute Press, 1943.

Lewis, Lloyd. *Captain Sam Grant*. Boston: Little, Brown and Company, 1950.

———. *Sherman: Fighting Prophet*. New York: Harcourt, Brace & Co., 1932.

Liddel Hart, B. H. *Sherman, Soldier, Realist, American* (1929). New York: Da Capo Press, 1993.

Linderman, Gerald F. *Embattled Courage: The Experience of Combat in the American Civil War*. New York: The Free Press, 1989.

Litwack, Leon F. *Been in the Storm So Long: The Aftermath of Slavery*. New York: Vintage, 1980.

Livermore, Thomas L. *Numbers and Losses in the Civil War in America: 1861–65*. Boston: Houghton Mifflin Company, 1900.

Livermore, Mary A. *My Story of the War: A Woman's Narrative* (1887). New York: Da Capo Press, 1995.

Logan, Marie T. *Mississippi-Louisiana: A History of Rodney, Miss., St. Joseph, La., and Environs*. Baton Rouge, LA: Claitors Publishing Division, 1980.

Long, E. B., and Barbara Long. *The Civil War Day by Day: An Almanac*. New York: Doubleday, 1971.

Longacre, Edward G. *From Union Stars to Top Hat: A Biography of the Extraordinary General James Harrison Wilson*. Harrisburg, PA: Stackpole, 1972.

Lonn, Ella. *Desertion During the Civil War*. New York: The Century Co., 1928.

———. *Salt as a Factor in the Confederacy*. Tuscaloosa: University of Alabama Press, 1933.

Loughborough, Mary Ann Webster. *My Cave Life in Vicksburg, with Letters of Trial and Travel* (1864). Wilmington, NC: Broadfoot Publishing Company, 1989.

Loving, Jerome M., ed. *Civil War Letters of George Washington Whitman.* Durham, NC: Duke University Press, 1975.

Lowe, Richard. *Walker's Texas Division C.S.A.: Greyhounds of the Trans-Mississippi.* Baton Rouge: Louisiana State University Press, 2004.

Lumpkin, Martha Neville, ed. *"Dear Darling Loulie": Letters of Cordelia Lewis Scales to Loulie W. Irby during and after the War Between the States.* Boulder: Ben Gray Lumpkin, 1955.

Luraghi, Raimondo. *A History of the Confederate Navy.* Annapolis, MD: Naval Institute Press, 1996.

Lyman, Theodore. *Meade's Headquarters, 1863–1865: Letters of Colonel Theodore Lyman from the Wilderness to Appomattox.* Boston: Atlantic Monthly Press, 1992.

Macartney, Clarence Edward. *Mr. Lincoln's Admirals.* New York: Funk & Wagnalls, 1956.

Mahan, A. T. *The Gulf and Inland Waters.* Wilmington, NC: Broadfoot Publishing Company, 1989.

Maihafer, Harry J. *The General and the Journalists: Ulysses S. Grant, Horace Greeley, and Charles Dana.* Washington, D.C.: Brassey's, 1998.

Manning, Chandra. *Troubled Refuge: Struggling for Freedom in the Civil War.* New York: Alfred A. Knopf, 2016.

———. *What This Cruel War Was Over: Soldiers, Slavery, and the Civil War.* New York: Alfred A. Knopf, 2007.

Marshall, Albert O. *Army Life; From a Soldier's Journal.* Joliet, IL: privately printed, 1884.

Marszalek, John F. *Commander of All of Lincoln's Armies: A Life of General Henry W. Halleck.* Cambridge, MA: Belknap Press, 2004.

———. *Sherman: A Soldier's Passion for Order.* New York: The Free Press, 1993.

———. *Sherman's Other War: The General and the Civil War Press.* Kent, OH: Kent State University Press, 1983.

Marszalek, John F., ed. *The Diary of Miss Emma Holmes, 1861–1866.* Baton Rouge: Louisiana State University Press, 1979.

Mason, F. H. *The Forty-Second Ohio Infantry: A History.* Cleveland: Andrews & Company, 1876.

McCain, William D. *The Story of Jackson: A History of the Capital of Mississippi, 1821–1951,* vol. 1. Jackson, MS: J. F. Hyer Publishing Co., 1953.

McCluney, Larry Allen Jr. *The Yazoo Pass Expedition: A Union Thrust into the Delta.* Charleston, SC: The History Press, 2017.

McClure, Alexander K. *Abraham Lincoln and Men of War Times.* Philadelphia: Times Publishing Company, 1892.

McDonough, James Lee. *William Tecumseh Sherman: In the Service of My Country: a Life.* New York: W. W. Norton & Company, 2016.

McFeely, William. *Grant: A Biography.* New York: W. W. Norton, 2002.

McPherson James M. *Battle Cry of Freedom: The Civil War Era.* New York: Oxford University Press, 1988.

———. *Embattled Rebel: Jefferson Davis as Commander in Chief.* New York: The Penguin Press, 2014.

———. *For Cause & Comrades: Why Men Fought in the Civil War.* New York: Oxford University Press, 1997.

———. *The Negro's Civil War: How American Blacks Felt and Acted during the War for the Union*. New York: Ballantine Books, 1991.

———. *War on the Waters: The Union & Confederate Navies, 1861–1865*. Chapel Hill: University of North Carolina Press, 2012.

———. *What They Fought For, 1861–1865*. Baton Rouge: Louisiana State University Press, 1994.

May, Robert E. *John A. Quitman: Old South Crusader*. Baton Rouge: Louisiana State University Press, 1985.

Melville, Herman. *Battle-Pieces of Herman Melville*. New York: A. S. Barnes and Company, 1963.

Merrill, James M. *Battle Flags South: The Story of the Civil War Navies on Western Waters*. Rutherford, NJ: Fairleigh Dickinson University Press, 1970.

Milligan, John D. *Gunboats Down the Mississippi*. Annapolis, MD: United States Naval Institute, 1965.

Mitchell, Reid. *Civil War Soldiers: Their Expectations and Their Experiences*. New York: Simon & Schuster, 1988.

Monroe, Haskell M. Jr., and James T. McIntosh, eds. *The Papers of Jefferson Davis*, vol. 9. Baton Rouge: Louisiana State University Press, 2016.

Moore, Frank, ed. *The Rebellion Record: A Diary of American Events*, vol. 6. New York: D. Van Nostrand, 1861–1868.

Moore, John Hebron. *The Emergence of the Cotton Kingdom in the Old Southwest: Mississippi, 1770–1860*. Baton Rouge: Louisiana State University Press, 1988.

Morgan, Sara. *The Civil War Diary of a Southern Woman*, edited by Charles East. New York: Simon & Schuster, 1992 (originally published as *The Civil War Diary of Sara Morgan*, 1991).

Morris, Christopher. *Becoming Southern: The Evolution of a Way of Life: Warren County and Vicksburg, Mississippi, 1770–1860*. New York: Oxford University Press, 1995.

Morris, W. S., L. D. Hartwell, and J. B. Kuykendall. *History: 31st Regiment Illinois Volunteers, Organized by John A. Logan*. Carbondale, IL: Southern Illinois University Press, 1998.

Moss, A. Hugh. *The Diary of A. Hugh Moss*. New York: The Scribner Press, 1948.

Munn, Asa B., A. H. Miller, and W. O. Newton. *Military History and Reminiscences of the Thirteenth Regiment of Illinois Volunteer Infantry in the Civil War in the United States, 1861–1865*. Chicago: Woman's Temperance Publishing Association, 1872.

Murray, Thomas Hamilton. *History of the Ninth Regiment, Connecticut Volunteer Infantry, the Irish Regiment, in the War of the Rebellion, 1861–65*. New Haven, CT: Price, Lee & Co., 1903.

Musicant, Ivan. *Divided Waters: The Naval History of the Civil War*. New York: Harper-Collins, 1995.

Nevins, Allan. *Ordeal of the Union*, vol. 3, *War Becomes Revolution, 1862–1863* (1960). New York: Macmillan Publishing Company, 1992.

Newsome, Edmund. *Experience in the War of Great Rebellion by a Soldier of the Eighty-First Regiment Illinois Voluntary Infantry*. Carbondale, IL: Edward Newsome, 1879.

Newton, James K. *A Wisconsin Boy in Dixie: The Selected Letters of James K. Newton*, edited by Stephen E. Ambrose. Madison: The University of Wisconsin Press, 1961.

Niven, John. *Gideon Welles: Lincoln's Secretary of the Navy*. New York: Oxford University Press, 1973.

Niven, John, ed. *Salmon P. Chase Papers*, vol. 3. Kent, OH: Kent State University Press, 1993.

Nolan, Cathal J. *The Allure of Battle: How Wars Have Been Won and Lost*. New York: Oxford University Press, 2017.

Oakes, James. *Freedom National: The Destruction of Slavery in the United States, 1861–1865*. New York: W. W. Norton, 2013.

Oldroyd, Osborn H. *A Soldier's Story of the Siege of Vicksburg from the Diary of Osborn H. Oldroyd*. Springfield, IL: privately published, 1885.

Osbon, B. S., ed. *Cruise of the U.S. Flagship Hartford, 1862–1863 . . . From the Private Journal of William C. Holton*. New York: L. W. Paine, 1863.

Paine, Albert Bigelow, ed. *A Sailor of Fortune: Personal Memoirs of Captain B. S. Osbon*. New York: McClure, Phillips, 1906.

Parker, John. *His Promised Land: The Autobiography of John P. Parker, Former Slave and Conductor on the Underground Railroad*, edited by Stuart Seely Sprague. New York: W. W. Norton, 1996.

Parrish, William E. *Frank Blair: Lincoln's Conservative*. Columbia: University of Missouri Press, 1998.

Pease, Theodore C., and James G. Randall, eds. *The Diary of Orville Hickman Browning*, vol. 1. Springfield: Illinois State Historical Library, 1925.

Pemberton, John C. *Pemberton: Defender of Vicksburg*. Chapel Hill: University of North Carolina Press, 1942.

Pena, Christopher G. *Scarred by War: Civil War in Southeast Louisiana*. Bloomington, IN: Author House, 2004.

Perret, Geoffrey. *Lincoln's War: The Untold Story of America's Greatest President as Commander in Chief*. New York: Random House, 2004.

———. *Ulysses S. Grant: Soldier & President*. New York: Random House, 1997.

Phelps, Elizabeth Stuart, et al. *Our Famous Women*. Hartford, CT: The Hartford Publishing Company, 1884.

Phillips, Christopher. *The Rivers Ran Backward: The Civil War and the Remaking of the American Middle Border*. New York: Oxford University Press, 2016.

Porter, David Dixon. *Incidents and Anecdotes of the Civil War*. New York: D. Appleton and Co., 1891.

———. *Naval History of the Civil War*. New York: The Sherman Publishing Co., 1886.

Porter, Horace. *Campaigning with Grant* (1897). New York: Bantam Books, 1991.

Pratt, Fletcher. *Civil War on Western Waters*. New York: Henry Holt and Company, 1956.

Rainwater, Percy Lee. *Mississippi: Storm Center of Secession, 1856–1861* (1938). New York: Da Capo Press, 1969.

Rawick, George P., ed. *The American Slave: A Composite Autobiography*, supplement, series 1, vol. 8, *Mississippi Narratives*, part 3. Westport, CT: Greenwood Press, 1974.

Reed, Rowena. *Combined Operations in the Civil War*. Annapolis, MD: Naval Institute Press, 1972.

Reps, John W. *Cities of the Mississippi: Nineteenth Century Images of Urban Development*. Columbia: University of Missouri Press, 1994.

Richardson, Albert D. *A Personal History of Ulysses S. Grant*. Hartford, CT: American Publishing Co., 1868.

———. *The Secret Service: The Field, the Dungeon, and the Escape*. Hartford, CT: American Publishing Co., 1866.

Ringle, Denis J. *Life in Mr. Lincoln's Navy.* Annapolis, MD: Naval Institute Press, 1998.

Ritner, Jacob, and Emeline Ritner. *Love and Valor: The Intimate Civil War Letters Between Captain Jacob and Emeline Ritner*, edited by Charles F. Larimer. Western Springs, IL: Sigourney Press, 2000.

Rogers, Clifford, Ty Seidule, and Samuel J. Watson. *The West Point History of the Civil War.* New York: Simon & Schuster, 2014.

Roland, Charles P. *Albert Sidney Johnston: Soldier of Three Republics.* Austin: University of Texas Press, 1964.

Rose, Victor M. *Ross' Texas Brigade.* Louisville: Courier-Journal Book and Job Rooms, 1881.

Rowland, Dunbar, ed. *The Official and Statistical Register of the State of Mississippi.* New York: J. J. Little & Ives Co., 1908.

Rusling, James F. *Men and Things I Saw in Civil War Days.* New York: Eaton and Mains, 1899.

Russell, Willam Howard. *My Diary North and South* (1863). Baton Rouge: Louisiana State University Press, 2001.

———. *Pictures of Southern Life: Social, Political, and Military.* New York: James G. Gregory, 1861.

Sanborn, John B. *The Crisis at Champion's Hill: The Decisive Battle of the Civil War.* St. Paul, MN: privately published, 1903.

Sandlin, Lee. *Wicked River: The Mississippi When It Last Ran Wild.* New York: Pantheon Books, 2010.

Sarna, Jonathan D. *When Grant Expelled the Jews.* New York: Nextbook/Schocken, 2012.

Saunier, Joseph A. *A History of the Forty-Seventh Regiment Ohio Veteran Volunteer Infantry.* Hillsboro, OH: The Lyle Printing Co., 1903.

Scarborough, William Kauffman. *Overseer: Plantation Management in the Old South.* Athens: University of Georgia Press, 1984.

Shanks, William F. G. *Personal Recollections of Distinguished Generals.* New York: Harper & Brothers, 1866.

Shea, William L., and Terence J. Winschel. *Vicksburg Is the Key: The Struggle for the Mississippi River.* Lincoln: University of Nebraska Press, 2003.

Sherman, William Tecumseh. *Sherman: Memoirs of General W. T. Sherman* (1875). New York: The Library of America, 1990. (The Library of America edition prints the text of the revised edition of 1886, with maps and Sherman letters written in response to the 1875 edition.)

Sillanpa, Tom. *Annie Wittenmyer: God's Angel.* Hamilton, IL: Hamilton Press, 1972.

Simon, John Y. *Ulysses Grant Chronology.* Athens: Ohio Historical Society, 1963.

Simon, John Y., and John Marszalek. *The Papers of Ulysses S. Grant*, 32 vols. Carbondale: Southern Illinois University Press, 1967–2012. (There is a digital edition of the papers: http://library.msstate.edu/usgrantassociation. The digital edition contains a guide to over sixty-six thousand pieces of correspondence not in the published volumes. The digital version of the papers is maintained by the Ulysses S. Grant Association, which moved from Southern Illinois University in Carbondale, Illinois, to the Ulysses S. Grant Presidential Library at Mississippi State University in Starkville, Mississippi, in 2008 after the death of Mr. Simon. John Marszalek is executive director and managing editor of the Grant Papers.)

Simpson, Brooks D. *Ulysses S. Grant: Triumph Over Adversity, 1822–1865.* Boston: Houghton, 2000.

Simpson, Brooks D., and Jean V. Berlin, eds. *Sherman's Civil War: Selected Correspondence of William T. Sherman, 1860–1865.* Chapel Hill: University of North Carolina Press, 1999.

Smart, James G., ed. *A Radical View: The "Agate" Dispatches of Whitelaw Reid, 1861–65.* Memphis: Memphis State University Press, 1976.

Smith, David M. *Compelled to Appear in Print: The Vicksburg Manuscript of General John C. Pemberton.* Cincinnati: Ironclad Publishing, 1999.

Smith, Jean Edward. *Grant.* New York: Simon & Schuster, 2001.

Smith, Myron J. Jr. *The Fight for the Yazoo, August 1862–July 1864: Swamps, Forts and Fleets on Vicksburg's Northern Flank.* London: McFarland, 2012.

Smith, Timothy B. *Champion Hill: Decisive Battle for Vicksburg.* New York: Savas Beatie, 2004.

———. *Rethinking Shiloh: Myth and Memory.* Knoxville: The University of Tennessee Press, 2013.

———. *Shiloh: Conquer or Perish.* Lawrence: University of Kansas Press, 2014.

Solonick, Justin S. *Engineering Victory: The Union Siege of Vicksburg.* Carbondale: Southern Illinois University Press, 2015.

Stahr, Walter. *Stanton: Lincoln's War Secretary.* New York: Simon & Schuster, 2017.

Stanley, Henry Morgan. *The Autobiography,* edited by Dorothy Stanley. Boston: Houghton Mifflin, 1909.

Steiner, Paul E. *Disease in the Civil War: Natural Biological Warfare in 1861–1865.* Springfield, IL: Charles C. Thomas Publisher, 1968.

Stephens, Gail. *The Shadow of Shiloh: Major General Lew Wallace in the Civil War.* Indianapolis: Indiana Historical Society Press, 2010.

Stevenson, B. F. *Letters from the Army.* Cincinnati: W. E. Dibble & Co., 1884.

Stickles, Arndt M. *Simon Bolivar Buckner: Borderland Knight.* Chapel Hill: University of North Carolina Press, 1940.

Stone, Kate. *Brokenburn: The Journal of Kate Stone, 1861–1868* (1955). Baton Rouge: Louisiana State University Press, 1995.

Stone, Mary Amelia (Boomer). *Memoir of George Boardman Boomer.* Boston: Press of Geo. C. Rand & Avery, 1864.

Strausbaugh, John. *City of Sedition: The History of New York City during the Civil War.* New York: Twelve, 2016.

Sword, Wiley. *Shiloh: Bloody April.* New York: William Morrow & Co., 1974.

Sydnor, Charles S. *A Gentleman of the Old Natchez Region, Benjamin L. C. Wailes.* Durham, NC: Duke University Press, 1938.

Symonds, Craig L. *Joseph E. Johnston: A Civil War Biography.* New York: W. W. Norton, 1994.

Taylor, Richard. *Destruction and Reconstruction: Personal Experiences of the Late War.* New York: D. Appleton and Company, 1879.

Temple, Wayne C., ed. *The Civil War Letters of Henry C. Bear: A Soldier in the 116th Illinois Volunteer Infantry.* Harrogate, TN: Lincoln Memorial University Press, 1961.

Thompson, Robert Means, and Richard Wainwright, eds. *Confidential Correspondence of Gustavus Vasa Fox, Assistant Secretary of the Navy, 1861–1865,* 2 vols. Freeport, NY: Books for Libraries Press, 1972.

Todd, William. *The Seventy-Ninth Highlanders: New York Volunteers in the War of Rebellion, 1861–1865.* Albany, NY: Press of Brandow, Barton & Co., 1886.

Trollope, Anthony. *North America* (1862), edited by Donald Smalley and Bradford Booth. New York: Alfred A. Knopf, 1951.

Trowbridge, John T. *The Desolate South, 1865–1866: A Picture of the Battlefields and of the Devastated Confederacy,* edited by Gordon Carroll. New York: Duell, Sloan and Pearce, 1956.

Trudeau, Noah Andre. *Like Men of War: Black Troops in the Civil War, 1862–1865.* Boston: Little, Brown and Company, 1998.

Tucker, Phillip Thomas. *The Forgotten "Stonewall of the West," Major General John Stevens Bowen.* Macon, GA: Mercer University Press, 1997.

———. *The South's Finest: The First Missouri Confederate Brigade from Pea Ridge to Vicksburg.* Shippensburg, PA: White Mane Publishing Company, 1993.

Tucker, Spencer C. *Andrew Foote: Civil War Admiral on Western Waters.* Annapolis, MD: Naval Institute Press, 2000.

Tunnard, W. H. *A Southern Record: The Story of the 3rd Regiment, Louisiana Infantry, C.S.A.* (1866) Fayetteville: University of Arkansas Press, 1997.

Twain, Mark. *Life on the Mississippi* (1883). NY: Airmont Publishing Company, 1965.

Twombley, V. P. *Second Iowa Infantry at Fort Donelson, February 15, 1862.* Des Moines, IA: Plain Talk Printing House, 1901.

Varon, Elizabeth R. *Armies of Deliverance: A New History of the Civil War.* New York: Oxford University Press, 2019.

Venet, Wendy Hammond. *A Changing Wind: Commerce and Conflict in Civil War Atlanta.* New Haven, CT: Yale University Press, 2014.

Villard, Henry. *Memoirs of Henry Villard: Journalist and Financier,* vol. 1. Boston: Houghton Mifflin, 1904.

Walke, Henry. *Naval Scenes and Reminiscences of the Civil War in the United States on the Southern and Western Waters.* New York: F. R. Reed & Co., 1877.

Walker, Peter F. *Vicksburg: A People at War, 1860–1865.* Chapel Hill: University of North Carolina Press, 1960.

Wallace, Lew. *An Autobiography,* vols. 1–2. New York: Harper & Brothers, 1906.

Waugh, Joan. *U. S. Grant: American Hero, American Myth.* Chapel Hill: University of North Carolina Press, 2009.

Wearmouth, John, ed. *The Cornwell Chronicles: Tales of an American Life.* Bowie, MD: Heritage Books, 1998.

Weigley, Russell F. *The American Way of War: A History of United States Military Strategy and Policy.* New York: Macmillan Publishing Co., 1973.

Welles, Gideon. *The Diary of Gideon Welles, Secretary of the Navy under Lincoln and Johnson,* vol. 1. Boston: Houghton Mifflin, 1910.

Wells, Seth J. *The Siege of Vicksburg: From the Diary of Seth J. Wells.* Detroit: Wm. H. Rowe, 1915.

West, Richard S. Jr. *Mr. Lincoln's Navy.* New York: Longmans, Green, 1957.

———. *The Second Admiral: A Life of David Dixon Porter, 1813–1891.* New York: Coward-McCann, 1937.

Whitcomb, Caroline. *The History of the Second Massachusetts Battery (Nims Battery) of Light Artillery, 1861–1865*. Concord, NH: The Rumsford Press, 1912.

White, Deborah Gray. *Ar'n't I a Woman? Female Slaves in the Plantation South*. New York: W. W. Norton & Company, revised edition, 1999.

White, Ronald C. Jr. *A. Lincoln: A Biography*. New York: Random House, 2009.

———. *American Ulysses: A Life of Ulysses S. Grant*. New York: Random House, 2016.

Wild, J. C. *The Valley of the Mississippi, Illustrated*. St. Louis: J. C. Wild, 1841.

Williams, Frederick D., ed. *The Wild Life of the Army: Civil War Letters of James A. Garfield*. East Lansing: Michigan State University Press, 1964.

Williams, Gershom Mott. *Letters of General Thomas Williams, 1862*. Washington, D.C.: American Historical Association, 1909.

Williams, John. *Johnny Green of the Orphan Brigade: The Journal of a Confederate Soldier*, edited by Albert D. Kirwan. Lexington: University Press of Kentucky, 2002.

Williams, Richard Brady. *Chicago's Battery Boys: The Chicago Mercantile Battery and the Civil War's Western Theater*. New York: Savas Beatie, 2005.

Williams, T. Harry. *McClellan, Sherman and Grant* (1962). Chicago: Ivan R. Dee, 1991.

———. *P. G. T. Beauregard, Napoleon in Gray*. New York: Collier Books, 1962.

Willison, Charles A. *Reminiscences of a Boy's Service with the 76th Ohio* (1908). Huntington, WV: Blue Acorn Press, 1955.

Wills, Charles W. *Army Life of an Illinois Soldier: Letters and Diary of Charles W. Wills* (1906), edited by Mary Kellogg. Carbondale: Southern Illinois University Press, 1996.

Wilson, James Grant and Titus Munson Coan, eds. *Personal Recollections of the War of the Rebellion*. New York: The Commandery, 1891.

Wilson, James Harrison. *The Life of Charles A. Dana*. New York: Harper & Brothers, 1907.

———. *The Life of John A. Rawlins: Lawyer, Assistant Adjutant General, Chief of Staff, Major General of Volunteers*. New York: Neale Publishing, 1916.

———. *Under the Old Flag: Recollections of Military Operations in the War for the Union, the Spanish War, the Boxer Rebellion, etc.*, vol. 1. New York: D. Appleton and Company, 1912.

Wineapple, Brenda. *Ecstatic Nation: Confidence, Crisis, and Compromise, 1848–1877*. New York: HarperCollins, 2013.

Winschel, Terrence J. *Triumph & Defeat: The Vicksburg Campaign*. Mason City, IA: Savas Publishing, 1999.

Winters, John D. *The Civil War in Louisiana*. Baton Rouge: Louisiana State University Press, 1963.

Winters, William. *The Musick of the Mockingbirds, the Roar of the Cannon: The Diary and Letters of William Winters*, edited by Steven E. Woodworth. Lincoln: University of Nebraska Press, 1998.

Witt, John Fabian. *Lincoln's Code: The Laws of War in American History*. New York: The Free Press, 2012.

Wittenmyer, Annie. *Under the Guns: A Woman's Reminiscences of the Civil War*. Boston: E. B. Stillings & Co., 1895.

Woods, J. T. *Services of the Ninety-Sixth Ohio*. Toledo, OH: Blade Printing and Paper Co., 1874.

Woodward, William E. *Meet General Grant*. New York: H. Liveright, 1928.

Woodworth, Steven E. *Jefferson Davis and His Generals: The Failure of Confederate High Command in the West*. Lawrence: University Press of Kansas, 1990.

——. *Nothing But Victory: The Army of the Tennessee, 1861–1865*. New York: Alfred A. Knopf, 2005.

——, and Charles Grear. *The Vicksburg Assaults, May 19–22, 1863*. Carbondale: Southern Illinois University Press, 2019.

Woodworth, Steven E., ed. *Civil War Generals in Defeat*. Lawrence: University Press of Kansas, 1990.

Woolworth, S. *The Mississippi Scout*. Chicago: self-published, 1868.

Wooster, Ralph A. *The Secession Conventions of the South*. Princeton, NJ: Princeton University Press, 1962.

Wright, Henry H. *A History of the Sixth Iowa Infantry*. Iowa City: State Historical Society of Iowa, 1923.

Yacovone, Donald, ed. *A Voice of Thunder: The Civil War Letters of George E. Stephens*. Urbana: University of Illinois Press, 1997.

Young, John Russell. *Around the World with General Grant*, vol. 2, subscription news service (1879).

ARTICLES AND CHAPTERS IN BOOKS

"Civil War Letters of Brigadier General William Ward Orme—1862–1866." *Journal of the Illinois State Historical Society* 23 (July 1930).

"Descendant Clarifies Champion Hill History." *Jackson Daily News*, May 24, 1984.

"Grant's Pertinacity." *Army and Navy Journal*, vol. 31 (December 30, 1893).

"How Grant Got to Know Rawlins." *Army and Navy Journal*, vol. 6 (September 12, 1868).

"How the Steamboats Run Rebel Batteries." *Harper's Weekly*, vol. 59 (May 30, 1863).

"Our Army in the Southwest." *Harper's Weekly*, April 4, 1863.

"Vicksburg by New Years." *Civil War Times Illustrated*, vol. 16 (January 1978).

Affeld, Charles E. "From Milliken's Bend to Vicksburg with Private Affeld," edited by Edwin C. Bearss. *Louisiana Studies*, vol. 6 (1967).

Alexander, Robert Chrisolm. "The Shiloh Battle-Order and the Withdrawal Sunday Evening." BL, vol. 1.

Allen, Stacey D. "Shiloh! The Campaign and First Day's Battle." *Blue and Gray*, vol. 14 (Winter, 1997).

Ash, Stephen V. "Civil War Exodus: The Jews and Grant's General Orders No. 11." *The Historian*, vol. 44 (August 1982).

Bailey, Ann J. "A Texas Cavalry Raid: Reaction to Black Soldiers and Contrabands." *Civil War History*, vol. 35, no. 2 (June 1989).

Baker, Marion A. "Farragut's Demands for the Surrender of New Orleans." BL, vol. 2.

Ballard, Michael B. "Misused Merit: The Tragedy of John C. Pemberton." In *Civil War Generals in Defeat*, edited by Steven E. Woodworth. Lawrence: University Press of Kansas, 1990.

Bartlett, John Russell. "The "Brooklyn" at the Passage of the Forts." BL, vol. 2.

Bearss, Edwin C. "The Battle of Baton Rouge." *Louisiana Historical Association*, vol. 3, no. 2 (1962).

———. "Pvt. Charles E. Affeld Reports Action West of the Mississippi." *Journal of the Illinois State Historical Society*, vol. 60 (Autumn, 1967).

Bearss, Edwin C., ed. "Diary of Captain John N. Bell at Vicksburg." *Iowa Journal of History*, vol. 59 (April 1961).

Beauregard, P. G. T. "The Campaign of Shiloh." BL, vol. 1.

Bedford, H. L. "Fight Between the Batteries and Gunboats at Fort Donelson." *Southern Historical Society Papers*, vol. 13 (January–December 1885).

Berlin, Ira. "Who Freed the Slaves? Emancipation and Its Meaning." In *Union & Emancipation: Essays on Politics and Race in the Civil War Era*, edited by David W. Blight and Brooks D. Simpson. Kent, OH: The Kent State University Press, 1997.

Bierce, Ambrose. "What I Saw at Shiloh." In Ambrose Bierce, *A Sole Survivor: Bits of Autobiography*, edited by S. T. Joshi and David E Schultz. Knoxville: The University of Tennessee Press, 1998.

Bigelow, Martha Mitchell. "Freedmen of the Mississippi Valley, 1862–1865." *Civil War History*, vol. 17 (1962).

Blair, Montgomery. "Opening the Mississippi." *United Service*, vol. 4 (January 1881).

Bollet, Alfred Jay. "Scurvy and Chronic Diarrhea in Civil War Troops: Were They Both Nutritional Deficiency Syndromes?" *Journal of the History of Medicine and Allied Sciences*, vol. 47 (1992).

Brown, D. Alexander. "Battle at Chickasaw Bluffs." *Civil War Times*, vol. 9 (July 1970).

Brown, George W. "Service in the Mississippi Squadron and Its Connection with the Siege and Capture of Vicksburg." *The Commandery, State of New York, MOLLUS*, December 3, 1890.

Brown, Isaac N. "The Confederate Gun-boat 'Arkansas.'" BL, vol. 3.

Buell, Don Carlos. "Shiloh Reviewed." BL, vol. 1.

Burt, R. W. "Letters from the Trenches: A Contemporaneous Account of the Investment and Surrender of Vicksburg." *National Tribune* (July 3, 1902).

Byers, S. H. M. "How Men Feel in Battle." *Annals of Iowa*. vol. 2 (July 1896).

———. "Some Recollections of Grant." *Annals of the War*. Philadelphia: Philadelphia Times Publishing, 1879.

Cable, George Washington. "New Orleans Before the Capture." BL, vol. 2.

Cadwallader, Sylvanus. "Grant and Rawlins." *St. Louis Daily Globe-Democrat*, February 11, 1887.

Callender, Elliot. "What a Boy Saw on the Mississippi." In *Military Essays and Recollections*, vol. 1. Chicago: The Commandery of the State of Illinois, 1891.

Canfield, Eugene B. "Porter's Mortar Schooners." *Civil War Times Illustrated*, vol. 6 (October 1967).

Castel, Albert. "'Black Jack' Logan." *Civil War Times Illustrated*, vol. 15 (November 1876).

Catton, Bruce. "U. S. Grant: Man of Letters." *American Heritage*, vol. 19, no. 4 (June 1968).

Chambers, William Pitt. "My Journal." In *Publications of the Mississippi Historical Society*, Centenary Series, vol. 5. Jackson, MS, 1925.

Clarke, H. C. "Vicksburg, Mississippi." *Southern Illustrated News* (November 8, 1862).

Cockerill, John A. "A Boy at Shiloh." In *Papers of MOLLUS*, vol. 6.

Coleman, S. B. "A July Morning with the Rebel Ram *Arkansas*." In *Michigan Commandery of MOLLUS*. Detroit: Winn & Hammond, 1890.

Cox, LaWanda. "The Promise of Land for the Freedmen." *Mississippi Valley Historical Review*, vol. 45 (December 1958).

De Bow, J. D. "The Late Southern Convention Proceedings." *De Bow's Review*, vol. 17.

Deupree, J. D. "The Capture of Holly Springs, Mississippi, Dec. 20, 1862." *Publications of the Mississippi Historical Society*, vol. 4 (1901).

Dorris, J. T. "Michael Kelly Lawler: Mexican and Civil War Officer." *Journal of the Illinois State Historical Society*, vol. 48 (Winter, 1955).

Dorsett, Lyle W. "The Problem of Ulysses S. Grant's Drinking During the Civil War." *Hayes Historical Journal*, vol. 4, no. 2 (1983).

Douglass, Frederick. "U. S. Grant and the Colored People." *Elevator*, vol. 8, no. 20 (August 24, 1872).

Eads, James B. "Recollections of Foote and the Gun-Boats." BL, vol. 1.

Emerson, John W. "Grant's Life in the West and His Mississippi Valley Campaigns." *Midland Monthly*, vol. 6 (July–December 1896), vol. 7 (January–June 1897), vol. 8 (July–December 1897), vol. 9 (February–June 1898), vol. 10 (July–August 1898).

Erickson, Edgar L., ed. "With Grant at Vicksburg: From the Civil War Diary of Captain Charles E. Wilcox." *Illinois State Historical Society*, vol. 30 (1938).

Fingerson, Ronald L. "A William Tecumseh Sherman Letter." *Books at Iowa*, vol. 3 (November 1965).

Flaccus, Elmer W. "Commodore David Porter and the Mexican Navy." *Hispanic American Historical Review*, vol. 34 (August 1954).

Freemon, Frank R. "Medical Care at the Siege of Vicksburg, 1863." *Bulletin of the New York Academy of Medicine*, vol. 67 (September–October 1991).

Gallagher, Gary W. "Lee's Army Has Not Lost Any of Its Prestige." In *The Third Day at Gettysburg and Beyond*, edited by Gary Gallagher. Chapel Hill: University of North Carolina Press, 1998.

Gift, George W. "The Story of the *Arkansas*." *Southern Historical Society Papers*, vol. 12 (1884).

Glover, Frank. "Separation from the Union, 1854–1861." In *A History of Mississippi*, vol. 1, edited by Richard Aubrey McLemore. Oxford: University College Press of Mississippi, 1973.

Gosnell, Allen H. "Damn the Torpedoes—?" *U.S. Naval Institute Proceedings*, no. 517 (March 1946).

Grant, Frederick D. "A Boy's Experience at Vicksburg." *New York MOLLUS*, vol. 3, 1907.

———. "General Grant: His Son's Memories of Him in the Field." *National Tribune* (January 27, 1887).

———. "With Grant at Vicksburg." *Outlook*, vol. 24 (July 2, 1898).

Grant, Jesse R. "The Early Life of General Grant." *New York Ledger*, March 21, 1868.

Grant, Ulysses S. "The Battle of Shiloh." *Century Magazine*, vol. 29 (February 1885).

———. "Shiloh: General Lew Wallace and General McCook." *Century Magazine*, vol. 30 (October 1885).

———. "The Siege of Vicksburg." *Century Magazine*, vol. 30 (October 1886).

———. "The Vicksburg Campaign." BL, vol. 3.

Green, Anna Maclay. "Civil War Public Opinion of General Grant." *Journal of the Illinois State Historical Society*, vol. 22 (April 1929).

Gregory, Edward S. "Vicksburg during the Siege." In *The Annals of the War: Written by Leading Participants, North and South*. Philadelphia: The Times Publishing Company, 1879.

Hanson, Kathleen S. "Down to Vicksburg; The Nurses' Experience." *Journal of the Illinois State Historical Society*, vol. 97, no. 4 (May 2005).

Harrison, Robert W. "Levee Building in Mississippi before the Civil War." *Journal of Mississippi History*, vol. 32 (1950).

Henderson, Archibald. "Eads, Master Engineer." *Universal Engineer*, vol. 55 (1932).

Hess, Earl J. "The Mississippi River and Secession, 1861: The Northwestern Response." *Old Northwest*, vol. 10 (Summer, 1984).

Hickenlooper, Andrew. "Our Volunteer Engineers." In *Papers Prepared for the Ohio Commandery of MOLLUS*. Cincinnati, OH: Robert Clarke and Co., November 1889.

———. "The Vicksburg Mine." BL, vol. 3.

Hobbs, Charles A. "Vanishing Vicksburg: The Campaign which Ended in the Surrender of America's Gibraltar." *National Tribune*, March 10, 17, 24, 1892.

Hollandsworth, James G. Jr. "The Execution of White Officers from Black Units by Confederate Forces during the Civil War." *Louisiana History*, vol. 35 (Fall, 1994).

Hovey, Alvin P. "Pittsburg Landing." *National Tribune*, February 1, 1883.

Ingraham, Mrs. Alfred. "The Vicksburg Diary of Mrs. Alfred Ingraham, May 2–June 13, 1863," edited by W. Maury Darst. *Journal of Mississippi History*, vol. 44 (May 1982).

Jenney, William Le Baron. "Personal Recollections of Vicksburg." In *Papers of MOLLUS*, vol. 12 (1899).

———. "With Grant and Sherman from Memphis to Chattanooga: A Reminiscence." In *Papers of MOLLUS*, vol. 13.

Johnson, Robert Erwin. "The Quintessential Nineteenth Century Naval Officer." In *Captains of the Old Steam Navy*, edited by James C. Bradford. Annapolis, MD: Naval Institute Press, 1986.

Johnston, Joseph E. "Jefferson Davis and the Mississippi Campaign." *North American Review*, vol. 143 (December 1886).

Johnston, William Preston. "Albert Sidney Johnston at Shiloh." BL, vol. 1.

Joiner, Gary D. "Soul-Stirring Music to our Ears." In *The Shiloh Campaign*, edited by Steven Woodworth. Carbondale: Southern Illinois University Press, 2009.

Jones, Archer. "The Gettysburg Decision." *Virginia Magazine of History and Biography*, vol. 68, no. 3 (1960).

Jones, J. H. "The Rank and File at Vicksburg." *Publications of the Mississippi Historical Society*, vol. 7 (1903).

Jordan, Thomas. "Notes of a Confederate Staff-Officer at Shiloh." BL, vol. 1.

Jordan, Philip D., and Charles M. Thomas. "Reminiscences of an Ohio Volunteer." *Ohio State Archaeological and Historical Quarterly*, vol. 48 (1939).

Kautz, Albert. "Incidents of the Occupation of New Orleans." BL, vol. 2.

Kennon. Beverley, "Fighting Farragut below New Orleans." BL, vol. 2.

Kouwenhoven, John A. "James Buchanan Eads: The Engineer as Entrepreneur." In *Technology in America: A History of Individuals and Ideas*, edited by Carroll Pursell Jr. Cambridge, MA; MIT Press, 1990.

Lee, Chulhee. "Socioeconomic Backgrounds, Disease, and Mortality among Union Army

Recruits: Implications for Economic and Demographic History." *Explorations in Economic History*, vol. 34 (1997).

Lee, Stephen D. "The Campaign of Generals Grant and Sherman Against Vicksburg in December 1862 and January 1st and 2nd, Known as the 'Chickasaw Bayou Campaign.'" *Mississippi Historical Society*, vol. 8 (1902).

———. "Details of Important Work by Two Confederate Telegraph Operators . . ." *Mississippi Historical Society*, vol. 4 (1901).

———. "The Campaign of Vicksburg, Mississippi, in 1863—From April 15 to and Including the Battle of Champion Hills, or Baker's Creek, May 16, 1863." *Publications of the Mississippi Historical Society*, vol. 3 (1900).

Legan, Marshal Scott. "The Confederate Career of a Union Ram." *Louisiana History*, vol. 41, no. 3 (2000).

Livermore, William R. "The Vicksburg Campaign." In *Papers of the Military Historical Society of Massachusetts*, vol. 9. Boston: The Society, 1920.

Lockett, Samuel H. "The Defense of Vicksburg." BL, vol. 3.

Long, E. B. "The Paducah Affair: Bloodless Action That Altered the Civil War in the Mississippi Valley." *Register of the Kentucky Historical Society*, vol. 70, no. 4 (1972).

———. "Rawlins: Staff Officer Par Excellence." *Civil War Times Illustrated*, vol. 12, no. 9 (1974).

———. "Ulysses S. Grant for Today." In *Ulysses S. Grant: Essays and Documents*, edited by David L. Wilson and John W. Simon. Carbondale: Southern Illinois University Press, 1981.

Longstreet, James. "Lee in Pennsylvania." In *Annals of the War* (Philadelphia, 1879).

Loop, M. B. "Campaigning with the Buckeyes." *National Tribune*, November 15, 1900.

Lord, William W. "A Child at the Siege of Vicksburg." *Harper's Monthly Magazine*, vol. 118 (December 1908).

Lowe, John to Manorah Lowe, May 12, 1848, in Carl Becker, "Was Grant Drinking in Mexico?" *Bulletin of the Cincinnati Historical Society*, vol. 24, no. 1 (January 1966).

Lowe, Richard. "Battle on the Levee: The Fight at Milliken's Bend." In *Black Soldiers in Blue: African American Troops in the Civil War Era*, edited by John David Smith. Chapel Hill: University of North Carolina Press, 2002.

McGinnis, George. "Shiloh." In *Papers of MOLLUS*, vol. 24.

McPherson, James M. "Introduction" to the Penguin Books edition of the *Personal Memoirs of U.S. Grant*. New York: Penguin Books, 1999.

McWhiney, Brady. "General Beauregard." In *The Shiloh Campaign*, edited by Steven Woodworth. Carbondale: Southern Illinois University Press, 2009.

Maihafer, Henry J. "Mr. Grant and Mr. Dana." *American History*, vol. 35 (December 2000).

Marszalek, John F. "The Knox Court-Martial: W. T. Sherman Puts the Press on Trial (1863)." *Military Law Review*, vol. 59 (Winter, 1973).

Mason, George. "Shiloh." In *Papers of MOLLUS*, vol. 10.

Maury, Dabney. "Grant's Campaign in North Mississippi in 1862." *Southern Magazine*, vol. 133 (July–December 1873).

———. "Recollections of General Earl Van Dorn." *Southern Historical Society*, vol. 19 (1891).

———. "A Winter at Vicksburg." BL, vol. 3.

Meredith, William T. "Farragut's Capture of New Orleans." BL, vol. 2.

Messner, William F. "The Vicksburg Campaign of 1862: A Case Study in the Federal Utilization of Black Labor." *Louisiana History: The Journal of the Louisiana Historical Association*, vol. 16, no. 4 (Autumn, 1975).

Michael, W. H. C. "The Mississippi Flotilla," a Paper Read before the Nebraska Commandery of MOLLUS, October 6, 1886. In MOLLUS, *Civil War Sketches and Incidents*. Omaha, NE: The Commandery, 1902.

Milligan, John D. "From Theory to Application: The Emergence of the American Ironclad War Vessel." *Military Affairs*, vol. 48 (July 1984).

Moore, Frank, ed. "General Sherman's Expedition," January 3, 1863, published in the *Missouri Democrat* and reprinted in *Rebellion Record*, 1862–63, vol. 6. New York: G. P. Putnam, 1863.

Moore, Glover. "Separation from the Union, 1854–1861." In *A History of Mississippi*, vol. 1, edited by Richard Aubrey McLemore. Oxford: University College Press of Mississippi, 1973.

Morgan, "The Assault on Chickasaw Bluffs." BL, vol. 3.

Morton, Charles A. "A Boy at Shiloh." In *Personal Recollections of the War of the Rebellion: Addresses Delivered before the Commandery of the State of New York, MOLLUS*, edited by A. Noel Blakeman. New York: G. P. Putnam's Sons, 1907.

Murphy, Brian J. "Truth behind U. S. Grant's Yazoo River Bender." Weider History Group, 2012. http://www.historynet.com/truth-behind-us-rants-yazoo-river-bender.htm.

Myers, Robert C. "Mortality in the Twelfth Michigan Volunteer Infantry, 1861–1866." *Michigan Historical Review*, vol. 20 (Spring, 1994).

Neely, Mark E. "Was the Civil War a Total War?" *Civil War History*, vol. 37, no. 1 (1991).

Northrup, L. B. "A Hill of Death." *Civil War Times Illustrated*, vol. 30, no. 2 (May–June 1991).

O'Dea, John. "Reminiscences of the War." *Chicago Times-Herald*, May 30, 1897.

Owens, Jeffery Alan. "The Burning of Lake St. Joseph." *Louisiana History*, vol. 32, no. 4 (Fall, 1991).

Pemberton, John C. "The Terms of Surrender." BL, vol. 3.

Perry, Oran. "The Entering Wedge." A Paper Read Before the Indiana Commandery of MOLLUS, April 19, 1898.

Phillips, Christopher. "Earl Van Dorn." *American National Biography Online* (February 2000).

Pirtle, John. "Defence of Vicksburg in 1862—The Battle of Baton Rouge." *Southern Historical Society Papers*, vol. 8 (June–July 1880).

Pitkin, W. A. "When Cairo Was Saved for the Union." *Journal of the Illinois State Historical Society*, vol. 51 (1958).

Polk, Jack. "The Union's Trojan Horse." *Proceedings of the United States Naval Institute*, vol. 113, no. 6 (1987).

Porter, David Dixon. "The Opening of the Lower Mississippi." BL, vol. 2.

Post, Lauren. "Samuel Henry Lockett (1837–1891): A Sketch of His Life and Work." *Louisiana History*, vol. 5, no. 4 (Autumn, 1964).

Pratt, Harry E. "Lewis B. Parsons: Mover of Armies and Railroad Builder." Lewis B. Parsons Papers.

Ranlett, Seth A. "The Capture of Jackson." In *Civil War Papers Read Before the Commandery of the State of Massachusetts, MOLLUS*, vol. 1. Boston: The Commandery, 1900.

Reed, Lida L. "A Woman's Experience during the Siege of Vicksburg." *Century Magazine*, vol. 61 (April 1901).

Reps, John W. "Great Expectations and Hard Times: The Planning of Cairo, Illinois." *Journal of the Society of Architectural Historians*, vol. 16 (December 1957).

Richards, Dora (Miler). "A Woman's Diary of the Siege of Vicksburg." *Century Illustrated Monthly Magazine*, vol. 30 (September 1885).

Riggs, Davis F. "Sailors of the U.S.S. *Cairo:* Anatomy of a Gunboat Crew." *Civil War History*, vol. 28, no. 3 (September 1982).

Roberts, John C., and Richard H. Webber. "Gunboats in the River War, 1861–1865." *Proceedings of the United States Naval Institute*, vol. 91 (March 1965).

Robinson, Armstead L. " 'Worser dan Jeff Davis' ": The Coming of Free Labor during the Civil War, 1861–1865." In *Essays on the Postbellum Southern Economy*, edited by Thavolia Glymph. College Station: Texas A & M University Press, 1985.

Roland, Charles P. "Albert Sidney Johnston and the Loss of Forts Henry and Donelson." *Journal of Southern History*, vol. 62 (February 1957).

Rosecrans, William S. "The Battle of Corinth." BL, vol. 2.

Ross, Stephen J. "Freed Soil, Freed Labor, Freed Men: John Eaton and the Davis Bend Experiment." *Journal of Southern History*, vol. 44 (May 1978).

Sanborn, John B. "The Campaign Against Vicksburg." In *Papers of MOLLUS*, vol. 27.

———. "Remarks on a Motion to Extend a Vote of Thanks to General Marshall for Above Paper." In *Papers of MOLLUS*, vol. 29. Wilmington, NC: Broadfoot Publishing Company, 1994.

———. *"The Crisis at Champion's Hill, the Decisive Battle of the Civil War."* St. Paul, MN, 1903.

Sartin, Jeffrey S. "Infectious Diseases during the Civil War: The Triumph of the 'Third Army.' " *Clinical Infectious Diseases*, vol. 16 (April 1993).

Scarborough, William K. "Heartland of the Cotton Kingdom." In *A History of Mississippi*, vol. 1, edited by Richard Aubrey McLemore. Jackson: University & College Press of Mississippi, 1963.

Schnell, J. Christopher. "Mary Livermore and the Great Northwestern Fair." *Chicago History*, vol. 4 (Spring, 1975).

Schenker, Carl R. Jr. "Ulysses in His Tent: Halleck, Grant, Sherman, and the Turning Point of the War." *Civil War History*, vol. 56, no. 2 (June 2010).

Seaton, John. "The Battle of Belmont." In *Sundry Papers of the Kansas Commandery, MOLLUS*, vol. 1.

Sherman, William T. "An Address on Grant." In *Personal Recollections of the War of the Rebellion*, edited by James Grant Wilson and Titus Munson Coan. New York: The New York Commandery, 1891.

———. "The Battle of Pittsburg Landing: A Letter from General Sherman." *United States Service Magazine*, vol. 3 (January 1865).

———. "The Grand Strategy of the War of the Rebellion." *Century Magazine*, vol. 35 (April 1888).

———. Letter to John W. Draper, November 24, 1867, in "Vicksburg by New Years." *Civil War Times Illustrated*, vol. 16 (January 1978).

———. "Sherman's Estimate of Grant." *Century Magazine*, vol. 70 (May 1905).

———. "An Unspoken Address to the Loyal Legion." *North American Review*, vol. 142 (March 1886).

Simon, John Y. "Grant and Halleck: Contrasts in Command." Frank L. Klement Lecture. Milwaukee: Marquette University Press, 1996.

———. "A Marriage Tested by War: Ulysses and Julia Grant." In *Intimate Strategies of the Civil War: Military Commanders and Their Wives*, edited by Carol X. Blesser and Lesley J. Gordon. New York: Oxford University Press, 2001.

———. "That Obnoxious Order." *Civil War Times Illustrated*, vol. 26, no. 6 (1984).

———. "U. S. Grant: The Man and the Image." In *U.S. Grant: The Man and the Myth*, edited by James G. Barber. Carbondale, IL: Southern Illinois University Press, 1985.

Simon, John Y., and David L. Wilson. "Samuel H. Beckwith, Grant's Shadow." In *Grant: Essays and Documents*, edited by John Y. Simon and David L. Wilson. Carbondale: Southern Illinois University Press, 1981.

Simpson, Brooks D. "After Shiloh: Grant, Sherman, and Survival." In *The Shiloh Campaign*, edited by Steven Woodworth. Carbondale: Southern Illinois University Press, 2009.

———. "The Doom of Slavery: Ulysses S. Grant, War Aims, and Emancipation." *Civil War History*, vol. 36 (March 1990).

Smith, Morgan L. "The Assault on Chickasaw Bluffs." BL, vol. 3.

Smith, Myron J. "Gunboats in a Ditch: The Steele's Bayou Expedition, 1863." *Journal of Mississippi History*, vol. 37 (May 1975).

Smith, Timothy B. "'A Siege from the Start': The Spring 1862 Campaign against Corinth, Mississippi." *Journal of Mississippi History*, vol. 66, no. 4 (2004).

Snead, Thomas L. "With Price East of the Mississippi." BL, vol. 2.

Soule, Harrison. "From the Gulf to Vicksburg with 6th Michigan Infantry." In *War Papers Read before the Michigan Commandery of MOLLUS*, vol. 2 (1898).

Stansbury, F. Haydon. "Grant's Wooden Mortars and Some Incidents of the Siege of Vicksburg." *Journal of the American Military Institute*, vol. 4, no. 1 (Spring 1940).

Strong, William E. "The Campaign Against Vicksburg." In *Papers of MOLLUS*, vol. 11.

Sutton, Robert M. "The Illinois Central: Thoroughfare for Freedom." *Civil War History*, vol. 7 (September 1961).

Taylor, John T. "Reminiscences of Services as an Aide-de-Camp with General William Tecumseh Sherman." In *War Talks in Kansas: A Series of Papers Read before the Kansas Commandery of MOLLUS*. Kansas City: Franklin Hudson, 1908).

Thayer, John to, "My Dear Sir and Comrade," September 18, 1891. In *Military History and Reminiscences of the Thirteenth Regiment of Illinois Volunteer Infantry in the Civil War in the United States, 1861–1865*, edited by Asa B. Munn, Amos H. Miller, and W. O. Newton. Chicago: Woman's Temperance Publishing Association, 1872.

Thienel, Phillip M. "Bridges in the Vicksburg Campaign." *Military Engineer*, vol. 47 (November–December 1955).

Thorpe, Thomas Bangs. "Remembrances of the Mississippi." *Harper's New Monthly Magazine*, vol. 12, no. 67 (December 1855).

Throne, Mildred, ed. "An Iowa Doctor in Blue: The Letters of Seneca B. Thrall." *Iowa Journal of History*, vol. 85 (April 1960).

Walke, Henry. "The Gunboats at Belmont and Fort Henry." BL, vol. 1.

————. "The Western Flotilla at Fort Donelson, Island Number Ten, Port Pillow and Memphis." BL, vol. 1.

Wallace, Lew. "The Capture of Fort Donelson." BL, vol. 1.

Warmoth, Henry Clay. "The Vicksburg Diary of Henry Clay Warmoth: Part 1," edited by Paul H. Hess. *Journal of Mississippi History*, vol. 31 (December 1869).

————. *Ibid.*, part 2, vol. 32 (March 1970).

Welles, Gideon. "Admiral Farragut and New Orleans." *Galaxy*, vol. 12, no. 6 (December 1871).

West, Richard Jr. "The Relations Between Farragut and Porter." *Proceedings of the United States Naval Institute*, vol. 61 (July 1935).

Westwood, Howard C. "The Ellet Family Fleet." *Civil War Times Illustrated*, vol. 22, no. 6 (1982).

————. "War on the River: Running Past Vicksburg." *Civil War Times Illustrated*, vol. 2, no. 6 (1982).

Wheeler, Joseph. "Bragg's Invasion of Kentucky." BL, vol. 3.

Widney, Lyman S. "Campaigning with 'Uncle Billy.'" *Neale's Monthly*, vol. 2 (August 1913).

Wilson, Edmund. "Northern Soldiers: Ulysses S. Grant." In *Patriotic Gore: Studies in the Literature of the American Civil War*, by Edmund Wilson. New York: Oxford University Press, 1962.

Wilson, James H. "A Staff Officer's Journal of the Vicksburg Campaign, April 30 to July 4, 1863." James Harrison Wilson Papers, LC.

Winschel, Terrence J. "First Honor at Vicksburg: The 1st Battalion, 13th U.S. Infantry." In *Civil War Regiments: A Journal of the American Civil War*, vol. 2, no. 1 (1998).

————. "To Rescue Gibraltar: John Walker's Texas Division and Its Expedition to Relieve Fortress Vicksburg." In *Civil War Regiments*, vol. 3, no. 3 (1993).

Woodworth, Steven E. "Intolerably Slow: Lew Wallace's March to the Battlefield." In *The Shiloh Campaign*, edited by Steven E. Woodworth. Carbondale: Southern Illinois University Press, 2009.

————. "Vicksburg: Davis, Van Dorn, Pemberton—A Triangulation of Shortcomings." *Civil War*, vol. 46 (August 1994).

Wright. Michael F. "Vicksburg and the Trans-Mississippi Supply Line (1861–1863)." *Journal of Mississippi History*, vol. 43, no. 3 (1981).

"The Yazoo Pass Expedition." *New York Herald*, March 25, 1863.

OFFICIAL REPORTS

Adjutant General's Report for Illinois, revised. Springfield, IL: 1900.

Confederate States of America. *Joint Resolutions in Reference to the Treatment of Colored Troops, February 15, 1864*. In *Confederate Imprints, 1861–1865*. New Haven, CT: Research Publications, 1974.

Eaton, John. *Report of the General Superintendent of Freedmen, Department of the Tennessee and State of Arkansas for 1864*. Memphis: U.S. Government, 1865.

House of Representatives. *Report on the Treatment of Prisoners of War by the Rebel Authorities during the War of the Rebellion*, 40th Congress, 3rd session, 1869, serial 1391. Washington, D.C.: Government Printing Office.

Preliminary Report Touching the Condition and Management of Emancipated Refugees; Made to the Secretary of War by the African Freedman's Inquiry Commission, June 30, 1863. New York: John F. Trow, 1863.

Proceedings of the Mississippi State Convention Held January 7th to 26th, A.D. 1861. Jackson, MS, 1861.

Statistics of the Operation of the Executive Board of the Friends Association of Philadelphia . . . For the Relief of Colored Freedmen. Philadelphia: Inquirer Printing Office, 1864, 1; CT, November 6, 1863.

United States Surgeon-General's Office. *Medical and Surgical History of the War of Rebellion,* vol. 1, part 1, appendix. Washington, D.C.: Government Printing Office, 1861–1865.

UNPUBLISHED ARTICLES

Warren E. Grabau. "The Logistics of the Army of the Tennessee at Vicksburg," unpublished paper in the possession of the Grabau family.

DISSERTATIONS

Bercaw, Nancy. "Politics of Household during the Transition from Slavery to Freedom in the Yazoo-Mississippi Delta, 1861–1876." Ph.D. dissertation, University of Pennsylvania, 1996.

Slay, David H. "New Masters on the Mississippi: The United States Colored Troops of the Middle Mississippi Valley." Ph.D. dissertation, Texas Christian University, 2009.

ILLUSTRATION CREDITS

INDEX

abolitionists, 143, 183, 205, 323, 337, 456, 485, 488

Abrams, Alexander S., 440, 477

Absalom, Absalom! (Faulkner), xi–xii

Adams, Charles Francis, Jr., 16

Adams, Charles Francis, Sr., 118

Adams, Wirt, 397

African Americans, 485–92

  attacks on settlements of, xx

  marriages for, 210

  refugee camps for, 207n

  as servants for Union officers, 205

  in U.S. military, 179n, 201, 205n, 323–24, 325, 333, 336–38, 453–58, 485, 486n, 487, 489–90

  as workers on canal projects in Vicksburg campaign, 154–55, 165–67, 265–66, 267, 281

  as workers on Porter's ship, 151, 178–79

  work programs for, 208–11, 231, 323, 487–89

  see also slaves

Agnew, Samuel A., 232, 233

Ainsworth, Calvin, 335, 340, 384

Albatross, 301, 306, 307

Alcorn, James L., 277

Alden, James, 149

Alison, Joseph Dill, 439–40

Allaire, Charles B., 281

Allen, Charles, 164

Allen, Robert, 221, 238

American Notes (Dickens), 3

Anaconda Plan, 6–7, 163n–64n

Anchuca, 500

Anderson, Robert, 67

Antietam, Battle of, 190, 408, 444, 482

Appler, Jessie, 70, 74

Argonauts, 342, 343, 353

Arkansas, xiii, 32, 163, 193, 194

Arkansas, CSS, 124, 127, 157–62, 166–69, 176, 279, 427n

Arkansas Post, Battle of, 257–58, 263

Army, U.S., 54

  black soldiers in, 201, 323–24, 325, 333, 336–38, 453–58, 485, 486n, 487, 489–90

  Department of the Cumberland, 67

  Department of the Missouri, 32

  Department of the Ohio, 6

  Department of the Tennessee, 190, 210, 259, 264

  Department of the West, 192

  desertions from, 313

  Medals of Honor awarded by, 427

  Navy cooperation with, 11, 55, 94, 275, 285

  see also Union soldiers and officers

Army of Mississippi, 71, 193, 417

Army of Northern Virginia, 186, 193, 242, 408, 480

Army of Relief, 475

Army of Tennessee, 193

Army of the Cumberland, 189

Army of the Gulf, 461

Army of the Mississippi, 87, 92, 257

Army of the Ohio, 56, 74, 82–83, 87, 186, 189, 237

Army of the Potomac, 30, 54, 59n, 182, 190, 193, 205n, 214–15, 408, 477, 484

Army of the Tennessee, xii, xvi, 25, 52, 58, 92, 186, 201, 214–15, 238, 263, 274, 335–36, 339, 374, 379, 410, 416, 424, 456, 460, 479
   see also Vicksburg campaign; Vicksburg campaign, Grant's operations in
Arnold, Isaac, 414
Arnold, James R., 256
Ash, Stephen V., 204
Ashwood, 379
Atlanta, Ga., 436
Audubon, John James, 123
Autry, James L., 125–26

Bacon, Edward, 154, 165
Badeau, Adam, 7, 182, 190, 269, 270, 275–76, 317, 419, 485
Bailey, Theodorus, 112, 116–17
Bakers Creek, 394, 398, 401, 402, 405–6
Baldwin, William E., 372, 373, 474
Baldwin Ferry Road, 424
Balfour, Emma, 242, 416, 417, 437–39, 441
Balfour, William, 242, 416
Banks, Nathaniel, 221–22, 241, 257, 301, 321, 328, 376, 412, 445, 461, 481
   plan for Grant to partner with, 301, 328, 376, 377
   Grant's decision to move on without, 376–77
Baron De Kalb, USS, 283, 286
Barron, Samuel, 101
Bates, Edward, 7–8, 163
Baton Rouge, La., xv, 119–20, 129, 131, 132, 135–36, 165, 170, 175, 240, 257, 359
   Battle of, 167–69, 392
   evacuation of, 170
   Farragut at, xv
"Battle for the Mississippi, The" (Melville), 97
Bayou Baxter, 280, 282, 283, 317
Bayou Macon, 279, 282, 283, 317
Bayou Pierre, 374
Bayou Vidal, 351

Bear, Henry C., 240, 247, 248
Beauregard, P. G. T., 53, 56, 64, 186
   at Corinth, 87–89, 108
   "Lost Opportunity" of, 80–81
   at Shiloh, 64, 71–73, 78–81, 83, 84, 146
Beck, S. C., 215
Beckwith, Samuel H., 26, 27, 450
Bell, Henry H., 107, 113, 128, 132, 135, 150n, 153, 161
Bell, John (politician), 144
Bell, John N. (captain), 336
Belmont, Battle of, 27–34, 36, 38, 44, 55, 70, 86, 181, 213, 238, 318
Benedict, George G., 156
Ben-Hur: A Tale of the Christ (Wallace), 46
Bennett, Thomas W., 342–43
Benton, USS, 8, 10, 153, 162, 249, 345, 348, 361–65
Benton Barracks, 69
Bickerdyke, Mary Ann, 338–39
Bierce, Ambrose, 74, 80, 82–83
Big Black River, 375–76, 380–83, 388–90, 392, 393, 414, 445, 446, 461, 475, 495, 496
Big Black River Bridge, 406
   Battle of, 408–12, 415, 416, 417, 428, 460, 479
Biloxi, Miss., 107, 108
Bissell, Josiah, 283
Black Bayou, 289–90, 292–94, 296–97, 299
Black Hawk, USS, 236, 240, 249, 254, 300
Black Hawk War, 460
Blair, Francis "Frank," Jr., 239, 248, 251–54, 271, 273, 360, 380, 393, 396, 408, 445–47, 496
   in siege of Vicksburg, 422, 424, 426
Blair, Francis Preston, 239
Blair, Montgomery, 102, 223, 239
Blair family, 239
Blanchard, Ira, 201, 224, 229, 352, 375, 386, 477
Blood, James H., 254n

Blue Wing, 257
boats:
 mortar, xv, 10, 46, 55*n*, 153, 178, 283, 288
 ram, 89–90, 135, 283
 "turtle," 8, 10, 47
 see also gunboats; steamboats,
 steamships
Boggs, Harry, 21, 22
Bohemian Brigade, 38
Bolton, Miss., 382, 392–94
Boomer, George B., 403, 404
Boucher, George Oliver, 314
Bovina, Miss., 382
Bowen, John S., 344–45, 349, 353, 359–63,
 382, 394, 472–73
 at Big Black River, 409
 at Champion Hill, 399, 401, 402, 404,
 407–8
 Pemberton and, 374, 401
 at Port Gibson, 372–76
 in siege of Vicksburg, 421
Bower's Landing, 380
Boyd, Cyrus F., 266, 268, 281, 309, 314,
 336
Bragg, Braxton, 89, 186, 189, 193, 195, 226,
 241, 248, 250, 344–45
 at Shiloh, 64, 71, 80, 81, 83
Breckinridge, John C., 64, 137, 144, 145,
 167, 168, 170, 444–45
Bridgeport, Miss., 408, 412
Brierfield Plantation, 126, 304, 487
Brinton, John H., 26, 29, 42, 51, 52, 58,
 59, 215
Brokenburn, 124–25, 126, 356–57
Brooke, Walter, 144, 145
Brooklyn, USS, 106, 112, 115, 121, 131–32,
 135, 138, 150*n*
Brooklyn Navy Yard, 100, 104, 105
Bross, William, 33–34
Brown, Edwin Witherby, 231
Brown, George, 303–4
Brown, Isaac Newton, 157–61, 164–65,
 167, 279, 427*n*

Bruinsburg, Miss., 363–64, 369, 372, 373,
 376, 378, 379
Bruinsburg Road, 271–73
Brown, Will, 266
Browning, Orville H., 182
Buchanan, James, 23, 44, 51, 64
Buchanan, Robert C., 20
Buck, George, 456
Buckner, Simon Bolivar, 44, 48, 50–52,
 472
Buell, Don Carlos, 40, 56, 60, 68, 74, 87,
 92, 94, 163, 186, 189, 237, 321
 on Grant's battlefield preparation, 70–71
 Lincoln and, 189
 at Shiloh, 62, 63, 70–71, 75, 77–78,
 80–86
Bull Run (Manassas), 53, 63, 64, 67, 190,
 193, 405
Burnside, Ambrose, 257, 321
Butler, Benjamin, 102–3, 107, 117–18, 120,
 126, 134, 136, 170, 222
 canal project and, 153–55
 fugitive slaves and, 207*n*, 209*n*–10*n*
Butler, William D., 488–89
Byers, Samuel [S. H.M.] 187, 229–30,
 283–84, 300, 381–82, 384, 391, 396,
 403–4, 406, 432

Cable, George Washington, 98, 116, 117
Cadwallader, Sylvanus, 224, 226, 270,
 292, 296, 386–87, 392, 407, 410, 413,
 428, 429, 448–52, 496
 Three Years with Grant, 448
Cahill, Thomas W., 168
Cairo, Ill., xiii, xviii, 3–11, 12–15, 34, 37,
 38, 40–41, 42, 47, 55, 57, 58, 90, 123,
 177–81, 202, 207, 211, 213, 215, 264,
 323, 324, 330, 380, 413, 450, 478, 481,
 484
 drinking at, 32–33
 Grant at, xvi, xx, 12–13, 25, 32, 36, 123,
 191
 gunboats at, 6–11

Cairo, USS, 10, 179*n*, 237
Calhoun, USS, 308*n*
Cameron, Simon, 4, 33–34, 67–68
Campbell, John, 214
Camp Moore, 167
canal projects:
 black workers on, 154–55, 165–67,
  265–66, 267, 281
 on De Soto Peninsula, 136, 153–56, 163,
  165–67, 259, 280, 281, 299
 Duckport, 328–29, 351–52
 of Grant, 263–66, 269–71, 279, 316–17,
  328–29, 351–52
Canton, Miss., 388–90, 392, 409, 415, 443,
 446
Carolina Sea Islands, 210*n*
Carondelet, USS, 10, 39, 40, 43, 46, 153,
 159–60, 289, 345*n*
Carr, Eugene, 365, 369, 371, 373, 396, 406,
 408, 410
Carter, Hodding, 123–24
Catton, Bruce, 290, 329, 377, 484
cavalry, 217, 224, 226–27
Cayuga, USS, 112
Chalmette, La., 115
Chambers, William Pitt, 129–30, 156–57,
 409, 411
Champion, Matilda, 131, 139, 395–96, 399,
 499
Champion, Sidney S., 131, 139, 394–96,
 497, 499
 death of, 499
Champion Hill, 398–99, 411, 461, 499
 Battle of, 394–408, 414, 415, 417, 419,
  425, 480
Chancellorsville, Va., 381
Chase, Salmon P., 86, 175–76, 182, 184,
 318, 320, 477
Chattanooga, Tenn., 186, 192, 487, 492
Chernow, Ron, 260*n*, 318–19, 450, 452
Cherry, William H., 60
Chicago, Ill., 207
Chicago Times, 292, 314, 315–16, 448–49

Chicago Times-Herald, 427
Chicago Tribune, 30, 33, 41, 85, 149, 197,
 198, 204, 207, 213, 267, 273*n*, 282,
 315, 316, 454, 457, 478
Chickasaw Bayou, 245, 250, 254*n*, 288,
 432, 449
Chickasaw Bayou, Battle of (Battle of
 Walnut Hills), xvii, 242–58, 261, 263,
 271, 290, 302, 312, 313, 334, 338, 359,
 399, 413, 417–19
 map of, 244
Chillicothe, USS, 283, 286, 287
Choctaw, USS, 453–55
churches, 440–41
Cincinnati, USS, 10, 39, 90*n*, 153, 296, 442
Cincinnati Commercial, 68, 86
Cincinnati Gazette, 78, 85, 318
City of Alton, 268
City of Mississippi, 302
City Point, Va., 387
civilians, xix, 138, 139, 150, 416
 in caves, 138, 436–39
 evacuations of, 126, 130, 149
 women, 204–5, 217, 437–39, 441
Civil War:
 beginning of, 23
 Champion Hill as decisive battle of,
  408
 and confiscation of property, 207*n*
 disease and, *see* disease and sickness
 dug-in defenses vs. open field battles
  in, 256
 Emancipation Proclamation and, 201
 Lincoln's shift in policy for, 199, 333–34
 military enlistment and draft for, 146,
  183, 191, 201*n*, 272–73
 purpose of, 201
Clarke, Jim, 395
Clausewitz, Carl von, 484
Clay, Henry, 18
Clinton, Miss., 389, 394, 396–98
Cockrell, Francis M., 343–45, 372, 373,
 402, 404

Cold Harbor, Va., 31
Coldwater River, 277, 284, 285, 287
Columbus, Ky., 13, 16, 27–30, 35, 53, 118, 211, 212
Comstock, Cyrus, 432n
Conestoga, USS, 6, 15
Confederate River Defense Fleet, xvi, 108, 135, 158
Confederate States Army, xii, xix
    and confiscation of property, 207n
    desertions from, 313n
    Northwestern Confederacy and, 184
    number of soldiers in, xix
    revitalization of, 185–86
Confederate States Navy, 8, 90, 100, 101, 104, 108
Confederate States of America, 23, 313
    Congress of, 233, 457
    Kentucky and, 16
    Medals of Honor awarded by, 427n
    newspapers in, 4
    secession of, 23, 67, 143–46, 207n
Confederate War Department, 41, 471
Congress, U.S., 85, 86, 144, 169, 177, 200, 205, 261, 315
    1862 elections for, 183n, 272
Conkling, James C., 482
conspiratorial organizations, 183–84
Constellation, USS, 99
Constitutional Union Party, 144
Cooper, James Fennimore, 18
Copperheads, xvii, 183–84, 314–16, 337
corduroy roads, 353, 380
Corinth, Miss., 53, 56, 57, 70, 71, 91–94, 108, 118, 150, 186, 190–92, 198, 202, 231, 280, 321, 383, 404
    First Battle of, 60–61, 62–65, 87–89
    Grant at, 187–90, 227, 484
    Second Battle of, 186–90, 227
    train maneuver at, 88
Cormal, Thomas, 457
Cornwell, David, 453

cotton, xii, xv, 124, 139, 145, 207–8, 486
    Grant's work camps and, 208–11, 323
    traders of, Grant and, 259–60
    Vicksburg and, 139–41
cotton plantations, see plantations
Craven, Thomas T., 115, 121, 122, 124, 131–32, 135, 151
Crocker, Marcellus, 386
    at Champion Hill, 396, 403–5, 407
    at Jackson, 391
Crooke, George, 371
Crummer, Wilbur F., 401, 433, 435, 438
Crump's Landing, 63, 75
Cumberland River, xx, 13, 15, 16, 35, 36, 42–43, 46, 53, 55, 56, 213, 484
Curtis, Samuel R., 163

Dana, Charles A., 54, 330, 332, 325–26, 348, 349, 374, 386, 414, 429, 447–52, 456, 459
    Greeley and, 325
    on Hovey, 399–400
    on Logan, 401
    sent to spy on Grant, xviii, 322, 325–27
    Sherman and, 325, 326
Daniel, L. L., 242
Davis, Charles Henry, 89, 91, 94, 134, 135, 148, 151–53, 157, 161–64, 166, 167, 176, 178
    Farragut and, 153
    removed from command of Mississippi Squadron, 177
Davis, Eliza, 500
Davis, Jefferson, 5, 13, 35, 53, 64, 89, 101, 108, 126, 141, 144, 161, 167, 191, 193, 195, 232–34, 377, 382, 387, 395, 452, 461, 486, 487, 492
    Albert Sidney Johnston and, 64–65
    Grant's southward strategy and, 344
    Joseph E. Johnston and, 193–94
    Mississippi trip of, 234, 241, 247–48
    Pemberton and, 192, 410

Davis, Jefferson (*cont.*)
  plantation of, 126, 304, 487
  as prisoner, 500
  siege of Vicksburg and, 443–44
  speech of, 247–48
  sworn in as president, 145
  Van Dorn and, 137, 189, 191
Davis, Joseph Emory, 126, 141, 304, 461,
    486–88, 497
  flight from Mississippi, 499–500
  plantation of, 126, 486–87, 500
Davis Bend, Miss., 126, 487–88, 500
D-Day, 365
De Courcy, John F., 251–53
Deer Creek, 290, 293, 334–35, 395
Deitzler, George W., 279, 280
Delhi, La., 356–58
Democratic National Convention, 144
Democrats, 23, 142–44, 182, 184, 239,
    429
  Copperhead, xvii, 183–84, 314–16,
    337
  in elections of 1862, 183*n*, 272
Dennis, Elias S., 453
Dent, Frederick, Jr., 19
Dent, Frederick, Sr., 19–23
Desertion During the Civil War (Lonn),
    313*n*
De Soto, 303
De Soto Peninsula, 124, 162, 263–65, 306,
    346
  canal project in, 136, 153–56, 163,
    165–67, 259, 280, 281, 299
  floods and, 155–56
De Soto Point, 140, 147, 148, 153, 165–66,
    170, 242, 281, 289, 305, 312, 346, 416,
    439
Deupree, J. D., 225
Dewey, George, 114
Dickens, Charles, 3
Dickey, T. Lyle, 226
Diligent, 289, 447–50
Dillon's farm, 390

disease and sickness, xvii, xviii, 11, 89, 155,
    163–65, 167–68, 178, 268–69, 300,
    308, 309–12
  in Confederate army, 311*n*
  malaria, xv, 11, 62, 135, 151, 155–56, 164,
    178, 311, 437, 441, 468
  measles, xvii, 156, 311
  medicine and, 312
  pneumonia, 156–57, 311
  sanitation and, 311
  water and, 311
Disharoon's plantation, 363–64, 371
Dixon, William Y., 130, 138
Dodge, Grenville, 383
Donaldsonville, La., 169
"Donelson" (Melville), 42
Doolittle, James R., 315
Dorsett, Lyle, 34
Douglas, Stephen A., 23, 143, 144
Douglass, Frederick, 210–11
  "U.S. Grant and the Colored People,"
    xiii
Downing, Alexander G., 456
Drennan, William, 397, 398, 405, 440,
    442, 443, 469, 470
Duckport Canal project, 328–29, 351–52
Duff, William L., 280
Duff, William S., 386–87
Duke, Basil W., 74
Dunbar's plantation, 345
Duncan, Johnson K., 111
Dwight, William, 412

Eads, James, 7–11, 36, 47, 90, 153, 237, 288
Eagle Bend, Miss., 290
Eaton, John, 20, 208–11, 226, 231, 319,
    487–89
Eddington, William R., 312–13
Edmondston, Catherine, 483
Edwards, Miss., 382, 383, 387, 388, 392,
    394–97, 406, 408
Edwards Station, 382
Eiffel, Gustav, 432

elections:
  1860 presidential, 143–44
  1862 congressional, 183*n*, 272
Elements of Military Art and Science
  (Halleck), 36
Ellet, Alfred W., 90, 91*n*, 147, 158, 162,
  179, 180, 306–7, 439, 457
Ellet, Charles, Jr., 89–91, 135, 147
Ellet, Charles Rivers, 91, 147–48, 179, 180,
  255, 306–7
  Porter and, 302, 305
  on Red River, 302–6
Ellet, Edward, 307
Ellet, John A., 307
Ellet Horse Marines, 180
Emancipation Proclamation, xix, 183,
  200–201, 230–33, 240, 260, 266, 313,
  323, 337, 457, 482, 485
Emerson, John Wesley, 13, 37
Enterprise, Miss., 473, 491
Era No. 5, 303
Ericsson, John, 8
Essex, USS, 39, 99, 104–5, 153, 157, 162
Ewing, Hugh, 424–26
Ewing, Thomas, Jr., 67
Ewing, Thomas, Sr., 66, 183

Fall, Philip H., 242
Farragut, David Glasgow, xv, xviii, 93–94,
  97, 103–6, 119–29, 131, 132, 134,
  161–64, 167, 169–71, 175, 177, 212,
  265, 300–301, 330, 332*n*, 346, 376,
  441
  background and career of, 104–5
  at Baton Rouge, xv
  Davis and, 153
  Ellet and, 147–48
  at Natchez, xv, 120
  New Orleans expedition of, xiii–xv, 97,
    103–18, 119, 123, 131, 133, 134, 487
  Porter and, 300–302, 306, 307
  Red River blockade of, 306–8

  in siege of Vicksburg, 421
  Vicksburg advance of, 120, 124–28, 394
  Vicksburg departures of, xv, 128–29,
    131, 133, 163
  Vicksburg returns of, 133–34, 135–39,
    142, 146, 147–51, 153, 157, 161–63,
    306–8
  Vicksburg surrender demanded by, xv,
    128
Farragut, George, 104
Farragut, Loyall, 104, 114
Farragut, Susan, 129, 133, 134, 135
Faulkner, William, xi–xii
Fay, Edwin H., 496
Featherston, Winfield, 294–95
Fellman, Michael, 67
Ferguson, Samuel W., 294–95, 334–35,
  395
Fiske, John, 83, 280
Fleetwood, 500
Floyd, John B., 44, 45, 48–49, 51
Foner, Eric, 488
Foote, Andrew Hull, 9–11, 15, 36–41, 55*n*,
  87, 89, 100, 101, 107, 257, 301, 406
  death of, 89*n*
  at Fort Donelson, 43, 45–48
Foote, Shelby, 31, 35, 84, 448
foraging, 201–2, 217, 218, 228–30, 379,
  380, 384, 388
Force, Manning F., 385, 386, 414
Forest Queen, 348–49
Forest Rose, USS, 277
Forlorn Hope, 424–27
Forney, John H., 360, 419
Forrest, Nathan Bedford, 44–46, 48, 51,
  195, 226–27, 379
Fort Cobun, 361, 362, 376
Fort Donelson, 36, 185, 186, 280
  Battle of, xvi, 25, 31, 35, 40–41, 42–57,
    59–61, 63, 64, 69, 70, 86, 89, 93, 118,
    125, 137, 168, 182, 202, 213, 226, 227,
    238, 273, 280, 284, 319, 338, 346, 472,
    484

Fort Henry, 13, 45, 57–59, 185
Battle of, xvi, 35–41, 46–47, 53, 54–56, 64, 118, 125, 227, 238, 406, 484
Fort Hindman, 257
Fort Jackson, 128, 131
in Battle of New Orleans, 109
in Civil War, 98, 101–2, 109–11, 113
Fort Pemberton, 285–88, 300, 375
Fort Pickens, 100–101
Fort Pillow, 89, 118, 133
Fort St. Philip, 98, 101–2, 112, 113, 115, 128, 131
Fort Sumter, 3, 4, 7, 23, 67, 100, 101, 119, 191
Fort Wade, 361, 362, 376
Fort Wagner, 205n, 456
Foster, Henry "Coonskin," 463–65
Foster, James P., 287
Foster, Kate, 491
Foster, William Lovelace, 417, 469–70
Fourteen Mile Creek, 385
Fox, Gustavus Vasa, 101–3, 106, 107, 133, 134, 151, 176–78, 181, 212, 298, 306, 347, 354
Porter and, 103
Frank Leslie's Illustrated Newspaper, 266
Fredericksburg, Battle of, 444
Freedmen's Bureau, 205n
Frémont, John C., 8–10, 15, 23, 24, 27, 30, 32, 321
Friars Point, 240, 241
Fugitive Slave Law, 207n
Fuller, J. F. C., 64n, 274, 381, 419, 483
funerals for soldiers, 310, 340

Gage, M. C., 219
Galena, Ill., 22–24, 320
Gallagher, Gary, 483
Gardner, Franklin, 481
Garfield, James A., 203
Garland, Hamlin, 18, 21, 22, 34, 77, 85, 271
Galveston, Tex., xv

Gayoso House, 236
General Orders No. 11, 259–60
General Price, USS, 288–89
Generalship of Ulysses S. Grant, The (Fuller), 64n
Gettysburg, 408, 444, 477, 482–83
Gift, George W., 158
Gilmer, Jeremy, 35
Given, John G., 202, 203
Gone with the Wind (Mitchell), xii
Gorgas, Josiah, 482–83, 492
Grand Gulf, Miss., 131–32, 136, 328–30, 343–45, 349, 351, 353, 354, 358–61, 365, 369, 372, 373, 375, 376, 378–81, 390, 393, 413, 460
Battle of, 361–63, 479
Grant's cutting of supply line from, 387–88, 390
Grand Junction, Tenn., 191, 194, 198, 201, 207–9, 212, 215, 227
workers' camp at, 208–11
Grant, Frederick, 20, 322, 347, 349, 361–64, 374, 383, 391, 407, 461
Grant, Hannah Simpson, 17, 18, 23, 27
Grant, Jesse Root (father of Ulysses), 17, 18, 22, 27, 32, 85–86, 213, 260, 461
Grant, Jesse Root II (son of Ulysses), 215, 224–25, 347, 348
Grant, Julia Dent, 19–23, 25, 47, 57, 59, 60, 62, 86, 91–92, 215, 224–25, 260, 262, 272, 280, 314, 315, 321, 322, 347–48, 383, 461
Wittenmyer and, 339, 347–48
Grant, Mary, 40, 206, 223–24, 259
Grant, Orvil, 22, 23
Grant, Simpson, 22, 23
Grant, Ulysses S., 11, 17–27, 163, 186
on army subsistence in the country, 189
on art of war, 215
at Belmont, 27–34, 36, 38, 55, 86, 213, 318
birth of, 17

at Cairo, xvi, xx, 12–13, 25, 32, 36, 123, 191

cigars smoked by, 54, 80, 477

command positions of, 24, 54, 56–59, 87–88, 92, 190, 480

command style and skill of, 25, 31, 34, 49–50, 70, 290, 381, 414, 479–80

at Corinth, 187–90, 227, 484

criticisms and charges against, xvii, 224, 314–16, 318–22

Dana's spying on, xviii, 322

drinking of, and accusations of drinking, xvii, xviii, 12, 17, 20, 21, 32–36, 43, 56–57, 86, 197, 224, 315, 318–19, 327, 340, 383, 386–87, 447–52, 480

early life of, 17–18

Eaton and, 20, 208–11, 226, 319, 487

Emancipation Proclamation and, 200

as equestrian, 19

farm of, 20–21

first Civil War combat of (Belmont), 27–34, 36, 38, 55, 86, 213, 318

at Fort Donelson, xvi, 25, 31, 35, 40–41, 42–57, 59–61, 64, 69, 70, 86, 93, 118, 137, 213, 226, 227, 280, 319, 472, 484

at Fort Henry, xvi, 35–41, 53, 54–56, 118, 227, 484

Galena years of, 22–23, 320

Halleck and, 195–97

Halleck's accusation of insubordination by, 56–67, 59–60

Halleck's demotion of, 87–88

Halleck's orders to remain in defensive position, 185

Halleck's restoration of command of, 92

Halleck's support of, over McClernand, 196, 221, 222

Hamilton and, 314–15

Iuka battle and, 187, 222, 227

Jews expelled from military district by, 259–60

Kountz and, 318

Lincoln and, 24, 54, 59, 86, 227, 259, 260, 318–22, 414, 471, 484

Lincoln's letter to, after victory, 478–79

logistics and, 212, 221, 378, 381

maps of, xx, 13, 19, 218

McClernand and, 25, 31, 181–82, 184, 221, 318, 375, 429, 459–60

McClernand relieved of command by, 459–61

McClernand's congratulatory order and, 459–60

McClernand's orders and, 196–97

McPherson and, 282

memoirs of, 25–26, 28, 57, 190, 228–29, 260n, 275, 282, 290, 329, 331, 365, 378, 405, 410, 419, 462n, 473n, 474, 496

in Mexican War, 19–20, 22, 24, 25, 191, 212, 378, 472

migraine headaches of, 20, 281, 447

militia organized by, 24

name of, 17–18

newspapers and, 315–16

at Paducah, 13–16, 213

Pemberton and, 472

Pemberton's surrender to, 472–74

Shepard and, 458–59

Sherman's partnership with, 54, 69, 86, 91–93, 228, 259, 262

Sherman's talks with, 495

at Shiloh (Pittsburgh Landing), xvi, 31, 55, 60–61, 62–65, 69–87, 92, 93, 187, 213, 224, 226, 227, 280, 314, 334, 484

slaves and, 18, 21, 32, 52, 206, 323–24, 485–86, 490

as store clerk, 22, 24

swearing eschewed by, 26–27

turning point in career of, 377

at West Point, 16, 18, 19, 21, 22, 24, 37, 432

Grant, Ulysses S. (*cont.*)
  wounded soldiers and, 50–51
  writing of, 25–26
  see also Vicksburg campaign, Grant's
    operations in
Grant, Ulysses S., Jr., 20
Graveyard Road, 422–24
Great Redoubt, 427
Greeley, Horace, 325
Green, Martin E., 372, 374, 402
Greene, Francis Vinton, 321
Greenville, Miss., 334–37, 344, 345, 372,
  446
Greenwood, Miss., 285, 287
Gregg, John, 242, 387, 388
  at Raymond, 385, 386
Gregory, Edward S., 436, 442, 483
Grenada, Miss., 218, 221, 238, 241, 250,
  255, 275n, 285, 329–30
Grierson, Benjamin H., 314, 358–59,
  364
Griffith, John S., 225
Griffith, Joseph, 428
Grimes, James W., 319
Guelzo, Allen C., 55, 183n
guerrilla warfare, 132–33, 136, 179, 181, 210,
  229, 239, 482, 490, 491, 496
Gulf of Mexico, xiii, xviii, 97, 133, 163–64,
  183, 330
  map of Mississippi River from New
    Orleans to, 110
gunboats, 6, 38, 53, 55, 55n, 56, 89, 90, 128,
  150n, 178, 220, 241, 242, 255, 257,
  263, 264, 275, 287–91, 293, 329, 351,
  409, 413, 487
  at Fort Donelson, 45–48
  ironclad, xv, xvi, xviii, xx, 6–11, 38–41,
    43, 45–48, 55, 87, 90, 102, 133, 135,
    148, 151, 153, 179, 180, 213, 273, 283,
    285–87, 290, 308, 320, 345–47, 352,
    360, 362, 376, 452, 455, 481
  Sherman's flotilla on the Yazoo, 359–61
  timberclad, xv, 6, 15, 28, 45–46, 79–80

tinclad, 179, 283, 286
and Yazoo Pass opening, 288
Gwin, William, 159, 248–49

Hall, Winchester, 130, 156, 157, 252
Halleck, Henry Wager, 32, 36–38, 40, 42,
  43, 54, 56–61, 68–70, 83, 86–88, 91,
  92, 150, 153, 163, 175–77, 180, 182,
  184, 189, 202, 212, 213, 238, 264, 272,
  323, 328, 344, 376, 412, 445, 457, 461,
  478
change in Vicksburg invasion plan
  suggested by, 220–21
command of all forces assumed by,
  87
at Corinth, 87–88, 186
drinking of, 56–57
forces dispersed by, 93–94, 186
Grant and, 195–97
Grant accused of insubordination by,
  56–67, 59–60
Grant demoted by, 87–88
Grant ordered to remain in defensive
  position by, 185
Grant restored to command by, 92
Grant's correspondence with, 190, 235,
  259, 260, 270, 273, 283–85, 315–18,
  322, 331, 333–34, 338, 363, 375–77, 383,
  391, 429, 430, 460, 473n
Grant's drive to Mississippi and, 217
Grant supported over McClernand by,
  196, 221, 222
Grant's victory and, 479
and plan for Grant to partner with
  Banks, 301, 328, 376, 377
Sherman and, 68, 69
Steele's Bayou expedition and, 290
Yazoo expedition and, 285, 302
Halstead, Murat, 86, 318
Hamilton, Charles S., 190–91, 198, 214,
  314–15
Hampton Roads, Va., 151
Hardee, William J., 64, 73, 81

hardtack, 379, 384, 414, 432–33
Hard Times, 353–55, 360–62
Harlan, James, 30, 86
Harper's Weekly, 210, 241
Harris, Annie, 146
Harrison, Isaac F., 342, 343
Hartford, USS, 106–7, 109, 112–14, 116,
    117, 120, 121, 129, 132, 133, 134, 136,
    138, 147, 149, 160, 300–301, 306, 307,
    332n
Haynes' Bluff, 171, 246, 248–49, 255–56,
    271, 285, 288, 302, 320–22, 327,
    328, 359–60, 388, 413, 415, 445–47,
    461
Heath, Corydon, 457
Hébert, Louis, 463, 465
Helena, Ark., 163, 164, 194, 218, 221,
    238–40, 262, 264, 265, 277, 283,
    300
Henry Clay, 349
Henry Von Phul, 347–49, 352
Hickenlooper, Andrew, 353, 435, 462–65,
    467
Hill's plantation, 292–93, 295–97
Hillyer, William, 378
Hoge, Jane, 309, 310, 339, 466
Holly Springs, Miss., xvii, 194–95,
    212, 214–17, 219, 224, 227, 234–35,
    272
    Van Dorn's destruction of, 224–28, 234,
    239
Holmes, Emma, 192, 483
Holmes, Samuel A., 404
Holmes, Theophilus H., 193–95
Hooker, Joseph, 197, 214, 215, 316, 321,
    381, 446
Hopkins, Owen J., 384, 386, 426, 430
hospitals, xx, 18, 78, 82, 89, 165, 264,
    268–69, 309, 340, 364, 407, 466–67,
    475
    Bickerdyke and, 338–39
    in siege of Vicksburg, 439–40
Hough, A. H., 466

Hovey, Alvin P., 218, 373, 374, 391
    at Champion Hill, 396, 399–407
Howard, R. L., 369–71
Howe, Orion P., 422–23
Hurlbut, Stephen A., 63, 75, 77, 264, 269,
    315, 445
Hurricane Plantation, 126, 486–87,
    500

Illinois Central Railroad, 4
Indianola, USS, 303–6, 346
Ingraham, Alfred, 379
Ingraham, Elizabeth Meade, 232,
    379–80
Ione, 343–45, 350, 351
ironclad gunboats, xv, xvi, xviii, xx,
    6–11, 38–41, 43, 45–48, 55, 87, 90,
    102, 133, 135, 148, 151, 153, 179, 180,
    213, 273, 283, 285–87, 290, 308, 320,
    345–47, 352, 360, 362, 376, 452, 455,
    481
Ironton, Mo., 12–13
Iroquois, USS, 119, 129
Irving, Washington, 18
Island Mound, 455n
Island No. 10, 35, 55n, 87, 118

Jackson, Andrew, 115, 239
Jackson, Isaac, 314, 398
Jackson, Miss., xvii, 128, 190, 198, 212,
    247, 264, 272, 359, 369, 378, 386–89,
    392, 397, 406, 493–96, 499
    Battle of, 390, 391–92, 397, 413–14
    Southern Railroad and, 382, 383
Jackson, Tenn., 188, 190
Jackson Mississippian, 4, 144
Jackson Road, 394, 396, 398, 399, 401–3,
    406, 424, 462, 476
Jackson Semi-Weekly Mississippian, 135
James River, 176, 484
Jenney, William Le Baron, 220, 251, 266,
    299, 360, 429, 432, 433, 461
Jessee, James, 392

Jews, 259–60
John Adams, USS, 99
Johnson, Andrew, 488
Johnson, W. A., 247
Johnston, Albert Sidney, 35–36, 41, 48, 53, 56, 60, 64–65, 108
    death of, 79
    at Shiloh, 64, 65, 71, 73, 78–79, 84
Johnston, Joseph E., 192–94, 241, 248, 344–45, 349, 377, 378, 387–90, 392–94, 406, 409, 410, 443–46, 452, 475, 492–94, 499, 500
    at Canton, 388–90, 392, 415, 443, 446
    at Champion Hill, 397
    Longstreet and, 444
    Pemberton and, 389–90, 393, 394, 409–10, 415, 462
    siege of Vicksburg and, 419, 433, 439, 442, 443–44, 461, 462, 467, 471
Jolly, William H., 365
Jomini, Antoine-Henri, 36, 37
Jones, James Henry, 409, 468
Jones, Joseph, 311*n*
Jones, Joshua, 343, 344, 350
Jones, "Russ," 273*n*
Jones, William, 20, 21

Kangaroo shantytown, 141
Kansas cavalry, 217, 224
Kellogg, J. J., 419–22, 424, 426, 431, 433, 467
Kennebec, USS, 127, 132
Kentucky, 4, 13, 16, 32, 163, 186, 189, 190, 200, 237
    map of Kentucky-Tennessee theater, 14
Kimball, Nathan, 446–47
Kiper, Richard L., 223*n*
Kircher, Henry A., 251–52
Kittoe, Edward D., 319
Knights of the Golden Circle, 183–84

Knox, Thomas W., 157, 201–2, 206, 246, 249, 261–62
Kountz, William J., 318

Lafayette, USS, 345*n*, 348
La Grange, Tenn., 190, 191, 194, 195, 197, 198, 199, 201, 202, 204, 207, 213, 214, 227, 229–30, 358
Lake Providence, La., 242, 331, 333, 337, 344, 345, 453, 455
    expedition at, xviii, 274–76, 279–85, 299, 300, 317
Lake St. Joseph, 353, 355–56
    plantations of, 355–56
Lancaster, 307
Lawler, Michael Kelly, 410, 412, 428
Lead Mine Regiment, 464–65
Lee, Robert E., 186, 190, 192, 193, 234, 242, 257, 381, 408, 444, 477–78, 480, 482–84
Lee, Samuel Phillips, 120, 125, 128, 129, 134, 164
    Vicksburg surrender demanded by, 125–26, 421
Lee, Stephen Dill, 334–35, 344, 345, 414, 474
    at Champion Hill, 399, 401, 402, 414, 425
    at Chickasaw Bayou, 242–45, 247–52, 255
    in siege of Vicksburg, 425
Leggett, Mortimer, 464
Lexington, USS, 6, 28, 79–80, 455
Lick Creek, 64, 84
Lieb, Hermann, 453–54
Life on the Mississippi (Twain), xiii
Lincoln, Abraham, xiii, xv, xviii, 4, 6–8, 10, 23, 32, 34, 37, 54, 85, 92, 99, 100, 101, 103, 107, 122, 137, 145, 175, 177, 186, 207, 222–23, 239, 262, 264, 272, 306, 315–18, 328, 381, 427, 461, 482, 490
    and accusations against Grant, 318–21

assassination of, 358
Buell and, 189
canal project and, 136, 259, 270
congressional elections and, 183*n*, 272
Copperheads and, 183–84
Dana and, 322, 327
Emancipation Proclamation of, xix, 183, 200–201, 230–33, 240, 260, 266, 313, 323, 337, 457, 482, 485
eye-for-an-eye policy declared by, 458
Farragut and, 105, 133–34
Grant and, 24, 54, 59, 86, 227, 259, 260, 318–22, 414, 471, 484
and Grant's order expelling Jews, 260
Grant's strategy questioned by, 319
Knox and, 261–62
letter to Grant from, after victory, 478–79
McClernand as viewed by, 196, 332, 429
McClernand's Vicksburg campaign and, 181–85, 256, 258, 261, 262
McClernand's Vicksburg orders from, 185, 196–97, 222–23
military service and, 146, 183, 191, 201*n*, 272
New Orleans and, 102
opposition to administration of, 183
Porter and, 177, 180, 184*n*
in presidential election, 143, 144
Second Confiscation Act of, 199–200, 201, 207
shift in war policy of, 199, 333–34
Vicksburg surrender and, 471, 477–78
Yazoo expedition and, 301–2
Lincoln, Mary Todd, 137, 427
Liddell Hart, B. H., 75, 85*n*
Lindsay, Lazarus, 125
Lingerman, Gerald F., 313*n*
Lioness, USS, 255
Little Rock, Ark., 194, 258
Livermore, Mary, 339, 340, 466
Livermore, William R., 228
Lockett, Cornelia, 164, 167

Lockett, Samuel H., xvi, 137, 149, 155, 156, 164–65, 167, 170, 171, 194, 361, 389, 406, 463
at Big Black River, 408–11
in siege of Vicksburg, 421
Logan, John "Black Jack," 26, 29, 88, 282, 337, 374, 385, 475, 476, 491
at Champion Hill, 396, 400, 401, 407
Louisiana Redan crater and, 462–63, 465
at Raymond, 385–86
in siege of Vicksburg, 424
London *Times*, 110, 200
Long, E. B., 15–16, 157
Longstreet, James, 444
Lonn, Ella, 313*n*
Lord, Lida, 412, 417, 437, 441, 442, 476
Lord, Margaret, 476
Lord, William, 411, 412, 417, 437, 441, 476
Loring, William, 285–86, 288, 300, 372, 374, 375, 382, 390, 394, 406
at Big Black River, 409
at Champion Hill, 398, 399, 401, 404
Pemberton and, 398, 401
Louisiana, xii, xiii, xvii, xviii, 67, 118, 126, 151, 460, 482, 496–97
Grant's march through, 331, 340–42
map of Grant's march through, 341
Louisiana, CSS, 109, 112, 114–15
Louisiana Redan, 462–67, 472
Louisiana State Seminary of Learning and Military Academy, 66, 67
Louisville, Ky., 65, 186
Louisville, USS, 10, 46, 153, 236, 345*n*
Lovell, Mansfield, 108, 109, 116, 117

Magnolia, USS, 259, 267, 269, 273*n*, 274, 321
Magnolia Church, 372
malaria, xv, 11, 62, 135, 151, 155–56, 164, 178, 311, 437, 441, 468
Mallory, Charles, 207*n*
Manassas, CSS, 108, 113, 114

Manassas (Bull Run), 53, 63, 64, 67, 190, 193, 405

Manning, Chandra, 207n

maps:

Battle of Shiloh, 72

Chickasaw Bayou, 244

Grant's invasion of northern Mississippi (November–December 1862), 216

Kentucky-Tennessee theater, 14

Mississippi River from Gulf of Mexico to New Orleans, 110

Mississippi Valley, xiv

siege of Vicksburg (May 18–July 4, 1863), 418

Vicksburg (June–July 1862), 152

Vicksburg Campaign (April–July 1863), 370

Yazoo Pass and Steele's Bayou expeditions, 278

Marine Hospital, 439

Marshall, Thomas A., 144, 145

Marx, Karl, 201

Maryland, 186, 189–90, 200, 381, 483

Mason, Louis, 365

Maury, Dabney H., 227, 246, 250, 294, 312

McClellan, George B., 6, 8, 24, 30, 55–57, 92, 102–3, 151, 176, 189–90, 193, 215, 316, 321, 446, 482, 484

McClernand, John A., 25, 31, 38, 70, 175, 181–85, 195, 211n, 212, 220–22, 236, 239, 251, 256–58, 263–65, 267, 268, 270, 279, 317, 330, 331–35, 351–55, 364, 365, 373–75, 382, 383, 392, 393, 406, 415, 461, 480

advances on Vicksburg, 413

at Arkansas Post, 257, 258, 263

at Belmont, 29, 31, 70, 181

at Big Black River, 408, 409, 411

canal project and, 265, 269–70

Champion Hill and, 396–98, 400, 403–5

character of, 182, 184

clause in Vicksburg orders for, 185, 196–97, 222–23

congratulatory order of, 459–60

at Fort Donelson, 42, 43, 48, 49, 70, 182

Grant and, 25, 31, 181–82, 184, 221, 318, 375, 429, 459–60

Halleck's support of Grant over, 196, 221, 222

Lincoln and Vicksburg campaign of, 181–85, 256, 258, 261, 262

Lincoln's view of, 196, 332, 429

Porter and, 236

at Port Gibson, 373–75

at Raymond, 389

relieved of command of Vicksburg campaign, 258, 262, 459–61

remarriage of, 222, 256, 354

Sherman's meeting with, 256–57

at Shiloh, 63, 70, 75, 76, 182, 184n

in siege of Vicksburg, 423, 424, 428–31

southward push of, 332–35, 340, 342–44, 351–53

Wilson and, 460–61

Yates and, 354

McClure, Alexander K., 86

McCulloch, Henry E., 453–55

McFeely, William S., 25, 260, 448, 451

McGinnis, George F., 400–402

McKeever, Chauncey, 30

McPherson, James Birdseye, 43, 50, 190–91, 198, 199, 214, 234, 264, 280, 282–84, 315, 317, 333, 342, 353, 354, 364, 373, 375–76, 379, 380, 382, 383, 386, 415, 430, 460, 462, 464–66, 472, 477, 479, 481, 491, 493

advances on Vicksburg, 413

at Big Black River, 408, 411

career of, 280

at Champion Hill, 396, 408

character and appearance of, 282

Grant and, 282
at Jackson, 387, 391, 393
McClernand's congratulatory order
    and, 459–60
plundering by army of, 355–56
at Raymond, 385–87
in siege of Vicksburg, 423, 424, 427–29,
    432
McPherson, James M., 161, 313*n*
Meade, George Gordon, 380, 477–78,
    482, 484
measles, xvii, 156, 311
Mechanicsburg, Miss., 445–47, 461
Medals of Honor, 427
Medill, Joseph, 85, 315–16
Meigs, Montgomery C., 100
Melville, Herman, 42, 97, 347, 349
Memphis, Tenn., xv, xvi, 13, 56, 89–91, 94,
    97, 98, 118, 124, 133, 135, 139, 169, 185,
    195, 212, 213, 219, 220, 222, 223, 235,
    238, 239, 250, 264, 272, 280, 329, 330,
    345, 352, 380, 413, 466, 481
option to return to, from Vicksburg,
    272–73
Memphis and Charleston Railroad, 62,
    321
Memphis Daily Bulletin, 260
Meredith, William T., 112–13
Merrimack, USS, 8–9
Mexican War, 46, 56, 63, 120, 137, 192,
    285, 299, 375, 395, 472
Grant in, 19–20, 22, 24, 25, 191, 212,
    378, 472
Porter in, 99
Militia Act, 201*n*
Miller, Dora Richards, 411, 436
Miller, M. M., 456
Milliken's Bend, La., 241, 257, 264, 269,
    270, 284, 299, 312, 317, 326, 328,
    329, 332, 338–40, 344, 351, 352, 354,
    364, 371, 376, 378, 380, 381, 413, 432,
    452–53, 455–58, 480
Battle of, 453–55, 459

mines, 277
    naval, 237, 255
Mississippi, xii, 60, 150, 185, 186, 188–90,
    212, 213, 219, 264–65, 480, 482,
    496–97
Davis's trip to, 234, 241, 247–48
secession of, 145, 146
slaves in, 142, 206, 219, 230–32, 233*n*,
    298
state convention of, 144–45
Mississippi, CSS, 115–16
Mississippi, The (Greene), 321
Mississippi, USS, 109
Mississippi Central Railroad, 272
Grant's march down line of, xvii,
    190–91, 197, 212–13, 214–35, 272
Mississippi Delta, *see* Yazoo-Mississippi
    Delta
Mississippi Marine Brigade, 179–80, 306,
    439, 457
Mississippi Ram Fleet, 89–90
Mississippi River, xii, xiii, xvii, xviii,
    3–7, 11, 12, 13, 16, 35, 55, 62–63,
    89, 94, 97, 119–24, 128, 133, 134,
    140, 143, 164, 167, 170, 175, 182–84,
    195, 240, 257–58, 267, 271, 283,
    285, 302, 329, 349, 415, 475,
    480–82
Baton Rouge evacuation and, 170
changing course of, 121–22
Farragut's New Orleans expedition and,
    97, 103–18
Grant's crossing of, 328, 342, 344,
    363–65
Island No. 10 on, 35, 55*n*, 87, 118
map of, from Gulf of Mexico to New
    Orleans, 110
rising and falling of, 121, 123, 129, 170,
    316–17
sandbars in, 121
snags in, 121
Mississippi River Squadron, xvi, xx,
    177–78, 237

Mississippi Valley, xviii, xx, 4, 8, 25, 62, 92, 107, 118–20, 123–24, 175, 190, 238
  map of, xiv
  slaves in, 206
Missouri, 4, 13, 200
Mitchell, John K., 109, 115
Mitchell, Margaret, xii
Mitchell, Mary Elizabeth "Lise," 500
Mobile, Ala., 120, 133–34
Mobile and Ohio Railroad, 62
Mobile Bay, 103, 120, 121, 133, 158
Moltke, Helmuth von, 76
Monitor, USS, 8
Monroe, John T., 117
Monroe, La., 124, 264, 357–58
Montgomery, Ala., 145
Montgomery, Benjamin T., 486–88
Montgomery, Isaiah, 487
Montgomery, James, 90
Montgomery, Lewis M., 472–73
Moore, Thomas O., 108
Morgan, George Washington, 237, 240, 250–51, 253, 254n, 258
Morgan, Sarah, 119–20, 132–33, 136, 499
mortar boats, xv, 10, 46, 55n, 153, 178, 283, 288
Moss, A. Hugh, 349, 441, 492, 496
Mound City, Ill., 9, 40, 48, 178, 345n
Mound City, USS, 10, 90n
Mumford, William B., 117–18
Murfreesboro, Battle of, 499
Murphy, Robert C., 225, 226
My Story of the War (Livermore), 339

Napoleon, 189, 381, 479, 484
Nashville, Tenn., 13, 15, 53, 56, 57, 59, 60, 63, 118, 125, 392, 484
  Fort Donelson and, 48–50, 53
Natchez, Miss., 120, 121, 125, 142–44, 486
  Farragut at, xv, 120

Navy, U.S., 6, 8, 54, 94, 104, 133, 153, 177, 180
  Army cooperation with, 11, 55, 94, 275, 285
  black sailors in, 179n, 486n
  ranks in, 100n
  union of blue-water and brown-water navies, 153
Navy Department, U.S., 99, 101, 122, 148, 151, 176, 179–81, 212, 298, 347, 477
Nelson, Horatio, 97, 107, 162, 286
Nelson, William "Bull," 75, 80, 83, 87
Nevins, Allan, 76, 83, 184
New Carthage, La., 328–32, 342, 343, 345, 348, 349, 352, 376, 480
New Orleans, La., xvi, xviii, 4, 6, 7, 93, 94, 122, 134, 139, 141, 151, 158, 161–63, 169, 170, 183, 186, 222, 301, 481
  Battle of (1815), 109, 115
  Farragut's expedition to, xiii–xv, 97, 103–18, 119–20, 131, 133, 134, 487
  Fort Jackson and, 98, 101–2, 109–11, 113
  Fort St. Philip and, 98, 101–2, 112, 113, 115
  Fox's plan for, 101–2
  map of Mississippi River from Gulf of Mexico to, 110
  Porter and, 97–98, 101–3, 107, 111, 113, 115, 118
  Union capture of, 117–18, 125, 126, 130, 131, 134
Newport, R.I., 176, 177
newspapers and reporters, 4, 262
  Sherman and, 68, 91, 239, 261, 360
  Shiloh and, 85–86
  see also specific newspapers
New York, N.Y., 142, 183
New-York Daily Tribune, xviii
New York Herald, 31, 56, 109, 201–2, 261
New York Sun, 54
New York Times, 5, 26, 32, 202, 260, 270, 309, 334, 446, 450, 461
New York Tribune, 17, 53, 68, 201, 322, 325

New York World, 261, 314
Nims's Massachusetts artillery battery, 165
Nolan, Cathal J., 479–80
Norfolk, Va., 104–6
North America (Trollope), 3, 5
Northwestern Confederacy, 184

Oakes, James, 230
O'Brien, John, 458
O'Dea, John, 426–27
Oglesby, Richard J., 12
Ohio and Mississippi Railroad, 238
Ohio River, xiii, xx, 3, 5, 15, 16, 55*n*, 186, 238
Olmsted, Frederick Law, 265–66, 299, 321–22
Opossum, 343
Ord, Edward, 187, 188, 459, 461
Order of American Knights, 184
Orme, William Ward, 200, 439
Osbon, Bradley S., 109, 112–14
Osterhaus, Peter J., 340–42, 353, 373, 396, 400, 405, 408, 410, 445
Owen, Robert, 486
Owl Creek, 64, 84
Oxford, Miss., xi
    in Grant's march, xii, xvii, 197, 218–21, 222–25, 228, 233

Paducah, Ky., 13–16, 34, 38, 58, 213, 238, 484
Palmer, James S., 119–20, 129
Parker, John, 230
Parrott gunners, 439, 440, 463
Parry, Augustus, 426
Parsons, Lewis B., 238, 264–65, 289, 318
Peabody, Everett, 73
Pearl River, 388, 393, 493, 494
Pemberton, John Clifford, xvi, xvii, 191–95, 208, 212, 215, 218–21, 223, 225, 227, 228, 234, 238–39, 241–42, 254, 255, 262, 263, 264, 271, 279, 285, 300, 344–45, 349, 358–61, 363, 372,

375, 377–79, 385, 387–90, 393, 395, 396, 406, 407, 412–15, 452, 476, 491, 493, 499
    at Big Black River, 409–11
    Bowen and, 374, 401
    at Champion Hill, 394, 396–99, 401, 402, 404–5, 407, 408, 417
    Chickasaw battle and, 250
    Davis and, 192, 410
    Grant and, 472
    Grant's strategies to mislead, 334, 344, 358–60, 382
    Grant's supply line and, 388, 394, 397, 417
    Grant's surrender terms and, 472–74
    Grierson's raid and, 358–59
    Holly Springs and, 225
    Holmes and, 194
    Johnston and, 389–90, 393, 394, 409–10, 415, 462
    letter to, 471
    Loring and, 398, 401
    in Mexican War, 192
    Northern birth and upbringing of, 191–92
    paroled army of, 473–75, 492
    at Port Gibson, 372
    in siege of Vicksburg, 416–21, 430–31, 433, 434, 441, 443–45, 467–70
    surrender of, 471–75
    Tallahatchie line abandoned by, 218–19
Pemberton, Martha "Pattie," 191
Pen and Powder (Wilkie), 450
Peninsula Campaign, 55, 92
Pensacola, USS, 106
Perkins, George, 116–17
Perkins, John, Jr., 351
Perkins's plantation, 343, 351–54, 378, 457
Perrett, Geoffrey, 187
Perry, Oran, 313, 342, 343, 350
Pettus, John J., 7, 144, 234, 247
Phelan, James, 233, 234, 247
Pickens, Francis, 192

Pickett, Jane, 231
pillaging and raids, 217, 224, 281, 395, 496
  by Blair's army, 445–47, 496
  by Grant's army, xii, 198–99, 201–5, 214, 217, 218, 231, 334–36, 356, 379–80, 384
  by McPherson's army, 355–56
  Sherman and, 203, 229, 336, 392–93, 446, 484, 493–95, 497, 499
Pillow, Gideon, 13, 15, 16, 28, 31, 44, 45, 48–49, 51
Pirtle, John B., 138, 168, 170
Pitts, Florison D., 229
Pittsburgh, USS, 10, 46, 345*n*, 350, 362
Pittsburgh Landing, 60, 62, 63, 69, 71, 74–76, 80, 81, 84, 86, 87, 108, 125, 238
  see also Shiloh, Battle of
plantations, 281, 488
  Deep South, 206
  Lake St. Joseph, 355–56
  owners' flight from, 356–57
  ownership regained, 488
  Union soldiers' disgust toward, 203–4
Plum Point Bend, 90
pneumonia, 156–57, 311
Pointe Clear (Smith's plantation), 343, 351
Point of Rock, 344, 361
Polk, James K., 19
Polk, Leonidas, 13, 27–29, 64
Pook, Samuel, 8, 11
Pope, John, 55*n*, 87, 88, 92, 94, 190
Porter, David, 99
Porter, David, Sr., 104
Porter, David Dixon, xv–xviii, 93, 94, 97–105, 120, 121, 134, 135, 137–39, 149–51, 157, 176–82, 184*n*, 196, 219, 236–37, 239, 240, 241, 257, 258, 263–65, 273–75, 279, 285, 300–307, 322, 327–30, 332, 343–49, 351, 352, 354, 356, 360–64, 372, 376, 377, 380,

388, 409, 411, 413, 415, 447, 452, 455, 462, 473, 477–78, 480–82, 487
  at Arkansas Post, 257
  background and career of, 99–100
  at Chickasaw Bayou, 245, 247–49, 254–56
  Ellet and, 302, 305
  Farragut and, 300–302, 306, 307
  Farragut as brother of, 104
  and Farragut's loyalty to the Union, 105–6
  former slaves as workers on ship of, 151, 178–79
  Fox and, 103
  at Grand Gulf, 361–63
  Grant's co-direction of Vicksburg campaign with, 211–12, 265, 330
  journal and memoirs of, 112*n*, 184*n*, 211*n*
  Lincoln and, 177, 180, 184*n*
  McClernand and, 236
  in Mexican War, 99
  New Orleans expedition and, 97–98, 101–3, 107, 111, 113, 115, 118
  at Rolling Fork, 293–96, 298, 300
  Sherman and, 180, 181, 236–37, 259
  and Sherman's rescue march from Hill's plantation to Rolling Fork, 296–97
  in siege of Vicksburg, 416, 423, 432, 436, 438–40, 442, 468, 469
  slaves liberated by, 297–98
  at Steele's Bayou, 287–91, 292–300, 305, 307, 312, 320, 424
  Taylor and, 457–58
  Vicksburg fire planned by, 149
  wounding of, 363
Porter, William "Dirty Bill," 157, 162, 168
Porter, Horace, 26–27
Port Gibson, Miss., 137, 363, 365, 378, 379, 381, 382, 392
  Battle of, 369–76, 379, 402, 414, 420, 460, 479

Port Hudson, La., xiii, xv, 167, 169, 170, 182–83, 195, 222, 241, 257, 264, 274, 301, 304, 306, 328, 376, 412, 445, 456, 481

Port Royal, S.C., 102*n*, 273–74

Powhatan, USS, 97, 100, 101

Prentiss, Benjamin M., 5, 63, 73, 75, 77, 78, 81, 83, 86

presidential election of 1860, 143–44

Price, Sterling, 186–89, 222

Prime, Frederick E., 431–32, 436

Prospect Hill, 412

Queen of the West, USS, 159, 162, 237, 238, 302–6, 308*n*, 346

Quinby, Isaac F., 284, 286–87, 299–300, 315

Railroad Redoubt, 424, 428, 429

railroads, 7, 55, 62, 87–89, 129, 163, 185, 194, 275*n*, 358, 382, 445, 480, 484
   Grant's reliance on single railroad in Vicksburg campaign, 212–13, 228
   Memphis and Charleston, 62, 321
   Mobile and Ohio, 62
   Southern Railroad of Mississippi, 382, 383, 388, 392, 393, 421, 424
   Vicksburg, Shreveport & Texas, 124, 140, 246–47
   Vicksburg and, 124, 139, 140, 170, 246–47, 382, 388, 415

ram warfare, 89–90, 108–9, 135, 147, 180, 283, 307

Randolph, George W., 195

Randolph, Tenn., 180–81

rape, 204–5, 217, 458

Rawlins, John A., 23–26, 31–34, 37–38, 51, 78, 224, 258–60, 273–74, 319, 320, 325, 326, 330–31, 332*n*, 375, 387, 429, 447, 449–51

Raymond, Henry J., 32

Raymond, Miss., 390
   Battle of, 385–87, 414

Raymond Road, 396, 398, 399

Reagan, John, 444

Red River, xv, 167, 169, 170, 177, 274–75, 279, 282, 301–7, 317, 330, 376, 481
   Farragut's blockade of, 306–8

Reichhelm, E. Paul, 254–55

Reid, Whitelaw, 85

Republicans, 23, 143, 239, 316
   in elections of 1862, 183*n*, 272
   Radical, 239

Richardson, Albert D., xviii, 4, 17, 23, 41, 54, 82, 86, 88, 90, 91, 204, 214–15, 319

Richmond, La., 453

Richmond, USS, 106, 135, 149

Richmond, Va., 30, 54, 55, 89, 146, 151, 193, 285, 342, 408, 443, 482, 484

Richmond Dispatch, 200, 230

Richmond Examiner, 118

Ritner, Emeline, 335, 339, 478

Ritner, Jacob, 249, 266, 335, 337, 339, 478

Roach, Mahala, 146

road building, 353, 380

Robinson, Mary, 21

Rodgers, John, 6, 9, 11

Rodney, Miss., 363–64

Rodney Road, 369–74, 394, 406

Rolling Fork, 293–96, 298–300
   Sherman's rescue march from Hill's plantation to, 296–97

Rorer, W. R., 220

Rosecrans, William S., 307, 321, 344–45, 487
   at Corinth, 187–89, 191
   at Iuka, 187

Ross, Leonard F., 283, 284, 286–87, 289, 299

Roundaway Bayou, 329, 342

Ruffin, Edwin, 483

Ruggles, Daniel, 137, 167, 169

"Running the Batteries" (Melville), 347

Russell, William Howard, 145, 233

St. Louis, Mo., 177, 238, 264, 280, 289, 306, 330, 380, 481
St. Louis, USS, 10, 11, 46–48
Sanborn, John B., 396, 404, 429, 434
Sanders, Jared Young, 473, 474
Sandlin, Lee, 121
Sanitary Commission, 266, 309, 310, 338, 339, 466
sanitary fairs, 339
Satartia, Miss., 445–48, 450–52
Scales, Cordelia Lewis, 217–19
Scales, Dabney Minor, 158, 166
Scott, Walter, 18
Scott, Winfield, 6–7, 163n–64n
secession, 23, 67, 143–46, 207n
"Second Coming, The" (Yeats), 277, 292
Second Confiscation Act, 199–200, 201, 207
Seddon, James A., 195, 444
sexual assault, 204–5, 217, 458
Seward, William H., 100–102, 105, 143, 175
Shannon, Marmaduke, 127, 144–45, 149, 347
sharpshooters, 434–35, 462, 463
Shaw, Robert Gould, 456
Shenandoah Valley, 484
Shepard, Isaac F., 458–59
Sheridan, Phil, 484
Sherman, Ellen Boyle Ewing, 65–69, 87, 181, 213, 222, 249, 256, 258, 259, 261, 331, 338, 380, 381, 413, 423, 469, 497
Sherman, John, 53, 86, 220, 238, 258, 270, 290, 441
Sherman, Tommy, 68
Sherman, William Tecumseh, xvi–xvii, xviii, 3, 7, 21, 26, 37, 40, 43, 53–54, 58, 63, 65–69, 87, 88, 91–94, 163, 182, 184n, 186, 191, 196, 197, 202, 213, 214, 218–24, 228, 235, 236–41, 256–58, 263, 265, 267, 271, 272, 300, 302, 316, 317, 327, 330–32, 334, 338, 342, 345–46, 348, 354, 359–61, 364, 372, 376, 380–83, 408, 445, 447, 452, 460, 461, 475, 479–81, 485, 493–97
advances on Vicksburg, 412–13
at Arkansas Post, 257
Bickerdyke and, 338
at Bridgeport, 412
canal project and, 265, 269–70, 317
at Chickasaw Bayou (Walnut Hills), xvii, 243, 246, 248–41, 253–58, 261, 263, 290, 312, 399, 413, 417–19
Dana and, 325, 326
Emancipation Proclamation and, 200
emotional troubles of, 65–66, 68–69, 77, 87, 91, 92, 93, 258
on Grant's drinking, 452
Grant's meeting with, to finalize Vicksburg plans, 211–13
Grant's partnership with, 54, 69, 86, 91–93, 228, 259, 262
Grant's supply line and, 212–13
Grant's talks with, 495
Halleck and, 68, 69
at Haynes' Bluff, 255–56, 271
in Jackson battle, 387, 391, 393
Jackson campaign of, 493–96
Jackson infrastructure destroyed by, 392–93
Jackson left by, 396
hospitals and, 338, 339
idea to divide army into two wings, 212–13
Knox and, 261–62
Lake Providence expedition and, 279–80
Louisiana State Seminary and, 66, 67
marches of destruction by, 229, 446, 484, 493–95, 497, 499
marriage of, 66–67
McClernand's congratulatory order and, 459–60
McClernand's meeting with, 256–57
newspapers and reporters and, 68, 91, 239, 261, 360
pillaging and, 203, 336, 392–93, 494

Porter and, 180, 181, 236–37, 259
quitting considered by, 258–59
rescue march from Hill's plantation to
  Rolling Fork, 296–97
return to Memphis proposed by, 272
at Shiloh, 62–65, 69, 70, 73–77, 81–84,
  86–87, 91, 92
in siege of Vicksburg, 421–30, 432–34,
  436, 439–42, 443, 467, 469
slavery as viewed by, 67
at Steele's Bayou, 289–91, 292–98, 317
troop transports and, 238
Vicksburg plan of, 240–41
Vicksburg railroad raid of, 246–47
village burned by, 180–81
Yazoo flotilla of, 359–61
Sherman (Liddell Hart), 85*n*
Shiloh, xvi, 31, 55, 60, 63, 150, 280
Shiloh, Battle of (Battle of Pittsburgh
  Landing), 62–65, 69–87, 89, 92, 118,
  125, 146, 165, 168, 202, 238, 338, 344,
  386, 399, 484
  Beauregard in, 64, 71–73, 78–81, 83,
    84, 146
  Beauregard's "Lost Opportunity" in,
    80–81
  Bragg in, 64, 71, 80, 81, 83
  Buell in, 62, 63, 70–71, 75, 77–78,
    80–86
  Dill Branch in, 79–81
  Grant in, xvi, 31, 55, 60–61, 62–65,
    69–87, 92, 93, 187, 213, 224, 226, 227,
    280, 314, 334, 484
  Hornet's Nest in, 77, 78
  Johnston in, 64, 65, 71, 73, 78–79, 84
  map of, 72
  McClernand in, 63, 70, 75, 76, 182,
    184*n*
  Sherman in, 62–65, 69, 70, 73–77,
    81–84, 86–87, 91, 92
  Wallace in, 63, 75–77, 80, 81
Ship Island, 107, 120, 131
Shirley house, 462–63

siege guns, 10
Silver Wave, 289, 296, 298–99
Sinclair, Arthur, 116*n*
Sisters of Mercy, 156, 467
Sky Parlor, 349
slaves, xii, 18, 22, 23, 97, 123–26, 145, 175,
  205, 239, 314, 333, 407, 477, 486,
  487
  abolitionists and, 143, 183, 205, 323, 337,
    456, 485, 488
  Craven and, 124, 151
  curfews for, 127
  on Deep South plantations, 206
  emancipation of, 205, 206, 210, 314,
    456, 490
  Emancipation Proclamation and, xix,
    183, 200–201, 230–33, 240, 260, 266,
    313, 323, 337, 457, 482, 485
  expansion of slavery, 143–44
  and flight of plantation owners, 356–57
  fugitive, 154, 175, 199, 206, 207*n*, 210,
    230–32
  fugitive, as contraband of war, 207
  Fugitive Slave Law and, 207*n*
  Grant and, 18, 21, 32, 52, 206, 323–24,
    485–86, 490
  Grant's campaign and, xii, xix, xx, 198,
    200–201, 206–7, 229–33, 323–24,
    333–35, 379
  Grant's work camps for former slaves,
    208–11, 323, 487
  in Mississippi, 142, 206, 219, 230–32,
    233*n*, 298
  at Natchez, 120
  popular sovereignty doctrine and,
    143–44
  Porter's liberation of, 297–98
  refugee camps for, 207*n*, 210
  Second Confiscation Act and, 199–200,
    201, 207
  as servants for Union officers, 205, 491
  Sherman and, 67
  "twenty negro law" and, 233

slaves (*cont.*)
Union soldiers aided by, 205–6, 249,
286, 287, 295
Union soldiers' stealing of, 199, 205
in Vicksburg, 140–43, 145, 146
Vicksburg evacuation and, 126
in war service as laborers, 52
Williams and, 154–55
as workers on canal projects in
Vicksburg campaign, 154–55, 165–67,
265–66, 267, 281
as workers on Porter's ship, 151, 178–79
as workers on Vicksburg fortifications,
xvi, xix, 127, 131, 171
work programs for, 208–11, 231, 323,
487–89
Slay, David H., 454
Smith, Andrew J. "Whiskey," 237, 240,
247, 373, 396, 472
Smith, Charles Ferguson, 16–17, 27, 28,
38, 56–58, 60, 63
death of, 86
at Fort Donelson, 42, 43, 49–52, 54, 86
Smith, Edmund Kirby, 186, 452
Smith, Giles A., 289, 290, 292, 295–97,
424, 426
Smith, Jean Edward, 31
Smith, Martin Luther, 125–27, 242, 419,
421, 472
Smith, Morgan L., 222, 237, 240, 250
Smith, Timothy B., 79
Smith, T. Kilby, 424
Smith, Watson, 283, 285–87
Smith's plantation (Pointe Clear), 343, 351
snuff, 204
Sons of Liberty, 184
Soper, E. B., 384
Soule, Harrison, 131–32
South:
Grant's soldiers' hatred of way of life
in, 203–4
nationalism in, xix
secession of, 23, 67, 143–46, 207*n*

women in, 204–5, 217
see also Confederate States of America
South Carolina, 144, 145, 229
Southern Railroad of Mississippi, 382, 383,
388, 392, 393, 421, 424
Spiegel, Marcus M., 479
Springfield, Ill., 182
Springfield Republican, 200
Stanley, David S., 206
Stanley, Henry Morgan, 78–79
Stanton, Benjamin, 86
Stanton, Edwin, xviii, 59, 86, 90, 163, 170,
175, 180, 184, 209, 222–23, 323, 324,
325, 332, 338, 429, 456, 457, 459, 478
Dana sent to spy on Grant by, xviii,
322, 325–27
McClernand's Vicksburg campaign
and, 181, 185, 256
McClernand's Vicksburg orders from,
185, 196–97, 222–23
steamboats, steamships, xiii, xv, 4, 6, 8,
55, 98, 106, 121, 124, 169, 238, 263–65,
283, 289, 293, 308, 317, 351, 352, 378,
482
ram warfare and, 89–90, 108–9
snag boats, 8
Vicksburg and, 139–40, 169, 170
see also gunboats
Steele, Frederick, 238–40, 249, 253, 255,
330, 334–37, 344, 372, 395, 446
at Jackson, 391
Steele's Bayou expedition, xviii, 287–91,
292–300, 305, 307, 312, 317, 320, 321,
375, 424
map of, 278
Stephens, George E., 205
Stevens, Henry, 167
Stevenson, B. F., 267, 268, 313
Stevenson, Carter L., 294, 305, 346, 360,
382
at Champion Hill, 399, 401, 402, 407–8
Stevenson, John D., 401
Stockade Redan, 421–22, 423, 426

Stone, Amanda, 125, 126, 357
Stone, Jimmy, 357–58
Stone, Kate, 119, 124–25, 126, 129, 146,
    147, 151, 154, 166, 356–58, 456–57
Stone, William, 125
Stowe, Harriet Beecher, 231
Strong, William E., 420, 464–65
Sullivan, Jeremiah, 458
Sumner, Charles, 323
Sunflower River, 288, 293, 295
Swords, James W., 130, 469

Tallahatchie River, 194, 212, 214, 215,
    217–20, 227, 234, 262, 277, 285–86
Taylor, Richard, 452–53, 455, 457–58, 462
Taylor, Zachary, 19, 25, 453
Tennessee, 53, 58, 60, 84, 94, 150, 163,
    185, 186, 188, 190, 194, 195, 200, 259,
    344–45, 496–97
  Grant's army's stay in, 203–4
  map of Kentucky-Tennessee theater, 14
Tennessee River, xx, 13, 15, 16, 35, 36, 39,
    53, 55, 57, 62–63, 73, 78–81, 213, 238,
    347, 484
Tensas River, 282
Texas, xiii, 19, 126, 163, 170
Texas Lunette, 424, 425
Thayer, John M., 251–53, 434
Thomas, George H., 87, 323–24
Thomas, Lorenzo, 59, 325, 333, 335, 337,
    338, 455, 458, 485, 490
Thomas, Samuel, 487
Thrall, Seneca B., 198, 199, 201, 202, 214,
    215, 217, 219, 234, 263, 268–69, 281,
    353
Three Years with Grant (Cadwallader), 448
Tigress, USS, 62, 75–76, 78, 256, 258, 352
Tilghman, Lloyd, 39, 40, 406
timberclad gunboats, xv, 6, 15, 28, 45–46,
    79–80
Times (London), 111, 200
tinclad gunboats, 179, 283, 286
Todd, David H., 137, 427

Tomkins, Charles Brown, 281
Tomkins, Mollie, 281
Tracy, Edward D., 372–74
Trimble, H. M., 416
Trollope, Anthony, 3, 5
Trowbridge, John T., 437, 440, 487–88
Tunnard, William H., 440, 466, 469
Tupelo, Miss., 88
Tuscumbia, USS, 345n, 362
Tuttle, James M., 391
Twain, Mark, xiii, 25, 121, 438
Tyler, USS, 6, 7, 15, 28, 79–80, 158–60

Underground Railroad, 205n
Union soldiers and officers:
  black people as viewed by, 205
  black servants of, 205, 491
  disillusionment and defeatism among,
    312–14
  sharpshooters, 434–35, 462, 463
  slaves' aiding of, 205–6, 249, 286, 287,
    295
  slaves stolen by, 199, 205
  Southern ways hated by, 203–4
  Southern women and, 204–5, 217
Usher, John P., 175

Valley Forge, 312
Van Dorn, Earl "Buck," 137, 160–61, 167,
    169, 186, 194, 379, 417
  at Corinth, 186–89
  Davis and, 137, 189, 191
  Holly Springs raided by, 224–28, 234,
    239
Vick, Newitt, 139
Vicksburg, Miss.:
  black refugees in, 488–89
  cotton and, 139–41
  ethnic diversity in, 140
  history prior to Civil War, 139–42
  incorporation of, 139
  political reversal in, 139, 142–46
  saloons and bordellos in, 141

Vicksburg, Miss. (*cont.*)
slaves in, 140–43, 145, 146
steamboats and, 139–40
storekeepers and supplies in, 130–31
streets in, 141
violence in, 141
Whigs in, 142–43, 145
Vicksburg campaign, xv, xviii, 13, 35, 56, 63, 89, 91, 93–94, 97, 103, 107, 125, 139, 142–43, 146, 139–41, 186
CSA *Arkansas* in, 124, 127, 157–62, 166–69, 176
Arkansas Post battle in, 257–58, 263
Baton Rouge battle and, 167–69
and bluffs surrounding the city, xiii, xv, xvii, 127, 420
canal project in De Soto, 136, 153–56, 163, 165–67, 259, 280, 281, 299
casualties in, 501
Champion Hill battle in, 394–408, 414, 415, 480
Chickasaw Bayou battle in, xvii, 242–58, 261, 263, 271, 302, 334, 338, 359
Chickasaw Bayou battle map, 244
civilian evacuations during, 126, 130, 149
civilians in, xix, 138, 139, 150, 416
civilians living in caves during, 138, 436–39
Confederate reinforcements sent, 130, 134
Corinth and, 188–89
decisiveness of, 482
Farragut in, *see* Farragut, David Glasgow
Grant in, *see* Vicksburg campaign, Grant's operations in
Grant-Porter accord in, 211–12, 265
Halleck orders Grant to remain in defensive position in, 185
Halleck's suggested change in, 220–21
at Haynes' Bluff, 171, 246, 248–49, 255–56, 271, 285, 288, 302, 320–22

Louisiana Redan crater and, 462–67
map of (June–July 1862), 152
map of (April–July 1863), 370
McClernand in, *see* McClernand, John A.
McPherson in, *see* McPherson, James Birdseye
Medals of Honor for service at, 427
New Orleans and, 98, 102, 116, 117, 118
Pemberton in, *see* Pemberton, John Clifford
political forces and, 183–84
Porter in, *see* Porter, David Dixon
railroads and, 124, 139, 140, 170, 246–47, 382, 383, 388, 415
Red River and, xv, 167, 169, 170, 177, 274–75, 279, 282, 301–7, 317, 330, 376, 481
Red River blockade and, 308
Sherman in, *see* Sherman, William Tecumseh
Shiloh battle and, 146
steamboats and, 169, 170
strategic importance of, xiii, 133–34, 482
Union possession of Vicksburg, 473–77, 480
Vicksburg as overconfident in, 346–47
Vicksburg bombed in, 138, 436–40
Vicskburg refuses to surrender in 1862, 125–26, 421
Vicksburg's fortifications and, xvi, 127–28, 131, 137, 170–71, 420–21
Vicksburg's guns and, 346, 420–21
Vicksburg surrenders, xii, xviii, xix, 92, 198, 470, 471–75, 476–78, 480, 483, 485, 488, 500
Vicksburg campaign, Grant's operations in, xvi, xviii, xx, 25, 31, 34, 43, 55, 190, 212, 241, 254, 255, 259, 262, 312, 413–14
Big Black River Bridge battle in, 408–12, 415, 416, 417, 428, 460, 479

canal projects in, 263–66, 269–71, 279, 316–17, 328–29, 351–52

casualties in, 480, 501

Champion Hill battle in, 394–408, 414, 415, 417, 419, 425

Chickasaw battle and, 248

crisis in, 309–24

Dana and, 327

desertions and, xvii, 313

disease and, xvii, xviii, 268–69, 300, 308, 309–12; *see also* disease and sickness

Duckport Canal project in, 328–29, 351–52

engineering corps in, 353–54

foraging and, 201–2, 217, 218, 228–30, 379, 380, 384, 388

Grand Gulf and, 131–32, 136, 328–30, 343–45, 349, 351, 353, 354, 358–61, 365, 369, 372, 373, 375, 376, 378–81, 390, 413

Grand Gulf battle in, 361–63, 479

Grand Gulf supply line abandoned, 387–88, 390

Grant gives Sherman one of his divisions, 221

Grant's battlefield orders and, 290, 405

Grant's correspondence with Halleck during, 190, 235, 259, 260, 270, 273, 283–85, 316–18, 322, 331, 333–34, 338, 363, 375–77, 391, 429, 430, 460, 473*n*

Grant's decision to move on without Banks, 376–77

Grant's division of army in, 284–85

Grant's first view of Vicksburg, 271

Grant's improvisations in, 352

Grant's meeting with Sherman to finalize plans for, 211–13

Grant's preparations for the march south, 198, 206, 211

Grant's Special Orders No. 1 in, 202–3

Grant's Special Orders No. 140 in, 431

Grant's strategies to mislead Pemberton, 334, 344, 358–60, 382

Grant's stumbles in, 480

Grierson's raid in, 358–59, 364

at Hard Times, 353–55, 360–62

Haynes' Bluff and, 271, 285, 320–22, 327, 328, 359–60

health care and, 339–40

Holly Springs base in, xvii, 194–95, 212, 214–17, 219, 224, 227, 234–35

Holly Springs base destroyed, 224–28, 234, 239

Iuka in, 187, 222, 227, 321, 403, 404

Jackson battle in, 390, 391–92, 397, 413–14

lack of provisions and, 378–79, 384, 413, 414

Lake Providence expedition in, xviii, 274–76, 279–85, 299, 300, 317

Lincoln's questioning of strategy in, 319

logistics in, 381

Louisiana march, 331–32, 340–42

Louisiana march, map of, 341

map of invasion of northern Mississippi (November–December 1862), 216

march down the Mississippi Central Railroad line, xvii, 190–91, 197, 212–13, 214–35, 272

and McClernand's orders from Lincoln and Stanton, 185, 196–97, 222–23

Mississippi River crossing in, 328, 342, 344, 363–65

New Carthage and, 328–32, 348, 349, 352

news of Grant's victory in, 478–79

newspapers and, xvii, 262, 314

Oxford in, xii, xvii, 197, 218–21, 222–25, 228, 233

panic migration caused by, 356, 384

partnership with Banks planned in, 301, 328, 376, 377

pillaging, raiding, and burning in, xii, 198–99, 201–5, 214, 217, 218, 228–29, 231, 334–36, 356, 379–80, 384

Vicksburg campaign, Grant's operations in (*cont.*)

Porter's co-direction in, 211–12, 265, 330

Port Gibson battle in, 369–76, 379, 402, 414, 420, 460, 479

Raymond battle in, 385–87, 414

return to Memphis and, 272–73

roads and bridges built in, 353, 380

Sherman's idea to divide army into two wings for, 212–13

siege of Vicksburg, xix, 416–42, 443–45, 460–70, 471–72

siege of Vicksburg, map of, 418

slaves and, xii, xix, xx, 198, 200–201, 206–7, 229–33, 323–24, 333–35, 379

slaves in work camps in, 208–11, 231, 323

social upheaval ignited by, 231–33, 324, 333, 489

and soldiers' discontent with Grant, 314

soldiers' pay and, 313, 322, 339

Steele's Bayou expedition in, xviii, 287–91, 292–300, 305, 307, 312, 317, 320, 321, 375, 424

Steele's Bayou expedition map, 278

strategy session for, 271–74

supply lines in, 212–13, 220, 228, 378–82, 387–88, 390, 393, 394, 397, 413, 417

surrender of Vicksburg, xii, xviii, xix, 92, 198, 470, 471–75, 476–78, 480, 483, 485, 488, 500

terrain and, xvi, xviii, 271–72, 274–75, 280, 282, 293, 331–32, 352–53, 414

Thomas and, 323–24, 325, 333, 335, 337, 338, 485

turning points in, 320–21, 342, 377

weather and, xvii, 267–68, 274, 281, 302, 340, 414

wounded left behind in, 364, 414

Yazoo Pass expedition in, 275–76, 277–80, 283–85, 288–90, 292, 299, 312, 317, 320

Yazoo Pass expedition map, 278

Vicksburg, Shreveport & Texas Railroad, 124, 140, 246–47

Vicksburg Daily Citizen, 130, 139, 440, 469

Vicksburg Daily Whig, 127, 131, 144, 347, 440

Vicksburg-Under-the-Hills, 141

Villard, Henry, 68

Virginia, 104, 484

Voluntary Engineer Corps, 354

Von Phul, 347–49, 352

Wade, William, 362

Wadley, Sara, 358

Wadley, William, 358

Wailes, B. L. C., 144

Walke, Henry, 11, 28, 39, 47, 159, 160, 306

Walker, John G., 453–55

Walker's Greyhounds, 453–55

Wallace, Lew, 16, 58, 84

background and career of, 46

at Fort Donelson, 42, 44–50

at Shiloh, 63, 75–77, 80, 81

Wallace, W. H. L., 63, 75, 77, 78

Wallace, Zerelda Gray Sanders, 46

Walnut Bayou, 329

Walnut Hills, 139

Battle of, *see* Chickasaw Bayou, Battle of

War Department, U.S., 6, 8, 10, 36, 128, 177, 180, 285, 325, 381, 383, 459, 461, 478, 487

War of 1812, 99, 104–5

Battle of New Orleans, 109, 115

Warren County, Miss., 140, 142

Warrenton, Miss., 171, 271, 328–30, 346, 380, 382, 461

Washburn, Cadwallader C., 218, 262, 309, 319–21, 459

Washburne, Elihu B., 24, 32–34, 85, 86, 218*n*, 235, 260, 262, 273*n*, 285, 315, 316, 219–21, 361, 414, 490

Washington, Edward, 422

Washington, George, 422
Washington Hotel, 439
Washita River, 282
Watts, William O., 347, 349
Waud, Alfred, 210
Webster, Joseph D., 49, 79
Weigley, Russell F., 484
Weiss, Enoch, 284
Welles, Gideon, 6, 9, 99, 105, 132, 133, 134, 150, 161–63, 169, 170, 171, 176–78, 181, 197, 212, 223, 236, 287, 298, 301, 302, 304, 305, 329–30, 482
    New Orleans expedition and, 97, 99–107, 111, 114
    Vicksburg surrender and, 471, 477–78
Wells, Seth J., 337, 355
Western Blockading Squadron, 177
West Point, 16, 19, 22, 24, 37, 43, 52, 64–65, 66, 87, 137, 184, 192, 193, 212, 242, 280, 344, 354, 411, 434
    Grant at, 16, 18, 19, 21, 22, 24, 37, 432
West Virginia, 200
"What I Saw at Shiloh" (Bierce), 74
Whigs, 142–45, 495
Whitman, George Washington, 493, 494
Wilcox, Charles Edwards, 369, 374, 375
Wilkie, Franc B., 26, 32–33, 38, 39, 85, 182, 199, 239, 249–50, 253, 270, 288–89, 330, 334, 347, 391, 450, 451
    death of family witnessed by, 298–99
    William H. Webb, 303, 304
Williams, T. Harry, 17
Williams, Thomas, 120, 122–24, 128, 129, 131–33, 135–36, 150, 163, 165, 167
    African American workers and, 154–55, 165–67
    canal project and, 136, 153–56, 163, 165–67, 259, 263–64
    death of, 168
Willison, Charles A., 236, 253, 267–68
Wills, Charles W., 185, 204, 205, 214, 217, 229

Wilson, James H., 184, 217, 224, 227, 271–74, 275, 277, 279, 280, 282–84, 286–88, 299, 312, 319, 325, 326, 327, 330, 332n, 336, 347, 353, 362, 373–75, 386, 407, 414, 448, 451, 452, 460–61
Wissahickon, USS, 123
Wittenmyer, Annie, 339–40, 347–48, 466, 490–91
women, 204–5, 217, 437–39, 441
Wood, Charles, 431
World War II, 481
    D-Day in, 365
Worthington, Amanda, 336
Wyatt, Miss., 218–20

Yalobusha River, xviii, 218, 220, 223, 226, 275n
Yandell, D. W., 79
Yates, Richard, 4, 7, 24, 182, 354
Yazoo City, Miss., 158, 279, 288, 289, 293, 447
Yazoo-Mississippi Delta, xi–xii, xvi, xviii, 101, 131, 140, 189, 268, 271, 292, 372, 395, 417, 446
    waterways in, 274–75, 280, 284, 292
Yazoo Pass expedition, 275–76, 277–80, 283–85, 288–90, 292, 299, 312, 317, 320
    map of, 278
Yazoo River, xiii, xvi–xviii, 103, 124, 135, 143, 147, 157–60, 171, 182, 211–13, 219–22, 236, 237, 240–42, 245–48, 251, 255–58, 261, 263, 267, 268, 271, 275, 275n, 277, 279, 285, 287, 290, 297–99, 320, 327, 384, 413, 432, 442, 443, 445, 446, 452
    Sherman's flotilla on, 359–61
Yeats, William Butler, 277, 292
Young's Point, La., 259, 262, 263–69, 271, 273n, 274, 281, 282, 284, 289, 293, 294, 299, 305, 306, 309, 312, 317, 321, 326, 327, 329, 330, 347–49, 360, 380, 415, 453, 455

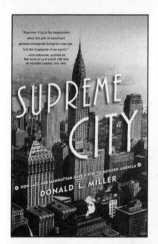

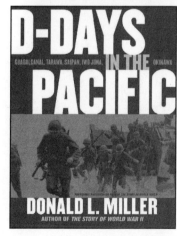
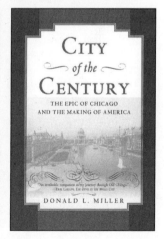